CONTENTS

PREFACE

One of the principal aims of the first edition of this book was to explain the doctrines of land law by reference to reason rather than to history. That approach is retained in this fourth edition, with the emphasis, however, that this refers to legal history only. Appreciation of social and economic background is essential to an understanding of land law and how it is likely to develop. For instance, almost the whole of the 1925 legislation can be explained by the national need to facilitate the transfer of land. This need was caused by the change from an aristocratic society, which aimed to keep land within the family, to an industrial one which required land for factories, houses and roads.

As in the case of previous editions, modern developments in the law and the problems of contemporary society have been accentuated. The recession has kept a steady stream of domestic mortgage repossession cases before the county and appellate courts. The increase in marital breakdown and unmarried cohabitation has continued to make co-ownership and occupational rights of property lively areas of study. Important legislative changes have affected the law of leaseholds and covenants.

Environmental law is also of enormous significance to land occupation in contemporary Britain, and no realistic study of land law can neglect at least an indicative survey of its range.

In accordance with the principal purpose of this book, which is to give students a confident understanding of the subject, as opposed to merely sound-bite knowledge, the study materials at the end of each chapter have been expanded in several ways. First, reproduction of primary sources has been increased. There is no substitute for reading appellate judgments and statutory extracts where the very words are citable law. Furthermore, the House of Lords and Court of Appeal judgments can explain in most expansive form the legal solutions to the most pressing problems and growth points in our society and expose the full intelligence of judicial policy.

These key judgements frequently subsume and outdate a mass of earlier decisions sometimes reported in text books out of a perhaps misguided conscience of legal scholarship.

Second, most students are less troubled by knowledge acquisition than by problem solution. This demands a prioritisation of such knowledge and calls for some separate study. To take an example from the law of tort, it would be futile to consider the quantum of damages even before it had been established that a duty of care existed towards the claimant. Where the complexity of the topic merits, therefore, this prioritisation is assisted by the use of algorithms. These plans simply indicate the order in which to apply legal rules in the solution of a problem. Third, some examples of problem solution are provided. Only occasionally is this by way of a 'model' answer, since such an answer is inappropriate in such a speculative subject as law at higher level of study. Generally the ways to solution are merely signposted or implied by the format of questions set for the student.

Fourth, practical precedents have been included at points where they bring theoretical principles to life. Examples are the *Standard Conditions of Sale* used by solicitors on the sale of land and the *Mortgage Conditions of Contract* of a leading building society.

Land law is not only an appropriate subject for academic study but, in modern times, has become a vital foundation for a growing number of disciplines such as conveyancing, town and country planning, estate management and housing law. This book therefore aims to provide not only a practically enlightened text for students on law degree and Common Professional Examination courses, but also a theoretical base for many non-law professional courses. Land law sometimes uses some rather strange terminology and a glossary has been provided to explain these.

I would like to thank all those who have so kindly helped me: my publishers for taking on this fourth edition; my colleague, Professor Patricia Woodward, for our discussions on the condition, dare I say plight, of legal education in this country; my brother Peter Dalton for his eagle eyed reading of proofs; Frances Walklate and Caroline Hughes for typing the manuscripts, often at very short notice; and of course my students, past and present, from whom I am still learning my trade.

I have attempted to state the law as it stood on 1 February 1996. All mistakes are, of course, mine.

Pat Dalton

TABLE OF CASES

TABLE OF STATUTES

1993
Leasehold Reform, Housing and Urban Development Act 1993 *124*

1994
Criminal Justice and Public Order Act 1994 *160*

1995
Agricultural Tenancies Act 1995 *125*
Landlord and Tenant (Covenant) Act 1995 *107, 115, 119*
s 3 *119*
s 5 *119*
s 6 *119*
s 7 *119*
s 8 *119*
s 16 *119*

TABLE OF STATUTORY INSTRUMENTS

1925
Land Registration Rules (SR&O SI 1925/1093) rr 34 and 35 *430–31*

1972
Town and Country Planning (Use Classes) Order (SI 1972/1385) *63*

1988
Town and Country Planning (General Development) Order (SI 1988/1813) *63*

CHAPTER 1

INTRODUCTION

LAND LAW AFFECTS ALL PEOPLE

The first message to students of land law is not to allow its reputation for quaintness to obscure that it is today, of all the subjects of the law, one of the most important to ordinary people: we must all have a place to live. For most people its importance has increased enormously in modern times. Approximately three-quarters of homes are now owned by their occupiers, and buying a house is the largest financial transaction of their lives. Even for those who rent accommodation the commitment is often crucial in terms of finance and personal well-being.

If land law is so fundamental to individual aspiration, it is no less significant in its social and economic contexts. The harmonious enjoyment of land in residential neighbourhoods and its availability for business enterprise are influences central to the quality of our lives, and import a measure of public control. In an even wider perspective, land is a national heritage which has influenced, and will continue to mould, our culture. As to the urban environment we shall see that the industrial revolution had a profound effect. As to the countryside, the sculptor Henry Moore, in his foreword to *The Theft of the Countryside* by Marian Shoard, remarked that it has shaped our characters.

> From the Beowulf poet to Shakespeare, Chaucer to the Brontes, our literature has sprung at our writers from the natural environment. Our painters and musicians too are inseparable from the landscape.

Even the homeless have a material interest, though regrettably small, in land law. The subject also defines the rights of lodgers and even visitors to premises such as cinemas and supermarkets.

While other forms of property, such as cars and shares, have expanded in volume to meet increased population and wealth, the surface area of our land has hardly changed since the end of the Ice Age. Space and, therefore, amenity are only two among many contemporary challenges to land law.

SUBJECT MATTER OF LAND LAW

Land law deals with the kinds of rights you can enjoy in land. Conveyancing deals with the transfer of these rights to others. If I am the owner of 'Blackacre' and have a right of way over my neighbour's property, 'Whiteacre', land law tells me how I may use my own land and in what way I may exercise the right of way over my neighbour's property. If we both retain our properties, land law continuously governs our behaviour to our own and each other's property. My neighbour might wish to build a greenhouse across that part of his land where I exercise my right of way; I might wish to build a high wall on my land which would threaten the flow of light to his kitchen; my oak tree might be sending branches and roots into his property; perhaps I have failed to pay my mortgage instalments. Land law provides the answers to the problems raised by all these circumstances.

Now let us say that my neighbour decides to sell his land to *P*. The problems that arise on the transfer of the property are dealt with by the rules of conveyancing. *P* will insist on proof that my neighbour really owns the land and so will investigate his title to it by examining the recent history of its ownership and use. He will also wish to know about any restrictions imposed upon the land such as the right of way. He might wish to raise the purchase money by means of a mortgage. In any case, he will want to ensure that the ownership is transferred to him in the manner demanded by the law. All this involves not only examining existing documents of title but also drafting new ones. This process is called conveyancing and is clearly of occasional occurrence only. The relationship between the two subjects is nevertheless very close and the study of land law frequently crosses the boundaries of conveyancing.

The rights in land with which land law is concerned are of two types. First, there are those rights which enable you to enjoy the land itself. Examples are *absolute ownership*, *tenancies* and *life interests*. In all these cases you may take exclusive possession of the land. Second, there are those rights which, while not empowering you to occupy the land itself, place restrictions on someone else's land in your favour: for example, the right of way over my neighbour's land, mentioned above, which is known as an *easement*. Other examples would be a right to prevent him carrying out certain activities on his land (a *restrictive covenant*), and a right to fish in the stream at the bottom of his garden (a *profit à prendre*). Both these kinds of rights are known as *interests*, although absolute ownership and tenancies are also called *estates* in land. This use of the word *estate* is peculiar to land law and must be distinguished from the everyday use of the word to mean a particular geographical portion of land.

History has exerted a powerful influence in land law and a few words are necessary to explain its role. Many of the statutes and cases which are still binding are old and untouched or only modified by modern legislation. The Prescription Act 1832 and the case of *Wheeldon* v *Burrows* (1879) are examples from the law of easements. These are not mere history but living law and must be appreciated as such. This obvious statement is intended to counteract a common early impression that a completely new law of land was created by the great property statutes of 1925. However, the effect of these Acts was more akin to the restoration of an old building than the construction of a new one. Although many cobwebby attics and passages were cut away, much of the building still stands, although refaced and modernised in many places. Much of the modernisation carried out in 1925 was actually aimed at the kitchen where the conveyancing is done: the reforms here were radical. Over much of the house, however, the structure is old and you must not be surprised to find the motor car in the stable.

Another application of history in land law is the study of old, but now defunct, law for the purpose of understanding the evolution of doctrines and terminology. History in this sense has been traditionally much pressed into service in the study of land law. Its role will be curtailed here and a rational, rather than narrative, account of doctrines and terms will be attempted. This will enable the reader to save his energies for the living law. Such an approach will, at times, demand a faithful acceptance of the quaint at its face value. One example may be given together with a readily comprehensible analogy from everyday life. The vehicle used for consolidating new road surfaces is still referred to by the unpedantic as a steamroller. Yet everyone knows that it works on diesel fuel, not on steam. When the roadman drives it, or when the mechanic services it, they do not do so less efficiently because they know nothing of steam engineering. In the same way in land law we shall find that the interest which entitles a person to the fullest ownership of land is called the *fee simple absolute*. The reason for the use of this term lies in history, as in the case of the steamroller, and both statutes and lawyers continue to use the term rather than 'ownership'. Yet there is no difference between the meanings of the two expressions.

COMMON LAW AND EQUITY

Some of the rights mentioned above were developed by the common law courts and some by the courts of equity. Originally, only the common law courts decided and enforced rights in land and such rights were frequently narrow in scope and dependent upon technicalities. On the other hand, when title to interests in land was based on these 'legal' rights the degree of protection given was high, for they were enforceable against everyone, not merely against particular individuals. They were known as rights *in rem*, or real rights, that is rights to the land itself, as opposed to rights *in personam*, or personal rights, such as contractual rights, enforceable only against specified individuals. For example, if *O*, the owner of land, leased it to a tenant, *T*, and concealing this transaction, sold the ownership to *P*, then *P* would buy the land subject to *T*'s lease, a legal interest, even though he knew nothing of this. Of course, *T* would be obliged to pay his rent to *P* and not to *O*.

Sometimes a person would be given such an interest in land on the understanding that he would, despite his own legal rights, allow someone else to enjoy the benefit of the land. This arrangement was known as a *use*, or, in modern times, a *trust*. The common law courts ignored it. Since all they were concerned with was the question 'Who has the legal interest or estate in the land?' only the conscience of the person who held that interest protected the intended beneficiary. Later, the Lord Chancellor and then the courts of equity did protect such a beneficiary by enforcing the arrangement. When this protection came to be granted regularly, and as a matter of course, the beneficiary was said to have the equitable right to the land.

Thus arose the *trust*. One person might have a legal interest in land but must allow a person having the equitable interest to enjoy possession of it. For historical reasons this was sometimes a convenient arrangement. If *A*, for instance, wished to make a gift of land to *X* who was a minor, he was faced with the problem that a minor could not hold a legal interest in land. He might overcome this difficulty, however, by transferring the legal interest in the land to *T* and directing that he hold it in trust for *X*, who would thus have the equitable interest. This would entitle *X* to the enjoyment of the land and, when he came of age, he would be able to demand that *T* should convey the legal interest to him. Even now that the courts of common law and equity have been merged, this distinction is still with us and gives us a 'two-faced' land law. A legal interest, if held in trust for another, gives no enjoyment of the land but merely imposes the duty to allow the beneficiary who has the equitable interest to enjoy it. A person who holds a legal interest in land not upon trust for another but for his own purposes might without artificiality be considered as holding both the legal and the equitable interests in the land. In short, when you find that someone has a legal interest in land you have only half the story. You must also ascertain who holds the equitable interest.

There have always been some differences between the enforceability of legal and equitable interests. Legal interests were perfectly secure and enforceable against all. Equitable interests became enforceable against more and more people but never reached the state of inviolability of the legal interest. At first, equity enforced them only against the person who was originally given the legal interest on trust, but later enforced them against all others whose consciences ought to be affected by the trust, like, for example, a purchaser of the legal interest who knew of the trust. Clearly it would be unfair and unconscionable to allow him to take the land free from the interest of the beneficiaries even though the latter could take action against the trustee. The purchaser would, therefore, be obliged to hold his legal interest on trust for the beneficiaries and thus involuntarily became a trustee. The scope of enforceability was widened as trusts became more common, the test again being that of good conscience and fairness, until the equitable interest was enforceable against nearly every person. This means that everyone who came to the land as donee or purchaser had to give effect to the trust. But equity stopped short of enforcing against a purchaser in good faith of a legal interest in the land for valuable consideration who had no notice of the trust. To deprive such a person of the enjoyment of the property would be as unfair as allowing the beneficiaries to lose their interest in the land. So, in such a case, the purchaser was allowed to hold the legal interest absolutely for himself. The land became discharged of the trust and the beneficiaries had to pursue personal remedies against the trustee. Furthermore, this discharge was permanent, so that if the purchaser resold the land to *X* who knew of the trust, *X* nevertheless took the land free of it.

Sometimes, however, the very terms of the trust are that the land should be sold and that the resultant purchase money should be divided amongst the beneficiaries. In these cases the purchaser takes the legal interest free from the trust although he knows of it because that is the purpose of the trust. Special provision is made for the protection of the purchase money.

An equitable interest gives much more than a personal right, but just less than a real right. The position is unchanged today and all that need be added at this stage is that the expression 'the purchaser in good faith of a legal interest for value without notice' referred to above has been carefully developed and defined in meaning by both case law and statute (this is described in more detail in Chapter 2). It must be emphasised that, in enforcing rights unknown to the common law, equity nevertheless paid full respect to the doctrines of the common law. It recognised legal rights, but merely directed that in some circumstances they should be exercised in favour of others. We shall see how, in fashioning the different types of interest which might be enjoyed by a beneficiary, it followed the law. Thus there were life interests in equity as at law. In some cases, equity went further and invented new interests in land unknown to the law. An example is the restrictive covenant.

HOW TRUSTS ARE CREATED

The trust is one of the greatest inventions of the English legal system and is found everywhere in the common law world. Continental systems have achieved analogous effects through different machinery, derived from their Roman Law structures. It provides a most flexible mechanism for the investment and settlement of all kinds of property. As regards land, it can take several forms, according to the purpose intended. These particular forms will be discussed in later chapters as they affect the topic then being explained. We must examine at the outset, however, the general ways in which they are created or arise by operation of law. Once an owner of property has set up a trust, as when *O* conveys her land to *A* and *B* to hold as trustees for *C*, that owner cannot change her mind. The trust provisions inexorably take effect. Trusts can arise by *express* grant, by *implication* or by operation of law. The last category includes *constructive, resulting* and *statutory trusts*.

An *express trust* of land arises when an owner clearly expresses an intention that his property is to be held on trust. To be enforceable, however, the following are necessary. If the owner wishes to retain the legal ownership and to hold it in trust for a beneficiary, thus making himself trustee, he must conform with the Law of Property Act 1925 s 53(1)(b) and evidence his intention by signed writing. If he wishes some other person to be trustee, the property must be formally transferred to that person for that purpose. This requires a deed if the transfer is to be during the owner's life, or a valid will if it is to occur on his death. The meaning of the word 'deed' is explained in the glossary.

An *implied trust* arises when property is conveyed to one person in circumstances which show an intention to benefit another person who is not expressly mentioned. For instance, if *A* and *B*, intending to own property jointly, both contribute to the purchase price but arrange for the property to be transferred into the name of *A* only, *A* will hold the legal interest in trust for himself and *B* jointly. This can occur in the context of couples sharing the cost of a home in which they wish to live together. It will be discussed more fully when co-ownership is examined in Chapter 11. Express and implied trusts thus arise from the intention of parties. Trusts can however arise, despite such intention, by operation of law. They fall into three categories, *resulting*, *constructive* and *statutory trusts*.

A *resulting trust* occurs when a donor's intentions fail, partially or totally. For instance if *O* transfers property to *T* to hold for the benefit of *L* for life, then on *L*'s death the benefit will *result* or spring back to *O*, who failed to dispose of his property exhaustively. *T* will then hold on a resulting trust for *O*.

A *constructive trust* arises when a person regards as his own some property which is in fact subject to a trust, irrespective of anyone's intentions. For example, if a trustee transfers trust property to a stranger to the trust, who is not a bona fide purchaser for value of the property without notice of the trust, that transferee will become an involuntary trustee of the property.

Finally, trusts sometimes occur by operation of a Statute. The most important is that *statutory trust* imposed by the Law of Property Act 1925 in all cases of land owned by two or more persons. We shall see, when we discuss co-ownership that this is a mere device of conveyancing and requires no further discussion at this stage.

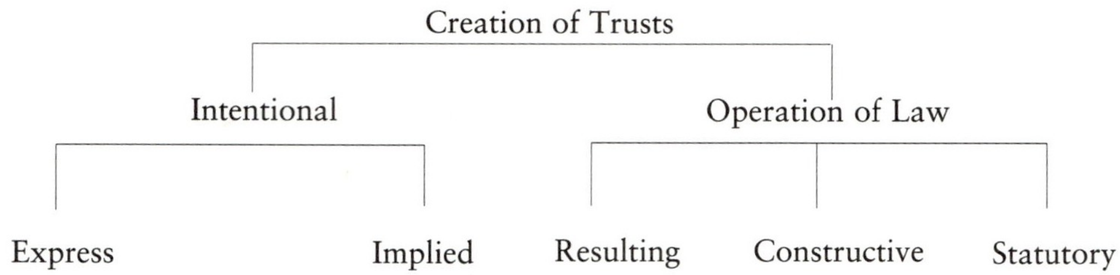

Figure 1.1 Summary of the methods of creating a trust.

The various categories mentioned above relate only to the ways in which trusts arise. Once a trust has arisen the rights of the beneficiaries and duties of the trustees are the same. There are several routes but only one destination.

This basic explanation of the trust will be developed in subsequent chapters in ways appropriate to the particular topic under discussion.

Figure 1.1 summarises the methods of creating trusts.

TENURE

There was a time following the Norman Conquest when only the King owned land. It was his because he had conquered it. All other persons enjoying land merely held it of him on certain conditions and, if these conditions were not fulfilled, the land could be reclaimed by the King; rather like, as between landlord and tenant today, the landlord might have the right to end the lease if the tenant breaks a condition in it. This conditional holding of land was called *tenure*. Several types of tenure developed and were named according to the conditions to be obeyed. The performance of these conditions amounted to a kind of rent. Thus tenure by knight service entailed supplying the King with soldiers for his army. Others include *frankalmoign, serjeanty, copyhold* and *socage*. All had their different types of rent as conditions but in time they tended to conform more to the pattern of socage, which came to have a money rent rather than services in kind. All these different forms of tenure have now been converted into socage by statute and, furthermore, with a few exceptions to be mentioned in Chapter 2, all the conditions and rents have been abolished. Since no such conditions exist to be broken, it follows that the monarch can never take the land back.

Although all land is in theory 'held' of the Queen on socage tenure, it is now quite proper to speak of owning it, or, to use the lawyer's phrase, which means the same thing, *owning the fee simple* in land. There is still one type of relationship which, although not feudal in origin, is called tenure. This occurs when the owner of land leases it to a tenant. Finally, it may be remarked that although the monarch does not own all land she is as capable of owning land in her private capacity as her citizens are.

Though of merely theoretical interest to English land law, the Australian case of *Mabo* v *Queensland* [1992] 66 ALJR 408 might be noted because of its considerable publicity. The Australian High Court held that aboriginal rights in land in the Murray Islands off the Queensland coast survived colonisation by the British Crown. Some specific act of appropriation or dealing with the land was necessary to achieve this result and had not occurred. Whether by force of fact or legal fiction such an appropriation and dealing occurred after 1066 in England when William the Conqueror is assumed to have granted all his conquered land to his tenants in chief. Further discussion can be found at 1995 Conveyancer and Property Lawyer 33.

THE DOCTRINE OF ESTATES

So *tenure* told the 'conditions' on which land was held, and is now, apart from the case of leaseholds, obsolete. The words *estate* and *interest* tell us for how long a person may enjoy land and this is extremely important today. When no time limit is placed upon your enjoyment of land, clearly you have absolute ownership of it.

This is the *fee simple* estate. It is the largest estate you can have in land in that it is potentially inexhaustible in duration. You may deal with it in the same way in which you may deal with an object absolutely owned by you. You may *alienate* it during your lifetime or leave it by will. If you die intestate it will pass to your close relations in the same way that your motor car will. Laymen refer to the fee simple as the *freehold*.

If you own the fee simple estate you can make grants of the enjoyment of the land to others for limited periods. Rights to enjoy land for these lesser periods are also called *estates* or *interests* and, like the fee simple estate, they have their own names to describe their duration. Examples are the *life interest* and the *term of years* or *leasehold*. Since the fee simple is of infinite duration any number of lesser interests may be granted by its owner. *C* may give a life interest to *A*, followed by a life interest to *B*. This would mean that *A* could occupy the land, to the exclusion of all other persons including the fee simple owner, for his lifetime. On *A*'s death, *B*, if still living, would be entitled to do the same. On the death of *B*, *C*, the fee simple owner, would again be entitled to enjoy the land. If he had died by that time the right would belong to the person to whom the fee simple has been conveyed by him or devised by his will. No matter how many lesser interests a fee simple owner grants, the fee simple remains his and will ultimately give the right to possession once again. In short, its owner is like the owner of a tap. Any number of buckets or barrels of water might be taken from it by various people but the ownership of the tap is unchanged, even though its owner may temporarily be denied the right of enjoying its water. This position only alters if he gives away the tap itself. Similarly the only way in which the owner of a fee simple can divest himself of it is to grant someone else the fee simple and not one iota less.

When an interest in land is owned by a person but does not entitle him to present possession, it is said to be *in reversion* if it is owned by the person who granted the lesser interest and *in remainder* if it is owned by someone else. Thus in the example above, during *A*'s life *A*'s interest is in possession, *B*'s is in remainder and *C*'s is in reversion. When *A* dies, *B*'s interest becomes an interest in possession and so on. The important point is that even if your interest is still in remainder or in reversion you presently own an interest in land which you can sell or give away. Thus, during the lifetime of *A*, *B* may sell his life interest to *P*. Upon *A*'s death *P* will then be entitled to possess the land for as long as *B* lives. In the same way *C* could sell his fee simple in reversion. The grant of successive interests in this way will create a *settlement* which will be more exactly defined later.

While terminology is being discussed, two terms, *freehold* and *leasehold*, frequently seen on advertisement boards, ought to be explained. The freehold, as we have seen, simply means the fee simple or absolute ownership. All land in England is freehold because someone somewhere always owns the fee simple of a particular piece of land. When that person has leased it, for instance for 50 years, and only the leasehold interest is being offered for sale, the land may be referred to as leasehold. There is a freehold to the land also: and consists of the landlord's fee simple, which of course is in reversion and will not entitle him to possession again until the lease has expired. Meanwhile, however, it does entitle him to receive the rent from his tenant. This freehold can be sold even while the lease is still running, whereupon the purchaser acquires the right to receive the rent for the remaining years of the lease and then the right to possession.

WHY REFORM WAS NECESSARY

Land law was well suited to the purposes for which it was originally most required, that is family endowment in a subsistence economy. Before 1926, when important changes were made to the law, there were three ways in which a person could settle his land for this purpose if, to take a very simple example, he wished to benefit his wife *W* and his son *S* only.

1 He could grant legal estates to both as follows: 'to *W* for life and then to *S* in fee simple'.

2 He could pass the legal fee simple to trustees and direct them to hold it for the benefit of *W* for life and then for *S* in fee simple. Here *W* and *S* have equitable interests for life and in fee simple respectively.

3 He could do exactly the same as in 2 above but order the trustees to sell the land and allow *W* and *S* to enjoy their interests out of the proceeds of sale. This arrangement is a 'settlement by way of trust for sale'. The life interest is satisfied after sale by allowing the owner of the life interest to take the annual investment income from the proceeds of sale for the period of his life. The capital sum in the form of investments represents the fee simple interest and in the present example will pass entirely to *S* after *W*'s death.

In these ways the needs of various members of a family can be satisfied as long as they live. Another example, however, will show that land law was not nearly so well suited to the world of commerce, which after the 18th century made increasing demands on land. What would be the position in the case of land settled as described above, if *X*, proposing to build a factory, wished to buy some of the land for that purpose? Certainly he would want land of which he could take immediate possession and which he and his successors could occupy for a very long time. He would therefore require either a fee simple in possession or a very long term of years in possession.

Suppose, in this instance, that the land was settled by the first method mentioned above, as was often the case in 18th century England. There is no person who can offer *X* the kind of interest he wishes to buy. *W*'s interest is of too indefinite duration. What is the good of building a factory on land and then being unable to use it because *W* has died? On the other hand, if he purchased *S*'s interest it might not give the right to possession for many years. In fact *X*'s purpose could only be achieved if both *W* and *S* were willing to sell their interests, or unless, as was often the case in well-drafted settlements, special powers of sale had been included.

Even if the land could be sold, the purchaser would have the expense of investigating not only his vendor's title to the land, but possibly that of several other owners of legal estates in the land. Even in the rudimentary example given above, both *W* and *S* might have dealt with their own interests in some way such as by sale or mortgage. Finally, in those cases where the land was rendered unsaleable by settlements, this inability to sell might be as harmful to the beneficiaries and to the land itself as it was inconvenient to the prospective purchaser, for there might be too much land and too little money to develop it. None of these difficulties existed, however, if the land had been settled by the third method. There was power, indeed a duty, to sell the fee simple owned by the trustees; a purchaser would have only the trustees' legal title to investigate and each has an identical title. The interests of the beneficiaries could be ignored by the purchaser since they were intended to be satisfied out of the purchase money paid to the trustees.

There were other reasons why land law was in need of an overhaul. Before 1926 it contained too many outmoded rules and fictions, such as the doctrine of tenure. Furthermore, the gulf between the law of freehold land on the one hand and that of leaseholds and ordinary objects on the other was unnecessarily wide. For instance, when a person died intestate, his freehold land went to his 'heir', which was usually his eldest son, whereas land which he held on lease went to his 'next-of-kin', who constituted a much wider class.

Reform did not come in one rush in 1925. Changes had been made throughout the 19th century. The Settled Land Act 1882 gave power to the owner of a life interest in possession under a settlement to sell the fee simple even though he did not own it. This helped to solve the problem of the unsaleability of land illustrated above. The life tenant of course could only take his life interest out of the resultant purchase money, the capital of which had to be carefully safeguarded for the other beneficiaries. This translation of rights in land into rights in the purchase money on sale is known as *overreaching*. Other reforms were carried out which were radical enough to have been left alone by the 1925 legislation. The Acts passed in 1925 were the culmination of the process but left a vast body of old law intact. They were primarily aimed at facilitating conveyancing but this involved changes in land law of a major kind. Further amendments and new principles of law have been brought into force by statutes passed since 1925. The changes made in that year, however, were so far-reaching that Chapter 2 will be devoted to a summary of their more fundamental effects. The detailed provisions of the Acts will be dealt with in the following chapters as and when they become appropriate to the particular topic under discussion.

THE IMPORTANCE OF A STUDY PERSPECTIVE

An overall perspective of any complex study is vital to its understanding. The main roads should be learnt before cul de sacs or housing estates. Ask any taxi driver. Table 1.1 attempts to provide an initial bird's eye view of the subject. You should, however, constantly refer to it during your study of individual topics. The layout is intended to integrate two fundamental themes in land law. The first theme is that interests in land can be divided into two classes. The first class contains all those interests which give you the right to occupy the land itself, such as ownership or a lease. The second class contains interests which do not give you occupation but merely a right to do or restrain something on another person's land, such as a right of way, which is one kind of easement.

The second theme is that of the difference between legal and equitable interests. We have already seen that equitable interests can be created under a trust. This can only occur in regard to interests giving the right to occupy the land itself. Thus *A* can convey a fee simple or lease to a trustee *T* to hold on trust absolutely for *B*. In such a case there will be an equitable fee simple, or lease, held by *B*, while *T* will hold the legal fee simple or lease.

We must now note that there is one other way in which equitable interests can be created. Generally, a legal interest, whether giving a right to the land itself or merely to rights in or over someone else's land, must be created by a deed. Failure to conform with this requirement might produce unfair results. For instance, if *A* agreed to grant *B* an easement such as right of way over his land in return for money, then paid, but the deed was not executed, at common law *B* could not exert his right against *A*. The common law recognised no easement in such a case. The courts of equity however at an early stage in our history, though recognising that no legal interest had arisen, considered *B* to have a right enforceable in the sense that they would order *A* to execute a deed to complete the transaction. Meanwhile *B* was considered to hold an equitable interest. Thus, there can be legal and equitable easements. The same principle applies to interests giving the right to the land itself. Therefore if *A* has contracted to sell his fee simple to *B*, but has not yet conveyed it by deed, *A* owns the legal fee simple and *B* owns the equitable fee simple.

There are two exceptions to this fundamental feature of land law – that all interests can exist in both legal and equitable modes. First, the *restrictive covenant*. This is the right to restrict the use of land occupied by another. It can only exist as an equitable interest. This is because it was invented late in our legal history by the Court of Equity and was unknown to the common law. Second, certain interests which formerly could exist both at law and in equity can, since 1925, exist only in equity. This will be explained in Chapter 2.

Table 1.1

	Interests capable of existing as legal interests	*Interests capable of existing as equitable interests*
Rights to the land itself	Absolute ownership (Fee simple absolute in possession) Leases	Absolute ownership (Fee simple absolute in possession) Conditional ownership (e.g. until marriage) } Only in equity since 1925 Life interests } Only in equity since 1925 Entailed interests Leases
Rights in or over another person's land	Easements Profits Mortgages	Easements Profits Mortgages Restrictive covenants

Reference to Table 1.1 should be made when the various interests are considered in later chapters. Detailed explanation will be given in those chapters.

CONSTANT DEVELOPMENT OF LAND LAW

Land fulfils so many needs in society that the law must constantly develop to balance those needs. Sometimes this evolution is reflected in entirely new codes of rules. The Housing Act 1980 and the Town and Country Planning Act 1990 are just two modern examples. They both respond to the problems of a large urbanised population in a highly industrialised country. But sometimes changes are more difficult to discern. They occur over a long period of time through judicial decisions or legislation less spectacular than that mentioned above. Changing values in society often affect judicial policy in the appellate courts. A few examples are mentioned below, though the topics are discussed in detail in later chapters.

1 There are signs that the rigid distinction between interests in land and personal rights relating to land is breaking down.

2 Occupation of property as a home attracts judicial and legislative attention.

3 While the married state still enjoys the greatest privileges under the law, other forms of cohabitation receive more recognition than formerly.

4 The impact of marital breakdown on home ownership and occupation is having a profound influence on land law.

The account of land law which follows attempts to provide a foundation of general principles, not only as a basis for the study of conveyancing but for the other specialised subjects which have sprung up in response to the modern role of land in our society. It is not possible to discuss these specialised codes in any detail in a book of this length. It is essential to an appreciation of land law as a living force, however, to recognise their enormous importance and to take account of new social needs and interests which might affect the future policy of judges and Parliament. It is also necessary to observe how existing legal rules are sometimes used for purposes for which they were not designed, by persons wishing to avoid certain legal consequences.

It is still possible to see strong connections between the old and the new. Freehold possession was protected over several centuries for the sake of peace and stability, pending some more permanent resolution of disputed ownership. This favour for the person presently under some roof continues today. Eviction of tenants by landlords, for instance, is generally prohibited except through court order, even though the tenancy has ended. Preservation of minor injustices can sometimes, paradoxically, keep a society at peace better than a too dynamic furtherance of abstract justice.

HOW PROPERTY IS ACQUIRED

Brief mention may be made here of how interests in land can be acquired and created. Further details will be given when those various interests are dealt with. Some methods of acquisition are of general application. Others are peculiar to certain interests only.

All interests in land, whether they give rights to the land itself or to rights in or over land belonging to another person, may be created or transferred by deed. The Law of Property (Miscellaneous Provisions) Act 1989 s 1 has abolished the requirement of a seal in the case of individual persons, as opposed to corporations, for deeds executed on or after 31 July 1990. The document must, however, be intended, from its face, to be a deed and be signed by the individuals in the presence of an attesting witness. If some other person, such as a purchaser, agrees to perform some act, then he must also sign the deed. Thus if I convey the fee simple in 'Blackacre' to you, I must sign the deed of conveyance. If you agree to do something in regard to 'Blackacre', however, such as not to use it for industrial purposes and this is expressed in the deed, you also must sign the document. The transaction is completed by delivering the deed to the person in whose favour the interest has been created. A deed of conveyance is shown on pages 16 and 17.

If the law insisted strictly upon the general rule that the appropriate way of creating an interest is by deed, unjust results would sometimes follow. Additional methods have therefore been allowed. Two of these apply to all interests in land. First, contracts must be considered. Although a valid contract to transfer or create an interest in land can save a transaction from being a nullity, it does not transfer the interest in question, but places the intended transferee in a position to demand that this be done. Sometimes such agreements are intermediate transactions only. Conveyances of land, for instance, are generally preceded by the exchange of contracts to convey. Sometimes, however, an owner will purport actually to convey his interest by a document which is not a deed. The law has been indulgent in such cases and treats such documents as contracts to convey the interests in question.

The second general exception concerns the doctrine of *proprietary estoppel*. This doctrine is discussed in Chapter 7 in regard to licences, since it has been particularly active in that field. Yet the principle can apply to the acquisition of any interest in land. It must be emphasised, however, that this is an exceptional manner of acquiring an interest. It is sufficient to note here that where an owner permits another person to spend money or to alter detrimentally his position in the expectation that he will enjoy some privilege in that land, the owner will be prevented by the court from acting inconsistently with this expectation, and might also be ordered to convey an interest in the land commensurate with that expectation.

Alternative methods to the deed sometimes apply only to certain types of interest. Certain short leases for instance can be created by mere writing or even orally. Easements and profits can be created by long enjoyment of the activity in question. Once again, the acquiescence of the landowner and the expectations of the person exercising the particular activity over his land lie at the foundations of the principle. Finally, interests giving rights to the ownership of land itself can be acquired by long possession adverse to the owner's rights. This principle has long been recognised by statute. The law on the topic is now contained in the Limitation Act 1980. This topic is discussed more fully in Chapter 8.

CAPACITY

Certain classes of persons are disabled from exercising some of the normal incidents of ownership over their property. The prohibition is usually imposed because the persons affected are considered to be in need of protection. This calls for discussion of minority, mentally disordered persons, corporations and charities.

Under the Family Law Reform Act 1969, a minor is a person who has not reached the age of eighteen (s 1). The following are the main restrictions upon a minor's powers in regard to land.

1 *Legal estates.* A minor cannot hold a legal estate in land (Law of Property Act ('LPA') 1925, s 1(6)). He can however own equitable interests. An attempt to convey a legal estate to a minor, or to two or more minors jointly, operates as an agreement for valuable consideration to execute a settlement in their favour and meanwhile to hold the land in trust for them (Settled Land Act 1925 s 27(1)). An attempt to convey a legal estate to a minor jointly with one or more other persons of full age vests the legal estate in those others on a statutory trust for sale for themselves and the minor as co-owners in equity (LPA 1925 s 19(2)). These matters are dealt with in Chapter 9.

2 *Wills.* A minor cannot make a will unless he is a serviceman in actual military service or a 'mariner at sea' (Wills Act 1837 s 7). The laws of intestacy apply to his property in the ordinary way except that under the Administration of Estates Act 1925 s 51(3), if a minor dies without having married and entitled to an equitable interest in fee simple, he is deemed to have died owning an *entailed interest*. Entailed interests are discussed in Chapter 5. This provision is designed on the assumption that the settlor would have, in such a case, preferred a reversion to himself rather than to have the property pass to a distant relation of the minor.

A mentally disordered person is generally capable of holding property. Wide powers relating to the property of such persons, when not so capable, are now vested in nominated judges of the Chancery Division under the Mental Health Act 1983, which should be consulted for further details.

Statutory corporations are subject to the *ultra vires* rule and therefore their powers to hold and deal with land must be discovered from their constitutions. Subject to this, corporations may acquire and dispose of land in the same way as natural persons.

The Charities Act 1992 has considerably liberated the powers of the trustees of charities to dispose of land subject to certain safeguards. Details should be sought in the Act.

A deed of Conveyance

THIS CONVEYANCE is made the 9th day of May 1983 BETWEEN JOHN QUINCE of 20 Athenia Wood Road Arden Warwickshire ('The Vendor') and MARY MOTH of 10 Starveling Lane Lysandford Warwickshire ('the Purchaser').

WHEREAS the Vendor is seised of the property hereby conveyed for an estate in fee simple absolute in possession free from incumbrances and has agreed with the Purchaser for the sale thereof to her for the sum of £30 000.

NOW THIS DEED WITNESSETH as follows:

1 In pursuance of the agreement and in consideration of £30 000 now paid by the Purchaser to the Vendor (receipt hereby acknowledged) the Vendor as beneficial owner hereby conveys unto the Purchaser ALL THAT property known as 20 Athenia Wood Road Arden Warwickshire and for the purpose of identification only edged by thick lines on the plan annexed hereto TO HOLD unto the Purchaser in fee simple.

2 The Purchaser hereby covenants with intent that this covenant shall enure to the benefit of the Vendor his successors and assigns and others claiming under him to that property owned by him adjoining the property hereby conveyed and known as 18 Athenia Wood Road Arden aforesaid that the property hereby conveyed shall not be used for the purposes of the trade of carpentry.

3 IT IS HEREBY CERTIFIED THAT the transaction hereby effected does not form part of a larger

transaction or a series of transactions in respect of which the amount or value or the aggregate amount or value of the consideration exceeds £30 000.

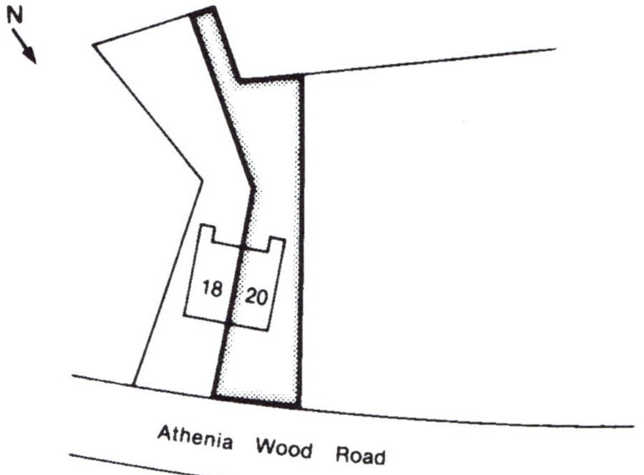

Scale 1:500

IN WITNESS whereof the parties hereto have hereunto set their hands and seals the day and year first before written.

Signed Sealed and Delivered by JOHN QUINCE — John Quince

in the presence of:– R Bottom
14, Wild Thyme Bank
Arden
Warwickshire

Mary Moth

Signed Sealed and Delivered by MARY MOTH in the presence of:– C. Mustardseed
2, Willowshop Pool
Lysandford

STUDY MATERIAL

The deed of conveyance

On pages 16 and 17 is a simple example of a deed of conveyance. You will notice that it contains a restrictive covenant because the Vendor wishes to protect neighbouring property retained by him against competition in the carpentry trade which he carries on in that property. Since the Purchaser is making the covenant she must also execute the deed.

The statement under Clause 3 of the conveyance is known as a 'certificate of value'. Stamp duty is payable on all property transactions in excess of the figure determined by current taxation law. The clause certifies that the transaction is a truly separate one and has not been broken up in order to evade this duty.

QUESTIONS

1 What is the importance of tenure in modern land law?

2 *O*, the legal owner in fee simple of land, created a restrictive covenant, an equitable interest, in favour of his neighbour, *N*. Later, *O* sold his legal fee simple in his land to *P*. Advise *P* as to whether he is bound by the restrictive covenant.

3 *O*, the owner in fee simple of 'Blackacre', created the following interests in that land:

(a) a life interest in favour of *A*, to be followed by
(b) a life interest in favour of *B*, to be followed by
(c) a life interest in favour of *C*.

Describe the nature of *O*'s interest in 'Blackacre' as a consequence of these transactions.

4 Why was English land law deficient in the face of the requirements of land transfer in the middle of the nineteenth century?

CHAPTER 2

THE GENERAL EFFECTS OF THE 1925 LEGISLATION

The following Acts comprise 'the 1925 legislation':

The unrepealed parts of the Law of Property Act 1922
The unrepealed parts of the Law of Property Act 1924
The Law of Property Act 1925
The Administration of Estates Act 1925
The Settled Land Act 1925
The Land Charges Act 1925
The Trustee Act 1925
The Land Registration Act 1925

All these came into force on 1 January 1926. The Acts of 1922 and 1924 contained many preliminary radical reforms but most of their provisions were repealed before they came into force and were absorbed into the Acts of 1925. As can be seen from their titles, each deals with a particular subject, with the Law of Property Act 1925 occupying a central position in the scheme of reform. Various amendments have been made to these Acts since 1925, but they will be mentioned later when the particular matters to which they refer are dealt with. The Land Charges Act 1925, as amended, has now been consolidated in the Land Charges Act 1972 and the Local Land Charges Act 1975.

The general manner of interpretation of the Acts was discussed by the House of Lords in *Grey* v *IRC* [1960] AC 1, at p 13. Although they are consolidating Acts, and the presumption is that consolidating Acts do not change the law, this presumption does not apply because they consolidate Acts which were themselves amending Acts. Accordingly the Acts of 1925, like the Acts of 1922 and 1924, must be construed simply so as to give each word 'the meaning proper to it in its context'.

The Acts achieved the following general effects: the final emasculation of the doctrine of tenures; the closer approximation of land law with the law of personalty; the reduction in number of legal estates in land; the extension of the systems of registration of charges and registration of title; and the abrogation of miscellaneous outmoded rules.

An appreciation of the general strategy of the Acts simplifies the understanding of their technical detail. This strategy was to reconcile two conflicting interests, the family and the market. The former was the aristocratic purpose of keeping land in the family. The latter was the modern need, brought about by the agrarian and industrial revolutions, that land should be available for sale on the commercial market.

THE FINAL EMASCULATION OF THE DOCTRINE OF TENURES

As explained in Chapter 1, apart from leaseholds, there is now only one tenure, socage. This was achieved by the Administration of Estates Act 1925 s 56, which abolished frankalmoign, already a dead letter, and the Law of Property Act 1922 s 128, which enfranchised all copyhold land by converting it into socage tenure. The other forms of tenure had already been abolished long before 1926. It has already been explained that, since the conditions and services on which land might be held had disappeared, and therefore land could not be claimed by the Crown for their non-performance, tenure is now obsolete and land may be considered as being susceptible to absolute ownership. It has been mentioned, however, that there are a few exceptional cases where incidents remain today. These must now be dealt with.

Some of the conditions or 'incidents' subject to which copyhold land was held before 1926 were, unlike other tenures, still very valuable either to the person who held the land or to the person of whom it was held. To have abolished all these peremptorily would have been an unjust act of confiscation. Some were extinguished at once and others were allowed to continue for a few more years, and all have now disappeared. The Act provided for the payment of compensation where appropriate. A third class, however, was allowed to continue permanently unless the persons entitled to the benefit and burden of the incidents agreed in writing in particular cases to discharge them upon payment of compensation. This class comprises:

1 any commonable right such as a right of pasture attached to the enfranchised land. Thus if such a right existed over other land in favour of copyhold land before 1926, it continues today, despite enfranchisement, until otherwise agreed between the parties;

2 any rights or liabilities existing in favour of or against the land in respect of mines, minerals, or rights of entry and way to win or search for minerals. The minerals in question may be under the enfranchised land or other land;

3 any liability of the enfranchised land to incidents in respect of fairs, markets, hunting or the taking of game, fish and fowl;

4 any right or liability in favour of or against the enfranchised land relating to the construction, maintenance or cleansing of any dykes, ditches, canals, sea

or river walls, ways and other works for the protection of land or preventing nuisances on them.

It should not be assumed, whenever rights and liabilities of the types mentioned above are met, that the land concerned was necessarily copyhold before 1926. Such rights may be created by landowners by ordinary private negotiation, in which case the Act does not apply. It only applies to these rights and liabilities when they are attributable to the fact that the land was once copyhold.

These are the only substantial remnants of the doctrine of tenure. Detached and inconsequential rootlets may still be unearthed which have a curiosity value (see 51 LQR 347 and 361 and *Re Lowe's Will Trust* [1973] 2 All ER 1136). We may now put the whole question of tenure to bed in the following way. All land in England may be absolutely owned. The only vestige of tenure is that there may be certain rights and liabilities, as described above, attaching to land which used to be copyhold. Enquiry must be made when buying land. There is now no question of land being forfeited as a result of them, though, of course, like any other legal liability, they must be observed.

THE FURTHER APPROXIMATION OF LAND LAW TO THE LAW OF PERSONALTY

Land law, so important in feudal society, developed precociously in comparison with other branches of law. But early development sometimes means early obsolescence and English land law in the 19th century still betrayed its feudal origins, whereas the law of personal property wore a more modern aspect. However, one part of land law, the law of leaseholds, developing later and outside feudal influence, reflected more of the modern rules. Indeed, even today, leaseholds are classified as *personalty*, though this strange classification merely reflects their historical origin and its implications do not go very deep. It is important mainly for descriptive purposes. Thus a gift by will of 'all my personal property' will carry land held by the testator on a lease. It does not mean that a leaseholder has a merely personal or contractual right to the land. Emphatically he has a real right, good against the whole world.

Complete identity of land law with the law of personalty is hardly possible considering the difference in subject-matter, but the 1925 legislation represents the culmination of the attempt to go as far in that direction as possible. The following steps were taken, although the significance of some of these may not be fully appreciated at this early stage of study.

1 *Descent on intestacy.* For centuries before 1926 a man had been able to dispose of land as well as personalty by will as he chose. Yet the destination of the two types of property differed if he died intestate. Personal property was distributed amongst the next of kin, which included a range of close relations, though the spouse and children were preferred. In the case of land,

excluding leaseholds, special rules of inheritance, which were feudal in origin but developed by common law and statute, dictated that it should descend upon the 'heir', a technical term which should never be used loosely. Suffice it to say here that they usually favoured the eldest son to the exclusion of all others including the wife and younger children of the deceased.

The Administration of Estates Act 1925 s 46 (as later amended) now applies a new code of distribution on intestacy to *realty* and *personalty* alike. It takes account of the close relations and in particular the surviving spouse and children. In the absence of such relations, property goes to the Crown as *bona vacantia*. The rules of inheritance, however, have been retained to govern the intestate succession to the entail (which interest will be described later), in deference to the traditions of aristocratic families who have employed entails in order to keep land descending to a single owner instead of being divided.

2 *Methods of mortgaging the fee simple and the term of years*. Mortgages of both types of interest are now carried out by conveying a term of years to the lender of the money as a security for the debt (LPA 1925 ss 85 and 86). In the case of a mortgage of a term of years this is achieved by creating a sub-lease, which is a term of years granted by the owner of a term of years and which is of less duration than the term he himself owns. The mortgage of a fee simple is carried out by granting the lender a term of, say, 3000 years, while the mortgage of a term of, say, 100 years' duration is effected by granting the lender a sub-term of, say, 99 years and 51 weeks. A new alternative method of mortgaging land called a 'charge by way of legal mortgage' is now possible under the Act and applies to mortgages both of the fee simple and of the term of years. This new method has gradually supplanted the mortgage by grant of a term of years. Before 1926 the fee simple was mortgaged by conveying the fee simple itself to the lender as a security until repayment of the debt.

3 *Personalty can now be entailed*. Before 1926 an entail could not be created in leasehold or other personal property. It may now be created in any form of property (LPA 1925 s 130). Here, therefore, the older law provided the example for reform.

4 *General abolition of the need for words of limitation*. When a fee simple or entail was conveyed by deed before 1926, special technical words, known as 'words of limitation', had to be used. A mistake could mean that the interest would fail to pass. In the transfer of other forms of property, what mattered was the intention of the grantor as gathered from the words used; no special form of words was necessary. The Law of Property Act 1925 s 60(1) provides that words of limitation are no longer necessary and that, on a conveyance of freehold land, the fee simple or other whole interest which the grantor had power to convey shall pass unless the contrary intention appears. The old strict rules have however been retained for the entail.

THE REDUCTION OF LEGAL ESTATES TO TWO

The difficulties caused by splitting the legal fee simple were considered in the previous chapter. Where land was granted 'to *A* for life with remainder in fee simple to *B*', there was no person for the time being independently capable of selling the absolute ownership of the land. The difficulties could be overcome however by conveying the fee simple to trustees with a direction or power to sell and to allow *A* and *B* to take equivalent benefits from the purchase money.

The policy of the 1925 legislation was to make it impossible to split the legal fee simple, so that the absolute ownership would always be available for sale. Accordingly, the Law of Property Act 1925 s 1(1), elemental in modern land law, enacts:

> The only estates in land which are capable of subsisting or of being conveyed or created at law are:
> (a) An estate in fee simple absolute in possession;
> (b) A term of years absolute.

So far as rights to the land itself are concerned, all others such as life interests, entails and even fees simple not in possession (such as *B*'s in the example above) may only exist in equity. The term of years absolute will be dealt with later, but the result is that there is always a fee simple presently available for sale in any land.

The part played by the Settled Land Act 1925 may be illustrated by referring again to the example above. The legal fee simple absolute in possession is held by a trustee in trust for *A* for life and for *B* in fee simple. Both *A*'s and *B*'s interests are equitable. This trustee holds and can, if desirable, sell what a prospective purchaser will want to buy – the absolute ownership. If a sale occurs, these equitable interests are satisfied out of the purchase money and no longer affect the land in the hands of the purchaser. They are overreached. The doctrine of overreaching was thus extended as a necessary corollary to the reduction in legal estates that may exist. Such a simplification of the law was achieved at a price. It clearly means that when land is settled there is no guarantee that the beneficiaries will enjoy the land in specie.

The Law of Property Act 1925 s 1(1) only refers to rights to the land itself. Certain rights in or over the land of another which may still exist both as legal and equitable interests are listed in s 1(2). Easements are an example. These interests, however, may not be legal unless they are created to endure for the equivalent of a fee simple absolute or a term of years; that is, they must be perpetual or for a definite time. Thus an easement to last for a lifetime must be equitable, while one to endure for ten years may be legal. As a matter of terminology, it is convenient to call the two rights in land named in s 1(1) *estates* and all other rights to the land itself, necessarily equitable, together with all rights in or over the land of another, whether legal or equitable, *interests*. An easement to last 100 years, therefore, is a legal interest; a right to occupy land for life is an equitable interest. The Act does not, however, stick scrupulously to this nomenclature. Finally, while the only estates which can be legal are the two in s 1(1), the Act does not say they must necessarily be legal. Both may be equitable. Thus a fee simple absolute in possession may be held by trustees on trust for *A* absolutely, in which case *A* will have an equitable fee simple absolute in possession.

Section 1 is fundamental to a mastery of modern land law. It must be applied word for word with the utmost rigour. If this is done it will be found to be a wonderful guide. Its implications are never contradictory.

DEVELOPMENT OF THE DOCTRINE OF NOTICE THROUGH REGISTRATION OF LAND CHARGES

One weakness of an equitable interest is that it does not bind a purchaser in good faith for value of a legal estate in the land without notice of the equitable interest. A legal interest is, however, enforceable against all. In establishing whether a person had notice of an equitable interest the courts employed tests which were difficult to apply. These rules were somewhat modified by statute. Notice could be of three kinds, namely: *actual notice*, *constructive notice*, or *imputed notice*.

Actual notice is almost self-explanatory. It simply means that the purchaser knows of the equitable interest. This knowledge however must be from a source sufficiently authentic to 'operate upon the mind of any rational man or man of business and make him act with reference to the knowledge he has acquired' (*Lloyd* v *Banks* (1868) 3 ChApp 488, at 491). Statements made in casual conversation, therefore, do not impart actual notice. Even though a person has no actual notice, however, the circumstances may affect him with constructive notice.

Constructive notice is knowledge which would have been revealed 'if such inquiries and inspections had been made as ought reasonably to have been made' (LPA 1925 s 199). Thus a purchaser has constructive notice of all rights which would have come to light if he had investigated the title to land for the period specified by the law for those cases where the parties to the transaction have not agreed otherwise. This period is a minimum of 15 years (LPA 1925 s 44, as amended by LPA 1969 s 23). A prudent purchaser should inspect the land as well as the vendor's title to it. The physical signs of a right of way for life over property might well be notice of this equitable easement, whether or not the purchaser inspects the land. In short, the rules as to constructive notice prevent a purchaser merely turning a blind eye so as to escape actual notice. On the other hand, the restricted form in which the Law of Property Act 1925 s 199 is expressed suggests that the doctrine will not be further expanded.

Imputed notice is the actual or constructive notice which an agent acting for a purchaser in that transaction receives in his capacity as agent (LPA 1925 s 199). Knowledge gained in this way by a solicitor acting for the purchaser of a house, for instance, will be deemed to be notice to that purchaser. If an agent acts for both parties in a transaction, such notice to the agent is normally imputed to both parties to the transaction.

Although these tests are based on sound ethical foundations, and have worked justly in many cases, they do lack precision and certainty. The Land Charges Act 1925 therefore introduced what was virtually a new system of safeguarding certain rights in land, and where it applies it dispenses with these tests. A state register – the *Land Charges Register* – was opened, and the registration of certain eligible interests in it is deemed to constitute notice to the whole world (LPA 1925 s 198). For instance, if a restrictive covenant was imposed on my neighbour's land before the Act, preventing him from building, and this covenant was intended to protect the amenities of my land, the covenant amounts to an interest of mine in the land of another, my neighbour. As we shall see later, it is an equitable interest. If my neighbour sells his fee simple to *P*, who gives value and has no notice of the covenant, *P* will take the land free of it and may therefore build upon it. Generally *P*'s notice will come from an inspection of the title deeds.

If, however, the covenant had been made after the Act, I could register it. Such registration would constitute permanent notice of my interest to all, so that no one will be able to buy my neighbour's land free of the covenant. Prospective purchasers of land, therefore, always search at the Land Charges Registry before completing a purchase. The request for a search is a simple process which may be carried out entirely by post for a small fee. Even if a purchaser does not carry out a search, he is nevertheless deemed to have notice of any entries against the land on the register. On the other hand, if a registrable interest is not registered a purchaser will not be affected by his own knowledge of that interest. We may therefore say that the fact of registration or non-registration at the time of the completion of purchase is conclusive as to notice.

In this way, precision and certainty were achieved, for whether an interest is registered or not permits no argument. They were gained, however, at the cost of some ethical principle, for it is now possible to take unscrupulous advantage of a person's carelessness in failing to register an interest. The process and effects of registration will be dealt with when the particular registrable interests are discussed, and a more comprehensive account will be given separately in Chapter 17. But the following matters must be mentioned at this stage. First, not all equitable interests are registrable and in these cases the old doctrine as to notice continues to apply, unless the interest is one which can be overreached, such as a life interest under a settlement. Equitable interests under a trust like this do not need the protection of the register because the Acts dealing with trusts provide their own special protection. We have already seen that a purchaser may take land free of such interests even though he knows of them, for they may be overreached and transferred to the purchase-money.

Second, a few legal rights are now registrable. Legal rights were always secure whether a purchaser of land knew of them or not, so that the system of registration was applied here not as a substitute for an existing doctrine of notice, but in order to provide a prospective purchaser with readily accessible information about third-party rights of which he might otherwise be unaware. Since the results of failing to register those legal rights which are registrable are similar to the results of failing to register eligible equitable interests, the position of such legal interests has been weakened by the Act. As failure to register them may result in a purchaser of the land taking free of them, this newly imposed risk might be considered a sharp incentive for the owners of such interests to make their existence known to the unwary purchaser through registration.

Finally, the Land Charges Act 1925 even created variations in the concept of the purchaser of the legal estate for value without notice. Sometimes the purchaser must take a legal estate in the land in order to take free of an unregistered interest; sometimes it is enough that he purchases any interest in the land, legal or equitable. Sometimes the price he pays must be 'valuable consideration'; sometimes it must be 'money or money's worth'. The application of these formulae will be considered later when the various registrable interests are being discussed.

'Money or money's worth' means all forms of consideration and also the payment of an existing debt. The consideration, however, need not represent the full value of the interest purchased. The consideration of marriage is not included. 'Valuable consideration' is a wider term including all that is meant by 'money or money's worth' together with the consideration of a future marriage. When a future marriage is the consideration given it is deemed to have been given not only by the parties to it, but also by the issue, as, for instance, grandchildren (*Macdonald* v *Scott* [1893] AC 642, per Lord Herschell, LC, at 650).

The purchaser can be affected by a registration entered at any time before completion of the purchase even after contracts have been exchanged. A purchase is not completed until the interest is finally transferred to the purchaser and, where the consideration consists of money or other payment, this has been paid over.

THE FURTHER DEVELOPMENT OF THE SYSTEM OF REGISTRATION OF TITLE

The Land Registration Act 1925 continued and developed the policy, begun in the last century, of applying by degrees the system of registration of title to the whole country. At this point the opportunity will be taken of giving a most elementary account of the unreformed system of conveyancing, first because it is necessary to an understanding of land law in any case, and, second, so that the reformed system of registered conveyancing may be appreciated.

Conveyancing is the transfer of interests in land. The study of conveyancing concerns the various methods of transferring these interests, the precautions that should be taken before they are purchased, and their protection after purchase. Ordinary chattels may be transferred from one person to another simply by delivery. Interests in land, however, are transferred by words. Sometimes these words must be contained in a deed but sometimes mere writing or even oral words may be enough. Let us take the common case of the transfer of a fee simple from *A* to *B*. All that is necessary is that a deed should be written stating '*A* hereby conveys unto *B* "Blackacre" in fee simple'. *A* then executes the deed. Before 31 July 1990 this was done by *A* putting his name to it with a seal and delivering it to *B*, whereupon the property passed. The Law of Property (Miscellaneous Provisions) Act 1989 s 1 abolished the need for a seal in any deed made on or after that date by individuals, as opposed to corporations. The instrument must, however, on its face be intended as a deed. Furthermore, the signature of the executor must be attested by a witness present at the time of signing. In practice, of course, the deed contains other information for the purposes of clarity, such as the full names and addresses of the parties, an accurate description of the property, the date, the purchase price and, preferably, a ground plan. Other matters are frequently added because they are part of the arrangement agreed between the parties. In short, while a conveyance primarily passes property, it may also be the occasion for other transactions and declarations.

Before *B* commits himself to buying the land, however, he will wish to be sure of two things. First, he will require proof that the fee simple is *A*'s to sell, for even though *A* is living in the property he may only own a life interest or a lease. Second, he must know whether there are any third-party rights already existing in or over the land, such as an easement. To a lesser extent, the same may apply when a chattel is purchased, but in that case much greater assumptions are made. If a person is in possession of a chattel and states that he owns it, then, unless there is positive ground for suspicion, you readily accept that he is owner. As for third-party rights over chattels, these are uncommon and may, in ordinary circumstances, be discounted. You cannot, for instance, have a right of way over a ship, and even if it is used as security for a debt, the creditor will not usually allow the owner to remain in possession of it.

Therefore what *B* will insist on seeing, before he buys the land from *A*, is proof that it was conveyed in the past to *A* by a conveyance and, to dispel doubt as to whether even the person who conveyed it to *A* owned it himself, a complete record of all the conveyances up to that time for such a period as to raise an irrebuttable inference that *A* really owns the land. Considering that the Limitation Act 1980, and similar statutes in the past, place a time limit on the recovery of land by a true owner, a purchaser does not really need to investigate the title, as outlined above, over a very long period. The vendor and purchaser can agree whatever period of investigation they like, but unless they agree otherwise the period is 15 years (LPA 1969 s 23). This minimum period, however, must commence with some particular transaction called the *root of title* so that in practice the period investigated might be considerably greater. As *B* also wishes to know of all third-party rights in or over the land he will make a search at the Land Charges Registry and will also wish to know the full contents of the deeds, but as noticed above, some rights in land are acquired even without writing, and do not require registration. *B* must therefore ask searching questions of *A* as to the existence of these.

Finally, there are many restrictions on land use which are imposed under statutory authority. Local authorities have power to refuse permission for developing land, to purchase property compulsorily and to require living accommodation to conform to certain standards. These matters are discussed in Chapter 4. A purchaser of land will wish to discover the extent of such restrictions before entering any agreement. Many such restrictions can be discovered by arranging for a search in the local land charges register which is maintained by the local district council. Such *local searches* will be accompanied by a questionnaire seeking information about such matters as responsibility for maintenance of roads adjoining the property, proposals for new roads in the vicinity, town and country planning decisions, proximity of sewers, building regulations, slum clearance plans and smoke control.

In regard to the inspection of the deeds, *A* does not simply hand them over to *B* for inspection, for *B* might use them for a fraudulent purpose. Instead, *A* will summarize the contents of all the deeds in an *abstract of title*, which is a kind of pedigree of the land. Before completing the purchase, *B* will check the accuracy of the abstract against the deeds and will take possession not only of the deed of conveyance to him from *A*, but also of all the earlier deeds and other documents.

The following example may help to illustrate the main process in a conveyance of the fee simple in 'Blackacre', which is unregistered land. First, we will set out the modern history of the land by showing the transactions that have occurred.

1920	*A* conveys 'Blackacre' to *B*	Deed 1
1930	*B* conveys 'Blackacre' to *C*	Deed 2
(*C* makes a restrictive covenant in favour of *B*)		
1980	*C* conveys 'Blackacre' to *D*	Deed 3
1985	*D* conveys 'Blackacre' to *E*	Deed 4
1987	*E* conveys 'Blackacre' to *F*	Deed 5

G now wishes, in 1996, to buy 'Blackacre' from *F* for £60 000. In very broad terms, this is how he goes about it.

He sees the land advertised, decides he would like it and approaches *F*, who says that he will accept £60 000 for it. Such an agreement is not made binding at that moment, but is simply a settlement of price. *G* and *F* now usually instruct their solicitors to act. The principal stages thereafter are as follows:

1 A search is made of the Land Registry index map to ensure that the title really is unregistered, for if the title to the land is registered, a different system of conveyancing is followed, as we shall shortly see. This is explained in Chapter 18 and need not detain us now.

2 An application for a mortgage will be made to a building society if *G* needs a loan.

3 A list of fairly standard questions (*Enquiries Before Contract*) is sent to *F*'s solicitor. The questions seek general information regarding boundaries, insurance policies, drainage and other services, shared facilities, adverse rights, fixtures, outgoings, possible completion date and other matters not likely to be revealed by searches and other enquiries mentioned later.

4 The land should be visited and inspected. Professional inspection of buildings will be required by building societies before they advance money.

5 A *local search* is made together with enquiries of the district council.

6 A search is made at the Land Charges Registry by the purchaser's solicitor.

7 *F*'s solicitor draws up a draft contract and sends it to *G*'s solicitor for approval. Most contracts for the sort of transactions we are considering here are in one of several standard forms, such as the *Law Society's Conditions of Sale*. These provide for such matters as the obligation of *F* to prove title, the deposit on purchase price, completion date, apportionment of outgoings, delivery of preliminary documents, date from which proof of title shall commence and other specially added conditions which the vendor wishes to impose.

8 If there is nothing in the answers to all the enquiries, searches and the terms of the draft contract to deter *G*, then the draft contract may be approved. Note carefully, however, that this does not yet signify the existence of a contract – merely that the terms are acceptable. A purchaser should never enter a contract until he has money available to finance the purchase price. Generally this means that the building society must have approved his application for a loan and, if he wishes to sell his present home, that the prospective purchaser has contracted to buy that property.

9 Assuming satisfactory responses to all *G*'s enquiries and applications, and that *F* is likewise ready to proceed, both parties may now sign their duplicate parts of the contract. When these are delivered to each other's solicitors, the contract is binding, provided that *F* can prove title to the land. Thus the parties are bound to buy and to sell; yet time is allowed for further work preparatory to sale. Upon *exchange of contracts* the purchaser generally pays a deposit (usually 5–10 per cent of the purchase price). The abstract of title is now delivered by *F*'s solicitor to *G*'s solicitor. Unless

otherwise agreed, *F* must show 15 years' history of the land's title ending with the conveyance to himself and beginning with a good root of title: the links in that title must be continuous. Since the proof of title must start with some transaction, on most occasions more than 15 years of ownership will be shown. In the present case, *F* may start with the 1980 conveyance. He must show how the land passed from *C* to *D*, from *D* to *E*, and from *E* to himself. If his proof simply showed the land passing from *C* to *D* and then from *D* to *E*, but no more, it would be unacceptable. He does all this by summarising these deeds in the abstract. He must also provide full information about the restrictive covenant even though it was entered into in 1930, for this will still be binding. Although it was initially entered into in 1930, a recital of its existence will probably be given in subsequent conveyances. If it was registered, as it should have been, under the Land Charges Act 1925, *G* will have to accept the burden of it. He will not be surprised by it because the preliminary investigations mentioned above will have revealed it. Such a matter should have been mentioned in the draft contract.

The establishment of contractual obligations by the exchange of signed duplicates can cause problems of timing in land transactions. Sometimes nowadays *chain transactions* demand a sharper definition of the time of acceptance of an offer. A chain transaction occurs when *P* is willing to buy 'Blackacre' once he possesses a signed acceptance for the purchase of his present home, 'Pinkacre'; and *V* is only willing to sell 'Blackacre' when he has a signed acceptance of his offer to buy 'Violetacre'. Such chains can involve several persons in regard to the properties of both the vendor and purchaser. It is clear that the whole line of vendors and purchasers can only safely conclude contracts when all are satisfied that their immediate vendors and purchasers are also ready to commit themselves to contractual obligations.

Where contract exchange depends upon the ordinary principle of 'last postage', there might be a failure by one party to post, thus causing a failure of contract. Meanwhile another party might have committed himself by postal acceptance. Such a person might be obliged to sell, but is legally incapable of buying, thus becoming homeless. To avoid such catastrophes the law has developed the refinement of 'telephonic' exchanges which avoids this problem. The problem and its partial resolution are fully explained in *Domb* v *Isoz* [1980] 2 WLR 565. The Law Society has provided guidance rules as to the conclusion of the contract in such cases.

10 *G*'s solicitor might now ask further questions by way of clarification of the title (*Requisitions on Title*). The abstract might, for instance, have shown a certain person as 'Florence White' in one transaction and as 'Florence Black' in another. The explanation will probably be that she married John Black at some time between the two transactions. The matter must however be cleared up.

11 If all matters of title appear to be in order the solicitors for both parties will arrange for completion on a certain day. The purchaser's solicitor will repeat his search at the Land Charges Registry shortly beforehand. The significance of this is explained in Chapter 17.

12 *G*'s solicitor meanwhile will have prepared a draft of the proposed conveyance. We will assume that this has been approved by *F*'s solicitor and that *G*'s solicitor has *engrossed* the draft, that is typed it in final form on durable paper.

13 On completion day, *G*'s solicitor will visit the office of *F*'s solicitor. The deed of conveyance transferring the ownership from *F* to *G*, which has been executed by *F*, is handed over in return for the purchase-money or the balance if part of the purchase-money was paid by way of deposit when the contract was completed. Thus another deed and link in the continuous chain of title is added and will be used in the future as the final link when *G* sells the land. The deed of mortgage will also have been prepared for this occasion. For the sake of simplicity explanation of this will be delayed until the mortgage is discussed in Chapter 15. Besides this deed conveying the land from *F* to *G* all the other deeds and documents relevant to the title are handed over to *G*'s solicitor. You will notice that *F* did not need some of the deeds, namely deeds 1 and 2, in order to prove his title. One of these, however, contains the restrictive covenant and is therefore of use for an indefinite period. It is clear, nevertheless, that some deeds become unnecessary as proof of title to land, as is the case with deed 1 here. The transaction is thus completed and *G* may enter the property.

The above account will suggest some of the shortcomings of this system. While new links in the title are being added at one end as transactions take place, and links at the early end gradually become redundant, nevertheless, on successive sales substantially the same documents are repeatedly investigated by different solicitors. This is wasteful of time and money. Furthermore, the purchaser's solicitor has to glean the information he requires in a cumbersome way and from various sources. Finally, proof of title through documents held in private custody is a system which might lend itself to fraud.

For these reasons, a new system of conveyancing was introduced and now extends to all parts of the country. Only a basic outline of the system will be provided here.

The fee simple must be registered after the first sale following introduction of the system to particular areas. Introduction has been carried out incrementally since 1925 but is now complete. Thus, in the example above, *G* would be required to register his title. It is assumed that registration did not apply to his neighbourhood in 1987. His solicitor will do this immediately after completion of the purchase by submitting the documents of title to the Land Registry where the title will be investigated for the last time. If this is satisfactory to the

Registry then the land is given a title number for identification and is placed on a register in the name of *G*. A certificate is then sent to *G* which henceforth constitutes his sole document of title to the land. The deeds are cancelled by the Registry. The state now guarantees the title, and any future conveyances of the land will be by a simple form of transfer. No investigation of title is necessary. All that is required is an inspection of the register to check who owns the land. The Registry not only records a person's right to the land itself, but also certain rights of other persons in or over the land. In this latter respect the Land Registry takes over the functions of the Land Charges Registry where registered land is concerned. In short, the Land Charges Registry is only used for registering rights in or over the land the title to which has not been registered. It may be mentioned here that while the Land Charges Registry is at Plymouth, the Land Registry has its headquarters at Lincoln's Inn Fields but it operates from various branch offices throughout the country.

While the system represents a considerable improvement in the method of transferring land, it must not be assumed that it is a perfect one. Some interests, for example, are not registrable, and a purchaser must still make an inspection of the land and search in the local land charges register. Indeed, it possesses many complexities of its own. It must be stressed that the Land Registration Act 1925 was not designed to change land law. It merely facilitates the mode of transfer of interests in land. It does not affect the nature of those interests. The system is discussed in more detail in Chapter 19. There we shall see that leasehold title to land can also be registered.

THE ABROGATION OF MISCELLANEOUS OUTMODED RULES

The 1925 legislation abolished a considerable number of rules which could not justify their place in modern land law and which in some cases produced unexpected and unfair results. To describe these rules would be contrary to the spirit of that legislation, which in this instance was to bury. Walk over the cemetery therefore by all means but there is no need even to remove the moss from the headstones to reveal the names.

We are shortly to proceed to a detailed study of the interests which give a right to the land itself. Before that, however, it is necessary to describe the meaning of a word which, up to this point, has been taken for granted, that is, the very subject matter of these interests – *land*.

STUDY MATERIAL

Law of Property Act 1925 s 1 (as amended)
Legal estates and equitable interests

1.—(1) The only estates in land which are capable of subsisting or of being conveyed or created at law are—

(a) An estate in fee simple absolute in possession;

(b) A term of years absolute.

(2) The only interests or charges in or over land which are capable of subsisting or of being conveyed or created at law are—

(a) An easement, right, or privilege in or over land for an interest equivalent to an estate in fee simple absolute in possession or a term of years absolute;

(b) A rentcharge in possession issuing out of or charged on land being either perpetual or for a term of years absolute;

(c) A charge by way of legal mortgage;

(d) . . . and any other similar charge on land which is not created by an instrument;

(e) Rights of entry exercisable over or in respect of a legal term of years absolute, or annexed, for any purpose, to a legal rentcharge.

(3) All other estates, interests, and charges in or over land take effect as equitable interests.

(4) The estates, interests, and charges which under this section are authorised to subsist or to be conveyed or created at law are (when subsisting or conveyed or created at law) in this Act referred to as 'legal estates', and have the same incidents as legal estates subsisting at the commencement of this Act; and the owner of a legal estate is referred to as 'an estate owner' and his legal estate is referred to as his estate.

(5) A legal estate may subsist concurrently with or subject to any other legal estate in the same land in like manner as it could have done before the commencement of this Act.

(6) A legal estate is not capable of subsisting or of being created in an undivided share in land or of being held by an infant.

(7) Every power of appointment over, or power to convey or charge land or any interest therein, whether created by a statute or other instrument or implied by law, and whether created before or after the commencement of this Act (not being a power vested in a legal mortgagee or an estate owner in right of his estate and exercisable by him or by another person in his name and on his behalf), operates only in equity.

(8) Estates, interests, and charges in or over land which are not legal estates are in this Act referred to as 'equitable interests', and powers which by this Act are to operate in equity only are in this Act referred to as 'equitable powers'.

(9) The provisions in any statute or other instrument requiring land to be conveyed to uses shall take effect as directions that the land shall (subject to creating

or reserving thereout any legal estate authorised by this Act which may be required) be conveyed to a person of full age upon the requisite trusts.

(10) The repeal of the Statute of Uses (as amended) does not affect the operation thereof in regard to dealings taking effect before the commencement of this Act.

QUESTIONS

1 Discuss the significance of *personalty* as applied to leasehold interests.

2 What was the general effect of the Administration of Estates Act 1925 upon the law of intestacy?

3 How did the Land Charges Act 1925 facilitate the sale of land?

4 Why does a sale of land demand more preliminary investigations than a sale of chattels?

5 What is meant by a good *root of title*?

6 What are the principal disadvantages of the unregistered system of conveyancing?

7 On pages 28–31 a conveyance of land from *F* to *G* has been described. The legal fee simple has been conveyed to *G*. He would like to build a house on the land, but the restrictive covenant entered into by *C* in 1930 states that no building operations shall be carried out on the land. Advise *G* as to whether this covenant is enforceable against him.

CHAPTER 3

THE MEANING OF LAND

The principal message of this chapter is simple to state though difficult to apply. The meaning of 'land' is not fixed but varies according to the context in which it is found.

The appellate courts frequently find that words have been misinterpreted by judges at first instance. Such misinterpretations are not necessarily 'mistakes'. They might merely show a divergence in policy between one judge and another. This is particularly so with words in new statutes, where the first tracks of precedent are being put down. Sensitivity to the meaning of recently enacted words is thus built up.

The word 'land' has been appearing in a host of statutes, cases, wills, deeds, contracts and other transactions for centuries. Lawyers therefore should have achieved considerable knowledge of it. Before proceeding further, let us examine a modern decision of the Court of Appeal.

The facts of *Cedar Holdings Ltd* v *Green* [1979] 3 WLR 31 were as follows. *H* and *W*, husband and wife, were joint owners of their home. After their divorce, *H* wished to mortgage the house and, by concealing the interest of *W*, appropriate all the loan proceeds. He therefore represented another woman, *X*, as being *W*. *H* and *X* thus purported to mortgage the house to *M* as a security for a loan. *M* later sought a declaration that the house was subject to a mortgage of *H*'s share in the property. It was conceded that the total interest in the house had not been effectively mortgaged because *X*, however convincing the deception, could not mortgage, sell or give away that which she did not own. That is a brute fact of property law, subject to very few exceptions. Therefore, the question really in issue was whether *H*, though failing in his scheme to mortgage the total interest, had at least mortgaged his half-share. This was really a matter of intention, since he clearly was capable of dealing with his very own share.

In an attempt to prove this intention, the Law of Property Act 1925 s 63(1) was invoked. This reads as follows:

> Every conveyance is effectual to pass all the estate, right, title, interest, claim, and demand which the conveying parties respectively have, in, to, or on the property conveyed, or expressed or intended so to be, or which they respectively have power to convey in, to, or on the same.

A conveyance includes a mortgage.

The crucial part of the judgment of Buckley LJ on page 38 reads as follows:

> In my judgment, upon the true construction of section 63 a beneficial interest in the proceeds of the sale of land held upon the statutory trusts is not an interest in that land within the meaning of the section and a conveyance of that land is not effectual to pass a beneficial interest in the proceeds of sale.

We shall see in Chapter 11 that interests in co-owned property are not interests in 'land' but interests in *personalty*. This arises from a fictional, but sometimes useful, doctrine of equity. But the significant point is that Buckley LJ refers to 'land'. Yet that word is not mentioned in s 63; instead *property* appears. That would not matter if the two words were synonyms, but they are not. The definition of land in s 205 of the Act expressly excludes co-owned property by the insertion of 'but not an undivided share in land'. This, uncontroversially, alludes to co-ownership. However, the definition of *property* in the same section includes 'anything in action and any interest in real or personal property'. It is also uncontroversial that 'personal property' may include interests in co-owned property. All this will become clearer after co-ownership has been studied.

The only matter presently demonstrated is that a judge of the Court of Appeal assimilated 'land' with *property*, where both words possessed immediately relevant available and different definitions.

Following this caution, the next part of this chapter will be devoted to explaining why it is important to know whether a particular entity is land or not, and the second part to discussing how such a decision is reached.

THE SIGNIFICANCE OF THE WORD 'LAND'

Contracts

The Law of Property (Miscellaneous Provisions) Act 1989 s 2, which applies to contracts made on or after 27 September 1989, provides that:

> A contract for the sale or other disposition of an interest in land can only be made in writing and only by incorporating all the terms which the persons have expressly agreed in one document or, where contracts are exchanged, in each.

There are three exceptions to this rule which render non-conforming agreements void:

1 a contract to grant such a lease as is mentioned in the Law of Property Act 1925 s 54(2). These leases for three years or less in duration will be discussed in Chapter 6;

2 a contract made at a public auction;

3 a contract regulated under the Financial Services Act 1986.

Furthermore, nothing in the section affects the creation of resulting, implied or constructive trusts, or terms implied by law. On the other hand *interest in land* is widely defined so as to include any estate, interest or charge in or over land or over the proceeds of sale of land. We shall see in Chapter 11 that the section therefore applies to interests held under a trust for sale of land.

If all the terms are incorporated in a single document, this must be signed by or on behalf of each party. If duplicate documents are exchanged, then it is sufficient that each party signs one of them. The terms of a contract may be either set out entirely in the contract document itself or be incorporated by reference to some other document. Since the purpose of the section was to counteract ambiguity as to the terms of land contracts, presumably such reference must be express, or if implied, patently clear.

Finally, this section repeals the Law of Property Act 1925 s 40 which it now replaces but which continues to affect contracts entered into before 27 September 1989.

The rules affecting contracts made before 27 September 1989 are clearly of diminishing importance and will not be discussed in detail here. A brief description is necessary however since the new law might contain a shortcoming similar to one contained in the law it has replaced. The problem illustrates a tension between two qualities desirable in any legal system, certainty and fairness. The origins of the old rule lay in the Statute of Frauds 1677 which, like the 1989 Act, strove primarily for certainty and the avoidance of fraud in establishing what was agreed by the parties. It provided that no action may be brought upon a land contract unless evidenced by writing signed by the party against whom it was brought. Although it did not require contracts actually to be in writing, but only evidenced by writing, its sanctions were as draconian. A brief example will illustrate these possible consequences. A landowner *L*, might orally agree to grant *T* a lease on condition that *T* first carried out improvements to the property. *T* might do so, only to find that he could not enforce the contract in court because there was no written evidence of the agreement. Certainty would thus be achieved at a monstrous cost to justice.

In succeeding centuries the courts of equity in effect negatived the statute in such cases. If the plaintiff had even partly performed the contract there was no need to provide written evidence. The Statute of Frauds was not to be allowed to become itself an 'engine of fraud'. So established was this 'judicial legislation' that the Law of Property Act 1925 s 40, substantially re-enacting the Statute of Frauds, provided that the section did not 'affect the law relating to part performance . . .' The 1989 Act has simply repealed s 40 without mention of the doctrine of part performance.

We must consider whether, in circumstances similar to those mentioned above, the new provisions might become an 'engine of fraud'. There are several grounds for believing that this will not be so:

1 The purpose of the Law of Property (Miscellaneous Provisions) Act 1989 s 2 was to effect the tightening of a technicality; contracts are to be in writing, not merely evidenced by writing. Surely such a section could not by implication alone cast aside the jurisdiction of equity? Section 40 itself merely acknowledged a jurisdiction already in being. To remove such an acknowledgement in passing, as s 2 does, can hardly abolish that which already had an independent existence.

2 Even if the doctrine of part performance has disappeared there are alternative equitable remedies to hand. Indeed it was stated in the *Law Commission Report on Formalities for Contracts for Sale etc of Land* (Law Com No 164, HC: 1987) at para 5.5:

> We see no cause to fear that the recommended repeal and replacement of the present section as to the formalities of contracts for sale or other disposition of land will inhibit the courts in the exercise of the equitable discretion to do justice between parties in individual otherwise hard cases.

A strong cadidate for this role would be the doctrine of proprietary estoppel which is discussed in Chapter 7.

3 Judicial interpretation of the section to date has been described as purposive (Cheshire and Burn's *Modern Law of Real Property* (15th edn) p 123). The cases cited however merely help to define the limits of s 2, not the consequences of its operation. In *Spiro* v *Glencrown Properties Ltd* [1991] 2 WLR 931 it was held that an option exercised in response to a written agreement obviously need not itself be signed by both parties. See also *Record* v *Bell* [1991] 1 WLR 853. Similarly, in *Pitt* v *PHH Asset Management Ltd* [1993] 1 All ER 961 it was held that an oral agreement that a seller would not negotiate with other prospective purchasers for two weeks after the buyer received a draft contract was not required to be in writing. Such 'lock-out' agreements are not contracts to sell land; indeed, they are contracts not to sell land.

Finally, in order to set the requirements of s 2 in perspective, we should note that contracts for the sale of interests in land are in practice almost invariably contained in one of the standard printed forms.

Requirement of deeds for legal interests

The second reason why it is important to know whether the subject with which you are dealing is 'land' is that the transfer of ownership in it, or of any other legal interest in or over land, can generally be carried out only by deed.

Furthermore, even if the interest is not a legal one, its creation or disposal must be in writing. Likewise declarations of trusts of land must be proved by writing, though this rule does not apply to the creation of resulting, implied or constructive trusts (LPA 1925 s 53; and see *Hodgson* v *Marks* [1970] 3 All ER 513). The significance of this will be appreciated later when we see how wide the definition of land is, but it may be mentioned, by way of example only, that deeds are necessary for the transfer of a fee simple, the grant of a lease or the grant of an easement. Furthermore, once a lease has been granted, the transfer of it to someone else must also be effected by a deed. An important exception to the rule is the grant of certain short leases which may be carried out by writing or orally. These will be discussed later along with leases in general, but it should be noticed that while the grant of such leases may be oral, contracts for this grant must nevertheless be in writing for the purposes of the Law of Property (Miscellaneous Provisions) Act 1989 s 2.

If an attempt is made to dispose of or create interests in land otherwise than by deed, equity will, in certain circumstances, regard the transaction as a contract to convey the interest, for 'equity treats that as done which ought to be done'. This is only so, however, if the transaction is for value and satisfies the requirements of the Law of Property (Miscellaneous Provisions) Act 1989 s 2.

Wide rights carried by a conveyance

If *V* sells his land to *P*, *P* would certainly expect the house standing upon it to pass to him along with the fences and the trees. Equally certainly and correctly, he would not expect the car which happens to be standing in the garage to pass to him. Nevertheless, the definition of land we are shortly to discuss is such that *V* may well be surprised at what rights would pass unless he took positive steps to exclude them from the sale at the contract stage. Otherwise, to give but a few examples, his prize-winning rose bushes may pass to *P*, and on the other hand *P* may be in for an unpleasant surprise when he finds that neither the greenhouse nor the valuable antique birdbath, which *V* always takes from house to house with him, is his on completion.

The Law of Property Act 1925 s 62 names the different classes of objects and rights which pass on a conveyance and it should be studied carefully. Some of the items, however, such as 'fixtures' are mentioned without explanation and call for discussion. It may seem odd that while 'land' is defined in s 205(1)(ix) of the Act, a separate section, namely s 62, should state what is deemed to pass on a conveyance of 'land' and proceed to give an independent, though similar, list of things and rights. Perhaps we can say that s 205 helps us to classify the totality of our property whereas, s 62 gives us a more magnified definition of a particular piece of physical property which is admittedly land.

Nomenclature in documents distributing a variety of property

The last paragraph stressed the importance of the distinction between land and other forms of property when land only is being conveyed. When, however, the whole or a wide variety of a person's property is being distributed according to his or another person's instructions, and the word 'land' is used to describe one of the classes of property, even more serious results may follow from a misunderstanding of its meaning. Thus, if I make a will leaving my 'land' to *L* and the 'rest of my property' to *R*, I shall certainly expect 'Blackacre', of which I own the fee simple, to pass to *L*, and it is perhaps not too catastrophic if I failed to realise that a particular object would go his way too, but my plans will go seriously wrong if I used the word 'land' without qualification, not realising that it includes a rentcharge of, say, £2,000 owned by me at death and payable out of someone else's land, yet perhaps not land which is subject to a trust for sale. A rentcharge is a periodical sum of money charged on land and is classified as land by s 205. If land is held upon trust for sale, equity, regarding that as already done which ought to be done, considers it to be, for some purposes, already sold. An interest in it, therefore, might be caught by the description *personalty* but not 'land' (*Re Kempthorne* [1930] I Ch 268). This rule is an example of the doctrine of conversion, which applies whenever there is a binding obligation to convert freehold land into money by a sale. The duty to convert may rise under a trust, as mentioned above, under a contract or under a statute. The topic will be further discussed later in this chapter.

This is a convenient place to note that the expression *real property* or *realty* means the same as 'land' except that, for historical reasons, *leaseholds* are excluded. *Leaseholds*, therefore, though not *realty*, are 'land'.

Equitable interests arising from contracts

> The moment you have a valid contract for sale the vendor becomes, in equity, a trustee for the purchaser of the estate sold and the beneficial ownership passes to the purchaser, the vendor having a right to the purchase money, a charge or lien on the estate for the security of that purchase money, and a right to retain possession of estate until the purchase money is paid . . . (per Jessel, MR, in *Lysaught* v *Edwards* (1876) 2 ChD 499, at 506).

The same principle applies to agreements for the creation or disposition of other interests in land such as leases or easements. The effect of this will be examined in the context of the various interests when they are dealt with later. A decree of specific performance will usually be granted to compel a recalcitrant vendor to pass the legal estate.

This doctrine does not apply to contracts for the sale of goods, for specific performance is applied much more sparingly since damages are usually an adequate remedy. On the other hand, the legal ownership in goods frequently passes at the time of the contract under the Sale of Goods Acts.

Application of various other special rules of land law

Finally, it is important to distinguish between land and other property because there are still large areas of law which apply to land and not to goods and vice versa. One important one, namely the Law of Property (Miscellaneous Provisions) Act 1989, has been noted already but others will be met. One example may be given here. If I settle 'Blackacre' on *A* for life and on *B* in fee simple in remainder, the technical rules of the Settled Land Act 1925 apply. If I made a similar settlement of my shares it would not. Similarly, the Sale of Goods Act 1979 applies to goods but not to land, though there is a slight skirmishing for territory on the boundaries of these two empires.

WHAT IS 'LAND'?

The meaning of 'land' varies according to its context. That context can be a particular statute, deed, will or other transaction, or a particular line of judicial decisions. Its meaning might even vary within a single statute. An example will demonstrate this.

The definition of 'land' for the purposes of the Law of Property Act 1925 is contained in s 205(1)(ix).

> Land includes land of any tenure, and mines and minerals, whether or not held apart from the surface, buildings or parts of buildings (whether the division is horizontal, vertical or made in any other way) and other corporeal hereditaments; also a manor, an advowson and a rent and other incorporeal hereditaments, and an easement, right, privilege, or benefit in, over, or derived from land; but not an undivided share in land.

We noticed earlier in this chapter that beneficial interests in co-owned property are considered for certain purposes not to be 'land' but personalty. The words 'undivided share' in the statutory definition simply refer to co-owned property. That definition as it stands above therefore appears to exclude such co-owned property from any provision in the Act which refers to 'land'.

Next, turn to s 40 of the Act, which was discussed earlier in this chapter. Though its provisions have now been replaced by the Law of Property (Miscellaneous Provisions) Act 1989 s 2, it nevertheless illustrates the point: it required contracts for the sale or other disposition of interests in 'land' to be evidenced in writing. The result of a rigid interpretation would be to produce the absurd result that if a single owner contracts to sell his house he is caught by the section, whereas a co-owning married couple would not be. If that fixed meaning were carried beyond the Act to other statutes, even stranger consequences would occur. The single owner would be obliged to apply for permission under the Town and Country Planning Act 1971 if he wished to develop his 'land', whereas the co-owning couple would be free of such restraints.

The reason why such results do not occur is that 'land' has a flexible meaning. The preamble to s 205 reads:

> In this Act unless the context otherwise requires, the following expressions have the meanings hereby assigned to them . . .

Clearly the context of s 40 requires an extended meaning of 'land' so as to embrace co-owned property. (See *Cooper* v *Critchley* [1955] 1 All ER 520). In the case of the Town and Country Planning Act 1971, the Act provides its own definition of land which similarly embraces both types of interest.

The word 'land', therefore, must be interpreted sensitively in the context of the particular statute in which it appears. Sometimes there will be a statutory definition; sometimes there will not be. The general purpose of the Act must be considered in all cases.

If the word appears in a deed or will or other instrument the same approach is necessary in order to discover the true intention of the parties. Surely one of the fundamental purposes of law is to protect lawful designs, not to frustrate them. In short, an interest might be 'land' for some purposes and not for others. The subject is further discussed in relationship to co-ownership in Chapter 11.

Turning from the potential meaning of 'land' in law, recognising the importance of the Law of Property Act 1925 to land law, we must briefly examine the meaning of the word in that particular Act, remembering however that its meaning even within that Act can vary.

In modern terms, this definition contains two categories. The first part of the definition mentions the cases where the subject matter of the ownership or other interest is physical. These are the things which the layman would expect to be within the meaning of 'land'; the ancient legal term for this class is *corporeal hereditaments. Hereditament* is simply an archaic word for 'land'. In short, the soil and its accoutrements are 'land'.

The second part contains the cases, such as easements, where the subject of ownership or other interest is not physical. These items are called *incorporeal hereditaments* because you cannot see or touch them. Yet they are either so inseparably linked in their use with land, or imitate its characteristics so closely, that they are treated as land. What matters today is that the full force of land law, as described in the first part of this chapter, applies as much to incorporeal as to corporeal hereditaments. This twofold division will now be used for a more detailed explanation, but since the incorporeal matters can be treated more briefly, they will be taken first. 'Land', therefore, consists of the following.

Incorporeal hereditaments

These constituted a large class in the old law. The only important examples today are *easements*, *profits* and *rents*. These are to be discussed individually later but a few general remarks may be made here. A *rent* includes a rent service, which is the rent received by a landlord from his tenant. Since the leasehold itself is included amongst *corporeal hereditaments*, both landlord and tenant own 'land'. Rent also includes other periodical payments made out of land such as rentcharges.

Corporeal hereditaments

This second category concerns physical land. It does not spell out, but takes for granted, much of the meaning given to the expression by the common law. Its full meaning will therefore be explained by reference to the decided cases and also to the Law of Property Act 1925 s 62.

In the first place it means the earth itself to an indefinite depth and also the air space to such height as is necessary for the ordinary use and enjoyment of the land and structures upon it, not above that (see *Bernstein (Baron)* v *Skyviews and General Ltd* [1977] 3 WLR 136). This includes all the natural and permanent features, ranging from minerals and ponds to trees and buildings. Even horizontal or other sections of this earth or space are land, whether or not they are owned separately from the surface. Thus, I can sell a seam of minerals in fee simple to *P*, who thereupon owns land. More quaintly, such a section may be carved out above the surface. If I build a three-storey block of flats on my land I can convey the upper two in fee simple to *A* and *B* and retain the ground floor flat myself. In this case, all three of us own land, even though I am the only one who owns any soil. Enjoyment of land above the earth in this way by means of *flying freeholds* is clearly dependent on the existence of easements of support and way, which, however, would readily be implied by law. Also included in the meaning of land are growing things generally such as grass and shrubs, but not annual crops such as corn.

Next, 'there is no doubt that the general maxim of the law is that what is annexed to the land becomes part of the land . . .' (per Blackburn J, in *Holland* v *Hodgson* (1872) LR 7 CP 328, at 334). An object which, by such attachment to land, becomes part of that land is hereafter called a *fixture*. The test whether it has become a fixture is not simply this physical one, and Blackburn J gave classic expression to it in that case in the following way at p 334.

> When the article in question is no further attached to the land, than by its own weight, it is generally considered to be a mere chattel . . . But even in such a case, if the intention is apparent to make the articles part of the land, they do become part of the land . . . On the other hand, an article may be very firmly fixed to the land, and yet circumstances may be such as to show that it was never intended to be part of the land, and then it does not become part of the land.

In short, two matters have to be examined in the following order: (1) the degree of annexation; and (2) the purpose of annexation. The first is a question of fact only and raises a presumption. If the object is attached otherwise than by its own weight, it is *prima facie* land; if it is merely resting by its own weight, it is *prima facie* a chattel. Whatever presumption is thus raised may be rebutted by showing what the intention was of the person who placed it: that is, whether, in the case of an object merely resting, it was intended to benefit the land, or whether, in the case of annexation, it was only so annexed the better to enjoy it as a chattel.

The same object may indeed be chattel or land according to the circumstances (see *Rogers (Inspector of Taxes)* v *Longsdon* [1967] Ch 93). For instance, let us say I own a statue of Venus which I have always taken with me when I have moved house. It is a massive statue for outdoor use. In the house I presently own, the terrace is very uneven so that I have had to screw the base to the ground for security. *Prima facie*, the statue is a fixture, but this presumption is clearly rebutted once the second test is applied. Conversely, if in planning my new garden I place a statue of Venus as part of the landscape on a balustrade, and find that it stands quite securely there by its own weight, then, although on the first test it is *prima facie* a chattel, this is reversed on applying the second, for the intention was to enhance the land as such.

Although the test of degree of annexation is applied first, 'it is not always the most important – and its relative importance is probably not what it was in ruder times' (per Lord Macnaghten in *Leigh* v *Taylor* [1902] AC 157, at 162). In that case, a tapestry was fastened to a wooden frame which was then screwed into a wall. It was held that it remained a chattel, for the intention was to fix it to the wall the better to enjoy it as a chattel. In other circumstances a tapestry might well be part of the land, as for instance the tapestry in Coventry Cathedral. It is important to note, particularly in view of modern building techniques, that a superstructure might remain a chattel, while its base becomes a fixture. Thus in *Dibble* v *Moore* [1970] 2 QB 181, greenhouses standing on concrete dollies merely by their own weight were held not to be fixtures, particularly in view of evidence that it was customary to move such greenhouses to fresh sites every few years. The law of fixtures was invoked in an unusual context in *Simmons* v *Midford* [1969] 2 Ch 415, where the owner of 'Blackacre' had, with his neighbour's permission, laid a drain under that neighbour's land. Some years later the ownership of the drain was contested. It was held to be the property of the present owner of 'Blackacre'; because, said Buckley J, it was 'appurtenant to' 'Blackacre'. Unfortunately for our present purpose, he did not have to determine whether the drain was land or personalty. He did, however, find that it had not become part of the land in which it was embedded, but had either remained a chattel or become part of the land it served, rather like a protruding limb upon that land, to which, however it was connected. This latter suggestion is, of course, consonant with the definition of land, which embraces horizontal sections of it.

Finally, where one object, which is part of a series or system fulfilling a common purpose, has become land, it does not follow that other parts of the apparatus have done so, even though they are physically connected with it. For instance, in *Jordan* v *May* [1947] 1 All ER 231, a generating plant set in concrete was held to be a fixture but a battery helping to run it was not.

Some of the practical results of these rules might now be considered. The owner of land may, of course, detach any fixture, whereupon it becomes a chattel again. If, however, he devises land to *L*, and leaves the rest of his property to *P*, all fixtures will pass to *L* and neither *P* nor the personal representatives may detach them (*Re Whaley* [1908] 1 Ch 615). Similar principles apply between vendor and purchaser. No fixtures existing at the time of the contract may be removed by the vendor. If he wishes to do so, he must reserve the right in the contract. If land is mortgaged, all fixtures are affected by the mortgage, as are any later added fixtures (*Monti* v *Barnes* [1901] 1 KB 205). This last rule may create serious difficulties these days when much valuable equipment belonging to third parties is taken onto mortgaged premises under a hiring or hire-purchase agreement. It might be thought that the existence of the agreement would show a contrary intention sufficient to prevent the machinery becoming a fixture, and so allow its original ownership to continue. A view that this is not, however, borne out by the decided cases, but that, where the agreement gives the hirer the right to seize the object on breach of the agreement, an equitable interest arises in his favour, may be found at *27 Conveyancer 30*.

The rules as to annexation might have worked great injustice to the owners of limited interests in land, such as life tenants or lessees. A tenant would certainly be discouraged from annexing valuable objects to the land if there were no exception to the rule that on annexation they become part of the land and must enure to the benefit of the owner. The law has therefore long given the right for lessees and life tenants, under certain conditions, to remove some classes of fixtures annexed by them. This does not mean the objects have not become fixtures. It means that such tenants may detach certain parts of the land. These rights will be discussed when those interests are dealt with.

STUDY MATERIAL

Berkley v *Poulett* (1976) 241 Estates Gazette 911; 242 Estates Gazette 39

The judgment of Scarman LJ is given below. Stamp LJ agreed with Lord Scarman's conclusions but gave a separate judgment. Goff LJ dissented.

This was an appeal by Rowland John Berkley, the sub-purchaser of Hinton House, part of Earl Poulett's estate at Hinton St George, Somerset, from the decision of Sir Anthony Plowman, then Vice-Chancellor, dismissing his claim for the delivery up of pictures and other objects, which he alleged to be fixtures passing to him on the sale of the house, and for compensation for loss and damage, and other relief. The respondents were the 8th Earl Poulett (and after his death his personal representatives), Sothebys and T R G Lawrence & Son, Crewkerne, Somerset.

Giving the first judgment, SCARMAN LJ said: In opening the appeal for the plaintiff Mr Millett QC said that the basic issue in the case was whether some pictures, some prints, a statue and a sundial were fixtures or chattels. If fixtures, they passed, he submitted, to the subpurchaser when Hinton House was sold: if chattels, he conceded they did not. The case has many complexities, which counsel have done their distinguished best to unravel, but ultimately we have to return to the issue identified by Mr Millett in the first few words of an address which, though it took five and a half days, lasted not a moment too long.

On 11 November 1971 Mr Berkley (the plaintiff and appellant) issued a writ naming Earl Poulett, Sothebys, and a firm of surveyors, T R G Lawrence & Son, who practise in Crewkerne, Somerset, as defendants. Put briefly, the claim was for delivery up of certain fixtures which it was claimed passed with Hinton House when Lord Poulett sold the house, compensation for the loss of, or damage to, the fixtures, together with appropriate consequential relief. The claim was, and remains, strongly contested by all the defendants. Lord Poulett died in 1972, since when his personal representatives have carried on as defendants in his place. The plaintiff was a subpurchaser of Hinton House. He bought from Lord Poulett's purchaser. The history of the sale was as follows. Lord Poulett, the 8th Earl, decided to put up for sale by public auction his ancestral estate at Hinton St George in Somerset. Hinton House, with its gardens and grounds comprising some 23 acres, was part of the estate and included in the sale. The Poulett family had lived in the house for 500 years. The south wing, said to have been designed by Inigo Jones, was built for the reception of a queen who never arrived – Queen Anne. The wing includes two rooms which feature in the case, the Queen's Dining Room and the Queen's Ante-Room. The Queen's Dining Room is described in the auction particulars as follows: 'The Queen's Dining Room, facing south and measuring about 39 ft 3 in by 29 ft, with oak panelling around picture recesses; open stone fireplace; magnificent moulded and decorated ceiling with egg and dart cornice and large casement windows overlooking the sunken garden.' The Queen's Ante-Room is described in the same particulars as follows: 'The Queen's Ante-Room, facing south and measuring about 28 ft 9 in by 27 ft 6 in, with oak panelling around picture recesses; large open stone fireplace; three-quarter glazed doors to sunken garden; doors to staircase hall and two communicating doors.'

In the Queen's Dining Room there were six pictures, which the plaintiff claims passed with the house on its sale to him. These pictures were firmly fixed into the recesses in the panelling of the room. They were: a framed oil painting of the Marquis of Hamilton, attributed to Mytens; a framed oil painting of Elizabeth, Countess of Essex, attributed to Mytens; a framed oil painting, said (but not believed) to be of James II, attributed to Kneller; a framed oil painting of the 1st Duke of Leeds, attributed to Gibson; a framed oil painting of Montague, Lord Willoughby, attributed to Old Stone; a framed oil painting of 'The return of the Poulett family from the war', artist unknown.

In the Queen's Ante-Room, there were a number of pictures, only two of which were affixed to a wall, namely two portraits by Wood, of the 7th Earl and his countess respectively, each in coronation robes. The plaintiff claims them because, like the pictures in the Queen's Dining Room, they were fixed into the recesses of a panelled wall. On the first floor of the house there is a suite of rooms known as the

Chinese Suite. These rooms contained a number of Chinese prints done on rice paper and stuck to the wall. It is conceded that these were fixtures and passed with the house. Finally, there were in the grounds two objects which the plaintiff claims: a white marble statue of a Greek athlete, weighing approximately half a ton and standing on a plinth which was (and remains) fixed into position on the West Lawn; and a sundial which rested on a stone baluster (or pedestal) outside the South Wing. Neither the statue nor the sundial nor any of the eight pictures came to the plaintiff. He did get the Chinese prints all tattered and torn – severely damaged by someone who had tried unsuccessfully to remove them intact from the wallpaper to which they were stuck. The plaintiff's case is that all these items were fixtures; that they passed to him, the purchaser, by subpurchase of the house, garden and grounds; that he is entitled to their delivery up in good condition, damages for their detention, and compensation for their loss or damage.

The Hinton St George Estate was put up for sale by auction on 2 August 1968. The auctioneers were Knight Frank & Rutley, who prepared the particulars of sale. There were 24 lots. Hinton House with its gardens, grounds and entrance lodge was lot 1, approximately 23 acres. The plaintiff was interested in lot 1 and also lot 4 (the park, 40 acres). A company, Effold Ltd, was prepared to bid for the whole estate, but was particularly interested in the forestry. A tenant farmer was interested in buying his farm. Such was the coincidence of their interests that, not surprisingly, a syndicate was formed. Mr Simon Lawrence was instructed to bid on their behalf. Mr Lawrence is a partner in the third defendants but at the auction sale on 2 August was acting for the syndicate which included the plaintiff and Effold. On the morning of the sale (which itself took place in the afternoon) the plaintiff contracted with Effold to buy lots 1 and 4 from them if their bid for the whole estate was successful. Later, by mutual agreement, he withdrew from the purchase of lot 4. Effold's bid for the estate was successful at a figure of £225 000 whereupon the plaintiff's contract to buy the house and grounds (lot 1) from Effold became unconditional. Effold were due to complete on 30 September, but completion was delayed until 4 November.

Meanwhile there occurred other events of some importance. On 5 August the plaintiff, having told Lord Poulett that he was the purchaser of the house, paid a visit to the house. The plaintiff's reason for buying the house and grounds was that he hoped to be able to develop Hinton as a tourist attraction; Longleat was in his mind's eye. Naturally he wanted to secure as many of its historic ornaments as he could. On his visit he sought to discuss with Lord Poulett the possibility of buying the contents of the house, or some of them. But the Earl would not be drawn.

The Earl had in mind not only an auction of the contents but also the sale by private treaty or otherwise of such of the treasures as he might be advised to sell separately, that is to say, otherwise than at a contents auction. He arranged for an auction on 23 October, with 22 October as the viewing date. The plaintiff did not visit the house between 5 August and 22 October – almost certainly because Lord Poulett did not wish him to do so. On 14 August upon the Earl's instructions, five of the six paintings were taken from the Queen's Dining Room, namely: 'Lord Willoughby' removed by Rogers instructed by Sothebys (subsequently, that is to say on 19 February 1969, sold by Sothebys at auction for £100); 'Duke of Leeds' removed by Rogers instructed by Sothebys (who subsequently, on 11 June 1969, sold it at auction for £180); the alleged 'King James II' removed by Rogers instructed by Sothebys (who subsequently, on 11 June 1969, sold it by auction for £250); 'Elizabeth Countess of Essex' removed by Rogers instructed by Sothebys (not sold); 'Marquis of Hamilton' removed by Rogers instructed by Sothebys, who sold it by auction on 5 March 1969 for £550. 'The Return' was left in position.

On 22 October the plaintiff, armed with a sale catalogue, the contents of which had disturbed him, came to view. He found the two Poulett coronation portraits in place in the Queen's Ante-Room but the five pictures gone from the Queen's Dining Room: only 'The Return' was in its place. The statue was on its plinth on the West Lawn, but the sundial had been removed from its baluster. In the Chinese Suite he noticed that several prints were missing. The catalogue upset him because it listed for sale 'The Return,' the two coronation portraits, the statue, the sundial, and a chandelier (about which there is no longer any dispute). He made complaint and sought advice the upshot of which was that Mr Simon Lawrence, now acting for Lord Poulett as auctioneer of the contents, withdrew from the sale the two coronation portraits and the plinth but not the statue which stood on it. The sundial and the statue were sold at the auction on 23 October. So also was 'The Return'; its frame was also sold on the same day to the same purchaser, but privately. A few days later the plaintiff went again to Hinton House only to find that all he claimed had gone save the Chinese prints, and these he found in bad shape. He refused to complete his subpurchase on the day agreed for completion that is to say 31 October. We now know that 'The Return' and its frame were removed on 24 October by a local builder, Mr Ash, after being sold (total price £700) by Mr Simon Lawrence on the 23rd; that the coronation portraits were also removed by him on Mr Lawrence's instructions; that the statue was sold for £225 at the auction and removed shortly thereafter by the purchasers; and that the sundial was sold at the auction for £40 and taken away by the buyer.

Despite the plaintiff's claims, of which Lord Poulett and Effold had notice before their completion, Effold completed their purchase of the whole estate without reservations or conditions on 4 November, and the plaintiff, likewise, his purchase of the house and grounds on 19 February following. Thus all the objects (other than the Chinese prints) which the plaintiff claims as his property were removed on Lord Poulett's instructions after sale and before completion by Effold. The conveyances which followed were silent as to the matters in dispute.

I have recited enough of the history to show that, if the pictures, statue or sundial, or any of them, be fixtures, very difficult questions arise as to the entitlement of the plaintiff to sue the head vendor, Lord Poulett. But if none of them was a fixture, the plaintiff is non-suited at the outset, save for his claim in respect of the Chinese prints, which are admitted to have been fixtures and did come into his possession. The first question, therefore, is whether the objects (other than the Chinese prints) were fixtures. On this preliminary, but fundamental, issue I confess that my mind has wavered. But at the end of the day, after listening to prolonged and painstaking argument upon the facts and reflecting upon counsel's submissions in the course of the tranquillity obtained by reserving judgment, I find myself in agreement with the Vice-Chancellor. None of the objects (other than the Chinese prints) was, in my judgment, a fixture. I shall now endeavour to explain how I have reached this conclusion. Lord Poulett sold as an absolute owner. He was in a position to decide what he would offer for sale and what he would exclude from his offer. One turns therefore first to the contract of sale for the terms of his bargain. They are to be found in the following documents: a memorandum of agreement signed by the purchasers, Effold Ltd, and dated 2 August 1968; printed stipulations which were bound up with the auctioneers' particulars of sale; some printed special conditions of sale; and the National Conditions of Sale (17th ed) with one or two express modifications. Effolds bought the whole estate (lots 1 to 24). Lot 1 was the house, garden and grounds. The particulars of sale contained a description of the lot, but, as is usual, the particulars were not incorporated into the contract. The printed stipulations, which were of contractual force, included the following clause:

Fixtures and fittings. Fixtures and fittings usually denominated tenant's fixtures and fittings belonging to the vendor shall be taken by the purchaser, according to an inventory to be prepared by the auctioneers and paid for at a valuation to be made in the usual way and the decision of the valuer or umpire as to what are tenant's fixtures and fittings shall be conclusive in the event of any dispute. Certain items are however specifically excluded from the Sale – see Special Conditions of Sale No 14.

I need not read the rest of the stipulation. Special condition no 11 reserved to the vendor the right to sell by auction at Hinton House 'household goods, effects, chattels or . . . other possessions of the vendor' prior to completion. Special condition no 14 specifically excluded certain items from the sale – two sets of tapestries, two statues, some ornamental stonework, some bookcases and the cornice cupboards and curtain rails of the Grand Saloon. None of the items in dispute was specifically excluded under this condition. The contract was therefore for the sale of the realty – Hinton House, garden and grounds; certain specifically mentioned fixtures were excluded, but an inventory was to be prepared of 'tenant's fixtures', which were to be taken by the purchaser and paid for at a valuation. No inventory has in fact ever been taken and, though the point is mentioned in the respondents' notice, no submissions based on this provision have, as I understand the litigation, been advanced to this court by either side. In my judgment, since the contract was silent as to the items in dispute, it is necessary to determine whether under the general law they are to be considered as fixtures, which pass with the realty, or as chattels, in which event they remain the property of the vendor.

As so often, the difficulty is not the formulation but the application of the law. I think there is now no need to enter into research into the case law prior to *Leigh* v *Taylor* [1902] AC 157. The answer today to the question whether objects which were originally chattels have become fixtures, that is to say part of the freehold, depends upon the application of two tests: (1) the method and degree of annexation; (2) the object and purpose of the annexation. The early law attached great importance to the first test. It proved harsh and unjust both to limited owners who had affixed valuable chattels of their own to settled land and to tenants for years. The second test was evolved to take care primarily of the limited owner, for example a tenant for life. In *Leigh* v *Taylor* the House of Lords invoked it to protect the interest of the tenant for life who had affixed large and valuable tapestries to the walls of the house for the purpose of adornment and enjoyment of them as tapestries. As I read that decision, it was held that she had not made them fixtures. 'They remained chattels from first to last', said Lord Lindley at p 164 of the report. In the law of landlord and tenant the law's protection went further: even if the chattel affixed by the tenant must be held to have become a fixture, that is to say part of the realty, a rule was evolved that it was to be treated as the property of the tenant and could be removed by him if it fell into a class recognised by law as 'tenant's fixtures', that is to say, if it be a trade, agricultural, or an ornamental fixture. We are not concerned, on the view I take of the case, with 'tenant's fixtures'. The governing relationship with which this case is concerned is that of a beneficial owner of the legal estate selling the freehold to a purchaser. Such a seller can sell as much or as little of his property as he chooses. Lord Poulett excluded certain named objects from the sale, but the contract was silent as to the objects claimed by the plaintiff. I think it was conceded by the defendants – certainly I so read the contracts of sale – that, if the pictures, statue, and sundial were fixtures at the time of the contract, they were included in it as part of the freehold (subject of course to a valuation if they should prove to be tenant's fixtures). The preliminary, and basic, question is therefore whether these objects were at that time fixtures.

Since *Leigh* v *Taylor* the question is really one of fact. The two tests were explained in that case by the Lord Chancellor (see the report at pp 158 and 159), who commented that not the law but our mode of life has changed over the years; that what has changed is 'the degree in which certain things have seemed susceptible of being put up as mere ornaments whereas at our earlier period the mere construction rendered it impossible sometimes to sever the thing which was put up from the realty'. In other words, a degree of annexation which in earlier times the law would have treated as conclusive may now prove nothing. If the purpose of the annexation be for the better enjoyment of the object itself, it may remain a chattel, notwithstanding a high degree of physical annexation. Clearly, however, it remains significant to discover the extent of physical disturbance of the building or the land involved in the removal of the object. If an object cannot be removed without serious damage to, or destruction of, some part of the realty, the case for its having become a fixture is a strong one. The relationship of the two tests to each other requires consideration. If there is no physical annexation there is no fixture. *Quicquid plantatur solo solo cedit*. Nevertheless, an object, resting on the ground by its own weight alone, can be a fixture, if it be so heavy that there is no need to tie it into a foundation, and if it were put in place to improve the realty. *Prima facie*, however, an object resting on the ground by its own weight alone is not a fixture (see *Megarry and Wade*, p 716). Conversely, an object affixed to realty but capable of being removed without much difficulty may yet be a fixture, if, for example, the purpose of its affixing be that 'of creating a beautiful room as a whole' (Neville J in *In Re Whaley* [1908] 1 Ch 615 at p 619). And in the famous instance of *Lord Chesterfield's Settled Estates* [1911] 1 Ch 237 Grinling Gibbons carvings, which had been affixed to a suite of rooms 200 years earlier, were held to be fixtures. Today so great are the technical skills of affixing and removing objects to land or buildings that the second test is more likely than the first to be decisive. Perhaps the enduring significance of the first test is a reminder that there must be some degree of physical annexation before a chattel can be treated as part of the realty.

When one seeks to apply the law to the facts of this case, it is necessary to discriminate between what is relevant but not decisive and what is decisive. Investigatory expertise of a high order has been devoted by both sides to discovering how the pictures were affixed to the panelling and the wall in the two rooms. Fascinating though the investigation was, its conclusion (whether it be, as Mr Millett contended, that the pictures were really put up as an integral part, with the panelling, of the wall-covering, or, as Mr Browne-Wilkinson contended, were put into recesses left for them) is not, in my judgment, decisive. It is enough to say that the pictures were firmly fixed and that their removal needed skill and experience if it were to be done without damage to the wall and panelling. Certainly they were firmly enough fixed to become fixtures if that was the object and purpose of their affixing. But, if ordinary skill was used, as it was, in their removal they could be taken down, and in the event were taken down, without much trouble and without damage to the structure of the rooms. The decisive question is therefore as to the object and purpose of their affixing. Pictures had hung in the two rooms for centuries. 'The Return' had been in the anteroom for a very long time – perhaps ever since it was painted. The 7th Earl decided in the early part of the 20th century to install in the two rooms the panelling and so designed it that there were recesses for pictures. It is this feature which lends plausibility to the suggestion that the pictures, fitted into the recesses left for them, were not to be enjoyed as objects in themselves but as part of the grand architectural design of the two rooms. The Vice-Chancellor rejected this view. So do I. When the panelling was installed in the two rooms the design was either panelled walls with recesses for pictures to be enjoyed as pictures, or rooms having walls which were a composite of panelling and pictures: in other words, the pictures were to be part of a composite mural. I think the former was the truth. The panelling was Victorian, the pictures a heterogeneous collection. According to Sothebys' expert they were of different dates in the 17th and 18th centuries, of different styles, by different hands, the sort of set anyone could put together at any time – very different, I would comment, from that unity of design, the 'Elizabethan Room' in the case of *In re Whaley*. There was a particular Poulett family interest in 'The Return' and in the two coronation portraits, but this interest focused attention not on the design of the room but on the pictures themselves. Notwithstanding the painstaking and attractive arguments of Mr Millett for the plaintiff, I find, applying the second test, that the pictures were not fixtures. They were put in place on the wall to be enjoyed as pictures. The panelling presented a technical problem in putting them up. The way the carpenter, or whoever it was, solved the problem is not decisive in determining their legal character. But the purpose in putting them there is.

The statue and the sundial give rise in my judgment to no difficulty. Neither was at the time of the sale physically attached to the realty. The sundial was a small object and, once the Earl had detached it (as he did many years earlier) from its pedestal, it ceased to be part of the realty. The statue was heavy. It weighed 10 cwt and stood 5 ft 7 in high on its plinth. There is an issue as to whether it was cemented into the plinth or rested on its own weight. The question is not decisive, for, even if it was attached by a cement bond, it was (as events proved) easily removable. However, upon the balance of probability, I agree with the Vice-Chancellor in thinking it was not attached. The best argument for the statue being a fixture was its careful siting in the West Lawn so as to form an integral part of the architectural design of the west elevation of the house. The design point is a good one so far as it goes: it explains the siting of the plinth, which undoubtedly was a fixture. But what was put upon the plinth was very much a matter for the taste of the occupier of the house for the time being. We know that at one time the object on the plinth had been a sundial. At the time of the sale it was this statue of a Greek athlete. The plinth's position was architecturally important: it ensured that whatever stood on it would be correctly positioned. But the object it carried could be whatever appealed to the occupier for the time being. Sundial or statue – it did not matter to the design, so long as it was in the right place – a result ensured by the plinth which was firmly fixed into the ground. Being, as I think, unattached, the statue was, *prima facie*, not a fixture, but, even if it were attached, the application of the second test would lead to the same conclusion.

As for the Chinese prints, I agree with the Vice-Chancellor. Even if the plaintiff could prove a title to sue in conversion, detinue or trespass, there is no evidence that it was by the hand or upon the instructions of Lord Poulett that the prints were damaged. And, if the plaintiff's case is put in equity as a breach of trust by a vendor when he was constructive trustee for the purchaser, the plaintiff (always assuming he can prove his entitlement to sue the head vendor, a question upon which I express no opinion) has failed to prove any act or omission by the defendant which could amount to a breach of trust.

Accordingly, I agree with the Vice-Chancellor. The action fails *in limine*. The plaintiff cannot show either that the pictures, statue and sundial were fixtures or that Lord Poulett, his executors, or anyone acting on their behalf were guilty of any acts or omissions in respect of the Chinese prints which, assuming the plaintiff could make title, could amount either to trespass, conversion or detinue or to breach of trust. Accordingly, I would dismiss the appeal.

After I had prepared this judgment, I had the advantage of reading the judgment about to be delivered by Goff LJ. I would make two comments. First, without in any way disagreeing with the possibility, in logic, of drawing the distinction I understand my brother to be making between chattels and removable fixtures, I think it would be illogical to overlook the possibility that an object fixed to realty may yet remain a chattel. In my judgment, the pictures, statue and sundial did so remain. Second, upon my understanding of the way the case has been fought, Mr Millett for the plaintiff submitted that these objects were fixtures and part of the realty, while the defendants submitted that they were chattels. Having declared myself in favour of the defendants on this issue, I have not thought it necessary to consider the possibility of the objects being fixtures but not part of the realty, that is to say removable fixtures.

QUESTIONS

1 John co-owned 'Oak House' in fee simple with his wife Jane. It was their home. He also independently held a lease of 'Blythe Meadows' which had 50 years to run. He had built a wooden shed at 'Oak House' in which he carried out his hobby of pottery making. He recently died. His will, which he had made without legal advice, contained only the following dispositions:

> '1. I would like Jane to take all my land.
> 2. I would like all my money and other goods to go to my friend Peter.'

Who is entitled to 'Oak House', 'Blythe Meadows', the shed, and the rest of his property?

2 John and Sarah signed a contract for the sale by John to Sarah of 'Panorama', a hardware shop. A clause in the contract stated: 'It is hereby agreed that the purchaser shall restrict her trade in accordance with the terms set out in the conveyance by the vendor to the purchaser of 'Venus Hair Salon' on 1 May 1994'. John now refuses to convey 'Panorama', claiming that the contract is void under the Law of Property (Miscellaneous Provisions) Act 1989 s 2. Advise Sarah.

3 What exceptions are there to the general rule that legal interests in land can only be created by deed?

4 Compare the meanings of *land* and *realty*.

5 Consider the policy influences possibly operating in the case provided in the study material.

CHAPTER 4

LIMITATIONS ON THE ENJOYMENT OF LAND

The legal restraints upon land use today are sometimes nostalgically contrasted with the freedom of former ages. The validity of the comparison depends upon which former age is considered. If the Middle Ages are chosen the criticism is surely misplaced. Communal agriculture, subsistence economy and formidable agrarian custom would have inclined an entrepreneur to deal with goods rather than land. Yet such choice of time is a little unfair. Enormous liberation of land use occurred during the hundreds of years which elapsed before Victorian times. This is when modern memory begins. Let us however go back to 1750 as our point of comparison. Villages were mostly tuned to agriculture still partly communal in nature. Sowing, weeding and harvesting tolled the year. Economics, though even then gravely affected by national and international events, still had a distinct local role. The problems of public health were unrealised. The houses of a few dozen families clustered together enjoyed the benefits of community and security. Aesthetic judgements were probably not so visually biased as our own. Indeed aesthetic appreciation was perhaps not so distilled a value as for us. The prevalence of settled traditions, with unconscious local variations, produced a balanced, even static environment. It has been remarked that 12 hovels can be a delight, but 12 000 a menace.

Spaced through these hamlets were market towns. Stratford, Derby and a hundred others supplied the more sophisticated elements of business. Finally, there were a few towns where commercial and social activities were much more intense. London, Bristol, Oxford and a few others were centres of metropolitan stature to the counties surrounding.

The important common factor in this society, however, was that all these communities were of centuries-old growth and common experience. Slow growth bred long tradition. The countryside was still nearby. There was little mobility of population. The influence of large landowners was strong and lasting. 'Welfare' was largely a private matter.

Then, in the second half of the eighteenth century, came the industrial revolution, inclining the angle of industrial, social and intellectual development so steeply that, two centuries later, we have not caught up with the problems posed by it. The intensive growth of industry, migration to the towns and the sudden incompetence of medical and sociological management to cope with it, brought up problems of such size that only the state could influence events. Twelve thousand hovels bred not only cholera but also grave moral problems. Reformists persuaded Parliament to pass Acts concerned with public health, factories and the urban environment.

Much of that legislation has now been overtaken by later Acts. What is significant is that the habit of social legislation, once seized by Parliament, has never been put down. The subject matter of that legislation has however moved on to new fields. Education, social security and the provision of a huge range of other benefits are the stuff of modern politics and administrative law. Land law has been crucially affected by it.

It seems that rapid growth and mixture of population must be associated with an increase in legislation and regulation. Perhaps this is not only because of the physical problems caused by large numbers of people living close together, but also because the powerful bonds of custom and tradition no longer hold sway. Any contrast drawn between the freedom to enjoy land in 1750 and the restrictions in force today should take account of the destruction of the environment which occurred when both social and legal restraints were lacking during the eighteenth century.

Uninhibited enjoyment of property is also sometimes incompatible with wider public needs. Once it is decided, for instance, that education shall be available for everyone, it follows that authorities must be empowered to buy land for schools compulsorily. Similarly, if we demand healthy towns and the preservation of our countryside, some restrictions on the use of land must be accepted. It is in this field of administrative law that enormous incursions into property rights have been made during the last century.

The rest of this chapter is given over to some of the more important restrictions on the enjoyment of land which affect all occupiers, whether they own fees simple or lesser interests. Owners of lesser interests are bound not only by these rules but often by further restrictions which prevent them abusing the land to the detriment of the absolute owner in reversion. The restrictions placed upon land use by these developments are sometimes complex and quite beyond the scope of a book of such general aims as this. Some of the subjects, such as planning, compulsory purchase, housing and security of tenure amount to statutory codes. The following accounts are therefore little more than signboards pointing in their directions. Yet the first constitutional principle must not be neglected. A landowner may do what he wishes with his property except insofar as the law positively restricts him from so doing.

RESTRICTIONS AFFECTING THE OWNERS OF ALL INTERESTS IN LAND

Self-imposed restrictions

A landowner may voluntarily inhibit the use of his land by private transaction with another owner. He may, for instance, grant his neighbour the right to lay a drain through his property, or agree not to build on certain parts of the land. Such transactions, if carried out in the correct way, frequently affect the land permanently, even when the ownership changes. Important examples are restrictive covenants and easements.

The law of tort

A landowner must not use his land so as to commit a tort against another person. He must not, for example, commit nuisances such as allowing harmful vapours to escape from his property (*St Helen's Smelting Co* v *Tipping* (1865) 11 HLC 642), or permit the accumulation and escape of mischievous things generally (*Rylands* v *Fletcher* (1868) LR 3 HL 330). Neither must he deny his neighbour the natural rights in his own land. One of these is the right of support of that neighbour's land against his own at their respective natural levels. This applies whether the two properties are vertically adjacent or horizontally so, as in the case of a separately owned mine (*Backhouse* v *Bonomi* (1861) 9 HL Cas 503). This duty does not, however, extend to supporting buildings or structures or the extra stresses they cause on land. In *Wyatt* v *Harrison* (1832) 3 B&Ad 871, a man who dug foundations for his house so close to his neighbour's house that the walls of the latter sank was held not liable. An injunction is the appropriate remedy to prevent an infringement of such rights. Yet this might not be granted on the simple terms that the damage should be completely reinstated if this would cause injustice. Thus, in *Redland Bricks Ltd* v *Morris* [1969] 2 All ER 576 the quarrying of clay had caused adjacent land to slip. This adjacent land was worth £12 000, whereas the cost of stabilizing it completely would have been £30 000. It was held that the county court judge should have ordered specific works to be done, rather than have granted an unqualified mandatory injunction. Although support for artificial structures is not a natural right, it can come into being by act of parties as an easement as mentioned in the section on self-imposed restrictions above, either expressly or by implication.

Another example of a natural right, needing no act of parties for its creation, is the right to have a stream that has always flowed through land continue to do so, subject to the water rights of other riparian owners. Diversions and obstructions would be obvious examples of infringement of this right.

Nationalisation of certain minerals

The Crown has long been entitled to gold and silver occurring in land. In the modern state, central regulation of vital mineral resources has been considered necessary in the national interest, though in recent years government policies of privatisation have diversified the agencies exploiting these resources in some cases. Natural petroleum vested in the Crown under the Petroleum (Production) Act 1934, and coal in the National Coal Board under the Coal Act 1938, and the Coal Industry Nationalisation Act 1946. Under the Atomic Energy Act 1946, and the Atomic Energy Authority Act 1954, the Minister may order the vesting in himself, or the United Kingdom Atomic Energy Authority, of the right to win from any land any mineral from which uranium, thorium, plutonium, neptunium, or other producers of atomic energy might be obtained.

Restrictions on the use of water

Water which stands on land, as in a pond or lake, is part of the land and belongs to the owner of the land (LPA 1925 s 62). Water which is moving through land, whether in defined channels above or below the surface, or merely percolating, is ownerless, though it is capable of ownership when drawn off. The owner of land containing water has the following rights of abstraction.

1 *Standing water*. The owner may use this without limit. The Water Resources Act 1991, dealt with below, does not apply since static water does not constitute a 'source of supply'. Even small groups of such waters which are interconnected are exempt from its provisions if they do not discharge out of the group.

2 *Percolating water*. Subject to the Water Resources Act 1991 the landowner may abstract as much percolating water as he pleases. Thus in *Chasemore* v *Richards* (1859) 7 HL Cas 349, the use of the Wandle stream was lost to a millowner because an adjoining owner sank a well and intercepted oozing water before it could reach the stream. In *Langbrook Properties Ltd* v *Surrey County Council* [1969] 3 All ER 1424, a similar decision was given when percolating water had been taken to such a degree that it had desiccated neighbouring land and caused settlements in buildings there.

   Abstraction of percolating water now, however, is subject to the Water Resources Act 1991, replacing the Water Resources Act 1963 (as amended). This Act, which aims at safeguarding the water supply of the country for the future, forbids abstraction without a licence granted by the National Rivers Authority. There are some exceptions to this requirement, including abstractions not exceeding 5 cubic metres, or 20 cubic metres in any 24 hours. The Environment Act 1995 provides for transfer of functions from this authority to the newly constituted Environment Agency.

3 *Flowing water*. A riparian owner, who is a person owning land which is both reasonably close to a river and abutting upon it at least at one point (*Attwood* v *Llay Main Collieries* [1926] Ch 444), may take water in unlimited quantities for 'ordinary' purposes connected with the riparian tenement. These purposes include drinking, washing, cooking and the needs of cattle on the land. Provided that these conditions are fulfilled, it does not matter that the use exhausts the stream. Second, he may take water for

> 'extraordinary' purposes connected with the riparian land, provided that the use is reasonable and that it is returned to the river substantially undiminished in both quality and quantity. Such purposes include ditch irrigation and manufacturing. In *McCartney* v *Londonderry Rly* [1904] AC 301 it was held that a railway company may not take water from a stream simply because locomotives were standing on their land nearby. Such a use was not connected with the riparian land at all, for the water would have been used over many miles of railway, not merely on that land. These principles were explained in the leading case of *Swindon Waterworks Co* v *Wilts & Berks Canal Co* (1875) LR 7 HL 697.
>
> In *Rugby Joint Water Board* v *Walters* [1966] 3 All ER 497 it was held that large-scale spray irrigation was not an ordinary use. Neither was it a valid extraordinary use, because the water was not returned in substantially undiminished quantity. Buckley J, however, remarked that no judge had yet attempted to define 'ordinary' use. It is to be hoped that when the opportunity for sharper definition arises the court will not induce it merely from the precedents of a technologically primitive society but will recognize that the ox has now yielded to the motor.

Apart from these rules, the use of flowing water is subject to the Water Resources Act 1991. The same rules apply generally as apply to percolating water, but a further exemption from licences exists. A riparian owner does not need a licence for taking water for agricultural purposes other than spray irrigation.

Licences under the Act may extend as well as restrict the common law right of extraction and may affect the defences available in civil actions between landowners for interference with water rights.

The same rules apply to the abstraction of water from an underground river as from one on the surface, provided that it is a reasonable inference from known facts that the water keeps to a bounded course. This knowledge must be present at the time when any act complained of was committed, and not merely established before the hearing. Entry of a stream below ground and its later re-emergence are an example of facts from which such inference may be made (*Bleachers Association Ltd* v *Chapel-en-le-Frith RDC* [1933] Ch 356, per Luxmoore J, at 363).

Other restrictions on the use of water include the public right of navigation in tidal waters up to the ebb and flow point of the mean tides. In non-tidal waters this right only exists where it can be proved to have arisen by immemorial use or under statute. Where it does exist, the riparian owner must not interfere with it either by physical obstruction or by abstraction of too much water. Thus in *AG* v *Terry* (1874) LR 9 Ch App 423, the extension of a wharf by three feet into a navigable width of 60 feet was held unlawful.

A few words may be added about the ownership of river beds and shores. The bed of a tidal river is vested in the Crown or its grantee up to the normal ebb and flow point; so is the foreshore. Boundaries which vary as a result of natural forces, such as the shift of a shoreline over the years, pose the question whether there can exist a *movable fee simple*. It seems that there can be (see *Baxendale* v *Instow PC* [1981] 2 All ER 620). As to the non-tidal parts of rivers, a riparian owner may in the nature of things own to the near bank, to some point under the river or to the far bank. It is a simple question of how much was conveyed to him and his predecessors in title. Frequently, however, a river is the boundary of property and such boundaries have, in the past, been all too vaguely drawn or described in conveyances. Where there is lack of positive evidence in such cases there is a useful presumption that the owner of each bank owns up to the midstream point in the bed. It is, however, a presumption only. The change of course of a river does not affect the ownership of land.

Objects and living things

The general rule is that if an object is embedded in the land so as to become a fixture it belongs to the landowner. As to objects that remain chattels, there is probably a presumption that the occupier is entitled against all but the true owner unless the circumstances show that he intended to exercise no control over them. The question should be pursued in the books on tort (see, for instance, *Re Cohen* [1953] Ch 88). In any event the following exceptions stand aside from this general principle.

1 *Treasure trove*. Under common law, the Crown has a prerogative right to treasure trove. An object is treasure trove only if it consists of gold or silver in the form of bullion, coin or trinket, if it has been hidden as opposed to having been abandoned or merely lost, and if the true owner is unknown. The second of these conditions, since it relates to an intention, must be inferred from the circumstances. It will readily be fulfilled for instance where several valuable objects are found placed together. Thus in *AG* v *Trustees of the British Museum* [1903] 2 Ch 598, gold ornaments lying together underground inside a hollow collar and dating from about AD 300 were held to be treasure trove. Speculation upon intention, however, tends to open the door to extravagant arguments 'more suited to the poem of a Celtic bard than the prose of an English law reporter'.

2 *Wild animals and birds*. These are ownerless unless they are too young to move away, or have been tamed. The landowner, however, or the person to whom he has granted sporting rights, has the exclusive right to catch them or to take eggs, whereupon they become his property. This is so even though they are killed by a trespasser (*Blades* v *Higgs* (1865) 11 HL Cas 621). White swans, unmarked and in open rivers, belong to the Crown. Apart from these and 'royal fish', any prerogative right of the Crown to wild creatures was abolished by the Wild Creatures and Forest Laws Act 1971. These remarks, of course, relate merely to ownership. The taking of wild animals and birds is also subject to the game laws and the laws protecting wildlife (*see*, for instance, the Wildlife and Countryside Acts 1981–1991).

3 *Fish.* Fish in rivers and sea, with a few exceptions, are ownerless. The owner of the river bed has, however, the exclusive right to catch them. The public have no such right even though there is a public right of navigation. The public have, however, a right to fish in tidal waters. All these rights must be exercised subject to the general law relating to fishing.

4 *Plants.* These belong to the landowner. Again attention is drawn to legislation protecting certain species of growing things.

5 *Conservation of nature.* During this century the enormous increase in agricultural technology and the exigencies of two world wars have led to the exploitation of land as an economic resource on a scale formerly impossible. Destruction of natural habitats for wild creatures and plants and pollution of soils and water have threatened not only the ecology but our natural culture. A new relationship between landowner and land has been engendered by public opinion and legislation, national and European. The details of this legislation should be sought in specialist books (e.g. Ball and Bell, 1994).

Interference with air space

The Civil Aviation Act 1982 empowers aircraft to fly over property at a reasonable height. These provisions must be taken to give a defence against actions in nuisance rather than in trespass, since considering the height at which even low-flying aircraft fly, no trespass would be committed. A landowner's rights of property are no longer believed to go beyond the height necessary for ordinary use of enjoyment (*Bernstein (Baron)* v *Skyviews Ltd* [1977] 3 WLR 136). In other cases of interference, as for instance by projections or missiles such as bullets from a rifle range, actions will lie in nuisance and trespass (see *Clifton* v *Bury* (1887) 4 TLR 8; see also *Woolerton and Wilson Ltd* v *Richard Costain Ltd* [1970] 1 All ER 483).

Control of activities on land

This head of restraint is not intended to be exclusive since some types of such control have already been mentioned, and others, in particular planning control, will shortly be dealt with separately. However, some examples of the huge residue of inhibitions are given here to illustrate the social responsibility which now attaches to land ownership. An activity is controlled in order to protect interests which might be quite external to the land. Riding schools, for instance, must conform to certain statutory standards for the welfare of horses. An owner or prospective purchaser of land cannot afford to ignore these laws even though they have not always been considered part of land law. It is much more important today for the ordinary landowner to be acquainted with certain aspects of public health law than with some of the more remote sidings of the Settled Land Act 1925 (see, for instance, the Environmental Protection Act 1990). The Environment Act 1995 establishes the Environment Agency and confers upon it important powers of control regarding contamination of land, air quality and protection of hedgerows and the National Parks.

The details of some of these subjects amount to codes in themselves. Furthermore, legislation is generally active on these fronts, quickly outdating ordinary textbooks. Fortunately, publishers have produced loose-leaf encyclopaedias on some of the topics to which anyone seeking detailed information should refer. Some of the most important of these subjects are the laws of: housing; public health (property aspects); pollution and health and safety at work. Yet some of the most specialised uses of land are also controlled by the law. From pub to private nursing home Parliament has been active. Finally, local bye-laws often have a bearing on land use.

Compulsory disfigurement of land

Certain statutes empower authorities to enter land and place apparatus there. Sometimes the bodies are local authorities or other public bodies; sometimes they are privatised bodies. Examples of such apparatus are sewers and electric pylons.

Compulsory purchase

A host of statutes enable various authorities to acquire land compulsorily for their purposes. These range from the provision of housing accommodation to the building of aerodromes. Like all administrative powers, they are strictly subject to the *ultra vires* rule. While the powers of acquisition are to be found scattered in many statutes, the procedure for acquisition is laid down as a common code for most of these cases in the Acquisition of Land Act 1981. Briefly this is as follows: the authority makes a compulsory purchase order and notifies the owners of all interests in the land and the general public of the order and of the time limits for objections. It then submits the order to the Minister for confirmation. If there are objections, the Minister must hold a local enquiry, and may then confirm or refuse the order. If it is confirmed, the authority serves a notice to treat under the Compulsory Purchase Act 1965, which invites the owner to make a claim for compensation. If the price is agreed, this agreement, together with the notice to treat, constitutes the contract of sale. Thereafter the procedure follows that of an ordinary conveyance. The district valuer, an independent person, normally assists agreement, but, failing this, the compensation is settled by the Lands Tribunal.

The principles of compensation are complex but are based on the open market value of the land, compensation for disturbance or other matters not based on the value of land and compensation for severance of lands. Detailed rules for assessment are contained in the Land Compensation Acts 1961 and 1973.

Protection of tenants

In this century, three classes of tenants have been given a large measure of security of tenure so that their tenancies continue indefinitely, despite the terms of their leases, unless landlords could prove specified reasons for termination. In some cases the rent that may be demanded is controlled. These classes are most business tenancies under the Landlord and Tenant Act 1954 Pt II (as amended by the Law of Property Act 1969), most agricultural tenancies under the Agricultural Holdings Act 1986 and certain residential tenancies under the 'Rent Acts'. Furthermore, under the Leasehold Reform Act 1967, certain tenants can demand either to buy the freehold reversions to their leases or to be granted new leases of 50 years. Much deregulation has now occurred. The law in this area is of a technical nature and will be considered in outline in Chapter 6. It is referred to here merely to show that legislation may restrain the contractual freedom of landlords in their dominion over land.

Town and country planning

This is the most important of all the influences on land use discussed in this chapter.

The account of the law given below amounts to little more than a thumbnail sketch of the complex body of rules, now principally contained in the Town and Country Planning Act 1990 and the large volume of delegated legislation. Even a detailed knowledge of the legal rules, however, would provide a very incomplete understanding of the subject. A real appreciation can be gained only by examining the purpose of planning and by recognising that the balancing of conflicting aims, sometimes private, sometimes public, turns more upon political, social and economic factors than upon law. The discretions exercised by planning authorities are enormous, and can seldom be controlled by law. (For such an open-textured approach see *Land Law and Planning* by Patrick McAuslan, 1975).

The local planning authorities are now the councils of counties and districts. These authorities are unified in the case of the metropolitan counties. Under former legislation each planning authority had to prepare a 'development plan' for its area and periodically to review it. These plans and reviews were subject to review by the Secretary of State. These plans forecasted the kind of development envisaged for the future and allocated areas for residential, industrial, cultural and other uses, including those of comprehensive redevelopment. These plans were superseded by 'structure plans' and 'local plans'. The structure plan outlines the large-scale development policy for the area, including traffic management and improvement of environment, and relates this policy to the policies of other authorities. The local plan consists of a map and a more detailed description of development proposals for land use in that area. The structure plan, consisting of a written statement with diagrams only, as opposed to the detailed maps of the old system, is less precise and therefore attracts few objections. Its approval is thus subject to less delay.

Before submitting its structure plan to the Secretary of State for confirmation, the county council, which is the planning authority for this purpose, must advertise the results of a preparatory survey, so that representations might be made in regard to it by members of the public and various bodies. After this stage, the council puts the plan into its final form for submission. The Secretary of State then conducts a public examination at which matters he considers ought to be discussed are considered. Only persons who are invited by him to participate may do so. He may then approve the plan, with or without modification, or reject it. The validity of the plan may be tested in the High Court within six weeks of approval on the grounds either that it is partly or wholly *ultra vires*, or that some procedural requirement has not been complied with.

The authority for the preparation of the local plan is, unless the structure plan provides otherwise, the district council. When the structure plan has been made, this authority must consider whether to make a local plan for any part of its area. It must, in any case, make such a plan if the Secretary of State orders it to do so or, if the structure plan has defined any part of the area as an *action area*, that is, due for comprehensive development. The preparatory stages of the local plan are similar to those of the structure plan. In certain circumstances a local enquiry must be held to consider objections. Finally, the authority sends a copy of its plan to the Secretary of State who may order that it be submitted for approval. Otherwise the authority may adopt it.

So far as the landowner is concerned the essence of the Town and Country Planning Act 1990 is s 55(1) which defines 'development' as 'the carrying out of building, engineering, mining or other operations in, on, over or under land, or the making of any material change in the use of any buildings or other land'.

There are thus two distinct facets to 'development', namely, *operations* and *uses*. *Operations* are acts which change the physical characteristics of the land or what is under or over it (see *Cheshire CC* v *Woodward* [1962] 1 All ER 517 and *Planning Law and Procedure* by A E Telling). *Use* denotes the purposes to which property is put. A change of use can therefore occur without any physical change in the land (see *Sunbury-on-Thames UDC* v *Mann* (1958) 9 P&CR 309). For clarification, certain matters are declared to constitute development, such as the tipping of waste or the use of a single dwelling-house as more than one separate dwelling, and certain other matters are stated not to be development, as, for instance, internal improvements to a house, the use of land for agriculture or forestry, road repairs and improvements, or a change from one use to another within any of the *use classes*. These *use classes* have been set out in a statutory instrument – the Town and Country Planning (Use Classes) Order SI 764/1987. This provision enables owners to change from one use to another one similar in kind without permission. An example might illustrate the operation of these: Class A1 includes most shops. A shopkeeper may thus change from selling groceries to selling toys since this does not constitute 'development' as both kinds of shop fall within the same use class.

The Minister is empowered to grant blanket permission for activities which do constitute development. He does this through statutory instruments known as General Development Orders (*see* the Town and Country Planning (General

Development) Order SI 1813/1988, as amended). This is known as *permitted development*. Examples of permitted development are the erection of a fence up to two metres high, or up to one metre where it abuts on a vehicular road, the use of land for any purposes, except as a caravan site, on not more than a total of 28 days in a calendar year, or the erection of buildings within the curtilage of and incidental to the enjoyment of a dwelling-house. It should be added as a caution here that these permissions are subject to conditions mentioned in the Order. The legislation itself must be consulted in this, as in other planning matters, for it is an extremely detailed code. Special development orders may also be made. These are limited to particular areas or subjects. It is possible that these will increase in importance in the future.

Apart from permitted development, no development is lawful without consent. Application for development is made to the distict planning authority. The authority must consult with a wide range of public bodies and publicise the application. They may grant permission unconditionally or subject to 'such conditions as they think fit', or refuse it.

An appeal against the decision of the local planning authority, or its failure to give a decision within two months of the application, lies to the Secretary of State, who, after considering the written representations of both sides, or holding a local enquiry, may dismiss or allow the appeal or substitute his own decision.

Control of development is exercised in other ways, too. Unauthorised development is remedied by means of *enforcement notices* in the long term and by *stop notices* in the short term. Such notices must be served within four years of its occurrence in the case of building, engineering or mining operations, or the failure to comply with any conditions regarding such operations. Even authorised development may be removed by a *discontinuance order* but compensation is then payable. Appeals lie to the Secretary of State in all these cases. Special kinds of control are provided for the preservation of certain kinds of amenities in town and country. There is a code for the control of advertisements. Trees can be protected by *tree preservation orders*, which may apply to single trees or woods. Such orders may provide for replanting after felling operations where these have been permitted under the order. Lists of buildings of special architectural or historic interest are compiled or approved by the Secretary of State, and the demolition, alteration or extension of such *listed buildings* requires consent. Planning applications affecting their setting require special publicity. Every planning authority must determine which areas are of special architectural or historic interest. There is machinery for their designation as conservation areas. Within these areas no building may be demolished without consent. Proposals for the preservation and enhancement of such areas must be publicised by the authority. There is special protection for trees in these areas. Orders to abate may be served where waste land is seriously spoiling amenity.

RESTRICTIONS WHICH MAY AFFECT THE OWNERS OF LIMITED INTERESTS

Subject to the heavy restrictions described above, a fee simple owner can use land as he pleases. He may pull valuable buildings down and neglect the land. Legally he has only himself to consider. When a person has a lesser interest, however, other people must be considered. If land is settled on *A* for life with remainder in fee simple to *B*, and that land holds a fine house, an oak forest and a seam of unnationalised minerals, it would be unjust if *A*, unless specially authorised by the settlor, cut down and sold the trees, won and sold the minerals and misused the house, so that on his death all that passed to *B* was a shack in a blasted landscape. The law has, therefore, developed rules calculated to balance the accounts fairly when limited owners are in possession. This is not to say that these rules always necessarily apply. A settlor may, if he wishes, countenance the result described above. The rules merely categorise certain acts and omissions as constituting a permanent alteration in the character or value of land, leaving it to the settlor or lessor to decide whether the owner of the limited interest be allowed to indulge in them. These rules are known as the laws of *waste*. Whether or not the owner of a limited interest is liable for, or, to use the technical term, 'impeachable for' waste, he is nevertheless bound by the general restrictions on the enjoyment of land described in the first part of this chapter. How to discover whether a particular limited owner is impeachable for waste will be discussed when the various limited interests in land are dealt with. There are three kinds of waste. Finally it should be borne in mind that one large class of limited owners, namely lessees, may suffer special restrictions on the use of land imposed under the lease.

Voluntary waste

This is the commission of any positive act which results in a change in the character of the land or injury of a lasting kind. Examples are pulling down or altering buildings, opening new pits or mines (though not merely working those already opened), and changing the course of husbandry, as for instance by changing woodland into arable land by cutting timber.

Acts which, though technically waste, have a beneficial effect on the land constitute *ameliorating waste* and will not be actionable. Thus an injunction was refused in *Doherty* v *Allman* (1877) 3 App Cas 709, where a tenant converted an old storehouse into a dwelling. Under the general law 'timber' is oak, ash or elm from the age of 20 years upwards but not so old that they cannot provide 'a good post' (per Sir George Jessel, MR, in *Honywood* v *Honywood* (1874) LR 18 Eq 306, at 309). Other trees may be timber, however, by local custom, as for instance, birch in Yorkshire. Custom may also provide a different qualifying age, or even require that girth should be the test. The cutting of other trees is not waste unless it amounts to such an improvident act, such as felling trees which would be timber when mature, as to constitute *equitable waste*, dealt with below.

In three cases, however, even the cutting of timber is not waste. First, in the case of timber estates, the taking of the proper periodic crop is not waste, because there will be a planned rotation of cropping and replanting which ensures constant replenishment of the trees. Second, there may be a local custom to cut timber in the ordinary course of husbandry (*Dashwood* v *Magniac* [1891] 3 Ch 306) and then proper cutting of it is not waste. Third, it is not waste to take *estovers*, which consists in the reasonable and thrifty cutting of timber for the following present needs, namely *housebote* for fuelling and repairing houses, *ploughbote* for making and repairing agricultural implements, and *haybote* for repairing boundaries.

Permissive waste

This is a mere failure to act which results in buildings and lands falling into decay. Failure to cultivate, however, does not constitute permissive waste (per Parke B, in *Hutton* v *Warren* (1836) 1 M&W 466, at 472).

Equitable waste

A limited owner who was not impeachable for either of the types of waste mentioned above had considerable scope for abusing his position by committing improvident and wanton acts for which there was no remedy at common law. Equity, therefore, developed restraints which are now recognised by statute (LPA 1925 s 135).

Examples of equitable waste are stripping or pulling down a house (*Vane* v *Barnard* (1716) 2 Vern 738), and cutting ornamental timber, unless of course there is good horticultural reason.

Restrictions imposed by leases

A tenant's use and enjoyment of land may be considerably curtailed by the terms of his lease, which might, for instance, forbid him to use the premises for business purposes, or to play musical instruments there after midnight.

STUDY MATERIAL

Extract from McAuslan's *Land Law and Planning*

(Weidenfeld and Nicolson, 1975 p 94)

Decision making: an introduction

It is easy to underestimate the complexity of the process of decision making. For lawyers the typical decision-making process is the judicial decision, publicly made after carefully phrased oral and written submissions, and based on a finding of the 'facts' of the case, followed by the application of law to those facts. We may be aware that beneath the surface, things are not quite what they seem, but apart from discussions of the finer points of precedent, we rarely explore beneath the surface. Yet we must try to do so in this book, because the typical decision-making process in planning takes place not in a court, but in a local authority committee or a department, and involves the interaction of experts with experts, experts with amateurs, amateurs with amateurs, and the bringing to bear of a host of considerations, both relevant and irrelevant, all of which we must try to take account of in assessing the efficacy of the planning process. The comments which follow are no more than the barest introduction to administrative decision making, designed to highlight the following points:

(a) Making a decision is not something which takes place in a short space of time, in an afternoon committee meeting for instance. Much evidence shows that the typical decision is made by a gradual process of whittling down alternatives, of perceiving issues with greater clarity, of taking up positions from a variety of motives, not all of them rational, or possibly respectable, and of responding to outside pressures over a period of time. Thus the people who appear to the public as being those who have 'taken the decision' are almost always at the end of a chain of lesser decisions which have crucially shaped the final decision. Decisions, in other words, are not and cannot be taken in isolation from what has gone before, or what is likely to transpire, from the values of the decision makers, and from what Simon has called organisational loyalties, that is the values of the group or organisation to which the decision makers belong. Indeed as Brown emphasises,

> Decisions in large organisations belong to the organisation as a whole and are not attributable to any one individual . . . The negotiations between individuals, the communication system, the formal rules – these and other factors interact to produce the decisions of the organisation.

(b) Both civil servants in a department and officers in a local authority are engaged in a process in which clear lines between policy and administration, and between policy making and fact finding are not easy to perceive. Nor are rules about the responsibility of ministers or local councillors for decisions they have taken clear to perceive, let alone base controlling devices or reforms of organisational structures on. The literature on decision making stresses the difficulty of pin-pointing who makes decisions, yet the theory of control over the administration is that *someone* can and must be held responsible for decisions that are taken, otherwise people at large will cease to have any say in their daily lives or any influence over the decisions that affect them. Part of the drive behind public participation in planning and in other fields is precisely because there is a general *feeling* that traditional methods of control of administrative decision making are less effective than of old at a time when more and more vital decisions are being taken which will affect our future. Is the problem that the controlling devices have failed to increase in scope and sophistication as fast as decision-making processes, or that potential controllers, and the public at large, are too easily mesmerised by the jargon of decision makers into believing that decisions are in some way inevitable and therefore uncontrollable?

(c) Taking this last point further, what is the role of the Minister and local councillor in the typical administrative decision-making process? How realistic is it to talk of ministerial responsibility for planning decisions when the minor decisions never reach the Minister, and the Minister can never hope to see more than a part of the information on the major ones before he announces 'his' decision? If anything, it is more difficult to see the role of the local councillor in decision making. Friend and Jessop's study of decision making in Coventry provides one of the clearest and most sympathetic accounts of local authority decision making that has been produced for some time, and that certainly makes a case out for the influence of councillors on decisions and the manner in which they are reached, but the general conclusions of the Maud Report on the Management of Local Government are less sanguine. My own view, based admittedly on very little experience, is that one can exaggerate the helplessness of the average councillor. However, there is no substitute for local councillors (and ministers for that matter) becoming familiar with a particular field, and then being prepared to spend a great deal of time on the major issues and problems in that field, and their effect on the councillors' locality so that they can hold their own with the officers. This is a counsel of perfection – it may even be thought rather naive – and unlikely to be realised except in a very small number of cases, but at least it will serve as an antidote to the 'Bains' philosophy which is sweeping local government: that a reorganisation of the management structure of local authorities to take account of the corporate approach to their activities is the key to more effective and accountable local government. Arguably, the corporate management approach to government was behind the reforms that led to the DoE; while that might result in a more co-ordinated approach by the administration to the problem of the cities, will it lead to more accountability to Parliament and the electorate at large?

(d) The last point to bear in mind arises not so much from the readings that follow as from what has gone before. We must add to our awareness of the general complexities of decision making our awareness that in planning, as in other spheres of government, particular legal constraints and constitutional conventions and practices exist and have to be followed; some reforms might not be possible because they conflict with the law or the conventions, neither of which can, as a matter of practical politics, be altered; some reforms might be introduced which are thought to be necessary politically, but do not always make sense from the point of view of the student of decision making. Law and politics in short affect the procedures of planning as much as they do the substance; an obvious point, but one that is sometimes overlooked by lawyers and planners alike.

Extract reproduced by permission of Professor J P W B McAuslan.

QUESTIONS

1 How does a solicitor acting for a prospective purchaser of land discover the extent to which the restrictions on land use discussed in this chapter affect that land?

2 Advise the owner of a retail grocery shop whether he requires planning permission in order to change the use of the shop to that of a launderette.

3 Consider the influences which might operate when local planning authorities make decisions in respect of applications to develop land.

4 Advise a market gardener whose premises are adjacent to a river as to his rights, if any, to use river water for irrigating crops; centrally heating greenhouses; and selling it in containers to purchasers of plants requiring the particular mineral qualities of the water.

5 You have heard that the owner of Victorian house at the end of your street is about to apply for planning permission to convert it into a keep-fit centre for the general public. You believe that this would be seriously detrimental to the amenity of the street, which consists of private residences only. What steps would you take to persuade the local planning committee to refuse permission? Assume that it would be within the legal powers of that authority to grant permission.

CHAPTER 5

FREEHOLD INTERESTS

THE FEE SIMPLE ABSOLUTE IN POSSESSION

Apart from the lease, this is the only interest giving a right to the land itself which can be a legal estate (LPA 1925 s 1).

To qualify, the description 'fee simple absolute in possession' used in s 1 must be perfectly satisfied. The expression, therefore, must be closely examined. Then the nature and the method of transfer of this estate will be described.

It must be observed here that the minute examination of the expression which follows is essential, given the present state of the law, since it imports serious consequences in the transfer of land. It will be explained in Chapter 9 that radical reform of the law relating to settlements of land, discussed in that chapter, could obviate the need for this detailed examination. There is, however, no immediate prospect of such reform. A full comprehension of the principles described in this chapter is therefore crucial to an understanding of modern land law.

The meaning of *fee simple absolute in possession*

1 *Fee simple*. The meaning of this may be disposed of quickly. It means ownership. In short, it is, of the interests we are now discussing, the only one which has no time limit placed on its potential endurance.

2 *Absolute*. This means free from any determining event or condition. It may seem strange, after establishing that *fee simple* means ownership, to suggest that limitations may be placed on its endurance, but it is possible to give ownership to a person yet provide that this ownership shall pass to someone else on the happening of a particular event. If, for instance, I give my land to *X* in fee simple 'so long as it is used for agricultural purposes' the interest passed is potentially of infinite duration. If, however, the use of the land is changed, then the interest ends and the land will pass back to me or my successor. Such an interest is not a legal estate because it is not *absolute*. Qualified fees simple like these are of two types, *determinable* and *conditional*. They are dealt with later in this chapter. What must be emphasised now is that any inhibition, however slight, on the endurance of a

fee simple prevents it from being a legal estate. Since it is, therefore, an equitable interest (LPA 1925 s 1(3)), it involves a trust.

A person who grants a fee simple subject to a condition may do so in such a way that the ownership automatically shifts on the occurrence of the event, as in the case of a grant 'to *A* in fee simple but, if he should marry *X*, then to *B* in fee simple'. In other cases, the shift in ownership does not happen automatically, for the grantor reserves to himself the right to take the land back on the breach of the condition, which he may or may not decide to exercise. This reservation is known as a right of re-entry. The former method might be used in cases of family endowment, the latter in ordinary commercial conveyances.

Since the meaning of *absolute* is so crucial, s 7 of the Act, as amended, resolves possible doubt in three cases. First, statutes enabling authorities to acquire land compulsorily for certain purposes frequently provide that, if the land is not used by the authority for those purposes, it shall revest in the original owner or the owners of the land adjoining. This possibility of the determination of the fee simple in the hands of the authority might seem to have prevented the interest from being absolute. The section, however, declares that it is absolute (*see also* the Revester of Sites Act 1987). Second, and on the same principle, a fee simple vested in a corporation which is liable to determine by reason of the dissolution of that corporation is declared to be absolute. The third case was not originally envisaged by the section and had to be clarified by amending legislation. In parts of England, particularly Manchester, it is sometimes the practice, on the sale of a fee simple, to take the purchase money not as a lump sum but as a permanent annual payment. To secure the prompt payment of this a right of re-entry is reserved in the grant. As explained above, this means that the vendor may take back the fee simple, if that sum is not paid. Following the enactment of the Law of Property Act 1925, such a fee simple clearly was not absolute. Being equitable, it attracted all the machinery of a trust, which was contemplated neither by the parties nor by the legislators, for the circumstances lacked all the ordinary characteristics of a trust. The Law of Property (Amendment) Act 1926 (Schedule), accordingly enacted that 'a fee simple subject to a legal or equitable right of entry or re-entry is for the purposes of the Act a fee simple absolute'.

The terms of the amendment appear wider than was necessary to remedy the particular difficulty. The Schedule applies whenever a condition is secured by a right of entry or re-entry, whether the condition is the payment of a rentcharge or some other obligation or factor. In the opinion of some (see, for example, Megarry and Wade, *The Law of Real Property*, 1966), it embraces all cases of determining factors expressed in the form of conditions, since the imposition of a condition gives rise to a right of re-entry. This view appears to be modified in later editions (1975). It is suggested that this is not so since it is based on principles which have been overtaken by the 1925 legislation. If the view is correct it would mean that, in the case of a grant 'to *A* in fee simple but if he remarries then to *B* in fee simple', *A* has a legal estate, whereas, as we shall see when settlements are discussed, the Settled Land Act 1925 s 1(1)(ii)(b) clearly marks out such a disposition as a settlement. The 1926 Act was aimed at commercial arrangements which had been inadvertently transformed into trusts, not at settlements which were admittedly and consciously intended to be trusts.

Finally, *absolute* does not mean that the land is free from the rights of other persons. The fact that it is subject to a mortgage for instance does not prevent it from being absolute.

3 *In possession.* A fee simple, even though absolute, cannot be legal unless it is in possession and not in remainder or reversion. Thus if a grant is made 'to *X* for life with remainder to *Y* in fee simple', *Y*'s interest, during *X*'s life, is equitable. *Possession*, however, has unexpectedly wide meaning, for under the Law of Property Act 1925 s 205(1)(xix), it means not only physical occupation but also 'receipt of rents and profits or the right to receive the same, if any'. If *A* owns a fee simple, therefore, and has leased the land to *L*, who is in occupation, *A*'s fee simple is in possession because he has the right to receive any rent payable. If the land is subject to a trust, and the fee simple is vested in trustees, the fact that those trustees do not themselves enjoy physical occupation of the land does not prevent their fee simple being in possession, for legally they have the right to possession even though equity directs that they exercise their rights in favour of the beneficiaries.

General

For every square inch of land in this country, someone holds the fee simple absolute in possession, even though there may be another person in occupation of that land. The case of a lessee in possession has just been explained. If possession is being enjoyed by the owner of a life interest, entail, or other limited interest, the fee simple absolute resides in one or more trustees in trust for that person in occupation, whose interest of course is merely equitable. The case of a person owning the fee simple absolute in possession for his own purposes, and not in trust for anyone else, is one of the commonest situations in land law. It is the case of the ordinary *owner occupier*.

A person who owns such an estate can create any number of lesser interests out of it, as was illustrated in Chapter 1. These are examined below.

Method of transferring the fee simple absolute in possession

No special words are necessary to pass the estate to another person, whether by deed or by will (LPA 1925 s 60). If I own such an estate in 'Blackacre' and execute a deed in which I 'hereby convey "Blackacre" to *P*', the fee simple absolute passes unless the contrary intention appears. In practice the words 'in fee simple' are added after the description of the property to avoid any doubt.

THE LIFE INTEREST

Nature and creation

A life interest is an interest which lasts only for so long as a particular person lives. No special words are needed to create it, either by deed or by will, though the intention to do so must, of course, be apparent. The grant of a merely personal privilege to occupy land is inconsistent with such an intention, for a life interest is property and has the essential characteristic of alienability possessed by all interests in land (see *Binions* v *Evans* [1972] 2 All ER 70 where the judgment of Lord Denning, MR, is surely to be preferred upon this point). Such words as 'to *A* for life' will leave no room for doubt. In home-made wills, however, the intention may have to be gleaned from the instrument as a whole. Instructions such as 'I give my house to my son but he must allow my widow to live there, if she wishes, for the rest of her days' might well create a life interest in favour of the widow, the son taking the fee simple in remainder. The owner of a life interest is usually referred to as a *life tenant*. The use of the word 'tenant' has no connection with its use in the relationship of landlord and tenant. It simply means 'owner' of a life interest. Life interests can only be equitable (LPA 1925 s 1).

Usually the life which measures the length of time for which the interest is to endure is that of the grantee. Thus, in a grant 'to *A* for life', *A*'s life does this. Other lives may be used, however, as in a grant 'to *A* for the life of *B*'. In this case, *A*'s interest will last as long as *B* lives, whether or not he outlives *A*. *B* takes no interest in the land but is used only in the capacity of an egg-timer. He is called a *cestui que vie*. Such life interests are called *interests pur autre vie*. An *interest pur autre vie* also arises where the owner of a life interest, say *A*, assigns it to *B*. *B*'s interest will last as long as *A* lives. It is not within the power of *A* to assign more because that is all he has to assign. Life interests may, though rarely these days, arise by operation of law in the form of 'curtesy' which is relevant only to entails.

A life tenant may dispose of his interest as he pleases during his lifetime. When he dies, however, his interest ends, so that there is nothing for him to leave by his will. In the case of a tenant *pur autre vie* the position is different if the *cestui que vie* is still living at the death of the tenant. Thus, if land is granted to *A* for the life of *B*, then *A* may on his death dispose of his interest as he pleases, or allow the laws of intestacy to act upon it. The beneficiary will then be entitled to enjoy the land for the rest of *B*'s lifetime.

The rights and duties of a life tenant

Rules are necessary to regulate the beneficial enjoyment of land by a life tenant for two reasons. First, his behaviour towards the land might otherwise prejudice the remainderman. Of course, this might well be within the contemplation of the person who settled the land, and in practice he often empowers the life tenant to act in this way. Second, and conversely, his interest being of uncertain duration, he might spend money of a capital nature on the land which, if no special rules existed, would fall undeservedly into the lap of the remainderman to the detriment of the life tenant's next-of-kin. In short, he has certain special duties and he, or his personal representatives, have certain special rights which must now be dealt with.

Duties of a life tenant

The nature of these duties is governed primarily by the instrument of creation, for it is quite open to a settlor creating the interest to decide what these duties shall be, even though in the outcome the remainderman is prejudiced. After all, the latter is receiving his interest, too, from that settlor. The weight of these duties will usually be described by reference to the law of waste. The settlor may make the life tenant impeachable, or otherwise, for the various types of waste as he thinks fit. As a matter of construction, 'without impeachment of waste', without more, will be interpreted so as to allow the life tenant to commit both permissive and voluntary waste. Some additional and clear words will be necessary if equitable waste also is to be allowed (LPA 1925 s 135).

If the instrument of creation is silent on the question the general rules as to impeachability must be invoked. These are that a life tenant is liable for equitable and voluntary waste but not for permissive (*Re Cartwright* (1889) 41 ChD 532). He will, however, be liable even for repairs if his life interest is in leasehold property and the lease contains a covenant to repair (*Re Betty* [1899] 1 Ch 821). This kind of settlement will be explained shortly. In any case, this is not strictly a question of waste.

We shall see later that the Settled Land Act 1925 empowers life tenants, even when impeachable for waste, under certain conditions, to cut and sell timber (s 66) and to grant mining leases (s 41), but since any profits of these transactions are deemed to represent the products of the land the fundamental basis of impeachability remains undisturbed. Thus, on a sale of timber by an impeachable life tenant, three-quarters of the proceeds are set aside for the benefit of the remainderman in fee simple. The purposes of the power is to enable land to *be* exploited to its best advantage in the absence, for the time being, of a beneficial absolute owner.

Rights of a life tenant and his personal representatives

The life tenant has the right, subject to his responsibilities to the remainderman described above, to occupy the land and enjoy its profits. If the land has been leased, he is usually entitled to the whole of the rent, for this is only a vicarious way of enjoying occupation. Two special rights, however, must be explained. They arise on the death of the life tenant and so will be exercisable by his personal representatives unless he is a tenant *pur autre vie*, in which case they may be exercised by the life tenant himself.

The first is the *right to emblements*. This is the right to enter the land after the end of the life interest and take crops which the tenant sowed. It extends only to annual crops such as corn and not to fruit trees. Only one growth of each crop may be taken. See generally *Graves* v *Weld* (1833) 5 B&Ad 105. Since the right is based on the principle that the end of a life interest cannot be foreseen, it cannot be exercised where the life tenant ends his interest by his own act. This might happen in the case of determinable life interests, dealt with later in this chapter, when, for instance, land is granted 'to *A* for life until he marries' and *A* later marries.

The second of these rights is the right of the next-of-kin, or the tenant himself if he is a tenant *pur autre vie*, to take certain fixtures from the land after the end of the life tenancy. The meaning of 'fixtures' was explained in Chapter 3. A life tenant may bring objects to the land in such circumstances that they become fixtures. The general rule is that all these must be left for the person next entitled to the land, since they have become 'land'. Such a rule would work unjustly, however, if applied without exception. It would certainly discourage a life tenant from improving the property if he thought he was making a gift of such improvements to a remainderman who might be a complete stranger to him, while his widow, who might be entitled to his property generally, would be unable to touch them. We shall see later that a similar problem arises between landlord and tenant and it is in that sphere that the law developed exceptions which make large inroads into the general rule. These exceptions, apart from one, that of agricultural fixtures, apply equally to life tenancies. Certain objects may be detached from land notwithstanding that they have become fixtures, during and at the end of the tenancy. These are *trade, ornamental* and *domestic fixtures*.

Trade fixtures are those fixtures attached by the life tenant for the purposes of carrying on his trade (*Poole's Case* (1703) 1 Salk 368). Such items are too numerous to list but machinery (*Re Hulse* [1905] 1 Ch 406) and petrol pumps at a garage (*Smith* v *City Petroleum Co Ltd* [1940] 1 All ER 260) are examples. Agricultural fixtures may not be removed on a life tenant's death because they are not trade fixtures. Market gardening is, however, classified for this purpose as a trade, and so fixtures used in connection with it, such as shrubs (*Wardell* v *Usher* (1841) 3 Scott NR 508), may be removed. *Ornamental* and *domestic fixtures* have been held to include a wide assortment of objects ranging from ornamental chimney-pieces to panelling (*Spyer* v *Phillipson* [1931] 2 Ch 183). A less indulgent approach is taken by the courts to ornamental and domestic fixtures, so that they cannot be removed if substantial damage would be caused. In any case the person removing must reinstate damage caused by removal and restore a similar article where the fixture has been placed by way of substitution. Redecoration is not, however, necessary (*Re De Falbe* [1901] 1 Ch 523).

A new role of the life tenant

So far we have been considering the beneficial position of the life tenant. The Settled Land Act 1925, perfecting earlier legislation, now casts him in the role of land manager. Since the very existence of a life tenant, or other limited owner, means that there is no absolute owner in occupation for the time being, many of the important decisions affecting the land and the persons entitled under the settlement such as sale, leasing and mortgaging could not be taken for a very long time. The Act, therefore, gives a wide range of such powers to the life tenant or certain other limited owners in possession. These powers do not affect the life tenant's beneficial position, for he is not entitled to the money accruing from such transactions. They are simply powers of decision making given to the person who ought to be in the best position to make such a decision, the man on the spot in occupation.

Subject matter of life interests

A life interest ordinarily results from a grant by a fee simple owner of land. It is possible, however, for the owner of a long lease, say for 150 years, to grant it to one person for life, and then for the remainder of its duration to another. Furthermore, it is even possible for pure personalty to be settled in the same way. I may, for instance, settle £10 000 on *A* for life and then to *B* absolutely. In that case, the money must be invested and the annual dividends of the investment represent the life interest, whereas the invested capital awaits the absolute owner, *B*, who may take it on *A*'s death. It will now be apparent how the owners of successive interests in land enjoy those interests when a sale of that land has taken place under the powers given the life tenant by the Settled Land Act 1925 and described above.

THE ENTAIL

Nature

This is an interest in land which lasts as long as the donee or any of his descendants live. Its origin lies even before the statute De Donis 1285, which perfected it, and it has been admitted into the twentieth century, by the 1925 legislation, still clanking much of its medieval armour. Its complexities rather outweigh its usefulness, for it is seldom met with now. It can exist only as an equitable interest (LPA 1925 s 1) and so involves a trust. It is the only interest of inheritance left and represents the only context of any importance in land law in which the term 'heir' may properly be used. Since it does not end until the donee's descendants die out, it is an interest of indefinite duration but, of course, a lesser interest than a fee simple because a break in that chain of descent assuredly brings it to an end. It is, moreover, an unstable interest in that it can be ended by *barring* with rather startling results as will be seen later. On an intestacy it does not go to the next of kin, as a fee simple and a motor car do, but to the descendant heir. As long as there exists a descendant heir unto whom it can descend, the entail will continue. It is important, therefore, to establish what the rules of descent are for this interest.

The rules of descent

1. *Descent is traced from the original donee.* On the death of the owner of an entail descent is not necessarily traced from that owner but from the first owner even if the grant was originally made a very long time ago.
2. *Males have priority.* Where there are members of both sexes in equal degree in the class from which the heir is to come, males are preferred to females unless special provision is made to the contrary in the terms of the grant. Thus, if a grant is made to *A* in tail and he has two children, a girl and a boy, the boy will be the heir irrespective of seniority. These rules can be varied.
3. *Primogeniture.* Where there are two or more males of equal degree the oldest takes exclusively as heir. If there are no males then a female may inherit. If there are two or more females, however, they all take together as *coparceners.*
4. *Representation.* This important rule enables descendants to represent a deceased ancestor *ad infinitum*. Thus, if *A* has two sons, B^1 and B^2, and B^1 has died leaving a son, C^1, then on *A*'s death C^1 represents his deceased father B^1, who would have inherited had he lived. C^1, therefore, inherits and not B^2.

Figure 5.1 may illustrate the operation of these rules. *D* denotes a daughter, *S* denotes a son, *GS* a grandson and so on. Age in a particular degree, that is a family of children, diminishes from left to right. *A* has just died and we must find his heir. He was the original donee, so that descent must be traced from him. His heir would have been *S*, had he lived, because, being male, he would have been preferred to his older sister *D*. *S*, however, is dead himself, but the representation rule may be applied, which brings us to GS^1, who would have been preferred to GS^2 and GS^3 because he was older. GS^1 is dead but he is represented by his heir GGS^1. The heir of *A* is therefore GGS^1 despite the existence of older descendants of *A*. If GGS^1 dies childless, descent will again be traced from *A* and GS^2 will be the heir.

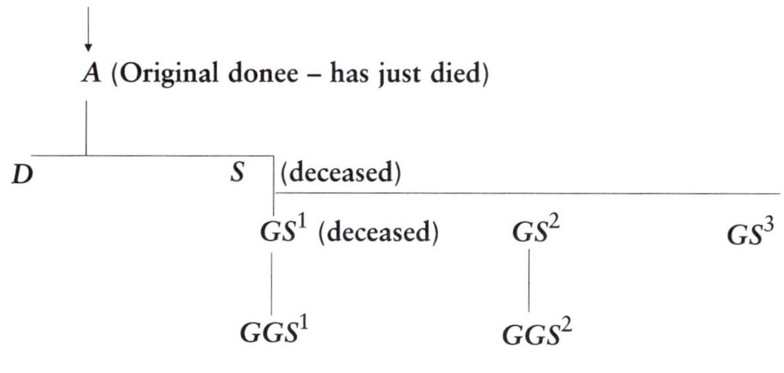

Fig. 5.1

The right of an illegitimate child to succeed, on the intestacy of its parents, to the property of those parents, contained in the Family Law Reform Act 1969 s 14 does not apply to entails. Fuller discussion of the entail is to be found in the reference books on land law. The rarity of the interest today requires us merely to notice its principal characteristics.

Principal characteristics

Creation

While words of limitation for all other purposes have been rendered unnecessary (LPA 1925 s 60), the rules have been tightened for entails. There are sound reasons for this. The entail is uncommon today and if its existence could be implied from informal expressions there would be a danger of it arising in cases where it was not intended. The ordinary testator will hardly wish to employ such an aristocratic method of disposing of his property. The person who wishes to use it will not make his will without legal advice. The rules for the creation of entails after 1925 are contained in the Law of Property Act 1925 s 130.

The right to bar the entail

Under the Fines and Recoveries Act 1833, a tenant in tail of full age in possession can execute a deed of disentailment which has the effect of converting the entail into a fee simple absolute (s 15). The result is that the interests not only of his own descendants but also any subsequent interests, including those of the fee simple owner in reversion or remainder are defeated. The Act merely rationalised a fiction which had facilitated this confiscatory act since the Middle Ages. A tenant in tail of full age in remainder can bar his own descendants only. His resultant interest is called a *base fee*, which will endure for so long as descendants of his survive, even though they are of course disentitled. A base fee is convertible to a fee simple absolute once events have occurred which would have brought the entail into possession if it had not been thus partially barred.

Entitlement to an entail thus provides potential for present or future ownership of the fee simple absolute estate in the land. The role of the entail however has been that of dissolving and recasting family interests during the heyday of the strict settlement of land.

DETERMINABLE INTERESTS AND INTERESTS UPON CONDITION SUBSEQUENT

Nature

Fees simple and life interests are sometimes made subject to special provisions which might bring them to a premature end. One reason for doing this was seen in the case of the fee simple made conditional upon the payment of a rentcharge.

Another example might now be added from the sphere of the family settlement. When a landowner makes his will he will obviously wish to provide for his wife and children. This he can do by leaving the land to his wife, *W*, for life and then in fee simple to his son, *S*. If *W* remarries, however, she will be provided for by her new husband and in that case there is a strong case for accelerating the interest of *S*. The testator could take account of this by framing his disposition 'to *W* for life until she remarries and then to *S* in fee simple'. If she never remarries she enjoys the land for the rest of her life; if she does, her life interest will end on the marriage. There are many other reasons, which will be seen from the decided cases, why fees simple and life interests are sometimes modified in this way.

The law has developed rules governing the nature and effect of these modifications, but, in doing so, has classified them into two types, namely, *determinable interests* and *interests upon condition subsequent.* Both types contain a terminating factor, but the way in which this factor is expressed decides whether a particular interest is classified as one or the other. There are some crucial differences between the two types of interest, so it is essential to know how to distinguish them.

The distinction between the two types of interest

In the case of an interest on condition subsequent, which will now be called a *conditional interest*, the terminating factor is expressed as a confiscatory proviso, as in a grant 'to *A* for life on condition he does not remarry'. The interest is granted in its ordinary full terms but might be interrupted before its course is run. In the case of a determinable interest, the terminating event is used to mark the natural end of the interest, as in a grant 'to *A* for life until he remarries'. Conditional interests are usually created by such expressions as 'on condition that' and 'but if', whereas *determinable interests* are created by 'until', 'during', 'while', and 'for as long as'. In short, in conditional interests the terminating event interrupts and is confiscatory, whereas in determinable interests it delineates and expresses duration. There is of course no difference between the intentions of the grantors in the examples of the gifts to *A* above, although their motives may differ. Remarriage in both cases is to end the interests. It is the mere mood of the language used which is effective. However, this can reflect motive so the distinction between the two types of interest is not entirely verbal or arbitrary.

Now that the identifying features have been highlighted, the differences in the law applying to the two types of interest must be explained.

Effects of conditional and determinable interests

Time of determination

There seems to be no conclusive modern authority as to whether all conditional interests become merely voidable, as opposed to void, on the occurrence of the terminating event. No doubt they are voidable only in the case of fees simple on condition supported by a right of re-entry. On breach of the condition, the interest is not divested until the grantor, or his successor in title to the right of re-entry, re-enters. This type of conditional fee simple does not involve a trust (Law of Property (Amendment) Act 1926). Many conditional interests, however, operate by way of gift over to another person rather than by re-entry (see *Re Dugdale* (1888) 38 ChD 176, at 179, per Kay J), as, for instance, in a grant 'to *A* in fee simple, but if he remarries to *B* in fee simple', in which case, we shall see, there is a settlement and, therefore, a trust. Once a trust has been constituted, the interest of a remainderman, such as *B* in the example above, can hardly be dependent on the whim of the grantor. It is submitted, therefore, though without positive judicial authority, that it is only in the case of conditional fees simple caught by the 1926 Act that the interest is merely voidable after the happening of the terminating event, and that in all other cases the interest ends spontaneously.

In the case of determinable interests the position is clear. They end automatically when the event occurs. This is to be expected, for that event is used as part of the limitation and serves to measure the time for which the property may be enjoyed. Just as an interest granted 'to *A* for life' ends naturally on *A*'s death, so one given 'to *B* for life until marriage' ends naturally upon *B*'s marriage without any steps being taken by anyone.

Existence at law

A fee simple on condition subject to a legal or equitable right of entry or re-entry may, provided it is in possession, exist as a legal estate (Law of Property (Amendment) Act 1926). Other conditional interests must be equitable.

A determinable interest must always be equitable (LPA 1925 s 1).

Effect of void terminating event

It will be explained below that the events used to mark the ending of determinable and conditional interests may sometimes be void. Here we are only concerned to notice that the results of such voidness vary according to whether the interest is conditional or determinable. In the case of a conditional interest the result is to make the interest absolute. This is also the case if the condition is or becomes impossible (*Re Croxon* [1904] 1 Ch 252). Thus, a grant 'to *A* for life, but, if he fails to murder his wife this year, to *B* for life', creates an unconditional life interest in *A*. In the case of determinable interests, the result is to make the whole interest fail (*Re Moore* (1888) 39 ChD 116). This is a rational result of the function that the terminating event performs in the two different cases. Pluck out the void event from a conditional interest and that interest still has a beginning and an end. Do the same with a determinable interest and you have taken its end away so that the whole fails.

The one exception to this is that if the event is void because it infringes the rule against perpetuities then even a determinable interest becomes absolute (Perpetuities and Accumulations Act 1964 s 12). This problem is dealt with in Chapter 10.

Grounds for voidness of terminating events

These will be noticed primarily in relation to conditional interests, which they affect more, and any differences applying to determinable interests will be pointed out in each case.

Repugnancy to the interest granted

It is really self-contradictory to grant an interest in land and then to take away some of the natural characteristics of ownership. These characteristics include the right of alienation, the availability of the property for the satisfaction of debts and the right to the fullest enjoyment of the land in those cases where the doctrine of waste has no application. In the case of an entail it includes the right to bar (*Mildmay's Case* (1605) 6 Co Rep 40a). Originally all forms of repugnancy to these principles may have been void, but exceptions have developed which are difficult to classify and give rise to unforeseeability (per Pearson J, in *Re Rosher* (1884) 26 ChD 801). One of the commonest forms of such repugnancy is a restriction on alienation. In the nature of things, such a restriction may apply either to the form of alienation, to the period of time before alienation shall be free or to the classes of persons to whom the land may be alienated. The present state of the law may be somewhat glibly summed up by saying that any condition which substantially affects the power of alienation is void, though partial restrictions may be valid. A few examples, beginning with the more restrictive and tapering to the less restrictive, may provide at least a rough guide. A condition against all forms of alienation either voluntary or otherwise was held void in *Re Dugdale* one against alienation to all but the donee's brothers, who were of course a small and diminishing class, was held void in *Re Brown* [1954] Ch 39; a condition that the property should be divested on bankruptcy was held void in *Re Machu* (1882) 21 ChD 838. So were restrictions on particular kinds of alienation. On the other hand, partial restraints have been held valid. Probably the widest which has been allowed was a devise to *A* 'on condition he never sells out of the family' (*Re Macleay* (1875) LR 20 Eq 186). This was criticised in *Re Rosher*, though it should be noticed that only one form of alienation, namely, sale, and not others such as leasing and mortgaging, was forbidden, and then only for the lifetime of *A*. Furthermore, he was not restricted from selling to his own family. There might be a distinction between limiting alienation to named persons and merely to an indeterminate class, because the numbers of the former are bound to diminish with time and reduce the market to such an extent as to lower the ordinary selling price, thus denying all real chance of selling (see 70 LQR 15).

Determinable interests, however, are almost completely free from the doctrine of repugnancy. Thus a grant 'to *X* until he attempts to alienate or becomes bankrupt' is valid, for during the subsistence of the interest no restrictions can be said to have been imposed. This advantage is used in the *protective trust*, discussed in Chapter 9. There is, however, one exception. Although a person may grant his property to another so that the interest terminates naturally on bankruptcy or attempted alienation, and may even settle his own property upon himself until attempted alienation, he cannot, even by a determinable limitation, limit his own property to himself until his bankruptcy so as to defeat his creditors (*Re Brewer's Settlement* [1896] 2 Ch 503).

It has been assumed above that the restriction has been framed as a condition which, if valid, would confer a right of re-entry or cesser of the interest granted. If, however, it has been expressed as a covenant only, giving the covenantee no more than the right to damages on its breach, it is not repugnant to the interest granted (*Caldy Manor Estate Ltd* v *Farrell* [1974] 1 WLR 1303).

Uncertainty

The condition must, said Lord Cranworth in *Clavering* v *Ellison* (1859) 7 HL Cas 707, at 725, 'be such that the court can see from the beginning, precisely and distinctly, upon the happening of what event it was that the preceding vested estate was to determine'. Not only must the language in the limitation be clear, but the operation of the terminating event must be susceptible of reasonably certain observation. The following examples may illustrate the standard of certainty needed, but it should not be assumed that decisions on the same subject matter in the future must follow these decisions, for not only circumstances but also the meaning of words are liable to change over many years. A condition that the donee should 'provide a home' for a certain person has been held too vague, for a home is something more than a mere protection from the weather and the other elements implicit in the expression were too elusive (*Re Brace* [1954] 2 All ER 354). The same decision was reached in the case of conditions requiring donees 'to conform and be members of the Church of England' (*Re Tegg* [1936] 2 All ER 878), and to 'continue to reside in Canada' (*Sifton* v *Sifton* [1938] AC 656).

On the other hand, the courts are usually practical rather than pedantic in their insistence upon reasonable certainty, so that a condition that a donee should become 'a convert to the Roman Catholic faith' was held to be valid in *Re Evans* [1940] Ch 629, since baptism is necessary for conversion in the ordinary usage of the expression, and there can be no reasonable doubt as to whether a person has been baptised. A condition requiring the assumption of a surname was upheld in *Re Neeld* [1962] Ch 643, because use of a name is a discernible fact. Finally, in *Bromley* v *Tryon* [1952] AC 265 a condition to operate when the beneficiary became entitled to 'the bulk' of certain other property was not void for uncertainty because 'the bulk' was taken to mean any proportion greater than 50 per cent.

Since breach of a condition brings about forfeiture of the interest it may be that a higher standard of definition is required of the terminating event than in the case of a determinable interest but in matters of definition and construction it is dangerous to venture sweeping statements.

Contrariness to public policy

A condition will be void if it provokes an illegal or immoral act, or prevents or discourages a person from carrying out his legal or moral duty, but the meaning of public policy embraces demands even beyond those of the law and morals. Thus, a condition aimed at preventing marriage altogether will be void, although this will not be so if the intention is merely to provide for a person until marriage (*Jones* v *Jones* (1876) 1 QBD 279). Partial restraints on marriage, such as conditions against marrying certain persons or forbidding second marriages, are always valid (see, for instance, *Jenner* v *Turner* (1880) 16 ChD 188). Other examples of conditions being against public policy are those which might induce spouses to separate (*Re Moore* (1888) 39 ChD 116) or influence parents' duties in the upbringing of children.

In this context may be mentioned an unusual application formerly made under the Variation of Trusts Act 1958 which empowers the court to order the rearrangement of trust provisions in favour of future beneficiaries under certain conditions. The court ordered the removal of a condition against practising the Roman Catholic religion on proof that its removal would benefit those on whose behalf the application was made. The condition was held to be 'undesirable' (*Re Remnant's Settlement Trusts* [1970] 1 Ch 560). The condition would not of course have been void as being against public policy.

An infringement of the rule against perpetuities is one which needs special watchfulness in drafting settlements. Racial discrimination in itself would not be unlawful for the reasons now being discussed, although a limitation framed with that motive might often fail for uncertainty.

Determinable interests are affected by the rules of public policy in the same way as conditional interests, except that they are completely free of the rules regarding marriage. An interest granted until marriage is valid in all circumstances and is often used in settlements.

Beneficial position of owners of modified interests

The owner of a determinable or conditional interest may enjoy the land to the same extent as if he owned the equivalent absolute interest. Thus, in the case of a determinable life interest, his position is controlled by the law of waste, subject to any express provision in the instrument of creation, and in the case of a modified fee simple, he may use the land in the same way as the owner of a fee simple absolute, except that equitable waste will be restrained if there is a gift over to another person following a breach of condition (*Re Hanbury's Settled Estates* [1913] 2 Ch 357, per Eve J, at 363 and 365). If there is no gift over but the grantor reserves a right of re-entry, the reasons for restraining equitable waste do not seem to be so strong. If there is no gift over or right of entry reserved in the instrument of creation, the court might be led to construe an expression as a mere request to the grantee rather than a condition of forfeiture (*Re Evans*, see p 82).

Apart from these beneficial rights, the owner of a conditional or determinable interest will often be in the position of a 'land manager', as we saw, earlier in this chapter, is the case with a tenant for life. This will be discussed with the settlement.

INTEREST UPON CONDITION PRECEDENT

Interests upon condition subsequent have been discussed above and their outstanding feature is that they are liable to be ended on the occurrence of a particular event. The main characteristic of an interest upon condition precedent is that the interest does not arise at all until the occurrence of an event, whereupon the interest which arises behaves just like other interests of its kind. Thus in a grant 'to *A* in fee simple when he marries' *A* owns no interest at all until he marries, but then the fee simple absolute which has sprung up in his favour is no different from any other fee simple absolute. Any interest in land may be subject to a condition precedent. They are sometimes called *contingent interests*.

The condition itself must not be void for any of the reasons mentioned in relation to conditions subsequent. If a condition precedent is void the interest fails to take effect. Just as a determinable interest fails if its terminating event is void because it then possesses no end, so an interest subject to a condition precedent is deprived of its beginning once a void condition is struck out, and therefore collapses completely. A common cause of voidness in conditions precedent is infringement of the rule against perpetuities.

STUDY MATERIAL

(1954) 70 LQR 15

Re Macleay (1875) LR 20 Eq 186 belongs to the group, select and small, of those decisions of Sir George Jessel MR which have not been approved by posterity. Land was devised to a brother of the testator 'on the condition that he never sells it out of the family.' The Master of the Rolls held that the condition did not infringe the rule against total restraint upon alienation because it bound only the devisee personally, it applied only to sales and not other modes of alienation, and within the 'family' (an expression which was construed as meaning 'blood relations', and comprehended many persons) even sales were permissible. The judgment was somewhat critical of the decision of Sir John Romilly MR in *Attwater* v *Attwater* (1853) 18 Beav 330, but in turn Pearson J in *Re Rosher* (1884) 26 ChD 801 was critical of *Re Macleay*. As John Chipman Gray pointed out, in *Re Macleay* 'there was no argument of opposing counsel,' and he added that 'the obvious ease of evading such a condition, if allowed to exist, renders it doubtful whether Sir George Jessel will have a following in this matter, beyond what he already has in the Province of Ontario' (*Restraints on the Alienation of Property* (2nd edn, 1895) pp 28, 43: for a modern Ontario instance, see *Re Noble and Wolf* [1949] OR 503, in which, incidentally, *Re Drummond Wren* [1945] OR 778 (noted (1948) 64 LQR 19) came under fire). On the other hand, Professor Glanville Williams has attacked the whole basis of the doctrine that total restraints against alienation are bad for repugnancy to the interest given, urging that any such invalidity should be based on grounds of public policy rather than repugnancy: (1943) 59 LQR 343.

In *Re Brown* [1953] 3 WLR 877, the point arose again. The testator gave land to trustees in trust for his widow for life, and thereafter (subject to an intermediate trust) in trust for his four sons as tenants in common. The will then provided that if any son executed any assurance whereby his share might become vested in any person except one or more of his brothers, that son's share should be held on certain discretionary trusts for the son, his wife and his children. Harman J held that the doctrine laid down for realty applied equally to the son's interests under the trust for sale which would arise on their mother's death (a point upon which it is useful to have authority), and then proceeded to a discussion of the cases. As between *Attwater* v *Attwater* and *Re Macleay*, the learned judge plainly inclined in favour of the former; but although the headnote records that *Re Macleay* was 'not followed', it could be said that in reality that case was distinguished. 'It is pertinent that a number of named persons as in this clause is in essence different from a class consisting, for instance, as Sir George Jessel's did in *Re Macleay*, of members of the family, which he said was a large indeterminate class of people and might, of course, increase as time went on; whereas, if alienation be restricted to three or four or five named persons, the class is bound to diminish as death takes its toll of the members' (p 885). The proviso accordingly in substance amounted to a general prohibition against alienation, so that both on the authorities and in accordance with the increasing modern tendency to curtail the extent to which the dead hand of a testator may rule the living, it was held to be void. This conclusion accords with the decision in a somewhat similar Australian case which does not seem to have been cited. In *Grayson* v *Grayson* [1922] QSR 155, a testator specifically devised certain lands to his four sons, subject (inter alia) to a condition against any son during his life selling any of the land except to one or more of the other sons. After a full examination of the authorities and literature on the subject, McCawley CJ (at p 163) said that the power of alienation was 'restricted within limits so narrow as to constitute a substantial taking away, not of the whole power of alienation, but of a valuable portion of it, subjecting it to fetters which inevitably, by limiting the market, diminish the ordinary selling value of the land, and which might, in fact, destroy all opportunity of selling.' The condition involved 'such a substantial restriction of the power of alienation' that it could not be regarded as falling within any recognised exception to the rule against such restrictions, and so was void.

R.E.M.

QUESTIONS

1 What is meant by *in possession* in the expression *fee simple absolute in possession* as used in the Law of Property Act 1925 s 1?

2 Under what circumstances might a fee simple subject to a condition subsequent be an equitable interest?

3 Explain the nature of the doctrine of 'repugnancy to the interest granted' and its limits in regard to determinable interests and interests upon condition subsequent.

4 Can you discern the reason for any distinctions made by the 1925 legislation between family and commercial interests in land?

CHAPTER 6

LEASEHOLD INTERESTS

The lease is the final interest to be discussed which gives a right to the land itself. *Lease, tenancy, demise, term of years*, and *leasehold interest* have the same meaning, although *tenancy* is often used to describe a lease of shorter duration. The order of treatment of leases will be their nature, types, creation and contents, the remedies of landlords and tenants, the remedies of assignees of landlords' and tenants' interests and the determination of leases. Finally, the statutory protection of certain classes of tenants is considered.

THE NATURE OF A LEASE

Definition

A lease is the grant of the right of exclusive possession of a defined piece of land for a fixed maximum period of time, or series of fixed periods of time, with the intention that the grantee shall have an estate in the land. Some of the elements of this definition must now be examined.

The intention to create an estate, included in this definition, has been retained despite the decision of the House of Lords in *Street* v *Mountford* [1985] AC 809, as explained below.

The right of exclusive possession

There can be no lease unless the right of exclusive possession is granted. The tenant must have the right to exclude all persons including the landlord himself. In a true lease, the landlord commits trespass if he enters the property without authority. Where the grantor retains some degree of authority over the land therefore, or where he has the right to enter at will, or where the grantee has not true dominion but merely the right to use the land for a certain limited purpose, possession is not exclusive. Thus a lodger is not usually a tenant (see *Wells* v *Kingston-upon-Hull Corporation* (1875) LR 10 CP 402). Restrictions imposed by the lease or otherwise against using the property for certain purposes are, however, quite compatible with exclusive possession; so is a right reserved by the landlord to enter at times for certain purposes, such as to view the state of repair.

An owner granting possession for profit will sometimes wish to represent the transaction as a licence rather than a tenancy since, as we shall see later in this chapter, a tenant's occupation and rent are generally protected by the Rent Acts, whereas in the case of a licensee this is generally not so. Superficial attempts to this end, such as the use of words denoting licences, have long failed to persuade the courts, which ask whether the parties really intended that the grantee should enjoy exclusive possession, not whether some sham words theoretically allow the owner to impose himself on some other person as joint possessor.

The possible gulf between express words and real intention is crucial. One owner might really intend to reserve the right to share possession; another might wish merely to exclude the Rent Acts. In such a broth of uncertainty the personal policies of particular judges can become rather fertile.

In *Street* v *Mountford* [1985] 2 All ER 289 a woman was given exclusive possession of residential accommodation. She did not dispute this. She signed a statement in the agreement, however, that no tenancy was intended, excluding protection under the Rent Acts. The House of Lords held that a tenancy had been created.

Lord Templeman identified three requirements for a tenancy: (1) exclusive possession; (2) fixed or periodic term; and (3) rent. If these are present then only in 'exceptional circumstances' will the possibility of a licence be considered. It is on account of this last concession that reference to the intention to create an estate is retained, in modified form, in the definition at the beginning of this chapter. It should be noted however that Lord Templeman emphasised that the intention of the parties as to the nature of the transaction, as opposed to whether exclusive possession was being granted, is irrelevant:

> The manufacture of a five-pronged implement for manual digging results in a fork even if the manufacturer, unfamiliar with the English language, insists that he intended to make and has made a spade.
>
> (at p 294)

The case represents an attempt to clarify the boundaries between leases and licenses in face of the mass of sham agreements which purport to create licences but are, in reality, tenancies. The following criticisms might be ventured however:

1 The judgment might be socially retrograde. The idea of an estate is rooted in the Middle Ages and status. The more sophisticated relationships in modern land contracts demand more flexible response to individual needs in residential and business accommodation. Even the lease was a licence only in those feudal times. Civil courts should follow rather than lead legitimate social trends. If the ingenuity of private draftsmen avoids, though not evades, specific legislation then perhaps the ball is in the court of Treasury draftsmen. The development of broader concepts of land should not be hindered by the courts.

In the bucolic imagery of Lord Templeman's opinion, for many years there have been in the garden shops spades with spikes on them and forks with blades. Society is less interested in dictionary definitions than good turnips.

2 There are too many escape routes for a 'round up' judgment. Lord Templeman's speech was a notable attempt to achieve some certainty in a flood market. Unfortunately for this design several areas of doubt remain:

(a) *Street* v *Mountford* concerned residential accommodation. Nice questions of *ratio decidendi* were allowed into play. In business land contracts even more complex relationships might arise (*see*, for instance, *Dresden Estates Ltd* v *Collinson* [1987] 1 EGLR 45; 50 MLR 655).

(b) The 'exceptional' circumstances in which, despite the satisfaction of the three requirements mentioned by Lord Templeman, a licence might arise are uncertain and were insufficiently described in his judgment. Too much discretion is left with the courts for the robust rule of law to prevail.

(c) The reference to 'rent' as being a hallmark of a lease is misleading. Rent is not necessary to constitute a lease (see *Ashburn Anstalt* v *Arnold* [1988] 2 All ER 147). Lord Templeman was confusing the definition of legal principle with the indicators or evidence of its application in particular cases. This is closely related to the following point.

3 The decision has further promoted confusion of findings of fact and of law. There has been a profusion of reported cases in recent years, most of which have not developed the law in the least. They merely illustrate the courts going about the humdrum task of applying legal principle to the facts and circumstances of particular cases, which of course are infinitely variable. For this reason citation of these cases has been spare here. The current wariness of the courts is well illustrated by *AG Securities* v *Vaughan* and *Antoniades* v *Villiers* [1988] 3 WLR 1205, decided together by the House of Lords. A discussion of the tension between the words of agreement and the ultimate reality of its purposes may be found at (1995) Law Teach 352.

4 Lord Templeman's speech blurs the line between intention and motive. In a later case, no doubt inadvertently, he illustrated that the House of Lords had merely transferred this problem to another area. In *Prudential Assurance Co Ltd* v *London Residuary Body* [1992] 3 All ER 504 at 511 he stated:

> In my opinion . . . a grant for an uncertain term does not create a lease.

It is interesting to speculate on a decision on facts identical to those in *Street* v *Mountford* save that the period of possession is 'for the duration of peace between the United Kingdom and Portugal'.

Defined piece of land

There can be no lease unless the property is defined. If the land or premises which are to be used are determinable from time to time by their owner there is no lease but merely a contract or licence. This might be the case, for instance, where a resident in a house is obliged by his agreement to change his rooms when asked to do so (see *Interoven Stove Co Ltd* v *Hibbard* [1936] 1 All ER 263).

Fixed maximum period of time

The duration of a lease may be as long or as short as the parties wish, but it must have a certain beginning and a certain maximum duration, though it is enough that these requirements are satisfied before the lease takes effect, even if they are not settled when the lease is executed (see *Harvey* v *Pratt* [1965] 1 WLR 1025). These dates may be expressly stated or determined collaterally as in a lease to *L* 'to commence upon his birthday this year'. If either of these two events is uncertain the transaction is void. Thus, an attempt to make a lease 'for the duration of the war' failed in *Lace* v *Chantler* [1944] KB 368.

This principle was reaffirmed by the House of Lords in *Prudential Assurance Co Ltd* v *London Residuary Body*, cited above. It is notable however that Lord Browne-Wilkinson agreed only reluctantly with Lord Templeman's leading opinion. He remarked:

> This bizarre outcome results from the application of an ancient and technical rule of law which requires the maximum duration of a term of years to be ascertainable from the outset. No one has produced any satisfactory rationale for the genesis of this rule.
>
> (at p 602)

The fixed period of time in a tenancy need not be continuous. Thus a grant of possession for a period of one or more weeks in the year, as in a timeshare, can constitute a lease (see *Cottage Holiday Associates Ltd* v *Customs and Excise Commissioners* [1983] QB 735).

Provided that the maximum duration is ascertained, an intermediate terminating event, which itself might happen at an uncertain time, does not invalidate the lease. A grant to *T*, for instance, for 50 years, terminable upon his marriage, is good.

Two forms of occupation which bear the name of *tenancy* are difficult to reconcile with this aspect of the definition. First, a *tenancy at will* has no ascertainable duration. It arises when a person occupies land, supposedly as tenant, on the understanding that either he or the owner may determine the occupation at any time. Despite the violence the suggestion does to accepted legal terminology, this form of occupation is better considered to be no tenancy at all. It is essentially a *licence*, that is a personal permission to occupy land which negatives trespass. The fact that it mixes in the company of tenancies, in that it sometimes arises before or after true leases, does not make it one itself. Nevertheless, for the purposes of the Limitation Act 1980, it must be distinguished from a licence (see *Cobb* v *Lane* [1952] 1 All ER 1199). Perhaps the tenancy at will is now obsolescent and the only purpose it can serve is as a midwife, in certain circumstances, to a periodic tenancy (see p 97 and *Heslop* v *Burns* [1974] 1 WLR 1241 and *Hagee* v *Erickson* [1976] QB 209).

Second, there is a *tenancy at sufferance*. This arises where a person whose tenancy has ended continues in possession of the property without the consent of the owner and without statutory authority. Clearly, the maximum duration of such occupation is uncertain. Once again, we can say that this is not a tenancy at all. Since, under the Limitation Act 1980, time begins to run against the owner from the inception of this form of occupation, it is clearly a simple case of adverse possession.

Series of fixed periods

Some leases are granted for a single fixed period such as for ten years. Others are granted on a periodic basis as from month to month or from year to year. These continue indefinitely until ended by a notice to quit. Thus a monthly tenancy might last 20 years and then be terminated by a month's notice. The requirement of certainty of duration is satisfied in these cases provided that the periodic unit itself has fixed bounds. The chain's length might be uncertain but the link must be measured. This is so even if restrictions have been placed on the right to serve notice to quit, such as that it may only be served by the tenant and not by the landlord. In such cases, however, even though the term itself is valid, the clause restricting determination might be held repugnant to the interest granted (*Centaploy Ltd* v *Matlodge Ltd* [1973] 2 All ER 720; and *see* 89 LQR 457).

Intention to create an estate

An estate in land gives a right to the land itself and not merely a right against particular persons. A person who owns an estate owns property which is defensible and recoverable *in specie*, and which is valid against the whole world. An estate is not restricted to the grantee, for it may be alienated both during his life and on death. This contrasts with a mere personal permission to use land either to the extent of full occupation or for some limited purpose, which amounts to a licence only, whether unilateral or contractual. The effect of such a licence is to create a relationship only between the parties to it. It is not contemplated that it shall give rights of property defensible against the whole world. Neither is it intended to be alienable like an estate.

Licences are, in most cases, easily distinguishable from leases but there have been several cases in the last century in which, in particular circumstances, they have been held to be binding upon third parties (*see,* for instance, *Errington* v *Errington and Woods* [1952] 1 KB 290). Where limited occupation is given, or when possession is merely transitory as when, for instance, you allow your neighbour to repair his car in your garage, the factors distinguishing them from leases stand out clearly: there is either no exclusive possession, or no definite duration. Since it is however now settled that licences may possess both these attributes (see *Marcroft Wagons Ltd* v *Smith* [1951] 2 KB 496), the really critical distinction between a lease and a licence must now be isolated. The distinction is that in a lease there is the intention to create an estate in land with the effects described above. This intention must be deduced from what the circumstances show the parties wished substantially to achieve, rather than from the terms in which they clothed the transaction. Some cases must be examined to illustrate this test. First, exclusive possession raises a presumption of a tenancy. Second, this presumption may be rebutted by circumstances showing a contrary intention.

In *Errington* v *Errington and Woods*, above, Denning, LJ, said

> Although a person who is let into exclusive possession is *prima facie* to be considered to be a tenant, nevertheless he will not be held to be so if the circumstances negative any intention to create a tenancy. Words alone may not suffice. Parties cannot turn a tenancy into a licence merely by calling it one. But if the circumstances and the conduct of the parties show that all that was intended was that the occupier should be granted a personal privilege, with no interest in the land, he will be held to be a licensee only.

In a licence the intention is to accommodate a particular person only in particular circumstances, and this intention does not embrace other persons, such as alienees. Thus in *Crane* v *Morris* [1965] 1 WLR 1104, a farm worker was allowed to occupy a cottage so long as he remained an employee. Later he went to work elsewhere. It was held that he was a licensee only, or *service occupant.*

The same conclusion was reached in *Abbeyfield (Harpenden) Society Ltd* v *Woods* [1968] 1 All ER 352n, where a resident in an old people's home had exclusive possession of a room. The provision of services, meals and other attention, including that of a housekeeper, led to the inference that the occupation was personal in nature despite the use of the words 'rent' and 'tenancy' in the agreement. (See also *Binions* v *Evans* [1972] 2 All ER 70.) To highlight the distinction, we might imagine the surprise of the owners of the home if that resident had attempted to assign his occupancy to a person aged 16 years. An inference that a licence only was intended is also likely in cases of family arrangement (see *Cobb* v *Lane*, p 91). The question of intention must be explored anew in each case and the deductions made from the circumstances of one case cannot be applied automatically to another one exhibiting similar conditions.

The intention to create an estate was not mentioned as one of the three major indicators of a lease in the leading case of *Street* v *Mountford* [1985] 2 All ER 289. Its inclusion here must therefore be justified as follows:

1 There is no doubt that transferability and enforceability against third parties are hallmarks of a lease. This is recognised in *Street* v *Mountford* itself where Lord Templeman cites the statutory foundations of the leasehold estate in the Middle Ages and its confirmation by the Law of Property Act 1925 s 1. Is it to be supposed that two parties can transact such a distinctive and binding relationship without intending it, and even intending to avoid it? To relegate what must be at the forefront of intention to a mere consequence of a transaction would be a real trap. Sleepwalking into contract is no part of English law. There are countless occasions when parties might justifiably wish to transfer possession without estate.

2 One of the terms of the contract was 'this personal licence is not assignable'. What becomes of such covenants in an unintended lease, say for ten years? It is not difficult to envisage licences transacted in all good faith suffering complete subversion of their individual terms.

3 It is submitted however that the solution lies in the misplacement of *Street* v *Mountford* as an authority. It does not even purport to be definitive of the nature of a lease. The decision represents a local 'firefighting' exercise in the area of high combustibility – 'sham' agreements. Its authority lies principally in the field of construction of documents. It instructs the courts to be wary. It was not within the intention or the power of the House of Lords to limit the individual's freedom of contract.

Legal and equitable leases

Legal

A lease can exist as a legal estate only if two conditions are satisfied. It must be *a term of years absolute* under the Law of Property Act 1925 s 1(1), and be created in the way laid down by ss 52 and 54 of that Act. The creation of leases is separately discussed below.

The expression *term of years absolute* is not as demanding as it appears and is defined in s 205(1)(xxvii). The effect is that if a grant satisfies the test as to duration outlined above it is a term of years. A monthly tenancy and one for 100 years are equally *terms of years*, for the definition includes terms of less than a year. The word *absolute* seems to have no meaning, for the definition expressly includes terms which are liable to terminate through notice to quit, by operation of law, or by re-entry. A right of re-entry by the landlord is inserted in a lease in order to bring about its premature forfeiture for breach of some covenant. In short, factors which would prevent a fee simple being absolute do not do so in the case of a lease.

There is no requirement that a lease shall be in possession. Thus a lease granted today to take effect in possession next year may be a legal estate. A sub-lease may equally be a term of years absolute and therefore a legal estate. These are described below. Several legal estates can therefore exist in land at the same time (LPA 1925 s 1(5)).

Equitable

Equitable leases may arise in two ways. First, a specifically enforceable contract for a lease creates an equitable lease which will be described below under creation of leases. Second, a lease, like any property, may be held upon trust by trustees for a person, in which case the beneficiary holds an equitable interest in it.

Sub-leases

If a lessee transfers to another person the whole of the unexpired term, the transaction is called an *assignment* (see *Milmo* v *Carreras* [1946] 1 All ER 288). Thus, if *L* leased land in 1960 to *T* for 20 years and in 1970 *T* transferred all the remaining term of ten years to *A*, an assignment has been made. *A* now becomes the owner of the lease and holds of *L*.

If, however, *T* transfers to a person something less in duration, even by a single day, than the unexpired term which he holds, he has granted a sublease out of the lease. If, in 1970 *T* granted to *S* a term of nine years, or even ten years minus one day, *S* would take a sub-lease. In that case *S* would hold of *T*, who would continue to hold of *L*, although only *S* would be entitled to present possession of the land. In such circumstances *L*, if he owns the fee simple, is said to hold the *freehold reversion*, while *T* holds a *leasehold reversion*, although it is, in this case, only of one day's duration. If *L* assigns his interest the transaction is a conveyance of his fee simple subject to *T*'s lease, which entitles the purchaser to receive the rent from *T*, or from *T*'s assignee if *T* has assigned his interest.

TYPES OF LEASES

There are two types of lease. First, there is a lease for a fixed term such as two years or 200 years. This kind does not normally end before the end of the specified period, unless a right to end it is expressly reserved. Second, there is the periodic tenancy, which might be granted on a monthly, quarterly, annual or other such periodic basis. These tenancies continue indefinitely until ended by notices to quit. There is thus a huge range in the length of leases. Certain other types of grant were possible before 1926, but these have been brought into line with the two types mentioned above. These cases, together with certain other related restrictions upon the types of lease which may be created, must now be considered.

Leases for life or until marriage (Law of Property Act 1925 s 149(6))

A lease at a rent, or for a fine for life or lives, or for a term of years determinable with life or lives or the marriage of the lessee, or a contract therefor, takes effect as a lease, or contract therefor, for ninety years. It is, however, terminable after such death or marriage by either party – by one month's written notice to determine it on one of the quarter days applicable to the tenancy – or, if there are none, on one of the usual quarter days. A fine is a premium. Such leases are uncommon.

The general effect is simply to equip such leases with a formal fixed duration, without affecting the substantial intentions and rights of the parties. In a few cases, however, the effects might interfere in a way probably not contemplated by the section. An example would be if the lessor only wished to make a grant of a few years to a person who he thought would not live long. Thus a lease for five years to *T*, if he should live so long, might not be terminable until more than that period has elapsed if *T* should outstay his welcome.

The application of this principle only where a rent or fine is payable is aimed at drawing a sharp line between a profit-making life term which leaves the fee simple still *in possession*, and one which is a truly gratuitous endowment, returning no profit, which therefore pushes the fee simple into remainder, thus creating a real element of succession. In the latter case, such as a grant 'to *A* for 100 years if he should live so long' free of rent or fine, a settlement arises. Such a lease is clearly equivalent in every substantial way to a life interest. The lessee becomes the life tenant under the Settled Land Act 1925 s 20(iv). (But see *Re Catling* [1931] 2 Ch 359). This will be discussed further in Chapter 9.

Perpetually renewable leases (Law of Property Act 1922 s 145)

A perpetually renewable lease is one which contains a clause entitling the tenant to a new lease on the same terms as the old one, including the clause for renewal, thus entitling the tenant to stay in the property forever. This must be distinguished from a lease which is 'simply' renewable, for in that case the original lease does not give the right to demand a lease which is the mirror image of itself, but simply another lease, without the renewal clause.

Perpetually renewable leases existing at the end of 1925 were converted into leases for 2000 years, calculated from the time when the existing term began. Fines payable on renewal became payable as additional rent. A purported grant of or contract for such a lease after 1925 takes effect as a term of 2000 years, or contract therefor, but free from any obligation to pay renewal money (see *Caerphilly Concrete Products Ltd* v *Owen* [1972] 1 WLR 372). These statutory terms are subject to the terms of the original lease but with the addition of the following provisions:

1 the lessee for the time being may end the lease by giving at least ten days' notice in writing before any date at which it would have expired had there been no conversion and if it had not been renewed;

2 the lessee must register every assignment or devolution with the lessor or his agent within six months of its occurrence;

3 a lessee who assigns the term ceases to be liable on the covenants even though privity of contract still exists between him and the lessor.

Once again, it should be observed that the substantial position of the parties is unchanged. The lessee has complete control over his future occupation, for the landlord is not entitled to serve the notice mentioned above.

There is a reluctance today to interpret words in a document as creating a perpetually renewable lease. See *Marjorie Burnett* v *Barclay* [1980] 258 EG 624.

Reversionary leases

A reversionary lease is one which is expressed to commence at some future date. Formerly, there was no limit as to this time lapse between creation and commencement. Under the Law of Property Act 1925 s 149(2) any term at a rent or for a fine, limited after 1925 to take effect more than 21 years from the date of the instrument purporting to create it, or any contract to create such a term, is void. The subsection does not apply to leases taking effect in equity under a settlement.

Thus a lease limited under an instrument executed in 1970 to take effect in 1992 is void. A contract for a lease is not void merely because the lease takes effect more than 21 years after the date of the contract, so that the exercise at the end of the lease of a right of renewal in a lease for 100 years is valid, because there will be no unlawful lapse between the execution of the lease and its operation (*Weg Motors Ltd* v *Hales* [1962] Ch 49). A contract, however, to grant a lease which when granted will not become effective for more than 21 years is void. Where contracts and options are in question, the rule against perpetuities must also be borne in mind.

Duration of renewed leases (Law of Property Act 1922 s 145)

A contract for the renewal of a lease or sub-lease for a term exceeding 60 years from the end of that lease or sub-lease is void. This provision affects simple renewals and must not be confused with the rules as to perpetual renewals mentioned above.

THE CREATION OF LEASES

All leases, legal or equitable, must conform to the essential requirements of a lease mentioned earlier. That being so, however, there are certain formalities necessary in the creation of some leases, upon the observance of which will depend whether a legal or equitable lease, or indeed any interest at all, arises. Frequently, however, the parties enter the landlord and tenant relationship under a contract for a lease only, and never contemplate the formation of a legal lease. Such equitable leases have most, though not all, of the attributes of legal leases. Finally, there are certain conditions which result in the formation of both legal and equitable leases of different durations simultaneously between the same parties in the same land. This happens because the formalities required for legal and equitable leases differ. The problem in these cases as to which of the two conflicting leases shall prevail has now been settled.

The subject of creation will therefore be discussed in the following order: the creation of legal leases; the creation of equitable leases; the solution of conflicts between them; and the advantages of a legal lease over an equitable one.

The creation of legal leases

A *periodic tenancy* such as a monthly or annual one may be created, and is in fact presumed, merely by a tenant going into possession and the landlord accepting rent. The particular period which is applicable will depend upon the period by reference to which the rent is calculated and not upon the mere frequency with which it is paid. Thus no formalities are required for these tenancies, a common law principle now preserved by statute (LPA 1925 s 55(c)).

Next, under s 54(2) of the Act, a lease taking effect in possession for a term not exceeding three years, whether or not the lessee is given power to extend the term, at the best rent which can be reasonably obtained without taking a fine, may be created orally. Of course, as is the case with periodic tenancies, the parties may carry out the transaction in writing or by deed if they wish. The three elements present in this rule should be carefully noted. A *reversionary lease*, for instance, no matter how short, can never qualify. On the other hand, these requirements do not affect the periodic tenancies mentioned above, which may be created by possession and payment of rent, even though they eventually last for more than three years.

Finally, all other legal leases must be created by deed (LPA 1925 s 52(1)). Furthermore, all leases, however created can only be assigned by law by deed (*Crago* v *Julian* [1992] 1 All ER 744).

The creation of equitable leases

An equitable lease is created by an enforceable agreement for a lease. Two matters are essential to enforceability. First, and this is a question of the ordinary law of contract, the parties must have reached final agreement upon the essential terms (see *King's Motors (Oxford) Ltd* v *Lax* [1970] 1 WLR 426). Second, as stated in Chapter 3, an agreement for the sale or other disposition of land such as a lease, if entered into on or after 27 September 1989, must comply with the formalities required by the Law of Property (Miscellaneous Provisions) Act 1989.

Provided that these rules are satisfied, in most cases the agreement can, if desired, be specifically enforced by the court, in which case a legal lease must be executed. In some cases, however, a decree of specific performance might not be granted because the party seeking it has infringed the maxim that 'he who seeks equity must do equity'. A tenant who has entered a specifically enforceable contract for a lease has an equitable lease, pending the grant of specific performance. He frequently seeks no legal lease.

Finally, although there is clearly a distinction between the intention to grant a lease and the intention to make a contract for a lease, it is quite settled that a purported lease which fails to create a legal estate, because it is not by deed, may be treated as a contract for a lease, provided that it satisfies the formal requirements mentioned above.

Where contradictory legal and equitable leases result, the equitable lease prevails

The discrepancy between the methods of creating legal and equitable leases can lead to contradictory results. This conflict and its solution is illustrated by *Walsh* v *Lonsdale* (1882) 21 ChD 9. *L* agreed in writing to lease a mill to *T* for seven years with a term that, on demand, *T* should pay a year's rent in advance. No deed was executed in accordance with this, but *T* took possession and paid rent quarterly. The question arose whether *L* could demand a year's rent in advance and use the remedy of distress to enforce it.

Clearly the possession coupled with payment of rent was sufficient to create a legal yearly tenancy; equally clearly the written agreement created an equitable lease for seven years. It was argued that distress was a legal and not an equitable remedy, and that the only legal interest *T* held was an annual tenancy, subject to those terms of the agreement that were consistent with such a tenancy. The payment of a year's rent in advance was not consistent with it because a yearly tenancy can be ended by half a year's notice. This being so, it was pressed, the advance payment could not be demanded because it was not a term of the legal tenancy.

It was held, however, that there were not two separate interests created by two independent codes of rules, as was the case before the fusion of the courts of equity and common law. The court must apply all the rules, legal and equitable, but if there should exist any incompatibility between them, the rules of equity must prevail. Therefore, *T* was holding under the equitable and not the legal lease, and since equity treated that as done which ought to be done, *T* and *L* must have all the rights and responsibilities which would have been theirs if the seven years' lease had been granted by deed. In short, the distress was lawful.

The case may be cited to support two propositions. First, if there is an enforceable equitable lease, this will stifle any legal tenancy which would otherwise have arisen from the incidents of possession and payment of rent. Second, a contract for a lease is for many purposes as good as a legal lease. This doctrine will be discussed below. However, the first of these propositions presupposes that the equitable lease is valid and enforceable. If for some reason it is not – because, for example, specific performance will not be granted – then advantage may nevertheless be taken of any legal tenancy that arises through taking possession and paying rent.

So, if *T* enters possession of land and pays rent upon a monthly basis after *L* has purported to grant him a term of five years under a written document which is not a deed, his rights and duties will be those expressed in that document, because the imperfect lease is treated as a contract for a lease: that is an equitable lease for five years. If, however, he has failed to perform some covenant in that document, he might not be able to claim specific performance. In that case, he would not be entitled to a lease for five years, although he might be entitled to sue *L* for damages for breach of contract. He would, however, have the advantage of a legal monthly tenancy.

The advantages of legal leases over equitable leases

Despite the doctrine of *Walsh* v *Lonsdale*, there are some important differences between a legal lease and an equitable lease arising from a contract for a lease. They are as follows:

1 *Specific performance is a discretionary remedy.* The doctrine in *Walsh* v *Lonsdale* presupposes that specific performance would be ordered of the contract. There are cases, however, when it might be refused (see *Coatsworth* v *Johnson* (1886) 55 LJQB 220 and *Warmington* v *Miller* [1973] 2 All ER 372). The parties will then be left with the mere right to sue upon the agreement for damages. Of course, in many cases a legal periodic tenancy will have arisen and they may then fall back on their rights under that.

2 *A contract for a lease does not create privity of estate.* There exists between a lessor and lessee under a legal lease *privity of estate*, a relationship which continues to exist between all assignees of the lease on the one hand and all assignees of the reversion on the other. Its significance is that some of the most important covenants in a lease are binding not only as between persons enjoying privity of contract, but also between persons who have privity of estate, and that the liabilities as well as the rights under such covenants pass into the hands of assignees. In the case of a contract for a lease, however, no privity of estate exists between the parties or their assignees, so that the ordinary rule of contract applies (except insofar as statute has altered this position) that the benefit but not the burden of the covenant may be assigned (*Purchase* v *Lichfield Brewery Co* [1915] 1 KB 184). This difference, however, has perhaps now disappeared. It will be considered further shortly.

3 *Equitable leases are liable to be overridden.* We have already seen that a legal interest is a real right, good against all persons. A legal lease, therefore, prevails against any purchaser of any interest in the land, whether or not that purchaser has notice of it and whether or not he gives value. This is not so with an equitable lease, which may in some circumstances be overridden by purchasers of legal estates in the land. Their position has been modified by the 1925 legislation if the contract was entered into after that date.

If the contract was made before 1926, and there has been no assignment after 1925, the equitable lease will be overridden by a purchaser for value of a legal estate in good faith for value without notice. Possession under the lease, however, constitutes notice. A contract for a lease entered into after 1925 is registrable as an estate contract under the Land Charges Act 1972 or, in the case of registered land, as a minor interest. If it is not registered, it is void against a purchaser for money, or money's worth, of a legal estate in the land – even though that purchaser had actual or constructive notice of the lessee's rights. If the interest is registered, therefore, it is quite as secure as a legal estate.

4 *The Law of Property Act 1925 s 62 does not apply to a contract.* It will be explained in a later chapter that this section may operate in a *conveyance* to convey unexpectedly wide rights in the form of easements or profits to a purchaser unless its effects are excluded by the conveyance. A contract for a lease, however, is not a *conveyance* for this purpose, whereas legal leases, provided that they are in writing, are (see LPA 1925 s 205(i),(ii), and *Borman* v *Griffith* [1930] 1 Ch 493).

THE RIGHTS AND DUTIES OF THE PARTIES UNDER A LEASE

The rights and duties of the parties under a lease are governed by two factors. First, there are certain rights and duties of a fairly rudimentary kind which apply when no express agreement has been made between the parties, beyond such really essential matters as the duration of the term, without which indeed the lease could not exist at all. Some of these may be displaced by express terms but others apply in certain circumstances, even in the face of express terms to the contrary. Second, it is open to the parties over a wide field to fix their own rights and duties by express covenants. Nevertheless, in view of the wide application of certain important statutory rules, which prevail irrespective of express terms, there is some truth in the observation that the relationship of landlord and tenant now owes much less to contract than it used to do, and much more to statute.

Such restrictions upon freedom of contract illustrate a more general protection of the consumer in the modern state. The development has affected contracts of employment and dealings with goods and mortgages. Later, however, we shall see that in the case of landlord and tenant there has been considerable deregulation during recent years, particularly to encourage the letting of domestic premises.

Rights and duties in default of effective express covenants upon the issue

Rights and duties are correlative notions and for simplicity they will be considered from the point of view of the tenant.

Rights of the tenant

Implied covenant for quiet enjoyment

Even if there is no express provision dealing with the matter, there is implied in every tenancy a covenant that the lessor shall put the lessee into possession and then shall not himself make, nor authorise any other person nor permit any person claiming under him to make, physical interference with the enjoyment of the premises (*Browne* v *Flower* [1911] 1 Ch 219 at 228). There is no liability, however, for the acts of persons claiming by a paramount title such as that of a superior landlord. Examples of breach of this right are the erection of scaffolding in front of the access to a shop (*Owen* v *Gadd* [1956] 2 QB 99), conduct threatening physical eviction and removing belongings of the tenant (*Kenny* v *Preen* [1962] 3 All ER 814). Even an easement granted for the enjoyment of the property may be within such an implied covenant (*Miller* v *Emcer Products Ltd* [1956] Ch 304). On the other hand, mere interference with personal comfort by noise or invasion of privacy does not constitute a breach.

There is no room for the implication of such a covenant if there is an express term covering the matter (*Line* v *Stephenson* (1838) 4 Bing (NC) 678), but the doctrine applies to all kinds of tenancies, whether created by deed, by writing, orally, or by agreement only (*Markham* v *Paget* [1908] 1 Ch 697).

The right to enjoy his grant without derogation

The terms and circumstances of the grant of a lease will determine the total rights to which a lessee is entitled, including any easements to be enjoyed with the premises and the purposes for which the property is let. This might involve difficult problems of construction, but it is a general principle applying to all grants that the grantor must not later derogate from that grant by acts which contradict or are inconsistent with it, so that the grantee cannot enjoy it to its full extent.

The doctrine is concentric with that of the implied covenant for quiet possession, in that breaches of the latter will constitute a derogation from grant, but the doctrine of non-derogation from grant is wider and may include obligations beyond the reach of the covenant for quiet possession. There is no need, for instance, to prove any physical interference with the property leased. It is frequently invoked in cases where the landlord retains property nearby and frustrates the enjoyment of his tenant's premises by the use of his own. There must, however, be some act which renders the property 'unfit or materially less fit to be used for the particular purpose for which the demise was made' (*Browne* v *Flower*, per Parker J, at 226). (See also *Port* v *Griffith* [1938] 1 All ER 295).

Examples of breach of this obligation are a landlord building on adjacent land so as to obstruct ventilation to land leased to a timber merchant, thus interfering with the drying of wood (*Aldin* v *Latimer Clark* [1894] 2 Ch 437); changing the environment of a flat leased for residential purposes by subsequently letting the surrounding flats for business purposes (*Newman* v *Real Estate Debenture Corporation Ltd* [1940] 1 All ER 131); and even the prevention of a tenant from entering the landlord's land to carry out repairs upon the leased property (*Ward* v *Kirkland* [1966] 1 All ER 609, at 617). See now, however, the Access to Neighbouring Land Act 1992.

Implied covenants for repair and fitness for habitation in certain residential lettings

The general rule is that there is no implied covenant by the landlord to repair or even that the property is fit for habitation. There are, however, exceptions to this.

First, in the absence of an agreement to the contrary, there is an implied condition that, upon the lease of a furnished house, it is fit for human habitation (*Collins* v *Hopkins* [1923] 2 KB 617). Breach of the obligation entitles the tenant to repudiate the tenancy. There is no implied covenant, however, that the house shall remain habitable, provided that it was so at the beginning of the tenancy. The principle could be justified under the doctrine of non-derogation from grant but seems to lead an independent existence.

Second, under the Landlord and Tenant Act 1985 ss 8–10 there is an implied condition, which cannot be excluded by the parties, that, on the letting for human habitation of a house at a rent not exceeding £80 a year in London, or £52 elsewhere, the house is fit for human habitation at the beginning of the tenancy and will be kept so by the landlord throughout it. The rule does not, however, apply to leases which are not terminable within three years and under which the tenant is obliged to make the house fit for human habitation. If the letting was made before 6 July 1957, smaller maximum rentals apply. The Act provides tests for deciding whether a house is fit for human habitation. The landlord is not in breach of the implied covenant unless he knows of the defect in question. Few houses are now within these provisions.

Third, in any tenancy of a dwelling-house made after 24 October 1961, for a term of less than seven years, there is an implied covenant by the landlord to keep in repair the external fabric of the house, the installations for supplying water, gas, electricity and sanitation, and for space heating or heating water (Landlord and Tenant Act 1985 s 11, as extended by the Housing Act 1988). (See *Brown* v *Liverpool Corporation* [1969] 3 All ER 1345). A term is to be treated as a term of less than seven years if it is 'determinable at the option of the lessor before the expiration of seven years from the commencement of the term'. *Determinable* has been held to mean determinable irrespective of the happening of any event (*Parker* v *O'Connor* [1974] 1 WLR 1160). A landlord, therefore, who makes the option exercisable only upon some event which is theoretically uncertain, but practically certain, avoids the responsibilities laid down by the Act. Under the 1988 Act the landlord's duty extends to any parts of the building in which he has an interest if the disrepair affects the tenant's occupation of the house or of common parts.

The landlord's obligation does not arise until he knows of the need for repairs or at least has been put on enquiry as to such need (*O'Brien* v *Robinson* [1973] 1 All ER 583). The parties cannot contract out of these obligations but the county court may modify them if it is reasonable to do so. The standard of repair required depends upon the age and character of the building and the neighbourhood. The landlord is not liable if the house cannot be rendered fit for human habitation at reasonable cost. Public law remedies are often available to tenants in these circumstances. See *McClean* v *Liverpool CC* [1987] 20 HLR 25 and *Newham BC* v *Patel* [1979] JPL 303. For a more comprehensive discussion see *Housing Law: Materials and Commentary*, Partington and Hill.

Under the Defective Premises Act 1972 s 4, when a landlord owes a duty of maintenance or repair to a tenant he also owes a duty to all persons, who might reasonably be expected to be affected by defects in the premises, to take reasonable care that they are reasonably safe from personal injury or from damage to their property caused by a failure in his duty under the tenancy of which he knows or ought to know. This provision applies whether the obligation to repair arises by agreement or by virtue of statute.

Implied covenant for repair of easements necessary to a demise

This doctrine was boldly established by the House of Lords in *Liverpool City Council* v *Irwin* [1976] AC 239. In the absence of contrary agreement, a landlord has a duty to maintain to a reasonable standard those parts of the premises retained in his possession over which the tenant has easements necessary to the enjoyment of his tenancy, such as stairways and lifts in high-rise lettings, and rubbish chutes.

The right to estovers

A tenant for years has the right to take estovers. This right was explained in Chapter 4.

The right to remove certain fixtures

A tenant has the right to remove trade, ornamental and domestic fixtures during, though not after, the term. Where a lease terminates by operation of law, such as by effluxion of time, rather than by act of parties, and even though replaced by a new lease, then, assuming the original lease is silent on the point, it is inferred that it was intended that the tenant does not give up his right to fixtures installed by him. The right of removal in those respects is the same as in the case of a life interest, which was dealt with in Chapter 4. A further right is given to tenants of agricultural holdings by the Agricultural Holdings Act 1986 s 10. Agricultural fixtures annexed by the tenant may be removed before or within two months after the end of the term, provided that one month's written notice is given to the landlord before the end of the tenancy (upon which the landlord acquires the option to purchase the fixtures at a fair price), and that the tenant has performed all his covenants.

The right to security of tenure and restriction of rent in certain cases

As mentioned in Chapter 4 most agricultural and business tenants enjoy a large measure of security of tenure under statute and many residential tenants have both security of tenure and protection against rent increase. These statutory rights cannot be excluded by the parties. Finally, the Leasehold Reform Act 1967 gives certain classes of lessees the right to buy the freehold or to demand an extended lease. These topics are considered in outline later in this chapter.

Duties of the tenant

The duties for which a tenant will be liable even when there is no express agreement upon the matter are as follows. (In the case of rent there must, of course, be agreement between the parties as to the amount payable.)

The duty to pay rent, rates and taxes

These payments must be made by the tenant except insofar as statute provides that a tax must be paid by the landlord.

The duty to use the premises properly and in certain cases to repair

In the absence of express covenants the tenant's duties in this field are governed by the doctrine of waste. A tenant for a fixed term of years is liable for both voluntary and permissive waste and thus has a duty to keep the property in repair (*Yellowly* v *Gower* (1855) 11 Exch 274).

A periodic tenant is liable for voluntary waste but not for permissive waste (*Warren* v *Keen* [1954] 1 QB 15), except that a yearly tenant probably has a duty to keep the premises wind and watertight (*Wedd* v *Porter* [1916] 2 KB 91), though this was doubted by Somervell, LJ, in *Warren* v *Keen*. Weekly and probably other periodic tenancies of less than a year only carry a duty to use the property 'in a tenant-like manner' (*Warren* v *Keen*). This duty merely involves doing those things which a good housekeeper would do and which, if left undone, could lead to a deterioration of the premises. Examples are sweeping the chimney, unblocking the sink and turning the water off when going away in the winter. A tenant at will is not liable for permissive waste but the commission of voluntary waste terminates his tenancy.

The duty to allow a landlord to view, if liable for repairs

The landlord generally has no implied right to enter the demised property to view the state of repair. If, however, he is under a contractual or statutory obligation to repair, such a right is implied.

Rights and duties of the parties where there are express covenants

It is not possible in a book of this length either to deal with all the covenants commonly used in leases today, or even to make a detailed study of those which are mentioned. The covenants in leases for specialised purposes might extend to several pages. Here we shall restrict ourselves to some general remarks about some of the more common covenants.

Covenant to pay rent

The rent payable by a tenant is called *rent service* because there is tenure between him and the person to whom it is paid, his landlord. It may be expressed in money or in kind. Unless otherwise provided, it is payable in arrears at the end of each period with regard to which it is calculated (see *Coomber* v *Howard* (1845) 1 CB 440). Payment is overdue if the tenant has failed to pay by midnight at the end of the day upon which the rent fell due.

It was formerly considered that the duty to pay the rent is absolute and continues despite the occurrence of some catastrophe which renders the property unusable, such as destruction by fire. Thus, in *Cricklewood Property and Investment Trust Ltd* v *Leighton's Investment Trust Ltd* [1945] AC 221, rent was held to be payable in respect of a building lease although government restrictions had made building impossible.

There is yet no reported case of the doctrine of frustration being applied to the lease itself and therefore to the rent covenant. Until recently, the prevalent view was that it could not apply. This view has now been dispelled by the House of Lords in *National Carriers Ltd* v *Panalpina Ltd* [1981] 1 All ER 161. The lessee in that case was, on the particular facts, unsuccessful in his submission that a ten years lease of a warehouse had been frustrated by the closure for about two years of the highway leading to it. It was held, however, that the doctrine is capable of applying to leases if frustrating events prevented any substantial use of the property permitted by the lease and in the contemplation of the parties.

On the other hand, the rent agreed cannot be unilaterally increased by the landlord even if inflation or other circumstances have rendered it unrealistically low. For this reason modern leases often contain a 'rent review' clause. These supply the machinery for revision of rent at stated intervals of time. Their Lordships noted that events qualifying as frustrating factors in the case of leases are likely to be rare; the 'never' school of thought has given way to the 'hardly ever' principle. Yet Lord Wilberforce's rejection of the argument that the floodgates of litigation might be opened was surely most welcome. 'It is said that to admit the possibility of frustration of leases will lead to increased litigation. Be it so, if that is the route to justice' (at p 172).

It is appropriate to note here that, within strictly confined limits, a tenant may recoup out of forthcoming rent the cost of repairs where the landlord has breached his duty to repair (see *Lee-Parker* v *Izzet* [1971] 3 All ER 1099).

Covenant to repair

Apart from the statutory duty of the landlord to repair in certain cases, the parties may make what arrangements they wish regarding repairs. Unless otherwise agreed, this covenant also imposes an absolute duty so that the defaulting party will be liable even though he is prevented from carrying out the repairs by circumstances outside his control, such as by the refusal of a building licence (*Eyre* v *Johnson* [1946] KB 481), for he can always pay damages. It is a question of degree whether work carried out on a building is 'repair' or work of a more radical kind which changes its essential character (see *Ravenseft Properties Ltd* v *Davstone (Holdings) Ltd* [1980] QB 12).

While the duty to repair does not involve any obligation to rebuild, it does demand replacement of parts of a building even if those parts are sizeable, but an ordinary covenant to repair does not include reinstatement so substantial as to be out of proportion to the value of the premises (see *Brew Bros Ltd* v *Snax (Ross) Ltd* [1970] 1 QB 612). The standard of this repair depends upon the character of the premises and the nature of the locality at the time of the letting. This does not mean that after a long lease the property must be in the same condition as when it was first let. It means that it must be retained in a condition in keeping with that type of property, accepting the fact that its age will show (see *Anstruther-Gough-Calthope* v *McOscar* [1924] 1 KB 716). It would, for instance, be contrary to this duty to replace a worn-out oak door with one of cheap deal which, though effective, was out of character with the building.

In all cases, the extent of the duty of repair is a matter of construction of the words used in the lease. The use of expressions, however, such as 'good repair' or 'tenantable' repair are not taken to add anything to the simple duty to repair. One qualification of the duty is that 'fair wear and tear' are excepted. This exempts the party concerned from liability for damage which results from ordinary use of the premises or from the weather. A tenant need not, for instance, repair floorboards worn away near a door, or point mortar which has been eroded by rain. Yet if damage occurs through such a cause and, if left unattended, will cause further serious damage, the exemption will not exonerate a person who allows the original damage to remain unrepaired. Thus, if a tile falls from a roof as a result of ordinary wear and tear, a tenant will be responsible for the consequent damage to the interior of the building (*Regis Property Co Ltd* v *Dudley* [1959] AC 370).

The measure of damages for breach of a repairing covenant is governed by the Landlord and Tenant Act 1927 s 18. In no case are the damages to exceed the diminution in value caused to the reversion. If, at the end of the term, the lessor intends that the premises are to be pulled down or to undergo such structural alterations that the repairs contemplated by the covenant would have been valueless, no damages are recoverable (see *Hibernian Properties Co Ltd* v *Liverpool Corporation* [1972] 3 All ER 1117). For proposed reforms to this area of the law see the Consultation Papers of the Law Commission, 1992 (No 123).

Covenant against assignment or underletting

Unless otherwise provided in the lease, a tenant may assign, sub-lease or grant a licence. This covenant is therefore frequently included in case the possession should come into the hands of an undesirable person. These covenants are, however, construed by the courts in favour of alienability. Such covenants are of two types. First, the covenant might be absolute, in which case the tenant cannot assign or sublet unless the landlord waives the benefit of the covenant. This he may refuse to do and his decision, however unreasonable, is binding.

Second, the covenant might be qualified in that assignment and subletting are only forbidden without the landlord's consent. Such covenants are, except in the case of agricultural holdings, subject by statute, despite any agreement to the contrary, to the proviso that the landlord's consent is 'not to be unreasonably withheld' (Landlord and Tenant Act 1927 s 19). The result is that, if a landlord unreasonably refuses consent, the tenant commits no breach if he assigns or sub-lets. If, however, he fails to ask for consent, the tenant commits a breach no matter how unreasonable it would have been for the landlord to refuse.

The Landlord and Tenant Act 1988 obliges landlords, in the case of written requests under qualified covenants made after 28 September 1988, to give consent within a reasonable time, unless he can show that it is unreasonable. The landlord must forward copies of the requests to other persons having an interest in his reversion. Thus the burden of proof of unreasonableness now lies on the landlord and delays in decisions are prevented. This Act is varied by the Landlord and Tenant (Covenants) Act 1995 which came into effect on 1 January 1996 and provides that in the case of new commercial, though not residential, leases landlords may in certain circumstances prescribe the conditions upon which they will consent to assignment. Whether the grounds for refusal must concern either the personality of the sub-lessee or assignee, or the purposes for which he intends to use the property, or whether it may be for some other reason, is uncertain (see *Swanson* v *Forton* [1949] Ch 143). Unless the terms of the covenant are qualified in some way, the latter view is probably preferable (see *Tredegar* v *Harwood* [1929] AC 72, at 79). It is, of course, open to the parties to restrict the grounds of refusal to narrower or broader reasons than these by an express qualification to that effect. The crucial question is whether the landlord's refusal is designed to achieve the true purpose of the covenant (*Bromley Park Garden Estates Ltd* v *Moss* [1982] 2 All ER 890). Under the Race Relations Act 1965, however, it is unreasonable to refuse consent on grounds of colour, race or ethnic or national origin. This does not apply where part of a dwelling-house is let and part of the house is shared with the landlord. It is of course possible to evade the effect of the Act if an absolute covenant against assignment and sub-letting is included in the lease, and discrimination then exercised by waiver. In *Bickel* v *Duke of Westminster* [1976] 3 WLR 805 it was held by the Court of Appeal that refusal of an assignment which would afford the assignee, unlike the assignor, the benefit of leasehold enfranchisement was reasonable. In *Adler* v *Upper Grosvenor Street Investment Ltd* [1957] 1 WLR 227 it was held by the Court of Appeal that a covenant requiring a tenant to offer to surrender the lease to the landlord before seeking consent to assignment or sub-letting was not caught by the section and was thus enforceable (see *Bocardo* v *S and M Hotels Ltd* [1980] 1 WLR 17). The correctness of this decision was doubted by the Court of Appeal in *Green* v *Church Commissioners for England* [1974] Ch 487. The latter case was, however, decided on different grounds. Many leases today contain such covenants because they are intended to enable landlords to take advantage of a rise in rents. It is, therefore, important that the question should be settled in the near future.

Finally the covenant is not breached by a bequest of the lease nor by involuntary alienation such as occurs upon bankruptcy.

'The usual covenants'

In agreements for leases the parties sometimes summarise their intentions by declaring that the lease is to contain 'the usual covenants'. What covenants are included in this description depends upon the circumstances of the case, trade practice and local custom (*Flexman* v *Corbett* [1930] 1 Ch 672). The question is one of fact and to be solved by examining the nature of the premises, their situation and the purpose for which they are being let. The evidence of conveyancers, including their books of precedents, is therefore in point. (*Chester* v *Buckingham Travel Ltd* [1981] 1 All ER 386.)

It has been suggested that what is essentially a question of fact can in particular cases, through notoriety and judicial knowledge, attain the status of law. Such elevation would often enable a court to reach a speedy decision and would screen many claims from the courts (97 LQR [1981] 385). In that case the list mentioned above must be supplemented by reference to current case law in regard to the many forms of specialised leases. Reported precedents are however scarce. Fifty years elapsed between the decisions in *Flexman* v *Corbett* and *Chester* v *Buckingham*. In any case, it appears from the latter case that the same test will be applied in deciding what covenants are usual whether the question arises in relation to an express reference to 'usual covenants' in a lease or contract, or in relation to cases where the term is implied.

The following covenants, however, are certainly included in such a description, namely covenants by the tenant to pay the rent, rates and taxes, to keep and deliver up the premises in repair, and to allow the landlord to view the state of repair, a condition that the landlord may re-enter if the rent is not paid, and a covenant by the landlord for quiet possession.

REMEDIES

We must now examine the remedies which are available when covenants are broken. The remedies for breach of a rent covenant differ from those for breach of all other types of covenant and will therefore be dealt with separately.

Remedies for breach of rent covenant

Action for arrears

No action may be brought to recover arrears of rent after the expiration of six years from the date when it fell due (Limitation Act 1980 s 19). Where, however, the tenant makes an acknowledgement of the claim or makes a payment of part of the rent, the six-year period runs from that time. Rent under a lease continues to fall due no matter how long a time has elapsed since the last payment and no matter how much rent has been rendered irrecoverable under the statute. If however the rent has been paid for 12 years to some third person who claims the reversion, as opposed merely to not being paid at all, the landlord's rights are determined.

Distress

Distress is a remedy which entitles the landlord to take and ultimately to sell chattels present upon the demised land, and to satisfy his claim out of the proceeds. The rules of distress are complicated and only a certificated bailiff can execute this remedy. Only a few brief remarks will therefore be made here.

A landlord cannot levy distress and bring an action for arrears at the same time. In all cases he must own the reversion both at the time the rent falls due and when the distress is levied. Only six years of arrears may be recovered (Limitation Act 1980 s 19). In the case of an agricultural tenancy only one year's arrears are recoverable (Agricultural Holdings Act 1986 s 16).

Re-entry under an express proviso for re-entry or for breach of condition

A breach of covenant does not itself enable a landlord to end a lease prematurely. Of course, in the case of a periodic tenancy, he may serve a notice to quit upon an unsatisfactory tenant, but if the lease is for a fixed term this will not be possible. Since it would be very inconvenient to bring successive actions against a persistently defaulting tenant, special provisions are included in most leases to enable landlords to end them prematurely by forfeiture. This may be achieved in two ways.

First, the duty in question may be expressed as a condition, in which case the lease may be forfeited when a breach of the obligation has occurred. Whether a duty amounts to a condition or not depends upon the intentions of the parties and might involve difficult problems of construction. Second, if the duty has been expressed as a covenant only, the right of forfeiture only follows upon its breach if the lease contains an express proviso for re-entry upon breach of those covenants to which it is expressed to apply. If the terms of the lease confer upon the landlord the right to serve notice to quit in case of breach of covenant, this right has the character of a right of forfeiture and the tenant may seek relief as described below (*Richard Clarke & Co* v *Widnall* [1976] 1 WLR 845).

In either case the landlord may waive his right of forfeiture either expressly or impliedly. Waiver will only be implied, however, if the landlord both knows of the facts constituting the breach and

> does some unequivocal act recognising the continued existence of the lease . . . Therefore, though an act of waiver operates with regard to all known breaches, it does not operate with regard to breaches which were unknown to the lessor at the time when the act took place (*Matthews* v *Smallwood* [1910] 1 Ch 777, per Parker J, at 786 and see *David Blackstone* v *Burnetts (West End) Ltd* [1973] 3 All ER 782).

Neither does it operate as a waiver of future breaches (LPA 1925 s 148). Typical examples of acts which imply waiver are demands for or acceptance of rent accruing after the breach and distress for rent whenever it fell due. No waiver can be implied, however, if the landlord does not know of the breach at the time of the alleged act of waiver. Furthermore, a statement or act by the landlord not communicated to or not having any impact on the tenant will not constitute waiver (*London and County (A & D) Ltd* v *Wilfred Sportsman Ltd* [1970] 3 WLR 418, per Russell, LJ, at 427). Once a landlord has, moreover, finally taken a step to forfeit the lease, such as by bringing an action for possession (see *Canas Property Co Ltd* v *KL Television Services Ltd* [1970] 2 All ER 795), acts which would usually constitute waiver do not amount to waiver. A landlord may, however, waive his rights by accepting rent even though it was stipulated that any waiver must be in writing (*R* v *Paulson* [1921] 1 AC 271).

Before proceeding to forfeiture, the landlord must make a formal demand for the rent unless he is exempted from doing so either by the terms of the lease or by statute. A formal demand is one made upon the demised premises between sunrise and sunset specifying the amount due. This requirement is usually excluded by the lease by the provision that forfeiture will ensue if rent is in arrear for more than a specified time 'whether formally demanded or not'. Even if there is no such provision, however, no formal demand is necessary if 'one half year's rent shall be in arrear' and there is not sufficient distress on the premises (Common Law Procedure Act 1852 s 210).

The exercise of a power of forfeiture can bring harsh results but equity gave relief against it – provided that the tenant paid the rent due together with interest and any costs which had been entailed to the landlord; for then a just position had been restored and it could be said that forfeiture was unnecessary. This jurisdiction has been regulated by the Common Law Procedure Act 1852 (ss 210–212) and the Supreme Court Act 1981 (s 38). Under the 1852 Act, if the landlord brings an action for forfeiture and the tenant makes the payments mentioned above to the landlord or into court before the trial, all proceedings are stayed. It was held in *Standard Pattern Co Ltd* v *Ivey* [1962] Ch 432 that, because of the unfortunate drafting of the three sections, this relief cannot be claimed by a tenant unless 'one half year's rent shall be in arrear'. (For a criticism of this result see 78 LQR 168.) This restriction only applies, however, to actions in the Supreme Court.

If the tenant does not make payment, so that judgment is given against him he can still apply for relief within six months after the execution of the judgment, and the court may then grant him relief subject to the same conditions as to rent and costs as could formerly be imposed under the equitable principles employed by the former Court of Chancery. There is thus a discretionary power to refuse relief in light of the conduct of the tenant or the possible hardship to the landlord. For instance, this might be so where the tenant has delayed his application until so late within the six months period that the landlord has changed his position upon the assumption that forfeiture was to ensue (see *Stanhope* v *Haworth* (1886) 3 TLR 34). It seems to be a corollary of the Standard Pattern case that the six months time limit would not apply to a tenant who has less than 'one half year's rent' in arrear.

The landlord might enforce forfeiture by re-entry rather than by action. In that case, relief may still be granted (*Howard* v *Fanshawe* [1895] 2 Ch 581). In such cases, however, relief would be granted under the court's inherent equitable jurisdiction since the Act only applies where the landlord takes proceedings to recover possession.

Finally, when relieved, the tenant holds under the terms of the original lease. An underlessee may also apply for relief from forfeiture when a head lessor is proceeding against that underlessee's own landlord, whereupon the court may vest the property in that underlessee for part or the whole of the remainder of the term upon such conditions as it thinks fit (LPA 1925 s 146(4)). The effect here, however, is the creation of a new lease in favour of the person who had been the underlessee.

Remedies for breach of covenants or conditions other than rent

The initial focus will be on the landlord's remedies, since this affords the opportunity to discuss some of the more complex problems affecting this topic. The remedies of the tenant are, however, of equal importance and are discussed subsequently insofar as they are not referred to the landlord's remedies.

Action for damages, injunction or specific performance

The landlord can sue for damages or for an injunction if the tenant breaks a covenant. In the case of a covenant to repair premises other than an agricultural holding, where the lease is for seven years or more, of which at least three are unexpired, the landlord must first serve a notice upon the tenant under the Leasehold Property (Repairs) Act 1938 (as amended by the Landlord and Tenant Act 1954 s 51), specifying the breach, requiring it to be remedied, if that is possible, and asking for compensation. The tenant may then serve a counter-notice within 28 days, in which case the landlord cannot proceed with an action without the leave of the court. In the case of failure by the landlord of an obligation to repair, the tenant may, after giving notice, carry out the repairs himself and set-off the costs against his rent (see *Lee-Parker* v *Izzet* [1971] 3 All ER 1099.

The remedy of specific performance can be awarded where appropriate. Its incidence as between landlord and tenant, however, is not necessarily mutual. Thus, while it is available to a tenant against a landlord who has broken a repairing covenant, a landlord could not obtain it against a tenant for such a breach (*Jeune* v *Queens Cross Properties Ltd* [1973] 3 All ER 97).

Re-entry under express proviso for re-entry or breach of condition

As in the case of a rent covenant, the remedy for forfeiture cannot be used unless there is an express proviso for re-entry relating to the covenant in question, or unless the obligation is expressed as a condition. The rules discussed above governing waiver of the right of forfeiture apply equally here. The provisions for relief against forfeiture are different; for equity only assisted where the covenant breached was for payment of rent. Eventually, relief was made available by statute. The law is now contained in the Law of Property Act 1925 s 146; this section operates despite any stipulation by the parties to the contrary (*Plymouth Corporation* v *Harvey* [1971] 1 All ER 623).

Before enforcing a right of forfeiture by action or otherwise, the landlord must serve a notice specifying the particular breach, requiring it to be remedied, if it is capable of remedy, and requiring the lessee to make compensation. In the cases to which the Leasehold Property (Repairs) Act 1938 applies, the landlord cannot take any proceedings without the leave of the county court if the tenant serves a counter-notice. This was explained above in relation to an action for damages, to which it also applies.

As to the three factors to be specified in the notice, the breach must be described sufficiently to enable the tenant to know with reasonable certainty what he has done wrong. The landlord need not however demand compensation if he does not want it, nor ask for the breach to be remedied if it is not remediable. Thus, in *Rugby School (Governors)* v *Tannahill* [1935] 1 KB 87, where premises had been used for prostitution, it was held that omission to demand compensation did not invalidate the notice, for the landlord understandably would not wish 'to touch money coming from a tenant in such circumstances'.

Furthermore, there was no need to require the breach to be remedied, for mere cessation of such a use would not cure the bad reputation which the property would have acquired in the neighbourhood. A breach of covenant by unlawful subletting has been held not to be capable of remedy for it is a breach once and for all and not a continuing breach. Accordingly, no time need be given for its remedy and the tenant's only recourse will be to apply for relief (*Scala House and District Property Co Ltd* v *Forbes* [1973] 3 All ER 308).

Where the unlawful use is by a subtenant, and the head landlord is proceeding against the tenant for allowing the breach, it does not follow that the breach is incapable of remedy so far as the tenant is concerned, provided that he had no previous knowledge of it and takes steps, including forfeiture proceedings, against the subtenant (*Glass* v *Kencakes Ltd* [1966] 1 QB 611).

After service of the notice, the landlord must allow the tenant 'a reasonable time' to remedy the breach and then may proceed to forfeiture if no remedy is forthcoming. When he is proceeding to enforce forfeiture, by action or otherwise, the tenant may, either in the landlord's action or in proceedings brought by himself, apply for relief which the court may grant or refuse as it 'thinks fit', considering the conduct of the parties and all other circumstances. Unlike the case of rent covenants, there is no power to grant relief after forfeiture has been accomplished by court action. It was held, however, in *Billson* v *Residential Apartments Ltd* [1992] 2 All ER 141 that, where a landlord has re-entered without court action the tenant can still apply for relief after repossession. As to mortgages of leasehold interests and their rights to apply for relief on the forfeiture of their leasehold securities see *United Dominions Trust Ltd* v *Shellpoint Trustees Ltd* [1993] 4 All ER 310. On the other hand, the provision enabling sublessees to apply for relief applies equally here (s 146(4), as amended by the Law of Property (Amendment) Act 1929 s 1). Furthermore, this applies in the exceptional cases mentioned below where the tenant himself cannot apply for relief.

These exceptional cases under the section in which the landlord need not serve a s 146 notice but may proceed immediately to forfeiture, and where no relief may be granted, are as follows:

1 Breach of covenant for inspection of records, machines or workings in the cases of a mining lease.

2 Breach of condition against bankruptcy of the tenant or the taking of his interest in execution where the lease is of agricultural land, mines, a public house, a furnished house, or any property with respect to which the personal qualifications of the tenant are important in preserving its value or character or important because the landlord or other tenants of his have premises nearby (see *Earl Bathurst* v *Fine* [1974] 2 All ER 1160).

In all other cases of breach of condition against bankruptcy, apart from those mentioned above, relief may be applied for at any time at all provided that the lease is sold within one year of the bankruptcy. If it is not sold within the year, then no relief may be sought after the expiration of that year. These rules are designed to give the trustee in bankruptcy a reasonable chance to decide whether to sell the lease and, in case of sale, to give the purchaser the chance to have his title confirmed.

Quite apart from statutory provisions and the Rules of the Supreme Court, the rules of natural justice demand that notice of proceedings must be given to a tenant when a landlord is seeking possession in the courts (*Fleet Mortgage and Investment Co Ltd* v *Lower Maisonette, 46 Eaton Place Ltd* [1972] 2 All ER 737).

Finally, it is appropriate to mention some specific remedies and rights of the tenant insofar as they have not been discussed in the account above. Under the Landlord and Tenant Act 1985 the court has a discretion to grant specific performance in favour of residential tenants for breach of covenant by the landlord where damages would not be an adequate remedy. Where a landlord has broken covenants of repair, the tenant, after giving notice, may carry out the repairs and set the cost off against future rent. See generally *Chiodi* v *Demarney* [1988] 2 EGLR 64. The tenant's rights under public law, mentioned earlier, are of considerable practical significance.

In 1994 the Law Commission recommended a restructuring of the law relating to the termination of tenancies, including the abolition of forfeiture in its present form because of its potential for injustice (see Law Com No 221, HC 135).

THE PERSONS AS BETWEEN WHOM THE COVENANTS ARE ENFORCEABLE

Before mentioning the persons by and against whom the covenants in a lease are enforceable, certain terms which are necessary to an understanding of this topic must be explained.

When a lease is made two major legal results occur. First, an estate in land is created. This is the only estate today which involves tenure in that land is held of a landlord in return for a rent and upon certain agreed conditions. The fact that a lease may be free of rent does not disturb this doctrine of tenure. This estate can of course be transferred to other persons, as can the landlord's reversion. The relationship between the persons entitled, at any particular time, to the reversion and to the lease, whether they are the original parties or not, is called *privity of estate*. In the case of transfer of the landlord's and tenant's estates there is only privity of estate between the transferees, however, if there is an assignment of the whole of the unexpired term of the lease or the entire reversion. Thus, if *L* leases land to *T* for 10 years and on the next day *T* grants *S* a term of nine years there is no privity of estate between *L* and *S*, because *S* only takes a sublease and not an assignment of the whole term of the lease. Successful adverse possession against a lessee under the Limitation Act 1980 does not operate to *assign* that lessee's title to the claimant. The Act does not transfer titles but merely extinguishes them, leaving claimants to establish their own independent titles (*Tichborne* v *Weir* (1892) 67 LT 735).

The second result of the creation of a lease is that the covenants contained in it are contractual between the parties to it. The original parties to a lease are bound together by privity of contract. This privity of contract continues between them throughout the term of the lease even though the estates of both the parties are transferred to other persons. The transferees of these estates neither interrupt nor partake of this privity of contract of the original parties. Figure 6.1 illustrates these relationships.

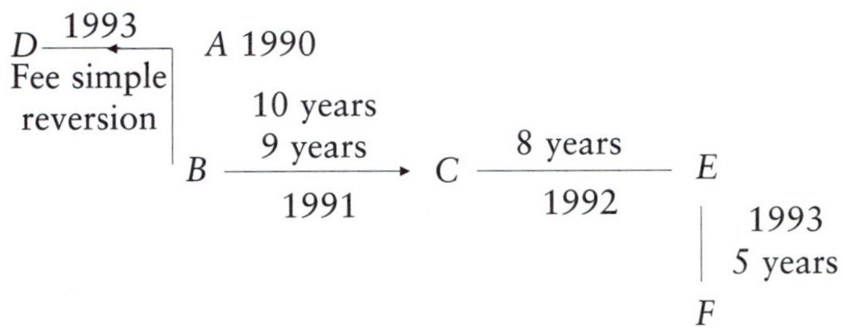

Fig. 6.1

In 1990, *A* leased land to *B* for ten years. Between these two at that time there exists both privity of contract and privity of estate. In the next year *B* assigned the whole of the unexpired lease to *C*. At this stage there is privity of contract between *A* and *B* but no privity of estate. Between *A* and *C* there is privity of estate but not of contract. In the next year *C* assigns the lease to *E*. There is still privity of contract between *A* and *B* but no relationship between *A* and *C* either in estate or contract. Privity of estate exists however between *A* and *E*.

Finally, let *E* sublease to *F* and *A* assign the reversion to *D*. Privity of contract continues between *A* and *B*. There is privity of estate between *D* and *E* since one holds the lease and the other holds the reversion to it. There is neither privity of contract nor privity of estate between *D* and *F* because *F* does not hold the lease of which *D* has the reversion. The same result would follow if *F* had been a mere licensee or trespasser upon the land. A new relationship, however, has sprung up. *E* now enjoys both privity of estate and privity of contract with *F*, for a sublease is just as much a lease as a headlease is.

In short, persons only enjoy privity of contract in regard to the covenants in a lease if they are the original parties to that lease. Yet this privity lasts throughout the lease. They only enjoy privity of estate if one holds the entire unexpired term of the lease while the other holds the reversion to it. This relationship does not outlast the period for which they are simultaneously held.

We are now equipped to consider the extent to which covenants contained in a lease bind third parties coming to the land, apart from the original landlord and tenant. Important changes were made to the law however by the Landlord and Tenant (Covenants) Act 1995 which came into effect on 1 January 1996. The principal changes affect only leases granted on or after that date. Some provisions, however, affect leases created before that date.

In these circumstances the strategy adopted below is to describe first the law as it stood up to that date and then to graft the changes on to that stock.

The law prior to 1 January 1996

Privity of contract between the parties: all covenants in lease mutually enforceable

The original parties to a lease can enforce against each other all the covenants in the lease. This rule is the ordinary law of contract and the only restriction therefore is that the covenant must not be illegal. Thus if *L* leases property to *T*, who assigns the lease to *A*, *T* remains liable to *L* upon all the covenants even though he no longer occupies the land. So if the liquidator of a company disclaims a lease which has been assigned to the company, the original lessee remains liable for the rent falling due even after the assignment (*Warnford Investments Ltd* v *Duckworth* [1978] 2 WLR 741). The principle applies equally if *L* assigns his interest.

Privity of estate between the parties: covenants 'having reference to the subject matter of the lease' mutually enforceable

Where there is no privity of contract but only privity of estate between the parties in question, only covenants 'having reference to the subject matter of the lease' are mutually enforceable. If this requirement is satisfied, however, it does not matter whether the covenant is positive or negative. The phrase 'having reference to the subject matter of the lease' is the modern expression of the requirement used by the Law of Property Act 1925 (ss 141 and 142), and is preferable to the older description of such covenants as 'touching and concerning the land'.

A test which has judicial approval for ascertaining whether a covenant is of such a kind is whether it 'affects either the landlord *qua* landlord or the tenant *qua* tenant'. A covenant may have reference to land without being referable to the lease (*Breams Property Investment Co Ltd* v *Stroulger* [1948] 2 KB 1 at 7). Furthermore, covenants which, though included in a lease for convenience, are of a merely personal nature do not satisfy the requirement.

A more recent test was suggested in *Swift Investments* v *Combined English Stores* [1988] 2 All ER 885 where Lord Oliver highlighted the test as whether the covenant could benefit later assignees, whether it could affect the use of the land and whether the covenant was expressed to be personal. The uncertainty of the various tests has led to the abolition, for new leases, of the distinction between covenants which do and do not have reference to the subject matter of the lease. These are to be considered later. Examples of covenants which do satisfy it are to pay rent, to repair, not to assign or underlet, to use property in a certain way, to buy beer from the landlord for sale on the demised premises and to renew the lease. On the other hand, examples of covenants which do not satisfy the requirement are to sell the reversion and not to open another public house near the demised property.

If the covenant has reference to the subject matter of the lease in this way, then both the benefit and burden pass to the assignee either of the tenant (*Spencer's Case* (1583) 5 Co Rep 16a), or of the landlord (LPA 1925 ss 141 and 142). The liability of the assignee is limited, however, to breaches committed while he holds the lease or the reversion. His right to sue for breaches is limited in the same way except that in the case of an assignment of the reversion the assignee is the only person who can sue, even though the breach occurred before the reversion came into his hands, unless the damage is suffered by the assignor exclusively (*Re King* [1963] Ch 459). The new reversioner is also entitled to remedy such breaches of covenant occurring before assignment by any right of re-entry contained in the lease provided that the right has not been waived. The assignment of the reversion, 'subject to and with the benefit of' the lease, does not impliedly waive previously committed breaches by admitting that the lease still exists, for the words are merely performing a mechanical conveyancing function (*London and County (A & D) Ltd* v *Wilfred Sportsman Ltd* [1970] 3 WLR 418).

There is now no need for the lease to be created by deed for the covenants to run with the estates in this way. In a case concerning an assignment by the tenant, the judge said: 'I assume that it does not matter that there was here only an agreement under hand and not a lease by deed, since the tenant took possession under the agreement' (per Evershed, MR, at p 242 in *Boyer* v *Warbey* [1953] 1 QB 234). Probably, therefore, a specifically enforceable contract for a lease suffices and it may now be that no writing at all is necessary in those cases in which tenancies can be created orally. Similarly relaxed rules apply equally when the landlord assigns, for the word 'lease' used in ss 141 and 142 includes a 'tenancy' (see s 154).

Where part only of a reversion is assigned the covenants and any conditions or rights of re-entry are apportioned and remain enforceable by the owners of the severed parts of the reversion against the lessee. If *L* leases houses numbered 1, 2, 3 and 4 to *T* and then assigns the reversions of numbers 1 and 2 to *A*, *L* could enforce a repairing covenant, for instance, against *T*, in respect of numbers 3 and 4, and *A* could do likewise in respect of numbers 1 and 2 (LPA 1925 s 140).

The operation of the two doctrines of privity of contract and privity of estate might give a lessor the choice of two defendants in the event of a breach of covenant. He may sue the original lessee, because the privity of contract continues throughout the lease, and, assuming that the covenant has reference to the subject matter of the lease, he may also sue an assignee who holds the lease at the time of the breach, because of his privity of estate with that assignee. In such cases, however, the lessor can only recover once and, furthermore, it is the assignee who is primarily liable. The original lessee, if sued, may claim indemnity from the guilty assignee. Lessees frequently took an express covenant for indemnity from their assignees at the time of assignment and those assignees would similarly cover their own contractual liability by taking covenants of indemnity from persons to whom they later assigned.

Such an indemnity against all breaches of covenant in the future is implied in any assignment for valuable consideration made after 1925 (LPA 1925 s 77(1)(c) and Sch 2, Pt IX). Thus if *A* leases property to *B*, who assigns to *C*, who assigns to *D*, who assigns to *E*, who commits a breach, *A* can sue either *B* or *E*. If he sues *B*, the latter can join *C* in the action because of the implied indemnity. Likewise, *C* can then join *D* and *D* can join *E*, so that ultimately liability is satisfied by the person who was in breach of the covenant in the lease.

Neither privity of contract nor privity of estate between the parties: covenants enforceable only if they run with the land

Before explaining what covenants 'run with the land', we must notice in what circumstances there might be neither privity of contract nor privity of estate between the parties. Neither form of privity exists between landlord and sub-lessee, nor between a landlord and the licensee of his tenant, nor between a landlord and a person who is a trespasser or an adverse possessor upon the demised premises. Yet all these persons might do acts which are contrary to the terms of the lease and, although the landlord might have his remedy against his tenant, it might often be more convenient to proceed directly, if possible, against the wrongdoer himself.

In such cases, it is not sufficient that the covenant 'runs with the estate' under *Spencer's Case*, because none of these persons takes the estate of the lease. What we must ask is whether there are any covenants which 'run with the land', so that persons coming to the land, though not the estate, through whatever right or claim, will be bound by them? There are indeed covenants which are so enforceable in certain circumstances and are effective even outside the sphere of leases as, for instance, when *A* sells land to *B* in fee simple and *B* later sells the land to *C*. The role of covenants in land law generally, and not merely in the province of leaseholds, is dealt with in Chapter 12. It is sometimes possible for *A* to enforce covenants contained in the conveyance to *B* against *C*, even though neither privity of contract nor privity of estate exists between *A* and *C*. Before mentioning those covenants, we must notice one other method, of particular importance in the law of leases, by which remedies are available against persons irrespective of privity of contract or estate.

A right of re-entry in case of breach of covenant in, or in respect of, a lease may be a legal interest in land (LPA 1925 s 1(2)(e)). As such, it is effectively enforceable against all occupiers of the land, even though there is no privity of contract or privity of estate between the parties concerned: a landlord may enforce it against a sub-lessee who has done acts which are contrary to a covenant to which the right of re-entry relates.

Restrictive covenants are discussed in Chapter 12. It is sufficient for present purposes to say that a restrictive covenant creates an equitable interest in land and is enforceable against persons irrespective of privity of contract or estate.

They may be created on the sale of land or by independent transactions. They may also be created by a landlord and tenant within a lease. Since they are capable of running with the land itself, as opposed to the estate of the lease merely, they affect persons coming to the land irrespective of privity of contract or estate and thus may be enforced, for instance, by the landlord against sublessees and licensees under the rule in *Tulk* v *Moxhay*.

The law prevailing on and after 1 January 1996

The Landlord and Tenant (Covenants) Act 1995 is revolutionary in its effect upon leases granted on or after 1 January 1996. Its effects may be summarised as follows.

The principle of privity of contract disappears after assignment

A tenant who assigns is released from his covenants and ceases to enjoy the benefits of the landlord's covenants (s 5). The provision does not apply to assignments by operation of law. This new freedom is however modified when the tenant needs the landlord's permission to assign. The landlord is then authorised to require the tenant to guarantee performance of the covenants by the assignee where it is reasonable to do so (s 16).

A landlord who assigns however is not automatically released from his covenants (ss 6–8). To achieve this result he must serve a prescribed form of notice on the tenant before the assignment or within the four following weeks. Release occurs if the tenant serves a notice of consent, or fails to serve an objection within four weeks and, in the latter case, the county court declares that release would be reasonable. The landlord, if unsuccessful, may apply again when the reversion is next assigned.

In order to redress the balance a little in favour of landlords of commercial leases only, in new leases landlords will be more free to prescribe in the lease the circumstances in which it will be 'reasonable' to refuse licences to assign leases as required by the Landlord and Tenant Act 1927 s 19. There are restraints upon the operation of this freedom however, for which the new Act should be consulted.

Distinction between covenants 'having reference to the subject matter of the lease' and merely 'personal' covenants disappears for new leases

The benefit and burden of all covenants will carry with assignments of the lease and the reversion unless expressly limited to any person (s 2).

Certain provisions apply to both new and existing leases

A landlord may no longer recover arrears of fixed charges or rent from a former tenant or sureties unless he serves a prescribed notice within six months of the sum becoming due. This is a safeguard against accumulation of these debts at high interest rates against him without his knowledge.

Another useful reform also applying to old leases is that a former tenant who has been held responsible for payment of money on account of the default of his assignee may demand an overriding lease which will constitute him landlord of the defaulting tenant with associated powers of enforcement. For a discussion of the possible effects of the Act on capital and rental values, see the *Solicitors Journal*, 1 December 1995 at p 1213.

DETERMINATION OF LEASES

Leases may end through effluxion of time, forfeiture, surrender, notice to quit, merger, enlargement (see LPA 1925 s 153) disclaims and, rarely, by frustration (*National Carriers Ltd* v *Panalpina (Northern) Ltd* [1981] AC 675). The last three are of minor importance and will not be considered here. Forfeiture has already been discussed. The death of one of the parties does not determine a lease even in the case of an ordinary short periodic letting, such as a weekly tenancy. The personal representatives must serve notice to quit in order to end the tenancy (*Youngmin* v *Heath* [1974] 1 All ER 461).

Effluxion of time

A lease for a fixed period of years ends naturally at the end of that term and no notice to quit is necessary unless expressly stipulated. This general principle has, however, been greatly affected by modern legislation which has given security of tenure to certain classes of tenants even though the contractual term of the lease has ended.

Surrender

A surrender is a return of the estate to the landlord immediately in reversion, whereupon it is extinguished by merger with that reversion. Surrender may be express or by operation of law. It will occur by operation of law, if, for instance, the tenant gives up possession of the premises to the landlord and the landlord accepts this or the parties otherwise show by their conduct their intention to end the lease. If express, surrender must be by deed (LPA 1925 s 52). If the transaction is supported by consideration and conforms with the Law of Property (Miscellaneous Provisions) Act 1989 s 2(1), however, specific performance would no doubt be ordered.

Notice to quit

Periodic tenancies may be ended by notice to quit which must conform to any agreement made by the parties to the tenancy as to its length and form, subject of course to mandatory statutory provisions. It is of the essence of a periodic tenancy that both landlord and tenant should be capable of terminating the contractual tenancy by notice to quit (see *Prudential Assurance Co Ltd* v

London Residuary Body [1992] 2 AC 386 at 394). It must name the date of the termination of the tenancy or refer to it in such terms that it can be ascertained without doubt (*Addis* v *Burrows* [1948] 1 KB 444), and there must be no ambiguity as to its purpose, which is to end the tenancy. Conditions in the notice will therefore invalidate it unless they can be construed as merely offering a new tenancy, as where it is stated that the tenancy may nevertheless continue if a new rent is paid. On the other hand, provided that the landlord's intentions are made clear, he is not prejudiced merely because he makes concessions to the tenant. Thus in *Dagger* v *Shepherd* [1946] KB 215 a notice to quit 'on or before the 25 March next' was construed as an unambiguous notice to quit upon the day mentioned coupled with an offer to accept an earlier termination.

In *Hammersmith and Fulham Borough Council* v *Monk* [1992] 1 AC 478 the House of Lords held that a periodic tenancy held by two or more joint tenants may be terminated at common law by the notice of only one of the joint tenants unless the tenancy agreement provides otherwise. Clearly this decision might be mischievously exploited, particularly by cohabitees who have fallen out. It was ingeniously avoided in such circumstances by the Court of Appeal in *Hounslow LBC* v *Pilling* [1993] 25 HLR 305. The *Hammersmith* case profiles again the question discussed earlier in this chapter. To what extent is a lease an estate of singular identity? To what extent can its coastlines be determined by contract?

We must now discuss the length of notice necessary to end the various types of periodic tenancy. First, quite apart from the statutory protection of tenure mentioned above, there is a statutory provision that no tenancy of a dwelling house, whenever let, may be ended by less than four weeks' notice to quit (Protection from Eviction Act 1977 s 5). All dwelling houses and not merely those otherwise protected by the Rent Acts are affected by this.

Unless otherwise agreed, a yearly tenancy may be ended by not less than half a year's notice. If the tenancy began on one of the usual quarter days the period of notice must be at least two-quarters, so that a tenancy begun on Midsummer Day, 24 June, may be ended by a notice served on or before Christmas Day. If, however, the tenancy began on some other day, the period of notice must be at least 182 days. Agricultural tenancies stand outside these rules.

The date upon which a tenancy should be ended is the day before the anniversary day of its commencement or the anniversary day itself. A tenancy begun on Lady Day, 25 March, should therefore be required by the notice to end on 24 or 25 March, for which purpose the notice should be served on Michaelmas Day, 29 September, at the latest.

Other periodic tenancies can be ended by notices governed by similar principles except that the period of notice is not half the duration of the period in question but the full duration: unless otherwise agreed, a weekly tenancy begun on a Saturday may be ended by a notice given on or before a Friday requiring the tenancy to end on the following Friday.

Merger

A lease signifies a relationship between two people. A person cannot hold land of himself. When the lease and the reversion become vested in one person in the same right, therefore, the lease becomes merged in the greater estate and disappears. This does not happen if the person who takes the two interests intends otherwise.

THE STATUTORY PROTECTION OF TENANTS

In modern times, Parliament has been prepared to combat social and economic problems by legislation over a wide field. We noticed in Chapter 4, where limitations on the use and enjoyment of land were discussed that, under various statutes, many tenants enjoy considerable security of tenure and sometimes protection against increases in rent. This topic will now be considered in outline, but it must be emphasised that this account is given only for the purpose of a general appreciation of the subject. The legislation is complex and at times highly developed by case law, so before any practical problem is considered, reference should be made to the books which deal with it in detail and, of course, to the primary sources of the law.

The Rent Acts

A chronic housing shortage during this century, sharpened by war, caused Parliament to intervene by passing the first of the 'Rent Acts' in 1915. This was the first of a series of Acts controlling rent and providing security of tenure for large numbers of residential tenants. The present law is mainly contained in the Rent Act 1977 and the Housing Act 1988. The 1988 Act provided that no new tenancies could be created under the Rent Act on or after 15 January 1989, and introduced a new regime for residential tenants in the private sector. It abolished rent control for new tenancies but retained a measure of security of tenure for some tenants. Thus there are two codes in operation, the earlier one diminishing in importance with the passage of time. Only the new one will be outlined here. Then a new form of control of residential tenancies in the public sector will be briefly described.

The Housing Act 1988

The Rent Acts placed such strong controls on rent and afforded tenants such security of tenure that owners were reluctant to let residential property. The purpose of the Housing Act 1988 was to release more rented accommodation on to the market. Some of the categories and expressions used in the Act are the same as those used in the Rent Acts. In those cases the existing case law clustering around these are useful in the interpretation of the new Act. The Act employs two new forms of tenancy to achieve its aims.

The assured tenancy

This is a periodic tenancy granted to an individual person or persons as opposed to a corporation, of a dwelling house 'let as a separate dwelling' as a sole or principal home (ss 1 and 3). Certain tenancies are excluded by Sch 1 Pt I. Examples are: houses having a rateable value of £1500 or less in Greater London or £750 elsewhere; student lettings; holiday lettings; council houses; lettings arranged by local authorities under their statutory duties for homeless persons. (If the tenancy was entered into on or after 1 April 1990, when rating was abolished, the values are rents not exceeding £1000 per annum in Greater London or £250 elsewhere.)

The terms of the tenancy include those expressly agreed by the parties and some implied by the Act. The latter class includes a prohibition against assignment without the landlord's consent and a right of the landlord to enter to carry out repairs. Rent is not generally regulated as under the Rent Acts. There is machinery however for its increase during the term including final determination by a rent assessment committee.

An assured periodic tenancy may be terminated by the landlord only by order of the court for one of the reasons specified by the Act (s 3). Examples are breach of covenant by the tenant and the intention of the landlord to demolish or substantially redevelop the property (see generally Sch 2, Pt II).

The assured shorthold tenancy

The general features are similar to the assured periodic tenancies described above but there are the following key differences which often make such a letting a more attractive proposition for the landlord.

It must be for a fixed term for a period of at least six months, with no power on the part of the landlord to determine it during the first six months, except through forfeiture for breach of covenant, and must be preceded by a prescribed notice served before the tenancy is granted (s 20).

The general effect is that the tenant has no security of tenure once the tenancy has expired by effluxion of time. The landlord must however give the tenant at least two months' notice before the end of the fixed term that he requires possession.

The rent payable under the tenancy is that agreed by the parties. The prescribed notice preceding the tenancy however informs the tenant of the right to apply to a rent assessment committee if he considers the rent is excessive. The committee's terms of reference however are more designed to take account of market values than was the case under the Rent Acts regime.

Public sector tenants

Public sector tenants, notably tenants of council houses formerly enjoyed no statutory protection. Under the Housing Act 1985, reconstituting the Housing Act 1980 on this point, however, they enjoy protection analogous to that provided by the Rent Acts under the new category of *secure tenants*. There is however no equivalent rent regulation but there are other controls under local government law which are beyond the scope of this book. Part V of the Act also confers on tenants the right to buy their houses in certain circumstances.

The Leasehold Reform Act 1967 (as amended)

This Act gives the opportunity to certain leaseholders of houses at low rents to buy the freeholds or to obtain extensions of their leases by 50 years. The conditions under which an application may be made under the Act are as follows. The Act in no way affects the ordinary free negotiation of a sale of the freehold reversion or a grant of an extension of a lease by a landlord and his tenant.

1 The rent must be less than two thirds of the rateable value specified or if the lease was created after 1 April 1990, when domestic rates were abolished, the rent must not exceed £1000 in Greater London or £250 elsewhere. The Leasehold Reform, Housing and Development Act 1993 has now empowered tenants of leases formerly excluded by these conditions to buy the freehold on more expensive terms.

2 The lease must have been granted for a term of more than 21 years.

3 The property must have been occupied by the lessee as his main or only house of residence for the last three years or for periods totalling three years in the last 10 years.

4 The lease must be of the whole house. The Act does not apply to flats or maisonettes, though it does apply in certain cases where the house has been sublet. The Leasehold Reform, Housing and Urban Development Act 1993 has improved the position of such tenants. The Act should be consulted carefully on these matters. There is machinery for the transmission of the lessee's rights under the Act in certain circumstances.

A qualified lessee has the following alternative rights:

1 After serving a notice he may acquire the freehold. There are now three different methods of calculating the price depending on rateable value and rent. Specialist books should be consulted for details.

2 He has the right to an extension of his lease by 50 years with a rent revised and based on the letting value of the site. This rent may be reviewed after 25 years. Once again, disputed cases are settled by the Lands Tribunal.

A landlord may resist applications of both kinds if he reasonably requires the house as a residence for himself or for a member of his family and, in certain cases where he owned a housing estate, could apply to the High Court for a scheme under which he retains powers of control over houses on the estate in the interests of the estate as a whole; the time for such applications has now passed. He may resist an application for an extended lease on the additional ground that he wishes to demolish or reconstruct the house. A Crown tenant cannot apply under either head and certain public authorities may apply to the Government for exemption if the land will be required for development within ten years.

Agricultural holdings

During the present century, the economic difficulties of the farmer and the crises of food supply produced by two world wars have made governmental influence in agriculture inevitable. Here we are concerned only with that aspect of the resulting legislation which has affected the farmer's security of tenure and the rent he pays. The law is now contained principally in the Agricultural Holdings Act 1986 for lettings made before 1 September 1995. For lettings made on or after that date, a new code is provided by the Agricultural Tenancies Act 1995. The law applying to lettings made before 1 September 1995 will be described first.

An agricultural holding is one let and used for the business of farming, horticulture, fruit growing or market gardening. If the tenancy was created substantially for one or more of those purposes the Act applies, even though the land or parts of it can be put to uses of a subsidiary nature. A notice to quit is invalid if it attempts to terminate the tenancy before the expiration of twelve months from the end of the current year of tenancy. A tenancy or licence for a period of one year certain or less becomes a tenancy from year to year.

Security of tenure

With some exceptions, a periodic tenancy can only be ended by 12 months' notice to quit expiring at the end of a tenancy year.

If, however, the tenant, within one month of receiving such a notice to quit, sends the landlord a counter notice, he has security of tenure unless one or more of the following conditions apply, in which case the notice to quit is effective. The notice to quit must specify the grounds:

1 The tenant of a smallholding has attained the age of 65 years.

2 Where the land is stated to be required for some non-agricultural use for which planning permission has been given or is, with certain exceptions, not required.

3 Bad farming.

4 Where the tenant has failed, within certain time limits, to remedy in full a breach of contract after the landlord has notified him of it.

5 Where the landlord's interest has been materially prejudiced by breach of some term which is incapable of remedy.

6 Where the tenant has become bankrupt.

7 Where the tenant, or the last survivor of joint tenants to whom the property was originally let, has died within three months of the notice. There is however provision for members of the deceased tenant's family to apply to the Tribunal for succession.

8 Amalgamation of farms with Ministerial consent.

9 Where the Agricultural Land Tribunal consents:
   (a) That the landlord's purpose in requiring possession is in the interests of good farming.
   (b) That the purpose is in the interests of the sound management of the estate.
   (c) That the purpose is in the interests of agricultural research, education, experiment or demonstration or for the provision of allotments or small holdings.
   (d) That greater hardship would be caused by withholding consent than by giving it.
   (e) That the land is required for some non-agricultural use not falling within (2) above.

Rent

On the granting of a tenancy, the parties may agree on whatever rent they please. Either party may, however, submit the matter not more than once every three years to an arbitrator who may increase or decrease the rent as from the time the tenancy could be ended by a notice to quit served when the request for arbitration was made. No revision is therefore possible where the tenancy is for a fixed term.

An entirely new code for the letting of agricultural land has been introduced by the Agricultural Tenancies Act 1995 for lettings made on or after 1 September 1995. The economic background to the Act was the depreciation in value of the landlord's interest due to the statutory protection of the tenant, who enjoyed virtually lifelong security of tenure. Consequently owners of agricultural land became reluctant to let their land. Here, as elsewhere in our economic life, deregulation and greater flexibility of contract were provided as a solution. Only the general principles of the Act can be provided here. They are briefly as follows.

1 Freedom is given to negotiate the length of term of the tenancy.

2 Security of tenure is generally reduced and notice to quit is not dependent upon the default of the tenant.

3 There are safeguards against the merging of agricultural tenancies with business tenancies as regulated by the Landlord and Tenant Act 1954 Part II.

4 The Act provides for review of rents and generally for arbitration on failure to resolve disputes.

Business tenancies

The Landlord and Tenant Act 1954 Pt II, as amended, affords protection in the two ways described below, where the property or part of property comprised in a tenancy is occupied by the tenant for the purposes of any trade, profession or employment. There are some exceptions such as agricultural holdings, public houses, mining leases, certain service tenancies and tenancies of not more than six months. 'Business' has been interpreted widely by the courts and may even apply to clubs and land where no buildings stand.

Security of tenure

Business tenancies continue under the Act even after the expiration of the term, unless ended in accordance with it or ended by a tenant's notice to quit, by surrender or by forfeiture.

To end the tenancy, the landlord must give not less than six nor more than 12 months' notice in the form required, expiring no earlier than the tenancy would have ended apart from the Act, or could have been ended by notice to quit. If the tenant serves a counter notice within two months informing the landlord that he is not willing to give up occupation, he may, not less than two nor more than four months after the landlord's notice, apply to the court for a new tenancy. There is an alternative procedure under which tenants for fixed terms exceeding one year can initiate matters by serving a statutory request for a new tenancy (see generally ss 25 and 26).

A new tenancy must be granted by the court unless the landlord establishes one of the following grounds mentioned below (s 30). The new term is not to exceed 14 years; the rent is based on market value; and the other terms are, in default of agreement between the parties, to be settled by the court. The statutory protection described above in no way affects the competence of the parties to negotiate a new lease without having recourse to the Act. The grounds for possession are:

1 breach of repairing covenant;

2 persistent delay in payment of rent;

3 other breaches of covenant or mismanagement of the property;

4 reasonable offer of alternative accommodation by the landlord;

5 the applicant is a subtenant of part of the premises and the whole could be let substantially more profitably than the parts;

6 the landlord intends at the end of the tenancy to demolish or reconstruct the whole or a substantial part of the premises and could not reasonably do so

THIS LEASE made the 9th day of May 1995 between John Snug of 14 Theseus Way Arden Warwickshire (hereinafter called 'the Landlord') and Peter Wall of 9 Philomel Creek Arden aforesaid (hereinafter called 'the Tenant')

WITNESSETH as follows:

1 The Landlord hereby demises unto the Tenant ALL THAT property known as Humblebee Cottage Shirley Warwickshire TO HOLD the same unto the tenant from 9th day of May 1995 for the term of 2 years in consideration of the yearly rent of £5000 clear of all deductions payable by equal instalments twice yearly on the 1st day of November and the 31st day of March in each year of the tenancy.

2 The Tenant hereby covenants with the Landlord as follows:

(i) To pay the rent on the days mentioned and all taxes assessments and other outgoings payable in respect of the property during the term.

(ii) At the Tenant's cost to repair and paint the interior of the property during the last six months of the tenancy.

(iii) At the expiration or sooner determination of the tenancy to yield up the property to the Landlord.

(iv) To use the property only as a dwelling house.

(v) Not to assign charge underlet or part with the possession of the property without the previous written consent of the Landlord.

3 The Landlord hereby covenants with the Tenant as follows:

(i) That the Tenant paying the rent hereby reserved and observing the covenants on his part shall enjoy peaceable possession of the property during the tenancy without disturbance on the part of the Landlord. The Landlord shall come on to the premises for the purposes of inspection at a date and time convenient to the Tenant.

(ii) That the Landlord will keep the property insured against loss or damage by fire in the sum of £30000 and if the property is destroyed or damaged by fire will reinstate the property fit for habitation within 6 months of the occurrence of the fire.

4 PROVIDED ALWAYS and it is hereby agreed that if the rent or any part thereof shall remain unpaid for 21 days after becoming payable (whether formally demanded or not) or if any covenant on the part of the Tenant shall not be performed or if the Tenant shall become bankrupt the Landlord may at any time thereafter re-enter upon the property and the tenancy shall absolutely determine.

IN WITNESS whereof the parties hereto have hereinto set their hands and seals the day and year first before written.

Signed and Delivered by John Snug
JOHN SNUG

in the presence of: Fred Flute
FRED FLUTE 9, Moonshine Glade
Bellows Mender Monks' Walk,
Warwickshire

This is a model lease prepared by the author based on commonly used forms.

without obtaining possession. There is no obligation on the landlord, however, to carry out his plans once he obtains possession;

7 the landlord wishes to occupy the premises wholly or partly for his own business or for his own residence. In this case, however, the landlord must not have purchased his interest nor must his interest have been created within five years before the end of the term. This provision protects tenants against speculative purchases of reversions of business tenancies when the terms have but short times to run.

Compensation

The Act provides for modest compensation where possession is granted on one or more of the last three grounds and, in certain cases, for improvements made by evicted tenants.

STUDY MATERIAL

The lease

On pages 128–9 is an example of a lease.

QUESTIONS

1 Who is responsible for the external repairs of the property?

2 Peter Wall has sublet the property without the landlord's permission. Advise the landlord as to his rights.

3 Suppose that Peter Wall has sublet the property with the landlord's permission and that the subtenant receives planning permission to use the house for business purposes. Will he be liable for breach of any covenant in the lease?

4 Peter Wall's neighbour, Jorrocks, keeps a pack of foxhounds. The hounds bark and bay so incessantly that Peter cannot sleep. Does he have any remedy against Jorrocks?

QUESTION AND GUIDELINES FOR ANSWER ON LEASES

The purpose here is not to provide a 'full' answer; it is explicitly to address method in tackling problems. Once sound technique is appreciated and practised, then completely decorated answers can be attempted. The guidance which follows might be classified as: (1) question analysis and isolation of the relevant issues; (2) assembly of pertinent legal principles; and (3) indication of solutions.

QUESTION

Larry orally agreed to grant a lease of Blackacre (which has unregistered title) to Terry for 10 years at a rent of £X pa payable monthly. Terry went into possession. He has paid rent regularly since. Terry has now discovered that Larry sold and conveyed the fee simple in Blackacre to Paula last week.

Advise Terry.

Would your answer differ if:

(a) the agreement had been in writing?

(b) Blackacre had been registered land?

GUIDANCE FOR ANSWER

1 Analysis of the question

Here we are asking 'in what waters is the examiner fishing?' The intended transaction is stated to be a lease. The word 'lease' is not in quotation marks. It is, therefore, your examiner speaking and providing you with data. Your examiner does not wish you to consider, for instance, whether a lease or a licence was intended. In that case the word 'lease' would have been put into Larry's mouth. Once this point is excluded, it is clear from the data that the relevant issues are the mode of creation of leases, and the possible consequences of imperfect creation and protection. Only these areas of the law relating to leases should be in focus.

2 Assembly of relevant legal principle

(a) Section 2(1) of the Law of Property (Miscellaneous Provisions) Act 1989 provides that all contracts for the sale or other dispositions in land shall be in writing. Thus an oral contract for a lease is void.

(b) Under s 52 of the Law of Property Act 1925, leases, as opposed to contracts for leases, must generally be created by deed. Important common law exceptions are, however, preserved. In particular, entry into possession of property under an ineffective lease or agreement for a lease can create a tenancy at will at common law. On the payment of rent on a periodic basis a legal periodic tenancy can arise, without the formalities of a deed or even writing (see s 55). Such a legal tenancy is enforceable against all persons coming to the land, whether or not the title is registered. No registration of the interest is required in either case.

(c) A written contract for a lease creates an equitable lease if the contract is specifically enforceable (*Walsh* v *Lonsdale* 1882). Such equitable interests, though fully enforceable against the grantor of the equitable lease, are vulnerable as against a purchaser for value of a legal estate in the land without notice of the equitable interest. This possibility can be avoided by registration of the equitable lease as a land charge in the case of unregistered land or as a minor interest in the case of registered land.

(d) In the case of registered land only, if the equitable tenant fails to register the equitable lease as a minor interest, the interest will be enforceable as an overriding interest under s 70(1)(g) of the Land Registration Act 1925, if the tenant is in actual occupation. Chapter 18 should be consulted for details of the effect of this.

3 Indication of solutions

(a) Oral agreement for 10 years:
  (i) Unregistered land: void.
  (ii) Registered land: void.

(b) Written agreement for 10 years:
  (i) In the case of unregistered land, enforceable against Paula only if registered as a land charge before the conveyance to her was completed.
  (ii) In the case of registered land, enforceable against Paula if registered as a minor interest before the conveyance to Paula was completed. If not so registered, the interest will still be enforceable as an overriding interest, as described above.

(c) Periodic legal tenancy:
  (i) In the case of unregistered land, this is enforceable against Paula on the common law principle of a legal interest being enforceable against the whole world.
  (ii) In the case of registered land, the tenancy would be enforceable against Paula as an overriding interest.

CHAPTER 7

OCCUPATIONAL RIGHTS WITHOUT ESTATE

INTRODUCTION

During the thousand years of history of English land law there has been a slow evolution of personal rights to estates. The principal features of an estate or interest in land are enforceability against all or most persons and assignability. To illustrate the former, suppose that a fee simple owner *F* grants a lease to *L* and later sells his fee simple to *P*. If *L* then sells his lease to *X*, the latter can enforce his interest against *P* and vice versa, whether or not either knows of the rights of the other. There is no need to prove any personal nexus.

No doubt, in the early days of feudalism rights in land were of a personal nature, that is enforceable only between grantor and grantee. The relationship of loyalty implied that the grant was personal and that free alienation was not contemplated. In practice, however, since land was the basis of the national economy as well as the object of political fealty, assignment of interests was later allowed. Thus arose estates in land enjoying the distinguishing features mentioned above.

This accolade of estate was bestowed on a limited range of grants, the fee simple, the entail, the life interest and the variants of these. The reason was that feudal land law was created by and for the aristocracy. The events which tolled the passage of aristocratic life were births, deaths and marriages. Estates were fashioned for the family.

The lease enjoyed a similar but later career. At first it sounded only in contract. It concerned only the landlord and his tenant. If the landlord assigned the fee simple and the new owner refused to confirm the lease, the tenant's only remedy lay in damages and not for recovery of occupation. Yet just as the social and economic factors of feudal England shaped the first estates, so did the developing commercial influences of the fifteenth century allow the lease to graduate from contract to estate. The tenant, usually a farmer and a stalwart of the economy, needed security of tenure against all persons for his term. The calendar rather than family events registers time for the trader. The leap to estatehood was brought about through technical developments in the law centred around the writ of ejectment.

We might also anticipate how social and economic need in the nineteenth century enabled the restrictive covenant to make that same leap with the guiding hand of equity.

Since the eighteenth century, the United Kingdom has changed from a centuries-old agrarian society to a community of such complex family and work patterns that it would be strange to find the old system of estates unrestrained by new influences. Human activity continuously outgrows the law which constantly tries to catch up upon, classify and control it. Examples of such influences in the contemporary UK are divorce and marital separation, cohabitation on the part of unmarried people, mobility of the population, greater incidence of home ownership, state protection of the underprivileged, the housing shortage and the leisure industry.

A complicating factor in regard to the relationships we are about to discuss is that they have not made any uniform leap towards estatehood. Sometimes enforceability of an arrangement has expanded beyond the immediate parties, but falls short of affecting all persons. Often the power of assignment is absent. Only time will confirm whether they will attain the two hallmarks of interests in land. Perhaps, however, this classical concept of the estate is outmoded and a more finely graduated system of occupational rights is called for. Between the rigid bone of estate and the soft muscle of contract there is needed, and is growing, a cartilaginous sinew which combines the capacity for youthful flexibility with some capacity for endurance.

Sometimes these rights have developed through precedents; sometimes they have been enacted. As to the former, while they are disparate they appear to spring from very general equitable principles. In *Re Sharpe* [1980] 1 All ER 195, Browne-Wilkinson J remarked at page 201:

> I do not think that the principles lying behind these decisions have yet been fully explored and on occasions it seems that such rights are found to exist simply on the ground that to hold otherwise would be a hardship to the plaintiff.

Here two elements of justice confront each other. The law ought to be reasonably certain and foreseeable; on the other hand, it should respond to the infinitely variable circumstances of the case in issue.

Land law has been accustomed to distinct interests with distinct names. These modern rights to occupy land possess some but not all the features of the older interests. Consequently they tend to be classed as merely personal rights, the result only of the brake of equity being applied to prevent the owner of an *interest* asserting his full *rights* against some person. The old legal maxim 'Where there is a right there is a remedy' is clearly appropriate where rights are precisely defined and well established. Yet what is a right but the claim to a remedy? The even older truth that 'Where there is a remedy there is a right' is appropriate in regard to these new relationships to land. Merely because the remedy is available against a narrower range of persons or for a shorter time than in the case of the older interests surely ought not to forbid their classification amongst rights to land.

It is, however, permissible to distinguish them from the older interests provided that we remember that the differences are of degree only. The scheme will be first to describe the nature of each right, then to silhouette it against the two hallmarks of estatehood, range of enforceability and assignability.

LICENCES

Nature

A licence gives permission to do some act, otherwise unlawful, in regard to land belonging to another. The permission might be express or implied. An example of the latter is the implied consent of a householder to members of the public to call at his door to make lawful enquiries, provided that he has not signified that such calls are forbidden. Licences generally lack the hallmarks of interests in land, namely assignability and enforceability against third parties. They merely authorise the licensee to do some act which would otherwise be a tort. During this century, however, it has become clear that in certain circumstances licences can possess these attributes.

The subject matter of licences is universal, spanning activities which are compatible with the existence of leases, easements, life interests and even profits, as shown below.

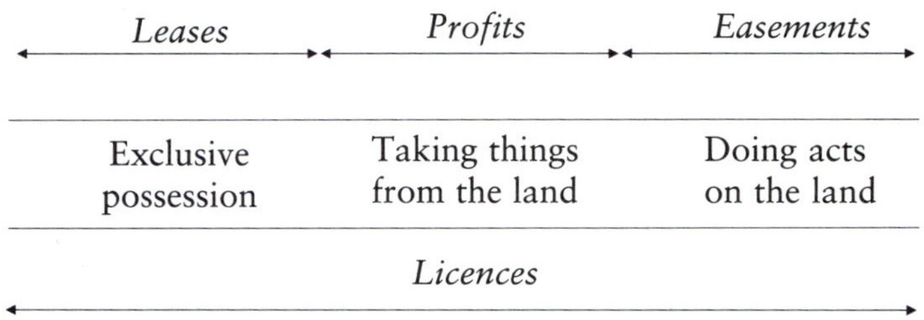

Fig. 7.1

A licence may authorise taking your seat in the cinema, going to a friend's house for a drink, putting an advertisement sign on another person's property or even enjoying exclusive occupation of land for an indefinite period. In short, any act can be the subject matter of a licence. In practice, the two interests from which it is important to distinguish it are leases and easements.

A licence is distinguishable from an easement in that the latter exists for the benefit of another piece of land, whereas the former exists for the benefit of a person only. This factor also distinguishes it from a profit which, we shall later see, is an interest in land analogous to an easement.

Generally there will be no confusion between a licence and a lease because licences usually concern doing some act upon land, whereas a lease demands exclusive possession. It is now beyond question, however, that a licence can confer exclusive possession (see *Errington* v *Errington and Woods* [1952] 1 KB 290), so that when this is present some conclusive test must be applied. The test is that, if exclusive possession is given, then *prima facie* there is a lease: but if the circumstances and conduct of the parties show that only a personal privilege, not an interest in land, was intended, then there is only a licence (per Lord Denning LJ in *Errington's Case*).

The criterion, imprecise though it might be, is that of the intentions of the parties. This intention must be deduced from all the circumstances. The most common cause for confusion is whether a licence or lease has been created. This was considered at the beginning of Chapter 6.

Association with land law and its precisely defined estates has fostered some prematurely rigid classification of licences. An attempt to distinguish them according to their range of enforceability has, however, produced a fourfold classification which is rooted only in mode of creation, namely bare licences, contractual licences, licences coupled with grants and estoppel licences. It is submitted that this classification is spurious as to its intended purpose and has been a principal cause of the confusion in this subject. It has failed to detect the true reasons why the courts have afforded durability to some licences but not to others.

The classification has failed fully to observe that a licence is a means only and, unlike an estate or interest, not an end in itself, whereas the remedies supplied by the courts have frequently been tuned to the ultimate aims of the parties.

A licence is merely one means through which occupation of land occurs. Its end or purpose must be sought by examining the precise terms of each individual licence and all the circumstances surrounding its offer and acceptance. Its mode of creation is not without significance but constitutes only one of these surrounding factors. A licence can, for instance, lead to the licensee becoming entitled to an estate in land. This is so in the case of proprietary estoppel. Such licences are more appropriately considered as means through which interests in land are acquired. They are accordingly dealt with as such in Chapter 1. Here we are only concerned with licences which confer rights of occupation falling short of 'interests', as described at the beginning of this chapter. Speaking in terms of remedies, such rights attract 'negative' injunctive relief, whereas the positive relief of specific performance is more appropriate in the case of interests.

There are signs that the rigid fourfold classification is crumbling in the face of modern authorities. The dictum of Browne-Wilkinson J noted on page 134 illustrates a more general approach. The older classification will be described below when the range of enforceability of licences is discussed. This is done not only because its rationale, faulty though it might be, is enshrined in high judicial authority, but also because the manner of creation possesses some genuine significance in attracting equitable remedies. More detailed criticism of the older approach will be reserved for that discussion.

It is submitted that general equitable principles and remedies ultimately measure all licences irrespective of manner of creation but according to all the circumstances of the case.

Range of enforceability of licences

Enforceability against the licensor

This is a question of revocability.

1 *Bare licence.* This is a licence given otherwise than for consideration and not coupled with a grant of property in the land. It is revocable at the will of the licensor at any time, even if given by deed. The licensee must however be given a reasonable time to leave. Subject to that he becomes a trespasser (see *Minister of Health* v *Bellotti* [1944] 1 KB 298).

The grant of exclusive occupation to a person, for example a mistress, with the intention of providing security of occupation even for a long period, may nevertheless be merely a bare licence, devoid of the contractual element qualifying it to be dealt with under (3) below. Even an intention that ownership shall pass will not alter this position if no conveyance of the property has been made (*Horrocks* v *Forray* [1976] 1 WLR 230). While some of the constituents of contract might be present, such as agreement to terms, the intention to create legal obligations might be absent.

2 *Licence coupled with a grant.* If the licence is ancillary to the grant of some proprietary right in the land or chattels on the land, such as a permission to enter and take a tree or a heap of bricks which the licensor has sold or given to the licensee, then it is irrevocable (*James Jones and Sons Ltd* v *Tankerville* [1909] 2 Ch 440).

3 *Licence for value.* This is simply an ordinary contract and revocability depends upon the particular terms. Whether the right to enter the land is the primary purpose of the contract or is merely secondary is immaterial (*London Borough of Hounslow* v *Twickenham Gardens Development Ltd* [1970] 3 All ER 328, at 343). Examples are admissions to cinemas and sportsgrounds for payment and entry upon property to do building or other work. Sometimes the contract will expressly state how long the licence is to last; sometimes it will clearly imply it.

In the earlier days of this century the rights of the licensee rang only in contract. The licence could be revoked at any time, the licensor being liable in damages only if revocation amounted to breach of contract. There could be no damages in tort. Damages in tort would depend upon the licensee having an interest in land, which, being property, the licence is irrevocable by the grantor. If the licensee's rights were merely contractual, however, the licence could be revoked effectively though wrongfully. The consequence would be breach of contract only.

This doctrine has been changed by modern developments, notably by the willingness of the courts to apply equitable remedies. In *Winter Garden Theatre (London) Ltd* v *Millennium Productions Ltd* [1948] AC 173 Lord Uthwatt said

> The settled practice of the courts of equity is to do what they can by an injunction to preserve the sanctity of a bargain.
>
> (p 202)

His statement was *obiter*, however, because the licence in question was held to have been properly revoked.

In *Hurst* v *Picture Theatres Ltd* [1915] 1 KB 1 it was held by the Court of Appeal that the ejection of the plaintiff from a cinema on the mistaken grounds that he had not paid for his ticket amounted not merely to breach of contract but to assault. The basis of the decision was that he had gained an interest in the land through his contract, for in equity he would have been entitled to decree of specific performance of his contract. Notionally, a Chancery judge was sitting by his side at the performance. The comparative age of this case is reflected by the old-fashioned requirement of an interest for securing occupation of the land itself, and the inference that, although contracting parties 'may' not break their contracts, they nevertheless 'can' do so. See *Wood* v *Leadbitter* (1855) 13 M&W 838. The *dicta* from *Winter Garden* cited above, although *obiter* only, point to a more sophisticated formula for modern development. A right to the land itself results from a remedy and not vice versa.

The view of Megarry J in *London Borough of Hounslow* at 343 that

> I find it difficult to see how a contractual licensee can be treated as a trespasser so long as his contract entitles him to be on the land

surely points the way for the future. In short, revocation depends upon the terms of the agreement.

4 *Estoppel licence*. The principle upon which this licence rests is that if an owner permits another person to spend money or detrimentally to alter his position in the expectation that he will enjoy some privilege in the land, the owner will be prevented from acting inconsistently with this expectation. The fundamental basis of the doctrine, however, is the otherwise unconscionability of the outcome rather than conduct alone. (See *Taylor Fashions Ltd* v *Liverpool Victoria Trustees Co Ltd* [1982] 1 All ER 897 and *Lim Teng Huan* v *Ang Swee Chuan* [1992] 1 WLR 113).

Thus, relief has been given against an owner where a person was allowed to spend money on a watercourse running through the owner's land (*Duke of Devonshire* v *Eglin* (1851) 14 Beav 530), where a territorial concession was made in the expectation of a right of way (*Ives Investment Ltd* v *High* [1967] 1 All ER 504), and where a son was encouraged to build a bungalow on his father's land, partly at his own expense, with the expectation of living there as long as he wished (*Inwards* v *Baker* [1965] 2 QB 29). While none would disagree with the justice of these decisions, the nature of the remedy and the rationalisation of the right by the judges have varied. The remedy has sometimes been of a positive kind, where the anticipated right has in reality amounted to a quantifiable interest in land. Thus, in *Dillwyn* v *Llewelyn* (1862) 4 De GF & J 517, where the facts were similar to those of *Inwards* v *Baker*, it was held that the son, having built the house, was entitled to a conveyance of the land. This decision was, however, criticised in the Court of Appeal in *Dodsworth* v *Dodsworth* (1973) 228 EG 1115, where it was remarked that such a positive remedy might sometimes presuppose wider rights than contemplated by the parties. Similar problems might arise from the recent development of *rental purchase* of property, when the purchaser pays the price by instalments while in occupation. Such purchasers are sometimes referred to in their contracts as licensees (*see* 36 Conveyancer 325). In other cases, with which this chapter is more concerned, the remedy has been of a negative kind, the court ruling that the licence has created a proprietary estoppel which the licensor is not allowed to deny (*Ives Investment* v *High*, above). The court looks at all the circumstances of each case to decide by what kind of remedy the equity can be satisfied (see *Plimmer* v *Wellington Corporation* (1884) 9 App Cas 699). Thus in cases such as *Ives Investment* v *High*, above, where decrees of specific performance are not appropriate because the substantive right is unenforceable through failure to register, the court may give negative procedural protection which is not founded upon a positive right. As to the rationalisation of the right to protection, it would surely be possible to classify these cases as contracts. The licensee has acted to his detriment in return for an undertaking by the licensor which amounts to a promise not to obstruct the licensee when he has altered his position. The question of consideration should cause no difficulty since it is clearly established that this only requires a detriment to the promisee, and not necessarily a benefit to the promisor. This is one of the branches of land law which needs bracing with stronger and clearer concepts. If the medieval lawyers had been concerned with the licence, things might have been different (see, generally, 37 Conveyancer 402).

This class of licence has often received separate treatment in the decided cases. There appears to be no good reason for this. Estoppel licences have been classified as 'equities', as for instance in the judgment of Lord Scarman in *Chandler* v *Kerley* [1978] 2 All ER 942. Yet the two features entitling them to be so called can apply equally to contractual licences. These are susceptibility to equitable remedies and the capability, in appropriate circumstances, of binding third parties. To the extent that they can claim these characteristics all licences are 'equities'.

The *constructive trust* is a principle which has also been used to justify decisions in deserving cases in this area. This has led to complications. First, as a matter of mere terminology it has been used to describe relationships of *common intention.* These are more appropriately called *implied* trusts. Attention was drawn to this possible confusion in Chapter 1. Second, it has raised distinctions between 'rights', automatically founded in the case of trusts, and 'remedies' discretionally granted by the courts in their equitable jurisdiction in the case of estoppel licences.

This question has been more fully explored by David Hayton (*see* 1993 LQR 108) and the study materials on p 148. Although his broad approach of 'unconscionability' is to be preferred to the reliance upon narrow categories of traditional trust law, two possible misconceptions should be borne in mind. First, his use of the term 'common intention constructive trusts' is questionable. Second, the distinction between *automatic* and *discretionary* rights appears faulted. On the one hand the *discretionary* remedies of equity are applied on principles as stable as the trust itself. On the other hand disputes as to the existence of an *automatic* trust postpone settled outcomes as much as do remedial applications.

Enforceability against third parties

1 *Bare licence.* This is not binding on third parties.

2 *Licence coupled with a grant.* If the subject matter of the grant is an interest in the land, and the legal interest has passed, then the licence, like the interest itself, will be binding on all third parties. If there is merely a contract to create such an interest, then its enforceability against third parties will depend upon whether this has been registered as an estate contract under the Land Charges Act 1972.

3 *Contractual licence.* On the principle that since contractual licences can, in appropriate circumstances, enjoy protection through equitable remedies in the same way as estoppel licences do, they ought to bind third parties to the same degree as the latter. This would mean that they are enforceable against third parties other than purchasers for value of a legal estate in the land without notice. There appears to be no good reason why contractual licensees, as such, should be denied this stability for their rights. They are as vulnerable and deserving of protection as estoppel licensees. The only distinction is that they act to their detriment at the time of the licensor's promise, whereas the estoppel licensee acts to his detriment after it.

It would appear fairer if the distinction between the two categories were forsaken and all forms of relief were based on the substantial merits of the case. The basis of relief could be developed by precedent to the point only of reasonable certainty yet so as to retain some elasticity. The law of tort managed to burst out of technical categories into broader standards of liability in the development of negligence. Perhaps this is an example to be followed. The existing authorities on the question however are less promising. The older cases infer that contractual licences do not bind third parties (see *King* v *David Allen and Sons, Billposting Ltd* [1918] 2 AC 54 and *Clore* v *Theatrical Properties Ltd* [1936] 3 All ER 483). Yet in *Errington* v *Errington* [1952] 1 KB 290 the Court of Appeal held that a contractual licence bound a third party volunteer and it was suggested that it might also bind a third party purchaser. The authority of this decision is weakened by *dicta* of the House of Lords in *National Provincial Bank* v *Ainsworth* [1965] AC 1175, and by the fact that it can be considered as a case of estoppel licence. (*See* also the judgment of Lord Denning, MR, in *Binions* v *Evans* [1972] 2 All ER 70; (1972) 35 MLR 551 and *DHN Food Distributors* v *Tower Hamlets* [1976] 1 WLR 852.) It is clear that mode of creation is obscuring the more fundamental question of whether all the circumstances of the case invoke a remedy *in specie* rather than mere damages. The need for a resolution of these difficulties was stressed by Browne-Wilkinson J in *Re Sharpe* [1980] 1 All ER 195.

4 *Licence by estoppel*. In *Errington* v *Errington,* a father bought a house with the aid of a mortgage from a building society, paying part of the purchase price as a down-payment, and leaving the rest on mortgage. He let his son and daughter-in-law live in it, telling them the house would become theirs when they paid off the building society instalments. Before these were fully paid off the father died, leaving the house to the widow. The Court of Appeal held that the married pair were licensees with an equitable right to remain in the house as long as the instalments were paid, whereupon they would have an equitable title to the house itself. Accordingly, the widow had no right to the house. The case is clear authority for the enforceability of this type of licence against third parties other than purchasers for value of a legal estate in the land without notice. Once again, the question must be asked why this problem cannot be considered as one of ordinary contract. The rights under it would be registrable as an estate contract, though upon the facts of *Errington* v *Errington* this would not have been necessary as against the widow, who was not a purchaser.

In the case of registered land, there appears no good reason why such licences to occupy should not constitute overriding interests. The unsettled state of the law makes difficulties for a landowner who wishes to grant occupation to a person without creating a commercial arrangement or a life interest. It has been suggested that the solution is to grant a short periodic tenancy rent free with an absolute covenant against assignment and subletting and with the landlord contractually postponing his right to serve notice to quit (36 Conv 266). This appears, however, to be open to two objections. First, persons attempting to accommodate friends and relations in this way frequently do not take legal advice and might not even be aware of the problem. Second, the highly personal nature of the terms and relationships might still lead the court to find that, despite the terms, a licence was intended rather than an estate.

Assignability of licences

Up to this point, we have been discussing the enforceability of licences against third parties. A brief word may now be added as to whether the benefit of a licence may be assigned by the licensee. A bare licence clearly cannot be assigned without the consent of the licensor. A licence coupled with a grant may be assigned along with the grant. As to contractual licences, the ordinary rule of contract law that the benefit is assignable applies, subject to the exclusion of this factor, expressly by the terms of the licence, or impliedly by the nature of the contract. Similar principles probably apply to licences by estoppel. There is a shortage of authority on the subject generally. The range of possibilities can be appreciated by a comparison of *Inwards* v *Baker* [1965] 2 QB 29 and *ER Ives Investment Ltd* v *High* [1967] 2 QB 379.

A table representing the enforceability and assignability of licences might be helpful in conclusion. The orthodox categorisation of licences has been adopted.

Table 7.1

Type of licence	*Revocable by licensor*	*Enforceable against third parties*	*Assignable by licensee*
Bare licence	Yes	No	No
Licence coupled with a grant	No	Yes, in certain circumstances	Yes
Contractual licence	No	Possibly, but some doubt here	Yes
Estoppel	No	Yes, in certain circumstances	Yes

Occupational rights of spouses

A spouse may be entitled to occupy the matrimonial home, irrespective of his or her status of husband or wife, because of a proprietary interest in the property. This will be so where spouses co-own the property. It is shown in Chapter 11 that this proprietary right exists, even though the legal estate is improperly vested in one of the spouses only, provided that it can be established that there is co-ownership in equity. The circumstances under which equitable co-ownership arises need not be repeated here. A proprietary right of occupation similarly arises where the spouses take a joint lease. In such cases, the right of occupation of a spouse is a result of the ordinary principle of co-ownership which was illustrated in another context by *Bull* v *Bull* [1955] 1 QB 234.

We must now consider the right of a spouse to occupy the matrimonial home by virtue of the status of spouse, even if that spouse has no proprietary interest in the property.

At common law, a husband is under a duty to his wife to allow her to occupy the home he has provided for her unless he provides suitable alternative accommodation for her (see *Lee* v *Lee* [1952] 2 QB 489). Where it is necessary to protect the wife's right, the court may compel the husband to leave the matrimonial home, pending divorce proceedings, even though he owns it or is a tenant of it (*Jones* v *Jones* [1971] 2 All ER 737). This right is *sui generis* and is not a species of licence or 'an equity' (*National Provincial Bank Ltd* v *Ainsworth* [1965] AC 1175). Even a husband who, during the subsistence of the marriage, remains in the matrimonial home after his wife has left, does not become a trespasser (even though the home is owned by her) until the court has determined that he has no right to stay (*Morris* v *Tarrant* [1971] 2 All ER 920).

Ainsworth, above, which settled that the right was not enforceable against third parties, placed the deserted wife who held no proprietary interest in the home in a vulnerable position. If her husband disposed of the property, her right of occupation could not be enforced against the purchaser, even though an injunction might prevent the dealing in appropriate cases when the wife, knowing of the intended transaction, acted in time. To mitigate these harsh consequences the Matrimonial Homes Act 1967 was passed. The current law is contained in the Matrimonial Homes Act 1983.

However, a right to occupy the matrimonial home can be futile if one of the partners suffers under a threat of violence from the other. Recognition in recent years of the scale of violence in the family has resulted in the Domestic Violence and Matrimonial Proceedings Act 1976. The provisions of that Act have an influence upon the right to occupation of the matrimonial home. The two Acts will be dealt with separately.

It must be emphasised that, although the 1983 Act applies only to married couples, the 1976 Act applies also to a man and woman living together as man and wife in the same household.

The principal provisions of the 1983 Act are as follows:

1 Where one spouse is entitled to occupy a dwelling-house by virtue of any estate or interest or contract, or under any enactment, and the other spouse is not, then the spouse not so entitled has a right, if in occupation, not to be excluded from occupation of any part by the other spouse without a court order, and, if not in occupation, the right, with the leave of the court, to enter possession of the house. Where these *rights of occupation* exist, either spouse may apply to the court for an order

> . . . declaring, enforcing, restricting or terminating those rights or regulating the exercise by either spouse of the right to occupy the dwelling house.
>
> (s 1)

Section 1 clearly could not as it stood be invoked in cases where the spouses are co-owners. If both spouses hold legal estates they have no such need for protection, though problems of a different kind might still arise, such as the spouses finding it intolerable to live under the same roof (see *Phillips* v *Phillips* [1973] 2 All ER 423). Then the court might order one spouse, even though a part-owner, to leave the property (see [1973] CLJ 227). If one spouse merely has an equitable interest, while the other alone holds the legal estate, there is clearly a danger that the one with only an equitable interest might have his rights overridden upon a sale by the other. Accordingly, the owner of an equitable interest in the house who does not hold a legal estate is now empowered to claim. In exercising this jurisdiction, the court may have regard to the conduct of the spouses, their needs and financial resources, the needs of any children and all the circumstances of the case and make such order as it thinks just and reasonable.

2 The effect of the statutory right of occupation is that of a charge on the interest of the spouse owning the estate or interest in the house, having priority as if it were an equitable interest created at the date of the acquisition of the estate or interest upon which it is charged, or the date of the marriage, or 1 January 1968 (the commencement date of the 1967 Act), whichever is the latest. The right is registrable. A deserted spouse in occupation, who has not registered, need not be joined in an action for possession by a prior chargee so as to give the opportunity of paying off the debts of the other spouse; such a deserted spouse would, of course, have no other means of retaining possession as against the prior chargee (see *Hastings and Thanet Building Society* v *Goddard* [1970] 3 All ER 954). The charge lasts for the duration of the marriage, unless the court directs otherwise in the event of a matrimonial dispute, and is void against a purchaser of the property, or of any interest in it, unless it is registered before the completion of the purchase. The right of a spouse not in occupation to re-enter is a continuing one and, though it is only to be exercised with the leave of the Court, may be registered at all times, even when still conditional in this way (*Watts* v *Waller* [1973] 3 All ER 257).

3 If the owner-spouse contracts to sell the house with vacant possession, a statutory term is implied in the contract that he or she will procure the cancellation of the charge, but breach of this implied term will not entitle the person who has agreed to purchase to obtain a decree of specific performance, since an owner will not usually be required to embark on a difficult and uncertain litigation (*Wroth* v *Tyler* [1973] 1 All ER 897). If the protected spouse knowingly stands by or assists while the owning spouse contracts to sell with vacant possession, that protected spouse may, however, be estopped from asserting the rights of occupation under the Act.

4 Where the title to the property is registered, a spouse's right of occupation may be protected by a notice under the Land Registration Act 1925 (Chapter 18). The registration of a class F land charge, the appropriate procedure for unregistered land, would be of no avail (*Miles* v *Bull* [1968] 3 All ER 632). Rights of occupation do not constitute overriding interests.

5 The rights of occupation will only be binding on a mortgagee of the home if

registration occurs before the mortgage is made. Such registration will not often take place. When it does, it might well discourage a prospective mortgagee from lending on the security of the home.

6 The Act also provides for the payment of rent by a spouse protected by the Act, where the other spouse is a tenant. The details of these provisions cannot be dealt with here.

7 Rights of occupation are not assignable.

The Domestic Violence and Matrimonial Proceedings Act 1976

Recognition in recent years that violence in the home is common led to the passing of this Act. Even before the Act, the divorce court occasionally granted injunctions excluding a spouse from the home for this reason, but the jurisdiction was exercised only incidentally to substantive matrimonial proceedings. The criminal law has not been effective as a deterrent since the police are reluctant to interfere in any but the more serious assaults between spouses.

Section 1(1) enacts:

> Without prejudice to the jurisdiction of the High Court on an application by a party to a marriage a county court shall have jurisdiction to grant an injunction containing one or more of the following provisions, namely:
>
> (a) a provision restraining the other party to the marriage from molesting the applicant;
> (b) a provision restraining the other party from molesting a child living with the applicant;
> (c) a provision excluding the other party from the matrimonial home or a part of the matrimonial home or from a specified area in which the matrimonial home is included;
> (d) a provision requiring the other party to permit the applicant to enter and remain in the matrimonial home;
>
> Whether or not any other relief is sought in the proceedings.

Section 1(2) enacts:

> Subsection (1) above shall apply to a man and a woman who are living with each other in the same household as husband and wife as it applies to the parties to a marriage and any reference to the matrimonial home shall be construed accordingly.

In *Davis* v *Johnson* [1978] 2 All ER 1132, an unmarried couple cohabited as joint tenants of a council flat. The man had been violent to the woman. She therefore left the flat, but wished to move back. She applied to the county court for an injunction excluding the man from the flat. The House of Lords held that such an injunction could be granted. It had been argued that the Act was procedural only in its effect and could not affect property rights. The House held that the Act did not affect property rights but did affect the way in which such rights could be enjoyed. Lord Scarman stated that the injunction confers a

> right of occupation which can for a period override the property rights of her family partner.
>
> (p 1156)

Discussion upon the interpretation of the Act, the procedures to be followed and the matters weighed by the court in deciding whether to grant an injunction must be sought in the textbooks on family law. The Domestic Proceedings and Magistrates' Courts Act 1978 should also be consulted. The significance of this legislation to land law is the nature of the right which accrues to a person who successfully applies for an injunction. In the first place, the injunctive relief is of short term duration only, a few months during which the relieved party can secure accommodation.

Of course, this prolonging of the status quo as against the other spouse or cohabitee is an augmentation of the original rights of the applicant in the scale of time. The Act does not, however, enlarge such rights in the 'horizontal' spheres of enforceability against third parties or disposability. In these last respects they remain what they were before. If an applicant spouse, for instance, has statutory rights of occupation under the Matrimonial Homes Act 1983 which, being registered, are enforceable against third parties, these rights remain so. If the rights of a cohabitee did not enjoy this capacity before the grant of injunction, presumably they will not acquire them under the grant.

The effect of an injunction is to put existing legal relations into a temporary freeze, not to change the right which is put into that freeze. Land law must surely be concerned with the rights to enjoy land, however precarious, as well as the rights to sell it. The effect of the Act is comparable with Acts which confer security of tenure in the field of landlord and tenant.

Condominium and time-sharing

The topics considered in this chapter show that important changes are taking place in the content and emphasis in land law. Even a short book such as this should greet new developments briefly, although they are only on the horizon.

In some parts of the world, notably in America and parts of Continental Europe, new kinds of community ownership are growing fast. Causes have been diverse. Sometimes the single family dwelling in its own grounds has become too expensive; sometimes the need to share the costs of purchasing and maintaining holiday accommodation enjoyed for only brief periods of the year has become crucial. The principal methods of meeting these difficulties have emerged during the last 20 years or so. They offer a challenge to expand our existing pattern of estates and licences.

Condominium

A condominium is an area of land of which a part is designated for separate ownership and part for common ownership by the owners of the separate parts.

In the context of a residential condominium, an owner might enjoy exclusive use of a house or apartment together with rights in common with other owners over gardens and other places of resort comprised in the holding. In the United States, condominia are run under statutory provisions which facilitate their management and funding. In the more complex structures, social organisation approaches the municipal function of local government.

Certain features of these schemes, such as multiple ownership by legal tenants in common and the running of positive covenants with land, present considerable technical difficulty to the introduction of condominium to England. For general reading see [1979] JPL 505 and study materials on p 343.

Time-sharing

Some applications of this concept have already reached this country in the context of holiday accommodation. Participants in a time-sharing scheme purchase the right to occupy an apartment and to enjoy the use of surrounding facilities for a limited period in recurring years. Matters such as insurance, rates and property maintenance are cared for by a management team. These rights can be transferred, let or bequeathed by the purchaser. Despite the description of 'interval ownership' sometimes applied to such arrangements, the legal title of the units will generally be vested in a company which is responsible for general management.

Although such schemes vary considerably in detail, generally the participants purchase a bundle of contractual rights including assignable licences to occupy the land during a particular week or weeks in each year. The general intention of assignability suggests a new form of lease or sublease. Alternatively, we must accept an expanded view of the contractual licence as a transmissible right. (See generally the Timeshare Act 1992 and [1992] Con V 301.)

Statutory tenancies

In Chapter 6 we saw that during this century the occupational rights of residential tenants have been controlled by legislation. The degree of control has varied according to the political philosophy of the Government of the day. The Housing Act 1988 marks a pronounced and progressive change towards deregulation of tenancy agreements. For some time, however, there will be earlier tenants who enjoy some protection of occupational rights. Their statutory rights entitle them to a mention in this chapter, although more precise detail can be sought in Chapter 6.

STUDY MATERIAL

Constructive trusts of homes – a bold approach [1993] LQR 485

Recently[1], Patricia Ferguson has sought to reject my view[2] that the common intention constructive trust should be regarded as indistinguishable from equitable proprietary estoppel and to support the view that, while an estoppel only entitles the plaintiff to prospective rights originating in the order of the court, such a constructive trust automatically gives rise to an independent proprietary right in the plaintiff effective from the date of the plaintiff's detrimental conduct and retrospectively recognised by the order of the court. It follows that a plaintiff, F, in occupation of the quasi-matrimonial home held on such a constructive trust for her by the defendant, M, is fully protected against a third party, like a mortgagee, X, to whom M may have granted a proprietary interest after the date of her detrimental conduct. Her protection should not be weakened by subsuming common intention constructive trusts within proprietary estoppel principles. She should only be subordinated to X if she knew of and expressly or impliedly consented to M's transaction with X[3]. Ferguson's illuminating article has stimulated me to develop further the question of priorities between F and X.

Of course, one accepts that the traditional or classic constructive trust[4] automatically confers on the plaintiff a proprietary interest which is retrospectively recognised by the court, e.g. where a trustee acquires trust property for himself or uses trust property to make a profit for himself, where a third party acquires trust property with notice of the trust and in the cases of secret trusts and mutual wills and trusts imposed to prevent a killer benefiting from his crime. However, the common intention constructive trust was recently invented in *Gissing* v *Gissing*[5] by a House of Lords Judicial Committee whose members did not include a Chancery lawyer and who were concerned just with M and F. They gave no thought to the possible impact of such a common intention constructive trust on third parties. Indeed, the speeches reveal some confusion with resulting trusts, though traditionally resulting trusts are based on presumed intention and constructive trusts are imposed against a wrongdoer's intentions[6]. Moreover, as *Re Densham*[7] reveals, while F's

---

[1] (1993) 109 LQR 114.

[2] [1990] Conv 370, developed in Hayton and Marshall, *Cases and Commentary on the Law of Trusts* (9th ed) pp 497–510 and by Browne-Wilkinson V-C (as he then was) in his Birmingham University Holdsworth Lecture on 'Constructive Trusts and Unjust Enrichment' (1991).

[3] Ferguson, *op cit* at p 130, fails to make it clear that any original proprietary interest of F will, irrespective of her knowledge or consent, be automatically subordinated to the first legal mortgage without which M could not have acquired the home in the first place, and to any replacement mortgage for such first mortgage: *Abbey National Building Society* v *Cann* [1991] 1 AC 56; *Equity & Law Home Loans Ltd* v *Prestridge* [1992] 1 WLR 137.

[4] See Hayton and Marshall, *op cit* at pp 440–441.

[5] [1971] AC 886 (Lord Reid, Lord Morris of Borth-y-Gest, Viscount Dilhorne, Lord Pearson and Lord Diplock).

[6] *Carl Zeiss Stiftung* v *Herbert Smith (No 2)* [1964] 2 Ch 276 at 301; *Allen* v *Snyder* [1977] 2 NSWLR 685; Hanbury and Maudsley, *Modern Equity* (13th ed), pp 69, 70, 280–281; Snell's *Equity* (29th ed), Pt II, Chs 4, 5.

[7] [1975] 1 WLR 1519; Bankruptcy Act 1914 s 42; Insolvency Act 1986 ss 339–342.

share in a home under a constructive trust is a gift which can be void against M's trustee in bankruptcy, her share as a purchaser on resulting trust principles will be valid, so that it can be crucial whether a share arises under a resulting or a constructive trust.

No argument as to the application of proprietary estoppel giving rise to a remedial constructive trust at the date of the court order was put in *Gissing* v *Gissing* where it seems that the Lords, in effect, reinvented proprietary estoppel in the guise of a common intention constructive trust. Do not the elements necessary for a common intention constructive trust correspond to the elements necessary to found a proprietary estoppel claim? It suffices for estoppel that M led F to have the expectation or belief that she had an interest in the home and that on the basis of such expectation or belief F acted to her detriment, M encouraging this or standing by while she so acted[8]. Moreover, where M made the representation of ownership to F, calculated to influence her, it is presumed that any detrimental acts of F were in reliance upon such representation[9]. Are not these elements present where a common intention constructive trust arises where M talked[10] with F, so that they are found to have a common intention as to F acquiring an interest in the home, and on the basis of such intention, F then acted to her detriment, M encouraging her or standing by while she so acted? Technically, the 'common intention' should be seen as a shorthand composite expression to cover both the donor M's unilateral intention to make a gift of a share of the home to F and her knowledge of that intention, making it possible for there to be detrimental reliance on that knowledge, such reliance being presumed where there are detrimental acts[11]. The extent of such detrimental reliance is crucial to the extent of the remedy provided on either estoppel or common intention constructive trust principles[12].

---

[8] *Taylor Fashions Ltd* v *Liverpool Victoria Trustees Co* [1983] QB 133; *Crabb* v *Arun DC* [1976] Ch 179; *Pascoe* v *Turner* [1979] 1 WLR 431; *Lim* v *Ang* [1992] 1 WLR 113.

[9] *Greasley* v *Cooke* [1980] 1 WLR 1306.

[10] *Lloyds Bank Plc* v *Rosset* [1991] 1 AC 107 at 132–133 indicates that evidence of express discussions will be required to establish a common intention constructive trust except that where there are direct contributions to the purchase price (overlooking that this, anyhow, creates a presumed purchase-money resulting trust) there will be an inferred common intention constructive trust in the absence of evidence of an express intention. But, otherwise, it is extremely doubtful whether any such inferred trusts can ever arise. On this basis one can ignore the category of inferred common intention constructive trust as an empty, unnecessary category. One should simply consider whether F has an interest under a resulting trust, arising directly or indirectly from separate or pooled financial contributions, or under an equitable estoppel (including express common intention constructive trusts): see the approaches of Lord Upjohn in *Pettitt* v *Pettitt* [1970] AC 777 at 818 and Lord Pearson in *Gissing* v *Gissing* [1971] AC 886 at 902–903.

[11] See *Grant* v *Edwards* [1986] Ch 638 at 657; *Maharaj* v *Chand* [1986] AC 898 at 907; *Lloyds Bank Plc* v *Rosset* [1989] Ch 350 at 381, 388; indeed, in *Gissing* v *Gissing* [1971] AC 886 at 905 Lord Diplock states 'An express agreement as to their respective beneficial interests in land conveyed into the name of one of them obviates the need for showing that the conduct of the spouse in whose name the land was conveyed was intended to induce the other to act to his or her detriment on the faith of the promise . . . and that the other so acted with the intention of acquiring that beneficial interest'.

[12] If F's detrimental conduct on a scale of one to 100 only registers 10 she should not necessarily obtain a promised half share: see *Grant* v *Edwards* [1986] Ch 638 at 659. Where the promise is that she will have a fair share as in *Stokes* v *Anderson* [1991] 1 FLR 391 then the fair share obviously reflects the extent of detrimental conduct. Equity is not in the business of perfecting imperfect gifts but of providing the minimum equitable relief to remedy unconscionable conduct: *Crabb* v *Arun DC* [1976] Ch 174 at 198–199; *Commonwealth of Australia* v *Verwayen* (1990) 170 CLR 394 at 429; *Amalgamated Investment and Property Co Ltd* v *Texas Commerce International Bank Ltd* [1982] QB 84 at 122.

Only where there are detrimental acts will reliance be presumed[13] and there is scope for uncertainty as to such acts unless the parties have agreed[14] what are to be regarded as the requisite detrimental acts. A broad view seems to be taken for estoppel purposes[15] and should also be taken for common intention constructive trusts[16] which should be subsumed within estoppel principles. This will provide flexibility for the Courts to tailor the remedy to fit the wrong and prevent M getting away with unconscionable behaviour or being unjustly enriched, so protecting F's position as much as possible.

Ferguson ripostes that the court's prospective remedy will not do F much good against the likes of X, so that F will instead need to rely on resulting trust principles, her equitable interest automatically arising thereunder as soon as she provides part of the purchase-money. Because X in dealing with M will be bound by any equitable interest that F has under a resulting trust if F is in actual occupation[17], X must ask her whether she claims any interest in the home. If she makes no claim to an interest under a purchase-money resulting trust[18] but claims that she has the foundation for a proprietary estoppel remedy to be declared by the court, whether a co-ownership share or a life interest or an equitable charge for a sum of money, the only sensible precaution for X, if he is to proceed, is to obtain F's written consent to his dealing with M.

If F is opposed to the grant of X's interest her only sensible precaution is to have M grant her a prior interest or to issue a writ (protected as a *lis pendens*) claiming a proprietary estoppel interest in the land against M and an injunction restraining him from proceeding with the proposed transaction with X. She will thus safeguard against X whatever interest the court eventually orders in her favour.

If X deliberately or recklessly failed to take the elementary conveyancing precaution of asking the occupier, F, whether she claims any interest in the home, so as to divest her of the opportunity she would otherwise have had to take the only sensible precautions set out in the last paragraph, is it not clearly unconscionable if

---

[13] *Coombes* v *Smith* [1986] 1 WLR 808 at 821: *Re Basham* [1987] 1 All ER 405 at 411–413; *Hammersmith London BC* v *Top Shop Ltd* [1989] 2 All ER 655 at 670; *Watts* v *Storey* (1983) CA Transcript 319, quotation in Maudsley and Burn, *Land Law: Cases and Materials* (6th ed) pp 575–576.

[14] *Grant* v *Edwards* [1986] Ch 638 at 650–651 *per* Mustill LJ.

[15] *Greasley* v *Cooke* [1980] 1 WLR 1306; *Pascoe* v *Turner* [1979] 1 WLR 431; *Re Basham* [1987] 1 All ER 405 (but *cf Coombes* v *Smith* [1986] 1 WLR 808).

[16] *Grant* v *Edwards* [1986] Ch 638; *Re Basham* [1987] 1 All ER 405 at 410; *Lloyds Bank Plc* v *Rosset* [1989] Ch 350 at 381, 388; and see Lord Bridge of Harwich apparently equating constructive trusts and proprietary estoppels, *Lloyds Bank Plc* v *Rosset* [1991] AC 107 at 132G and also *Gillies* v *Keogh* [1989] 2 NZLR 727 at 730–733; *Commonwealth of Australia* v *Verwayen* (1990) 170 CLR 394 at 410–413.

[17] *Kingsnorth Finance Co Ltd* v *Tizard* [1986] 1 WLR 783; *Williams & Glyn's Bank Ltd* v *Boland* [1981] AC 487.

[18] Where M pays all the mortgage instalments and F pays all the household outgoings in circumstances where, but for such substantial expenditure by F, M would not have been able to pay all the instalments and maintain their joint standard of living, it is to be hoped that F will be protected by a court holding that F has an interest under an indirectly purchased resulting trust as indicated in *Burns* v *Burns* [1984] Ch 317 at 329, 344–345 and *Gissing* v *Gissing* [1971] AC 887 at 903, 909 (restricting Lord Bridge's remarks in *Lloyds Bank Plc* v *Rosset* [1991] 1 AC 107 at 132–133 as *obiter dicta* concerned only with constructive trusts) or by finding some evidence of discussion between M and F to support an express constructive trust.

X can then take advantage of his own wrong (such failure being inherently reckless) to have priority for his interest over whatever interest the court subsequently confers on F? Surely, a remedial constructive trust can be imposed upon X to accord priority to F's interest because X's conscience is affected, as recognised by the Court of Appeal in *Ashburn Anstalt* v *Arnold*[19], where it was pointed out that a constructive trust could be imposed on a purchaser otherwise taking free of a contractual licence, as a personal and not a proprietary interest, if there were circumstances where it would be unconscionable if he were not bound by such licence. Thus, the court can make its normal prospective relief for F against M retrospective where the state of the defendant's conscience justifies this.

To help support a court decision in favour of F against X, it may also be possible to argue that M was in a fiduciary relationship with F, placed in a vulnerable position by M where he had led her to expect that he would at least act in their joint interest in respect of the legal estate to the exclusion of his own separate interest[20]. In breach of M's fiduciary duty X received an interest in the fiduciary property with notice[21] (if not also 'Nelsonian' or 'naughty' knowledge[22]) of such breach and so took subject to F's rights as subsequently crystallised by the court[23].

Chancery judges can thus do more to safeguard the interests of women like F than Ferguson's narrow approach supposes. In the bold visionary era ushered in by House of Lords' decisions like *Lipkin Gorman* v *Karpnale*[24], *Woolwich Equitable Building Society* v *IRC*[25] and *Lord Napier and Ettrick* v *Hunter*[26], which emphasise the courts' readiness to intervene to prevent unconscionable conduct, the Law Lords can be expected to uphold the Chancery judges, especially in view of the policy[27] to protect disadvantaged occupiers against the monied might of persons, like

---

19 [1989] Ch 1. In *Commonwealth of Australia* v *Verwayen* (1990) 170 CLR 394 at 441 Deane J states that 'unconscionable conduct will commonly involve the use of or insistence upon legal entitlement to take advantage of another's special vulnerability in a way that is unreasonable and oppressive to an extent that affronts ordinary minimum standards of fair dealing.'

20 See the bold extension of fiduciary relationship in *English* v *Dedham Vale Properties* [1978] 1 WLR 93; *Norburg* v *Wynrib* (1992) 92 DLR (4th) 449; *KM* v *HM* (1993) 96 DLR (4th) 289 at 323–328; S. Gardner, (1993) 109 LQR 263 at 287–289. Also see Meagher, Gummow and Lehane: *Equity Doctrines and Remedies* (3rd ed) Ch 5; Mason J in *Hospital Products Ltd* v *United States Surgical Corporation* (1984) 156 CLR 41 at 96–97; Sopinka J in *LAC Minerals Ltd* v *International Corona Resources Ltd* (1989) 61 DLR (4th) 14 at 26–32, and P. Finn in *Equity, Fiduciaries and Trusts* (ed T G Youdan), concluding at p 54 'A person will be a fiduciary in his relationship with another when and insofar as that other is entitled to expect that he will act in that other's or in their joint interest to the exclusion of his own several interest.'

21 Actual, constructive or imputed: *Polly Peck Plc* v *Nadir (No 2)* [1992] 4 All ER 769. This approach will help F if X is merely negligent rather than reckless.

22 Such knowledge *a fortiori* justifies X's conscience being bound. 'Nelsonian' knowledge arising where a Nelsonian blind eye is turned to what otherwise would be obvious and 'naughty' knowledge arising where deliberately or recklessly X fails to make the inquiries an honest reasonable man would make: *Agip Africa Ltd* v *Jackson* [1990] Ch 265, [1991] Ch 547; *Cowan de Groot Properties Ltd* v *Eagle Trust* [1992] 4 All ER 700 at 754.

23 *Cf Elders Pastoral Ltd* v *Bank of New Zealand* [1989] 2 NZLR 180.

24 [1991] 2 AC 548.

25 [1992] 3 All ER 737.

26 [1993] 1 All ER 385.

27 *Williams & Glyn's Bank* v *Boland* [1981] AC 487; *Kingsnorth Finance Co* v *Tizard* [1986] 1 WLR 783.

mortgagees, who can so easily help themselves. The court's function is surely not to help those who deliberately or recklessly fail to take simple steps to protect themselves.

Hopefully, it should not be too long before we have a case with appropriate facts to justify a judgment[28] clearly distinguishing between the exclusively proprietary institutional constructive trust, that arises and exists independently of the court order retrospectively recognising it, and the remedial constructive trust declaring at the time of the court order the extent of the proprietary or personal relief tailored to remedy the relevant unconscionable conduct. For ease of reference one should, perhaps, distinguish between 'automatic' and 'discretionary' constructive trusts, the former being an automatic incident of the institution of the express trust of property, and the latter involving discretionary relief of a proprietary or personal nature imposed on a defendant because of the poor state of his conscience.

DAVID HAYTON
Professor of Law, Kings College, London University

Extract reproduced by permission of the Law Quarterly Review.

[28] E.g. *Muschinski* v *Dodds* (1985) 160 CLR 583 at 612–617; *LAC Minerals Ltd* v *International Corona Resources Ltd* (1989) 61 DLR (4th) 14 at 50–51; *Rawluk* v *Rawluk* (1990) 65 DLR (4th) 161 at 183–188.

QUESTIONS

1 Why should not any contract affecting land be enforceable against third parties, if not limited in terms to the period of the licensor's ownership or control of the land?

2 Jane cohabits with Rockie, though she is not his wife. She comes to your office in distress, stating that she has been evicted from the house where they live after much violent treatment. She claims no interest in the house. What action can be taken? How, if at all, would your advice differ if she were married to him?

3 Your principal has asked you to set out, in the form of numbered points, a précis of the article by David Hayton provided in the study materials (see pp 148–52) in not more than 100 words. Do so.

CHAPTER 8

EXTINGUISHMENT OF INTERESTS IN LAND UNDER THE LIMITATION ACT 1980

INTRODUCTION

Entitlement to land in English law is based upon priority of possession. If *A* possesses land he has a better right to it than anyone else, except one who can prove a superior right by showing previous possession of the land or its profits. If *A* occupies land and *B* dispossesses him, *A* has a superior right based upon previous possession and may retrieve the land. However, if *A* does not do this, and later *C* dispossesses *B* and then *D* dispossesses *C*, *C* may evict *D* because of his superior title. Similarly B may recover the land as against both *C* and *D*, and *A* has the best right of all these persons.

Since land exists permanently, the life story of a particular plot might, if discoverable, reveal several such acts of dispossession over the centuries. It might show that even *A*'s title was based upon the dispossession of *X* over a hundred years ago. Perhaps the persons who today would have been entitled to the land through *X* under the laws of succession have now learned of these events. If there were no restrictions on the doctrine that possession is the basis of title, then ancient claims of this kind would constantly empower speculators to disturb long-accepted rights to land, so that indeed no fee simple owner could sleep tight in his bed at night. There is a social need for certainty of title to land.

For centuries, therefore, statute has placed a limit on the time after which a claimant to an interest in land may bring an action to establish it in the face of the possession of another person holding under a later title. The present law is contained in the Limitation Act 1980. The general effect of the Act is not to confirm any particular claim to land but merely to extinguish stale titles to it. In the example given above, the title of *X* would be extinguished simply, leaving *A*'s claim as superior. It is most important to realize that the Act does not transfer *X*'s title to *A* (see *Tichborne* v *Weir* (1892) 67 LT 735). A man of 90 suddenly finds himself the oldest man in the village not necessarily because he is 90 but because a man of 91 died yesterday. The scythe of time creates superiority of title as it does seniority of age. Title is never extinguished because of its age, of course. Quite the contrary. It is only extinguished or *barred* because the claim it gives to land has been allowed to remain unpressed for a long time in face of a rival title.

Thus the effect of the Act is to eliminate. This is in contrast to the Prescription Act, which is acquisitive in its approach to easements and profits. Even though the Limitation Act works negatively, once a person, through his own occupation and that of his predecessors in title, can show possession for such a time and in such circumstances that the risk of a successful rival claim may be discounted, the element of relativity of title disappears for practical purposes, and that person may consider that he has an absolute title to the land.

It might appear that while the law punishes theft of chattels it rewards theft of land but acquisition of title under the doctrine is seldom attributable to a single and conscious act of confiscation. In many cases there has been misunderstanding as to boundaries, perhaps due to mistakes or lack of definition in conveyancing documents. The role of the Act in quietening claims and rendering title certain in such instances is clearly beneficial.

It is sometimes suggested that when an owner, *A*, is dispossessed by *B*, both *A* and *B* own fee simple estates in the same land, only one of which will prevail of course if the parties put their rights before a court. Inviting though the notion is for the speculative thinker, it is surely misconceived. The fee simple estate simply denotes ownership. There cannot be two conflicting ownerships of the same piece of land; neither can there be two fee simple estates in the same land at the same time. What there can be is two or more rival claims to one fee simple estate or to ownership. One claimant only owns it.The other is a trespasser as against that person (see 80 LQR 63).

THE LENGTH OF THE LIMITATION PERIOD

The general rule under s 15(1) is that

> no action shall be brought by any person to recover any land after the expiration of twelve years from the date on which the right of action accrued to him or, if it first accrued to some person through whom he claims, to that person.

The period for recovery by the Crown or by a charitable corporation or corporation sole is thirty years from the date when the right of action accrued to it, or, if it first accrued to some person through whom it claims, to that person. The period for the recovery of foreshore by the Crown is 60 years (see s 15(7)).

THE POINT FROM WHICH THE LIMITATION PERIOD RUNS

The fundamental rule is that the period runs from the date of the accrual of a right of action against some person. The identification of that date is dealt with in Part I of Schedule 1 of the Act.

Initially, two provisions must be examined. Paragraph 1 enacts:

> Where the person bringing an action to recover land, or some person through whom he claims, has been in possession of the land, and has while entitled to the land been dispossessed or discontinued his possession, the right of action shall be treated as having accrued on the date of the dispossession or discontinuance.

Paragraph 8(1) provides:

> No right of action to recover land shall be treated as accruing unless the land is in the possession of some person in whose favour the period of limitation can run (referred to below in this paragraph as 'adverse possession'); and where under the preceding provisions of this Schedule any such right of action is treated as accruing on a certain date and no person is in adverse possession on that date, the right of action shall not be treated as accruing unless and until adverse possession is taken of the land.

In short, there must be some person in possession and that possession must be 'adverse'. No right of action can accrue, for instance, if land is merely vacated by the owner. The meaning of 'adverse' has been the subject of some controversy.

So often in English civil law confusion has been caused by the failure to distinguish between the rhetorical framing of a legal rule, which creates precedent, and its application to the infinitely variable circumstances of everyday life, which does not. In early times the former was a question for the judge, the latter for the jury. The absence of the jury in civil litigation has no doubt fostered this confusion.

The principles of law are that possession, in order to generate title under the Limitation Act 1980, must be exclusive, intentional and adverse. In testing whether these criteria are satisfied in fact

> . . . it must be considered in every case with reference to the particular circumstances. The acts, implying possession in one case, may be wholly inadequate to prove it in another. The character and value of the property, the suitable and natural mode of using it, the course of conduct which the proprietor might reasonably be expected to follow with a due regard to his own interests – all these things, greatly varying as they must, under various conditions, are to be taken into account in determining the sufficiency of a possession.
>
> [Lord O'Hagan in *Lord Advocate* v *Lord Lovat* [1880] 5 App Cas 273 at 288; approvingly cited by Sir John Pennycuick in *Treloar* v *Nute* [1976] 1 WLR 1295 at 1299]

Two factual circumstances which in the past have pretended to the status of legal principles have been rehabilitated in modern times. First, in *Leigh* v *Jack* [1879] 5 ExD 264 it was held that the deposit of industrial materials on land set aside for a highway but temporarily unused was not 'adverse' because such entry was not inconsistent with the enjoyment of the owner. In *Buckinghamshire County Council* v *Moran* [1989] 2 All ER 225 the Court of Appeal held, on very similar facts, that adverse possession had occurred. The crucial issue was the intention and accomplishment of factual possession, judged in light of all the circumstances.

Second, although a licence by the owner to possess land is clearly fatal to 'adversity' of possession, in a series of cases possession by a squatter, if not inconsistent with the future intended use of the owner, was held to be by virtue of an 'implied' licence and therefore not adverse (see the judgment of Lord Denning MR in *Wallis's Clayton Bay Holiday Camp Ltd* v *Shell-Mex and BP Ltd* [1975] 1 QB 94). This presumption which was acquiring the status of legal principle was reestablished as an issue of fact by Sch 1 Pt I para 8(4) of the Act which enacts:

> for the purpose of determining whether a person occupying any land is in adverse possession of the land it shall not be assumed by implication of law that his occupation is by permission of the person entitled to the land merely by virtue of the fact that his occupation is not inconsistent with the latter's present or future enjoyment of the land.
>
> This provision shall not be taken as prejudicing a finding to the effect that a person's occupation of any land is by implied permission of the person entitled to the land in any case where such a finding is justified on the actual facts of the case.

The doctrine of the implied licence therefore remains available as a possible channel of judicial policy in relation to squatters; but the channel now runs only through the medium of fact, not law. In *Hyde* v *Pearce* [1982] 1 All ER 1029, the Court of Appeal held that the possession of a person who had been in occupation of land for 14 years following a contract to purchase never completed by conveyance, was not adverse because he had a defence to any action for possession. This seems to suggest that only trespassers can enjoy adverse possession. In that case one of the functions of the Limitation Act, that of ironing out little problems based on informal agreements, will be thwarted. (See 46 MLR 89.)

Adverse possession is therefore necessary before an action can accrue. Provided that it is present, the Act identifies the time when actions shall accrue, and the period thus begin running, for various types of circumstances as follows. (The Act should be consulted, however, for an exhaustive list of these.)

Present interests

We have seen that when the person bringing the action was in possession of the land and either was dispossessed or abandoned his occupation, and this abandonment was followed by another person taking possession, the right of action accrues when that act of adverse possession takes place. When a person is in occupation at his death, however, and a squatter takes the land after his death, the right of action accrues at the date of death and not at the time when the adverse possession begins. (Sch 1 Pt I para 2.)

Future interests

When the adverse possession occurs while an interest is in reversion or remainder, and the owner of the prior interest was in possession when that prior interest ceased, the right of action accrues on the determination of the preceding interest. If the person entitled to the preceding interest, not being a lease, was not in possession at the determination of that interest, then two alternative periods are available during which the owner of the remainder or reversion may bring an action, namely, twelve years from the time when the right of action accrued to the owner of the preceding interest, or six years from the date when the right of action accrued to the person entitled to the remainder or reversion, whichever is the longer (s 15(2) and Sch 1 Pt I para 4).

Trust property (s 18)

A trustee's title to trust property is not barred until the rights of all the beneficiaries have been barred. Thus twelve years' adverse possession against a tenant for life will bar his title to the life interest, but will not affect his right to the legal estate so long as the interest of any remainderman still exists and is unbarred. Trustees can never bar the interest of the beneficiaries by adverse possession no matter how long. This of course applies to statutory trusts for sale as well as to express trusts and therefore affects cases of co-ownership (see 35 Conveyancer 6). Neither can a beneficiary under a strict settlement or trust for sale extinguish the title of any trustee, statutory owner, life tenant or other beneficiary under the trust.

Leases (Sch 1)

The right of action does not accrue to a reversioner until the end of the lease, even though a right of forfeiture has occurred before that time and has not been enforced. If a tenant is dispossessed, although his title to the lease may be extinguished after twelve years, time will not begin to run against the landlord until the end of the lease (see *Fairweather* v *St Marylebone Property Co Ltd* [1963] AC 510). Failure by a tenant to pay rent does not, with one exception (*see* LPA 1925 s 153), affect his landlord's title to the reversion unless, in the case of a lease in writing under which a yearly rent of at least £10 is reserved, it is received by some other person wrongfully claiming the reversion. In this case the reversioner's right of action is deemed to accrue at the time of the first wrongful payment (para 6).

In the case of a tenancy at will the cause of action accrues against the landlord at the end of one year after its beginning or after its determination, whichever event occurs first. (But see *Hughes* v *Griffin* [1969] 1 All ER 460). In the case of a tenancy at sufferance it accrues at its beginning because the possession is immediately adverse. Where there is a periodic tenancy but no written lease, it accrues at the end of the first period (para 5). If there is a written lease, however, it accrues upon the determination of the tenancy.

EXTENSION, POSTPONEMENT AND RECOMMENCEMENT OF THE PERIOD

The normal running of the limitation period is modified in certain special circumstances as follows.

1 *Extension of the period (s 28).* If the person to whom a right of action accrues is a minor, or suffering from a mental disability when it accrues, the period is extended to six years, from the cessation of the disability or his death, whichever event occurs first, notwithstanding that the ordinary period of limitation has expired. In no case, however, is the period to be extended for more than 30 years from the date when the right of action accrued.

   This privilege does not apply to a disability which occurs after the right of action accrues, such as when a person becomes a mental patient after dispossession, but it may be claimed where one disability succeeds another in the same person, provided that there is no interval between the ending of one disability and the beginning of the next. When a disabled person dies while still suffering from a disability, the person next entitled must bring any action within six years of that death, even though he himself was under a disability upon his succession to his interest.

2 *Postponement of the period.* Section 32(1) enacts that where
   (a) the action is based upon the fraud of the defendant; or
   (b) any fact relevant to the plaintiff's right of action has been deliberately concealed from him by the defendant or
   (c) the action is for relief from the consequences of a mistake; the period of limitation shall not begin to run until the plaintiff has discovered the fraud, concealment or mistake (as the case may be) or could with reasonable diligence have discovered it.

   There is protection for innocent third parties.

3 *Recommencenent of the period (s 29).* The period of limitation may be stopped in two ways and, in both cases, if adverse possession recurs, the period of time which has already run is discounted and time must start afresh.

   First, the owner may end the period by taking back possession of the land or by bringing an action for its recovery.

Second, the period is ended if a written signed acknowledgement of title is made by the person in possession of the land to the person whose title is being acknowledged, or if any part-payment of principal interest or rent is made by the person from whom it is due to the person to whom it is due (s 29) (see *Edginton* v *Clark* [1964] 1 QB 367). Once the period of limitation has run its course, no repossession, acknowledgement or part-payment can revive the rights of the person against whom it has run, for his title is extinguished.

Finally no recommencement of the period occurs if a person enjoying adverse possession transfers his possession to another either *inter vivos* or by will, or even if he himself is dispossessed. In all such cases the new occupier may aggregate the original period of possession with his own as against the owner (*Asher* v *Whitlock* (1865) LR 1 QB 1), but if adverse possession is abandoned and later another enters the land, the limitation period must start afresh.

THE NATURE OF THE TITLE ACQUIRED BY POSSESSION

The general effects of acquisition of title by possession and the elimination of title under the Limitation Act have already been considered. Certain qualifications of these principles must now be discussed briefly.

First, even if an adverse possessor or 'squatter' acquires a supreme title to the land, rights in or over that land which existed before his possession will continue to affect it unless they are ended independently by some form of extinguishment to which they are susceptible. Thus a restrictive covenant will remain in force, for a squatter is not a 'purchaser' and therefore cannot override even such an equitable interest (*Re Nisbet and Potts' Contract* [1906] 1 Ch 386).

Second, when the title to a lease is extinguished by a squatter, that lease nevertheless remains valid as between the lessor and lessee, so that the latter can repossess the land if the squatter leaves, and the lessor can re-enter to enforce forfeiture for breach of covenant if the lease allows this (*Fairweather* v *St Marylebone Property Co Ltd* [1963] AC 510). In such circumstances, the effect of the Act is considerably diminished (*see* 37 Conveyancer 85).

The Land Registration Act 1925 s 75 enacts that the Limitation Act shall apply to registered land in the same way as to unregistered land, except that when an interest would have been extinguished in the case of unregistered land, then in the case of registered land it shall not be extinguished, but shall be deemed to be held on trust by the proprietor for the person who has acquired title against him. This provision was not intended to affect the substantive position of the parties but merely to provide machinery to apply the law to registered land (per Lord Denning in the *Fairweather* case at 548). In *Spectrum Investment Co* v *Holmes* [1981] 1 All ER 6 however, Browne-Wilkinson J held that if a squatter registered his rights under the Land Registration Act 1925, once the limitation period has run, those rights could not be defeated by subsequent surrender of the lease between the original documentary lessee and the landlord. In the *Fairweather* case the House of Lords held that a surrender of the lease enabled the landlord forthwith to evict the Squatter. It was not open to the House however to consider the effect of registration of a squatter's title.

REMEDIES

Possession may be recovered by an owner, before his title is barred, under RSC Ord 113 in the High Court and under CCR Ord 24 in the county court. The procedure is swift. Squatting in residential premises is, under certain circumstances, a criminal offence under the Criminal Law Act 1977 (see s 7 as amended by the Criminal Justice and Public Order Act 1994). It is also an offence to use or threaten violence to gain entry into premises where there is known to be someone present and therein opposed to such entry (see s 6). This provision applies to owners re-entering as well as to squatters entering, though there are certain defences, in particular, in favour of a displaced residential occupier.

ALGORITHM FOR PROBLEMS OF ADVERSE POSSESSION

1 Was the possession adverse in law? Answer 'yes' only if the answers to all the following questions are 'yes'. — Yes | No → Exit. No Claim.

(a) Was the possession exclusive?
(b) Was there an intention to possess exclusively?
(c) Was there an absence of permission of the owner, express or implied?

2 Did such possession continue for an uninterrupted period of 12 years? — Yes | No → Exit. No Claim.

3 If the period of possession was extended through disability, postponement or land belonging to the Crown, have the additional requirements been satisfied? — Yes | No → Exit. No Claim.

↓ Yes

The title of the 'paper' owner is extinguished

STUDY MATERIAL

Buckinghamshire County Council v *Moran* [1989] 2 All ER 225; [1990] 1 Ch 629

SLADE LJ This an appeal by the Buckinghamshire County Council ('the council') from a judgment of Hoffmann J given on 19 February 1988, whereby he dismissed the claim by the council to recover possession of a plot of land situated at Chenies Avenue, Amersham, Buckinghamshire ('the plot'). By a conveyance of 20 October 1955 the plot was conveyed to the council, which indisputably still has the paper title to it. However, the judge held that Mr Christopher Moran, the defendant to the action and respondent to this appeal, had been in adverse possession of it for more than 12 years before the proceedings were commenced on 28 October 1985, and that the council's title to it had therefore been extinguished under sections 15 and 17 of the Limitation Act 1980.

I can take the primary facts of the case largely from the judge's judgment, where they are stated very clearly. The plot fronts on to Chenies Avenue, which runs from north to south. It is one of a number of plots of roughly equal size on the west side of the road. By 1955 houses had been built on the plots immediately to the north and south of the plot, but the plot itself remained vacant. The house immediately to the north was called Westward Way; the house immediately to the south was called Croft Edge. The council acquired the plot for a proposed diversion of the A404 road around Amersham, but it was contemplated that the construction of that road would not take place for many years. Meantime, the council has no use for the land.

In 1955 there was a laurel hedge separating the plot from the garden of Croft Edge, a chain link fence and a privet hedge along the western boundary and a fence in poor condition with an old gate along the road frontage. There was no fence between the plot and Westward Way.

In 1962 the council acquired Croft Edge also for the purposes of the proposed new road. It let the house to a tenant. At about the same time, Mr Builith, the then owner of Westward Way, complained about the state of the fence on the road frontage to the plot. He said that children were using the plot as a playground and as a means of access to some recreation grounds beyond the western boundary and that they were causing him annoyance. In response to his complaint the council put up a chestnut paling fence along the whole length of the road frontage and re-erected the gate at the road, which had fallen down. Mr Wherry, the district surveyor at the time, said in evidence that, when making inspections during the 1960s, he used occasionally to climb over the gate or fence; he thought that the gate was wired up, but not locked.

On 15 June 1965 Mr Builith wrote another letter of complaint to the council and suggested that the only solution was for the council to fence off the plot completely from his garden. The council, however, declined to do so. At about the same time, Mr Builith built another house on the western side of his plot, which was Dolphin Place.

Early in 1966, Mr Builith sold off Dolphin Place, together with most of the garden, to a Mr and Mrs Swabey. The southern boundary of their garden abutted the north boundary of the plot along the whole of its length. Mr and Mrs Swabey, in turn, conveyed Dolphin Place to a Mr and Mrs Wall. They took over the maintenance of the plot, mowing the grass, trimming the hedges and treating it as part of their garden. In August 1970 the Divisional Roads Surveyor noted in a memorandum to the County Surveyor that the plot was being cut and maintained in a tidy condition by Mr Wall. Thereafter, the road surveyor's department, being spared the need to maintain the plot itself, did no more than inspect it regularly by looking over the fence from the road, usually from a car window. Mr Wherry, who was responsible for these inspections in the 1960s and early 1970s, said that so far as he knew no one from the council had gone upon the land since the late 1960s.

In 1971, Mr and Mrs Wall sold Dolphin Place to the defendant, Mr Moran. The judge found that there had not been any substantial change in appearance of the house and garden since the time when the defendant bought it. On inspection, he said, the plot would appear to be part of the garden enclosed on all sides except the north, where there is nothing to indicate any boundary between it and the garden contained within the paper title of Dolphin Place. He also found, however, that the defendant was aware that the paper title to the plot was vested in the council, and that the council had acquired the land in order to construct a road at some time in the future.

It seems fairly clear that at the time of his purchase of Dolphin Place, the defendant and his legal advisers were well aware of the possibility that Mr and Mrs Wall had acquired, or were in the course of acquiring, a possessory title to the plot. They procured the making of a statutory declaration by Mr and Mrs Wall dated 15 July 1971, in which they said that since 1967 they had occupied the plot and cultivated it to the extent of tending and cutting the grass and trimming hedges and had from time to time parked a horse box on the plot. They said that no person had challenged their right to occupy it, and their permission had been requested for the laying of an electricity supply across it, by parties owning or occupying the tennis courts at the rear. The conveyance of Dolphin Place to the defendant dated 28 July 1971 was expressed to include not only the land comprised in the vendor's paper title, but also: 'all such estate, right, title and interest that the vendor's may have in or about the remaining part of the plot formerly numbered 206 as aforesaid,' that is, the plot.

Following the conveyance to him of Dolphin Place, the defendant took possession of that property and for the next 18 months or so lived there with his mother, Mrs Moran. After that time he moved out, but his mother has remained there ever since and he returns occasionally for weekends and other visits. In argument on this appeal no reliance had been placed on the fact that since about 1973 the defendant has not been personally residing at Dolphin Place.

The defendant said in evidence that he thought that the gate which the council had re-erected in the early 1960s might have had a lock which had been placed upon it by Mr Wall. Subject to this, the judge found that the state of the fences when the defendant bought the property was as has been described earlier in this judgment. Whether or not there was already a lock on the gate when the defendant bought the property, the judge accepted the defendant's evidence that when he moved in he bought a new lock and chain and fastened the gate; he also found that he kept the key. The judge also found that since then there has been no access to the plot other than by climbing over the fences or through the hedges, except via the driveway of Chenies Avenue and through the garden of Dolphin Place.

In 1975 the local tennis club, whose courts lay over the boundary to the west of the plot, had a scheme for laying a drain which would be connected with the drainage arrangements of Dolphin Place. They applied to the council for permission. As a result, the council got in touch with the defendant. A telephone conversation took place between the defendant and Mr Harris of the county valuer's department on 10 November 1975. Mr Harris made an attendance note of that conversation which, so far as material, read:

> Mr Moran . . . discussed with [Mr Harris] the use of the land immediately to the north of the property known as 'Croft Edge'. Mr Moran indicated that he had been the owner of Dolphin Place for five years and that the land in question was incorporated within the garden of his property. He indicated that he had purchased the property form a Mr Wall of Westward Way, in whose garden Dolphin Place was built. He stated that the previous owner had obtained a right to use the county council land when Dolphin Place was built and that this right had been passed on to himself. He believed that the right to use this land had been arranged as part of the granting of planning permission for the erection of Dolphin Place. He also stated that he was of the opinion that he had first option to purchase the land if the road was not constructed. He believes that the county council had asked the previous owners for permission to lay an electricity cable across his land. This was actually carried out by the tennis club. Mr Moran requested details of the works proposed by the tennis club.

The defendant said in evidence that, while he did not remember this conversation, he had no reason to believe that it had not taken place. He did not accept some of the things which Mr Harris recorded him as having said. The judge, however, thought it right to treat the attendance note as representing a substantially accurate account of the conversation and it has not been suggested that he was wrong to do so.

Correspondence between the defendant and the council followed that telephone conversation. On 18 December 1975 the County Secretary and Solicitor wrote to the defendant a letter saying:

> I understand from the County Valuer and Land Agent that you have been exercising certain rights over the council's land shown coloured pink on the attached plan [the plot] and that you have laid this land to grass and planted trees thereon. Would you please let me know how long you have been exercising this right and also let me have a copy of the document granting you permission to use the same. The County Valuer and Land Agent informs me that you were going to send him a copy of the document granting you permission to use the land, but to date he has not heard from you. I await hearing from you as soon as possible.

Following a reminder the defendant, on 20 January 1976, wrote to the County Secretary and Solicitor a letter acknowledging the letter of 18 December 1975 and saying:

> I enclose herewith a copy of the sale agreement between myself and Mr G Wall dated 28 July 1971, upon which I have marked the relevant part which I believe

> relates to the piece of land in question. I also enclose herewith, a copy of a signed statement regarding the piece of land, which I obtained from the vendor at the time of the sale. You will notice from the documents, that the previous owner laid the land to grass in April 1967 and ever since then either the previous owner or myself have occupied the land and it has therefore, been kept as part of the garden for the last 11 years. It was my understanding with Mr Wall, that he had the right to this ground and that he only lost this right, if and when the Little Chalfont by-pass was built, so much so that as you can see I went to the trouble to get an extra declaration document from him. I notice your enclosed plan is to do with an underground cable and I believe that Mr Wall was asked for and had given permission for this to be put under the land concerned.
>
> I do not know whether you know the property itself, but the piece of land concerned forms an integral part of the garden and the whole situation of the house itself, in fact, without it, the house I think, would be unbearable to live in. I would reiterate, that it has always been my firm understanding that the land should be kept by the owner of Dolphin Place, if and until the proposed Little Chalfont by-pass was built. Since the owner of Dolphin Place has been the occupier of the land for the last 11 years, I have never had any doubt as to the situation indeed many local functions, mainly Conservative Party ones, which local councillors have attended, have been held there. I have not discussed this matter with my solicitor as yet and I await your reply before doing so.

After the defendant's signature, this letter appended the words 'Without prejudice.'

On 3 February 1976 the County Secretary and Solicitor wrote to the defendant acknowledging his letter of 20 January, and continued:

> The council purchased [the plot] in 1955, for an estate in fee simple. At no time since that date has the council given any permission for the land to be used for any purpose whatsoever, except for the laying of an electricity cable by the Little Chalfont Sports Club. The council totally disclaims your purported right to use the land, and admits that at no time have you been entitled to the use and occupation of the land. I note your claim that the land has been kept as part of the garden of Dolphin Place for the last 11 years, but the statutory declaration made by Mr and Mrs Wall states that the land has only been used since 4 April 1967. This is, therefore, a period of nine years at the present time. No doubt you will be consulting your solicitor in this matter, and I await hearing from you further as soon as possible.

The defendant then consulted solicitors, who on 22 March wrote a letter to the council making a claim that he had acquired title to the plot by adverse possession, a claim which was debated in further correspondence during 1976.

However, the council allowed a further nine years or so to elapse before it took any steps with a view to excluding the defendant from the plot. At last, on 28 October 1985, it issued proceedings seeking an order for possession and ancillary injunctions.

During the course of the trial a question arose as to the admissibility in evidence of the letter of 20 January 1976. The judge held that it was inadmissible in evidence on the basis that it was written 'Without prejudice'. He gave his reasons in a short judgment on this point delivered in the course of the trial in which he said:

> In the recent case of *South Shropshire District Council* v *Amos* [1986] 1 WLR 1271, Parker LJ, giving the judgment of the Court of Appeal, said that the use of the words 'without prejudice' prima facie meant that the letter was intended to be a part of negotiation. It would not of course be conclusive because it might be plain from the contents of the letter that it was not so intended and, in addition, the rule that 'without prejudice' documents are inadmissible is qualified by, for example, the ruling in *In re Daintrey, Ex parte Holt* [1893] 2 QB 116, that a document which might prejudicially affect the recipient cannot be excluded from evidence.
>
> The letter in question does not specifically propose any terms of settlement to the council but it is clear that Mr Moran recognised that the council might be making claims adverse to those which he was putting forward and therefore that there was a possibility of dispute. That is, of course, confirmed by his statement that he might have to go to his solicitor.
>
> The *South Shropshire* case also decided that a letter which purported to initiate some sort of negotiation ('an opening shot') is not necessarily excluded from the privilege. Negotiations have to begin somewhere. The question really is whether this letter contemplated any kind of negotiation at all. It did not, as I have said, put forward any offers or make any proposals of compromise. It merely stated what Mr Moran, without yet having obtained legal advice, thought that his rights might be.
>
> I do not think that a letter of that kind can be characterised as incapable of being a negotiating document. Looking at the public policy expressed in the privilege, it would seem to me advantageous that parties should, under cover of privilege, be able to offer to discuss the case, not necessarily putting forward any immediate compromise terms for settlement but with a view to seeing whether either side can persuade the other that he is right. I think that that was what Mr Moran was trying to do and I think it is clear from the last line of his letter that he was telling the council that, if as a result of this correspondence neither side could persuade the other, he would have to seek legal advice.
>
> In my view, the prima facie inference that the document was intended to be a negotiating document which is derived from the 'without prejudice' label has not been displaced in this case and the document is therefore not admissible.

In his judgment on the substantive issue, the judge held in effect that the defendant had for more than 12 years before the institution of proceedings had sufficient physical control of the plot and sufficient animus possidendi to constitute possession in law and that such possession had been adverse within the meaning of the Limitation Act 1980. He accordingly held that the defence based on ss 15 and 17 of the Act of 1980 succeeded.

With the leave of the judge, the council now appeals from his order made during the course of the trial whereby he held that the letter of 20 January 1976 written by the defendant to the council was inadmissible in evidence. The council further appeals from his judgment on the substantive issue relating to the Act of 1980.

The letter of 20 January 1976

In *In re Daintrey, Ex parte Holt* [1893] 2 QB 116, 119, Vaughan Williams J, delivering the judgment of the court, stated the conditions for the application of the 'without prejudice' rule as follows:

> In our opinion the rule which excludes documents marked 'without prejudice' has no application unless some person is in dispute or negotiation with another, and terms are offered for the settlement of the dispute or negotiation, and it seems to us that the judge must necessarily be entitled to look at the document in order to determine whether the conditions, under which alone the rule applies, exist. The rule is a rule adopted to enable disputants without prejudice to engage in discussion for the purpose of arriving at terms of peace, and unless there is a dispute or negotiations and an offer the rule has no application.

If this statement represented the outer limits of the 'without prejudice' rule, there could be no question of its availing the defendant, since by his letter of 20 January 1976, he was not offering terms for the settlement of any dispute or negotiation subsisting between him and the council. Later authorities, however, have expressed the principle in rather wider terms. This court in *South Shropshire District Council* v *Amos* [1986] 1 WLR 1271 held that privilege can attach to a document headed 'without prejudice' even if it is merely an 'opening shot' in negotiations. As Parker LJ said, at 1277–1278:

> It attaches to all documents which are marked 'without prejudice' and forms part of negotiations, whether or not they are themselves offers, unless the privilege is defeated on some other ground as was the case in *In re Daintrey, Ex parte Holt* [1893] 2 QB 116.

More recently the House of Lords in *Rush & Tomkins Ltd* v *Greater London Council* [1989] AC 1280 has stated the general principle that the rule applies 'to exclude all negotiations genuinely aimed at settlement whether oral or in writing from being given in evidence:' see *per* Lord Griffiths, at 1299.

I think the judge was right to regard the relevant question as being whether or not the letter of 20 January 1976 could properly be regarded as a negotiating document. But I respectfully disagree with his conclusion that it could. As the judge himself said, and as the letter itself indicated, the defendant was writing the letter in an attempt to persuade the council that his case was well founded. As I read the letter, it amounted not to an offer to negotiate, but to an assertion of the defendant's rights, coupled with an intimation that he contemplated taking his solicitor's advice unless the council replied in terms recognising his asserted rights. I cannot derive from the letter any indication, or at least any clear indication, of any willingness whatever to negotiate.

If, as in my view, the letter of 20 January 1976 cannot fairly and properly be read as an 'opening shot' in negotiations, the attribution of the protection of 'without prejudice' privilege to it would in my opinion go beyond the bounds of that privilege established by existing authority and would not in my opinion be justifiable. The public policy on which the privilege rests does not in my judgment justify giving protection to a letter which does not unequivocally indicate the writer's willingness to negotiate. Though I think this will make no difference to the result on the substantive issue, this head of appeal is in my judgment accordingly well founded.

The substantive issue

Section 15(1) of the Limitation Act 1980 provides:

> No action shall be brought by any person to recover any land after the expiration of 12 years from the date on which the right of action accrued to him or, if it first accrued to some person through whom he claims, to that person.

Subject to certain irrelevant exceptions, s 17 of the 1980 Act provides for the extinction of a person's title to land after the expiration of the relevant time limit.

As is stated in s 15(6) Schedule 1 Pt I to the 1980 Act contains provisions for determining the date of accrual of rights of action to recover land in the cases there mentioned. Schedule 1 para 1 provides:

> Where the person bringing an action to recover land, or some person through whom he claims, has been in possession of the land, and has while entitled to the land been dispossessed or discontinued his possession, the right of action shall be treated as having accrued on the date of the dispossession or discontinuance.

It is clear that, under the Act of 1980 as under the previous law, the person claiming a possessory title must show either (1) discontinuance by the paper owner followed by possession, or (2) dispossession (or, as it is sometimes called 'ouster') of the paper owner: compare *Treloar* v *Nute* [1976] 1 WLR 1295, 1300,

> the difference between the dispossession and the discontinuance of possession might be expressed in this way – the one is where a person comes in and drives out the others from possession, the other case is where the person in possession goes out and is followed into possession by other persons.

see *per* Fry J in *Rains* v *Buxton* (1880) 14 Ch D 537, 539–540.

In the present case the judge found that the council had never discontinued its possession of the plot, and this finding is not challenged on this appeal. The defendant's claim is that the council had been dispossessed of the plot by him more than 12 years before it instituted its proceedings.

If the law is to attribute possession of land to a person who can establish no paper title to possession, he must be shown to have both factual possession and the requisite intention to possess (animus possidendi). A person claiming to have 'dispossessed' another must similarly fulfil both these requirements. However, a further requirement which the alleged dispossessor claiming the benefit of the Act of 1980 must satisfy is to show that his possession has been 'adverse' within the meaning of the Act. Schedule 1 para 8(1) defines 'adverse possession' as follows:

> No right of action to recover land shall be treated as accruing unless the land is in the possession of some person in whose favour the period of limitation can run (referred to below in this paragraph as 'adverse possession'); and where under the preceding provisions of this Schedule any such right of action is treated as accruing on a certain date and no person is in adverse possession on that date, the right of action shall not be treated as accruing unless and until adverse possession is taken of the land.

Schedule 1 para 8(2) provides:

> Where a right of action to recover land has accrued and after its accrual, before the right is barred, the land ceases to be in adverse possession, the right of action shall no longer be treated as having accrued and no fresh right of action shall be treated as accruing unless and until the land is again taken into adverse possession.

On this appeal Mr Douglas, on behalf of the council, has accepted that if the plot was in adverse possession of the defendant more than 12 years before action was brought (i.e. on 28 October 1973) it has not ceased to be in adverse possession since that time. Ultimately, therefore, the crucial question will be: was the defendant in adverse possession of the plot on 28 October 1973?

Possession is never 'adverse' within the meaning of the 1980 Act if it is enjoyed under a lawful title. If, therefore, a person occupies or uses land by licence of the owner with the paper title and his licence has not been duly determined, he cannot be treated as having been in 'adverse possession' as against the owner with the paper title.

Before the passing of the 1980 Act, certain decisions of this court (in particular *Wallis's Cayton Bay Holiday Camp Ltd* v *Shell-Mex and BP Ltd* [1975] QB 94 and *Gray* v *Wykeham Martin & Goode* (unreported), 17 January 1977; CA (Civil Division) Transcript No 10A of 1977) were thought to have established a general doctrine that in one special type of case there would be implied in favour of the would-be adverse possessor, *without any specific factual basis for such implication*, a licence permitting him to commit the acts of possession upon which he sought to rely; the effect of implying such a licence would, of course, be to prevent the squatter's possession from being 'adverse'. That special type of case was broadly one where the acts of an intruder, however continuous and far-reaching, did not substantially interfere with any plans which the owners might have for the future use of undeveloped land.

The doctrine of implied licence, in my view, raised substantial conceptual difficulties as a matter of law for reasons which I stated in *Powell* v *McFarlane* (1979) 38 P&CR 452, 484, where I said:

> I do not find it easy to see how the words 'possession' or 'dispossess' can properly be given anything but their ordinary meaning in the context of the 1939 Act and I doubt whether this has been done in any decisions before the *Wallis* case. I am not sure how one can justify the imputation of an implied or hypothetical licence for the purpose of applying or defeating the provisions of that Act in circumstances where the fact would not admit the imputation of a licence for any other purposes.

The doctrine has now been abrogated by Schedule 1 para 8(4) to the 1980 Act which provides:

> For the purpose of determining whether a person occupying any land is in adverse possession of the land it shall not be assumed by implication of law that his occupation is by permission of the person entitled to the land merely by virtue of the fact that his occupation is not inconsistent with the latter's present or future enjoyment of the land. This provision shall not be taken as prejudicing a finding to the effect that a person's occupation of any land is by implied

permission of the person entitled to the land in any case where such a finding is justified on the actual facts of the case.

In the light of this provision, it would at first sight appear that there is now no reason why the words 'possess' and 'dispossess' or similar expressions should not be given their ordinary legal meaning in the context of the Act of 1980. However, Mr Douglas, on behalf of the council, while accepting that the implied licence doctrine is now abrogated, nevertheless submits that para 8(1) (I quote from his skeleton argument):

> leaves intact the special rule formulated by Bramwell LJ in *Leigh* v *Jack* (1879) 5 ExD 264 and Sir John Pennycuick in *Treloar* v *Nute* [1976] 1 WLR 1295 that where land is acquired or retained by the owner for a specific future purpose, then acts of trespass which are not inconsistent with such purpose do not amount to dispossession.

The origin of the suggested 'special rule' is said to be the often cited statement of Bramwell LJ in *Leigh* v *Jack* 5 ExD 264, 273, where he said:

> in order to defeat a title by dispossessing the former owner, acts must be done which are inconsistent with his enjoyment of the soil for purposes for which he intended to use it: that is not the case here, where the intention of the plaintiff and her predecessors in title was not either to build upon or to cultivate the land, but to devote it at some future time to public purposes.

Superficial support for the existence of the 'special rule' is to be found in a passage in the judgment of this court delivered by Sir John Pennycuick in *Treloar* v *Nute* [1976] 1 WLR 1295, 1300–1301, where he said:

> The literal application of the statutory provisions has been adapted by this court to meet one special type of case. It sometimes happens that the owner of a piece of land retains it with a view to its utilisation for some specific purpose in the future and that meanwhile some other person has physical possession of it. When that state of affairs exists, the owner is not treated as dispossessed: see *Leigh* v *Jack* 5 ExD 264, where factory materials were placed upon a strip of land intended by the owner to be dedicated as a road . . .

Sir John Pennycuick went on to refer to the judgment of Cockburn CJ in *Leigh* v *Jack* 5 ExD 264, 271, and cited the passage from Bramwell LJ's judgment, at 273, above. He also referred very briefly to the decision of this court in *Williams Brothers Direct Supply Ltd* v *Raftery* [1958] 1 QB 159.

All the observations of Sir John Pennycuick in *Treloar* v *Nute* [1976] 1 WLR 1295, to which I have referred, were obiter because they were made in the absence of any evidence of 'special purpose' on the part of the plaintiff: see 1302E. The court below had found that the defendant's father took possession of the disputed land outside the limitation period, but that this possession was not adverse by reason that it caused no inconvenience to the plaintiff. The actual decision of this court was that, in the absence of any evidence of special purpose, the absence of inconvenience to the plaintiff was an irrelevant consideration, and that time began from the taking of possession by the father, whether or not the plaintiff suffered inconvenience from such possession.

The other members of this court in *Treloar* v *Nute* were Ormrod LJ who had been one of the majority in *Wallis*'s case [1975] QB 94, in which Lord Denning MR had introduced the doctrine of implied licence, and Stamp LJ, who had dissented in that case. In giving judgment, the court [1976] 1 WLR 1295 1302F, referred to the considerable disadvantage which it had suffered from the absence of any legal argument on behalf of the appellant. It was faced with a further difficulty that the ratio of the majority decision in *Wallis's* case, so far as that ratio extended, was binding on it, since the 1980 Act had not been passed. I respectfully agree with the actual decision in *Treloar* v *Nute*, but respectfully disagree with the obiter dicta to which I have referred.

On any footing, it must, in my judgment, be too broad a proposition to suggest that an owner who retains a piece of land with a view to its utilisation for a specific purpose in the future can never be treated as dispossessed, however firm and obvious the intention to dispossess, and however drastic the acts of dispossession of the person seeking to dispossess him may be. Furthermore, while it may well be correct to say that the implied licence doctrine (so long as it survived) itself involved the 'adaptation' of the literal application of the statutory provisions 'to meet one special type of case,' I do not think it correct to suggest that the decisions in *Leigh* v *Jack* 5 ExD 264, or *Williams Brothers Direct Supply Ltd* v *Raftery* [1958] 1 QB 159 (or indeed any other decisions prior to *Wallis's* case [1975] QB 94) authorise or justify an application of the statutory provisions otherwise than in accordance with their ordinary and natural meaning.

In the course of my judgment in *Powell* v *McFarlane* 38 P&CR 452, 472–474, I considered in some detail the decisions in *Leigh* v *Jack* and *Williams Brothers Direct Supply Ltd* v *Raftery* and *Tecbild Ltd* v *Chamberlain* (1969) 20 P&CR 633. I do not propose to embark on a similar analysis in this judgment, but would venture to repeat certain conclusions about these cases which I expressed, at 484–485:

> I incline to the view that the ratio decidendi of all the various judgments in cases, such as *Leigh* v *Jack*, the *Williams* case and *Tecbild Ltd* v *Chamberlain* was either (a) that the necessary *animus possidendi* had not been shown or (b) that the acts relied on had been too trivial to amount to the taking of actual possession; some members of each court seem to have relied on the first ground and others on the second. I venture to think that all these three decisions are readily explicable, not so much on the basis of any imputed licence, but merely on the grounds that in circumstances where an owner has no present use for his land but has future plans for its use (for example by development or by dedication to the public as a highway), then the court will, on the facts, readily treat a trespasser, whose acts have not been inconsistent with such future plans, as having not manifested the requisite animus possidendi or alternatively, as not having acquired a sufficient degree of exclusive occupation to constitute possession.

On re-reading the relevant authorities, the view to which I then inclined has become a firm one. The statement of Bramwell LJ in *Leigh* v *Jack* 5 ExD 264, 273, on which so much reliance has been placed on this appeal was made in the context of a case in which, it would appear, the defendant would have had knowledge of the intention of the owner to dedicate it to the public as a highway. (It was marked as a street on a plan of his estate, which he hung up in his estate office and this fact was presumably common knowledge among those interested in the property.) If in any given case the land in dispute is unbuilt land and the squatter is aware that the owner, while having no present use for it, has a purpose in mind for its use in the future, the court is likely to require very clear evidence before it can be satisfied that the squatter who claims a possessory title has not only established factual possession of the land, but also the requiste intention to exclude the world at large, including the owner with the paper title, so far as is reasonably practicable and so far as the processes of the law will allow. In the absence of clear evidence of this nature, the court is likely to infer that the squatter neither had had nor had claimed any intention of asserting a right to the possession of the land.

I agree entirely with the following passage from the dissenting judgment of Stamp LJ in *Wallis's* case [1975] QB 94, 109–110:

> Reading the judgments in *Leigh* v *Jack* . . . and *Williams Brothers Direct Supply Ltd* v *Raftery* [1958] 1 QB 159, I conclude that they establish that in order to determine whether the acts of user do or do not amount to dispossession of the owner the character of the land, the nature of the acts done upon it and the intention of the squatter fall to be considered. Where the land is waste land and the true owner cannot and does not for the time being use it for the purpose for which he acquired it, one may more readily conclude that the acts done on the waste land do not amount to dispossession of the owner. But I find it impossible to regard those cases as establishing that so long as the true owner cannot use his land for the purpose for which he acquired it the acts done by the squatter do not amount to possession of the land. One must look at the facts and circumstances and determine whether what has been done in relation to the land constitutes possession.

In the present case, the defendant was well aware that the council had acquired the plot in order to construct a road on it at some time in the future and meantime had no present use for the land. This factor, which Mr Douglas naturally stressed in the course of his argument, should make the court the more cautious before holding that the defendant had had both a factual possession and animus possidendi sufficient to confer on him a possessory title. Nevertheless, every *Leigh* v *Jack* type of case such as this must involve questions of fact and degree. I would, for my part, reject the submission that since the Act of 1980 there remains any 'special rule' which requires the words 'possessed' and 'dispossessed' or similar words to be given anything other than their natural and ordinary meaning in the *Leigh* v *Jack* type of case.

Thus far, therefore, I conclude that (1) if by 28 October 1973 the defendant had taken possession of the plot, his possession must have been adverse to the council; (2) the question whether or not the defendant had taken possession of the plot by 28 October 1973 falls to be decided by reference to conventional concepts of possession and dispossession and not by departing from the ordinary and natural meaning of the relevant statutory provisions merely because this is a *Leigh* v *Jack* type of case.

I turn then to consider the first of the two requiste elements of possession. First, as at 28 October 1973 did the defendant have factual possession of the plot? I venture to repeat what I said in *Powell* v *McFarlane* 38 P&CR 452, 470–471;

> Factual possession signifies an appropriate degree of physical control. It must be a single and (exclusive) possession . . . Thus an owner of land and a person intruding on that land without his consent cannot both be in possession of the land at the same time. The question what acts constitute a sufficient degree of exclusive physical control must depend on the circumstances, in particular the nature of the land and the manner in which land of that nature is commonly used or enjoyed.

On the evidence it would appear clear that by 28 October 1973 the defendant had acquired complete and exclusive physical control of the plot. He had secured a complete enclosure of the plot and its annexation to Dolphin Place. Any intruder could have gained access to the plot only by way of Dolphin Place, unless he was prepared to climb the locked gate fronting the highway or to scramble through one or other of the hedges bordering the plot. The defendant had put a new lock and chain on the gate and had fastened it. He and his mother had been dealing with the plot as any occupying owners might have been expected to deal with it. They had incorporated it into the garden of Dolphin Place. They had planted bulbs and daffodils in the grass. They had maintained it as part of that garden and had trimmed the hedges. I cannot accept Mr Douglas's submission that the defendant's acts of possession were trivial. It is hard to see what more he could have done to acquire complete physical control of the plot by October 1983. In my judgment, he had plainly acquired factual possession of the plot by that time.

However, as the judge said, the more difficult question is whether the defendant had the necessary animus possidendi. As to this, Mr Douglas accepted the correctness of the following statement (so far as it went) which I made in *Powell* v *McFarlane* 38 P&CR 452, 471–472:

> the animus possidendi involves the intention, in one's own name and on one's own behalf, to exclude the world at large, including the owner with the paper title if he be not himself the possessor, so far as is reasonably practicable and so far as the process of the law will allow.

At least at first sight the following observations of Lord Halsbury LC in *Marshall* v *Taylor* [1895] 1 Ch 641, 645, which were referred to by Hoffmann J in his judgment, are very pertinent to the present case:

> The true nature of this particular strip of land is that it is enclosed. It cannot be denied that the person who now says he owns it could not get to it in any ordinary way. I do not deny that he could have crept through the hedge, or, if it had been a brick wall, that he could have climbed over the wall; but that was not the ordinary and usual mode of access. That is the exclusion – the dispossession – which seems to me to be so important in this case.

As a number of authorities indicate, enclosure by itself prima facie indicates the requiste *animus possidendi.* As Cockburn CJ said in *Seddon* v *Smith* (1877) 36 LT 168, 169: 'Enclosure is the strongest possible evidence of adverse possession.' Russell LJ in *George Wimpey & Co Ltd* v *Sohn* [1967] Ch 487, 511A, similarly observed: 'Ordinarily, of course, enclosure is the most cogent evidence of adverse possession and of dispossession of the true owner.' While Mr Douglas pointed out that the plot was always accessible from the north where no boundary demarcation existed, it was only accessible from the defendant's own property, Dolphin Place. In my judgment, therefore, he must be treated as having enclosed it.

Mr Douglas, however, submitted that even if enclosure had occurred, the defendant's intention must be assessed in the light of the particular circumstances of this case. The defendant knew that the council had acquired and retained the plot with the specific intention of building a road across it at some future time. The council had no use for the land in the interim. It was for all practical purposes waste land. None of the defendant's acts, he submitted, were inconsistent with the council's known future intentions. He invoked, inter alia, the words of Cockburn CJ in *Leigh* v *Jack* 5 ExD 264, 271, which, he submitted, applied in the present case:

> I do not think that any of the defendant's acts were done with the view of defeating the purpose of the parties to the conveyances; his acts were those of a man who did not intend to be a trespasser, or to infringe upon another's right. The defendant simply used the land until the time should come for carrying out the object originally contemplated.

If the defendant had stopped short of placing a new lock and chain on the gate, I might perhaps have felt able to accept these submissions. Mr Douglas submitted that this act did not unequivocally show an intention to exclude the council as well as other people. (It is well established that it is no use for an alleged adverse possessor to rely on acts which are merely equivocal as regards the intention to exclude the true owner: see for example *Tecbild Ltd* v *Chamberlain* 20 P&CR 633, 642, *per* Sachs LJ). In my judgment, however, the placing of the new lock and chain and gate did amount to a final unequivocal demonstration of the defendant's intention to possess the land. I agree with the judge in his saying (1988) 86 LGR 472, 479:

> . . . I do not think that if the council, on making an inspection, had found the gate newly padlocked, they could have come to any conclusion other than that [the defendant] was intending to exclude everyone, including themselves, from the land.

The other main point which Mr Douglas has argued in support of this appeal has caused me slightly more difficulty. In his submission there can be no sufficient *animus possidendi* to constitute adverse possession for the purpose of the 1980 Act unless there exists the intention to exclude the owner with the paper title in *all* future circumstances. The defendant's oral statements to Mr Harris in the conversation of 10 November 1975, as recorded in the attendance note, do appear to have constituted an implicit acknowledgement by the defendant that he would be obliged to leave the plot if in the future the council required it for the purpose of constructing the proposed new road. The letter of 18 December 1975, which I have concluded should be admitted in evidence, contains an express acknowledgement of this nature. If the intention to exclude the owner with the paper title in all future circumstances is a necessary constituent of the *animus possidendi*, the attendance note and the letter of 18 December 1975 show that this constituent was absent in the present case.

There are some dicta in the authorities which might be read as suggesting that an intention to *own* the land is required. Sir Nathaniel Lindley MR, for example, in *Littledale* v *Liverpool College* [1900] 1 Ch 19, 23, referred to the 'acts of ownership' relied upon by the plaintiffs. Russell LJ in *George Wimpey & Co Ltd* v *Sohn* [1967] Ch 487, 510, said:

> . . . I am not satisfied that the actions of the predecessors in bricking up the doorway and maintaining a lock on the gate to the roadway were necessarily referable to an intention to occupy the [land] as their own absolute property.

At one point in my judgment in *Powell* v *McFarlane* 38 P&CR 452, 478, I suggested:

> any objective informed observer might probably have inferred that the plaintiff was using the land simply for the benefit of his family's cow or cows, during such periods as the absent owner took no steps to stop him, without any intention to appropriate the land as his own.

Nevertheless, I agree with the judge that 'what is required for this purpose is not an intention to own or even an intention to acquire ownership but an intention to possess' – that is to say, an intention for the time being to possess the land to the exclusion of all other persons, including the owner with the paper title. No authorities cited to us establish the contrary proposition. The conversation with Mr Harris, as recorded in the attendance note and the letter of 18 December 1975, to my mind demonstrates the intention of the defendant for the time being to continue in possession of the plot to the exclusion of the council unless and until the proposed by-pass is built. The form of the conveyance to the defendant and of the contemporaneous statutory declaration which he obtained from Mr and Mrs Wall, are, of course entirely consistent with the existence of an intention on his part to take and keep adverse possession of the plot, at least unless and until that event occurred.

In the light of the line of authorities to which we have been referred, beginning with *Leigh* v *Jack* 5 ExD 264, I have already accepted that the court should be slow to make a finding of adverse possession in a case such as the present. However, as the judge pointed out, in none of those earlier cases, where the owner with the paper title successfully defended his title, was there present the significant feature of complete enclosure of the land in question by the trespasser. On the evidence in the present case he was, in my judgment, right in concluding that the defendant had acquired adverse possession of the plot by 28 October 1973 and had remained in adverse possession of it ever since. There is no evidence that any representative of the council has even set foot on the plot since that date.

This appeal, which has been well argued on both sides, should in my judgment be dismissed.

NOURSE and BUTLER-SLOSS LJJ agreed, NOURSE LJ adding some views of his own.

QUESTIONS

1 The doctrine of the implied licence has been abrogated by the Limitation Act 1980. The possibility of a licence being implied from the facts has been preserved however. Discuss whether this enactment commits the question too openly to the personal proclivities of the judge.

2 Patience has occupied 'Folornacre' for 13 years, so that Peregrine, the original owner, has lost his title. Patience now discovers that Peregrine entered into a restrictive covenant 15 years ago with the neighbouring landowner, Green, not to build. The covenant was registered at the Land Charges Registry at the time of its creation. Advise Patience as to whether she is bound by the covenant.

3 A group known as 'occupants militant' consult you as to their rights if they break into and occupy an empty dwelling house owned by Gwen. Advise them generally.

4 'Greyacre' is a strip of land between 'Blackacre' and 'Whiteacre'. 'Blackacre', owned by Black, is grazed by beasts. 'Whiteacre', owned by White, is under the plough. There is no fencing between 'Blackacre' and 'Whiteacre'. 'Greyacre' has long been unused because it comprises steep inclines into a central ditch. Black now wishes to claim 'Greyacre'. What investigations will you make?

5 The Limitation Act 1980 legitimates the tort of trespass in the public interest of security of title to land. Consider whether there is an equally strong private interest worthy of protection when homeless persons enter unoccupied residential accommodation. For this purpose refer to the defence of 'necessity' in the standard textbooks on the law of tort. Also consider what liberties might be afforded to New Age Travellers.

CHAPTER 9

SETTLEMENTS

In Chapter 5, we were concerned with various interests in land and the problems they raised individually. When two or more of these interests occur consecutively, new kinds of difficulty arise. These will be examined in this chapter. Leases, however, do not raise the same difficulties and may be left out of the account at this stage. When interests in land, other than leases, occur consecutively, the whole structure of interests is called a *settlement.* A grant as simple as 'to *A* for life, remainder in fee simple to *B*' creates a settlement, but some of the settlements met in practice are of great complexity. There are two kinds of settlement, strict settlements and settlements by way of trust for sale. The former is dealt with by the Settled Land Act 1925, the latter by the Law of Property Act 1925. Since they are mutually exclusive it is vital to distinguish them. That is easy: in a settlement by way of trust for sale the settlor gives an instruction to sell the land. This instruction must be mandatory; a mere power of sale is insufficient. In a strict settlement this instruction is absent.

STRICT SETTLEMENTS

Strict settlements reached their heyday in the classical England of the eighteenth and early nineteenth centuries, the England of the gavotte, Mr Capability Brown and Bath. In those days a single settled estate might consist of thousands of acres, for not only was land a most secure form of wealth, but affection for the country life was strong. Yet a strict settlement can arise at the present time from a home-made will disposing of a tiny cottage. Although applying equally to large and small estates, the special body of law which applies whenever there is a strict settlement contemplates sizeable ones, so here the machinery employed in the traditional strict settlement of a large estate will be described. This will be done in a much simplified way since, for reasons of taxation planning, strict settlements are rarely created where professional advice is taken. Yet simple settlements can easily arise in other circumstances.

Let us say that O, owner in fee simple of a large estate, intends to marry shortly and wishes to endow future members of his family. He would find the doctrine of estates admirably suited to his purposes, and could dispose of his fee simple absolute in the following way. First O himself would take the fee simple until his marriage, a determinable fee simple, then, upon marriage, a life interest, which is contingent of course. Next, an entail would be limited to his first son, and then, in case that son should die without an heir, entails would be limited to other sons in order of age. These entails are contingent because no sons yet exist. All these provisions are made in a single grant and their purpose is to keep the land in the family for as long as possible. O wishes to provide for other members of the family too, so the settlement also includes an annual rentcharge, known as a *jointure*, payable out of the profits of the land to O's wife, if she should survive him, and capital sums, known as *portions*, payable to younger children of the family. These are secured on the land. Despite the grant of all these interests, the fee simple absolute still remains to be disposed of. The final limitation in the instrument therefore is that the ultimate reversion in fee simple shall belong to O. After the failure or exhaustion of all the other interests, the land will pass absolutely to him or his successors in title, who would, of course, be identified by the general law without reference to the settlement. It has been the tradition in the case of large settlements to resettle the land before such a result occurs. In this way, the property is kept within the family for generation after generation.

Whether a settlement is of a complex nature, or as simple as 'to *A* for life, remainder to *B* in fee simple', the greatest problem it has presented is that of inalienability. Sometimes a power of sale was included in a settlement but where it was not, since the fee simple was in reversion, there was no person who owned what the ordinary purchaser wished to buy, namely a fee simple absolute in possession. The Settled Land Act 1882 brought reform and many of the cases still relevant to the subject were decided on that Act. It has now been re-enacted and perfected in the Settled Land Act 1925, which will be our starting-point.

The essence of the reform is that all the beneficial interests under a settlement are now equitable following the Law of Property Act 1925 s 1. The fee simple absolute in possession is held on trust for the various beneficiaries, can never be divided in any way, and is always available for sale. On sale, the interests of the beneficiaries are overreached and are satisfied out of the purchase money. Furthermore, powers of leasing, mortgaging, improvement and management are also given to the life tenant by the Settled Land Act – otherwise he would not be able to carry out a transaction of this nature which transcended his own life interest. A prospective lessee, for instance, would think little of a lease which would end suddenly on the life tenant's death. If these powers are to be granted, a strict and delicate machinery is necessary to safeguard the interests of all the beneficiaries. Trustees are needed to take care of purchase money and their appointment and duties require regulation; rules for the management of the land during a minority must be provided, together with the control of many other activities. In short, a special and elaborate code of rules is necessary to govern all the activities of a settlement. This is contained in the Settled Land Act 1925. These rules must now be discussed systematically, beginning with the crucial question of how to diagnose a settlement, for it is the existence of a settlement only which invokes these rules. Statutory citations, unless otherwise stated, will be from the Settled Land Act 1925.

Definition of a settlement

Under s 1, a settlement exists when land is

1 limited in trust for any persons by way of succession; or

2 limited in trust for any person in possession:
   (a) for an entailed interest, whether or not capable of being barred or defeated;
   (b) for an estate in fee simple, or for a term of years absolute, subject to an executory limitation, gift, or disposition over, on failure of his issue or in any other event;
   (c) for a base or determinable fee or any corresponding leasehold land;
   (d) being an infant, for an estate in fee simple or for a term of years absolute; or

3 limited in trust for any person for an estate in fee simple or for a term of years absolute contingently on the happening of any event; or

4 charged, whether voluntarily or in consideration of marriage or by way of family arrangement, and whether immediately or after an interval, with the payment of any rentcharge for the life of any person, or any less period, or of any capital, annual or periodical sums for the portions, advancement, maintenance, or otherwise for the benefit of any persons, with or without any term of years for securing or raising the same.

This definition need not intimidate. It could have been expressed in much shorter form, but the Act, in order to save doubt in the minds of busy practitioners, spells out the individual occasions which produce settlements. If we go to the root of the section and understand its policy, there will be no need to memorise it. Its purpose is to round up all the cases which produce the problem of inalienability, in preparation for the treatment in store for them in the Act. On examination, this inalienability is caused in most cases by the beneficial interest, that is the equitable fee simple absolute, being put into remainder by the creation out of it of limited interests. Thus, if a grant is made to *A* for life, with remainder in fee simple to *B*, there is, for the present, no single person capable of offering for sale the type of interest a purchaser will wish to buy, for *A*'s interest might end suddenly and early, whereas *B*'s does not give possession at all for the moment. In short, the common element in all the cases mentioned in the definition except 2 (d) and 4 is that of succession. Apart from these two, all the other instances are implicit in 1 and are really superfluous. A few examples will illustrate this.

Take, for instance, 2 (a), the entail. Whenever an entail exists, there must be an element of succession because its grant does not exhaust the grantor's ownership. There must be a fee simple owner in reversion or remainder. One interest is thus followed by another. Second, take 2(b), which is a conditional fee simple. An example of this would be a grant 'to *A* in fee simple, but, if he shall remarry, to *B* in fee simple'. Although the interest of *B* is only contingent on *A* remarrying, it constitutes a clear possibility of one interest following another. Finally, in the case of 3, there is an element of succession. This is a contingent interest and an example would be a grant 'to *A* at the age of 30 in fee simple'. Here we must ask what happens to the land during the time before *A* has reached 30. The answer is that it remains with the grantor, *G*, so that a description of the interests really reads, 'to *G* in fee simple until *A* reaches 30 and then to *A* in fee simple', whereupon the elements of succession becomes obvious. So we can both shorten and rationalise all this part of s 1 by deducing that, leaseholds apart, whenever any person is entitled to any interest less than a fee simple absolute in possession there exists a settlement, for in all such cases there must be an interest in remainder or reversion, and therefore an element of succession. This does not embrace fees simple on condition subject to rights of entry or re-entry, because these have been declared absolute by the Law of Property (Amendment) Act 1926. However, these must be sharply distinguished from conditional fees simple subject to gifts over, which do create settlements under 2(b) above.

The two additional cases where settlements arise must now be explained, and first that of minority under 2(d). Minority does not involve succession, but it does involve a problem of inalienability. A person under 18 years of age cannot hold a legal estate. Thus, if I grant the fee simple absolute in possession of 'Blackacre' to *A*, a minor, while he alone is entitled to enjoyment because he owns the land absolutely in equity, he himself cannot sell the land because he cannot own it at law. Since minority posed this problem of inalienability in common with the cases where there was an element of succession, it was constituted a settlement by the section so that it could partake of the same solution for its problems provided by the Act. Next is the case of charges under 4. The requirement that they are voluntary and are for no consideration unless it be marriage or other family arrangements divides them sharply from the rentcharges which are sometimes payable as the result of the purchase of a fee simple estate. In those cases, there is clearly consideration. Settlements are instruments of family endowment, not commercial transactions, and the Act follows this natural boundary. The presence of land charged in this particular way in the settlement fold can be justified in two ways. First, such a charge is a natural and common incident of settlements. Second, and more significantly, land subject to charges may be difficult to sell if those charges are to continue to affect the land. If, however, they can be overreached and be satisfied out of the purchase money, this problem can be overcome. Since a settlement must contain all the necessary machinery for overreaching, including trustees, it was a convenient solution to classify these cases as settlements (*Lord Henry Bruce* v *Marquess of Ailesbury* [1892] AC 356, per Halsbury LC, at 361).

While this provision would serve usefully where the land had been rendered difficult to sell, it did impose a burden where the existence of the charge did not have this effect, because all the elaborate rules which must be observed when settled land is sold applied. To release vendors from compliance with these rules, where purchasers are willing to buy the land even subject to the charge, the Law of Property (Amendment) Act 1926 therefore enacted that an estate owner may sell subject to the charge as if the land were not settled (s 1). Of course this privilege only applies when the existence of the charge is the only reason why a settlement exists, and not where there are other grounds too, such as the presence of a life interest.

Before summing up the total effect of these remarks, it should be explained that the existence of a lease does not create an element of succession so as to constitute a settlement. It is true that strictly speaking the right to possession of a tenant is followed by that of his landlord, but since the right of the landlord to receive the rent, if any, amounts to *possession* under the Law of Property Act 1925 s 205(1)(xix), there is no *succession* for present purposes, and the landlord's fee simple remains absolute and *in possession*. Yet a lease can be instrumental in the creation of a settlement in two ways. First, it might be a lease itself which is settled, as, for instance, if I, the owner of a 100 years' lease, bequeath it to *A* for life with remainder of the term to *B*. Here, the subject matter of the settlement is a lease, and the fee simple is unaffected. Second, if a fee simple owner grants land to a person for a term of years determinable on death, and no rent is payable, this creates a settlement of the grantor's interest. This is really only a foreshortened life interest rather than a lease, because no one is receiving rent and presumably the fee simple in reversion is not *in possession*.

In short, a settlement exists whenever any person is entitled to any interest less than the fee simple absolute in possession, and, even if entitled to the fee simple absolute in possession, if he is a minor or if the land is subject to charges of the type described above.

The life tenant in possession holds the legal estate

We have seen that, apart from leases, no limited interest in land can exist at law, and that such interests as determinable fees simple and life interests can exist only in equity (LPA 1925 s 1). It was explained in Chapter 2 that effect is given to these equitable interests by vesting the legal fee simple absolute in possession, or term of years absolute if a leasehold is being settled, in some trustee who holds it on behalf of the various beneficiaries. Thus, the absolute ownership is always available for sale in the hands of one person. This trustee is the person who is currently entitled in possession to the life interest or other interest under the settlement (Settled Land Act 1925 s 4). Where, for instance, land stands settled on *A* for life, then to *B* for life and then to *C* in fee simple, the legal fee simple absolute in possession is held by *A*. A few remarks must be made about this rather surprising rule.

First, he is given the legal estate because the legislature designated him the land manager and as such he may take decisions on major matters such as the sale, leasing, mortgage or improvement of the land, which will affect not only himself but future beneficiaries under the settlement. When you consider that he will often be the father, husband, or grandfather of many of the other beneficiaries, his claims to this role are clearly stronger than those of an outsider with no interest, beneficial or otherwise, in the land. Second, although the life tenant thus finds himself in two capacities, these are quite distinct. As to the legal estate, he holds it only as trustee for himself and the other beneficiaries, and his own beneficial entitlement is not altered in the least. In disposing of it in any way, he is strictly bound by the terms of the Act. His life interest is his very own, and he can dispose of it as he wishes. Third, while it is, in view of certain safeguards provided by the Act, quite safe to allow him to hold the fee simple absolute while the land remains unsold, it would be dangerous to allow him to hold the purchase money on sale, for a person can abscond with money, though not with land. Because of this, in every settlement there must be special trustees for the purposes of the Act. This trusteeship is quite distinct from the trusteeship of the life tenant. Such trustees have many functions to perform, but the main one is to hold the purchase and other capital moneys which result from the sale or other disposition of the land. They never, as such, hold the legal estate in the land, although we shall see that they do, in certain other capacities, hold it temporarily when there is presently no life tenant, or when it is in transit on the termination of a life tenant's interest.

There are two exceptions to the rule that the legal estate and its associated statutory powers must be held by the tenant for life.

Where the life tenant is a minor

A minor cannot hold a legal estate and the Act is concerned to ensure that there is no abeyance of the power to dispose of the land. The legal estate is therefore vested in the *statutory owner*, a term used to describe the makeshift body who exercise the statutory powers in such an interim period (see s 117(1) (xxvi)). The beneficial interest of the minor is affected in no way. The statutory owner in this case is

> (a) if the settled land is vested in a personal representative, the personal representative, until a principal vesting instrument has been executed pursuant to the provisions of this Act; and (b) in every other case, the trustees of the settlement.
>
> (s 26)

An example of (a) would be if a landowner settled his land by will, for then the legal estate would vest in his personal representative. If the first person entitled is a minor, that personal representative is a statutory owner, but under s 26(2) the trustees may require him to vest the legal estate in them and meanwhile he shall give effect to the directions of the trustees, irrespective of their 'propriety', provided that they appear to be legal. Finally, the section does not apply if the minor is one of joint life tenants and one of the others is of full age, for then the person of full age may hold the legal estate.

Where there is no life tenant presently entitled

An example of this would be if, as in *Re Frewen* [1926] Ch 580, land is settled upon trust to pay *A* two-thirds of the income, the other third to go on different trusts, for, as we shall see, *A*'s interest does not amount to a life interest. Once again, to enable the land to be dealt with, the statutory owner is brought to the helm. In this case, under s 23, this is: '(a) any person of full age on whom such powers are by the settlement expressed to be conferred; and (b) in any other case, the trustees of the settlement'.

Who is the tenant for life?

It is the policy of the Act that the legal estate and the wide statutory powers of disposal and management of the land should be in the hands of the tenant for life. It is essential therefore to know who this very important person is. Since the intention was to confer these powers upon the person beneficially entitled in possession, the *tenant for life* would ordinarily be too narrow a term to use for this purpose, for a person might be in possession, for instance, by virtue of an entail. Sections 19 and 20 bestow these powers not only on the tenant for life properly so called, but upon other persons interested in possession. To save laboriousness of reference, these are all called *tenants for life* (s 117 (xxviii)). This does not in any way affect their various beneficial interests and perhaps 'land manager' would have been a happier description. As in the case of the definition of a settlement, these sections are rather superfluous in their expression and the general characteristic present here is that all the persons described are presently entitled to possession or to the whole of the net income of the land. More specifically, however, the tenant for life may be one of the persons mentioned below, provided he is of full age, and presently and beneficially entitled under the settlement (*Re Jemmett and Guest's Contract* [1907] 1 Ch 629). It was held in *Re Johnson* [1914] 2 Ch 134 that the personal representative of a deceased beneficiary is beneficially entitled so as to have the powers of a tenant for life, provided, of course, that the interest of the beneficiary is one which is not extinguished by his death. Finally, an assignee of a life tenant's beneficial interest does not take 'under the settlement', so that the legal estate remains in the hands of the life tenant, even though he is no longer beneficially entitled (*Re Earl of Carnarvon's Chesterfield Settled Estates* [1927] 1 Ch 138).

1 The person entitled to possession of the land for life. This refers to the owner of an ordinary life interest. It was held in *Re Anderson* [1920] 1 Ch 175 that where a person had been given an option to take possession of property, or part of it, she would not become a tenant for life until she had

exercised the option by informing the trustees of her intention to take up possession. Occasionally the existence of a life interest might depend upon the construction of ambiguous words in a document or even upon the conduct of persons (see *Ungurian* v *Lesnoff* [1990] Ch 206).

2 A tenant in tail in possession.

3 An owner of a fee simple or lease subject to a gift over. An example would be 'to *A* in fee simple, but if he marries *B*, to *C* in fee simple'.

4 An owner of a determinable or base fee or a corresponding interest in leasehold land.

5 A tenant for years determinable on life, not holding merely under a lease at a rent. The Act aims at cases of endowment, not of profit return. This was strictly applied in *Re Catling* [1931] 2 Ch 359, where a woman was given such a term at a nominal rent of £1 per year. It was held that she was not a tenant for life. Where rent is payable in this type of lease terminable upon 'family' events, such as death and marriage, the interest is converted into a ninety year lease under the Law of Property Act 1925 s 149(6). In that case, there is no settlement at all. This was considered under leasehold interests.

6 A tenant for the life of another, not holding merely under a lease at a rent.

7 A tenant for his own or other life, or for years determinable on life, whose interest is liable to cease in any event during that life, or is subject to a trust for accumulation of income.

8 A tenant by curtesy.

9 A person entitled to the income of land for his own or other life, whether or not subject to expenses of management, or to a trust for the accumulation of income, or until some other event. Thus a person who is not entitled to physical possession of the land, because, for instance, it is leased, but only to its income, becomes tenant for life and can demand the legal estate. It does not matter if this income is reduced by outgoings such as repairs (*Clarke* v *Thornton* (1887) 35 ChD 307) and annuities, even though they exhaust the income as they did in *Re Jones* (1884) 26 ChD 736, where the beneficiary was held to have the powers of a life tenant, even though he received no benefit; but he must have the right to the whole net income, not merely even a large fraction of it (*Re Frewen* [1926] Ch 580) or a hope only that a discretion will be exercised in his favour (*Re Atkinson* (1886) 31 ChD 577). If, on the other hand, the net profits are divisible between two or more beneficiaries, this will constitute them joint life tenants (*Re Bennett* [1903] 2 Ch 136).

10 A person entitled to a fee simple or lease subject to any estates, interests, charges, or powers of charging, subsisting or capable of being exercised

under a settlement. If land is charged under a settlement with the payment of charges and the fee simple absolute belongs beneficially to *X*, then *X* has the powers of a life tenant and has a right to the legal fee simple absolute and to exercise the powers of a life tenant. We have seen, however, that if he does not wish to overreach the charges, but to sell subject to them, he can deal with the land irrespective of the Act (Law of Property (Amendment) Act 1926 s 1).

Despite such a wide range of eligible life tenants, there might still be circumstances where, for the time being, there is no life tenant. One example is during a minority. Another is in the circumstances presented by *Re Frewen*, above, where the beneficiary was entitled only to two-thirds of the income of land, the other third going on different trusts and not to another person so as to constitute joint life tenants. In such cases, the statutory owner holds the legal estate and statutory powers.

Who are the trustees?

The trustees are a vital part of the furniture of a settlement and without them none of the major statutory powers granted to the life tenant may be exercised. Section 30 provides who they shall be and in what order of precedence. We must follow that 'queue order' rigidly.

If the settlement arises under a will or intestacy and there are otherwise no trustees, then the deceased's personal representatives may be trustees until others are appointed. If there is only one personal representative, not being a trust corporation, he must appoint another trustee to act with him. If the settlement is created *inter vivos* and otherwise there are no trustees, an application may be made to the court under the Trustee Act 1925, for appointments to be made. These last two provisions are for use as a last resort, but they ensure that a settlement need never be crippled through lack of trustees.

Formalities of creation

It was seen in Chapter 1 how simple a deed of conveyance can be, but it can be complicated by further additions, such as covenants, which will affect the purchaser and future owners. At one time, a further complicating factor was the existence of a settlement, because all the various interests and charges occurring under it were recited. This was so even when a power of sale existed, despite the fact that such family interests were of no interest to the purchaser, because they would be overreached. As a result he had to examine large quantities of material which were to him irrelevant, in order to find the comparatively small amount of information which concerned him. The nuisance to him may be compared with that presented to a motorist who, travelling along a fast major road to his destination, suddenly finds in the middle of the journey that he has to drive through a busy town, full of minor roads and culs-de-sac which do not concern him and present him with confusion. How much more convenient if the town can be bypassed by the major road. The policy of the Settled Land Act is to bypass the settlement because now, under its provisions, all the family interests arising thereunder can be overreached. This it achieves by providing that only matters necessary to the proof of the legal title, or otherwise concerning the purchaser, shall appear on the deed of conveyance, and that the interests which are overreached and concern only the beneficiaries shall be contained in a separate document which need not, and in most cases cannot, be inspected by the purchaser. This is known as the *curtain principle.*

Accordingly, s 4 enacts that every *inter vivos* settlement of a legal estate shall be made by two deeds, a principal vesting deed and a trust instrument, and if effected in any other way, shall not transfer the legal estate. Under s 6, if a settlement is created by will, the will becomes the trust instrument and the personal representatives must, when required, convey the land to the person entitled to the legal estate by a vesting assent, which is tantamount to a vesting deed except that, being made by personal representatives, it needed no seal. Sections 4 and 5 lay down what these two instruments must contain.

The principal vesting deed or assent must:

1 Describe the settled land.

2 Declare the land to be vested in the person to whom it is conveyed, or in whom it is declared to be vested, upon the trusts of the settlement. This rather strained expression covers not only cases where the settlor conveys to another person as tenant for life, but also where he himself is to be the first tenant for life and the legal estate is thus already vested in him.

3 Name the trustees.

4 Name the persons empowered to appoint new trustees.

5 Describe any powers conferred in addition to those provided by the Act.

Additional land is brought into a settlement by a subsidiary vesting deed (see s 10).

In short, the vesting instrument is like an ordinary conveyance except that it advertises that a settlement exists, even though its terms do not appear. The purchaser is therefore alerted to pay the purchase money to the trustees, whose identities are also discoverable from the deed. He can see what land has passed from whom to whom. He has need for no more. The trust instrument must:

1 Declare the trusts. This refers to the detailed beneficial provisions of the settlement.

2 Appoint the trustees.

3 Contain any power to appoint new trustees.

4 Set out any powers granted in addition to those in the Act.

5 Bear any *ad valorem* stamp duty which is normally carried by a conveyance.

Some of the information is common to both instruments, and in these cases the vesting instrument is merely recording something effected by the trust instrument.

Figure 9.1 might illustrate the effects of the sections.

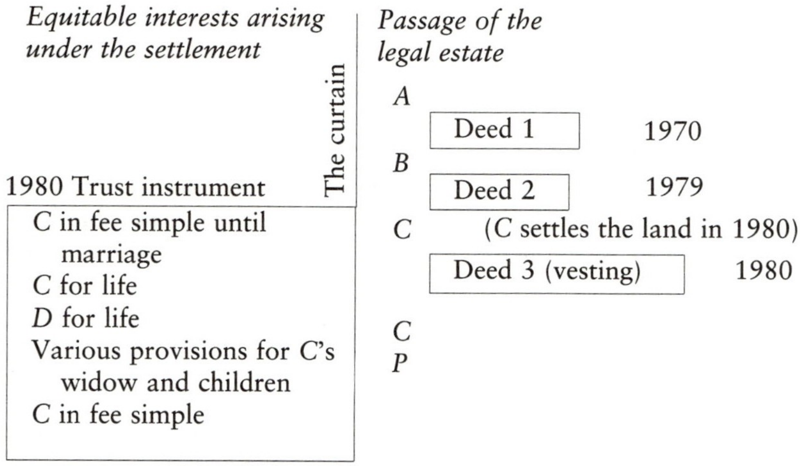

Fig. 9.1

P, a purchaser, now wishes to buy the settled land from C, the tenant for life. He will require proof of title from a root at least 15 years old. This root will be provided by the conveyance of 1970, which was before the settlement. The title is traced in the ordinary way by inspection of deeds 1, 2 and 3. The settlement provisions are bypassed and overreached on sale, so that the trust instrument is not seen. Deed 3 announces the existence of the settlement because it is a vesting deed, so that *P* pays the purchase money to the trustees named in it, or to their successors.

Absence of vesting instrument

The Act had to provide sanctions if the requirement that all settlements must be created by two instruments was to be observed. These are provided by s 13, known as 'the paralysing section', although, as we have already seen, s 4 prevents the legal estate passing in cases where it is not obeyed. Section 13 enacts that once a tenant for life or statutory owner has become entitled to have a vesting instrument executed in his favour, then, until this is done, any purported disposition *inter vivos* by any person of the legal estate shall operate only as a contract for valuable consideration to carry out the transaction after the vesting instrument has been executed. In short, no legal estate passes; but there are the following exceptions to the provision:

1 Personal representatives may pass the legal estate even if a principal vesting instrument was not executed in favour of the person entitled. So if C, above, had created the settlement only by one instrument, and then died, his personal representatives would nevertheless be able to deal with the land.

2 If a person purchases the legal estate without notice that the tenant for life or statutory owner has become entitled to a vesting instrument, then s 13 does not apply. For instance, if C had made his settlement by one instrument and then concealed from a purchaser that he had settled the land, by showing him deeds 1 and 2 only, the purchaser would take the legal estate (Law of Property (Amendment) Act 1926 Sched). The language of s 13 is not really satisfactory here, because in referring to a purchaser of *the legal estate*, it presupposes the exception which the section itself created.

3 If the settlement has ended before a vesting instrument has been created, s 13 does not apply. In *Re Alefounder's Will Trusts* [1927] 1 Ch 360 it was held that a tenant in tail in possession, with no prior trusts or incumbrances which could independently keep the settlement alive, could, on disentailment, dispose of the land, although he had obtained no vesting deed.

4 Where land is settled land merely because it is subject to family charges – it has already been seen that the land may be conveyed, still subject to the charges, as if it were not settled land (Law of Property (Amendment) Act 1926 s 1).

Where an *inter vivos* settlement is attempted by a single document, this document becomes the trust instrument. The general effect, therefore, of s 13 is not to invalidate a settlement, but to immobilise it until it has been regularised by the execution of a vesting instrument. However, a settlor who has lapsed in this way cannot correct his own mistake. Under s 9, it is the trustees who must then execute the deed.

The curtain principle

A purchaser of a legal estate in settled land cannot, with a few exceptions, demand to see the trust instrument (s 110(2)). Furthermore, he is bound to assume that the facts recited in the vesting deed are correct, although the Act provides no solution to the problems which might arise if they are not. The exceptions under which a purchaser may look behind the curtain include the case of the imperfectly constituted settlement which was originally created *inter vivos* by a single deed. Here the purchaser may look at the trust instrument to make sure that the corrective vesting deed is faithful to the original act of settlement, which, though formally incorrect, is the authentic record of the transaction.

Subsequent transfer of the legal estate within the settlement and at the end of it

The essential difference between an ordinary conveyance and a vesting deed is simply that the latter, by showing the existence of a settlement, flashes a warning sign to prospective purchasers. Since such a warning is necessary throughout the subsistence of the settlement, then when one life tenant gives way to another, the legal estate must be passed to the next person entitled by an instrument which continues to transmit this warning, namely, by a further vesting instrument. We must see how, and on what occasions, this need arises (see s 7).

1 *Death of a life tenant.* The legal estate devolves upon the special personal representatives, who are the trustees of the settlement under the Administration of Estates Act 1925 s 22, and when required, they must convey it to the next person entitled, either by vesting deed or vesting assent.

2 *Termination of life tenant's interest before death.* An example would be if, under a settlement upon '*A* for life until he marries, then to *B* for life with remainder in fee simple to *C*', *A* married, thereby ending his beneficial interest. The settlement, of course, continues, and *A* must convey the legal estate to *B* by a vesting deed.

3 *Minor reaching full age.* During his minority, a life tenant cannot hold a legal estate. When he reaches full age, the person in whom it is vested, usually the statutory owner, must convey it to him by the appropriate vesting instrument.

4 *Person of full age absolutely entitled.* An example would be when, under a settlement on '*A* for life, remainder to *B* in fee simple', *A* dies. Provided that there are no charges, powers of charging or other limitations, the settlement ends, for *B* is beneficially entitled to the fee simple absolute in possession. In this case, the legal estate vests in the general personal representatives of the deceased, and not in the trustees as special personal representatives (*Re Bridgett and Hayes' Contract* [1928] Ch 163). They must now convey the land to the person entitled by an ordinary conveyance or assent, and not by a vesting instrument. Since the land can now be dealt with outside the terms of the Settled Land Act, the warning sign to purchasers is, so to speak, turned off. The same is true if the person last entitled is entitled as a trustee for sale, personal representative or otherwise.

Requirement of deed of discharge

It will be explained later that although the tenant for life holds the legal estate, he cannot dispose of it just as an absolute owner can, but only as laid down in the Act (s 18). Furthermore, purchase money must be paid to the trustees and not to the life tenant. The vesting deed makes a purchaser aware of this. We have seen how, when a settlement ends on a death, the legal estate is transmitted to the person entitled by an ordinary assent, and this does not mention trustees. The purchaser may then assume that the person holding that legal estate owns it absolutely and not upon trust (s 110(5)). The same rule applies if the settlement ends with an ordinary conveyance; where land is settled on *A* for life until marriage, then to *B* in fee simple, and *A* marries. *B*'s title will derive from an ordinary conveyance from *A*. In such cases, the inhibiting effect of the last vesting instrument is thereby cancelled. Similarly, if a settlement ends before a vesting deed has been executed, the legal estate may be freely dealt with, because there is no vesting instrument to inhibit dealing (*Re Alefounder's*, p 187).

In some cases, however, even when a settlement has ended, the last document of title is a vesting instrument; an example being if land stood limited to *E* in tail in possession and there were no prior interests existing but a vesting deed has been executed in *E*'s favour. If *E* now barred the entail, the settlement would be at an end. Yet, since the land is still subject to a vesting deed, s 18 makes any dispositions subject to the stringent terms of the Act, including the necessity of paying the purchase money to the trustees. The person absolutely entitled may require the trustees to execute a *deed of discharge*, which has the result of cancelling the restraining effect of the vesting deed by declaring that all the trusts are discharged (s 17). He may then deal with the land as an ordinary absolute owner and the deed of discharge will be proof of this to a purchaser.

Duration of settlements

The Administration of Estates Act 1925 s 3 (as amended by the Law of Property (Amendment) Act 1926 s 7) hardly adds anything new to s 1, which defines a settlement, but emphasizes that not until the final wisp of its tail has disappeared is the settlement over. It enacts that land remains settled so long as:

1. any limitation, charge, or power of charging under the settlement subsists, or is capable of being exercised; or

2. the person who, if of full age, would be entitled as beneficial owner to have the land vested in him for a legal estate is an infant, provided in either case that under the terms of the settlement a trust for sale has not come into operation. If land has been settled on *A* for life, then to *B* for life, then to *C* in fee simple with a power given to *X* and *Y* to charge the land in favour of the widow of *B*, and *A* and *B* have both died, then, even though *C* is of full age, the power given to *X* and *Y* keeps the settlement alive.

Ultra vires transactions

Although the life tenant or statutory owner holds the legal estate, he holds it as trustee. Unlike a person who owns it beneficially for himself alone, he cannot deal with it as he wishes, but only as authorised by the Act, unless wider powers are given under the settlement or by the court. In short, he is subject to the *ultra vires* rule. Section 18 defines his position, where the land is still subject to a vesting instrument and the trustees have not been discharged.

1 Any disposition not authorised by the Act or other statute or made under additional powers mentioned in the vesting instrument 'shall be void' except for the purpose of disposing of his equitable interest.

2 If capital money is payable in respect of a transaction, the transaction only takes effect if it is paid to or by the direction of the trustees, or into court. Notwithstanding anything to the contrary expressed in the settlement, such payment shall not be to less than two trustees unless a trust corporation has been appointed.

These restrictions do not affect the right of personal representatives to deal with the land for the purposes of administration, or the right of a person who has become absolutely entitled at the end of a settlement to have the land conveyed to him. The relationship between ss 13 and 18 is as follows. Section 13 prevents, with a few exceptions, any dealings at all with the legal estate until a vesting instrument has been executed. Section 18 prevents any dealings with the legal estate beyond the limits authorized by statute or by the settlement, even when a vesting deed has been executed. Section 13 places a muzzle upon the goat so that he cannot graze at all. Section 18 fixes a tether on him which confines him even when that muzzle is off. The extent of his pasture will be described in the next section.

The operation of s 18 is well illustrated by *Weston* v *Henshaw* [1950] Ch 510. *G* sold land to *F*, his son, who later sold it back to *G*. *G* then settled it upon *F* for life, then to *F*'s son, *S*. *F* then purported to mortgage the land to *M*. He presented himself not as a tenant for life, who can mortgage the settled land only for the purposes mentioned in the Act, but, by concealing all the documents of the settlement and the deed of conveyance from himself to *G*, as absolute beneficial owner, which of course he once had been. His motive was to raise money for his own purposes. After his death, the question arose whether the mortgage to *M* was good as against *S*, both of whom were innocent of the fraud. It was held that the mortgage was void as against *S*. The fact that *F* could show a deed which once vested the land in him absolutely was a matter of mere history and no longer entitled him to deal with the land at all, because it had since been reconveyed to *G*. His only power to dispose of a legal estate in the land, therefore, was by virtue of his status of tenant for life under the settlement. Since, however, his purpose was not one of those listed in the Act for which a life tenant may deal with the legal estate, but his own personal purpose only, the mortgage was void under s 18. The doctrine of the purchaser of the legal estate without notice is not in point in such cases, because the legal estate itself does not pass at all. It should be noted that this situation can arise only in relation to unregistered land. (See 1991 Conv 601.)

The powers of the tenant for life

The extent of the life tenant's powers must now be discussed. These rules confining his powers of dealing with the legal estate do not affect his right to dispose of his beneficial interest. This he can do in any way he wishes, because it is his very own and not held upon trust for anyone else.

As a safeguard against abuse of his powers, the tenant for life must, before exercising most of his powers, give notice to the trustees (*Wheelwright* v *Walker (No 1)* (1883) 23 ChD 752), and in a few cases he must obtain the permission of the trustees or a court order. Where notice is necessary it must be given by a registered or recorded delivery letter to at least two trustees, or all of them if there are more than two, or a trust corporation, and to the solicitor to the trustees if known, at least one month before the transaction or the contract for it. A person dealing in good faith with the tenant for life is not concerned to enquire whether such notice has been given (s 101(5)). A general notice that the life tenant intends from time to time to exercise his statutory powers is enough, except in the case of a mortgage or charge. However, the trustees may demand information as to completed or impending transactions (s 101). On the other hand a trustee may, by writing, accept less notice or waive it altogether. In authorising the following transactions, the Act confers powers, not duties, so that if there are joint life tenants, one life tenant cannot, at least in the absence of bad faith on the part of the other, insist upon a transaction against the wishes of the other (*Re 90, Thornhill Road, Tolworth* [1970] Ch 261).

It is not the function of a textbook concerned with general principles to reprint statutory provisions. Signposting only of these powers will be given here therefore. What must be emphasised is that the powers authorised by the Act can only be exercised to the extent and in the manner allowed by the Act. The tenant for life can exercise most of the powers of an absolute owner of land but only in the way permitted by the Act. These powers include sale (ss 38–40); exchange (ss 38 and 40); leasing (ss 41–48); acceptance of leases (s 53); mortgaging (s 71); granting options (s 51); improvement of settled land (ss 83–89, Sched 3); investment of capital money (ss 75 and 73) and *see* also the Trustee Investments Act 1961 and some minor powers.

Enlargement of powers

We shall see that the life tenant's statutory powers cannot be inhibited in any way. They can, however, be increased in two ways:

Under the settlement

The Administration of Estates Act 1925 s 109 provides that powers wider than or additional to those conferred by the Act may be granted to the tenants for life, and when the settlement authorises such greater powers, they are exercisable as if they were conferred by the Act. Furthermore, any power, other than a power of appointment or revocation, which the settlement attempts to give to the trustees or any other person, whether or not provided for in the Act, becomes exercisable by the life tenant or statutory owner (s 108(2)). If, for instance, powers of mortgaging, whether or not for one of the purposes authorised by the Act, were in terms conferred upon the trustees by the settlement, they would be exercisable by the life tenant.

Under an order of court

The Administration of Estates Act 1925 s 64 empowers the court to authorise the life tenant to carry out any 'transaction', not being one which is authorised by the Act or the settlement, concerning the settled land or other land, if, in its opinion, it would be for the benefit of the settled land or the persons interested under the settlement, provided that it is a transaction which could validly be effected by an absolute owner.

The section, as amended, gives a wide meaning to the word 'transaction', so that besides its more obvious meanings such as leasing, it includes a covenant, an application of capital money, a purchase and any compromise or other arrangement. Its provisions have been used, for instance, to permit a mortgage for the purpose of paying debts incurred in running the estate (*Re White-Popham Settled Estates* [1936] Ch 725). It can even be used to authorise schemes on behalf of persons under a disability or who are unborn, which would change the beneficial interests under the settlement. The motive will frequently be the saving of tax. (See also *Re Simmons' Trusts* [1956] Ch 125). It has, however, been largely overtaken in this role by the Variation of Trusts Act 1958. For a contemporary illustration of the unrestricted interpretation of the word 'transaction' see *Hambro* v *Duke of Marlborough* [1994] 3 All ER 332, which concerned the management of the Blenheim Palace estate by the Marquis of Blandford.

The inviolability of the life tenant's powers

The policy of the Act in choosing the life tenant to exercise the statutory powers, and in making these powers inviolable, is reinforced in several ways.

The Act prevails (s 108)

While nothing in the Act restricts powers given to the life tenant and while the powers in the settlement and in the Act are cumulative, if the Act and the settlement conflict, the Act shall prevail. So if a settlement purports to make the consent of another person necessary before a life tenant or statutory owner can sell, there is a direct conflict between the settlement and the statutory power of sale, and the life tenant may sell without consent (*Re Jefferys* [1939] Ch 205).

Inhibiting provisions void (s 106)

Section 108 above deals with cases where there is an express or overt conflict between the Act and the settlement, but a life tenant might be prejudiced against exercising his powers by the use of indirect provisions in the settlement which dissuade rather than forbid or restrict. If a settlor wished, for instance, to prevent a sale of the settled land, he might provide that on its sale some other benefit given to the life tenant under the settlement should terminate. Section 106 develops the theme set in s 108 and enacts in its first subsection that if any provision is inserted in a settlement:

> (a) purporting or attempting, by way of direction, declaration, or otherwise, to forbid a tenant for life or statutory owner to exercise any power under this Act, or his right to require the settled land to be vested in him;
> or
> (b) attempting, or tending, or intended, by a limitation, gift, or disposition over of settled land, or by a limitation, gift, or disposition of other real or any personal property, or by the imposition of any condition, or by forfeiture, or in any other manner whatever, to prohibit or prevent him from exercising, or to induce him to abstain from exercising, or to put him into a position inconsistent with his exercising, any power under this Act, or his right to require the settled land to be vested in him;
> that provision, as far as it purports, or attempts, or tends, or is intended to have, or would or might have, the operation aforesaid, shall be deemed to be void.

This strong and rather difficult section should be studied with the help of decided cases. In *Re Ames* [1893] 2 Ch 479, a fund was left for the maintenance of the settled land and any surplus income was to be given to the tenant for life, unless he ceased to be entitled to possession of the land, whereupon that fund was to be denied to him. It was held that even after sale of the settled land, he would still be entitled to the income. Otherwise, he might be discouraged from exercising his statutory power by the prospect of losing this benefit. The section strikes at such inhibiting factors even if they involve property apart from the settlement or are expressed in documents outside the settlement. Thus in *Re Smith* [1899] 1 Ch 331 there was a provision in a settlement that, if the land were sold, personalty settled under a different settlement should not go to the life tenant of the land, but to someone else. It was held that the gift over was ineffectual.

The section is often infringed by conditions in settlements that the life tenant's interest shall determine when he ceases to live on the settled land. Clearly the prospect of enjoying no interest in the purchase money could dissuade him from exercising any powers such as the power to sell which must result in his giving up possession. In *Re Simpson* [1913] 1 Ch 277, a leasehold house was bequeathed to *W* during her widowhood, and rents, taxes and repairs were to be paid for out of a general fund by trustees during her occupation. It was held that there was no infringement of s 106, because the fund was from the beginning bestowing a benefit on the land, not on the tenant for life, and therefore was not a deterrent to the exercise of the statutory powers, because *W* would suffer no direct loss on a sale of the property. The fact that the provision of the fund in the first place might obliquely deter her from selling because in her new home she would have to pay her own outgoings did not invoke the section.

This distinction made by the judge may perhaps be further explained by remarking that all the settlor did was to leave her a desirable property which she might be reluctant to leave. If this had been a transgression of the section, it might have been argued with equal strength that the grant of a life tenancy in a house so beautifully situated and appointed that a person would never wish to move from it would also infringe it. A leading modern case which discusses this and other decisions is *Re Aberconway's Settlement Trusts* [1953] Ch 647. In all such cases, however, if the life tenant decides to leave the property for some reason other than that he wishes to exercise his statutory powers, the forfeiture condition is effective and his interest ends (*Re Trenchard* [1902] 1 Ch 378). The rather cynical moral to be drawn by a life tenant who is subject to such a condition and who, while not wishing in any case to reside on the settled property, yet wishes to retain a live interest in the purchase money, is that he should exercise the statutory power of sale.

To the extent that a provision deters exercise of the statutory powers, it is an illegal determining factor, whether employed in a condition subsequent or in the delineation of a determinable interest. Such illegal conditions were dealt with in Chapter 5, but it may be added here that its illegality does not cause a determinable interest to fail, as illegal terminating events usually do.

A life tenant cannot relinquish his powers (s 104)

A life tenant cannot assign or release his powers or contract not to exercise them. Even when he assigns his beneficial interest, or when assignment of his interest occurs by operation of law, it is he and not the assignee who may exercise them. Only in three exceptional cases do they become exercisable by someone else. These are dealt with below. If the assignment of the interest occurred after 1925, no consent of the assignee is needed. If the assignment so provides, or if it takes effect through bankruptcy and the trustees have notice of this, the assignee's consent is required for the application or investment of capital money affected by the assignment, unless the investment is to be in trustee securities. Notice of intended transactions must be given to the assignee unless otherwise provided in the assignment. On sale of the land, the rights of the assignee are transferred to the purchase money just as the life tenant's rights would have been if he had not transferred his interest. The exceptional cases where the statutory powers cease to be exercised by the life tenant are as follows:

1 *Surrender of life tenant's interest to next remainderman* (s 105). When the life tenant's interest has been assured, with intent to extinguish it to the next person entitled under the settlement (see *Re Maryon-Wilson's Settlements* [1969] 3 All ER 558), the powers become exercisable as if he were dead. In *Re Shawdon Estates Settlement* [1930] 2 Ch 1, the trustee in bankruptcy

sold a life tenant's beneficial interest to the next remainderman and it was held that there had been such an assurance. Indeed, the language of the section is in the passive voice, so that the assurance need not be by the life tenant, and the intention to extinguish need only be that of whoever assigns. Accordingly, he has to execute a vesting deed in favour of the remainderman.

2 *Tenant for life a mental patient.* In this case, the powers may be exercised by the life tenant's Receiver under the provisions of the Mental Health Act 1959.

3 *Court order under s 24.* If the life tenant has by reason of bankruptcy, assignment, incumbrance or otherwise ceased, in the opinion of the court, to have a substantial interest in his estate or interest in the land or part of it, and either has unreasonably refused to exercise any of the statutory powers, or consents to an order under the section, the court may, on the application of anyone interested in any part of the land affected, make an order authorising the trustees to exercise any of the powers in the name and on behalf of the life tenant, either generally or in such way or for such period as it thinks fit.

While the order is in force, the life tenant must not exercise his powers, but a person dealing with him is not affected unless it is registered under the Land Charges Act 1972 (s 6), or, in the case of registered land, by a notice or caution. The legal estate and the powers remain vested in the life tenant, for the words of the section merely forbid and do not disable him. The combinations of factors which will satisfy the section should be carefully noted. Thus, even a deplorable failure to exercise his powers is not enough. He must also have ceased to have a substantial interest in the land and either unreasonably refused to exercise the powers or consented to an order. (*See* generally *Re Thornhill's Settlement* [1941] Ch 24). Finally, 'substantial interest relates to the right to proprietary enjoyment of the land and not to a concern for its welfare, so that a life tenant who merely neglects or absents himself from the property is no candidate for the section for those reasons.

Legal estate remains in life tenant even on bankruptcy (s 103)

Even though his beneficial interest may be taken in bankruptcy, the legal estate of a life tenant does not vest in the trustee in bankruptcy as long as the settlement subsists. This is a further illustration of the general inviolability of his statutory powers.

The life tenant as trustee (s 107)

This section enacts that a life tenant or statutory owner, in exercising his statutory powers, shall 'have regard to the interests of all parties entitled under the settlement' and 'be deemed to be in the position and to have the duties and liabilities of a trustee for those parties'.

Two views have been expressed as to the extent to which the section enables the court to examine the motives of a life tenant in exercising his statutory powers. The first favours an objective view. Provided that the terms of the Act are obeyed in such matters as obtaining the best price reasonably obtainable on a sale, the court cannot inquire into motives, which might even be malicious. To take an example, if the life tenant wished to sell, in order to thwart the remainderman who he knew was anxious to enjoy the land *in specie*, the court could not interfere, provided that the transaction was properly carried out (*Wheelwright* v *Walker (No 1)* (1883) 23 ChD 752, per Pearson J). The weakness of this view is that s 107 is just as much part of the Act as are the more specific sections regulating the exercise of the powers and its language seems capable of supporting the second view.

This view is that the life tenant must consider all interests, whether they are pecuniary or sentimental, and mere compliance with the more particular statutory obligations is not in itself enough. This would allow the court to make a more subjective approach to a life tenant's decisions. Perhaps the two views may be compromised. Both accept that, to whatever extent the interests of other beneficiaries must be considered, once they have been considered they may be overridden by the life tenant, although it could be argued that the beneficiaries may thus find themselves at the mercy of an autocrat.

The operation of the section may be illustrated by *Middlemas* v *Stevens* [1901] Ch 574, where a woman, entitled for life until her remarriage, proposed to grant a lease to her intended husband. She was restrained by an injunction on proof that her sole purpose was to ensure that she could continue to live in the property after her marriage. Where the life tenant wishes the statutory powers to be exercised in favour of himself in his private capacity, for example where he wishes to buy the settled land, special provision is made so that his trusteeship does not place him in an ambivalent position. Section 68 enacts that in such cases the trustees shall have all the powers of the life tenant in negotiating and completing the transaction (see *Re Pennant's Will Trusts* [1969] 2 All ER 862).

Protection of purchasers (s 110)

The Act has greatly facilitated dealings with settled land, but of course such transactions are subject to more rules than dispositions by an ordinary absolute owner. The purchase price must be the best reasonably obtainable, capital money must be paid to trustees and the obligations regarding vesting instruments and notice must be obeyed. Such complications might well deter a person from buying settled land if the Act did not exonerate him from establishing whether they had all been observed. Otherwise, he might be placed in a false position. For example he can hardly be expected to ensure that the best price reasonably obtainable is paid, since his purpose is clearly to acquire the land as cheaply as possible. Section 110, therefore, provides as follows:

1 On any disposition, a purchaser dealing in good faith shall, as against all the beneficiaries, be conclusively taken to have given the best price, rent, or other consideration reasonably obtainable by the life tenant, and to have complied with all the requisitions of the Act (s 110 (1)). The subsection applies even though the purchaser does not realise he is dealing with a tenant for life. It applies to executory as well as to completed transactions (*Re Morgan's Lease* [1971] 2 All ER 235). Section 101 more specifically enacts that a person dealing in good faith with the life tenant is not concerned with the question whether notice of an intended transaction has been given to the trustees.

2 With some exceptions, mentioned earlier in this chapter, the purchaser of a legal estate may not call for the trust instrument, and is entitled to assume that statements made in the vesting instrument are correct.

3 If a conveyance or assent relating to land formerly settled does not state who are the trustees, a purchaser of the legal estate may assume that the person in whom it was thereby vested was entitled to the land free of the settlement, and that the facts in the conveyance are correct.

Although this is, in the ordinary case, a reassuring section to a purchaser, it operates on the assumption that every statement is correct. It does not provide for cases where mistakes or misrepresentations are made, such as where the person stated to be life tenant in the vesting deed, although originally entitled, has ceased to be life tenant (see Megarry and Wade, *The Law of Real Property* (3rd edn) p 315 and 22 Conveyancer 78).

The duties of Settled Land Act 1925 trustees

The various duties of the trustees have been mentioned from time to time in this chapter. It may be convenient to collect them at this point for appreciation, but without further comment:

1 to receive capital money;

2 to receive notice of transactions;

3 to consent to certain transactions;

4 to execute deeds of discharge;

5 to act as statutory owner;

6 to negotiate transactions when a life tenant takes a disposition of the settled land;

7 to exercise the statutory powers in the name of the life tenant under s 24;

8 to act as special personal representatives;

9 to execute vesting deeds in imperfectly constituted settlements;

10 to oversee the settlement and to intervene in cases of illegality or where responsible initiative is desirable, as for instance under s 24 (see, however, s 97).

Overreaching of interests (s 72; see also Law of Property Act 1925 s 2)

The meaning of overreaching has already been explained. It must now be explained in more detail what interests can be overreached when a life tenant completes a transaction under the Act, whether by way of sale, mortgage, lease or other disposition. The broad policy is to overreach all the beneficial interests under the settlement and a few others arising independently of it where they lose nothing by being expressed in money. The following interests are overreached:

1 'All the limitations, powers, and provisions of the settlement and all estates, interests and charges subsisting or to arise thereunder', with the following exceptions:
   (a) legal estates and charges by way of legal mortgage prior to the settlement;
   (b) legal estates and charges by way of legal mortgage created for securing money actually raised at the date of the disposition by the life tenant;
   (c) all leases, easements, profits or other rights which are at the date of the disposition binding on the successors in title of the life tenant and protected by registration, if registrable.

2 Limited owners' charges, general equitable charges and certain annuities, whether arising under the settlement or prior to it, and whether or not they are registered.

An example may illustrate the working of the section:

1970 – *O*, absolute owner of land, creates a general equitable charge, such as an equitable mortgage not protected by deposit of deeds in favour of *A*.
1980 – *O* creates a restrictive covenant in favour of *B*.
1982 – *O* settles the land upon *C* for life and *D* in fee simple in remainder.
1987 – *C*, under statutory powers, creates a lease in favour of *E*.
1991 – *C*, under statutory powers, sells the land to *P*.

The interests of the following will be overreached: *A* under 2 above; *C* under 1; *D* under 1. The interests of the following will not be overreached: *B* under 1(c); *E* under 1(c); so that *P* will not be entitled to occupy the land during the lease, but will be entitled to receive the rent from *E*.

The strict settlement in modern times

The strict settlement has lost most of its attractions as a means either of family endowment or of ensuring that a particular landed estate should remain in the ownership of members of one family. Its role has largely been taken up by the settlement by way of trust for sale. Modern tax legislation has been partly the cause of decline in the first of these purposes, and, as we have seen, the statutory powers given to the life tenant might often frustrate the latter. Ironically, it is easier to ensure that land remains unsold by creating a settlement by way of trust for sale, for the persons holding the legal estate may in that case be instructed to obtain consents before selling land: this will be explained below. This obligation cannot, of course, be imposed upon a life tenant under a strict settlement, even though he might be a poor land manager. It must be emphasised that taxation is a crucial issue when family endowment is being contemplated and the type of settlement being selected. Guidance on this must be sought in specialist revenue law texts which are up to date with the most recent budget.

Another disadvantage of the strict settlement is the cumbersome machinery imposed by the Act. These complicated and expensive safeguards might perhaps be expected where a large estate is being settled, but they apply equally to land of the smallest dimensions and testators might be completely unaware that they are creating strict settlements. As remarked at the beginning of his chapter, a simple gift of a cottage to a testator's widow for life and then to his son attracts all the provisions of the Act, including, for instance, those regarding vesting deeds, trust instruments, trustees and deeds of discharge.

Since the only difference at inception between a strict settlement and a settlement by way of trust for sale is that the latter contains a mandate to sell, and since the words used by a settlor might not always make it clear whether such an imperative instruction is being given, there is the possibility of confusion. Such confusion could be very inconvenient, for the two categories are governed by very different rules.

These considerations have led to the suggestion that the two types of settlement ought to be fused, or that the trust for sale should be the only method allowed for settling land (see 54 LQR 576).

The Law Commission has recommended that the present system of strict settlements and settlements by way of trusts for sale should be replaced by a new, single system of trusts, which would also embrace statutory trusts for sale (see Chapter 11). (Law Com No 181, 1989). Surely we hear the death knell of the strict settlement.

SETTLEMENTS BY WAY OF TRUSTS FOR SALE

Nature

If, in a strict settlement, the settlor were to give one additional instruction, namely that the land must be sold, a trust for sale and not a strict settlement would arise. So a simple statement in a will such as 'I wish 'Blackacre' to be sold and its rents and profits until sale, and the proceeds after sale, applied for the benefit of my wife *W* during her life, and then for my son *S* absolutely', creates a settlement by way of trust for sale. This small addition has extremely important results, for a completely different code of rules applies to a trust for sale.

Trusts for sale are wider in their scope than strict settlements, for they can exist even when there is no element of succession in the disposition, nor a minority, nor a family charge in existence. For instance, land can be ordered to be held upon trust for sale for *A* absolutely. Such are the advantages of a trust for sale, that statute has copied from it and imposed some of its basic rules upon certain transactions where there is no express instruction by the settlor to sell. These are called *statutory trusts for sale* and do not concern us here. Those we are now to examine are called *express trusts for sale*, because the sale has been expressly ordered by a settlor. The hallmark of an express trust for sale is simply an imperative instruction by the settlor to sell the land.

The trust for sale came into common use in the nineteenth century. Because it was used by the new rich rather than by the aristocracy, it was known as the *trader's settlement*. When a successful businessman wished to settle his wealth upon his family he would naturally look for some secure and profitable investment wherein his money would be protected against the constant fall in the value of the pound while his family grew up. In those days land satisfied these requirements admirably, for, provided its site was wisely chosen, it was in growing demand in a rapidly advancing industrial society.

The land chosen, however, might differ sharply from that subject to a strict settlement, because the settlor was only interested in its potential value on sale and did not intend that the beneficiaries should live there. It was simply a treasure chest for his wealth and might consist of some very unattractive and undeveloped areas near towns which would soon be ripe for development. Such land would be purchased and conveyed to trustees upon trust that they should sell it and hold the proceeds for the beneficiaries of the trust. This did not oblige the trustees to sell at once. Indeed, such an exercise would have been pointless. The purpose was that they should sell when they considered it profitable to do so.

The usual disposition of interests under a trust for sale is quite different from that under the traditional strict settlement. Since land held on trust for sale is personalty, because of the doctrine of conversion, the entail could not be used in such a trust before 1926; the reason for this being that personalty could not be entailed until that time. Although it is now possible to entail personalty, it is unlikely that anyone would wish to do so under a trust for sale, for the modern approach is to divide the settled property equally between the issue. Under a typical trust for sale there would probably be a determinable interest to *H* until marriage, then to *H* for life, then to his wife *W* for life, if she should survive him, and then absolutely to such of their children or other issue in such shares as *H* and *W* should appoint, or, in default of appointment, to the children equally on reaching a specified age or on marriage. In case there were no children there would be an ultimate limitation to *H*, the settlor.

A device frequently used in trusts for sale is the protective trust, which is a combination of limitations designed to safeguard a family in case the life tenant becomes bankrupt or attempts to alienate his interest. It hinges on the use of the determinable interest. For instance, if property is being settled on a husband, *H*, and his family, *H* would be granted a life interest determinable on his bankruptcy or attempted alienation. In that event, the trustees are given a discretion as to how they will then apply the income during the rest of *H*'s life amongst certain specified beneficiaries, which will include *H* himself, his wife *W* and the children. After *H*'s death the property will probably be limited to pass to *W* for life, if she should survive *H*, and finally to the children or other issue in such shares as *H* and *W* shall appoint, and in default of appointment to the children equally, with ultimate remainder, if there should be no children, to the settlor. The protective nature of this trust may now be appreciated. When a husband is granted the first life interest under a settlement, although the interest is legally speaking entirely his own, it is naturally anticipated that he will maintain his wife and children out of it. There is always the risk, however, that this means of support will be snatched away from the family either by the husband's bankruptcy or by his capitalization of it by a sale. Once a steady income is thus converted into a lump sum there is obviously a danger that it might soon be dissipated, leaving the family without its main source of income for the rest of the husband's life. In a protective trust this cannot happen. Any attempted alienation or a bankruptcy automatically ends his interest, so that there is no longer anything to sell, or anything which can be taken into bankruptcy. Therefore the husband has no longer any property in the trust, but merely the hope that the trustees will from time to time exercise their discretion in his favour. This they will usually do, but it is only the subject matter of each of these individual applications of income which falls into the ownership of the husband. Of course, a person cannot settle his own property upon himself until bankruptcy and then upon another, as this would be contrary to the bankruptcy laws. This was explained in Chapter 5.

The protective trust has been used so frequently that a settlor need not now set out its detailed machinery. If he declares that any periodical payment shall be held on *protective trusts* for any person, the Trustee Act 1925 s 33 now provides a model similar to that described above, the terms of which are incorporated into a trust by such a reference. These terms of course may be varied as the settlor wishes by a contrary provision in the settlement. Trusts of this nature have been used in recent years to save estate duty.

The machinery of trusts for sale

The detailed rules as to the operation of trusts for sale are to be found mainly in statutes, in particular in the Law of Property Act 1925 ss 22–23. The definition of a trust for sale is contained in s 205 of that Act. These detailed rules will be considered later in this chapter. At this point, two of the outstanding features of a trust for sale must be considered. Throughout the remainder of this chapter, references to sections will be from the Law of Property Act 1925, unless otherwise stated.

The legal estate is held by trustees

The settlor constitutes the trust by conveying the legal estate to trustees who are instructed to hold it upon trust for sale and to give effect to the beneficial interests described. The legal estate remains with the trustees throughout the trust. There is no provision, as there is in the case of strict settlements, requiring or allowing a life tenant to hold it. In practice, the trust has always been created by two instruments, the one conveying the land to the trustees stating that it must be held on the trusts which are declared in a second instrument. This second deed contains the beneficial interests. The advantage in this is that since the trust envisages the satisfaction of these interests out of the proceeds of sale, and since they therefore do not concern a purchaser, they do not appear in the documents of legal title. Conveyancing is thus simplified. It was this practice in trusts for sale which provided the example for the introduction of vesting deeds and trust instruments in the case of strict settlements under the Settled Land Act 1925, but strangely there is still no statutory provision that a trust for sale shall be constituted by two instruments.

The fact that in strict settlements the legal estate must be vested in the life tenant, whereas in trusts for sale it must be vested in the trustees for sale, provides just one of the several important reasons why the two categories must be sharply distinguished. Since it remains with the trustees in the case of trusts for sale, the death of life tenants or the cessation of their interests calls for no transfers of the legal estate. Conveyancing is thus facilitated.

The doctrine of conversion applies

Under the principle that equity treats that as done which ought to be done, the interests of the beneficiaries are considered to be interests in the purchase money from the very creation of the trust, even before the land is sold (see *Irani Finance Ltd* v *Singh* [1970] 3 All ER 199, but distinguish *National Westminster Bank Ltd* v *Allen* [1971] 2 QB 718). The settlement therefore is one of personalty. This is known as the doctrine of conversion and will be explained in Chapter 11.

We shall see later that when the trustees eventually sell the land the purchaser takes it free from the interests of the beneficiaries. In the case of strict settlements this process is known as overreaching because these interests are transferred from land to money. In the case of trusts for sale, however, it is hardly correct to use this expression because, since the interests are in money from the beginning, there is no such transference and therefore no overreaching in the real sense. The purchaser takes the land free of the interests because they never affected the land at all. Nevertheless the fact that the result, if not the cause, is the same in both cases has led to the somewhat improper use of the term 'overreaching' even in the case of trusts for sale.

The definition of a trust for sale (s 205(1)(xxix))

Although the distinguishing feature of an express trust for sale is the instruction to sell, we must now take a much closer look at the nature of this obligation by examining the definition in the Act, which enacts that a trust for sale in relation to land means:

> An immediate binding trust for sale, whether or not exercisable at the request or with the consent of any person, and with or without a power at discretion to postpone the sale.

Some of the elements of this definition must now be discussed.

Trust for sale

As is sometimes unfortunately the case in the 1925 legislation, this definition attempts to describe something by reference to itself. Leaving that aside however, the word 'trust' means that there must be a duty to sell as opposed to a mere power. Unless the very phrase 'trust for sale' is used by the settlor, the matter is one of construction and the whole instrument must be examined to discover whether he was issuing an imperative instruction to sell. The difficulty will be most commonly met in home-made wills, because few testators even know that there is such a thing as a trust for sale. A person making a will might vaguely feel that a sale of certain property would be wise, but perhaps is not even sure himself. He might therefore write in his will: 'I think it would probably be a good idea if "Blackacre" were sold' or "Blackacre" is a valuable property; sell it if you think fit'. In short it might sometimes be difficult to decide whether a duty is being imposed.

The Act does assist in just one case of difficulty of interpretation and that is where the settlor leaves the scales so equally balanced that it would, without such help, be impossible to decide whether a duty is conferred. Section 25(4) enacts that in instruments coming into force after the Act 'a trust either to retain or sell land' shall be construed as a trust for sale, though with power to postpone the sale.

Immediate

The fact that the trust for sale must be immediate does not mean that there must be a duty to sell the land immediately, for, as we shall see, there may still be a trust for sale when there is power to delay sale, or even when consents have to be obtained before sale. It means that the mandate to sell is presently operative and capable of exercise, even though some person may have the discretion to delay it, and is not merely to arise at some future date. If land is settled upon *A* for life, then upon trust for sale, with *X*'s consent, for *B* for life, and then to *C* in fee simple, there is a strict settlement followed by a future trust for sale (*Re Hanson* [1929] Ch 96). The strict settlement persists throughout *A*'s life because during that time there is no duty to sell, only a power to do so under the Settled Land Act 1925. The legal estate must therefore be vested in *A*. The terms of settlement clearly show, however, that on *A*'s death the duty to sell arises. At this point, the trust for sale becomes 'immediate' so as to satisfy the definition. This is so despite the need for *X*'s consent, which might indeed be long delayed. After *A*'s death the legal estate must therefore be vested in the trustees for sale.

Thus the trust for sale is immediate if the duty to sell is presently exercisable apart from the power to delay given to any persons.

Binding

This word has given rise to conflict of opinion among judges and writers. Probably the word was inserted to emphasise the mandatory character which a trust for sale must possess, so as to distinguish it from cases where a mere power of sale is given. Some have been unable to accept this natural interpretation because, since the word 'trust' itself imports imperative duty, the word would become mere surplusage (see *Re Leigh's Settled Estates* [1926] Ch 852; *Re Parker's Settled Estates* [1928] Ch 247; Megarry and Wade, *The Law of Real Property* (4th edn)). Yet the 1925 legislation, masterly though it is, contains many superfluous words and phrases. Furthermore, if it had been intended to bear the meaning that some judges have given it, the legislature would surely not have allowed this one frail and somewhat ambiguous word to stand alone. It would have been out of character with the Act, which is not self-consciously concise but mindful of the busy practitioners who have to operate it. Nevertheless, the view persists that a trust for sale does not exist unless there is power to overreach all interests affecting the land. Insofar as this incompetence might be caused by a previous strict settlement, however, the continuance of the latter is secured by the Law of Property (Amendment) Act 1926 s 7, discussed on page 189.

Consents, requests and power to postpone

Provided that there is a duty to sell, neither the need for requests or consents before the duty may be exercised, nor the power to postpone the sale indefinitely, prevent a trust for sale from arising. Thus if land is conveyed upon trust to sell when the consents of *A, B, C, D, E* and *F* have been obtained, and to hold the profits pending sale and the proceeds after it for the benefit of *X* for life and then for *Y* absolutely, there is a presently operative trust for sale even before any consents are given. It is thus possible for a settlor to ensure that a beneficiary in remainder can enjoy the land in specie if he wishes, by making his consent necessary to a sale (*Re Herklot's Will Trusts* [1964] 2 All ER 66). This of course cannot be done in a strict settlement because the life tenant's powers cannot be restricted. The requirement for such a consent may even be implied from the tenor of the instrument.

The power to postpone sale (s 25)

It has just been explained that this is quite compatible with a trust for sale, and this section enacts that this useful power to postpone sale is implied in every trust for sale unless the contrary intention appears. Furthermore, subject to any express directions to the contrary in the instrument, the trustees are not liable in any way for their exercise of this discretion. Neither is a purchaser of a legal estate concerned with any directions regarding postponement of sale.

An example of a contrary intention is provided by *Re Rooke* [1953] Ch 716, where land was devised to trustees with the instruction to sell it 'as soon as possible after my death'. It was held that this prevailed over the trustees' desire to delay sale. Even where there is a power to postpone sale, moreover, the trustees must be unanimous in their decision to exercise it. If only one wishes to sell, then in the absence of bad faith the land must be sold. All must agree before a power may be exercised, whereas one can insist upon a duty being carried out (*Re Mayo* [1943] Ch 302). If a settlor, therefore, wishes to allow one person to delay a sale, he would be advised to make that person's consent necessary.

The power to retain the land unsold for an indefinite period has helped to make the trust for sale a more popular way of settling land than a strict settlement.

Consents to sale (s 26)

It has been explained that the need for prior consents to sale is compatible with a trust for sale. We must now consider whether there are any limits upon the need for consents. When consents are made necessary, they may be the consents of beneficiaries, of trustees, or of persons quite external to the trust. The question of limitation of consents necessary may be considered under two heads.

From the standpoint of the trustees

The rule is that the trustees must obtain all the consents specified, no matter how many in number and how difficult to secure. If this is not done before sale they will be guilty of a breach of trust, and of course will be restrained by the court if the transaction has not been completed. This rule is however relaxed in two instances. First, if a person whose consent is necessary is subject to a disability, or is a minor, then the trustees must obtain a consent of the receiver, if any, in the case of the former and the parent or testamentary or other guardian in the case of the latter. Secondly, if any requisite consent cannot be obtained, 'any person interested' may, under s 30, apply to the court, which may make 'such order as it thinks fit'.

From the standpoint of a purchaser

If the consent of more than two persons is required by the trust, then, in favour of a purchaser, the consent of any two of these will be enough. The same applies if more than two consents are needed for the exercise of any other powers vested in the trustees by statute or otherwise. Furthermore, a purchaser is not concerned at all with the consent of a person who is a minor or under a disability.

Thus, if the consents of *A*, *B*, and *C* are required under an instrument, and *B* is a minor and *C* is a mental patient, the trustees must obtain three consents, namely those of *A*, *B*'s parent and *C*'s receiver. A purchaser, however, needs simply to ensure that *A*'s consent has been given.

Other powers of the trustees besides sale (s 28 (as amended))

The possible need for consents and the power to delay sale will frequently mean that the land will remain unsold for a considerable period of time. It is clear therefore that powers to make interim dispositions of the land less than sale and to manage the property pending sale are desirable. These are generously bestowed upon the trustees, as holders of the legal estate, by the Act.

The trustees have, in regard to both the land and the proceeds of sale, all the powers of a life tenant under the Settled Land Act 1925, together with those of the settlement trustees, including the powers of management exercisable during a minority. The section (which was amended by the Law of Property (Amendment) Act 1926 s 7 and Schedule) incorporates by reference the wide powers dealt with in the previous chapter. These include, for example, leasing, mortgaging and making improvements within the limits described in the Settled Land Act 1925, and all the powers also which a life tenant under a strict settlement could only exercise with the consent of the trustees. Furthermore, the powers of Settled Land Act trustees under s 102 of that Act are available to trustees even though no minority exists, whereas under a strict settlement they are only exercisable where there is a minority. Such powers include entering into possession and cutting timber, rebuilding and repairing property and continuing the working of mines and quarries which have usually been worked.

These powers must be exercised with the consents of any persons whose consents would be required for a sale of the land, and presumably the same provision for vicarious consents and the relaxations in favour of purchasers also applies. With strict settlements, the powers are capable of enlargement under statute. First, it was held in *Re Simmons' Trusts* [1956] Ch 125 that the incorporation of Settled Land Act powers included the power to seek a court order under s 64 of that Act. The wide powers given by this section, which even enable the court to adjust beneficial interests, have been considered in connection with strict settlements. Second, a further provision is available in the case of trusts for sale which does not apply to strict settlements, but which, however, does not countenance variation of beneficial interests. This is the

Trustee Act 1925 s 57, under which the court may authorize the trustees to carry out a wide range of transactions where power to do so is not otherwise available to them, where this is expedient for the trust.

Subject to any express provision to the contrary, all capital money arising from the exercise of these powers must be treated in the same way as proceeds of sale, unless applied for a purpose authorised by the Settled Land Act 1925.

An interesting illustration of the operation of the section is provided by *Re Wellsted's Will Trusts* [1949] Ch 296, where it was held that after trustees for sale had sold the land they could invest the proceeds of sale in the purchase of other land because this was within the powers of the life tenant and trustees under the Settled Land Act 1925 (see ss 75 and 73).

Finally, there remains the question whether these statutory powers may be curtailed in any way by the trust. We have seen that they may be subjected to consents. Such restrictions are valid because the Act says they are. As to other kinds of restrictions, since the trustees are given 'all the powers of a tenant for life . . .', presumably these powers have the same protection in the hands of trustees for sale as they have in the hands of the life tenant under a strict settlement. So the Settled Land Act 1925 s 106 applies, and such other types of restriction are invalid. There is no direct authority on the point, though the problem was touched upon in *Re Davies' Will Trusts* [1932] 1 Ch 530.

Delegation of certain powers by the trustees (s 29)

The Act recognises that the beneficiary presently entitled to the income of the land is likely to take a keen interest in its management. That is why the Settled Land Act 1925 chooses the life tenant to exercise the wide powers contained in that Act. In the case of a trust for sale, some outlet is provided in this respect for the beneficiaries, although the legal estate remains vested in the trustees.

The section enables the trustees, revocably and in writing signed by them, to delegate from time to time to any person of full age, other than a mere annuitant, for the time being beneficially entitled in possession to the net rents and the profits of the land during his life or for any less period, the powers of and incidental to leasing, accepting surrenders of leases and management. When delegated, such powers are exercisable only in the names and on behalf of the trustees delegating the powers, but it is the person exercising the powers, and not the trustees, who is liable for any consequences of their exercise. He is deemed to be in the position of a trustee for this purpose. In the absence of express powers, the trustees could not delegate these powers to a beneficiary under a discretionary trust because his enjoyment of any benefits or even of occupation of land derives not from *entitlement* but from the changeable wish of trustees.

Although these powers may be delegated, there is no obligation for the trustees when they exercise their powers and duties to consult any beneficiaries unless the trust provides that they shall do so.

Satisfaction of the beneficial interests (s 28(2))

Subject to any contrary direction in the trust, the net rents and profits of the land until sale, after keeping down outgoings such as repairs, are to be applied in the same way as income from investments would be payable after a sale of the land. If, however, some transaction has been carried out under Settled Land Act powers and this has produced capital money, such proceeds must be treated as capital.

If all the potential beneficiaries are of full age and capacity and have become absolutely entitled to the property, they may decide to put an end to the trust altogether, and direct the trustees not to sell but to convey the land according to their wishes (see s 23). Such a direction may ultimately give rise to a division of the land between the beneficiaries, who will each own a part absolutely, or to a strict settlement. The former would occur if the beneficial ownership became entirely vested in two or more as co-owners. The latter would occur if the persons entitled to the entire beneficial interest were entitled in succession, as, for instance, where *A* had a life interest and *B* the absolute ownership in remainder. In the latter case a vesting deed would be necessary to give *A* the legal estate. The difficulties which might be caused by such an instruction given to trustees, and the solution to them provided by the Act, are dealt with below.

Duration of trusts for sale (s 23)

If a prospective purchaser knew that all the beneficiaries were of full age and capacity he might be unwilling to take a conveyance without the agreement of the beneficiaries in case a direction of the kind described above had been given to the trustees, thus terminating the trust for sale. It is therefore provided that as regards the safety and protection of a purchaser, a trust for sale shall be deemed to continue until the land has been conveyed to or under the direction of the beneficiaries. In short, if the legal title is still in the trustees, purchasers are protected and they may accept this fact at its face value. This however is without prejudice to an order of court restraining a sale.

Enforcement of duties and powers (s 30)

We have seen that the Act gives trustees for sale certain powers. Further powers of giving or withholding consents to sales might also be given to the trustees or other persons by the trust. It is the nature of a power that the person to whom it has been given may decide to exercise or not to exercise it according to his own discretion. In this way it differs from a duty which must be carried out irrespective of a person's private opinion. Nevertheless, a decision not to exercise a power might sometimes have serious effects on the wellbeing of the settlement and there should be some ultimate means of resolving deadlock. This is provided by the section, together also with appropriate machinery for enforcing duties as follows.

If the trustees refuse to sell, or to exercise their powers of management or dealing with the land under the Settled Land Act, or to exercise their powers of delegation under s 29, or, as we have already noticed, any consent cannot be obtained, any person interested may apply to the court, which may make such order as it thinks fit.

Overreaching (ss 2 and 27 (as amended))

Since the interests of the beneficiaries under a trust for sale are, under the doctrine of conversion, interests in the purchase money from the outset, a purchaser of the land takes free of these interests without reference to the doctrine of overreaching. This is so even if the interests appear on the documents of legal title. Section 27 declares that a purchaser of a legal estate from the trustees shall not be concerned with the trusts affecting the proceeds of sale or the rents and profits pending sale. It then provides (as amended by the Law of Property (Amendment) Act 1926 s 7 and Schedule), that, notwithstanding anything to the contrary in the terms of the trust, the proceeds of sale or other capital money shall not be paid to or applied by the direction of fewer than two trustees unless a trust corporation is trustee. This does not affect the right of a sole personal representative to give receipts. If no capital money is involved in a transaction there is need only for one trustee. If a purchaser fails to comply with these provisions he will not take the land clear of the rights of the beneficiaries, although it would be better if the Act had expressed itself more clearly at this point.

There is no power to overreach any interests other than those mentioned above. If, however, the trustees were appointed or approved by the court or are a trust corporation, certain prior interests can be overreached under s 2 (as amended by the 1926 Act s 7 and Schedule). This device, usually called an *ad hoc* trust for sale, is little used. Under the Settled Land Act 1925 *ad hoc* settlements may be created by absolute owners of land for the purpose of overreaching certain equitable interests to which this land is subject. This also is little used. In any case even under *ad hoc* settlements and *ad hoc* trusts for sale certain prior equitable interests can never be overreached.

Apart from the *ad hoc* arrangements under s 2, the *overreaching* effect under a trust for sale is thus less than that under a strict settlement, under which certain prior interests may be affected.

STUDY MATERIAL

Re Morgan's Lease [1971] 2 All ER 235

12 March. UNGOED-THOMAS J read the following judgment. This summons raises the question whether a tenant's option to renew a lease of settled property was varied and was duly exercised and the resulting contract is now enforceable by specific performance.

By a document of 12 November 1960, and described as a lease, David William Morgan purported to demise four rooms on the ground floor of 16 and 18 Pier Street Aberystwyth, to the plaintiffs for the term of seven years from an unspecified day of November 1960, at a yearly rent of £475 exclusive of rates and charges; and he purported to covenant with the plaintiffs that he would, on their written request made three months before the expiration of the term, grant to them a lease for a further term of seven years from the expiration of the original term, and containing the same provisions, with the exception of the covenant for renewal. The document was signed by the parties over a 6d stamp. The plaintiffs had been in possession with another under a 1950 lease to the three of them. That lease expired on 12 November 1960, and thereafter the plaintiffs continued in possession and paid the rent of £475 in accordance with the 1960 document. The rooms are shop premises and at all relevant times the plaintiffs have carried on the business of drapers there.

In March 1962, Mr Morgan died and the legal estate in reversion of the property vested in his daughter, the first defendant, as administratrix of his estate. In August 1965, she executed a vesting assent to herself and the other three defendants on trust for sale. The plaintiffs, in accordance with the provisions of the 1960 document, duly gave notice for the further lease from the expiration of the current lease, i.e. commencing 12 November 1967. Before that date the plaintiffs commenced proceedings in the county court for a new tenancy to avoid losing the protection of the Landlord and Tenant Act 1954; but those proceedings were stayed pending the decision of this action.

Apart from any question of adequacy of rent it is common ground that: (1) the 1960 document is void as a lease, but operated as an agreement for a lease, taking effect as a present demise in equity (*see*, in particular, the Settled Land Act 1925 s 42(1), the Law of Property Act 1925 ss 52(1) and 152(1)); (2) on service of the notice exercising the option, an executory contract arose in accordance with the terms of the option.

Consequently the case turns principally on the Settled Land Act 1925 s 110(1). It provides:

> On a sale, exchange, lease, mortgage, charge, or other disposition, a purchaser dealing in good faith with a tenant for life or statutory owner shall, as against all parties entitled under the settlement, be conclusively taken to have given the best price, consideration, or rent, as the case may require, that could reasonably be obtained by the tenant for life or statutory owner, and to have complied with all the requisitions of this Act.

The questions which arise are: (1) Assuming good faith within the meaning of the subsection, are the plaintiffs, as against the defendants, to be taken to have given the best rent that could reasonably be obtained by the tenant for life? (2) If the answer to (1) is Yes, then have the defendants shown absence of good faith, within the meaning of the subsection, on the part of the plaintiffs? (3) If the answer to (1) is No, (a) with reference to what date is such best rent to be ascertained? and (b) have the plaintiffs proved that the option rent is such best rent at such date?

Three issues arose on the first question. First, whether the section can be relied on only if there is no defect in the transaction apart from insufficiency of rent. The defendants raise this issue on the basis of *Kisch* v *Hawes Brothers Ltd*[1]. In that case a lease granted by a tenant for life was exposed to attack on two grounds under the

---

[1] [1935] Ch 102, [1934] All ER Rep 730

Settled Land Act 1925 s 42, i.e. (1) that it did not reserve the best rent that could reasonably be obtained; and (2) that it did not take effect in possession not later than 12 months after its date. Farwell J at first instance, assumed for the purposes of his judgment that the Law of Property Act 1925 s 152, would defeat the second ground of attack[2]. That left the first ground of attack, and in reply to that the lessee sought to rely on the Settled Land Act 1882 s 54, replaced, with immaterial alterations for present purposes, by the Settled Land Act 1925 s 110. Farwell J observed[3]:

> It is essential, in my judgment, for the defendants to prove that apart from the fact that the lease is to take effect more than twelve months after its date it is otherwise such a lease as Mrs Ramus [the tenant for life] could properly have granted on December 25, 1919, and in this respect s 54 of the Settled Land Act, 1882, does not assist them.

This observation is so compressed as to have caused difficulties. It was made in circumstances in which the lease was, on its face, granted by a tenant for life in contravention of the Settled Land Act 1882, because it was not to take effect in possession not later than 12 months after its date, with the result that the lessee did not satisfy the good faith required by s 54 (now s 110 of the 1925 Act). This appears quite clearly from counsel's submission[4] followed by Farwell J's interlocutory observation. Counsel, in the course of his argument as reported, said[4]:

> . . . the lease granted by Mrs Ramus is invalid, since it is one which was to take effect more than twelve months from its date . . . s 54 of the Settled Land Act, 1882, does not assist the lessee where the lease on the face of it is in contravention of the Act. The defendants say the lease takes effect in equity, and it is for them to show that the rent reserved was the best rent.

Then comes immediately Farwell J's interlocutoty observation[5]:

> The lease of 1919 was a lease which Mrs Ramus could not have granted, and it is on the face of it an invalid lease: the burden of proof is therefore on the defendants.

The interpretation of this case for which the defendants contend was frowned on by Somervell and Romer LJJ in *Davies* v *Hall*[6]. Romer LJ said[7]:

> . . . the tenant could not rely on s 110 of the Settled Land Act 1925 because, as I have already said, it could not be said of him that he was a person acting in good faith, the lease, on the face of it, being an improper one . . . Certainly I do not think that [FARWELL J] was suggesting as a general proposition that where an attack is made on a lease which has been granted by a tenant for life for reasons other than insufficiency of rent, the lessee cannot rely on s 110. In my opinion, he could do so, provided that he had acted in good faith.

I respectfully agree.

---

[2] [1935] Ch at 109, 110, [1934] All ER Rep at 733, 734
[3] [1935] Ch at 109, [1934] All ER Rep at 734
[4] [1935] Ch at 105, 106
[5] [1935] Ch at 106
[6] [1954] 2 All ER 330, [1954] 1 WLR 855
[7] [1954] 2 All ER at 334, [1954] 1 WLR at 861

The second issue on the first question was whether s 110 is only available where the transaction has been completed and is not still the subject of a contract which is executory. The defendants urged that in the clauses of the definition subsection of the Settled Land Act 1925, i.e. s 117(1), the clauses do not, in terms, extend to include or cover an executory contract in the definitions of the words 'lease' or 'disposition' appearing in s 110 (see s 117(1)(x) and (v)), or to include or cover a person who falls short of acquiring an interest in settled land in the definition of 'purchaser' (similarly appearing in s 110) under s 117(1)(xxi). So, if the defendants' submission were correct, the plaintiffs would not, in this case, be within the express words of the clauses defining the words 'lease', 'disposition' and 'purchaser' which appear in s 110(1).

Wilberforce J in *Re Rycroft's Settlements, Rycroft* v *Rycroft*[8] decided that the 'agreement for a lease', included in the definition of 'lease' in s 117(1)(x), meant such an agreement as takes effect in equity as a present demise, to the exclusion of an executory contract for a lease. It appears to me, however, that in accordance with the decision of the Court of Appeal in *London and South Western Ry Co* v *Gomm*[9], and especially from the observations of Sir George Jessel MR[10], the contract created by the exercise of the option would create an assurance of the interest in the property and, subject to good faith, constitute the plaintiff purchasers as persons who acquired an interest in settled land for value and thus fall within the words 'disposition' and 'purchaser' within s 110 (1).

The defendants sought to rely on the past tense appearing in s 110 in 'have given' and 'have complied with' as indications of a transaction that had been completed before the section spoke. But these clauses are not exclusive definitions, and each of the two words 'disposition' and 'purchaser' is described in its clause as a word which 'includes' what is thereafter stated; and the clauses themselves are governed by the introductory words of s 117(1), which provide that the expressions in the clauses have the meanings assigned to them 'unless the context otherwise requires'. Further, 'have given' must, in the context, be capable of including future payment, since a lessee cannot be said to have given the rent not yet due; and 'to have complied with' is capable of referring to having complied with whatever requisitions are applicable as at the date of the occurrence contemplated by the section.

This brings me back to the opening words of s 110(1), and in particular: 'On a sale . . . lease . . . or other disposition'. 'Sale' is not defined by the Act, but in the Settled Land Act 1882 'on a sale' are words which similarly appear in s 54 (corresponding to s 110 of the 1925 Act), and in s 5. Section 5 provided for transfer of incumbrances from settled land sold to settled land retained; and in *Re Knight's Settled Estates*[11] it was indicated that 'on a sale' in that section was not limited to cases where a sale had been made, and could even include a contemplated or intended sale. Certainly it appears to me that the words 'on a' governing sales and other transactions, as in ss 5 and 54 of the 1882 Act, and s 110 of the 1925 Act, do

---

[8] [1961] 3 All ER 581 at 584, [1962] Ch 263 at 268

[9] (1882) 20 Ch D 562

[10] (1882) 20 Ch D at 580, 581

[11] [1918] 1 Ch 211, [1916–17] All ER Rep 662

not merely mean 'after' a sale. If 'after' was meant then it would certainly have been clearer to have said so. 'On a' sale is a vague and wide expression; and presumably deliberately so. It bears, to my mind, a significance approaching more nearly to 'in connection with' or 'on the occasion of' than 'after', and is not limited to a completed sale; and 'on the occasion of' is one of the meanings given by the Oxford English Dictionary for 'on'. 'On a' lease or other disposition would have a corresponding meaning, and would include an executory contract for a lease.

The defendants, however, suggested that s 110 should be narrowly interpreted so as to be limited to completed transactions, on the ground that otherwise it would do what a court of equity would not do in any specific performance action, i.e. treat as best price or rent what was not so; and achieve performance of a contract in breach of a life tenant's trust duty. Words in Fry on Specific Performance[12], were relied on in support of this proposition on specific performance. But those words are cautiously phrased:

> The Court will not generally exercise its extraordinary power in compelling a specific performance, where to do so would necessitate a breach of trust.

Nor do the authorities quoted in support of the proposition in terms fully establish it. I need not and do not dissent from the quoted passage as a general proposition. It is not, however, directed specifically at all to the Settled Land Acts; nor, even more particularly, to the duties of the tenant for life under the Settled Land Act 1925 (or duties under its predecessor). The purpose of the 1925 legislation is, of course, to facilitate dealings in settled land, and it provides a complete scheme for that purpose. The terms of s 110, which I have analysed, the history of the section into which no such limitation as the defendants suggested has been imported by legislation or judgment, the meaning which the section on its face, so it appears to me, carries, and the omission to include such a limitation into a section which forms part of the comprehensive scheme which the Act establishes, convince me that s 110 should not be restricted to completed transactions as the defendants submit.

I come now to the third issue on the first question, whether s 110 only applies if the purchaser knows that the other party to the transaction is a tenant for life. The defendants' submission was founded on *Weston* v *Henshaw*[13]. I will now follow and paraphrase the headnote so far as material for present purposes. In 1921 a father sold certain property in fee simple to his son who, in 1927, sold it back to him in fee simple. By his will made in 1931 the father settled that particular property on his son for life with a remainder over. In 1944 the son charged the property by way of legal mortgage to secure certain advances, the charge reciting that he was seised in fee simple of it, and the schedule to the charge describing it and stating that it had been conveyed in fee simple to him by a conveyance dated 29 July 1921. In an action by the grandson for a declaration that the charge and further charges were void as against him, Danckwerts J observed[14]:

---

[12] 6th Edn, para 407
[13] [1892] 3 Ch 382
[14] [1950] Ch at 519

> I am satisfied, however, that that subsection [i.e. s 110(1)] applies only to a person who is dealing with the tenant for life or statutory owner as such, whom he knows to be a limited owner, and with regard to whom he might be under a duty.

The passage, unfortunately, does not set out the reasoning which led to the conclusion, and I confess to some difficulty in appreciating what was the relevant duty which the person dealing with the life tenant might be under to the life tenant, as contrasted with the limitation which was imposed on the purchaser by the section. Unfortunately, too, *Mogridge* v *Clapp*[15] was not brought to the judge's notice. The headnote of *Mogridge* v *Clapp*[15], so far as I need read it, states:

> In October, 1884, one *H*, purporting to demise as absolute owner (which he believed himself to be), granted a building lease of certain land to the Plaintiff for the term of 99 years. The Plaintiff made no inquiry as to *H*'s title but assumed that he was the absolute owner of the land demised. The Defendant afterwards agreed to purchase the lease of the demised land from the Plaintiff; but, on investigating the title, he discovered that the land had, under a will, belonged to *H*'s deceased wife, and that *H* was only tenant by the curtesy. A tenant by the curtesy has, under s 58(1)(viii), of the Settled Land Act 1882 all the powers of a tenant for life; but the lease, though complying with the enabling sections of the Settled Land Acts, contained no reference thereto; and at its date there were no trustees of the will, to whom the notices, required by s 45 of the Settled Land Act 1882 in the case of a lease by a tenant for life, could be given.

Kay LJ referred to s 54 of the 1882 Act, the predecessor of s 110 of the 1925 Act and said[16]:

> Section 54 provides that on a sale, lease, &c., a purchaser or lessee, dealing in good faith with a tenant for life, shall, as against the parties entitled under the settlement, be conclusively taken to have given the best price or rent 'and to have complied with all the requisitions of this Act'. This section confirms the view that in the case of a lessee dealing in good faith the remedy, if any, of the persons entitled under the settlement for any neglect of the provisions of the Act is to be against the tenant for life in his fiduciary character, not against the lessee, and is not to affect the validity of the lease . . . If the lessee knew that there were no trustees, or that the tenant for life had not given the trustees notice, he might, by accepting the lease under such circumstances, be implicated in the breach of fiduciary duty by the tenant for life. It might be said that he was not dealing then in good faith with the tenant for life. Good faith in that connection must mean or involve a belief that all is being regularly and properly done; and if the lessee has not that belief, it may be said that s 54 of the Act of 1882 does not protect him against an action by other persons entitled under the settlement . . . my present opinion is that if the lease were otherwise unobjectionable it could not be set aside because the lessee knew there were no

---

[15] [1950] Ch 510

[16] [1892] 3 Ch at 400, 401

> trustees . . . it is not necessary to give a decided opinion on this point, because I do not think that the lessee in this case had either knowledge or notice such as to make his acceptance of the lease a dealing not in good faith with the lessor.

Here Kay LJ, sitting in the Court of Appeal with Lindley and Bowen LJJ, seems to me to treat it as self-evident that a person dealing with a life tenant without knowing that he was a life tenant would be entitled to rely on s 110; and, with the greatest respect for the decision in *Weston* v *Henshaw*[17], that is the conclusion to which I would come independently of authority. There is, in the section, no express provision limiting its benefit to a purchaser who knows that the person with whom he is dealing is a tenant for life. On its face it reads as free of limitation and as applicable to a person without such knowledge as to a person who has it. There is a limitation, i.e. that the purchaser must act in good faith; but that limitation reads as applicable to a purchaser with such knowledge as without. So, despite the insertion of the limitation of good faith on the part of the purchaser, there is no insertion of the limitation for which the defendants contend. Thus my conclusion is that s 110 applies whether or not the purchaser knows that the other party to the transaction is tenant for life. That disposes of the first question.

The second question is whether the defendants have shown absence of good faith, within the meaning of s 110(1), on the part of the plaintiffs. The defendants have rightly disavowed any suggestion of dishonesty on the part of the plaintiffs. Quite clearly there was none whatsoever. It is submitted that the plaintiffs knew, in 1960, that the £475 rent provided for in the option was less than was or would be obtainable under a lease in the terms of the option lease. I am, however, satisfied that this is not so for reasons which, I trust, will sufficiently appear from my consideration of question 3 (b) when I deal with the quantum of rent. However, assuming that the defendants' submission so far is correct, they then, on that footing, suggest that it follows that the plaintiffs were not dealing in good faith. But the plaintiffs did not know that the life tenant was a life tenant, and thought that he was absolute owner. Therefore even if they thought that the option rent was or would be less than would be obtainable under a lease on the terms of the option lease, that would clearly not establish any lack of good faith on their part; and if, contrary to my view, knowledge that they were dealing with a person who was tenant for life was required to bring the plaintiffs within s 110(1), then they were not within it and this question does not arise at all.

It follows from the answers to questions 1 and 2 above that the plaintiffs are entitled to rely on s 110, and their option to renew the lease has been validly exercised and is enforceable by specific performance. Question 3, therefore, does not arise, but it may be helpful if I state briefly my conclusions on question 3(a) and deal at greater length with the questions of fact arising on question 3(b).

Question 3(a): at what date is the best rent to be ascertained? In 1887, in *Gas, Light and Coke Co* v *Towse*[18] it was decided that where there was a covenant for renewal in a lease made under a power of granting leases in possession at the best

---

[17] [1950] Ch 510

[18] (1887) 35 Ch D 519

rent, the best rent has to be ascertained as at the date of the new lease made under the covenant, and not at the date of the covenant. As I read the case, it turned on the construction of the power and the best rent to which it referred.

In 1889, the Settled Land Act 1882 was amended to enable any building lease, and any agreement for a building lease, to contain an option, exercisable within ten years, to purchase the land leased at the price fixed at the time of the making of the lease or agreement for the lease, and to be the best price reasonably obtainable. This seems to me to state clearly, in express terms, that the price is fixed at the time of the lease, or the agreement for a lease, and not at the time of the exercise of the option to purchase or of the purchase. The Settled Land Act 1925 s 51 replaces the Settled Land Act 1889 s 2, and extends it to options to take leases whilst preserving the ten year period, and the requirement of best price or, under the 1925 Act, rent 'fixed at the time of the granting of the option'. In *Re Rycroft's Settlements*[19] Wilberforce J held, on the construction of s 90(1)(iii), which empowered the tenant for life to contract to make a lease 'but so that the lease be in conformity with this Act', that it related to executory agreements, but that the lease had to be in conformity with the Act when it came to be granted. This decision was made in accordance with *Gas, Light and Coke Co* v *Towse*[18], to which Wilberforce J referred. It was not concerned with, and did not refer to, s 51 of the 1925 Act, or its predecessor, s 2 of the 1889 Act.

However, it follows from these cases, and the wording of the Settled Land Act 1925 s 90(1)(iii), that an executory contract for a lease can only be made if the lease conforms with the Act in respect of (inter alia) best rent reasonably obtainable when the lease is granted. Section 51, however, deals specifically with options and best price or rent under them, as contrasted with the more general provision of s 90(1)(iii) applicable to executory contracts and the requirements for leases thereunder. For my part, I have little difficulty in reading s 51 apart from, or if need be in the case of options, as prevailing over s 90(1)(iii). It is not difficult to see business considerations which would be to the advantage of those interested under the settlement in thus treating options exercisable subject to the safeguard of a limited period for their exercise. So my conclusion is that the best rent is to be ascertained as at 1960, when the option was granted.

Question 3(b): was the option rent the best rent at 1960? I had the advantage of evidence from two valuers, Mr Griffiths for the plaintiffs and Mr Hackett for the defendants. [His Lordship then reviewed the evidence of the valuers and concluded:] To estimate the best obtainable rent is certainly not free from difficulty, but doing the best I can I, for my part, conclude that £475 in 1960 satisfies the requirement of the Settled Land Act 1925 s 42(1)(ii) as being 'the best rent that can reasonably be obtained, regard being had . . . to the circumstances of the case'.

Order for specific performance.

Extract reproduced by permission of the All England Law Reports.

---

[19] [1961] 3 All ER 581, [1962] Ch 263

QUESTIONS

1 What is the authority of *Weston* v *Henshaw* [1950] Ch 510 in view of *Re Morgan's Lease* [1971] 2 All ER 235?

See Cheshire and Burn's (1982) *Modern Law of Real Property*, Butterworth, (15th edn) p 816.

2 What would be the advantages of merging the categories of the strict settlement and the settlement by way of express trust for sale?

3 Discuss the extent to which the 1925 legislation, as it affected strict settlements, was principally aimed at facilitating conveyancing.

4 John, sole fee simple owner of 1 Railway Crescent, has recently died. His will, drafted without legal advice, states: 'I would like my wife Lucy to stay on at the Terrace for as long as she wishes. After that it shall go to my daughter Isobel'. What are the rights of Lucy and Isobel?

CHAPTER 10

THE RULES AGAINST PERPETUITIES AND ACCUMULATIONS

INTRODUCTION: REASONS FOR THE RULES

The difference between vested and contingent interests

Where Peter, Jane and Hina live there is a tennis court. Some time ago, Peter and Jane were each given a tennis racquet. Hina was promised one if she passed an examination next year. At the moment Peter is playing tennis on the court with a friend. Jane would like to play with her friend also, but since there is only one court she must wait until later in the day. If I ask who owns a tennis racquet Peter and Jane will answer 'yes'. Hina will say 'no'. Now return to land law.

Suppose that land is settled upon Peter for life with remainder for life to Jane and remainder in fee simple to Hina when she marries, with ultimate remainder over. If I ask who owns an interest in the land at this moment Peter and Jane will answer 'yes', and Hina 'no'. It is true that Jane is not entitled to the possession of the land yet, by virtue of that interest, because Peter is now in occupation, but her interest is none the less a present one. She can, for instance, sell or mortgage it to another person, just as surely as she could sell or pawn her tennis racquet, even though there is someone else in possession of the court. Hina, however, has no interest at all in the land at the moment and might never have, in the same way that she has no tennis racquet. In both cases her acquisition of these things depends upon contingencies, namely getting married or passing an examination respectively. A mere prospect of having an interest in land in this way is called a *contingent interest.*

When, in the example given above, Peter dies, Jane's interest comes into, or *vests* in possession. When Hina marries her interest springs into being or *vests* in interest. This is the very nativity of her interest which she now for the first time owns, even though the law has long recognised that even a prospect of an interest is a saleable asset and may be disposed of (LPA 1925 s 4). When the word 'vests' is used without additional words it bears the latter of these two meanings and it will be so used throughout this chapter. In short, *vested* means the opposite of 'contingent', that is free of any conditions precedent to an interest coming into being. It will be explained how vitally important it is to know whether an interest is contingent and that special strict rules apply to such interests; the first task, however, is to learn how to discover whether an interest is contingent or not. In the example above, Hina's interest clearly is so, but in some cases the element of contingency is less obvious.

An interest is contingent unless three requirements are satisfied. First, the identity of the beneficiary must be ascertained. Second, the size of the interest which he is to take must be finally settled. Third, any conditions precedent imposed upon the grant of the interest must have been satisfied. These must now be discussed.

The beneficiary must be identified

It is not enough that the beneficiary is alive. He must be able to show that in every way he satisfies the description of the beneficiary used in the gift. Thus in the case of a grant to 'the survivor of *A* and *B*', neither owns the interest until the other has died. Similarly, if a grant is made to *A* for life with remainder for life to any wife he might marry, the second life interest does not arise until *A* has married even though he plans to marry *B* in a week's time.

The quantum of the interest must be finally settled

Two factors constitute the quantum of an interest in property. First, there is the nature or duration of the interest itself. This is lacking in a limitation such as 'to *A* for such interest as *X* shall appoint'. Not until *X* appoints a particular interest such as a life interest does *A*'s interest vest. Second, although the nature of the interest might be established, it might have to be shared amongst a certain class of beneficiaries. In that case, the size of the share of each will not finally be known until it is known how many persons will make up the class: if a gift is made 'to all the children of *A* equally for life', the size of each share will depend on how many children *A* ultimately has. Not until all his children are born, therefore, does the gift vest in favour of any of them.

Any conditions precedent must be satisfied

An example of this type of contingency was given above in the limitation to Hina in fee simple upon her marriage. The interest remains contingent until that condition is satisfied. Another common example of a condition precedent is the grant of an interest to a person when he reaches a certain age.

A gift might be subject to more than one of these three kinds of contingency. In that case it does not vest until the last of them has been satisfied. Sometimes, however, the one event might accomplish this, as in a grant 'to the first son of *A* to marry'. Here the marriage of a son identifies the beneficiary and fulfils the condition. When several interests follow each other consecutively each limitation must be separately and rigorously tested by applying all the three tests described above. Provided that this is done the diagnosis of a contingent interest is a simple matter.

The problem created by contingent interests

We have seen that in the past when successive interests were created in land a serious problem of inalienability could result because a long time might elapse before there was a person capable of disposing of the fee simple absolute in possession. So far as the land itself is concerned, the problem was solved by providing for the overreaching of those interests and by equipping the life tenant with a power of sale which cannot be fettered.

Overreaching does not eradicate the problem of inalienability; it merely transplants it from the land to the purchase money and the investments which represent it, so that the capital cannot be dealt with by anyone as absolute owner for a very long time, even though it may be dealt with by trustees. The general policy of the law has always been against removing property of any kind from free commerce for too long a period. Some examples of this policy have already been discussed, such as the barring of the entail and the illegality of conditions subsequent which prevent alienation. Before considering a further example which is the subject of this chapter, it must first be shown that where successive interests are created in property it is the contingent rather than the vested interests which cause serious inalienability.

In the case of vested interests the beneficiary is always in being and identified – see the first rule as to vesting discussed above. This means that there is a practical limitation upon the extent to which successive vested interests may be created and, therefore, upon the extent to which the property may be tied up. For instance, if a settlor wishes to keep property within his family for an indefinite time it is not through the grant of vested interests that he can do so. Having granted life interests to his children and such grandchildren as are already living, he has reached the limits to which he can go. If he wishes to grant any interest to unborn persons it follows that they must be contingent interests. That is not to say that there is any numerical limit to the number of vested interests which may be granted; he can give a life interest to *A*, followed by a life interest to *B* and so on successively to *Z*. All these 26 interests are vested; only possession is postponed in 25 of them. But the very fact that they are all given to living people necessarily means that they will all be exhausted in the space of an ordinary lifetime, give or take a few years, for 26 people do not live substantially longer than one or two. Many of them might not live to enjoy their interests in possession, but the application of the three tests clearly shows that even the interest given to *Z* was vested from the beginning.

While vested interests tie property up they cannot do so for a very long time. In the example above, if the ultimate remainder to *Z* had been granted to a living person, the property would have been fully disposable again within a human life span. The use of contingent interests, however, which have no such natural time boundaries, may, if unrestricted, cut deep into the future and tie land up indefinitely. One single example is enough to show this. A settlor might attempt to grant property 'to my son *A* for life, then to his eldest son for life, then to the eldest son of the eldest son of *A for life* . . .' and so on. The first interest to *A* is vested but, if *A* has no son yet, the next and all the following gifts given by reference to the formula of successive eldest sons are contingent because the intended beneficiary is unborn in each case. Such a settlement might delay the final vesting of the property in a beneficiary absolutely for hundreds of years and therefore constitute a most serious problem of inalienability.

The law has developed a rule designed to prevent this, known as 'the rule against perpetuities'. In so doing, it has recognised that settlors justifiably wish to endow their families, and that some kind of compromise as to the limits to which property may be fettered in this way is desirable. Such compromises illustrate that the law 'is not really about law' but is a mere resultant of social and economic forces. Since vested interests do not raise a serious problem of inalienability the rule does not apply to them at all. The rule took many years to develop, but the case of *Cadell* v *Palmer* (1833) 1 Cl&F 372 brought it to maturity. Some of the technicalities of the rule, however, have proved a trap and have caused hardship to beneficiaries. Some of these have been radically dealt with by the Perpetuities and Accumulations Act 1964 so that, although the substance of the rule is still the same, the considerable reforms justify us in referring to the changed law as the 'new rule'. Since the Act applies only to instruments coming into operation after 15 July 1964 (with the exception of two retrospective provisions), the old rule will be still needed for many years to come for assessing the validity of instruments operating before that date. Furthermore, the new reforms are engrafted onto the stock of the old rule, which must be mastered for this reason also. Both rules apply to all forms of property.

The old rule will be first considered; then the new rule will be examined separately, but by reference to it. Finally, the related subject of accumulations will be explained. In 1993 the Law Commission published a consultation paper with a view to the simplification or even abolition of the rule (Law Com No 133). See 1995 Conv 212 for a published response.

In some ways the rule illustrates the worst characteristics of common law jurisprudence in both practice and academy. Its rationale has been pronounced, in the broadest terms, the compromise between individual and family dominion over property and the public interest in its free alienability. In fact its verbal pedantry makes medieval schoolmen appear as free thinkers. For instance, even under the old rule the most preposterous aims could have been legitimated by careful drafting. Thus I might have left all my property to 'the first of my granddaughters to become Queen of Arabia during the lifetime of my last grandson born during my life and twenty one years after his death.' This internalised reasoning has damaged legal studies as a true discipline since it has delayed the realisation that law, of all subjects, is the least exclusive and perhaps even the most 'amateur'. Judicial decisions have favoured economic interests rather than the cultural investment of one generation in the next.

At least one writer of a leading textbook appears to opt for 'strike it down' (Gray, *Elements of Land Law* (2nd edn)).

THE OLD RULE AGAINST PERPETUITIES

The rule

An interest which is capable of vesting later than 21 years after the end of some specified life or lives in being when the instrument creating it came into operation is void. The two main components of the rule must now be analysed. The meaning of the word 'vest' has already been explained.

Life or lives in being

The period allowed by the rule is a compromise based on the ordinary settlement; a lifetime and the period of minority have been familiar working units of time in family affairs. All persons who are alive or conceived when the instrument creating the interest comes into operation are eligible lives in being (see *Long* v *Blackall* (1977) 7 Term Rep 100). A will only comes into operation on the death of the testator, even though it was executed many years before that. Only human beings and not animals or corporations may be lives in being (*Re Kelly* [1932] IrR 255).

Although all persons are eligible to be lives in being, the only people who may be considered in testing the validity of a gift are those who are expressly so designated in the grant, or whose length of life has such a bearing on the time at which the interests of the beneficiaries will vest that they are lives in being by implication; in short, those whose lives validate the gift (*see* 86 LQR 357, at 363). A person who is only casually mentioned in a grant may not be considered as a life in being. On the other hand, a person may be a life in being whether or not he is also a beneficiary under a particular limitation. For the purposes of the rule a conceived child may be treated as a life in being.

There is no limit to the number of lives in being that may be appointed or implied and persons of any age may be chosen, for it has been remarked that a hundred candles lit together will not significantly outlast one single candle. Thus in *Re Leverhulme (No 2)* [1943] 2 All ER 274 under a will coming into operation in 1925, the lives designated were those descendants of Queen Victoria living at the testator's death. These numbered over one hundred. The appointment was held valid. This particular device, used because it is relatively easy to ascertain whether royal persons are alive or dead, is known as the *Royal lives clause*. If, however, so many are designated that it becomes 'substantially impracticable to ascertain the date of the extinction of the lives' there will be a failure for uncertainty (see the remarks of Astbury J in *Re Villar* [1929] 1 Ch

243). If there are no valid express or implied lives in being the period for vesting is 21 years only. Where there are such lives the period lasts for 21 years from the death of the last survivor. These principles must now be illustrated by examples.

An example of expressly designated lives in being would be a grant 'to all the grandchildren of *X* who are alive 21 years after the death of the survivor of *A*, *B*, *C* and *D*'. Here the lives are clearly used to control the time at which the gift shall vest. But the mere mention of a person's name in a gift does not necessarily constitute him a life in being, as for instance where it appears merely casually or for some other function. In a gift 'to the first of my children to break *A*'s record for the 100 metres', *A* is not a life in being, even though he is alive, for his name is used to describe a standard of performance and not to control a time of vesting. Frequently there will be no express designation of lives in being and indeed sometimes this will not be necessary, for the persons in question, whether mentioned or not, will be very clearly involved by implication. If a testator leaves property 'to all my grandchildren equally', his children will all be lives in being, for they must all have been born by the time of his death and the reference to grandchildren presupposes children. There is no need for him to state the obvious by writing 'to such of my grandchildren as are born during the lives of my children'. Of course, such persons must be in existence at the time of the instrument coming into operation so that in a similar gift *inter vivos* children born after that time would not be lives in being.

In the same way a gift 'to the children of *A*' would constitute *A* a life in being, because his death is the event which finally enumerates the beneficiaries and marks the vesting time. Further examples will appear throughout this chapter.

Incapability of the interest vesting outside the period

The strangest characteristic of the old rule is that it is not enough that the interest vests within the perpetuity period; it must, from the very date on which the instrument came into operation, bear no possibility, no matter how remote or curious, of ever vesting outside the period. Even though you are examining the limitation many years after that date, you have to transport yourself back in time to the date when the instrument came into operation, ignore all subsequent events, and ask: 'Is there one single chance of this interest not being vested by the end of the period?'. If there is such a chance, the gift is void even though it did in fact vest within the period. In short, it is possible, not actual, events which count and you cannot 'wait and see' whether vesting takes place within the period. The vigour with which this principle is applied and the absurd results which it can produce can only be appreciated by examining some of the decided cases.

In *Re Wood* [1894] 3 Ch 381 a gift was made to such of the testator's issue as should be living when certain quarries were worked out. The gift was held void even though in the event they were worked out within six years. The lives in being by implication were his children. The contingency of the gift lay in the fact that the beneficiaries would not be identified until the quarries were exhausted. Ignoring the fact that the quarries were finished inside the perpetuity period, the judge, from the standpoint in time of the testator's death, had to ask whether there was a possibility, however remote, that the workings would not be completed during the lifetimes of these lives in being and a further 21 years, for not until that event occurred would the gift vest. There clearly was such a possibility.

The remoteness of the possibility was even more pronounced in *Re Dawson* (1888) 39 ChD 155. The relevant part of the gift was to such of the grandchildren of *A* as should reach 21. The gift was clearly contingent until all the grandchildren which *A* could possibly have had either reached 21 or died before that age, because not until the last born had done one or other of these would the shares of any beneficiary be finally ascertained. Your approach in testing the validity of limitations should be to discover just one single possibility of the gift vesting outside the period. One is enough to avoid the gift as one prick will collapse a whole balloon. Let us apply this method to this case.

If *A* had been dead at the date of the grant, the gift would have been good. All her children would have been implied lives in being, and, since she was dead, there would have been no chance of her having any more children after the date of the grant who would not have been lives in being. We could then have said that all the grandchildren must have been born within the lifetimes of the lives in being who were their parents. It follows that the contingency, the attaining of majority by the youngest of these, must have occurred within 21 years after the death of the last life in being.

A, however, was not dead at the date of the gift; so it was possible that she might have a child, *X*, after the date of the gift who would, therefore, not be a life in being. It was also possible that *A* and all the other lives in being might die, leaving *X* only alive. *X* might some time later have a child. Such a child, who would be a grandchild of *A*, clearly might not reach 21 until more than 21 years after the death of the last life in being, for *X* himself would not be a life in being. Even such a remote possibility of vesting outside the period made the gift void. Yet the case provides even more spectacular illustration that it is possibilities, not probabilities or even actualities, that count. The real cause for the failure of gifts to the grandchildren of a living person is, as shown above, that this living person might have a child after the gift who would not constitute a life in being. In *Re Dawson* it was argued that, although alive at the date of the gift, *A* could not have another child because she was in her sixties. The argument was rejected, but strangely, although under the old rule the law ignored physical impossibilities it takes account of legal ones, so that a person under 16 years of age is considered incapable of having children since it is not lawful to marry under that age (*Re Gaite's Will Trusts* [1949] 1 All ER 459).

A limitation which has frequently caused gifts to fail is that used in *Re Frost* (1889) 43 ChD 246. Land was devised to *A* for life, then to any husband she might marry for life, and then in remainder to such of their children as should be living at the death of the survivor of these two. Each gift must be scrutinised in the light of the rule. The gift to *A* is vested since none of the three elements of contingency is present. The beneficiary and the quantum of the interest are identified and there are no conditions precedent to be fulfilled. The second limitation is contingent because the beneficiary was not identified at the date of the instrument. The event which will cause the gift to vest is the marriage of *A*, for then a husband of *A* will exist. We must now ask whether this might possibly occur outside the period. The only life in being is *A*, who is so by implication. Her future husband is not a life in being, first because he might not even be born at that time, but also because even if born, he is not identified in the instrument. The gift cannot vest outside the period because the marriage of *A* cannot take place outside her lifetime. So, although contingent, the second limitation is valid. This validity, it need hardly be added, means only validity from the viewpoint of the perpetuity rule, for if *A* never marries at all, clearly no one benefits from the grant.

The third limitation is contingent because the beneficiaries do not even exist at the date of the instrument. Their identification will only be complete when *A* and the husband she might marry are both dead. The grant does not contemplate all the children of the marriage necessarily benefiting, but only those outliving both parents. This means that even after the death of one parent, the class is not finally enumerated because reductions might occur before the death of the survivor. *A* is the only life in being for the same reasons as stated above. The vesting event is the death of the survivor of *A* and her possible future spouse. The question is whether there is the remotest possibility of the survivor of the two dying more than 21 years after *A*'s death. There clearly is. *A* might marry *B* and they might have children. *A* might die first, thus reducing the perpetuity period to a further 21 years only. *B* might then die 22 years later, thus for the first time identifying the eligible children. This third limitation was, therefore, void.

If the third limitation had been simply in favour of 'the children of such marriage', rather than the children who survived both parents, it would have been valid. The vesting event would have been the birth of the last child of the marriage, and this, or, of course, its conception, must occur within the lifetime of *A*, who is a life in being. All the children, and hence all the shares, will be identified at that time. It is quite true that the children will not be able to enjoy their share until their father's life interest has run its course, and this might not occur until outside the perpetuity period. The rule against perpetuities is, however, completely unconcerned with the time at which interests fall into possession (*Re Garnham* [1916] 2 Ch 413).

Since a gift is not vested until the quantum of the interest is finally established, it follows that, in the case of class gifts, if there is any chance of the number of beneficiaries in a class being increased or decreased outside the period, the whole gift is void even though most of those beneficiaries must have been identifiable within the period. In other words, a class gift cannot be partly good and partly bad. It must either vest entirely within the period or be totally void. Some of the examples given above illustrate this. Careful drafting of instruments however can produce the effect of severing the gift and ensuring that those beneficiaries who must fulfil all the required conditions within the period can take an interest. Thus if, instead of leaving property 'to the grandchildren of *A*', which is a void gift if *A* is still living, the grant is limited to 'such of the grandchildren of *A* who shall be born within 21 years after the death of the last survivor amongst *A* and the children of *A* who are now living', it would be valid because by its own terms it only contemplates beneficiaries born within the period.

Even if this intention to limit the class is not express, a class gift might sometimes be construed to have been intended in this way. This construction might occur under the class-closing rules based upon the doctrine in *Andrews* v *Partington* (1791) 3 BroCC 401. These rules are no part of the rule against perpetuities, but are a convenient means through which a confined interpretation may be placed upon the class of beneficiaries intended to be benefited, with the aim not of making the gift valid under the perpetuity rule, but of distributing the property as soon as possible. The essence of the rule is that the class is closed when the time for distribution has arrived through one member of the intended class of beneficiaries having fulfilled all conditions for possession. Suppose property is devised to the grandchildren of *A*, a living person, at 21. If a grandchild has reached 21 at the death of the testator, then all grandchildren then living will be entitled to benefit provided they reach 21. Those born later will be excluded. With the class severed in this way, an accidental by-product of the interpretation will be that the gift is also good from the standpoint of the perpetuity rule. If, however, no grandchildren have reached 21 at the testator's death, then all grandchildren must be taken to constitute the intended class, whenever born. This would make the gift void.

The rationale of the rule may be said to be the solution of a dilemma caused by the appearance of two inconsistent intentions of the settlor. On the one hand, he seems to wish to benefit the whole class; on the other hand, he can hardly wish for the effects of his gifts to be stultified by having to wait for an inordinate period before all the beneficiaries are identified (*Re Kebty-Fletcher's Will Trusts* [1969] 1 Ch 339). Since the rule is one of construction, it may be excluded expressly or impliedly by the settlor. The strength of the policy underlying the rule means that it is only excluded if the tenor of the gift is inescapably incompatible with it (*Re Clifford's Settlement Trusts* [1980] 1 All ER 1013 at 1016). Independently of this rule, moreover, where there is a limitation which offers two possible and unstrained constructions, one of which would lead to an infringement of the perpetuity rule and one of which would not, the latter one should be followed (*Re Deeley's Settlement* [1973] 3 All ER 1127). Finally, if the share to be given to each member of a particular category is specified there is not a true class gift and some of the associated problems will not arise. Thus if a person grants ten acres of land to 'each of my children for life', the gifts can vest as soon as each child is born and before the settlor dies.

Even under the old rule, there is an exception to the principle that it is possible, not actual, events which must be considered, and where it is permitted to 'wait and see'. This occurs when a gift is subject to two alternative and separately expressed contingencies, one too remote under the rule, and the other valid. Such a gift is not void from the beginning and will remain good if the valid contingency is the one which actually happens. If property is granted to 'the first son of *A* to become a clergyman, but if *A* should either have no son who becomes a clergyman, or have no son at all, then to *B*' the first contingency is too remote, for it might not be finally known whether a son becomes a clergyman or not until more than 21 years after *A*'s death. *A* might, for instance, have a son after the date of the instrument, who would not be a life in being. That son might then become a clergyman 22 years after his father's death. The second contingency, however, cannot occur outside the period. On the death of *A*, a life in being, and not later, we shall certainly know whether he has a son or not. The validity of the gift to *B* will therefore not be settled until *A*'s death. If he dies without a son at all, the gift to *B* is good; if he dies leaving a son, then the gift to *B* is void, even though that son never becomes a clergyman.

However, this privilege is only extended to limitations where the two alternatives are explicit and not where they are merely implicit, as in a gift to 'the first son of *A* to become a clergyman, but, if he should have no such son, to *B*' (*Proctor* v *Bishop of Bath and Wells* (1794) 2 HyBl 358).

Validation of gifts by reduction of age

The condition that a beneficiary should reach a certain age before becoming entitled to a gift was such a common cause of voidness under the rule that the Law of Property Act s 163 made special provision for it. If a gift would otherwise be void for a beneficiary or class of beneficiaries because it is dependent upon them reaching an age greater than 21, then the age of 21 may be substituted for that age.

This relaxation only applies to age and not to a period of time which does not refer to age. If, therefore, a grant is made 'to the youngest son of *A* 22 years after the death of *A*' the gift is still void if *A* is alive at the date of the instrument of grant. If the gift, in similar circumstances, is to 'the youngest son of *A* at the age of 22' then the age of 21 may be substituted and the gift will be valid. If *A* is dead at the time of the grant and his youngest son is then one year old the limitation is valid without reference to the section, which therefore cannot be used. The gift will not vest until the child is 22. When the section applies the reduction is always to the age of 21, never more, never less. Although the section has now been repealed and replaced, the work it has already done is undisturbed, so that it will be employed in litigation for some time to come when the instrument in question came into force after 1 January 1926 and before 16 July 1964.

Application of the old rule to powers of appointment

The way in which the rule applies to powers depends upon whether the power in question is general or special. Since the meanings of 'general' and 'special' have been statutorily defined for the purposes of the rule, all other classifications of powers must be ignored in this context. Furthermore, since that definition contained in the Perpetuities and Accumulations Act 1964 s 7 is retrospective (s 15(5)) it must be applied to all powers, no matter when the instruments of creation came into operation. This means that it is part of the old rule. This vital definition must first be discussed and then the application of the old rule to the two types of powers of appointment will be explained.

Definition (s 7)

A power is only general if:

> (A) in the instrument creating the power it is expressed to be exercisable by one person only, and
>
> (B) it could, at all times during its currency when that person is of full age and capacity, be exercised by him so as immediately to transfer to himself the whole of the interest governed by the power without the consent of any other person or compliance with any other condition, not being a formal condition relating only to the mode of exercise of the power:
>
> Provided that for the purpose of determining whether a disposition made under a power of appointment exercisable by will only is void for remoteness, the power shall be treated as a general power where it would have fallen to be so treated if exercisable by deed.

All other powers are special. The principle of division taken by this definition is that in the case of a general power, the appointor can sit down and make the property his own by a mere stroke of a pen. This does not mean that he must appoint to himself; it simply means that he must be able to do so. By this test, some powers which might well be special powers for other purposes are general. Thus a power given to *A* to appoint amongst the children of *B* will be a general power if *A* is himself one of *B*'s children, because he could appoint to himself. The rationale of the definition is that whenever a person has complete powers of alienation over a particular interest there is nothing contrary to the rule against perpetuities because the interest is not tied up in anyway (see *Earl of Coventry's Indentures* [1973] 3 All ER 1). This is also the principle which operates in the proviso to the section. A person who is given complete freedom of appointment except that he can exercise the power by will only, has, during his life, no power of disposal at all, because a will only becomes effective on death; therefore during the appointor's life the power is special because the property is inalienable. At the moment of death, however, the appointor has complete freedom to give the property to any person in the world, provided the power would have been general if exercisable by deed. In short, the fact that at that time the fetters drop away from the interest, even though momentarily, means that it may then be treated as a general power. This type of testamentary power therefore changes its character, once executed.

Application of the rule to general powers

The rule applies to general powers in two ways:

1 The powers must be incapable of first becoming exercisable outside the perpetuity period beginning with the date when the instrument creating the power came into operation.

2 The interest eventually created by the appointment must be incapable of vesting outside the perpetuity period commencing with the date when the appointment was made. An example will illustrate these rules.

Suppose that in 1950 *T* devised 'Blackacre' 'to such person as my son *S* shall appoint after his marriage', and that immediately after his marriage in 1960 *S* appointed 'to my first son to reach 21 years of age in fee simple'. First, the power must be classified and this is done by reference to the 1964 Act, which is retrospective on this particular point. It is clear that from the moment the power is expressed to begin, namely, the marriage of *S*, until it is exercised, *S* could appoint to himself, if he wished, without referring to any other person or fulfilling any condition. This would not be so of course if the power had been given jointly to him and another person. The power may be exercised either by deed or will, for there is no requirement that it should be exercised by will only. The power is therefore general.

The next question is whether the power must become exercisable, if at all, within the period. The 1964 Act can now be tossed aside because, since the instrument in question came into operation in 1950, the old rule applies. In 1950, *S* was a life in being and the power was to become exercisable upon his marriage. This event clearly could not occur outside the lifetime of *S* and a further 21 years. The first rule set out above is therefore satisfied. Once *S* marries and the power becomes exercisable, since the power is general, it is tantamount to absolute ownership, so that the rule does not demand that *S* must actually exercise the power within the period. It is enough that he can exercise it as he likes, for at this time the property is out of its fetters and the perpetuity rule therefore loses interest in it (see *Re Fane* [1913] 1 Ch 404, at 413).

However, in exercising the power, *S* might do so in such a way that the interest created is contingent, as in the example given. The rule against perpetuities must be applied afresh, but since the property came out of its fetters completely on the marriage of *S*, who then acquired complete powers of alienation, the period may begin anew. Since the instrument creating the contingent interest came into force in 1960, the old rule still applies. On the other hand, we can take advantage of any lives in being expressly or impliedly so designated who are in existence in 1960, and we are not concerned with the 1950 instrument for this purpose. *S* is still the only life in being and to test the appointment we therefore ask whether it is possible for a son of *S* to reach 21 more than 21 years after the death of *S*. That is obviously not possible and the appointment is therefore valid.

Application of the rule to special powers

The rule applies to special powers also in two ways: to the power itself and to the resultant appointment, but in a more stringent way than is the case with general powers.

1 The power must be incapable of being exercised outside the perpetuity period commencing with the date of the instrument creating the power (*Re De Sommery* [1912] 2 Ch 622).

2 The appointed interest must be incapable of vesting outside the perpetuity period beginning with the date when the instrument creating the power came into operation. If a power is special merely because it is exercisable by will only, the period commences afresh and runs from the date of the appointment, as in the case of general powers.

The first requirement is more severe than in the case of general powers, for not only must a special power be incapable of becoming exercisable outside the period, but it must be incapable of being exercised outside it. Thus if property is left 'to such of the grandchildren of *A* as the first-born son of *B* shall appoint' and *B* is childless at the date of the grant, the power is void. It is true that it cannot become capable of exercise after the lifetime of *B*, who is a life in being, and a further 21 years. This would have been sufficient in the case of a general power. The power may, however, be capable of being actually exercised outside the period, for the first-born son of *B* might wait until more than 21 years after *B*'s death before deciding to exercise it. Once again it is possible, not actual, events which matter. The reason for this additional demand of a special power is that even when the power becomes exercisable the interest does not become absolutely disposable as in the case of ordinary ownership, for *B*'s son can only appoint to *A*'s grandchildren. In short, the property might be fettered not only during the period before it is capable of exercise but also during the period when it is capable of exercise but before the appointment is made. Accordingly the rule stretches its control over this period too.

On the other hand, the fact that it would be possible to make an invalid appointment under the special power does not invalidate it. Provided that the power itself is good, it is only the appointment made which must be considered, another concession to the 'wait and see' principle even under the old rule. Here again, the rule is stricter than it is for general powers, for the appointment must obey the rule from the standpoint of the instrument creating the power. Once again the reason is that in the case of special powers there is a continuing problem of inalienability from the time the power is created until the interest appointed itself vests. There is no intermediate hiatus of absolute freedom of alienation as with a general power and so there is no justification to begin a new period to run for the appointment. The following example will illustrate this.

Let us say that in a will operating from 1950 property was left 'to such of my children and upon such terms as my brother *B* shall appoint' and that in 1960 *B* appointed to child *C* 'when he marries'. The power itself is good, for since it is given to a life in being, *B*, an appointment cannot be made outside the period which begins in 1950. The interest of *C* must now be tested, but since the period for this purpose also begins in 1950 and not in 1960, only lives in being under the 1950 instrument may be used. Since the testator is dead, all his children are included in these. The appointment made may only be one which could validly have been made in 1950. The question to be asked is whether the testator himself in 1930 could have left the property 'to my child *C* on his marriage'. Since *C* was a life in being under the 1950 instrument he could do so, for *C* is incapable of marrying outside his own lifetime. The appointment, therefore, is good. (See also *Re Brown and Sibly's Contract* (1876) 3 ChD 156.)

Although the appointment is considered to be an extension to the instrument of creation and is said to be 'read back' into it, and although only lives in being under the original instrument may be taken into account, nevertheless factual circumstances existing at the date of the appointment may be considered. Thus in *Re Paul* [1921] 2 Ch 1, *T* left property to his daughter *D* for life and then to such of her children as she could appoint. *D* later by will appointed to her son *S* on attaining the age of 25. *S* was not a life in being at *T*'s death, but was 18 years of age at *D*'s death. The court held the gift to the son to be valid and took into account the fact that he was 18 years old. *T* could have left property to his daughter *D* for life and then to her son at 25 'provided that he should reach 25 within 21 years of his mother's death'. Similarly, if the appointment to *S* had been made conditional upon his marriage and he had married by the time the appointment came into operation, it would have been valid. If, however, he had been still single at that time, the gift would have been void even though he had married shortly afterwards.

Finally, an example may illustrate the proviso to s 7 of the 1964 Act. Suppose that in 1950 property was granted 'to such a person as *A* shall by his will appoint', and that in 1960 *A* died having by his will appointed to 'the last survivor of all my children'. The power is special because, since it is exercisable by will only, *A* cannot appoint to himself. Applying the appropriate test to this power, we find that, as *A* is a life in being in 1950 and since it is incapable of being exercised later than his death, the power itself is valid, but the only factor which prevented the power qualifying as a general one was that it was only exercisable by will. If it had been exercisable by a deed it would have constituted a general power. Under the proviso, having tested the power itself as special, we may now treat the appointment as if it had been produced under a general power. This enables us to take advantage of a new perpetuity period commencing in 1960. At that time all *A*'s children must have been born and were implied lives in being under *A*'s will. It follows that the death of the last-but-one child, the event which will identify the beneficiary, must occur during the period and the appointment is valid.

Before leaving the subject of powers of appointment, the application of the perpetuity rule to protective trusts should be mentioned. It was explained earlier that in such trusts the trustees are given a discretion to apply the income in favour of specified beneficiaries, usually upon the termination of a prior life interest. This power to apply income is akin to a power of appointment. Its exercise on one particular occasion does not once and for all exhaust the power however. Each application may be considered as a separate exercise of it. This must be borne in mind when deciding whether the power is capable of being exercised outside the period. If a life interest in property is given to A, and after his death trustees are to have a discretion to make grants of income to any widow he may leave, the latter disposition is void because the trustees might choose to make such applications in favour of *A*'s widow more than 21 years after his death. Of course, if a simple life interest had been granted to such a widow it would have been valid because it would vest, if at all, upon *A*'s death. On the other hand, if the right to an interest which consists of periodic payments must vest within the period it is not objectionable that the quantum of each payment might be variable outside the period (*Beachway Management Ltd* v *Wisewell* [1971] 1 All ER 1, but see *Re Whiteford* [1915] 1 Ch 347).

Exceptions to the old rule against perpetuities

The general principle is that the rule applies to all contingent interests in property. Thus the grant of an easement to use drains not only presently passing under land but also 'hereafter to pass' is void because it contemplates easements through drains which might be constructed outside the perpetuity period (*Dunn* v *Blackdown Properties Ltd* [1961] Ch 433). The rule, therefore, must be borne in mind when drainage and other easements are being negotiated preparatory to the construction of large estates which will take a long time to complete. The rule does not, however, apply to the duration or divesting of interests, but merely to their commencement. This is an integral part of the rule, and not an exception to it, but there are two cases in which, at first sight, the rule does not appear to apply to the duration of an interest.

The first is that the rule does apply to the determining event in an interest upon condition subsequent (*Re the Trustees of Hollis' Hospital* [1899] 2 Ch 540; and see LPA 1925 s 4(3)). An example of such an interest is a grant to '*A* in fee simple provided that the land is always used for agriculture'. When the condition is void under the rule, the effect is to make the interest absolute and not to invalidate it. Herein lies the justification for the application of the rule. What is a condition subsequent to the owner of one interest is really a condition precedent to the owner of the interest expectant upon it, and this is substantially so whether the second interest operates by way of gift over or by right of entry. If land is granted to '*A* in fee simple but if the land should ever become part of

Warwickshire then to *B* in fee simple', the rule is attacking the commencement of *B*'s interest, and not the duration of *A*'s.

Whether the old rule applies to determinable interests is controversial, but in one case it was certainly held to do so. In *Hopper* v *Liverpool Corporation* (1944) 88 SolJ 213, property was conveyed in fee simple until it should cease to be used as a library. It was held that the terminating event was void under the rule, that the possibility of reverter expectant upon it was void and that the fee simple accordingly became absolute. This decision presents no exception to the rule, for once again the terminating event is susceptible to the rule not because it marks the end of the determinable interest but because it marks the commencement of the possibility of reverter. Now the true exceptions to the rule must be mentioned.

Interests following entails

Since an entail may be barred so as to defeat all subsequent interests, the latter cannot cause property to be inalienable. To enjoy this privilege, the interest must be incapable of vesting after the end of the entail, as in a grant to 'A in tail and in default of such issue to such of the descendants of *B* then living'. The rule applies in full force to the grant of the entail itself, though not of course to the inheritance of it once it is vested. Thus a grant in tail to the first child of *A* upon his marriage would be void if *A* has no child at the time of the grant.

Certain gifts to charities

The rule applies to all original contingent gifts to charities such as 'to Charity *A* when it moves its premises to London'. If there is a gift over from one charity to another, such as a grant to Charity *A* to go to Charity *B* if Charity *A* fails to repair a family vault, then the gift over to the second or subsequent charity is exempt from the rule (*Re Tyler* [1891] 3 Ch 252).

Certain rights of entry

These include a right to re-enter and determine a lease for breach of covenant and certain remedies for enforcing rentcharges (LPA 1925 s 121(6)). We have already seen that the terminating event in an interest upon condition subsequent is subject to the rule and so a right of entry exercisable upon breach of such a condition is not an exception to the rule. Where, however, the condition is the payment of a rentcharge, the right of entry is not subject to the rule and may be enforced even though exercisable in perpetuity (see LPA 1925 s 4(3)).

Obligations arising from privity of contract

Between the original parties contractual obligations are not subject to the rule, even though they create contingent interests in land such as an option to purchase it in the future (*Hutton* v *Watling* [1948] Ch 398). But where a contract does create a contingent interest in land in this way, and the land is sold to a third person, then if the promisee attempts to enforce against that third person, he is basing his claim not upon a privity of contract but upon an interest in land alone. The existence of such a contingent interest of course attracts the rule. In *Woodall* v *Clifton* [1905] 2 Ch 257 it was held that a covenant in a 99-year lease to purchase the fee simple in reversion at any time during the lease was not enforceable by the assignee of the lease against the assignee of the reversion since the option was exercisable outside the perpetuity period.

Covenants to renew leases

Despite what has been said above, covenants contained in leases giving rights of renewal of such leases are exempt from the rule as between both the original parties and assignees (*Weg Motors Ltd* v *Hales* [1962] Ch 49). This valuable and practical exception should be sharply distinguished from a right in a lease to purchase the reversion, which is dealt with above and is not an exception.

Mortgages

The rule against perpetuities does not apply to the postponement of the right to redeem a mortgage.

Administrative powers

The rule does not apply to any administrative powers such as those of sale, lease, exchange or otherwise disposing of property for full consideration, which are sometimes conferred upon persons under settlements, in addition to their statutory powers, for the purposes of the better administration of the trust. Such powers, administrative only in nature, and not affecting beneficial interests, must be distinguished from powers of appointment, which are dispositive and do affect beneficial interests. This exemption was introduced by s 8 of the 1964 Act but, being one of the two retrospective provisions in that Act, applies to the old rule.

Pension and superannuation funds

This is of little theoretical interest for the private lawyer. See Cheshire and Burn's *Modern Law of Real Property* (15th edn) for further references.

The consequences of voidness under the old rule

A gift which infringes the rule is itself void but we are now concerned with any effect this might have on other limitations in the grant. First, we can say that an invalid limitation has no effect on prior interests. It might be anticipated that subsequent interests are also unaffected and can take effect provided they themselves do not infringe the rule. This unfortunately is not true in all cases, although conflicting decisions and *dicta* and the imprecise nature of the rules applied make the formation of any principle difficult. However, the following classification of subsequent interests into three categories is generally accepted.

1 *Vested.* If the subsequent interest is vested then it is always good no matter what limitation precedes it. An example would be 'to the first of my descendants for life who shall join the Royal Navy, remainder to *A* in fee simple' (see *Re Hubbard's Will Trusts* [1963] Ch 275).

2 *Contingent but independent.* If the contingency upon which the subsequent gift depends must not only occur within the period, but is quite unassociated with the void contingency in the prior gift, then the subsequent gift is good. Thus in *Re Coleman* [1936] Ch 528 property was left on discretionary trusts to *A* for life, then on similar trusts to any widow he might leave for life, then to *A*'s children equally at the age of 21. The discretionary trust to the widow was void but the gift to the children was good. The events upon which their shares were to vest could not occur outside the period and were not connected in any way with the void contingency of the prior gift. *Re Backhouse* [1921] 2 Ch 51 is a decision which runs contrary to this but is probably bad in law.

3 *Contingent but dependent.* If the subsequent gift is contingent and also dependent or expectant upon a prior void gift, it is itself invalid even though it is incapable of vesting outside the period. This is sometimes called the rule of *infectious invalidity*. The difficulty in distinguishing cases which fall under this class from those falling under 2 above is considerable because no precise objective meaning has been given to the word 'dependent'. A clear example would be 'to the youngest son of *A* on his marriage in fee simple, but if *A* should have no such son to *B* for life'. Although the gift to *B*, being for life only, is incapable of vesting outside the period because *B* is a life in being, the vesting event is clearly linked to that of the prior gift. The gift is therefore void. If the subsequent gift is capable of vesting outside the period, as would be the case if the second gift above had been for an interest in fee simple, it would have been void quite apart from the infectious invalidity principle (see *Proctor* v *Bishop of Bath and Wells*).

In short, whether a limitation is placed in the above category 3 and therefore rendered void, even though good in itself, or is classified as independent, is to a large extent a matter of construction for the judge, who will place it in the present category if he considers the gift was only to take effect upon the exhaustion of the prior interest (see the judgment of Buckley J, in *Re Hubbard's Will Trusts*, above).

THE NEW RULE AGAINST PERPETUITIES

Important changes have been made to the rule by the Perpetuities and Accumulations Act 1964, which affects all instruments coming into effect on or after 16 July 1964. The order of treatment below will, as far as practicable, follow that of the old rule, so that these changes can be appreciated more conveniently.

The rule

An interest which is capable of vesting outside the perpetuity period shall be void only if it does not in fact vest within the period prescribed by the Act. The implications of this statement must be examined.

Actual vesting within the period is sufficient

This is a result of s 3(1), which introduces the 'wait-and-see' rule under which actual, and not possible, events decide whether a gift is valid. A gift will no longer be void merely because it might vest outside the period; it is to be treated as valid until it is clear that it must vest outside the period. The new rule has no application unless the gift would have been void, although some slight differences in drafting could have made this preliminary reference to the old rule unnecessary (see 86 LQR 357, at 370). Thus, if a testator leaves property 'to my youngest son on his marriage' there is no need to wait and see because the gift is clearly good in any case. This illustrates how the new rule merely places a superstructure upon the old. If the gift does turn out to be void because, after waiting and seeing, it does not vest within the period, any advancement or application of intermediate income earned by the property is not thereby invalidated. Unless otherwise provided by the settlement, therefore, this income may generally be applied to the contingent beneficiary without fear that such application will be falsified by the subsequent failure of the capital gift to vest.

Recognising that all gifts must first be judged under the old rule, the Act seeks to prevent the need to invoke the 'wait-and-see' rule by negativing one of the most extravagant possibilities recognised by the old rule. It may now be presumed that a female can only have a child between the ages of 12 and 55 inclusive, and that a male can only do so over the age of 14 (s 2). These presumptions, where applicable, will enable a gift to be valid from the beginning without reference to the 'wait-and-see' rule. They may be rebutted positively or negatively by evidence to the contrary in the case of living persons. An example would be proof that a 56-year-old woman was expecting a child.

'Having a child' for the purposes of the presumption, includes having one by adoption, legitimation or 'other means' but, for the purposes of rebutting the presumption, only includes physically bearing or begetting one (s 2(4)). A woman of 60 may rebut the presumption that she cannot bear a child by conceiving one, but not by merely showing that she might adopt one. It may be remarked in passing here that in any disposition coming into force after 1 January 1970, any reference to the children of a person is presumed, unless the contrary intention appears, to include illegitimate children (Family Law Reform Act 1969 s 15).

These provisions clearly enable property to be distributed without reference to the 'wait-and-see' rule, and events might prove the presumptions, generous though they are, to have been wrong. In such a case, the court may make 'such order as it thinks fit' for making a just restoration of the position of a beneficiary. As to whether reversible sterilisation will create problems in this field in the future we shall have to wait and see.

The application of the new rule to class gifts must now be examined. First, the old class-closing rules based upon *Andrews* v *Partington* are not affected. They must, as rules of construction, be applied in the first instance, before invoking the Act. If they operate to limit the intended beneficiaries in such a way as to conform with the old rule the gift is good and there need be no reference to the Act. If they do not so limit the meaning of the class, and if as a result the gift would be void under the old rule, then the 'wait-and-see' principle must be applied under the Act. If the class is incapable of increase at the end of the period the gift is obviously completely saved. It might happen, however, that when the end of the period arrives there are potential class members who are either yet unborn or who still have to fulfil some condition. To meet this event, the Act introduces a class-closing rule in the true sense of the word without taking refuge in the subject of construction.

It provides in s 4(3) and (4) that those potential members in whose favour the gift has failed to vest at the end of the period shall be excluded from the class. Thus if a grant is made to the grandchildren of *A*, and *A* is still of child-bearing age, the gift is *prima facie* void, unless of course *Andrews* v *Partington* operates to save it, so that the 'wait-and-see' principle must be used. If, at the end of the period, three grandchildren exist, these alone take, to the exclusion of any grandchildren born later.

Finally, the Act provides for a new alternative form of perpetuity period which, like the *Royal lives clause*, may be used collaterally to a gift and thus make it incapable of vesting outside the period, and therefore necessarily valid from the standpoint of the law without reference to the 'wait-and-see' rule. It is now possible under s 1 to specify a number of years not exceeding 80. If used, this period should be expressly and clearly designated and cannot be combined with lives in being. An example of its use would be a gift to 'such of my great grandchildren who shall be alive 80 years from now which I hereby specify as the perpetuity period'. Such a gift is, through its own self-limiting drafting, valid from the beginning and needs no help from the 'wait-and-see' rule for this purpose, although of course the time must elapse before any distribution can take place.

The duration of the 'wait-and-see' period

In determining the validity of the gift initially, in order to discover whether it will be necessary to wait and see, the perpetuity period is the same as at common law, subject to the alternative period of 80 years. Once it has been found that it is necessary to 'wait and see', because the gift is void under the old rule, the lives in being which may be used for this purpose are those provided by the Act in s 3 and no others. Frequently, the lives in being so identified will be the same as at common law but this is not necessarily so. These statutory lives must not only be in existence but ascertainable at the time when the instrument comes into operation. If there are no lives in being under the section, the period during which you can wait and see is 21 years only. The persons mentioned by the section are as follows:

1 the donor;

2 the beneficiaries, their parents and grandparents. In the case of class gifts this includes any member or potential member. In the case of conditional gifts to individuals, any person who has satisfied some of the conditions and may in time satisfy the others is included;

3 objects of a special power of appointment, their parents and grandparents. Where there is only one object and he is ascertainable only on certain conditions being satisfied, any person who has satisfied some of the conditions and may in time satisfy the others is included;

4 a person on whom any power, option or other right is conferred;

5 the owner of an immediately prior interest.

Though all these persons must be alive and ascertainable to be eligible, parents and grandparents of beneficiaries under 2 and 3 qualify if their children or grandchildren respectively would be beneficiaries or objects when born, even if not born at the date of the gift. Of course, the parent or grandparent himself must be alive at that date.

Long though this list is, there is one common type of disposition to which it lends insufficient help. This is a gift 'to *A*, a bachelor, for life, remainder to any wife he might marry for life, remainder equally to such of their children as should be living at the death of the survivor'. The final limitation is void under the old rule (*Re Frost*, p 224). If the wife of *A* dies before *A*, the gift to the children will now be saved by the Act under the 'wait-and-see' principle, for *A* is a life in being. If *A* dies first, however, even this new rule would not necessarily save the gift. For the wife, not being ascertainable at the date of the gift, even though alive, is not a statutory life in being and she might die more than 21 years after *A*. Section 5 therefore provides that in this latter event the gift may be treated as if it had been limited by reference to the end of the perpetuity period. In short, if the 'wait-and-see' period has elapsed and the wife is still alive, all the children then living share the gift. This will not of course vest in possession until their mother's death; her life interest is unaffected and valid to the end of her life.

Validation of gifts by reduction of age

Section 4 replaces the Law of Property Act 1925 s 163, for instruments coming into force on or after 16 July 1964, and provides a rule for age reduction which is more capable of respecting a settlor's intentions. Where it is clear at the end of the 'wait-and-see' period that a disposition, limited by reference to the attainment of a specified age exceeding 21 years by any person, would otherwise be void merely because of the requirement that an age greater than 21 must be reached, then that age may be reduced as much as is necessary to save the disposition. A flaw in the drafting of this provision has now been corrected by the Children Act 1975 Sch 3 para 43.

Though the age still cannot be reduced below 21, it need not now be reduced arbitrarily to 21, but only to such age (nearest to that specified by the settlor) as will save the gift. The rule applies not only to cases where the beneficiaries themselves are required to reach a certain age, but where they are only to take when some collateral person does so. Now that the three major relaxations permitted by the Act have been explained – the 'wait-and-see' principle, the class-closing provision and the rule now under discussion – an example may be given to show how they operate together.

Suppose that property was granted in 1965 to the grandchildren of *A*, a living person, at the age of 30. The gift is void under the old rule so that the 'wait-and-see' rule may be invoked. The lives in being for this purpose must be ascertained from s 3. At the death of the last of these, a further 21 years must elapse. However, since no grandchild born after this date will be capable of reaching even 21, below which the qualifying age cannot be reduced, they will not be eligible beneficiaries. The extent to which the age must be reduced may now be determined. Let us say three grandchildren exist aged ten, eight and five. The age must be reduced for the whole disposition and not merely for each individual, unless separate ages are specified for different classes of beneficiaries. This means that the age requirement must be reduced for all three beneficiaries to 26, for that is the age which even the youngest will be capable of reaching. Since no later born grandchildren can even reach 21 they must now be excluded from the gift under the class-closing principle. In short the rules are applied in the following order: wait and see; reduce the age; close the class.

Application of the new rule to powers of appointment

The definition of general and special powers has already been discussed. It may simply be added that all the general reforms brought about by the Act apply equally to powers. Thus the 'wait-and-see' rule may be applied to the question whether a power will become exercisable or will actually be exercised within the period, as well as to the appointed interest when created. A few further matters of more special application to powers must be mentioned.

First, if the 80-year period or less is specified by the instrument creating the power, that period will also apply to any disposition made under the power as well as to the power itself (s 1(2)). Next it is important to remember that an instrument made in the exercise of a special power of appointment attracts the new rule only if the instrument creating the power does (s 15(5)), for it is deemed to come into force when its parent instrument did. If an instrument coming into force in 1950 gave a power to *A* to appoint to such of the grandchildren of *B* as he thought fit, and in 1970 *A* appointed to grandchildren G^1 and G^2, the rule against perpetuities must be applied in the following way. First, the power must be classified as general or special by reference to the 1964 Act because on this matter it is retrospective. Whether the power must become exercisable, if at all, and be exercised, if at all, within the period, must be decided under the old rule because the power was created in 1950. Furthermore, the appointment to G^1 and G^2, though made in 1970, attracts the old rule only, because it was executed in response to a 1950 instrument and the power was a special one. In such cases no advantage can be taken of the 'wait-and-see' rule.

Exceptions to the new rule against perpetuities

The new rule applies, like the old, only to the commencement of interests and not to their duration. As explained above, the application of the old rule to determinable interests and interests upon condition subsequent does not breach this principle. The new rule applies to both these interests and also to resulting trusts (s 12), and so the controversy as to the application of the rule to determinable interests is now settled for the future and the case of *Hopper* v *Liverpool Corporation* is confirmed. When the new rule applies, the 'wait-and-see' rule may of course be used to decide whether the terminating event is valid.

The effect of the Act upon the exceptions to the rule against perpetuities at common law must now be examined. First, the exceptions relating to entails, charities, covenants of renewal in leases and mortgages are unaffected, and of course the retrospective exception relating to administrative powers introduced by the Act applies under both the old and new rules. The other two exceptions have been affected in the following way.

Rights of entry

Section II broadens and clarifies the Law of Property Act 1925 s 121(6) by enacting that the rule shall not apply to any powers or remedies for recovering or compelling the payment of rent charges. As to the right of entry exercisable on breach of condition in an interest on condition subsequent, the rule still applies in the same way as it did under the old law, but of course the 'wait-and-see' rule may be applied.

Obligations arising from privity of contract

First, the Act has applied the rule even as between the original contracting parties to contracts *inter vivos* which create interests in land (s 10). Second, options to purchase any interest in land for valuable consideration are now, with the exception mentioned below, subject to a restricted perpetuity period of 21 years only. Neither lives in being nor the 80-year period can be used, although once again the 'wait-and-see' rule applies (s 9(2)). Third, one class of option is now totally exempt from the rule. This is an option to purchase for valuable consideration the reversion, immediate or otherwise, on a lease, provided that (1) it is exercisable only by the lessee or his successors in title; and (2) it ceases to be exercisable at or before the expiration of one year after the end of the lease (s 9(1)). The length of the lease is immaterial and the section applies to agreements for leases as well as to leases.

The consequences of voidness under the new rule

An important reform has been introduced by the Act. An interest is no longer to be void because it follows and is dependent upon a void limitation, and the voidness of the prior gift is not to prevent the acceleration of the later one (s 6). Of course, there might be other factors preventing acceleration. Thus the infectious invalidity rule is abolished and every limitation must be considered entirely on its own merits.

THE RULE AGAINST ACCUMULATIONS

The rule against perpetuities is one manifestation of a wider principle that property shall not be rendered inalienable. A further example must now be considered. Wealthy persons sometimes direct that the income derived from property shall be re-invested and accumulated for a very long period of time and finally shared out amongst beneficiaries. This might be done so that the vesting of the shares must take place within the perpetuity rule. Even though the rule might thus not be infringed, huge sums of money might be rendered inalienable for a very long time. A separate and even more severe rule has therefore been developed to place limits upon the period during which such accumulations, whether total or partial, may be ordered. If the instrument directing the accumulation came into force before 16 July 1964, the settlor may select one only of the periods permitted by the Law of Property Act 1925 s 164. If it came into operation on or after that date there are two additional possibilities available under the Perpetuities and Accumulations Act 1964 s 13.

The accumulation periods

The periods provided by the 1925 Act are as follows:

1. the life of the grantor or settlor;
2. a period of 21 years from the death of the grantor, settlor or testator;
3. the duration of the minority or respective minorities of any person or persons living or *en ventre sa mère* at the death of the grantor, settlor or testator;
4. the minority or respective minorities only of any person or persons who under the limitations of the instrument directing the accumulations would, for the time being, if of full age, be entitled to the income directed to be accumulated.

The two additional periods available for instruments coming into effect on or after 16 July 1964 are as follows:

5 a period of 21 years from the making of the disposition;

6 the minority or respective minorities of any person or persons in being at that date.

The fourth period includes persons who might not even be born at the death of the settlor (*Cattell* v *Cattell* [1914] 1 Ch 177). Susceptibility of a disposition to the accumulations rule, however, does not confer immunity from the perpetuities rule, and the vesting of a gift must obey the old or new rule as appropriate. If the purpose of the accumulation is that of purchasing land, then the fourth period alone may be chosen (LPA 1925 s 166), though this does not apply to accumulations to be held as capital money under the Settled Land Act 1925. Finally, under the Family Law Reform Act 1969 s 1, *minority* denotes an age less than 18 years, but this provision is not to invalidate any direction for accumulation in any instrument made before its commencement date (Sch 3).

The effects of excessive directions to accumulate

If the duration of the accumulation ordered exceeds the ordinary perpetuity period of a life or lives in being and 21 years the direction is completely void (*Curtis* v *Lukin* (1842) 5 Beav 147). This requirement is quite separate from the general rule that all interests must vest within that period which was mentioned above. However, if the accumulation is confined within that period, but is to exceed the statutory period which according to the construction of the instrument the settlor must be deemed to have selected, the direction is only void to the extent of the excess (see *Re Ransome's Will Trusts* [1957] Ch 348 at 361). The process of ascertaining which of the periods is applicable is necessarily rather an artificial one. If *S* orders the accumulation of income during the lifetime of X, the second or fifth period will most nearly fit his designs so that accumulation may last for 21 years. Which of these two is invoked depends upon whether the settlement was by deed or will. The first period is not appropriate because it is that of the lifetime of the settlor only. (See also *Re Watt's Will Trusts* [1936] 2 All ER 1555.)

Finally, if at the end of an accumulation period the beneficiary is a minor, the further accumulation necessary pending his majority is not aggregated to the original accumulation and so will not cause an infringement of the rule (LPA 1925 s 165).

The right to stop accumulations

Under the doctrine in *Saunders* v *Vautier* (1841) 4 Beav 115, where a beneficiary has an absolute and vested interest in property, but there is a direction to accumulate the income from it for him during a certain period, he may end the accumulation and call for a transfer of the property to himself, when he reaches his majority.

Since it is based upon the principle that because no other person is interested in the property he must be allowed to have full control over it if he wishes, it follows that if there is more than one such beneficiary, they may do the same, provided that together they constitute the total number of persons who have any interest, contingent or otherwise, in the property. There is no right to stop an accumulation if the class of beneficiaries is still capable of growing. In the case of instruments coming into operation on or after 16 July 1964, however, beneficiaries may take advantage of the presumptions relating to the ability to bear children contained in s 2 of the 1964 Act (*see* ss 14 and 2). If the beneficiaries in question are 'the children of *A*' and three such children have reached their majority, then if there are no other young children, and *A* is a woman of 56, the three children can claim that together they constitute the entire class of beneficiaries. They will accordingly be entitled to end an accumulation provided that the other requirements of the doctrine are fulfilled.

Exceptions to the rule against accumulations

Directions to accumulate income for the following purposes are exempt from the rule (LPA 1925 s 164(2)).

1 *Payment of debts*. Accumulations for this purpose need not be restricted either to an accumulation period or to the perpetuity period. Furthermore, the debts may be those of the settlor, the testator or any other person.

2 *Raising of portions*. If the portions are to be raised for any children or remoter issue of any grantor, settlor or testator, or any children or remoter issue of a person taking any interest under any settlement or other disposition directing the accumulations, or to whom any interest is thereby limited, a direction to accumulate need not be confined to a statutory period. No satisfactory definition of the meaning of 'portions' has been settled in the decided cases and in practice the word is used in several different senses in different branches of law.

3 *Timber or wood*. A direction to accumulate the produce of timber or wood is exempt from the accumulations rule but must be confined to the perpetuity period (*Ferrand* v *Wilson* (1845) 4 Hare 344). Various reasons have been suggested for this exception, such as that it is intended to encourage tree planting. There are certain other forms of accumulation which are not caught by the Act, which operates on dispositions or settlements of property only. Such exceptions lie outside the range of land law. Finally a direction to apply income for the upkeep of property is not a direction to accumulate at all, though its effect must be confined to the perpetuity period.

QUESTION

A testator who died in 1963 left a will by which he gave property on trust for all Jane's grandchildren, whenever born, who should attain 21. At the testator's death, Jane was 60 years old and all her children were dead, but she had one grandchild, Rebecca, aged 18. Consider whether Rebecca is entitled to the trust property. Would your answer be the same if the testator had died in 1983?

SPECIMEN ANSWER

This question concerns the rule against perpetuities which represents one of several different ways in which the law generally ensures that property shall not become inalienable. The rule was reformed by the Perpetuities and Accumulations Act 1964, though, with minor exceptions, only for instruments coming into effect after 15 July 1964. If the testator died in 1963, the dispositions attempted by his will must be considered in the light of the unreformed common law rule, whereas if he died in 1983 the new rule will apply.

The old rule, perfected by *Cadell* v *Palmer* [1833] requires that an interest in property must be incapable of vesting outside the lifetime or lifetimes of some life or lives in being at the time when the instrument attempting to create the interest came into operation plus a further 21 years.

Vesting means the precipitation of the right of an ascertained beneficiary to a defined piece of property or share of property. It demands that the beneficiary and the size of the interest be ascertained and that any conditions precedent imposed upon the gift be fulfilled necessarily within the period. In short, vesting means ceasing to be contingent. In the case of a class gift, the class of persons must be incapable of expansion outside the period because an increase in numbers must mean a reduction in the share of the other members. The lives in being may either be expressed or implied in the limitation. An example of the former would be 'to all my descendants living 21 years after the death of the last lineal descendant of King George V now living'. Such lives must, however, be ascertainable (*Re Villar* (1928)). An example of the latter would be a gift by will to all the testator's grandchildren, when all his children would be lives in being by implication. By definition, lives in being must be persons whose duration of life concerns and governs the vesting of the gift. In applying these principles, the rule at common law is that it is possible not actual events which count. If there is even the slightest theoretical possibility of the gift vesting outside the period the gift is void and the fact that it does eventually vest inside the period must be disregarded. Thus in *Re Dawson* (1888) a testator left property to his daughter and then after her death, *inter alia*, for her grandchildren at the age of 21. It was held that the gift was void. The daughter, herself of course a life in being, might have had a further child after the testator's death and that child would not have been a life in being. The other lives in being at the testator's death might then have died leaving perhaps the youngest child to have a child which would not reach 21 until more than 21 years after the death of the last life in being. That possibility prevented the shares of the existing members of the class from being finally ascertained within the period. The absurd stringency of the rule is, however, highlighted by the fact that the daughter was in her sixties at the testator's death. The court, regarding the authorities, refused to recognise, for the purposes of the rule, that she could have no more children and that the possibility mentioned above did not exist.

Applying these common law principles to this question, Jane is a life in being. She must be considered capable of having more children with the same results as were pointed out in *Re Dawson*. Sometimes, such a gift can be saved because of the limited construction placed by the court on the words used by the donor under the class closing rules, known as the rules in *Andrews* v *Partington*. Then the class of beneficiaries is a restricted one, the effect of which might be that no further beneficiary can enter it outside the period. In the present case unfortunately, the testator has ruled out such a confined interpretation because he has made the gift to all his grandchildren 'whenever born'. Therefore Rebecca is not entitled to the property. If the testator had died in 1983, then the will must be considered in the light of the Perpetuities and Accumulations Act 1964. This Act brought several important changes, but only some of these need be considered in the case of this question. Quite apart from the Act it may be mentioned that, if Jane had died between 1963 and 1964, the gift to Rebecca would be valid because there would not be even a theoretical possibility of children having been born to her after the commencement of the period.

Section 2 of the Act introduces the presumption that a female over the age of 55 cannot have a child, though this presumption is rebuttable by evidence that she would be able to do so. When this presumption has been acted upon, and has then been falsified by subsequent events, the High Court is empowered to make 'such order as it thinks fit' for placing the persons interested in the property 'so far as is just' in the position they would have held if the question had not been so decided. 'Having a child' generally means both having or begetting one physically or having one by adoption or legitimation or 'other means', but in the case of the presumption now being discussed its rebuttal can only be achieved by physically having or begetting one (s 2(4)). This means that it may be presumed that Jane will have no more children. There can therefore be no more grandchildren, so the gift will be valid from the standpoint of the perpetuity rule. Rebecca will be entitled to all the property, but only if she reaches 21, which she will clearly do within the period if at all.

In the most unlikely event of Jane giving birth to another child after Rebecca has received her share and of that child having a child, recourse may be had to s 2 mentioned above. If Jane has another child after the testator's death, but before the distribution of the property, then the personal representatives must not of course operate the presumption in s 2. Yet there will be a possibility of the birth of more grandchildren outside the period. Two further provisions in the Act may, however, be invoked.

First, the introduction of the 'wait-and-see' rule by s 3 has abolished the rule that possible not actual events must be considered. It is enough now that the gift actually vests fully within the period. The section specifies the lives in being available for this purpose which largely, though not completely, correspond to those available at common law. For present purposes, they would be Jane and Rebecca only, since no subsequently born child or grandchild of Jane would have been alive and ascertainable at the commencement of the period as demanded by the section.

The personal representatives may therefore wait until the dropping of these two lives and then establish how many grandchildren Jane has, for these will be capable of reaching 21 within the next 21 years. Any grandchild born after the death of the last life in being must be excluded, since s 4, which introduces a true class closing rule, enacts that any potential member of a class whose inclusion would prevent the disposition vesting fully within the period must be excluded. However, no grandchild of Jane may take until the age of 21.

AN ALGORITHM FOR SOLVING PROBLEMS OF PERPETUITIES

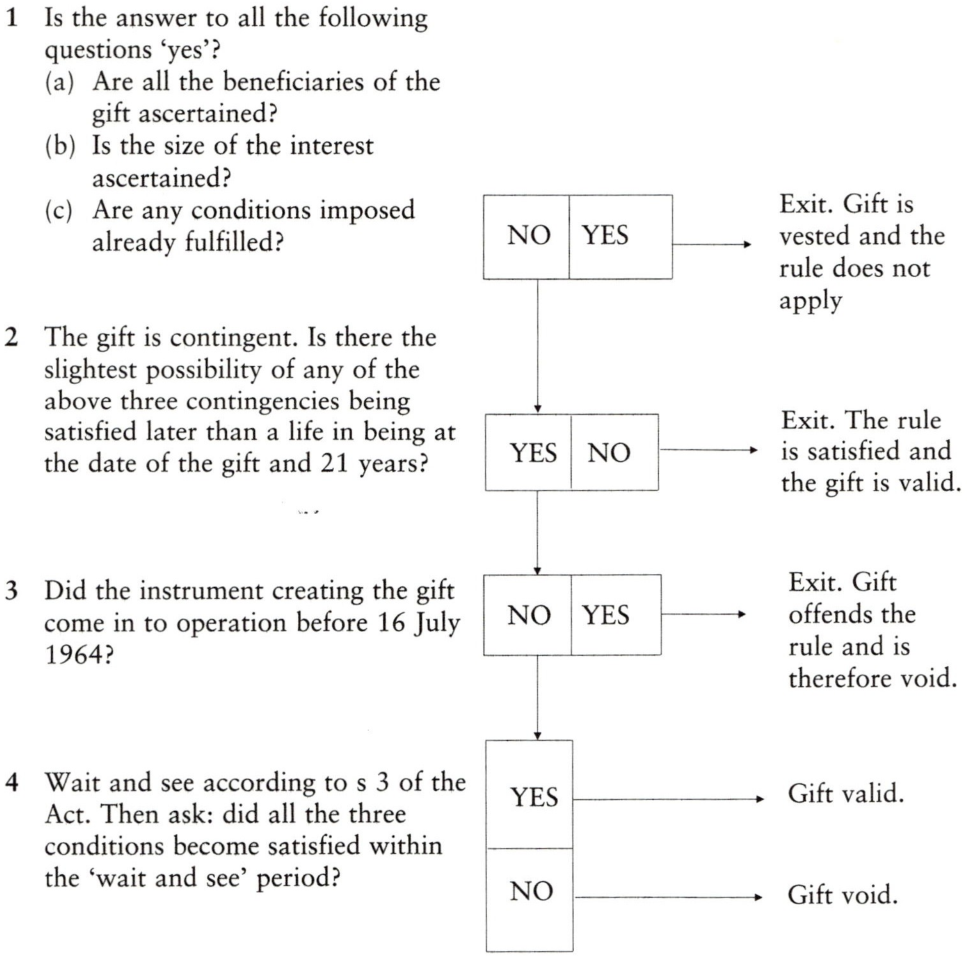

CHAPTER 11

CO-OWNERSHIP

We have seen that several persons maybe interested in land consecutively. It is also possible for two or more persons to be interested concurrently. A fee simple, life interest or other interest may be granted to *A* and *B* so that they both enjoy that interest together at the same time. Common examples of co-ownership are business partnerships, the family homes of married and cohabiting couples and houses let on short leases to students and others. The last example concerns leases which are dealt with in Chapter 6. The focus of this chapter will be on the matrimonial home. It is within this context that the greatest social and, consequently, legal developments have occurred. This shift in emphasis is justified as follows.

In Chapter 9 the settlement of landed property was examined. Whether as strict settlement or as settlement by way of trust for sale its purpose was to conserve land dynastically for an extended family, aristocratic or, in later days, the new industrial rich. Since the end of the second world war there has been a social revolution which has relegated the settlement to a relative specialism and promoted co-ownership to the bread and butter of high street practice.

The social axes of law are the key to any understanding of the rules and cases clustering around its problem centres. In the case of co-ownership today they are: the enormous increase in home ownership; the divorce and separation rate amongst married couples; cohabitation without marriage; the mortgage as a facilitator of home ownership; inflation of land prices during the 1970s and 1980s; depression of land prices during the 1990s; unemployment.

The appellate case law in this area of study appears to undervalue these influences and to overpromote law as a detached discipline.

TYPES OF CO-OWNERSHIP

There are three different types of co-ownership: joint tenancy, tenancy in common and coparcenary. The first two of these are much more important than the third, which is rarely met today. The word 'tenancy' here has nothing to do with leases and simply means 'ownership'. (It is quite possible of course for a lease, like any other interest, to be co-owned.)

It is crucial to distinguish between joint tenancy and tenancy in common because the doctrine of survivorship operates in joint tenancy but not in tenancy in common. This doctrine will therefore be explained first. Survivorship here means the coalescence, on the death of one joint tenant, of the entire interest in question in the surviving joint tenants. The joint tenants together constitute one single legal personality, rather like a body corporate whose existence remains unimpaired by the removal of one member. Thus a joint tenant does not own a share or proportion of value of the property as a tenant in common does. The group of joint tenants as such own it all. Despite this principle, however, the profits and enjoyment of the land are the property of all the joint tenants to the same extent.

If an interest in property is granted to *A, B, C* and *D* as joint tenants and *D* dies, the interest passes entirely to *A, B* and *C* and no part of the interest passes either under the will of *D* or upon his intestacy. When *C* dies the interest survives in *A* and *B* only. If *B* dies, the joint tenancy is ended and the interest belongs to *A* absolutely. If such a result is not desired, a joint tenancy can be converted into a tenancy in common by a joint tenant during his lifetime, though not by his will, since a will operates only immediately after death and upon that event survivorship will have already operated. On the other hand, the doctrine works very conveniently for certain other purposes such as trusteeships. When property is vested in trustees it is done by way of joint tenancy so that on the death of one trustee the entire interest survives in the remaining trustees, for it would obviously be undesirable if a share of the interest were to pass to the trustee's personal representatives.

When the doctrine operates it might sometimes be very important to know which of two or more joint tenants died last so as to ascertain who became entitled to the property by survivorship. To take an example: if joint tenants in fee simple, *A* and *B*, both die in circumstances where it is not known who died first – such as in a motor accident – there is the question whether the next-of-kin of *A* or *B* become entitled to the property. The rule is that if ordinary evidence can prove that one died before the other, even though by only a few seconds, this proved fact must predominate, for the doctrine does not require one to have survived the other by any substantial time. If, however, positive evidence fails to prove which survived the other then, subject to any order of court, the younger is presumed to have survived the elder (LPA 1925 s 184). Presumably such an order of court would be used where it is unknown which is the elder. In *Hickman* v *Peacey* [1945] AC 304 the rule was applied to discover survivorship where two persons were killed by a bomb. It seems therefore that the courts will not entertain the possibility of completely simultaneous deaths, because such an event is incapable of proof.

The rule is of general application and is not restricted to the establishment of priority of death in the case of joint tenants only. In the case of joint tenancies it applies even as between husband and wife, despite the exception introduced by the Intestates' Estates Act 1952 s 1(4), for the purposes of intestate succession generally as between husband and wife.

HOW TO DISTINGUISH BETWEEN JOINT TENANCY AND TENANCY IN COMMON

A joint tenancy only exists if the answers to all the following questions are positive. Otherwise there can only be a tenancy in common. We shall see later in this chapter that only joint tenancies can exist at law, though in equity there can be both joint tenancies or tenants in common. The questions should be asked in the following order:

1 Are the four unities present?

2 Are words of severance absent?

3 Is the transaction in question free of all the three characteristics any one of which would, on equitable principles, raise the presumption of a tenancy in common?

Of course what originated as a joint tenancy might later have been converted to a tenancy in common, so this must also be checked. The first two questions mentioned above can be answered by examining the face of the document creating the co-ownership. In the case of the third it will be necessary to go behind the instrument to discover the true nature of the transaction. These three matters must now be discussed in detail.

The four unities

The principle explained above that joint tenants are in many ways in the position of a single tenant necessarily means that there must be unity between them in the following four ways.

1 *Unity of time.* The interest of each tenant must vest at the same time. Some exceptions however grew up in this rule and it does not apply to wills, so that joint tenancy may arise on a devise 'to my grandchildren' even though the births and therefore the vesting of the interests of the beneficiaries might occur at different times.

2 *Unity of title.* The title of all the co-owners must derive from the same instrument or, in the case of title based on adverse possession, under a contemporaneous commencement of possession.

3 *Unity of interest.* The interest of each co-owner must be identical. Thus if one interest is leasehold and the other freehold, or if one is vested and the other contingent, this unity does not exist.

4 *Unity of possession.* Each co-owner is entitled to enjoy possession of every part of the property, yet cannot exclude any of the others from the same enjoyment. None of the co-owners can identify any particular part as his, for this would amount to separate independent ownership by them. If several

persons are joint tenants of property they might, and probably will, allow each other to occupy certain parts exclusively for the sake of their own privacy, but this does not affect their predominant right to universal possession. This unity is common to all forms of co-ownership. The right to possession must be distinguished from actual possession. Co-ownership can exist even though one or more of the co-owners is not in occupation. A co-owner out of occupation cannot generally claim rent from his fellow co-owners in occupation. If, however, one co-owner has been ousted by the other, the former is entitled to such compensation as could be claimed by a beneficiary against a trustee who had taken sole possession of trust property. The purpose to which the trustee has actually put the property in such cases is therefore irrelevant. (*Dennis* v *McDonald* [1982] 1 All ER 590).

Words of severance

Even if all the unities are present, there will still be a tenancy in common and not a joint tenancy if there are any words in the instrument creating the co-ownership which suggest that the co-owners are to take distinct shares in the interest. This does not mean that possession of particular divided parts must be intended, for that would amount to grants of separate ownership of various parts, and we have seen that unity of possession is necessary even in tenancy in common. It means that even the allocation of a proportion of value of the whole will be incompatible with a joint tenancy. In fact, any words which individualise shares necessarily deny the essential molecular singleness which joint tenancy demands. Examples of such words are 'equally', 'divided between', and 'as to one-third', etc. The sensitiveness of the rule is illustrated by *Re North* [1952] Ch 397, where land was granted to two persons on condition that they 'should pay in equal shares' ten shillings a week to another person. This identification of separate personalities was held to create a tenancy in common. A clear express provision, however, indicating that one form of tenancy or the other is intended will prevail despite the presence of words which are capable of producing severance. If this provision does not record the true intentions of the parties taking the conveyance, rectification of the conveyance can be obtained from the court (*Re Colebrook's Conveyances* [1974] 1 All ER 132).

Equitable presumption in favour of tenancy in common

Equity preferred equality and justice to the element of chance operating in joint tenancy through the doctrine of survivorship, and has left its mark upon co-ownership. Even though the four unities are present, and even though there exist no words of severance, tenancy in common will still be presumed in exceptional cases. The presumptions can of course be rebutted. It was emphasised in *Malayan Credit Ltd* v *Jack Chia – MPH Ltd* [1986] 1 All ER 711 (at 715) that the established exceptions, listed below, are not rigid categories but examples only of circumstances in which equity may infer tenancy in common.

1 *Purchase by business partners.* When two or more persons purchase land for the purposes of business or some other enterprise aimed at making profit, there is a presumption that the land is held by them as tenants in common because clearly such arrangements are not compatible with the rule of survivorship. Thus in *Lake* v *Craddock* (1732) 3 PW 158, the principle was held to apply where several persons had purchased land in order to improve it by drainage.

2 *Loan by co-morgagees.* When a person lends money on the security of land the borrower, or mortgagor, conveys to the lender, or mortgagee, a lease in the land or, alternatively, creates a legal charge in his favour, which, we shall see in Chapter 15, produces the same effect as a lease. The mortgagee will not ordinarily take possession under the lease, for its purpose is merely to endow the lender with what is one of the best forms of security, a legal estate in the land. When the money is repaid the mortgage ends, and it contains special provisions to this effect. When several persons together advance money to a borrower they take a conveyance as co-mortgagees. It is convenient for them to do so as joint tenants rather than as tenants in common so that if one mortgagee dies survivorship will make it unnecessary to involve his personal representatives in the discharge of the mortgage when the loan is eventually paid. This is often made quite clear on the face of the mortgage deed by the inclusion of a 'joint account clause'. There is, however, a presumption that where several persons advance money in this way, whether in equal or unequal shares, a tenancy in common is intended, because, as in the case of business enterprises, survivorship is clearly not intended to operate. But these apparently conflicting factors can live side by side. Under the Law of Property Act 1925 s 111, the money lent is, as between the mortgagees and mortgagor, deemed to belong to the mortgagees on a joint account, so that surviving mortgagees can give a valid receipt and discharge. However, this does not affect the presumption that there is a tenancy in common, as between the mortgagees themselves. In short, the right to discharge is joint, but the beneficial interest in the land and the repaid money is in common.

3 *Purchase money provided in unequal shares.* If land is purchased with money provided by two or more persons in unequal shares, there is a presumption that these persons are tenants in common even though there are no words of severance in the conveyance and the four unities are present. Their shares in the interest purchased will be in proportion to the amounts they advanced. There is no such presumption if the money is advanced in equal shares. This absurdity has not been consciously created by equity. It intervened where it could on the grounds of presumed intention, but in the case of equal advancement there was no initial fissure in the face of the unities to provide it with an occasion for severance. These circumstances raise presumptions of intention which may be rebutted by proof of

contrary intention. Such contrary intention may be expressed in the conveyance itself by a declaration of the beneficial shares of the co-owners. If the conveyance does declare the beneficial shares, this will be conclusive unless it is proved that the document, through fraud or mistake, does not faithfully record the true intentions of the co-owners at the time of the conveyance (see 34 Conveyancer 156).

4 *Separate business purposes.*

> Suppose that an accountant and an architect take a lease of premises containing four rooms, that the architect uses two rooms, and that the accountant uses two rooms. It is scarcely to be supposed that they intend if, for example, the architect dies first without having gone through the formalities of a severance the beneficial interest in the entire premises is to survive to the accountant.
>
> Lord Brightman in *Malayan Credit Ltd* v *Jack Chia – MPH Ltd* [1986] 1 All ER 711 at 715

Implied co-ownership

Up to this point, in distinguishing between joint tenancy and tenancy in common, it has been assumed that the co-ownership is at least expressed in the conveyance in that all the co-owners are mentioned. There are two circumstances where co-ownership arises in favour of a person without this. First, coparcenary arises only on intestacy and so there is no instrument of creation at all. This will be dealt with later. Second, persons sometimes advance money with which land is purchased and the conveyance is taken by one or some of the persons and no mention is made in the instrument of the others. In these cases co-ownership may arise by the presumed intention of the parties or by implication of law. It most commonly occurs in the case of husband and wife. In Chapter 1, a description of *implied*, *resulting* and *constructive trusts* was suggested, together with a diagram of their sources. These were intended to provide a rational vocabulary for guidance in the study of the decided cases. Appellate cases by their very nature however respond primarily to social pragmatism, so that reason in its tidiest sense must follow rather than lead judicial precedent. With this caution we must push out to the turbulent case law. That vocabulary will suffer strain.

The problem is well illustrated by *Bull* v *Bull* [1955] 1 QB 234. A mother and son provided the purchase-money for a house in which they were to live, the son advancing the greater proportion. The property was conveyed into the son's name only. After domestic strife the son tried to evict his mother by a notice to quit, as if she were his lessee only. It was held that they were both tenants in common in equity and so until sale both were entitled to possession. The mother was a co-owner and a notice to quit was quite out of place. We shall shortly see that in such cases the property cannot be sold, however, until a further trustee is appointed. The requirement under the Law of Property Act 1925 s 53(1), that interests in land must be created in writing does not prevent co-ownership arising by implication in this way, because it does not apply to constructive, implied or resulting trusts. See also *Hussey* v *Palmer* [1972] 3 All ER 744. The inferred trusts now to be discussed will be termed *implied trusts* in order to emphasise that they are based on the intention of the parties. They are however often classified as *resulting trusts*.

This inference of co-ownership in equity is not difficult where a direct contribution is made to the purchase price in circumstances which suggest that the persons contributing intend to take interests in the property, even though the conveyance is made into the name of one legal owner only. In recent years, however, in disputes as to ownership between husband and wife, the courts have inferred co-ownership when the contributions by one spouse have been of an indirect kind. A contribution might be made by one spouse to the general household expenses so as to leave the other spouse free to pay the mortgage instalments, or money might be spent upon improving the property, or personal time and skill might be spent carrying out alterations which would ordinarily be done by professional tradesmen. Indeed, there is at least moral strength in the argument that a wife, by spending her time in running the house and looking after her husband so as to enable him to earn the money with which to pay for the house, is equally deserving of a share in the property. In recent years the principle of the implied trusts, a 'cold legal question' of property law, has been strained in order to do substantial justice to a spouse who will be poorly provided for on the breakdown of a marriage which might have lasted many years.

Such provision is, however, more properly the function of the divorce court and should not be allowed to slur the lines of property law, according to *Gissing* v *Gissing* [1970] 2 All ER 780. In that case, the doctrine of the implied trust was returned to its native vigour and held to be based on the common intention of the parties at the time of purchase. Yet the conduct of the parties in relation to the payment of the mortgage instalments may be no less relevant to the proof of this common intention than their conduct in relation to the cash deposit (per Lord Diplock, at p 791). The House of Lords held that such an intention cannot be imputed to the parties where in reality it did not exist, no matter how much one party might evoke sympathy. What is required is evidence of the whole conduct of the parties from which it can be inferred that there probably was an agreement or common intention to share in the property.

The nature of this common intention is to be deduced on objective grounds as a reasonable man would discern it from words and conduct. (For an interesting though earlier insistence by the court upon original intention, see *Tinker* v *Tinker* [1970] 1 All ER 540.) Little purpose is served by discussing what evidence will or will not suffice to satisfy this test because it is the total inference in every individual case which weighs. Rules of thumb are sucker growths that enfeeble sound broad principles. Thus there is no distinction in law between a direct and an indirect contribution. In weighing contributions by a husband, there is little place in these days of women's liberation for the old presumption that they are intended as a gift to his wife (*Falconer* v *Falconer* [1970] 3 All ER

449). (See 86 LQR 98.) Furthermore, the mere fact that the quantum of contribution is difficult to assess does not justify taking refuge in the maxim *equality is equity*, for a fair estimate amounting to some other fraction might be a preferable allocation of shares in the property. (See also *Pettit* v *Pettit* [1969] 2 All ER 385.)

If express agreement can be shown, evidence of subsequent conduct might not be necessary, for the transaction might be effective by way of settlement rather than by purchase. Unlike a 'purchase' agreement this would not require consideration. An express trust is not effective unless proved by writing, as required by the Law of Property Act 1925 s 53. Yet equity would count such an arrangement as a constructive trust, and therefore exempt from this requirement, if it would be unconscionable to allow the legal owner to take refuge in the fact that the legal interest had been conveyed to him alone. The scope of the trust and the quantum of the shares of the parties in such cases would depend entirely upon the terms of the agreement actually made, and not upon the inference to be drawn from the subsequent conduct of the parties. (See *Re Densham* [1975] 1 WLR 1519 and 92 LQR 489.)

Unfortunately, the judgments given by the House of Lords in *Gissing* v *Gissing* vary in their statements of principle. Lord Diplock considered that where one party has made no initial contribution to the deposit and legal costs, and no direct contribution to the mortgage instalments, and has made no adjustment to her contribution to other household expenses which are referable to the purchase of the house, there is, in the absence of an express agreement, no material to justify the inference of a common intention to share the ownership (at 793). Yet in *Hazel* v *Hazel* [1972] 1 All ER 923, Lord Denning MR held in the Court of Appeal that it was enough that the party claiming a share had made a 'substantial contribution' to the family expenses, and that there need be no agreement, express or implied. He said that he was well aware that some speeches in the House in *Gissing* v *Gissing* were to different effect so that he had to choose between them, and he would follow Lords Reid and Pearson. Yet Lord Pearson had stated, only a few lines before his passage cited by Lord Denning, that contributions of a substantial nature would raise 'a presumption as to the intention of the parties . . .' (at 787), thus indicating that a common intention was always necessary. Lord Denning's interpretation of the case was wide enough to deny it any importance as a precedent.

Liberal views have now been stilled by the decision of the House of Lords in *Lloyds Bank* v *Rosset* [1990] 1 All ER 1111. The leading and unanimous judgment of Lord Bridge is provided in the study materials at the end of this chapter. This judgment should be read critically in light of the points numbered below. It does however present the contemporary judicial approach to the implied trust.

1 Lord Bridge sharply distinguished two mutually exclusive routes to its creation.

(a) An agreement, based on express discussions between the parties, prior to acquisition of the property and only exceptionally later, that the property is to be shared beneficially, followed by the claimant significantly altering his position in reliance. This would give rise to a a *constructive trust* or *proprietary estoppel*. An example is *Grant* v *Edwards* [1986] 2 All ER 426.

(b) When there has been no such prior agreement, however informal, but subsequent conduct of the parties leads the court to infer a *common intention* to share the property beneficially and to find a *constructive trust*. Probably only direct financial contributions will suffice for such conduct. *Gissing* v *Gissing* and *Pettit* v *Pettit* fall into this category.

The referability of conduct to some implied trust under (a) might be much weaker than under (b).

2 Although Lord Bridge contemplates oral agreement as founding the creation of an interest in land, he fails to address the requirement of the Law of Property (Miscellaneous Provisions) Act 1989 s 2(1) that such agreements must be in writing and the abolition of the doctrine of part performance. Perhaps this explains the 'remedial' solution of the constructive trust or proprietary estoppel which escape these requirements.

3 The technical vocabulary used in the judgment appears to be inaccurate. The mode of creation mentioned under 2(b) above sounds more happily in *resulting* than *constructive* trust. A resulting trust is robustly based on the equitable presumption that provision of money implies enjoyment of beneficial interest in the land purchased with it. This is a peacable operation, surely to be distinguished from the unconscionability of the rogues of constructive trusts.

4 The decision is not a good one for women, particularly if they are cohabiting but unmarried, or indeed for anyone who is uncalculating in his contribution towards co-occupied property maintenance or communal living.

As to unmarried cohabitation alone there might be three million or more people affected by these fine points of equity. The case also delays the development of any principles of family or community property expectations which, because they are based upon trust in the traditional sense of the word, are often undeclared.

5 The decision also vibrates in wider jurisprudence. Equity, the erstwhile protector of moral obligations, is now associated with money. Lord Bridge remarked (at 1118C):

> On any view the monetary value of Mrs Rosset's work expressed as a contribution to a property acquired at a cost exceeding £70 000 must have been so trifling as to be almost de minimis.

6 The notion of 'direct financial contribution' mentioned under 2(b) presents

problems of its own. Most family properties are not in reality purchased by a single payment but over may years by a mortgage. The implied trust thus requires an elongated view of 'conduct'. This is further complicated by matters of mere domestic administration. Suppose that one partner agrees to pay the mortgage instalments, while the other undertakes to pay other outgoings in the family budget, thereby enabling that other partner to undertake direct payments of the instalments.

The principle in *Lloyds Bank* v *Rosset* applies to all cases of implied co-ownership. Its potentially harsh effects for unmarried people who have cohabited even for 20 years are illustrated by cases such as *Burns* v *Burns* [1984] Ch 317. Cohabitation agreements declaring the rights of the partners should be drawn up before cohabitation begins. Family type relationships however develop more by gradual drift than business dispatch. Statute should surely provide a background code for a more equitable formula on breakdown of these relationships.

Such a provision was made for married persons by the Matrimonial Proceedings and Property Act 1970. The present law is contained in the Matrimonial Causes Act 1973 as amended by the Matrimonial and Family Proceedings Act 1984. Lord Denning's judgmemt as to how the 1970 Act should be applied, as delivered in *Wachtel* v *Wachtel* [1973] 1 All ER 829, has been a strong influence in the development of this jurisdiction. Appropriate extracts from the amended Act of 1973 are provided in the study materials at the end of this chapter. Their principal outlines are briefly considered below. Section 24 empowers the Court to make 'property adjustment orders' in cases of divorce, nullity or judicial separation. It is important to note that this enables the court to shift property rights, not merely to declare them as in the case of the equitable jurisdiction relating to implied trusts discussed earlier. The matters to which the Court can have regard include a wide range of considerations, well beyond the monetary boundaries envisaged by Lord Bridge in *Lloyds Bank* v *Rosset*.

In substance, the 'warm question' which flew out of the window of equity has returned through Statute's front door – but only if you are married and even then only if you are seeking divorce, nullity or judicial separation.

Discretions placed with courts, or administrative authorities, always create some frontal activity between reasonable foreseeability of outcome and the necessity to respond the infinite variety of circumstances confronting the judge. These are indeed 'warm questions', perhaps more closely related to administrative rather than judicial function. A more detailed discussion of this area of family property is to be found in Hoggett, BM and Pearl, DS, *The Family Law and Society Cases and Materials* (3rd edn), Butterworths.

There is a growing trend for couples, married or not, who are contemplating the purchase of homes, to take the property into their joint names, and this is encouraged by building societies and banks.

The question arises whether the legal profession plays too large and too early a part in marital conflict. Accustomed as it is to taking sides, claiming rights and representing the only route to the final demise of marriage, perhaps it is too naturally attuned to confrontation, upon which marital breakdown feeds. Perhaps reconciliation prospers best when there is no potential loser.

Questions as to the ownership of property concerning husband and wife can be settled by a convenient procedure of application under the Married Women's Property Act 1882 s 17, as amended, by spouses or by persons whose marriages have been dissolved or annulled within three years before the application. The judge is empowered to make such order regarding the property 'as he thinks fit'. Despite previous doubt, this last phrase does not empower the judge to vary property rights as is the case under the 1973 Act. It is now settled that the jurisdiction is procedural only. The court's function is simply to unravel and discover confused existing rights and to give effect to them, or, where this is impracticable, to give a fair ruling (*Pettit* v *Pettit*, above). It is to declare ownership and not to reallocate it.

In cases of divorce, nullity or judicial separation, it is now unnecessary to decide the property rights of the parties under s 17, since all appropriate orders can be made under the 1973 Act. Section 17 will still be appropriate in other cases such as where the parties are not seeking divorce, or where one of the parties is dead. Section 37 of the 1970 Act has a role to play here in assessing the shares in property to which a spouse is entitled.

The Law Commission's Third Report on Family Property (Law Com No 86) has now recommended that, subject to contrary agreement, spouses should become statutory equal co-owners of any interest in the matrimonial home.

THE LEGAL MACHINERY OF CO-OWNERSHIP

The problems of inalienability and complication in the investigation of title experienced in settlements existing before 1926 have already been discussed. The difficulties caused by successive legal interests were solved by making it impossible to split the legal fee simple and by giving the life tenant an inviolable right to sell it. These difficulties, which existed on the vertical plane in settlements, were present in even more acute form on the horizontal plane in co-ownership, for up to 1926 both joint tenancy and tenancy in common could exist either as legal or equitable interests.

Joint tenancy did not, however, cause hardship in conveyancing as tenancy in common did. An example will illustrate this. Suppose that *A*, *B* and *C* were legal joint tenants and *P* wished to buy the land. Since it is an unfailing characteristic of joint tenancy that there is unity of title, *P* would only have to investigate one title to the land. If, however, *A*, *B* and *C* were legal tenants in common this was not necessarily so and the title of each individual tenant had to be investigated. *A* might have died, leaving his share to his three children equally, *B* might have mortgaged his share and *C* might have sold his to another person. Any purchaser wishing to buy the land would in that case have to navigate his title through a delta of distributary legal interests.

The solution given by the Law of Property Act 1925 is, as in the case of settlements, of a twofold nature. First, simplicity of investigation of title and disposability of the legal estate were achieved by enacting that tenancy in common can no longer exist at law, only in equity. Second, the Act rendered land more saleable by imposing a trust for sale in all cases of co-ownership, although there is power to retain the land unsold for an indefinite time. Furthermore, upon sale a purchaser takes a title freed from all the interests of the co-owners whether they all agreed to the sale or not, for these interests are overreached and satisfied out of the purchase money. These provisions must now be examined in detail.

Legal tenancies in common abolished

Section 1(6) enacts that 'a legal estate is not capable of subsisting or of being created in an undivided share in land . . .' The expression 'undivided share' simply means *tenancy in common*, which may continue to exist as an equitable interest behind a trust. Joint tenancies are unaffected and may exist at law or in equity. Striking though this provision is, its purpose is only that of a conveyancing device, and exactly the same beneficial effects can be achieved after the Act as before it.

If, for instance, a grantor wishes to grant land to *A* and *B* as tenants in common he must convey the legal estate to trustees as joint tenants. These trustees may be *A* and *B*, the beneficiaries themselves. *A* and *B* then hold the legal estate according to the settlor's instructions, namely upon trust for themselves as tenants in common in equity. If he wishes to make them equitable joint tenants, he again conveys the legal estate to them; or other trustees, as joint tenants upon trust for them both as joint tenants in equity.

In either case, the number of trustees who hold the legal estate jointly must not exceed four (Trustee Act 1925 s 34(2)). Where an attempt is made to convey the legal estate to more than four persons as trustees, the first four named, who are able and willing to act, alone become trustees. Any attempt to constitute persons as legal tenants in common is blocked by the provision that this shall operate as if the land had been conveyed to them, or, if there are more than four, to the first four of them named in the conveyance, as joint tenants upon trust for all of them as tenants in common (LPA 1925 s 34(2)). Thus, if a conveyance expresses that land is conveyed to *A*, *B*, *D*, *E* and *F* as tenants in common, the legal estate vests in *A*, *B*, *C* and *D* as joint tenants at law upon trust for sale for the benefit of *A*, *B*, *C*, *D*, *E* and *F* as tenants in common in equity.

This new machinery will cause no confusion provided you remember that the true position of the beneficiaries is reflected in the equitable interests only, that joint tenancies, whether legal or equitable, and tenancies in common are still true to their old natures, as described earlier in this chapter, and that the devolution of the legal and equitable interests must be plotted completely separately. Table 11.1 might help to show this.

Table 11.1

Legal fee simple			*Equitable fee simple*	
1930	*ABCD*	JT	*ABCDE*	TIC
1940 (*D* dies)	*ABC*	JT	*ABCXE*	TIC
1950 (*C* sells beneficial interest)	*ABC*	JT	*ABPXE*	TIC

This shows land conveyed for the benefit of *A, B, C, D* and *E* in 1930 as tenants in common. The legal title is vested in *A, B, C* and *D* only as legal joint tenants upon trust for all of them in equity as tenants in common. When *D* dies in 1940 survivorship operates on the legal joint tenancy but does not affect the beneficial interests. *D*'s share goes to his next of kin *X*. Of course, if the five persons had been granted beneficial joint interests, survivorship would have operated in equity as well as at law, so that *X* would take no interest on *D*'s death. On the other hand, when *C* sells his beneficial interest in 1950 to *P* the legal joint tenancy is not affected. *C* remains a joint tenant at law but when the land is sold he will take no benefit. Nor will he enjoy any benefit before sale. The purchaser, however, will have the same single title to investigate as he would have done if he had bought the land in 1931. The changes in ownership mentioned above do not cause a ripple of disturbance on the surface of the legal title.

A trust for sale arises

Second, with one exception to be mentioned later, a trust for sale arises in all cases where land becomes vested in co-owners. This type of trust for sale, imposed by the statute and not by act of parties, is called a 'statutory trust for sale'. In the case of joint tenancies, the Law of Property Act 1925 s 36(1) imposes the trust for sale in all cases in an unambiguous way. When beneficial tenancies in common are dealt with by s 34, the wording does not seem wide enough to embrace all cases in which such interests might arise. Section 36(2) imposes the trust for sale where land 'is expressed' to be conveyed to persons in undivided shares. The word 'expressed' seems to demand that the tenancy in common must be apparent on the face of the instrument. We have already seen, however, that tenancies in common can arise without being so apparent, as where there are no words of severance but the beneficiaries are partners, or advance purchase money in unequal shares. Sometimes this even occurs when the legal estate is conveyed to one person only. This difficulty has not prevented the courts from finding that a trust for sale arises in all cases of tenancy in common. In *Bull* v *Bull* [1955] 1 QB 234, the court was able to justify this by having recourse to the Settled Land Act 1925 s 36(4), which provides, almost parenthetically in the particular context, that an 'undivided share in land shall not be capable of being created except under a trust instrument or under the Law of Property Act 1925, and then shall only take effect behind a trust for sale'.

The mere imposition of a trust for sale in cases of co-ownership would not of itself assist the alienability of the land if the purchaser took it still subject to the equitable interests of the beneficiaries. The essence of the new principle is that he is enabled to take free of them. As with the express trusts for sale, the doctrine of conversion applies to the statutory trust so that the beneficiaries' interests are interests in personalty and not interests in land (*Irani Finance Ltd* v *Singh* [1970] 3 All ER 199, at 203, but see *National Westminster Bank Ltd* v *Allen* [1971] 2 QB 718) and the Charging Orders Act 1979 s 2(1)(ii). Therefore, perhaps, it is technically incorrect to say that these interests are *overreached* on a sale. In any event, it is enacted by the Law of Property Act 1925 s 27, that the purchaser takes the land free of the rights of the beneficiaries – provided that the purchase money is paid to trustees who must be at least two in number or a trust corporation. This raises difficult problems in those cases where the legal estate was irregularly conveyed to one of the owners only and the beneficial interest of the other or others does not appear on the face of the conveyance but arises by implication. The question arises whether the legal owner has either a right or power to pass the legal estate to a purchaser so that the latter takes free of the beneficial interests.

First, it is clear that the sole trustee has no right to do so and may be prevented from selling or leasing the property if a beneficial owner takes the appropriate steps before the sale or lease is completed, even though the contract has been made. Thus in *Waller* v *Waller* [1967] 1 All ER 305 an injunction was granted against a husband at the insistance of his wife to prevent him selling until the appointment of a second trustee had been made. The legal estate was vested soley in him, but his wife was co-owner in equity.

If however the sale or other disposition of the legal estate goes through, the outcome varies according as whether the title is unregistered or registered. If it is unregistered the purchaser takes free of the undisclosed equitable interest only if he is a purchaser of a legal estate in good faith for value without notice. This requires an application of the historic doctrine of notice, since there is no provision for registration of the equitable interest, as such, on the Land Charges Register. The question then arises as to what constitutes adequate notice. In *Caunce* v *Caunce* [1969] 1 All ER 722 it was held that the mere presence of such an equitable owner on the premises was not adequate. This reflected the business interest since it was considered that otherwise unreasonable duties would be placed upon purchasers to enquire about the status of possibly many members of the household or other residents. This approach has been disapproved and is no longer followed and a more social or familial interest has voice.

In *Kingsnorth Trust Ltd* v *Tizard* [1986] 2 All ER 64 it was held that a purchaser (mortgagee) had notice of a separated wife's equitable interest even though, far from being in exclusive residence of the home, she only visited it to attend to her children. What constitutes notice is a question of fact not law. It is undesirable therefore to multiply precedents, but wiser merely to note general trends. The factual circumstances are infinitely variable.

The outcome in the case of registered land depends upon an entirely different theoretical test. First, even if the equitable interest has not been registered as legally co-owned, the interest may still be notified on the charges register. This is unlikely to occur however since a failure to protect rights by the most obvious means will probably not be corrected by a less evident process. So an identical situation is presented as that in *Caunce* v *Caunce*, save that the title is registered. An entirely different question is now asked. This is whether the owner of the concealed equitable interest is in *actual occupation* of the land so as to enjoy an *overriding interest*. See *Williams and Glyn's Bank Ltd* v *Boland* [1980] 2 All ER 408. These expressions will be explained more fully in Chapter 18 when registration of title is discussed. For present purposes the sharp distinction might be expressed as follows:

1 *Unregistered land*. 'Did the purchaser have notice of the interest?'

2 *Registered land*. 'Was the owner of that interest "in actual occupation"?'

The development of the case law has been aimed to produce the same practical outcome for the two distinct theoretical tests. Any other result would have been absurd in practical terms.

It is appropriate here to note a decision which illuminates the distinction between overreaching and overriding equitable interests in co-owned property. In *City of London Building Society* v *Flegg* [1988] AC 54 property was conveyed to and the title registered in the names of a husband and wife. The wife's parents made substantial contributions to the purchase price and became co-owners in equity. The parents also resided in the property. The husband and wife later created further mortgages without the knowledge of their parents and eventually defaulted in repayments. It was held by the House of Lords that on sale by the mortgagee the interests of all four co-owners would be overreachable on sale provided that the purchase money was paid to at least two trustees, that is the husband and wife.

The case is to be distinguished from cases such as *Williams and Glyn's Bank* v *Boland* where the capital money was advanced to a sole trustee, since this could not trigger the overreaching machinery at all. Thus where the overreaching mechanisms are conformed with, then the overreaching principle prevails. In such cases the equitable owners would of course retain their rights in the purchase money.

We must remember that if the legal estate is vested in two or more beneficiaries the overreaching provisions of the 1925 legislation apply, but also that no surreptitious dealing with that estate can occur (see 1980 Conveyancer 191).

THE OPERATION OF THE STATUTORY TRUST FOR SALE

In the case of an express trust for sale, the fundamental rule is that the trustees carry out the instruction of the settlor who has ordered a sale. The timing of the sale will also depend upon such instructions, although statute provides guides if they are lacking. In the case of statutory trusts for sale, such a mandate will frequently be lacking because the co-owners are probably contemplating anything *but* sale. The trust for sale is an imposition of statute, which clearly ought to supply a formula to enable the trustees to decide when the land must be sold in the absence of any other guide. This formula will be mentioned below, but it should be borne in mind that the purpose of the statutory trust is not to enforce a sale but merely to provide conveyancing liquidity and resolve deadlocks. The formula is contained in the Law of Property Act s 26(3), as amended by the Law of Property (Amendment) Act 1926. It does not apply to express trusts for sale, unless of course it is incorporated by the settlor in his instructions to the trustees. The trustees:

> shall so far as practicable consult the persons of full age for the time being beneficially interested in possession in the rents and profits of the land until sale, and shall, so far as consistent with the general interest of the trust, give effect to the wishes of such persons, or in the case of dispute, of the majority (according to the value of their combined interests) of such persons . . .

The section contains two elements: first, the general purpose for which the land is co-owned, and second, the desires of the co-owners. The first predominates, although sometimes, even when it has been present, the second might provide evidence as to whether it still exists. If the first element is not present then the second one operates.

The first rule is that if the land was taken into co-ownership for some particular purpose, such as for a matrimonial home, or for business, the land must not be sold while this purpose subsists. Such *collateral purposes* indeed account for the greater number of co-ownerships of land (see *Jones* v *Challenger* [1961] 1 QB 177; *Re Buchanan-Wollaston's Conveyance* [1939] Ch 738). Cases of doubt may be tested by an application to the court under s 30 of the Act, when the court will judge whether the purpose still exists (*Jackson* v *Jackson* [1971] 3 All ER 775). Since this section enables the court to make 'such order as it thinks fit', it is not restricted merely to deciding whether or not there shall be a sale, but may mould its decision to the circumstances, such as by ordering that, though the property may remain unsold and in the occupation of one co-owner, the other shall be entitled to periodical payments secured by a charge on the property, but shall lose all rights in the ownership. In *Re Holliday* [1980] 3 All ER 385 the sale of a former matrimonial home was postponed, even in face of the claims of the trustee in bankruptcy of one co-owner, so that the other owner and the children of the marriage might enjoy the home while the children grew up. Generally, however, the courts have preferred the interests of the trustee in bankruptcy. The Insolvency Act 1986 now provides guidance for the court in such applications under the section. Thus it confers limited rights of occupation on the bankrupt person as against the trustee in bankruptcy with regard to his dwelling house in which the spouse has a beneficial interest. It also protects a limited security of possession, which the spouse of a bankrupt might enjoy under the Matrimonial Homes Act 1983. The judgment of Nourse LJ in the case of *In Re Citro (Domenico) (A bankrupt)* [1990] 3 All ER 952 should be consulted generally.

The problem of deciding what order to make is capable of much variation in matrimonial cases, particularly in view of a husband's duty to allow his wife to enjoy accommodation he has provided for her (see Law Commission Working Paper No 42, and 36 Conveyancer 99). In deciding whether or not to postpone sale, the court can take into account all the personal problems affecting the owners of the beneficial interests, such as the provision of a home for their children. The most important factor, whether or not there are children to be considered, is that everyone concerned should have a roof over his head (*Martin* v *Martin* [1977] 3 WLR 101). Questions involving the matrimonial home should now be disposed of by the Family Division under the Matrimonial Causes Act 1973. There is greater responsiveness on the part of today's judges to the use of property for family purposes.

If there is no collateral purpose the trustees must, so far as practicable, consult the persons of full age for the time being beneficially interested in possession in the rents and profits of the land until sale, and give effect to the value of their combined interests. Thus if land is devised to *A*, *B* and *C* in shares of three-fifths, one-fifth and one-fifth respectively, *A*'s wish must be followed even if *B* and *C* disagree with him. Section 30 may be invoked here also, if, for instance, trustees failed in this duty. The meaning of the words 'in possession' in the section is simply 'not in remainder' so that physical occupation is not necessary (see also *Re House* [1929] 2 Ch 166).

Whether the duty to sell emanates from the first or the second of the two elements just discussed, a purchaser is not concerned to see that the provisions of s 26(3) have been complied with.

A short comparison of the duty to sell in express and statutory trusts for sale might be helpful at this point.

Express trust for sale:

1 Obey the express terms, taking any necessary consents. If these cannot be obtained, or a co-trustee will not agree to sale, an application to the court may be made under s 30.

2 If there are no instructions as to when to sell, the trustees may delay sale if they unanimously agree. There is no need to consult beneficiaries.

Statutory trust for sale:

1 If there is a collateral purpose the land must not be sold while this subsists. Of course, if all the beneficiaries wish to sell, this would be conclusive that the purpose has ended. Cases of doubt can be tested under s 30, when the court will be guided by the existence or otherwise of such purpose.

2 If there is no collateral purpose the trustees must be guided by the wishes of the majority of the beneficiaries according to value. If trustees do not obey this duty, s 30 can be used to force them to sell where applicable.

Apart from the duty to sell, the main features of a statutory trust for sale are similar to those of an express trust for sale. Thus the doctrine of conversion applies and the interests of the persons interested are *overreached* upon sale. Property granted to persons in equal shares may, of course, be subject to an express trust for sale by the grantor, in which case his instructions must be regarded. In one case, a grantor ordered sale as a priority, since he only intended the beneficiaries to receive a distribution of the sale money. Their interests in such cases might only be in the proceeds so that possession of the land cannot be claimed (*Barclay* v *Barclay* [1970] 2 All ER 676).

The differences between express and statutory trusts for sale also occur in relation to the right to occupy the land in question. In the case of express trusts, the doctrine has always been that the beneficiaries may only occupy the land at the discretion of the trustees, although they enjoy the right to receive the rents and profits pending sale. This principle reflects the managerial role to which trustees are appointed by a landowner setting up a settlement of what was lately his own property. Such a doctrine can hardly apply in the case of statutory trusts for sale for the following reasons. First, before the 1925 legislation co-owners had an unqualified right to occupy the land itself. The application of the trust for sale to co-ownership by the Law of Property Act 1925 was a mere device aimed at conveyancing liquidity, but not intended to affect substantive rights. Second, the vast majority of co-owners have purchased the land for themselves and therefore must have intended to receive full managerial powers. Indeed, in most cases, the legal estate and the beneficial interests are held by the same persons (see *Bull* v *Bull* [1955] 1 QB 234 at 237).

A contrary view is put forward by the learned authors Gray, KJ and Symes, PD, in (1981) *Real Property for Real People*, Butterworth, pp 262–73. The 1925 legislation indeed favoured land transfer at the expense, it now transpires, of land enjoyment. Suppose, for instance, that one co-owning spouse should sell his equitable share in the matrimonial home. May the stranger purchasing it move into possession with the spouse remaining in occupation?

Social developments in one decade sometimes carry their problems to the Court of Appeal in the next. The greater incidence of both divorce and home-ownership during the 1950s and 1960s gave rise to litigation which culminated in *Gissing* v *Gissing* and the Matrimonial Proceedings and Property

Act 1970. During the 1960s and 1970s another important social development occurred. Cohabitation without marriage, always present to some degree in most societies, increased considerably in this country. The problems arising on separation have gained litigiousness through the frequency of home-ownership by one or both parties. The waves of this development are now beginning to break upon judicial shores.

The Matrimonial Causes Act 1973 has no part to play in the settlement of property disputes of such unmarried couples, although we have seen that injunctive relief against molestation in the home may be afforded. At present property adjustment is not available. The court is restricted to declaring rights in such cases. Section 30 of the Law of Property Act 1925 is available, of course. Thus, sale of property may be delayed while illegitimate children of unmarried couples grow up during the separation of their parents (*Re Ever's Trusts* [1980] 3 All ER 399). Once marriage has taken place however, it appears possible, in appropriate circumstances, to take into account the circumstances prevailing during previous unmarried cohabitation in the judicial resolution of break-up (*Kokosinki* v *Kokosinki* [1980] 1 All ER 1106).

The commencement of an implied trust in the case of unmarried persons accords with the general principles laid down in *Gissing* v *Gissing*. To that extent, the legal principles are the same as in the case of married couples. The possibly different relationship between unmarried couples, however, might alter the factual inferences to be drawn from their behaviour (See *Bernard* v *Josephs* [1982] 3 All ER 162 at 169). One extraordinary decision suggests that this trust ends spontaneously on separation of the parties. In *Hall* v *Hall* [1982] 3 FLR 379 it was held that, as a result of this, the share of a wife who left the home had to be calculated as at the time of her leaving and not at the time of judgment. The decision infers that trusts can die as impliedly as they can be born, a novelty in English law. It also confirms the desire of judges to approve or disapprove of behaviour in particular cases without too much doctrinal constraint. That is certainly no novelty.

CONVERSION OF JOINT TENANCY INTO TENANCY IN COMMON

Although the doctrine of survivorship which characterises joint tenancy is convenient for some purposes, there will obviously be many instances when it is undesirable. It is possible, however, to convert a joint tenancy into a tenancy in common.

This process is known as *severance*. It has already been explained that tenancy in common cannot exist at law so that severance cannot affect the legal estate (see also LPA 1925 s 36(2)). What really matters is that the beneficial joint tenancy can be severed. Thus if *A* and *B* hold the legal estate jointly in trust for themselves jointly and *B* severs, the result will be that *A* and *B* still hold the legal estate jointly but on trust for themselves as tenants in common in equity. So although survivorship will operate upon the bare legal ownership, it will not affect the beneficial enjoyment of the interest: if *B* dies, his share will go to his next-of-kin or beneficiary under his will.

As a result of severance, the co-owner can for the first time say he holds a share in the property, whereas before he only had a potential share. This share is only a mathematical one, for even in tenancy in common there is unity of possession. This is why it is called tenancy 'in undivided shares'. The size of share which a severing tenant will own depends upon the number of co-tenants. If he is one of three he will own a third, if one of five a fifth and so on. The view expressed by Lord Denning MR in the Court of Appeal in *Bedson* v *Bedson* [1965] 2 QB 666 that a spouse cannot sever a joint interest in the matrimonial home while the other spouse remains in possession is surely wrong (see LPA 1925 ss 36(2) and 37; and 82 LQR 29, at 31).

Yet the learned judge was seeking to avoid a difficult and practical dilemma. If, for instance, one spouse deserted the other and severed the beneficial joint ownership, selling his interest to a stranger, that stranger would be entitled to go into possession with the other spouse. Against this, it has been argued that ownership of the equitable interest does not entitle a person to possession, for the right to possession belongs to the owners of the legal estate as trustees, and the purchaser from the deserting spouse would not obtain the legal estate (37 Conveyancer 270). This argument can hardly be valid because the right of the trustee to possession is cancelled, and has been so for the last three hundred years, by his duty to allow the persons beneficially entitled to enjoy their interests. The stranger would therefore be entitled to possession or compensation. The ultimate solution would be a sale of the property, an outcome which might well have occurred if the deserting spouse had made an application under the Law of Property Act 1925 s 30. In any case, a similar problem could arise if the original joint tenants were not husband and wife so that Lord Denning's remarks, aimed at co-ownership by spouses, hits all cases of joint ownership.

There are four ways of severing joint tenancy. The first three mentioned derive their authority from *Williams* v *Hensman* (1861) 1 John & H 546, which formerly applied only to personalty but was extended to land by the Law of Property Act 1925 s 36(2).

Inter vivos alienation

If a joint tenant alienates his interest in equity, severance occurs and his potential share thereby precipitates out of the joint tenancy in favour of the alienee. If there is more than one other co-tenant, however, their relationship between themselves is not changed. If there are three, *A*, *B* and *C*, and *C* sells his interest to *P*, *A* and *B* hold two-thirds as joint tenants as between themselves, but as tenants in common against *P*, who takes a one third share of the property, as tenants in common. Figure 11.1 expresses the change in relationships between these co-owners caused by disunity of titles following alienation.

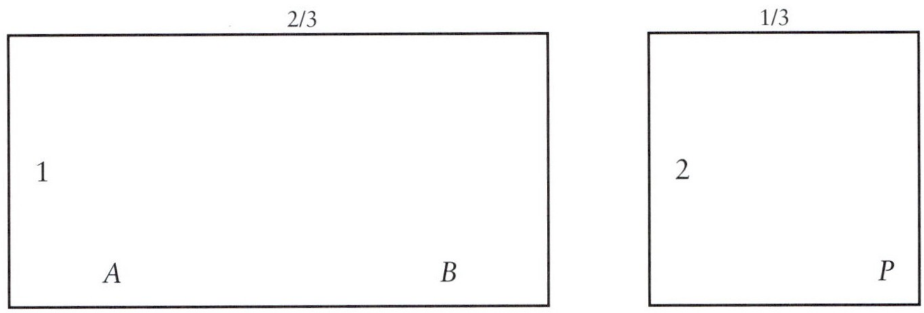

Fig 11.1

A and *B* are still joint tenants as to a two-thirds part so that survivorship will operate between them. If *A* dies, *B* will take a two-thirds share in common with *P*, who continues to own one-third. Severance also occurs upon other forms of alienation such as mortgage, and even upon contracts for alienation if specifically enforceable. Alienation, even though involuntary as in the case of bankruptcy, can sever joint tenancy (see *Re Gorman* [1990] 1 WLR 616).

Later acquisition of another interest in the land

If one co-owner acquires an additional interest, severance occurs as to his part, for the unity of interest is broken. Thus if *A*, *B* and *C* are joint life tenants and *C* subsequently acquires the fee simple in remainder, his life interest 'merges', that is coalesces, with his remainder. As in the example above, however, *A* and *B* continue to hold jointly as between themselves. Severance does not occur unless the additional interest is different in quantum from the one held in joint tenancy, neither does it result if the additional interest is granted at the same time as the joint interest, as in a gift to *A*, *B* and *C* jointly for life with remainder in fee simple to *C*.

Agreement by joint tenants to hold as tenants in common

Such an agreement might be expressed or implied from the conduct of the co-owners (*Jackson* v *Jackson* (1804) 9 Ves 591). A merely unilateral declaration or a course of conduct falling short of alienation is not sufficient (*Nielson-Jones* v *Fedden* [1974] 3 All ER 38), but if communication of intent is made it does not matter that the transaction in which it took place is otherwise legally ineffective, as, for instance, where there was an oral agreement for sale by one joint tenant of his share to the other lacking the requirements of section 40 of the Law of Property Act 1925 or the Law of Property (Miscellaneous Provisions) Act 1989 s 2 (see *Burgess* v *Rawnsley* [1975] 3 WLR 99). This doctrine has now been confirmed by statute which, since the section concerned also deals with severance by writing, is cited below.

Notice in writing (LPA 1925 s 36(2))

> . . . where a legal estate (not being settled in land) is vested in joint tenants beneficially and any tenant desires to sever the joint tenancy in equity, he shall give to the other joint tenants a notice in writing of such desire or do such other acts or things as would, in the case of personal estate, have been effectual to sever the tenancy in equity . . .

(See *Re 88 Berkeley Road, London, NW9* [1971] 1 All ER 254 and *Holwell Securities Ltd.* v *Hughes* [1974] 1 All ER 161.)

Two points should be highlighted. First, the language of the subsection requires that the legal owners and the owners in equity shall be exactly the same persons, as in the case of *A*, *B* and *C* holding the legal estate for *A*, *B* and *C* in equity. Severance by notice is perhaps not therefore possible by any co-owner where any person holds only at law, or only in equity, as where *A*, *B* and *C* hold the legal estate for *A*, *B*, *C* and *D* jointly in equity, or where trustees T^1 and T^2 hold the legal estate for *A* and *B* jointly in equity. The matter is open to doubt. Second, the provision excludes settled land. This topic will be mentioned later, but the result of the subsection is that co-owners, such as joint life tenants who hold land under a strict settlement, cannot sever a joint interest by written notice.

DETERMINATION OF CO-OWNERSHIP OF LAND

Co-ownership of land may end in the following ways:

Partition

When all the co-owners, whether in joint tenancy or in tenancy in common, being of full age, are beneficially absolutely entitled to the net proceeds of sale, the trustees may partition the land, with the consents of the persons (if any) of full age who are interested in possession in the net rents and profits until sale. Each co-owner becomes sole owner of a separate part of the land. The details of the process are to be found in the Law of Property Act 1925 s 28(3) (see 34 Conveyancer 123). The subsection in terms only applies to tenancies in common, but in fact also applies to joint tenants because of the assimilating effect of s 36(1). Cases of deadlock can be resolved through applications under s 30.

Sale

When the land is sold, we have seen that the purchaser takes it free of any of the interests of the co-owners, provided that the transaction is conducted in accordance with the Act. The co-ownership continues to exist in the purchase money.

Union of beneficial interest in one person

If a joint tenant becomes solely entitled in equity, either by survivorship or by acquiring the interests of his co-tenants *inter vivos*, or a tenant in common becomes similarly entitled by acquisition of the other shares, the co-ownership ends. In the two types of determination mentioned above, the end of the trust for sale will be marked by a conveyance from the trustees which will vest the land in the alienee as absolute owner and which will clearly purge the title of the trust. When the co-ownership ends through union, however (see *Re Cook* [1948] Ch 212), it might not be so apparent as to satisfy a purchaser.

Suppose land was held both at law and in equity by *A*, *B* and *C* as joint tenants in fee simple, and that *B* and *C* both died. Survivorship will have vested both the legal and equitable interest in *A* only. The co-ownership has ended, and with it the trust for sale. *A* is therefore entitled to dispose of the land as an absolute owner, without appointing a trustee to act with him to receive purchase money (*see* LPA 1925 s 36(2), as amended by the Law of Property (Amendment) Act 1926).

Even though *A* can make an ordinary conveyance, the purchaser might have misgivings. If, for instance, either *B* or *C* has severed his tenancy before his death, a fact which might not be easy to discover at once, then the co-ownership and therefore the trust for sale still subsists. *A* would therefore have to appoint another trustee before making a sale. Even if no severance had taken place, this negative fact might be difficult to prove. This problem has now been remedied by the Law of Property (Joint Tenants) Act 1964, which is retrospective to 1 January 1926; this provides that, in favour of a purchaser of the legal estate, the survivor of two or more joint tenants shall be deemed to be solely and beneficially interested if he conveys as 'beneficial owner' or the conveyance includes a statement that he is so interested, unless before the date of the conveyance either: (a) a memorandum of severance has been endorsed on the conveyance which vested the legal estate in the joint tenants or (b) a bankruptcy petition or receiving order has been registered. The relevance of this latter provision is that bankruptcy brings about a severance of joint tenancy because it involves an alienation, even though an involuntary one, in favour of the trustee in bankruptcy. There are circumstances, however, in which the trustee in bankruptcy may have a claim even against the share of the person who is in co-ownership with the bankrupt (see the Bankruptcy Act 1914 s 42, and in *re Densham* [1975] 1 WLR 1519). The Act does not apply to registered land. It is not stated what shall happen if a purchaser takes the legal estate with knowledge of a severance which has not been endorsed. In any case the owner who has severed will have an interest in the purchase money.

The main effect of the Act is to give peace of mind to a purchaser. It does not endow a sole owner at law with any additional powers.

CO-OWNERSHIP AND STRICT SETTLEMENTS

If two or more persons become entitled under a strict settlement beneficially as joint tenants, they together constitute the tenant for life, if of full age, and the settlement continues (Settled Land Act 1925 s 19(2)). The subsection refers to beneficial entitlement for life, but presumably the same applies if the beneficiaries are entitled for some modified interest less in quantum than a fee simple absolute, such as a determinable interest. If, however, they hold for a tenancy in common, or in coparcenary, as in the case of life tenants in common, the strict settlement ends and the statutory trust for sale supervenes (Settled Land Act 1925 s 36(1)). The Settled Land Act trustees become the trustees for sale and can demand the legal estate. This is so even when the element of succession has been exhausted and the land would have ceased to be settled in any case. Thus if land is limited to *A* for life with remainder in fee simple to *X*, *Y* and *Z* equally, on *A*'s death his personal representatives must convey the land to the settlement trustees and not to *X*, *Y* and *Z*.

STUDY MATERIAL

Lloyds Bank plc v Rosset [1990] 1 All ER 1113

LORD BRIDGE OF HARWICH My Lords, the subject matter of this dispute is Vincent Farmhouse, Manston Road, Thanet (the property). The property is registered land which the first respondent, Mr Rosset, contracted to purchase on 23 November 1982 and which was conveyed to him on 17 December 1982. On the same date Mr Rosset executed a legal charge on the property in favour of the appellant, Lloyds Bank plc, to secure an overdraft on his current account with the bank. The bank's charge was registered on 7 February 1982. The bank initially agreed to allow Mr Rosset to borrow up to £15 000, but later raised this limit to £18 000. The limit was in due course exceeded, the bank's demand for repayment was not met and the bank instituted preceedings in the Thanet County Court for possession of the property in July 1984 against Mr Rosset and his wife. Mr and Mrs Rosset, who had initially occupied the property as their matrimonial home, had by this time parted. Mr Rosset, who was no longer residing in the property, did not resist the bank's claim. Mrs Rosset, however, alleged by way of defence to the bank's claim and by way of counterclaim against her husband that she had been entitled, since the date when her husband contracted to purchase the property, to a beneficial interest in the property under a constructive trust which qualified as an overriding interest under s 70(1)(*g*) of the Land Registration Act 1925 because she was in actual occupation of the property both on 17 December 1982 and 7 February 1983, whichever was the relevant date to be considered in determining the existence of the overriding interest to which she alleged the bank's charge was subject.

At the trial his Honour Judge Scarlett found that Mrs Rosset was entitled as against her husband to a beneficial interest in the property in an amount to be determined at a future hearing. He held that, on the true construction of the 1925

Act, the proprietor of a legal charge takes subject to overriding interests which are subsisting on the date of *creation*, as opposed to the date of *registration*, of the charge. He accordingly asked himself whether Mrs Rosset was in actual occupation of the property on 17 December 1982 and, finding that she was not, concluded that her equitable interest was not protected as an overriding interest by s 70(1)(*g*) so as to prevail against the bank's legal charge. He gave judgment for possession in favour of the bank. Mrs Rosset appealed, but Mr Rosset has taken no further part in the proceedings.

The Court of Appeal unanimously affirmed the judge's decision that the relevant date on which Mrs Rosset had to show that she was in actual occupation in order to establish an overriding interest which would prevail against the bank was 17 December 1982, the date of creation of the bank's charge. But they differed on the facts whether she was in actual occupation on that date: Purchas and Nicholls LJJ held that she was; Mustill LJ held that she was not (see [1988] 3 All ER 915, [1989] Ch 350). The bank now appeals by leave of your Lordships' House against the majority decision of the Court of Appeal in Mrs Rosset's favour.

The important question arising under the 1925 Act as to the relevant date on which to ascertain whether an interest in registered land is protected by actual occupation so as to prevail under s 70(1)(*g*) against the holder of a legal estate has now been resolved by your Lordships' decision in *Abbey National Building Society* v *Cann* [1990] 1 All ER 1085, in favour of the view that it is the date when the estate is transferred or created, not the date when it is registered.

The primary ground of the bank's appeal challenges the judge's finding, which was also unanimously affirmed by the Court of Appeal, that Mrs Rosset had by the date of completion acquired a beneficial interest in the property.

The Rossets were married in 1972. There are two children of the marriage, a daughter born in 1972 and a son born in 1981. From 1976 until the events giving rise to the present dispute, the parties were living in premises which had been built as an extension to a bungalow in Broadstairs which was the home of Mrs Rosset's parents, Mr and Mrs Gardner. Mr Rosset had borne the cost of building the extension, but it was occupied on the terms of an agreement between the Rossets and the Gardners which provided that, on the Rossets vacating the extension, each should be paid a fixed sum by Mr and Mrs Gardner. Mrs Rosset's father had insisted on his daughter being joined in the agreement in this way.

Mr Rosset is a Swiss national. He was working in 1982 as a courier conducting coach parties of tourists on the continent of Europe and was away from home a great deal. Some time before 1982 he became entitled to a substantial sum of money under a trust fund established by his grandmother in Switzerland. In 1982 the Rossets were looking for a new home to be bought with Mr Rosset's inheritance. It was Mrs Rosset who first found the property. It had been unoccupied for seven or eight years and required substantial work to render it suitable for occupation. Mrs Rosset took her husband to see it. He liked it and made an offer to purchase it for the asking price of £57 500. This was accepted on 3 August 1982 subject to contract.

On 25 October 1982 Mr Rosset opened an account at the Broadstairs branch of the bank. He saw the manager and told him that he was intending to buy the property with money he had inherited Switzerland. On 2 November Mr Rosset received a payment of £70 200 from Switzerland of which £59 200 was paid into his account with the bank. On 23 November contracts for the purchase of the property were exchanged. On 14 December Mr Rosset saw the bank manager and asked to be allowed to overdraw on his current account up to £15 000 to meet the cost of the works of renovation which were needed to be undertaken to the property. The manager asked whether the property was to be acquired in joint names. Mr Rosset replied that the property was to be acquired in his sole name because his wife and children were living with her parents. The manager agreed the overdraft and Mr Rosset signed the bank's form of charge which was then sent to Mr Rosset's solicitor to be dated on completion and registered on behalf of the bank. Completion took place on 17 December with funds drawn from the account which required an initial overdraft of £2267. Mrs Rosset knew nothing of the charge to the bank or the overdraft.

Meanwhile, Mr and Mrs Rosset had been let into possession of the property by the vendors even before the exchange of contracts. The builder employed by them, a Mr Griffin, commenced work on 7 November 1982. It was originally hoped that the house would be ready for the Rossets to move in before Christmas, but this proved in the event to be impossible. Eventually the Rossets moved in about the middle of February 1983 when the work was substantially complete. By this time Mr Rosset's overdraft had risen to over £18 000 and the bank refused to extend further credit. Most of the additional funds from the account had been expended in paying for the renovation works. Both the purchase price of the property and the cost of the works of renovation were paid by Mr Rosset alone and Mrs Rosset made no financial contribution to the acquisition of the property.

The case pleaded and carefully particularised by Mrs Rosset in support of her claim to an equitable interest in the property was that it had been expressly agreed between her and her husband in conversations before November 1982 that the property was to be jointly owned and that in reliance on this agreement she had made a significant contribution in kind to the acquisition of the property by the work she had personally undertaken in the course of the renovation of the property which was sufficient to give rise to a constructive trust in her favour.

There was a conflict of evidence between Mr and Mrs Rosset on the vital issue raised by this pleading. The question the judge had to determine was whether he could find that before the contract to acquire the property was concluded they had entered into an agreement, made an arrangement, reached an understanding or formed a common intention that the beneficial interest in the property would be jointly owned. I do not think it is of importance which of these alternative expressions one uses. Spouses living in amity will not normally think it necessary to formulate or define their respective interests in property in any precise way. The expectation of parties to every happy marriage is that they will share the practical benefits of occupying the matrimonial home whoever owns it. But this is something quite distinct from sharing the beneficial interest in the property asset which the matrimonial home represents. These considerations give rise to special difficulties for judges who are called on to resolve a dispute between spouses who have parted and are at arm's length as to what their common intention or understanding with respect to interests in property was at a time when they were still living as a united family and acquiring a matrimonial home in the expectation of living in it together indefinitely.

Since Mr Rosset was providing the whole purchase price of the property and the whole cost of renovation, Mrs Rosset would, I think, in any event have encountered formidable difficulty in establishing her claim to joint beneficial ownership. The claim as pleaded and as presented in evidence was, by necessary implication, to an equal share in the equity. But to sustain this it was necessary to show that it was Mr Rosset's intention to make an immediate gift to his wife of half the value of a property acquired for £57 500 and improved at a further cost of some £15 000. What made it doubly difficult for Mrs Rosset to establish her case was the circumstance, which was never in dispute, that Mr Rosset's uncle, who was trustee of his Swiss inheritance, would not release the funds for the purchase of the property except on terms that it was to be acquired in Mr Rosset's sole name. If Mr and Mrs Rosset had ever thought about it, they must have realised that the creation of a trust giving Mrs Rosset a half share, or indeed any other substantial share, in the beneficial ownership of the property would have been nothing less than a subterfuge to circumvent the stipulation which the Swiss trustee insisted on as a condition of releasing the funds to enable the property to be acquired.

In these circumstances, it would have required very cogent evidence to establish that it was the Rossets' common intention to defeat the evident purpose of the Swiss trustee's restriction by acquiring the property in Mr Rosset's name alone but to treat it nevertheless as beneficially owned jointly by both spouses. I doubt whether the evidence would have sustained a finding to that effect. But the judge made no such finding. On the contrary, his judgment on this point amounts to a clear rejection of Mrs Rosset's pleaded case. He said:

> The decision to transfer the property into the name of [Mr Rosset] alone was a disappointment to [Mrs Rosset], but I am satisfied that she genuinely believed that [Mr Rosset] would hold the property in his name as something which was a joint venture, to be shared between them as the family home and that the reason for it being held by [him] alone was to ensure that [his] uncle would sanction the export of trust funds from Switzerland to England for the purchase. As so often happens [Mr and Mrs Rosset] did not pursue their discussion to the extent of defining precisely what their respective interests in the property should be. It was settled that the property should be transferred into the name of [Mr Rosset] alone to achieve the provision of funds from Switzerland, but *in the period from August 1982 to the 23 November 1982 when the contracts were exchanged, [the parties] did not decide whether [Mrs Rosset] should have any interest in the property.* On one occasion [Mrs Rosset] heard [her husband] say to her parents that he had put the house in their joint names, but she knew that he could not do that and treated what he said as an expression of what he would like to do. In these circumstances I am satisfied that the outcome of the discussions between the parties as to the name into which the property should be transferred did not exclude the possibility that [Mrs Rosset] should have a beneficial interest in the property.

I have emphasised the critical finding in this passage from the judgment.

Even if there had been the clearest oral agreement between Mr and Mrs Rosset that Mr Rosset was to hold the property in trust for them both as tenants in common, this would, of course, have been ineffective since a valid declaration of trust by way of gift of a beneficial interest in land is required by s 53(1) of the Law of Property Act 1925 to be in writing. But if Mrs Rosset had, as pleaded, altered her position in reliance on the agreement this could have given rise to an enforceable interest in her favour by way either of a constructive trust or of a proprietary estoppel.

Having rejected the contention that there had been any concluded agreement, arrangement or any common intention formed before contracts for the purchase of the property were exchanged on 23 November 1982 that Mrs Rosset should have any beneficial interest, the judge concentrated his attention on Mrs Rosset's activities in connection with the renovation works as a possible basis from which to infer such a common intention. He described what she did up to the date of completion as follows:

> Up to 17 December 1982 [Mrs Rosset's] contribution to the venture was: (1) to urge on the builders and to attempt to co-ordinate their work, until her husband insisted that he alone should give instructions; (2) to go to builders' merchants and obtain material required by the builders . . . and to deliver the materials to the site. This was of some importance because Mr Griffin and his employees did not know the Thanet area; (3) to assist her husband in planning the renovation and decoration of the house. In this, she had some skill over and above that acquired by most housewives. She was a skilled painter and decorator who enjoyed wall-papering and decorating, and, as her husband acknowledged, she had good ideas about this work. In connection with this, she advised on the position of electric plugs and radiators and planned the design of the large breakfast room and the small kitchen of the house; (4) to carry out the wallpapering of Natasha's bedroom and her own bedroom, after preparing the surfaces of the walls and clearing up the rooms concerned before the papering began; (5) to begin the preparation of the surfaces of the walls of her son's bedroom, the den, the upstairs lavatory and the downstairs washroom for papering. All this wallpapering was completed after 17 December 1982 but by 31 December 1982; (6) to assist in arranging the insurance of the house by the Minster Insurance Co Ltd home cover policy, in force from 3 November 1982; (7) to assist in arranging a crime prevention survey on 23 November 1982; (8) to assist in arranging the installation of burglar alarms described in a specification dated 3 December 1982.

Later the judge said:

> I am satisfied that in 1982 the common intention expressed by [Mr and Mrs Rosset] in conversation between themselves was that Vincent Farmhouse should be purchased in the name of [Mr Rosset] alone, because funds would not be made available from [his] family trust in Switzerland unless the purchase was made only in his name. In addition, however, it was their common intention that the renovation of the house should be a joint venture, after which the house was to become a family home to be shared by [the parties] and their children.

I pause to observe that neither a common intention by spouses that a house is to be renovated as a 'joint venture' nor a common intention that the house is to be shared by parents and children as the family home throws any light on their intentions with respect to the beneficial ownership of the property.

Reverting to Mrs Rosset's activity in connection with the renovation of the property the judge said:

> It is plain that she made every effort to make the house fit for occupation before Christmas 1982 and spent all the time she could at Vincent Farmhouse in between taking Natasha to school and fetching her from school . . . Obviously the extent of the work which [Mrs Rosset] did in preparation, clearing up before painting and decorating, and the painting and decorating itself, was valuable . . . In the result, having considered (1) the semi-derelict condition of Vincent Farmhouse in November 1982, (2) the absence of [Mr Rosset] abroad for ten days in November and early December 1982, (3) [Mrs Rosset's] special skills in painting and decorating over and above those of the average housewife and her direct contribution to reducing the cost of renovation of the farmhouse by carrying out certain painting and decorating herself, (4) the time she spent at the farmhouse from 4 November 1982 attempting to co-ordinate the work of the builders and her work in ordering and delivering materials to the site for the builders, and (5) the conversations between the parties concerning into whose name the property was to be transferred and the nature of the joint venture and the purpose of purchasing Vincent Farmhouse, I am satisfied that prior to 17 December 1982 there was a common intention between [Mr and Mrs Rosset] that [Mrs Rosset] should have a beneficial interest in the property under a constructive trust and that she did act to her detriment on the faith of such a common intention. Some, but not all, of her work at the farmhouse prior to 17 December 1982 falls into the category of work on which she could not reasonably have been expected to embark unless she was to have an interest in the house, namely the work to which she brought the special skills of painting and decorating and her work in ordering and delivering materials to the site for the builders in attempting to co-ordinate her work. These actions by [Mrs Rosset] must have reduced the cost of renovating the farmhouse and thus indirectly contributed to the acquisition of the property, albeit to a small extent.

At the very end of his judgment the judge pointed out that he had made no finding as to the extent of Mrs Rosset's beneficial interest in the property. He indicated that he would hear counsel as to what directions should be given for the determination of this issue at a later date. He concluded his judgment with the sentence:

> An area which the court would wish to explore is the extent to which the qualifying conduct of [Mrs Rosset] reduced the cost of the renovation of the farmhouse and its buildings.

It is clear from these passages in the judgment that the judge based his inference of a common intention that Mrs Rosset should have a beneficial interest in the property under a constructive trust essentially on what Mrs Rosset did in and about assisting in the renovation of the property between the beginning of November 1982 and the date of completion on 17 December 1982. Yet by itself this activity, it seems to me, could not possibly justify any such inference. It was common ground that Mrs Rosset was extremely anxious that the new matrimonial home should be ready for occupation before Christmas if possible. In these circumstances, it would seem the most natural thing in the world for any wife, in the absence of her husband abroad, to spend all the time she could spare and to employ any skills she might have, such as the ability to decorate a room, in doing all she could to accelerate progress of the work quite irrespective of any expectation she might have of enjoying a beneficial interest in the property. The judge's view that some of this work was work 'on which she could not reasonably have been expected to embark unless she was to have an interest in the house' seems to me, with respect, quite untenable. The impression that the judge may have thought that the share of the equity to which he held Mrs Rosset to be entitled had been 'earned' by her work in connection with the renovation is emphasised by his reference in the concluding sentence of his judgment to the extent to which her 'qualifying contribution' reduced the cost of the renovation.

On any view the monetary value of Mrs Rosset's work expressed as a contribution to a property acquired at a cost exceeding £70 000 must have been so trifling as to be almost *de minimis*. I should myself have had considerable doubt whether Mrs Rosset's contribution to the work of renovation was sufficient to support a claim to a constructive trust in the absence of writing to satisfy the requirements of s 51 of the Law Of Property Act 1925 even if her husband's intention to make a gift to her of half or any other share in the equity of the property had been clearly established or if he had clearly represented to her that that was what he intended. But here the conversations with her husband on which Mrs Rosset relied, all of which took place before November 1982, were incapable of lending support to the conclusion of a constructive trust in the light of the judge's finding that by that date there has been no decision that she was to have any interest in the property. The finding that the discussions 'did not exclude the possibility' that she should have an interest does not seem to me to add anything of significance.

These considerations lead me to the conclusion that the judge's finding that Mr Rosset held the property as constructive trustee for himself and his wife cannot be supported and it is on this short ground that I would allow the appeal. In the course of the argument your Lordships had the benefit of elaborate submissions as to the test to be applied to determine the circumstances in which the sole legal proprietor of a dwelling house can properly be held to have become a constructive trustee of a share in the beneficial interest in the house for the benefit of the partner with whom he or she has cohabited in the house as their shared home. Having in this case reached a conclusion on the facts which, although at variance with the views of the courts below, does not seem to depend on any nice legal distinction and with which, I understand, all your Lordships agree, I cannot help doubting whether it would contribute anything to the illumination of the law if I were to attempt an elaborate and exhaustive analysis of the relevant law to add to the many already to be found in the authorities to which our attention was directed in the course of the argument. I do, however, draw attention to one critical distinction which any judge required to resolve a dispute between former partners as to the beneficial interest in the home they formerly shared should always have in the forefront of his mind.

The first and fundamental question which must always be resolved is whether, independently of any inference to be drawn from the conduct of the parties in the course of sharing the house as their home and managing their joint affairs, there has at any time prior to acquisition, or exceptionally at some later date, been any agreement, arrangement or understanding reached between them that the property is to be shared beneficially. The finding of an agreement or arrangement to share in this sense can only, I think, be based on evidence of express discussions between the partners, however imperfectly remembered and however imprecise their terms may have been. Once a finding to this effect is made it will only be necessary for the partner asserting a claim to a beneficial interest against the partner entitled to the legal estate to show that he or she has acted to his or her detriment or significantly altered his or her position in reliance on the agreement in order to give rise to a constructive trust or proprietary estoppel.

In sharp contrast with this situation is the very different one where there is no evidence to support a finding of an agreement or arrangement to share, however reasonable it might have been for the parties to each such an arrangement if they had applied their minds to the question, and where the court must rely entirely on the conduct of the parties both as the basis from which to infer a common intention to share the property beneficially and as the conduct relied on to give rise to a constructive trust. In this situation direct contributions to the purchase price by the partner who is not the legal owner, whether initially or by payment of mortgage instalments, will readily justify the inference necessary to the creation of a constructive trust. But, as I read the authorities, it is at least extremely doubtful whether anything less will do.

The leading cases in your Lordships' House are *Pettitt* v *Pettitt* [1969] 2 All ER 385, [1970] AC 777 and *Gissing* v *Gissing* [1970] 2 All ER 780, [1971] AC 886. Both demonstrate situations in the second category to which I have referred and their Lordships discuss at great length the difficulties to which these situations give rise. The effect of these two decisions is very helpfully analysed in the judgment of Lord MacDermott LCJ in *McFarlane* v *McFarlane* [1972] NI 59.

Outstanding examples on the other hand of cases giving rise to situations in the first category are *Eves* v *Eves* [1975] 3 All ER 768, [1975] 1 WLR 1338 and *Grant* v *Edwards* [1986] 2 All ER 426, [1986] Ch 638. In both these cases, where the parties who had cohabited were unmarried, the female partner had been clearly led by the male partner to believe, when they set up home together, that the property would belong to them jointly. In *Eves* v *Eves* the male partner had told the female partner that the only reason why the property was to be acquired in his name alone was because she was under 21 and that, but for her age, he would have had the house put into their joint names. He admitted in evidence that this was simply an 'excuse'. Similarly, in *Grant* v *Edwards* the female partner was told by the male partner that the only reason for not acquiring the property in joint names was because she was involved in divorce proceedings and that, if the property were acquired jointly, this might operate to her prejudice in those proceedings. As Nourse LJ put it ([1986] 2 All ER 426 at 433, [1986] Ch 638 at 649):

> Just as in *Eves* v *Eves*, these facts appear to me to raise a clear inference that there was an understanding between the plaintiff and the defendant, or a common intention, that the plaintiff was to have some sort of proprietary interest in the house; otherwise no excuse for not putting her name onto the title would have been needed.

The subsequent conduct of the female partner in each of these cases, which the court rightly held sufficient to give rise to a constructive trust or proprietary estoppel supporting her claim to an interest in the property, fell far short of such conduct as would by itself have supported the claim in the absence of an express representation by the male partner that she was to have such an interest. It is significant to note that the share to which the female partners in *Eves* v *Eves* and *Grant* v *Edwards* were held entitled were one-quarter and one-half respectively. In no sense could these shares have been regarded as proportionate to what the judge in the instant case described as a 'qualifying contribution' in terms of the indirect contributions to the acquisition or enhancement of the value of the houses made by the female partners.

I cannot help thinking that the judge in the instant case would not have fallen into error if he had kept clearly in mind the distinction between the effect of evidence on the one hand which was capable of establishing an express agreement or an express representation that Mrs Rosset was to have an interest in the property and evidence on the other hand of conduct alone as a basis for an inference of the necessary common intention.

If Mrs Rosset had become entitled to a beneficial interest in the property prior to completion it might have been necessary to examine a variant of the question regarding priorities which your Lordships have just considered in *Abbey National Building Society* v *Cann* [1990] 1 All ER 1085 and, subject to that question, to decide whether, as a matter of fact, she was in 'actual occupation' of the property on 17 December 1982. Since these questions have now become academic, I do not think any useful purpose would be served by going into them.

For the reasons I have indicated, I would allow the appeal, set aside the order of the Court of Appeal and, as between Mrs Rosset and the bank, restore the order of the trial judge.

STUDY MATERIAL

Matrimonial and Family Proceedings Act 1984 – Provisions relating to powers of the High Court and county courts

Orders for financial relief after divorce, etc.

3. For section 25 of the Matrimonial Causes Act 1973 (in this Part referred to as 'the 1973 Act') there shall be substituted the following sections—

"Matters to which court is to have regard in deciding how to exercise its powers under ss. 23, 24 and 24A

25.—(1) It shall be the duty of the court in deciding whether to exercise its powers under section 23, 24 or 24A above and, if so, in what manner, to have regard to all the circumstances of the case, first consideration being given to the welfare while a minor of any child of the family who has not attained the age of eighteen.

(2) As regards the exercise of the powers of the court under section 23(1)(*a*), (*b*) or (*c*), 24 or 24A above in relation to a party to the marriage, the court shall in particular have regard to the following matters—

(*a*) the income, earning capacity, property and other financial resources which each of the parties to the marriage has or is likely to have in the foreseeable future, including in the case of earning capacity any increase in that capacity which it would in the opinion of the court be reasonable to expect a party to the marriage to take steps to acquire;

(*b*) the financial needs, obligations and responsibilities which each of the parties to the marriage has or is likely to have in the foreseeable future;

(*c*) the standard of living enjoyed by the family before the breakdown of the marriage;

(*d*) the age of each party to the marriage and the duration of the marriage;

(*e*) any physical or mental disability of either of the parties to the marriage;

(*f*) the contributions which each of the parties has made or is likely in the foreseeable future to make to the welfare of the family, including any contribution by looking after the home or caring for the family;

(*g*) the conduct of each of the parties, if that conduct is such that it would in the opinion of the court be inequitable to disregard it;

(*h*) in the case of proceedings for divorce or nullity of marriage, the value to each of the parties to the marriage of any benefit (for example, a pension) which, by reason of the dissolution or annulment of the marriage, that party will lose the chance of acquiring.

(3) As regards the exercise of the powers of the court under section 23(1)(*d*), (*e*), or (*f*), (2) or (4), 24 or 24A above in relation to a child of the family, the court shall in particular have regard to the following matters—

(*a*) the financial needs of the child;

(*b*) the income, earning capacity (if any), property and other financial resources of the child;

(*c*) any physical or mental disability of the child;

(*d*) the manner in which he was being and in which the parties to the marriage expected him to be educated or trained;

(*e*) the considerations mentioned in relation to the parties to the marriage in paragraphs (*a*), (*b*) (*c*) and (*e*) of subsection (2) above.

(4) As regards the exercise of the powers of the court under section 23(1)(*d*), (*e*) or (*f*), (2) or (4), 24 or 24A above against a party to a marriage in favour of a child of the family who is not the child of that party, the court shall also have regard—

(*a*) to whether that party assumed any responsibility for the child's maintenance, and, if so, to the extent to which, and the basis upon which, that party assumed such responsibility and to the length of time for which that party discharged such responsibility.

(*b*) to whether in assuming and discharging such responsibility that party did so knowing that the child was not his or her own;

(*c*) to the liability of any other person to maintain the child.

Exercise of court's powers in favour of party to marriage on decree of divorce or nullity of marriage

25A.—(1) Where on or after the grant of a decree of divorce or nullity of marriage the court decides to exercise its powers under section 23(1)(*a*), (*b*) or (*c*), 24 or 24A above in favour of a party to the marriage, it shall be the duty of the court to consider whether it would be appropriate so to exercise those powers that the financial obligations of each party towards the other will be terminated as soon after the grant of the decree as the court considers just and reasonable.

(2) Where the court decides in such a case to make a periodical payments or secured periodical payments order in favour of a party to the marriage, the court shall in particular consider whether it would be appropriate to require those payments to be made or secured only for such term as would in the opinion of the court be sufficient to enable the party in whose favour the order is made to adjust without undue hardship to the termination of his or her financial dependence on the other party.

(3) Where on or after the grant of a decree of divorce or nullity of marriage an application is made by a party to the marriage for a periodical payments or secured periodical payments order in his or her favour, then, if the court considers that no continuing obligation should be imposed on either party to make or secure periodical payments in favour of the other, the court may dismiss the application with a direction that the applicant shall not be entitled to make any further application in relation to that marriage for an order under section 23(1) (*a*) or (*b*) above."

QUESTIONS

1. Dylan and Dandelion, his girlfriend, do not believe in marriage. They wish to set up home together and to have children. They intend to pool their savings and buy 'Nettle Nook' as their family home, with the assistance of a loan from a building society secured upon that property. Dylan is a herbal scientist who intends to stay at home in order to carry out research into natural medicines. There is little prospect that he will earn any income. Dandelion is manageress of 'Fibrefoods Pantry', a very successful restaurant. Dylan is very domesticated but Dandelion has little time for household work. Advise them as to their material interests in the future if they should go ahead with their venture. Draft a cohabitation agreement for them.
2. Consider whether lawyers are suitable people to offer initial advice to married persons who contemplate divorce or separation.
3. Since cohabitation outside marriage is not forbidden by criminal law, should not the civil law be more ready to recognise unmarried unions?
4. In 1989 the Law Commission published a Report on Trusts of Land (Law Com No 181). See also (1989) 52 MLR 683. Consider the effects these proposals, if enacted, would have on the law relating to ownership of land.

CHAPTER 12

EASEMENTS

INTRODUCTION

An easement is traditionally defined as a right to use or restrict the use of another person's land in some way. This definition is unsatisfactory because it misses the purpose of a definition, which is to distinguish and identify. It attempts to describe easements by reference to their subject matter, whereas this is one of their least distinctive characteristics. There is no kind of advantage which one person can enjoy over another person's land by virtue of an easement which he cannot enjoy through some other means, even though the enforceability and stability of the right might be much more robust if achieved by an easement. Thus rights of ways and of light are commonly found as easements but may be enjoyed through licences or restrictive covenants respectively.

To give an analogy, I can go to a concert either on my bike or in my car. The concert will sound the same in either case. No one would describe a car by saying that it will take you to a concert, because so will a bike. To describe a car you must talk of the vehicle itself. Likewise, easements are vehicles, not destinations. It is true that there are some destinations I cannot reach by means of easements, just as there are certain destinations, such as mountain peaks, which are beyond the reach of my car. These forbidden destinations no more serve to identify easements than do the destinations they are capable of reaching.

Yet it is most important to know whether enjoyment of a particular advantage over another person's land is attributable to an easement as opposed to some other right, because, as mentioned above, the span of enforceability and the durability of the advantages will be affected by this. This is because an easement is an interest in land. It may be a legal interest if it is to endure forever or for a certain term of years (LPA 1925 s 1(2)(a)) and has been created in one of the ways required for legal easements. These methods of creation are dealt with below. It is an equitable interest if it is to endure for any other period, such as for life, or has not been created in the form appropriate for legal easements, even though it is to endure for a period which would ordinarily entitle it to exist as a legal interest.

In other words, an easement is very much more than a personal right such as a licence. If it is a legal easement it can be enforced against anyone coming to the servient land whether he has notice of it or not, and no matter what interest he takes in the land. Furthermore, a legal easement needs no registration to secure it. Indeed, it cannot be registered. The benefit is, moreover, as sturdy as the burden. It passes without mention on a conveyance of the dominant land to another person (LPA 1925 s 62). If it is an equitable easement then it possesses the Achilles' heel of all equitable interests and may be overridden by a purchaser of a legal estate in the servient land for value without notice. An equitable easement created after 1925, however, may be registered under the Land Charges Act 1972 as a Class D (iii) land charge or, in the case of registered land, as a minor interest under the Land Registration Acts. Once registered, it becomes universally enforceable just as a legal easement is. If not registered, it will be void as against a purchaser of a legal estate in the servient land for money or money's worth unless the principle of *proprietary estoppel* can be invoked. This will be explained below.

An easement, therefore, is a means by which certain advantages may be enjoyed over the land of another person. It is the means, or vehicle, which must be examined. The subject will be approached in the following way, which reflects the order in which a particular claim to an easement should be analysed so as to establish whether it really is an easement or some other right. First, since there are certain advantages which cannot be enjoyed through the medium of easements, these must be considered at the outset, for if the subject matter is not within the province of easements there is no purpose in exploring further. Second, given that the right can be achieved by an easement, certain conditions must exist before an easement can be created. Third, even if the first two conditions are satisfied, an easement can only be created in certain ways. The first requirement speaks of content, the second of conditions, and the third of form. To bake a pie the ingredients must be acceptable though the choice is wide, the oven must be correct, and the mixture contained within a dish.

So an easement is a means of acquiring against land, for the benefit of other land, a right which is enforceable as an interest in land.

Certain other rights which have some of the characteristics of easements must then be distinguished.

THE SUBJECT MATTER OF EASEMENTS

We may begin with the general principle that all kinds of advantages over another person's land can be the subject matter of easements, except insofar as the law has imposed restrictions to the contrary. The precise limits of these restrictions have not been conclusively settled, for all the possibilities have not been litigated, but the broad principles of exclusion can be identified. Within this somewhat ill-defined framework, new kinds of easements are quite capable of emerging, and two judicial *dicta* on the question must not be taken as contradictory. On the one hand, Lord Brougham said in *Keppell* v *Bailey* (1834) 2 My & K 517 (at 535) that 'it must not therefore be supposed that incidents of a novel kind can be devised and attached to property, at the fancy or caprice of any owner', while Lord St Leonards remarked in *Dyce* v *Hay* (1852) I Macq 305, that 'the category of servitudes and easements must alter and expand with the changes that take place in the circumstances of mankind'.

The first dictum means that there are restrictions in principle upon the subject matter of easements. These restrictions will be described below as precisely as the present condition of the law permits. The second statement means that, given that those principles of exclusion are not offended, new examples of easements are quite possible. Thus it is clear that the rights to drive a motor car over land or to attach a television aerial to a roof are both capable of being easements although obviously of modern origin.

Before examining these principles relating to subject matter, some examples of established easements may be given. *Positive easements*, which involve the dominant owner in doing some act, include rights of way whether on foot or otherwise; drainage through pipes; rights to fix boards; cables or other such items on or through property; to enter property of another in order to repair your own; to take water; to discharge roof water; to create nuisances such as emissions of liquids, gases or noises; the right to use a lavatory and many other rights of a miscellaneous character. These are only examples and reflect the activities of mankind in the past; they should not be taken to mark the boundaries of easements but rather to pave the way for new ones. Examples of *negative easements* which do not involve the dominant owner in the doing of any act, but merely restrict the activities of the servient owner, are rights of support and light.

The restrictions placed upon the subject matter of easements are as follows:

An easement cannot involve the servient owner in doing any positive act or expending money

In *Jones* v *Price* [1965] 2 All ER 625, at 628, Willmer LJ said: '. . . properly speaking an easement requires no more than sufferance on the part of the occupier of the servient tenement . . .' and approved a statement in Gale on Easements that an easement is 'either a right to do something or a right to prevent something'. (Gale, (1986) *Law of Easements*, Sweet and Maxwell.) There is no known case where an easement has obliged the servient owner either to do any positive act or to spend money in relation to an easement. The relationship of landlord and tenant, however, might import a contractual duty to maintain and repair the subject matter of an easement to a reasonable standard where that easement is necessary to the tenancy. Thus in *Liverpool City Council* v *Irwin* [1977] AC 239 the House of Lords held that unless there was express provision to the contrary, the landlord must so maintain stairways, lifts and rubbish chutes where these are not part of the letting but retained by him.

If *A* has a right of way over the land of *B*, *B* is under no duty to maintain the path or road which is used by *A* for this purpose. Nor can the right to a supply of hot water be the subject matter of an easement (*Regis Property Co Ltd* v *Redman* [1956] 2 All ER 335). Similarly, if *A* has a right to support for his buildings against those of *B*, *B* need not repair his own property even though his failure to do so threatens that support. He must, however, allow *A* to carry out these repairs. On the other hand, the servient owner cannot remove the existing means of support without substituting an equivalent one (*Bond* v *Nottingham Corporation* [1940] Ch 429, at 438–439). Although an easement cannot itself impose a duty to do a positive act or to spend money, once it is created, its very existence can constitute a financial loss to the servient owner, since the useful enjoyment of the land subject to the easement may be rendered more expensive because of it (*Saint* v *Jenner* [1973] 1 All ER 127).

A right to have fences, hedges, or boundary walls maintained is therefore said not to be a true easement, for it involves positive acts or expenditure of money by the servient owner. Yet when the conditions appropriate to the existence of easements exist, such a right enjoys enforceability similar to that of an easement. Although described as a 'spurious' easement, its status as a right analogous to an easement cannot now be questioned. (See *Jones* v *Price*, above, and *Crow* v *Wood* [1970] 3 All ER 425). Nevertheless, it offends the principle that an easement is a right against property as such and not against persons, for only persons can perform dynamic acts. The right is rare.

An occupier of servient land might however be liable in tort or public law for damage or personal injury caused by dangerous apparatus fitted to facilitate the enjoyment of an easement. An example is liability to visitors for a faulty manhole cover under the Occupiers' Liability Acts 1957 and 1984.

An easement cannot involve taking anything from the land apart from water

A right which involves taking away part of the land or the produce of land cannot be an easement, although it may be a *profit à prendre*. Thus the rights to pasture cattle, or to take peat, sand or game cannot be easements, though they may be profits (see p 323). However, water is not for this purpose deemed to be part of land so that a right to take water may be an easement (*Polden* v *Bastard* (1865) LR 1 QB 156).

An easement cannot give exclusive possession of the servient land

The four tests, described later, which define the conditions necessary to the existence of an easement, do not lay down to what extent the exercise of an easement may preclude the owner of the servient land from enjoying his land. Certainly all easements have this effect to some extent. A right of way, which can be an easement if anything can, may prevent an owner building on land. A right of way is a fairly elemental example and others must be examined to find out how near an easement may approach to an ouster of possession of the servient owner from his land.

In *Re Ellenborough Park* [1955] 3 All ER 667 it was held that the owners of several houses could enjoy such an easement over land nearby as entitled them to walk about in and have 'full enjoyment' of a pleasure garden. They were not restricted to a mere right of passage but could sit and linger. Of course, this did not exclude the owner, but it shows an easement of broader calibre than a mere right of way. Let us see how much broader it may be. In *Miller v Emcer Products Ltd* [1956] 1 All ER 237 the right to use another person's lavatory was held to be an easement. Here, we have an easement amounting to exclusive occupation, or so most people would expect. This represents a further stage towards ouster of the servient owner, but the exclusive use of the premises was of course temporary and occasional. Yet if there were many people residing at the dominant tenement their use of the lavatory might be so extensive as to be, if one might use the expression, an inconvenience to the servient owner. Still, it might be argued, even an ordinary right of way might, in its exercise, exclude the servient owner from a certain part of his land for the brief moment of time for which the dominant owner covered a given piece of land.

The next case is *Pye* v *Mumford* (1848) 11 QB 666, the facts of which are hardly more salubrious. The right of one farmer to enter the land of another to mix manure was held to be an easement. Here exclusive possession was taken of a part of land. The report tells us little except several different words for manure, and neither judge nor counsel gave any consideration to the point in question, although the dominant owner was held to be entitled to 'a certain small reasonable portion' of the close 'at all seasons'.

The next stage in the progression is the right to put small items on servient land on a permanent footing. Several rights of this type have been sanctioned by the courts as easements. One is the right to fix stones there to prevent earth erosion as in *Philpot* v *Bath* (1905) 21 TLR 634. There is some doubt as to whether the right to run telephone wires across another's land may be an easement, although one judge in *Lancashire Telephone Co* v *Manchester Overseers* (1884) 14 QBD 267, assumed it could be. In any case, this doubt is somewhat leapfrogged by the decision in *Moody* v *Steggles* (1879) 12 ChD 261, where it was held that the right to have a signboard fixed on a neighbouring property could be an easement. No mention was made that this amounted to exclusive and permanent possession of a small portion of that land. The same problem arises of course in the case of an easement of drainage through pipes. Is the easement merely the right to pass the effluent across the servient land, and the right to have the pipes there attributable to some other legal category? The pipe is necessary to prevent contamination of the land by sewage but does its presence turn a spasmodic and occasional activity into virtually permanent possession? Further complications may be caused by the question to whom does the pipe, as a physical thing, belong? Buckley J tangled with this latter problem in *Simmons* v *Midford* [1969] 2 All ER 1269. The answer to it depends on the circumstances of the particular case, but has its home more in the law of fixtures than that of easements. In other words if *S* allows *D* to lay pipes under his (*S*'s) land, those pipes, according to the arrangements made of course, may be fixtures appurtenant to the land of *D*, not *S*. In short they become part of *D*'s land. There is nothing particularly strange in this, for back in 1879 James LJ in *Wheeldon* v *Burrows* (1879) 12 ChD 31, at 60, discussing a similar problem, remarked

> . . . the whole of the conduit through which the water ran was a corporeal part of the house, just as in any old city there are cellars projecting under other houses. They thought it was not merely the right to the passage of water, but that the conduit itself passed as part of the house, just like a flue passing through another man's house.

This reasoning, however, would not justify the presence of things on another man's land where there is no physical connection between them and the dominant land.

In any case, two further cases suggest that an easement may go much beyond transient use and may amount not merely to a theoretical and inconsequential possession but to a considerable and territorially substantial and permanent one, which may even exclude the servient owner. In *Wright* v *Macadam* [1949] 2 All ER 565, a decision of the Court of Appeal, it was held that the right to store coal in a shed belonging to another was an easement, despite the fact that this would deny possession of part of the property to the owner. Neither judges nor counsel addressed themselves to this factor. In *A-G of Southern Nigeria* v *John Holt & Co* [1915] AC 599, a decision of the Judicial Committee of the Privy Council, *X* carried on business in Lagos from land of his which originally fronted directly on to the sea. Foreshore works, however, had enabled the recovery of the land between his land and the sea. He, believing this land to be his own, erected warehouses on it. It was held that, since the reclamation amounted to natural accretion, the land vested in the Crown but that an irrevocable licence should be presumed in his favour, allowing him to continue his business. There was held to be no easement, only a licence, but only because an easement can only be constituted over servient land which the dominant owner takes to be servient land – which was not so here. The Privy Council saw no objection to such a right being an easement on the grounds now under discussion.

Thus, on the cases so far considered, the fact that a substantial piece of land is permanently and to all intents and purposes exclusively possessed has not prevented a right being classified as an easement. But the next case, *Copeland* v *Greenhalf* [1952] Ch 488, a decision of the High Court, runs contrary to this. It was held that the right to store vehicle parts on part of a neighbour's land could not exist as an easement since it amounted to joint user. The remark by Upjohn J, 'I say nothing of course as to the creation of such rights by deeds or covenants; I am dealing solely with the question of a right arising by prescription', should not be taken as meaning that he thought such a right could be an easement if created by express grant. It probably means no more than that it is open to parties to confer such rights by way of licence or contract. To conclude that the subject matter of easements may vary according to the mode of creation would be dangerous since, fictionally, all easements are deemed to 'lie in grant'.

Wright v *Macadam* was not even cited in *Copeland* v *Greenhalf*. The way is therefore open for reconciliation on the grounds that one was wrongly decided, rather than leaving as the only explanation that there is some hairline distinction between the two that will cause such a blurring of the boundaries of easements as has occurred between leases and licences.

Nevertheless, it must be faced that the difference between the right to do something on someone's land and the right to occupy is a matter of degree, for they both involve possession, and sooner or later the questions 'How much?' and 'For how long?' must be decided. In *Grigsby* v *Melville* [1973] 3 All ER 455, Brightman J, considering the problem to be one of degree, was not convinced that there was any inconsistency between the two cases because, while the claim in *Copeland* v *Greenhalf* was to exclusive possession, it was not clear from the report of *Wright* v *Macadam* that a right to the whole of the coalshed was asserted. It was not, however, necessary for him to express any final view on the question.

In *London and Blenheim Estates Ltd* v *Ladbroke Retail Parks Ltd* [1993] 4 All ER 157, Baker J stated *per curiam* that the right to park motor cars was capable of being an easement, though the essential question is 'one of degree'. There have been unreported decisions suggesting that this is so even if the consequence were to be that the whole servient land might be occupied by cars. This approach is, however, surely wrong in principle. Such a right would be more appropriately achieved through a licence or lease. (As a matter of jurisprudence the role of the 'unreported' decision appears in need of some definition.)

The problem has sometimes been masked by authors who state that before a right can be an easement it must be 'within the general nature of rights capable of existing as easements'. This particular version is from Megarry's (1975) *Manual of the Law of Real Property* (4th edn), Stevens & Sons. It does not take a deep analysis to show that this falls into the trap of defining a thing by reference to itself. Occasionally things and ideas do not need defining because they are unique and no other things or ideas are proximate enough to need distinguishing. Thus there is no need to define a human being. But surely, in light of the cases mentioned above, this is not so with easements, which, it seems, may merge with licences and occupation.

The subject matter of an easement must be reasonably definite

We shall see that all easements, other than those arising under statute, must originate in grant. In many cases, however, such a grant is implied from the circumstances, or is presumed to have been made at some time in the past, when an alleged easement has been enjoyed for a long time, even though in reality there was no grant. This relaxation was developed in order to give legal validity to what had, by long user, become accepted as a fact.

The doctrine that the origin, real or fictional, of all easements lies in words has led to the contention that the subject matter of easements must be reasonably definite. Lack of definition is clearly a justifiable ground for the failure of a claim to an easement, as it is indeed for the failure of a claim to any other legal right. Several cases are traditionally cited to support this view. In *Bryant* v *Lefever* (1879) 4 CPD 172, it was held that the flow of air in undefined channels could not be the subject matter of an easement. In *Phipps* v *Pears* [1964] 2 All ER 35 the right to have a wall protected against the weather by the retention of an adjacent though not contiguous building was held incapable of being an easement. Nor can the right to an unspoilt view be an easement.

On the other hand, the right to a flow of light to a window, as opposed to land in its natural state, is a well-established easement. In *Wong* v *Beaumont Property Trust Ltd* [1965] 1 QB 173 the right to a flow of air through a defined channel was held to be capable of being an easement, as was the right to enjoy another person's garden in *Re Ellenborough Park* [1955] 3 All ER 667.

The reasons given by the judges in the cases of failure cited above do not always support the contention that certain kinds of rights are predeterminedly incapable of sufficient definition to be easements. Lord Denning's reason in *Phipps* v *Pears* seems to have been that the right claimed 'would unduly restrict your neighbour in his enjoyment of his own land'. A right to sunshine, as opposed to disseminated light, now appears capable of being an easement, provided it is enjoyed through defined apertures (*Allen* v *Greenwood* [1979] 1 All ER 819). Certainly an easement must be defined, but there seems no good reason for not even allowing a draftsman to try, particularly since the desired effect can in any case be produced by a properly drafted covenant (per Lord Denning in *Phipps* v *Pears*, at 38).

The rationale behind the exclusion of these rights from the category of easements is rather different from a congenital insusceptibility to definition. The truly common factor in the cases seems to be that, where an easement is being acquired by long user, the servient owner should be able to discern easily what rights are being obtained against him, so that he will be able to resist and nullify them before they become established as legal rights. This he is much less able to do in the case of a negative easement because its encroachment is not marked by events which strike the senses. A nascent positive easement, such as a way over the servient property, can be detected by seeing a man walking over the property, and therefore should not emerge insidiously and without warning as a fully fledged right. Perhaps this is why the right to use a garden, though open to the charge of indefiniteness, has been allowed to join the ranks of easements whereas 'the law has been very chary of creating any new negative easements' (per Lord Denning in *Phipps* v *Pears*, at 37).

Moreover, even a positive act must be identifiably adverse to the servient property to enable its owners to resist it. A blacksmith cannot acquire an easement to commit a nuisance in the middle of a barren moor, for his hammering will not constitute a nuisance until his neighbour develops his land (see *Sturges* v *Bridgman* (1879) 11 Ch D 852, at 858).

Yet even a negative right is only objectionable in this way when claimed through long user, for then a man's property might be besieged by a hundred emerging rights, such as those of his neighbour to light over all his property or to an unspoilt view. These the servient owner could neither individualise, nor indeed resist, unless he built up the whole of his land. Such negative rights, however, are hardly open to the same criticism if they are quantified and identified within the four corners of an express grant.

In short, the principle that certain kinds of rights are at the outset too indefinite to be easements ought only to be applied to the acquisition of negative easements by long user and should not affect positive easements by whatever means they are acquired, nor negative easements when they are acquired by express grant. In the case of positive easements, the acts of the dominant owner perform the act of definition. In the case of negative easements expressly granted, the skill of the draftsman should at least be allowed to have its tilt at moulding the right, no matter how intractable, into a definite form. If he fails, then let us say he failed because of faulty creation rather than because of ineligible subject-matter.

Curiously, however, the Fourteenth Report of the Law Reform Committee on Acquisition of Easements and Profits by Prescription (1966) Cmnd 3100 recommended that shelter of a building by an adjoining building should be treated in the same way as the long established easement of support. This illustrates the supremacy of policy over logic in law as an academic discipline. The argument against admission of weather protection as an easement has been that it would be too difficult for a potential servient owner to resist a claim based on long user by interruption. This is quite inconsistent with the approach to the long established easement of light. Light does not flow exclusively from its original source, the sun, but like flowing air, comes to a window from numberless reflecting surfaces. Indeed, we have daylight even on the most cloudy days. Furthermore, as we shall soon discuss, enjoyment of light to windows, even at multiple storey level, can be interrupted by registration of a notional physical obstruction.

The problem might well assume greater practical importance in the future as living accommodation becomes denser and more interdependent. The lack of an easement for protection against weather, for instance, might be felt when a lower freehold flat depends for its weather-proofing upon the roof of the flat above (see 80 LQR 321).

On the basis of the present authorities, however, certain rights, negative in nature, are excluded from the category of easements because of their subject matter, rather than their mode of creation. It is difficult to foretell what new rights will be admitted.

CONDITIONS NECESSARY TO THE EXISTENCE OF EASEMENTS

An easement involves a relationship between two pieces of land and, even though the subject matter of a right is eligible for the formation of an easement, it must also be shown that the particular right in question expresses such a relationship. If it does not, although capable in the abstract of being an easement, it cannot be one in the particular instance, even though it may be enforceable for some other reason, perhaps as a personal licence. The following conditions must be fulfilled before the right can be said to represent a relationship between two properties.

There must be a dominant and servient tenement

There must be two properties concerned with the right, one enjoying the benefit of it, and one carrying the burden. Thus in *Hawkins* v *Rutter* [1892] 1 QB 668, a man claimed, as a member of the public, an easement to ground his barge on the bed of a river although he owned no land for the benefit of which the right was claimed. It was held that there was no easement because there was no dominant land. This requirement is sometimes expressed by saying that an easement cannot exist 'in gross'. In short, it is helpful to forget about persons altogether and imagine one piece of land having rights over another. Thus, if I give permission to the postman to cross my land so that he can more easily reach the next street, he enjoys a licence only, because the privilege was not given for the benefit of any land. The dominant tenement is usually physical land, but it may also be an incorporeal hereditament, so that there can exist, for instance, a right of way over land for the benefit of a fishing right in a river. The identity of the dominant land must be established at the time of the creation of the easement, since land cannot be encumbered with burdens of uncertain extent (*London and Blenheim Estates Ltd* v *Ladbroke Retail Parks Ltd* [1993] 4 All ER 157).

It has been argued that this doctrine has been accepted on too flimsy authority and could be an obstacle to reasonable land use in the future (*see* 96 LQR 557).

The easement must 'accommodate' the dominant tenement and must bestow some benefit upon the dominant land

A right enjoyed by one over the land of another does not possess the status of an easement unless it accommodates and serves the dominant tenement, and is

> reasonably necessary for the better enjoyment of that tenement, for if it has no connection therewith, although it confers an advantage upon the owner and renders his ownership of the land more valuable, it is not an easement at all, but a mere contractual right personal to and only enforceable between the two contracting parties. (Per Evershed MR, in *Re Ellenborough Park* at 677.)

The essence of this requirement is that the dominant land as such must benefit. While the dominant and servient properties will frequently be close together, this need not necessarily be so (*Pugh* v *Savage* [1970] 2 All ER 353). It is possible, for instance, for a right of way to accommodate a dominant property, even though it does not lead all the way up to it. On the other hand, as remarked by Byles J, in *Bailey* v *Stephens* (1862) 12 CB (NS) 91, a right of way over land in Kent cannot accommodate land in Northumberland. Even this restriction, however, does not apply to all kinds of easements. A signboard on land facing a busy road in Kent advertising a holiday cottage in Northumberland might well accommodate the latter.

Hill v *Tupper* (1863) 2 H&C 121 illustrates the principle. The owner of a canal leased land adjoining it to *L* together with the exclusive right to sail boats upon the canal. This right was held to be a contractual licence only and not an easement. Pollock CB said: 'It is not competent to create rights unconnected with the use and enjoyment of land, and annex them to it so as to constitute a property in the grantee'. The result was that when a third party began to put boats on the canal, *L* could only sue his licensor in contract and not that third party, with whom he enjoyed no privity of contract, for *L* had no right of property in the canal. This highlights nicely the difference between a personal right acquired under a contract and real right enjoyed under an easement.

The reasoning in the decision seems to be that the land on the canal bank was really intended to serve an independent business enterprise upon the canal, rather than itself to be enhanced by the right of sailing. Far from being intended as the dominant land, it was subservient to the business venture. But the case must not be taken as deciding that the right to sail boats cannot accommodate land on the banks of water. In view of *Re Ellenborough Park*, above, such a right must surely be capable of being an easement.

It is not enough that the right increases the value of property unless it is also connected with the normal enjoyment of it (*Re Ellenborough Park*, at 173). This does not mean that a property has a fixed mode of enjoyment; merely that the right must be restricted to the needs of that particular piece of land and not embrace some collateral purpose as where a right of way is granted 'for all purposes' (*Ackroyd* v *Smith* (1850) 10 CB 164). The court will, if possible in the circumstances, construe 'for all purposes' as meaning all purposes connected with the dominant land. Perhaps the best test is to ask whether the right assists what goes on in the dominant property. The land in respect of which the easement is claimed and not merely some person or some other land must benefit, and this was not so in *Hill* v *Tupper*, above.

Finally a right can accommodate a business on the dominant premises (see *Clapman* v *Edwards* [1938] 2 All ER 507).

The dominant and servient tenements must not be both owned and occupied by the same person

'You cannot have an easement over your own land' (*Metropolitan Railway Co* v *Fowler* (1892) 1 QB 165, at 171). This is really an obvious fact, for it is indeed impossible for a person to have a right of any kind against himself. However, mere occupation of both properties without ownership of both is quite compatible with the existence of an easement, which would simply lapse temporarily until the unity of occupation ended. Neither is ownership of both without occupation of both objectionable, although in that case the easement will not be of permanent duration, but will last only until the occupation of the second of the properties returns to the common owner.

Actions constantly exercised by an owner over part of his land are sometimes called *quasi-easements*, although they are really nothing more than habits. Thus a farmer might consistently choose to reach the road from his field 'Blackacre' by crossing another of his fields, 'Whiteacre'. The significance of such habits is that under certain circumstances they become easements if part of the land is sold off. *Quasi-easements* is therefore not a satisfactory description for activities which are the simple result of ordinary ownership and which are, during that time, devoid of significance, but it is however widely used.

An easement must be capable of being made by a grant

The rule that all easements, other than those of statutory origin, must be created by deed of grant naturally means that the right in question must, in all the circumstances of its creation, have been capable of being granted by deed. This is equally so in those cases where it is fictionally presumed that a grant was made at some time. The rule gives rise to the following requirements:

1 There must have been a capable grantor and grantee – there can be no easement if at the time when it was alleged to have been created there was neither a person capable of making the grant on behalf of the servient land, nor person capable of receiving it on behalf of the dominant land. Thus in *Mulliner* v *Midland Railway Co* (1879) 11 ChD 611, a claim to an easement alleged to have been granted by a railway company failed because a grant would have been *ultra vires* that body. Similarly, a vague or fluctuating body of people, such as the inhabitants of a village, cannot claim an easement, because they cannot receive a grant. They might, however, be able to prove some enforceable customary right, or a public right of way.

2 The right must be reasonably well defined – the question of definiteness of subject matter has already been discussed and the argument advanced that it would be preferable not to pre-judge the problem of definition by treating it

as one of subject matter, but to treat it as one of mode of creation. In any event there can be no controversy about the rule that an easement must actually be defined in its creation. It is strange that such a fundamental asset as certainty, which is surely as necessary to other kinds of rights as to easements, should be attributed to the rule that easements lie in grant. Perhaps the real answer lies in the 'thinginess' of English land law. Easements are property which can be conveyed. A right of way and the way itself, for instance, are both frequently referred to in one breath (see LPA 1925 s 62). Both can be pointed to from a bedroom window. A negative right is hardly a thing in this sense and has only been allowed as an easement when it has geometric shape, such as a right of support or right of light to a window.

THE CREATION OF EASEMENTS

Even though the subject matter of the right in question is eligible to be an easement, and even though the right conditions exist for its formation as discussed above, there can be no easement unless the relationship between the two properties has been created in one of the legally accepted ways. These methods of creation are as follows.

By statute

Easements are occasionally created by statute. Such Acts are usually local ones.

Under the Access to Neighbouring Land Act 1992 the civil courts may make *access orders* to enable owners to enter neighbouring property in order to carry out works on their own properties where this is reasonably necessary for their preservation.

By express grant

An express grant may arise in any of the following ways:

By direct grant

An easement will arise by a direct grant when the owner of the servient property grants the right in so many words in the deed of creation. This is a commonplace form of express creation and needs no further discussion. It is important however to look at examples in the books of conveyancing precedents in order to gain a fuller contextual appreciation of the subject.

By reservation

When a landowner sells part of his land, he might wish to retain an easement over the part sold in favour of the part retained. He can secure such a right in the deed of conveyance to the purchaser, for, like restrictive covenants, easements do not require separate independent documents for their creation, but may arise as subsidiary features in larger transactions. The purchaser need not execute the document for the easement (LPA 1925 s 65(1)). Before 1925, reservations operated by way of implied re-grant to the vendor by the purchaser. Because the purchaser was granting a legal interest to the vendor, this had to be done by deed executed by the purchaser as grantor. Since 1925 this is not necessary, because the easement reserved is not now deemed to arise by way of an immediate re-grant (LPA 1925 s 65).

Since the vendor is therefore the 'grantor' of this easement to himself, the rule that grants, including any reservations contained in them, are construed against the grantor might be taken to run against him. There is, however, reluctance to accept this view (*St Edmundsbury and Ipswich Diocesan Board of Finance* v *Clark (No 2)* [1973] 3 All ER 902). The moral is that the vendor should precisely define and quantify any easements reserved by him upon sale, for he will not receive the benefit of any doubt (*Cordell* v *Second Clanfield Properties Ltd* [1968] 3 All ER 746).

Under the Law of Property Act 1925 s 62

This section provides that on a 'conveyance' of land there shall, subject to any expressed intention to the contrary, be deemed to pass to the purchaser, besides all the buildings and other fixtures, all 'liberties, privileges, easements, rights, and advantages whatsoever, appertaining or reputed to appertain to the land . . . or any part thereof, or, at the time of conveyance'.

The operation of this section is dealt with here under express grants because it 'speaks' between the lines, as a word-saving section, in every conveyance – unless it is expressly excluded. The section is mainly concerned with a statement of what would normally be the intention of the parties. We would all expect a conveyance to include buildings, fences and water-courses upon the land, and nineteenth-century conveyancers, in their verbosity, expressly mentioned such matters. Now we are saved the trouble. Similarly, we would expect easements already existing for the benefit of the land that we purchase to pass to us in the conveyance. Hence the mention of easements. Thus if *V*, the common owner of 'Whiteacre' and 'Greenacre in Fig. 12.1, sells 'Whiteacre' to *P*, the benefit of the

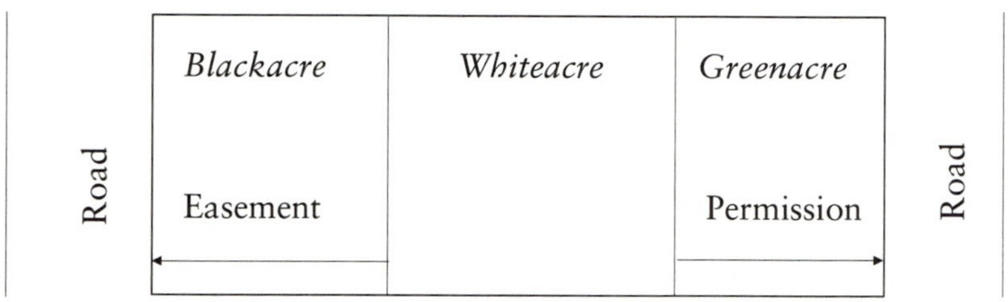

Fig. 12.1

right of way over a neighbour's property 'Blackacre', which had been created perhaps many years previously, will pass to *P* without any mention, just as the buildings and fixtures on 'Whiteacre' will. To this extent, the provision is only a word-saving section.

It is quite settled, however, that the later words of the section have a much wider effect than this and may create new rights, not contemplated by the parties, as well as transferring existing ones. Suppose that, before the sale of 'Whiteacre' by *V* to *P*, *V* had leased it to *P*, and later, as a matter of goodwill, had given *P* permission to cross 'Greenacre' to reach the road. The permission at this stage would be a mere licence revocable at the will of *V*. When *V* later sells 'Whiteacre' to *P*, however, the conveyance operates under s 62 to convert the licence into an easement in favour of 'Whiteacre'. This *V* can no longer revoke and it will permanently enure for the benefit of that property. Thus, in *Wright* v *Macadam* [1949] 2 KB 744, *T* became tenant of a flat and was later allowed by her landlord to use his shed for storing her coal. Later he granted her a new tenancy making no reference to the shed. It was held that the grant of the second tenancy turned the hitherto precarious right in the shed into an easement. See also *Ward* v *Kirkland* [1967] Ch 194. The effect of the section might even be to enlarge the area of benefit of the right, though not its burden. See *Graham* v *Philcox* [1984] QB 747. The requirements of the section must now be examined in some more detail.

First, there must be a *conveyance*. Under s 205(1)(ii) of the Act this includes 'a mortgage, charge, lease, assent, vesting declaration, vesting instrument, disclaimer, release and every other assurance of property or of an interest therein by any instrument, except a will'. The weight of judicial opinion holds that some form of written document is necessary to constitute a conveyance, even in cases where a legal estate can be created orally. Some doubt remains, however (*Rye* v *Rye* [1962] AC 496). It is settled that the document need not be under seal in those cases where mere writing is sufficient to pass the legal estate (*Wright* v *Macadam*, above). A conveyance does not include an agreement for a lease or sale (*Borman* v *Griffith* [1930] 1 Ch 493), even though specific performance would be granted. Presumably this restriction only applies to truly executory agreements and not to those cases where the document embodies the final arrangements of the parties but uses the expression 'the landlord agrees to let'. In any case, the exclusion of agreements from the definition is somewhat surprising, because even an agreement effects an 'assurance of property', though only of an equitable interest.

Second, the liberty will not be transformed into an easement unless it is by virtue of its subject matter capable of being an easement. There need not be any 'right' to do the act and even the most precarious of licences may be turned into easements (see *Goldberg* v *Edwards* [1950] Ch 247). Yet if permission has to be sought before every exercise of the act in question there will not even be a privilege in existence at the time of the conveyance upon which the section can operate, because each performance of the act exhausts the particular permission.

Thus in *Green* v *Ashco Horticulturist Ltd* [1966] 2 All ER 232 a tenant of shop premises was allowed from time to time to use his landlord's adjacent entry, but frequently had to ask on individual occasions that the gates be opened. It was held that a renewal of his lease did not create an easement of way. The distinction seems to be as follows. In the case of privileges which are given for an indefinite period, though subject to withdrawal, the nature of the privilege is not changed by the section. It is simply made permanent. In cases like *Green* v *Ashco Horticulturist Ltd*, where there is no continuing privilege but merely a series of frequent independent concessions, the section is excluded because its effect would be to change the nature of the privilege itself. It has now been held that a right to have a fence maintained is capable of passing under the section (*Crow* v *Wood* [1970] 3 All ER 425).

Third, it was until recently by no means clear whether the section only operates where there has been, before the conveyance, diversity of occupation of the part sold and the part retained. If, in the example given above, *V* had not only owned but occupied the land before the sale to *P*, then no 'rights', 'privileges' or 'advantages' could have existed over 'Greenacre' in favour of 'Whiteacre'. It is true that *V* might have been in the habit of crossing 'Greenacre' from 'Whiteacre', but this would have been attributable to his ownership and occupation of 'Greenacre' itself and not merely to rights in or over it. Furthermore, as a matter of brute jurisprudence and common sense, a person cannot have a 'right', 'privilege' or probably even an 'advantage' against himself (Fry J, in *Bolton* v *Bolton* (1879) 11 ChD 968). The clearest case in favour of this view was *Long* v *Gowlett* [1923] 2 Ch 177, where it constituted the *ratio decidendi*. Yet the question of diversity of occupation has been ignored altogether in other cases, so that doubt persisted (see *Godwin* v *Schweppes Ltd* [1902] 1 Ch 926). These cases were decided upon the Conveyancing Act 1881 s 6, which s 62 re-enacts (see 30 Conveyancer 346). It has now been confirmed in *Sovmots Investments Ltd* v *Secretary of State for the Environment* [1979] AC 144, that diversity of occupation is necessary to the operation of the section. We shall shortly see that quasi-easements may be converted into true easements under the doctrine of *Wheeldon* v *Burrows* (1879) 12 ChD 31 without previous enjoyment of the advantage by a second party.

As a fourth point, the section cannot operate to enlarge rights against third parties. Figure 12.2 illustrates this principle.

Fig. 12.2

If the owner of 'Blackacre', *B*, has been allowed by the owner of 'Whiteacre', *W*, to walk over 'Whiteacre', and *B* later sells 'Blackacre' to *P*, the licence never becomes an easement. The reason is that the only person capable of granting such an easement is *W*, and he has carried out no legal act whatsoever which can be taken to have done this, whereas when one person sells off part of his own land, the creation of an easement over the part retained is clearly within his power (*Quicke* v *Chapman* [1903] 1 Ch 659).

The drastic consequences of the section are avoided in most cases by excluding its operation to the extent desired, as occurs on standard forms of contract for the sale of land. Clear words are necessary (*Hansford* v *Jago* [1921] 1 Ch 322), although the circumstances preceding the conveyance may sometimes have the same effect. The fact that one right has been granted will not itself be sufficient to exclude the inference that others might pass. See *Pretoria Warehousing Co Ltd* v *Shelton* [1993] EGCS 120.

Under an agreement for an easement

An easement must be created by deed (LPA 1925 s 52), but under the doctrine of *Walsh* v *Lonsdale* (1882) 21 ChD 9 an equitable easement will arise where a purported grant is in writing only, or where there exists an agreement for an easement of which specific performance would be granted. Contracts for easements made before 27 September 1989 must conform with the formalities or part performance required by the Law of Property Act 1925 s 40. Thus where *A*, in reliance on *B*'s permission, laid waterpipes under *B*'s land, it was held that an equitable easement had been created although the permission was not granted under seal (*Duke of Devonshire* v *Eglin* (1851) 14 Beav 530; see also *McManus* v *Cooke* (1887) 35 ChD 681). Contracts made on or after 27 September 1989 must satisfy the formalities laid down in the Law of Property (Miscellaneous Provisions) Act 1989 s 2. These were discussed in Chapter 3.

Equitable easements which have arisen after 1925 are registrable as Class D(iii) land charges under the Land Charges Act 1972 or, in the case of registered land, as minor interests. If not so registered, they are void against purchasers of legal estates in the land for money or money's worth (LPA 1925 s 199). The practical effect of this rule can in certain circumstances be nullified where the owner of the servient property is estopped from denying the burden of an unregistered easement. In a modern case, the principle was described by Lord Denning in the following way:

> When adjoining owners of land make an agreement to secure continuing rights and benefits for each of them in or over the land of the other, neither can take the benefit of the agreement and throw over the burden of it. This applies not only to the original parties but also to their successors (*ER Ives Investment Ltd* v *High* [1967] 1 All ER 504, at 507).

While no one would deny that even technical legal rules must be applied in the light of justice, one of the elements of justice is certainty, and such a decision can sap the confidence of both practitioners and laymen in their interpretation of apparently straightforward statutory provisions.

> Remember, man, 'The Universal Cause
> Acts not by partial, but by general laws';
> And makes what happiness we justly call
> Subsist, not in the good of one, but all.
>
> (Pope's *Essay on Man*, Epistle IV)

In the *Ives* case, *A* built flats the footings of which extended slightly under the neighbouring land of *B*. The latter, however, agreed not to insist upon his rights, provided that *A* allowed him in return to have a vehicular right of way over his land. *A* accepted this arrangement. The right of way was not granted by deed and *B* did not protect it by registration as an estate contract or an equitable easement. Later the successors in title to *A*, who purchased with knowledge of the right, sought to prevent its exercise. It was held that although they were purchasers of a legal estate they must, since they enjoyed the benefit of the agreement, submit to the right of way. Alternatively, it could be said that a *proprietary estoppel* incapable of registration operated against them (see 32 Conveyancer 333).

Although the right had all the attributes of an easement, the court seemed at pains to steer it away from this category of right so that failure to register would not cause an unjust result. To achieve this, the arrangement between the original parties was substantially reduced by the court to mutual agreements not to sue, which would clearly have been incapable of registration. Alternatively we might say that, because of lack of registration, the easement was void against the purchasers, but because of the associated benefit they were enjoying, they were estopped from pleading lack of registration. The danger in the former explanation is that it could breed a species of right alongside easements; this might cause problems of identification as serious as in the case of leases and licences.

It is hardly surprising that the statutory code of registration should sometimes cause substantive rules to be warped. The old doctrine of notice was based upon good conscience, as is all sound law. The code of registration is not primarily so based. An honest layman is no more likely to be acquainted with that code than is a dishonest one. The same problem arose in regard to the requirement of written evidence for contracts concerning land under the Statute of Frauds 1677. The doctrine of part performance developed as a result to scavenge justice where the strict letter of the law failed to provide it.

By implied grant

When a landowner grants part of his land – or some interest in it – to another person, easements may sometimes be implied from the circumstances surrounding the transaction, even though there is no express mention of them. However, since a grant is usually construed against the grantor, they are implied more generously in favour of the grantee. The grantor must, with two exceptions, expressly reserve any easement which he wishes to exercise over the part sold.

Easements implied in favour of land retained by grantor

The two exceptional situations when easements will be implied in favour of the grantor are as follows:

Easements of necessity

An easement will be implied in favour of the grantor if it is essential to the mode of enjoyment of the retained land at the time of the disposal of part of it. The most obvious such case is when the land retained is totally encircled by the land disposed of, or partly by this and partly by land belonging to third parties. A right of way will then be implied in favour of the grantor, who may choose, once and for all, its route. This easement is limited by the necessity existing at the time of the grant. For example, if an island of agricultural land is retained, a right of way can be claimed only for agricultural purposes and not for other kinds of use or development (*London Corporation* v *Riggs* (1880) 13 ChD 798). Furthermore, mere difficulty of access does not constitute necessity.

Other examples of necessity exist besides that of access. A right of support for buildings is probably better classified in this category than in the second of the exceptions mentioned below. In *Wong* v *Beaumont Property Trust Ltd* [1965] 1 QB 173 an easement to maintain a ventilation duct through which to expel fumes from premises let for the purposes of a Chinese restaurant (and so comply with public health regulations) was implied in favour of a tenant against his landlord. This suggests that the necessity need not be a physical one but may be simply a legal one. This was an example of an easement implied in favour of the grantee, which will be mentioned below, but the principle of necessity is the same. The case also suggests that the doctrine of easements of necessity is perhaps not founded on the common intention of the parties because neither landlord nor tenant was aware of the necessity at the time of the letting. This factor, therefore, might separate true easements of necessity from the class mentioned below.

In *Nickerson* v *Barraclough* [1981] 2 All ER 369, however, the Court of Appeal rejected public policy as the basis of the doctrine. The decision exposes potential problems for the future in this part of the law (see *Current Legal Problems 1981*, p 133).

Easements particularly intended by the parties

If the circumstances are such as to raise a necessary inference that the common intention of the parties was to reserve to the grantor the right to exercise the right in question, an easement will be implied to this effect. Mere knowledge by the purchaser that the grantor was using the property disposed of in a certain way is not enough (*Re Webb's Lease* [1951] Ch 808). (But see also *Simpson* v *Weber* (1925) 133 LT 46, discussed in *Webb's* case.)

There is some overlap between this principle and that of implied easements, but the former has wider scope. For instance, the activity intended might be crucial to the particular purposes for which the claimant wishes to use the land, yet might not qualify under the demanding rules of easements of necessity. A more generous interpretation of 'necessity' might render the doctrine of common intention superflous. An illuminating example of this argument is *Wong* v *Beaumont Property Trust Ltd*, discussed above.

Easements implied in favour of land taken by grantee

The easements implied in favour of the grantee are as follows:

Easements of necessity

The principles discussed above in relation to the grantor apply equally in favour of the grantee. If the grantee takes a limited interest in the land the easement will of course be limited to that duration. Thus in *Wong* v *Beaumont Property Trust Ltd*, above, a leasehold easement resulted in favour of the tenant.

Easements particularly intended by the parties

Once again the same principles as discussed above apply in favour of the grantee.

Easements within the doctrine of Wheeldon *v* Burrows *(1879) 12 ChD 31*

Easements are more liberally implied in favour of the grantee upon the disposition by an owner of part of his land. For, in addition to easements of necessity and of common intention, there will also pass to the grantee all those *quasi-easements* previously exercised by the common owner which are 'continuous and apparent' and 'necessary to the reasonable enjoyment of the property granted' and which 'have been and are at the time of the grant used by the owners of the entirety for the benefit of the part granted'.

'Continuous and apparent' denotes some form of habitual enjoyment, the signs of which would reveal themselves on an inspection of the land by a person who is ordinarily capable of interpreting such signs. Examples are light going to windows, drains showing some marks on the land, and a made-up or worn path (*Hansford* v *Jago* [1921] 1 Ch 322). On the other hand, a route which leaves no indication of its use on the face of the land would not qualify. The word 'necessary' here is used in a softer sense than is 'necessity' in the term 'easements of necessity' and does not mean 'indispensable'. Yet in *Wheeler* v *J J Saunders Ltd* [1995] 2 All ER 697 the Court of Appeal appeared to interpret the word as meaning more than merely being occasionally convenient for the dominant land.

Comparison of the doctrines of Wheeldon *v* Burrows *and s 62*

The operation of the doctrine differs in several ways from that of s 62 of the Law of Property Act 1925. Section 62 only operates where there is a 'conveyance' and not, for instance, where an interest in land is passed by an agreement or by will. The doctrine of *Wheeldon* v *Burrows* is not confined in this way. In *Borman* v *Griffith* [1930] 1 Ch 493, *L* agreed to lease *T* a house in a large park which contained a mansion reached by a main drive which also served as access to the house. The agreement did not reserve *T* any right of way over the drive. It was held that a right to use the drive passed, however, under *Wheeldon* v *Burrows*, even though there had been no 'conveyance' to attract the operation of s 62.

It is also obvious that the doctrine in *Wheeldon* v *Burrows* operates, even though immediately before the transaction there was no diversity of occupation. *Quasi-easements* exercised by the person who commonly owned and occupied both pieces of land are capable of passing. *Borman* v *Griffith*, above, illustrates this.

On the other hand, s 62 embraces a wider class of potential easements than does the rule in *Wheeldon* v *Burrows*. For instance, the section does not require that the advantage should be of a continuous and apparent nature. Thus a right which has left no evidence of its exercise upon the servient land – such as that of entering a neighbour's property in order to carry out repairs on your own building – will pass under s 62, but not under *Wheeldon* v *Burrows* (see *Ward* v *Kirkland* [1967] Ch 194). When a conveyance is preceded by a contract, the rights of the parties are settled by the contract, and, unless otherwise agreed, easements will be implied in this contract as mentioned above. The conveyance should reflect these rights and s 62 should be excluded to the extent necessary to reflect the contract. These matters are often regulated by the general conditions in the printed forms used on the sale or leasing of land.

When an owner makes contemporaneous grants of two or more pieces of land to different persons, each new owner takes the same implied easements over the land of the others as he would have done if his grant had been made first. In other words, *Wheeldon* v *Burrows* applies. Conveyances will rarely be contemporaneous but gifts by will are governed by this rule. When the two conveyances are not contemporaneous but the order in which they are made is fortuitous, as in the sale of houses on an estate, the rule that only easements of necessity are implied in favour of the land reserved by the grantor works capriciously, for the vendor would often be surprised to learn that the purchaser of one plot has greater rights than another (see *Kwiatkowski* v *Cox* (1969) 213 EG 34).

By presumed grant

All the methods of creating easements described so far allude to a grant on some particular occasion. Often, however, an advantage capable of existing as an easement has been enjoyed over another person's land for a long time but cannot be traced to any grant. In certain circumstances the law protects such advantages and presumes fictionally that a grant was made at some time, but that the record of it has been lost. This method of acquisition, justified by the acquiescence of the servient owner, is known as prescription. The fiction can appear flimsy. Thus in *Cargill* v *Gotts* [1981] 1 All ER 682, the Court of Appeal considered that an easement could not be acquired through a criminal activity, even though recently made so by Act of Parliament (see also *Oakley* v *Boston* [1975] 3 WLR 478 at 490).

There are three forms of prescription, reflecting the development of the doctrine at common law and under statute over the centuries. The main difference between them is the period over which the enjoyment of the advantage must be proved. Long enjoyment alone, however, is not enough to found a claim under any of the three methods. The enjoyment must, with a few exceptions, occur under certain conditions. It must be 'continuous' and 'as of right'. Furthermore, since with one exception it can only result in the formation of a perpetual easement, it must be such as to bind the owner of the fee simple of the servient land. These three conditions must be considered before we discuss the three forms of prescription in detail.

Enjoyment must be continuous

Only advantages which require no personal participation, such as those of light, support or drainage, can strictly be said to be continuous, but this kind of continuity is not necessary in other cases. Moreover, there is no rule requiring any particular degree of frequency for individual types of advantages. It also seems that the site of a nascent easement need not, in certain circumstances, be constant during the prescription period (*Davies* v *Whitby* [1973] 3 All ER 403, at 405). Some kind of regularity in its exercise is necessary to suggest to the servient owner that a right of a permanent nature is being asserted rather than an isolated trespass or nuisance committed (see *Dare* v *Heathcote* (1856) 25 LJ Ex 245).

Enjoyment must be 'as an easement' and 'as of right'

The advantage must be enjoyed in such a way as would lead an observer, who is aware of the circumstances and behaviour of the parties, to the conclusion that an easement exists. This means that it must be enjoyed under a claim of an easement and not for some other reason, and that it must be enjoyed 'as of right'. This latter expression implies that, although the servient owner knows that the advantage is being enjoyed, and although he has given no permission for its exercise, he acquiesces in it. In technical language, the enjoyment must be *nec vi, nec clam, nec precario*. These elements must now be discussed.

1 *Enjoyment 'as an easement'* – The advantage must be exercised against one tenement for the benefit of another. The assumption of dominancy,

necessary to the existence of an easement, cannot arise if the advantage is enjoyed by virtue of some other legal claim. Thus no easement will arise where, for instance, one owner uses another person's land in a certain way because he mistakenly believes he owns it himself (*A-G of Southern Nigeria* v *John Holt & Co* [1915] AC 599). In such a case the advantage has been exercised not out of dominancy and serviency of two properties but out of sovereignty over one.

2 *Enjoyment 'as of right'* – The enjoyment must be *nec vi, nec clam, nec precario. 'Nec vi'* means without force. No easement can arise, therefore, if the user is exercised by force or in the face of clear and continuous protests or legal proceedings, for these would be incompatible with acquiescence, which is the basis of prescription. An observer would put the exercise down to trespass or nuisance.

'Nec clam' means not secretly. An owner cannot acquiesce in the exercise of advantages of which he does not know or which he cannot discern. Thus a secret discharge of liquids into a drain cannot found an easement by prescription. On the other hand, a person cannot claim ignorance of a fact of which a reasonably observant man ought to have been aware, such as that a building will normally demand some lateral support from adjacent ground (*Dalton* v *Angus* (1881) 6 App Cas 740). Long user raises the presumption that the servient owner has knowledge, but this can be rebutted by proof that he did not know. When a servient owner employs an agent to act for him in relation to the property, the burden of proving the agent's knowledge or means of knowledge rests on the claimant and depends upon the nature of the duties delegated (*Diment* v *N H Foot Ltd* [1974] 2 All ER 785). An activity is also *clam*, even though known to an owner, if he has for the time being no means of resisting it. This *constructive ignorance* is illustrated by *Sturges* v *Bridgeman* (1879) 11 ChD 852, where a confectioner created noise which obtruded into the back garden of a physician. No actionable nuisance existed until the physician built a consulting room in the garden, for it was only then that the noise began to interfere with the use and enjoyment of his land. It was held that the long period during which the noise had been emitted before the consulting room was erected, counted as nothing towards prescription because the physician was powerless to prevent the confectioner's activities by action or otherwise.

In *Union Lighterage Co* v *London Graving Dock Co* [1902] 2 Ch 557, the support of a dock by means of rods sunk invisibly under a neighbour's land was held to be unenforceable as an easement since, although originally lawfully placed, the rods were unknown to the person through whose land they passed. However, in view of the modern case of *Simmons* v *Midford* [1969] 2 Ch 415, their retention could surely be justified on the grounds that they had become fixtures attached to the dock so as to become an extension of it. In short, the issue was simply one of land ownership, not one of easements (see the dissenting judgment of Vaughan Williams CJ).

'Nec precario' means without permission. The enjoyment of an advantage by a permission which the grantor may give or refuse is inconsistent with a claim to such enjoyment 'as of right'. A user which begins permissively may, however, become *nec precario* in certain circumstances, for example when the advantage is exercised after the permission originally given has exhausted its authority (*Healey* v *Hawkins* [1968] 3 All ER 836). As a precaution against acquisition by prescription, a periodic payment is often demanded for the user to show clearly that permission is regularly sought and given. In *Gardner* v *Hodgson's Kingston Brewery* [1903] AC 229, such a payment clearly showed that a woman's use of a way from her stables through an inn yard to a road was *precario* even though it had been enjoyed for sixty years. The principles now being discussed are concerned with the acquisition of easements by prescription. When easements are granted expressly, the very grant itself is a permission to do the act in question; and there is no objection in law to the exaction of a payment in consideration of that grant.

Only perpetual easements can be prescribed for

Although easements may be expressly or impliedly granted for any periods of time, only perpetual easements can result from prescription. The reason for this is that the doctrine of prescription is based on immemorial enjoyment of a use. If the dominant tenement is occupied by the owner of a limited interest, such as a lessee, during some of the prescription period, the exercise of the advantage during this time still counts towards the development of a perpetual easement, and not for a leasehold one. The user is, so to speak, 'banked' for the benefit of the fee simple. We shall see later that there is an exception to this rule in the case of an easement of light.

Now that the conditions necessary for the operation of prescription have been explained, we must examine the three kinds of prescription.

Prescription at common law

At common law it is presumed that an easement has been granted if the advantage has been enjoyed under the conditions described above since 'time immemorial'. The date fixed by the Statute of Westminster in 1275 for this purpose was 1189. It has remained unchanged. With the passing of the centuries the burden of proving user dating back to 1189 became so great that the courts presume that fact if proof is given of enjoyment for twenty years. Yet even this presumption can be rebutted if it is shown that the advantage was, at some time between 1189 and the present day, incapable of being exercised. Thus a claim to a right of way on foot exercised for many generations might be defeated by proof that the servient land lay under water until, say, the seventeenth century. This factor obviously spells death to claims to easements of support for buildings, since very few have stood since 1189.

Lost modern grant

This doctrine, also evolved by the common law, remedies to some extent the frequently fatal flaw in common law prescription that a claim fails if it can be demonstrated that there was a time after 1189 when user would have been impossible. If enjoyment is proved for 20 years or more, this intermediate impossibility is rendered irrelevant by the presumption that a grant of an easement was made at some later date but has been lost. This desperate fiction prevails, even though the court has no shadow of a belief that any such instrument ever really existed (see *Bryant* v *Foot* (1867) LR 2 QB 161, per Cockburn CJ, at 181). Although the presumption cannot be defeated by proof that a grant was never made, it probably can be rebutted by evidence that it could not have been made because, for instance, there was no capable grantor, or because it would have been *ultra vires* (*Neaverson* v *Peterborough RDC* [1902] 1 Ch 557). Furthermore, a person resisting a claim is entitled to know whether it is claimed that the lost grant was fictionally made before or after a certain date, so that he can more conveniently assemble his evidence to rebut the plea (*Tremayne* v *English Clays Lovering Pochin & Co Ltd* [1972] 2 All ER 234).

Under the Prescription Act 1832

The Prescription Act was passed to overcome the difficulties of proving user since time immemorial. Its main effect is to shorten the time of legal memory. It leaves intact prescription at common law and under lost modern grant, which are still available for the establishment of easements, but provides a third alternative and more desirable method of proof. The Act applies special rules to the easement of light which must therefore be discussed separately.

Although the general purpose of the Act was to simplify the law, it has made it more complex by diversifying the prescriptive means of acquiring easements. Bad drafting also created ambiguities of interpretation.

Easements other than light

The Prescription Act 1832 provides two new ways of establishing easements other than light.

First, when an easement has been enjoyed as of right without interruption for 20 years next before some suit or action concerning the claim, it cannot be defeated by proof that it commenced after 1189, but may be defeated in any other way under the law. Second, where an easement has been enjoyed as of right without interruption for 40 years next before some suit or action concerning it, the right to it shall be considered absolute and indefeasible, unless it appears that it was enjoyed by some consent or agreement expressly given or made for that purpose by deed or writing. In neither case is a break deemed to be an interruption, unless it has been submitted to or acquiesced in for one year after the party interrupted has had notice of it and of the person making or authorising it (ss 2 and 4).

In both cases, the user must be 'next before some suit or action' so that an easement cannot be finally established under the Act until precipitated by an action. Since the user for 20 years or 40 years must be immediately before that action, it follows that potential easements which have been exercised for either of these periods without being finally constituted in an action are dissolved if they are later interrupted. Thus in *Hyman* v *Van Den Bergh* [1908] 1 Ch 167, user was exercised as of right between 1877 and 1899 but then was enjoyed by consent of the owner of the servient land. It was held that the enjoyment for the period of 22 years was of no avail since it was not 'next before' the action, which commenced in 1906.

Next, although the user must be uninterrupted, no interruption counts unless it is acquiesced in for one year. Furthermore, interruption means obstruction by the servient owner and not mere non-user (*Smith* v *Baxter* [1900] 2 Ch 138 at 143). In short, what must be proved to defeat a claim is an acquiescence lasting one year in an obstruction to the easement. A protest is enough to negative acquiescence and will be effective for this purpose for some time after it is made. If it is not repeated, silence and inaction may be interpreted as submission. The date when such acquiescence begins is a question of fact depending on all the circumstances (*Davies* v *Du Paver* [1953] 1 QB 184). Since an interruption is ineffective to defeat an easement unless it has lasted for one year, once an advantage has been enjoyed for more than 19 years or 39 years no interruption can prevent an easement being established, provided that the dominant owner clinches the right bringing an action as soon as the twenty or forty years have elapsed. Such an interruption could not then last one year even if acquiesced in. No action by the dominant owner, however, will be successful if commenced before the period in question has elapsed (*Reilly* v *Orange* [1955] 2 QB 112).

The interaction of the notions of 'as of right', 'uninterruption' and 'acquiescence' can produce some difficulties of interpretation in certain circumstances. (See 1989 Conv 356 discussing *Newnham* v *Willison* (1988) 56 P&CR 8.)

Prescription under both periods must be 'as of right', so that the enjoyment must be *nec vi, nec clam, nec precario* throughout those times. A permission given long before the prescription period begins to run will characterise the user even within the period as *precario*, for the principle is

> once permission has been given the user must remain permissive and not capable of ripening into a right . . . unless and until, having been given for a limited period only, it expires, or being general it is revoked or there is a change in the circumstances from which revocation may fairly be implied . . . (*Healey* v *Hawkins* [1968] 3 All ER 836, at 841).

The only exception to this rule under the section is that in the case of the 40 year period a permission given before the period commences will not defeat a claim unless it was given in writing expressly for the purpose.

The effects of consents may be summarised in the following way which has been judicially approved (see *Healey* v *Hawkins*, above, at 840).

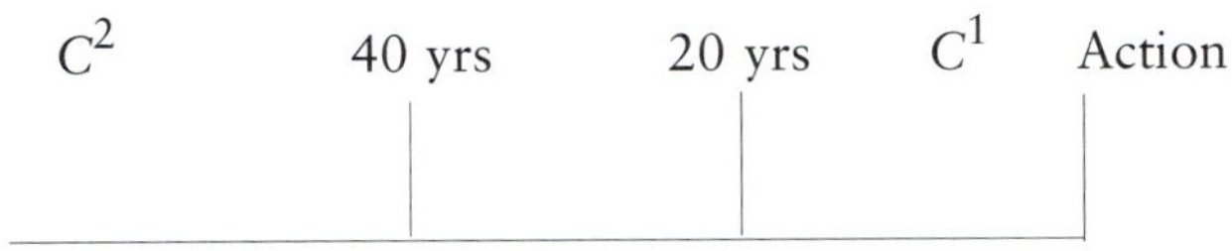

Fig. 12.3

Figure 12.3 represents the time running up to an action at the present time. C^1 and C^2 represent oral consents. If a claim is brought on account of user for 20 years, it will be defeated by proof of either C^1 or C^2 unless the latter consent had expired for some reason. If a claim is brought supported by proof of user for 40 years, it will be defeated by C^1 but not by C^2. A consent given at the stage when C^2 was given will only defeat a claim if it is in writing. In short, apart from this one exception in favour of the 40 year period, the section merely makes concessions as to the proof of the period of enjoyment and not as to the mode of enjoyment.

Finally, the Act recognises that in certain circumstances the owner of the servient land might not be in a position to resist the accrual of an easement against his property and it makes allowances in the following way. Under s 7, the period during which the person entitled to resist a claim is a minor, a mental patient or a tenant for life or during which an action has been pending and diligently prosecuted must be deducted in computing the 20-year period. A period of user enjoyed before such a deducted interval may, however, be aggregated with one enjoyed after it. Thus if 15 years of user were enjoyed against a fee simple owner and then there followed ten years during which there was a life interest running and this in turn was followed by a further five years of enjoyment against a fee simple owner, a claim could be established.

Section 8 then enacts that any period during which the servient land has been held for a life interest or a lease exceeding three years shall be deducted in computing the 40-year period, provided that the claim is resisted by the 'reversioner' within three years after the determination of the life interest or lease. The section applies to any 'way or other convenient watercourse or use of water' but it is thought that the word 'convenient' is a misprint for 'easement'. If it is not a misprint, the scope of the section is considerably reduced. This problem, raised as long ago as 1881 (see *Laird* v *Briggs* (1881) 19 ChD 22, at 33), is undecided even today. A strange result of the two sections should be noted. While periods for which the servient property was subject to a leasehold interest may be deducted in the case of a claim under the 40-year period, this is not so when a claim is made under the 20-year period (see *Pugh* v *Savage* [1970] 2 All ER 353).

The Law Reform Committee Report on Acquisition of Easements and Profits by Prescription (1966) Cmnd 3100, recommended the abolition of prescription as a means of acquiring easements and profits, or at least its radical simplification. None of these recommendations has been implemented.

Easements of light

Section 3 provides that

> when the access and use of light to and for any dwelling-house, workshop, or other building shall have been actually enjoyed therewith for the full period of 20 years without interruption, the right thereto shall be deemed absolute and indefeasible, any local usage or custom to the contrary notwithstanding, unless it shall appear that the same was enjoyed by some consent or agreement expressly made or given for that purpose by deed or writing.

An easement of light cannot be acquired for the benefit of open land. The section clearly shows that, as at common law, so under the Act, some building must exist for the benefit of which the right is prescribed for. Yet, provided that a window-opening exists, the fact that it was shuttered for long periods or that the house was uninhabited does not prejudice the dominant owner (*Cooper* v *Straker* (1888) 40 ChD 21).

The enjoyment must immediately precede the action, for s 4 governs s 3 as well as s 2, and an action is necessary to precipitate it into an easement. It need not, however, be 'as of right' because this requirement is significantly omitted from s 3. This is a most important factor which sets easements of light apart from other easements where prescription under the Act is concerned. Proof of the simple fact of actual enjoyment of the light over the period suffices, unless it is shown to be attributable to some written consent. Oral permissions are no obstacle to acquisition under the section (see *Mallam* v *Rose* [1915] 2 Ch 222). Similarly, the enjoyment may be *'vi'* or *'clam'* but these factors will have little practical application in the case of enjoyment of light.

The words of the section are strong and unqualified enough to enable a tenant not only to acquire an easement against another tenant of his landlord but also against the landlord himself (*Mallam* v *Rose*, above). Indeed, the fact that the servient land is leased does not prevent the running of the period. Sections 7 and 8, discussed above, deal with disabilities and do not apply to prescription for the easement of light under the Act. On the other hand, unlike other easements, a right of light cannot be acquired against Crown lands, for s 3 does not bind the Crown.

Like all other easements established in this way, an easement of light acquired by prescription is of perpetual duration. This is so even when it is acquired by a tenant against another tenant of his landlord. Such a result can be prevented by the inclusion in the lease of a clause amounting to a written consent.

Section 3 requires that the period of 20 years shall be 'without interruption' and the remarks made above as to the meaning of this expression in regard to the acquisition of other easements apply also to the easement of light. Similarly, the period must be next before some suit or action (s 4). If the owner of the servient land seeks to obstruct the passage of light to the dominant land, an alternative method to that of erecting unsightly hoardings is now available to him under the Rights of Light Act 1959 (as amended by the Local Land Charges Act 1975 s 17). He may register a notice as a local land charge in a prescribed form, which should describe by dimensions and location a hoarding notionally erected so as to interrupt the flow of light to the desired degree. The notice must be accompanied by a certificate from the Lands Tribunal stating that it has been given to all persons likely to be affected. The dominant owner is thereby placed in the same position that he would be in if the light had been physically obstructed. The Act should be consulted for further details, but it applies to acquisition of easements of light under all forms of prescription and not only under the Prescription Act.

The quantity of light which the dominant property is entitled to receive under an easement of light, by whatever means that easement is acquired, is no more than is sufficient to make a house comfortable or to enable any business to be carried on as beneficially as it was when the easement was created (see *Colls* v *Home and Colonial Stores Ltd* [1904] AC 179, at 187). This means that a reduction of the flow of light by the servient owner will not be a violation of the easement unless it constitutes a nuisance. On the other hand, the amount of light which is considered sufficient for the purpose in question changes with human progress and higher minimum standards are expected today than formerly. The court can also have regard to the locality (*Ough* v *King* [1967] 3 All ER 859). But see *Allen* v *Greenwood* [1979] 1 All ER 819.

A right to sunshine, as opposed to sunlight, is yet to be established as an easement.

THE EXTENT OF THE EASEMENT ACQUIRED

When an easement has been acquired by one of the various methods discussed above, the owners of the dominant and servient lands will sometimes wish to know the extent to which the right can be exercised. Two factors are particularly important in assessing the limits of an easement: the mode of user and the intensity of user. If a right of way is granted over 'Blackacre', in favour of a house on 'Whiteacre', the question might arise as to whether the right of way is exercisable on foot only, or by means of horses, or vehicles. Such a question would be one of mode of user, but if the problem was how frequently the right could be exercised, it would relate to intensity. Both these considerations depend upon the circumstances under which the easement was acquired.

Under statute or express grant

The extent of an easement created by statute or by express grant is a simple question of construction. The language of the document must be consulted to define the rights of the parties. If, however, their intentions are not clear upon some particular matter, the rule that a grant is construed against the grantor must be applied (per Willes J, in *Williams* v *James* (1867) LR 2 CP 577, at 581). One example only will be given here to serve as a caution when drafting easements. In *VT Engineering* v *Barland and Co* (1968) 19 P&CR 890, a right of way was granted 'for all purposes' over a road which the dominant owner used for carrying large structural units. The servient owner later began to erect a building on stilts over the road. It was held that a right of way for all purposes granted over land open to the skies includes reasonable vertical, though not lateral, 'swing space'. An injunction was accordingly granted to prevent the obstruction of the easement.

Under implied grants

Insofar as easements created under implied grant are based upon the intention of the parties, similar principles apply here as under express grant. But since there are no words expressing them, these intentions must be discovered from the circumstances prevailing at the time of the transaction. Easements of necessity are not, however, so clearly attributable to the intentions of the parties and the extent of these might be defined strictly by the necessity existing at the time of the transaction.

Under presumed grants

The extent of an easement acquired by prescription is defined by mode of user in fact enjoyed during the period. Therefore, a right of way for agricultural purposes cannot be used for industrial purposes (see *Bradburn* v *Morris* (1876) 3 ChD 812). Though the mode of user is finally cast in this way, intensification of that user may take place both during the prescription period and after it, provided that the increase in intensity is not so extreme as to amount to a user of a different kind. Thus in *British Railways Board* v *Glass* [1965] Ch 538 a way to a caravan site, originally used for only six caravans, was being used for 28 caravans immediately before the action. It was held that an easement had been acquired for this larger number. Furthermore, once an easement exists in favour of land, the identity of the persons making lawful use of it is immaterial (*Woodhouse & Co Ltd* v *Kirkland (Derby) Ltd* [1970] 2 All ER 587, at 590). It is of course possible that a right of way for certain purposes might even become generalized into a right of way for all purposes in certain circumstances.

Easements acquired for certain purposes will usually be taken to include other purposes which are less onerous on the principle that the greater includes the smaller. Thus a vehicular right of way includes a right of way on foot, though the contrary is not so. Furthermore, the nomenclature of an easement is not itself a restricting factor; it is the substance of the enjoyment which matters. This enables owners to take advantage of modern methods of enjoying advantages over the land of others. Thus a right of way for coaches and horses granted 100 years ago would entitle the dominant owner to drive motor vehicles over the servient land today.

The question of the extent of the easement of light has already been dealt with.

THE EXTINGUISHMENT OF EASEMENTS

By release

The dominant owner may extinguish an easement by releasing it. Release may be either express or implied.

Express release

A deed is necessary for an express release, but if the servient owner has prejudicially altered his position in reliance on a release informally granted, he will be protected by equitable principles (*Davies* v *Marshall* (1861) 10 CB (NS) 697). The case law on release and abandonment is however too tritely stated in the textbooks and in the cases. The passage or relinquishment of rights in English law is generally based upon the more fundamental concepts of contract, gift and limitation of actions. These have not been fully addressed by these sources. For instance, should an implied release not sound in a contract for release and therefore be subject to the provisions of the Law of Property (Miscellaneous Provisions) Act 1989?

Implied release

Behaviour by the dominant owner which shows an intention to abandon the benefit of the easement will release the easement. It is a question of fact to be gathered from the circumstances of each case whether a particular act or omission shows an intention to abandon (see *Swan* v *Sinclair* [1924] 1 Ch 254, at 266). Thus while mere non-user may be evidence of release, it is not in itself enough. In one context it might be explained as abandonment; in another merely as an interlude. In *Moore* v *Rawson* (1824) 3 B&C 332, where the owner of a building enjoying an easement of light rebuilt it without a window to receive the benefit of the easement, it was held that there was a clear intention to release the right. Destruction of a building alone, however, is not conclusive, for there might be an intention to rebuild and to continue the easement.

> Abandonment of an easement or of a *profit à prendre* can only, we think, he treated as having taken place where the person entitled to it has demonstrated a fixed intention never at any time thereafter to assert the right himself or to attempt to transmit it to anyone else (*Tehidy Minerals Ltd* v *Norman* [1971] 2 All ER 475, at 492). (See also *Benn* v *Hardinge* (1993) 66 P&CR 246.)

By unity of ownership and possession

If the dominant and servient properties fall into both the same ownership and possession the easement ends. Unity of ownership alone does not produce this result, for the easement continues in favour of, or against, the person who is enjoying possession without ownership. Neither is unity of possession enough, for then the easement is merely suspended during the time this unity lasts. There remains some doubt, however, as to whether this principle is of general application (see *Richardson* v *Graham* [1908] 1 KB 39 and *Buckby* v *Coles* (1814) 5 Taunt 311).

In any case, once an easement has been extinguished by unity of ownership and possession, it is not resurrected by a later alienation of one of the original tenements, although a new easement might arise under the doctrine of implied grant.

RIGHTS TO BE DISTINGUTSHED FROM EASEMENTS

We have already seen that, although there are some restrictions upon the subject matter of easements, this factor does not serve to distinguish them from other advantages over land. Such distinction lies rather in the circumstances in which the advantage was created. A few of the more common rights which might be confused with easements because of the common subject matter will now be very briefly distinguished from them. Some of these rights are separately discussed in other parts of this book.

Profits à prendre

Profits have many characteristics in common with easements. The factor which distinguishes them is that they give the right to take something from land, other than water.

Licences

A licence is a permission bestowed upon a person, whereas an easement is a right created in favour of a piece of land – the dominant tenement. It would indeed be quite possible for *A*, the owner of 'Blackacre', to give *B*, the owner of neighbouring 'Whiteacre', permission to cross 'Blackacre' and yet thereby create merely a licence, if the permission was personal only. There are other differences between the two rights which might sometimes be present in the comparison of particular examples of them, but this is the really telling difference.

Restrictive covenants

The elemental difference between an easement and a restrictive covenant is that a restrictive covenant imposes a duty not to do something whereas an easement imposes the duty to allow something to be done. There are several differences of more practical consequence which derive largely from the later advent of restrictive covenants into our legal system and from certain shortcomings in the law of easements. First, the subject matter of restrictive covenants, while negative only and narrower than that of easements, is complementary to it. Thus some of the effects which are denied to easements on the grounds of uncertainty of subject matter mentioned above can be achieved through restrictive covenants. A right to an unspoilt view, for instance, cannot constitute an easement, but a restrictive covenant can forbid alterations to land. Second, the methods of creating the two rights differ. Third, a restrictive covenant can only exist as an equitable interest.

Natural rights

Rights in law can arise in two ways. First, they might exist because the law applies them to all persons except insofar as they voluntarily restrict them. Examples of such 'natural rights' arise under the laws of tort and intestacy. Second, parties may themselves sometimes manufacture their own rights and obligations, within the framework of the law. Examples are the law of contract and the law of wills. Easements come into this second class, being created, actually or fictionally, by act of parties. However, there are certain other rights against the land of others which come into the class of rights ever present by operation of law, except insofar as they are altered by act of parties. One or two of these might be confused with easements.

A landowner has, for instance, a natural right of support of his land by that of his neighbour, which extends only to the support of land in its natural state. Any support required for building upon the land must be acquired by act of parties as an easement (*Dalton* v *Angus* (1881) 6 App Cas 740). Other examples of natural rights affecting land are the right to have water in a stream flow through land as it always has done, and the right not to have enjoyment of land spoilt by nuisances committed by other landowners. Once again, however, the natural right can be diminished by the acquisition of an easement to override it.

Public rights

Some public rights superficially resemble easements, such as the right to use a highway for passage, a river for sailing, or a park for recreation. The distinction between such rights and easements is that they are exercisable by all or certain sections of the public as such and without reference to any dominant land.

Customary rights

Customary rights which resemble easements are mentioned separately from public rights because, although they are often exercisable by a section of the public, their derivation is remarkable enough to earn special attention. A right can be established as a 'customary right' if it is certain, reasonable and applicable to a particular district, and if it has been exercised continuously since time immemorial (see *Mercer* v *Denne* [1904] 2 Ch 534). In practice, long use of the custom will raise the presumption of enjoyment since 1189, though this presumption can be rebutted.

Rights are from time to time established by custom which bear a resemblance to easements, such as the duty to fence against cattle on a common (*Egerton* v *Harding* (1974) 118 Sol J 565), or the right for fishermen in a village to dry their nets on certain land (*Mercer* v *Denne*, above) or to cross land to get to a church (*Brocklebank* v *Thompson* [1903] 2 Ch 344). These rights are of course not easements, because they benefit inhabitants of a particular area as such and have no reference to dominant land.

Rights arising from the doctrine of non-derogation from grant

This doctrine was discussed in Chapter 6. It applies to all grants, including easements. The importance of establishing whether a purported right is attributable to the doctrine is that the requirement of definition of subject matter is not so strict as in the case of easements.

STUDY MATERIAL

Liverpool CC v *Irwin* [1976] 2 All ER 39

Lord Wilberforce's speech is given in full below. It represented the prevailing opinion of the House.

LORD WILBERFORCE. My Lords, this case is of general importance, since it concerns the obligations of local authority, and indeed other, landlords as regards high-rise or multi-storey dwellings towards the tenants of these dwellings. This is a comparatively recent problem though there have been some harbingers of it in previous cases.

50 Haigh Heights, Liverpool, is one of several recently erected tower blocks in the district of Everton. It has some 70 dwelling units in it. It was erected ten years ago, following a slum clearance programme at considerable cost, and was then, no doubt, thought to mark an advance in housing standards. Unfortunately, it has since turned out that effective slum clearance depends on more than expenditure on steel and concrete. There are human factors involved too, and it is these which seem to have failed. The appellants moved into one of the units in this building in July 1966; this was a maisonette of two floors, corresponding to the ninth and tenth floors of the block. Access to it was provided by a staircase and by two electrically operated lifts. Another facility provided was an internal chute into which tenants in the block could discharge rubbish or garbage for collection at the ground level.

There has been a consistent history of trouble in this block, due in part to vandalism, in part to non-cooperation by tenants, in part, it is said, to neglect by the corporation. The appellants, with other tenants, stopped payment of rent so that in May 1973 the corporation had to start proceedings for possession. The appellants put in a counterclaim for damages and for an injunction, alleging that the corporation was in breach of its implied covenant for quiet enjoyment, that it was in breach of the statutory covenant implied by s 32 of the Housing Act 1961 and that it was in breach of an obligation implied by law to keep the 'common parts' in repair. The case came for trial in the Liverpool County Court before his Honour Judge T A Cunliffe. A good deal of evidence was submitted, both orally and in the form of reports. The judge himself visited the block and inspected the premises; he said in his judgment that he was appalled by the general condition of the property. On 10 April 1974 he gave a detailed and careful judgment granting possession to the corporation on the claim and, on the counterclaim, judgment for the appellants for £10 nominal damages. He found that the defects alleged by the appellants were established. These can be summarised as consisting of (i) a number of defects in the maisonette itself – these were significant but not perhaps of major importance; (ii) defects in the common parts, which may be summarised as continual failure of the lifts, sometimes of both at one time, lack of lighting on the stairs, dangerous condition of the staircase with unguarded holes giving access to the rubbish chutes and frequent blockage of the chutes. He found that these had existed or been repeated with considerable frequency throughout the tenancy, had gone from bad to worse, and that while some defects in the common parts could be attributed to vandalism, not all could be so attributed. No doubt also some defects, particularly the blocking of the rubbish chutes, were due to irresponsible action by the tenants themselves. The learned judge decided that there was to be implied a covenant by the corporation to keep the common parts in repair and properly lighted, and that the corporation was in breach of this implied covenant, of the covenant for quiet enjoyment and of the repairing covenant implied by the Housing Act 1961 s 32.

The corporation appealed to the Court of Appeal[1], which allowed the corporation's appeal against the judgment on the counterclaim. While agreeing in the result, the members of that court differed as to their grounds. Roskill and Ormrod LJJ held that no covenant to repair the common parts ought to be implied. Lord Denning MR held that there should be implied a covenant to take reasonable care, not only to keep the lifts and stairs reasonably safe, but also to keep them reasonably fit for use by the tenant and his family and visitors. He held, however, that there was no evidence of any breach of this duty. The court was agreed in holding that there was no breach of the covenant implied under s 32 of the Housing Act 1961; the appellants did not seek to uphold the judge's decision on the covenant for quiet enjoyment, and have not done so in the House.

I consider first the appellants' claim insofar as it is based on contract. The first step must be to ascertain what the contract is. This may look elementary, even naive, but it seems to me to be the essential step and to involve, from the start, an approach different, if simpler, from that taken by the members of the Court of Appeal. We look first at documentary material. As is common with council lettings there is no formal demise or lease or tenancy agreement. There is a document headed 'Liverpool Corporation, Liverpool City Housing Department' and described as 'Conditions of Tenancy'. This contains a list of obligations on the tenant – he

---

[1] [1975] 3 All ER 658, [1975] 3 WLR 663

shall do this, he shall not do that, or he shall not do that without the corporation's consent. This is an amalgam of obligations added to from time to time, no doubt, to meet complaints, emerging situations, or problems as they appear to the council's officers. In particular there have been added special provisions relating to multi-storey flats which are supposed to make the conditions suitable to such dwellings. We may note under 'Further special notes' some obligations not to obstruct staircases and passages, and not to permit children under ten to operate any lifts. I mention these as a recognition of the existence and relevance of these facilities. At the end there is a form for signature by the tenant stating that he accepts the tenancy. On the landlords' side there is nothing, no signature, no demise, no covenant; the contract takes effect as soon as the tenants sign the form and are let into possession.

We have then a contract which is partly, but not wholly, stated in writing. In order to complete it, in particular to give it a bilateral character, it is necessary to take account of the actions of the parties and the circumstances. As actions of the parties, we must note the granting of possession by the corporation and reservation by it of the 'common parts' – stairs, lifts, chutes etc. As circumstances we must include the nature of the premises, viz a maisonette for family use on the ninth floor of a high block, one which is occupied by a large number of other tenants, all using the common parts and dependent on them, none of them having any expressed obligation to maintain or repair them.

To say that the construction of a complete contract out of these elements involves a process of 'implication' may be correct: it would be so if implication means the supplying of what is not expressed. But there are varieties of implications which the courts think fit to make and they do not necessarily involve the same process. Where there is, on the face of it, a complete, bilateral contract, the courts are sometimes willing to add terms to it, as implied terms; this is very common in mercantile contracts where there is an established usage; in that case the courts are spelling out what both parties know and would, if asked, unhesitatingly agree to be part of the bargain. In other cases, where there is an apparently complete bargain, the courts are willing to add a term on the ground that without it the contract will not work – this is the case, if not of *The Moorcock* itself on its facts, at least of the doctrine of *The Moorcock*[2] as usually applied. This is, as was pointed out by the majority in the Court of Appeal, a strict test – though the degree of strictness seems to vary with the current legal trend, and I think that they were right not to accept it as applicable here. There is a third variety of implication, that which I think Lord Denning MR favours, or at least did favour in this case, and that is the implication of reasonable terms. But though I agree with many of his instances, which in fact fall under one or other of the preceding heads, I cannot go so far as to endorse his principle; indeed, it seems to me, with respect, to extend a long, and undesirable, way beyond sound authority.

The present case, in my opinion, represents a fourth category or, I would rather say, a fourth shade on a continuous spectrum. The court here is simply concerned to establish what the contract is, the parties not having themselves fully stated the terms. In this sense the court is searching for what must be implied.

What then should this contract be held to be? There must first be implied a

---

[2] (1889) 14 PD 64, [1886–90] All ER Rep 530

letting, i.e. a grant of the right of exclusive possession to the tenants. With this there must, I would suppose, be implied a covenant for quiet enjoyment, as a necessary incident of the letting. The difficulty begins when we consider the common parts. We start with the fact that the demise is useless unless access is obtained by the staircase; we can add that, having regard to the height of the block, and the family nature of the dwellings, the demise would be useless without a lift service; we can continue that there being rubbish chutes built in to the structures and no other means of disposing of light rubbish there must be a right to use the chutes. The question to be answered – and it is the only question in this case – is what is to be the legal relationship between landlord and tenant as regards these matters.

There can be no doubt that there must be implied (i) an easement for the tenants and their licensees to use the stairs, (ii) a right in the nature of an easement to use the lifts and (iii) an easement to use the rubbish chutes.

But are these easements to be accompanied by any obligation on the landlord, and what obligation? There seem to be two alternatives. The first, for which the corporation contends, is for an easement coupled with no legal obligation, except such as may arise under the Occupiers' Liability Act 1957 as regards the safety of those using the facilities, and possibly such other liability as might exist under the ordinary law of tort. The alternative is for easements coupled with some obligation on the part of the landlords as regards the maintenance of the subject of them, so that they are available for use.

My Lords, in order to be able to choose between these, it is necessary to define what test is to be applied, and I do not find this difficult. In my opinion such obligation should be read into the contract as the nature of the contract itself implicitly requires, no more, no less; a test in other words of necessity. The relationship accepted by the corporation is that of landlord and tenant; the tenant accepts obligations accordingly, in relation, *inter alia*, to the stairs, the lifts and the chutes. All these are not just facilities, or conveniences provided at discretion; they are essentials of the tenancy without which life in the dwellings, as a tenant, is not possible. To leave the landlord free of contractual obligation as regards these matters, and subject only to administrative or political pressure, is, in my opinion, totally inconsistent with the nature of this relationship. The subject matter of the lease (high-rise blocks) and the relationship created by the tenancy demands, of its nature, some contractual obligation on the landlord.

I do not think that this approach involves any innovation as regards the law of contract. The necessity to have regard to the inherent nature of a contract and of the relationship thereby established was stated in this House in *Lister* v *Romford Ice & Cold Storage Co Ltd*[3]. That was a case between master and servant and of a search for an 'implied term'. Viscount Simonds made a clear distinction between a search for an implied term such as might be necessary to give 'business efficacy' to the particular contract and a search, based on wider considerations, for such a term as the nature of the contract might call for, or as a legal incident of this kind of contract. If the search were for the former, he said[4]: 'I should lose myself in the

[3] [1957] 1 All ER 125, [1957] AC 555
[4] [1957] 1 All ER at 133, [1957] AC at 576

attempt to formulate it with the necessary precision'. We see an echo of this in the present case, when the majority in the Court of Appeal, considering a 'business efficacy term', i.e. a '*Moorcock*'[5] term, found themselves faced with five alternative terms and therefore rejected all of them. But that is not, in my opinion, the end, or indeed the object, of the search.

We have some guidance in authority for the kind of term which this typical relationship (of landlord and tenant in multi-occupational dwellings) requires in *Miller* v *Hancock*. There Bowen LJ said[6]:

> 'The tenants could only use their flats by using the staircase. The defendant, therefore, when he let the flats, impliedly granted to the tenants an easement over the staircase, which he retained in his own occupation, for the purpose of the enjoyment of the flats so let. Under those circumstances, what is the law as to the repairs of the staircase? It was contended by the defendant's counsel that, according to the common law, the person in enjoyment of an easement is bound to do the necessary repairs himself. That may be true with regard to easements in general, but it is subject to the qualification that the grantor of the easement may undertake to do the repairs either in express terms or by necessary implication. This is not the mere case of a grant of an easement without special circumstances. It appears to me obvious, when one considers what a flat of this kind is, and the only way in which it can be enjoyed, that the parties to the demise of it must have intended by necessary implication, as a basis without which the whole transaction would be futile, that the landlord should maintain the staircase, which is essential to the enjoyment of the premises demised, and should keep it reasonably safe for the use of the tenants, and also of those persons who would necessarily go up and down the stairs in the ordinary course of business with the tenants; because, of course, a landlord must know when he lets a flat that tradesmen and other persons having business with the tenant must have access to it. It seems to me that it would render the whole transaction inefficacious and absurd if an implied undertaking were not assumed on the part of the landlord to maintain the staircase so far as might be necessary for the reasonable enjoyment of the demised premises.'

Certainly that case, as a decision concerning a claim by a visitor, has been overruled (*Fairman* v *Perpetual Investment Building Society*). But I cite the passage for its common sense as between landlord and tenant, and you cannot overrule common sense.

There are other passages in which the same thought has been expressed. *De Meza* v *Ve-Ri-Best Manufacturing Co Ltd* was a case of failure to maintain a lift in which Lord Evershed MR, sitting with Denning and Romer LJJ, held the landlords liable in damages for breach of an implied obligation to provide a working lift. The agreement was more explicit than the present agreement in that there was an express demise of the flat 'together with the use of the lift', but I think there is no doubt that the same demise or grant must be implied here, and if so can lead to the same result.

In *Penn* v *Gatenex Co Ltd*, a case about a refrigerator in a flat, Sellers LJ said:

---

5 (1889) 14 PD 64, [1886–90] All ER Rep 530

6 [1893] 2 QB 177 at 180, 181, [1891–4] All ER Rep 736 at 738, 739

> 'If an agreement gives a tenant the use of something wholly in the occupation and control of the landlord, for example, a lift, it would, I think, be accepted that the landlord would be required to maintain the lift, especially if it were the only means of access to the demised premises. I recognise that a lift might vary in age and efficiency, but in order to give meaning to the words "the use of" and to fulfil them it should at lease be maintained so that it would take a tenant up and down, subject to temporary breakdown and reasonable stoppages for maintenance and repairs.'

That was a dissenting judgement but Lord Evershed MR made a similar observation as to lifts.

(Lord Wilberforce them emphasised that the landlord's obligation to repair only arose when the means of access retained by him was essential to the tenants, and where the duty had not been clearly imposed upon them.)

QUESTIONS

1 Consider what reform of the law of easements appears desirable, particularly in regard to:

subject matter;
s 62 of the Law of Property Act 1925;
prescription.

Compare your answer with the Law Reform Committee Report on Acquisition of Easements and Profits (1966) Cmnd 3100. See also the Law Commission's Working Paper No 36 of 1971.

2 What is meant by 'acquiescence' in regard to enjoyment of an easement 'as of right'?

3 Discuss the advantages and disadvantages to a fair and settled law of easements presented by *E R Ives Investments Ltd* v *High* [1967] 1 All ER 504.

4 In April 1970 Jane, owner and occupier of Ivy Cottage, began to cross Nettle Meadow, which belongs to her neighbour Jonocks, in order to take a short route to the village. Jonocks discovered this in May 1990 and immediately removed the gate through which she entered the field and replaced it with a high wall. In June 1990 Jane vigorously objected in a letter to Jonocks. In July 1990 she commenced an action against Jonocks for an injunction to prevent him further obstructing her use of Nettle Meadow.

Adjudicate. Then see 1989 Conv 356.

QUESTION ON EASEMENTS

In 1978 Angela built a pair of semi-detached houses, Conway and Sunnyside, and conveyed them to separate purchasers. In the conveyances she granted the purchasers the right to use a swimming pool on land she retained. Both Conway and Sunnyside were later sold and are now owned by John and Rajni respectively. John has now bought the land upon which the pool stands and proposes to demolish Conway so that he can build a new house on the site of the pool. Rajni fears that the wall of his house will become damp when exposed to the weather, objects to the loss of his right to use the pool and believes that the light to his windows will be obstructed and reception to his television set impaired by the tall new building. Advise Rajni.

SUGGESTED ANSWER

Since Rajni enjoys no contractual relationship with Angela or John, and since none of the claimed advantages exist as natural rights in land, all the rights claimed by him must be shown to be interests in land owned by John. An interest in land is capable of running in favour of land enjoying its benefit and against the land suffering its burden without any act or even knowledge of new owners coming to the properties subsequent to the creation of that interest. The interest which appears most appropriate for Rajni's claim is the easement. No right can be an easement, however, unless it satisfies the legal rules as to subject matter, conditions affecting the two pieces of land in question and manner of creation. These will be now discussed in relation to Rajni's claim.

'Subject matter' refers to the very nature of the particular activity or advantage claimed. The case law indicates four restrictions on subject matter. First, the claimed advantage must not be too vague or fluctuating, for the definition of a property right must be sufficiently precise to be expressed in a deed, which is the general vehicle of creation or alienation of interests in land. Thus in *Phipps* v *Pears* (1965) it was held that a right to protection against the weather is disqualified for that reason. Lord Denning emphasised the policy of the law against new 'negative' easements on the grounds that they might unduly inhibit the development of neighbouring land.

The right to the support of one building by another can exist as an easement (*Dalton* v *Angus* (1881)). If a claim could be established for an easement of support this would incidentally achieve the aim of protection against weather.

As regards the use of the swimming pool it might have been arguable at one time that the subject matter was also too imprecise to exist as an easement. In *Re Ellenborough Park* (1956), however, it was held that the right to enjoy a garden belonging to another was capable of being an easement. The use of a swimming pool is sufficiently analogous to that case to enable it to exist as an easement.

Two of the other three restrictions on subject matter, namely that an easement cannot afford exclusive possession of land and must not entail the taking of any substance from the servient land, are not in question in the present context. The fourth and final restriction is that generally the servient owner must not be obliged to spend money in regard to an easement. Thus in *Regis Property Co Ltd* v *Redman* (1956) it was held that there could not be an easement for a supply of hot water. If, therefore, it is established that Rajni has an easement to enjoy the pool, he will not be entitled to insist that the water is warmed.

Reception of light has long been recognised as capable of being an easement. Since it is a 'negative' right, however, an important constraint is imposed in case it might forbid new building on the servient land, which would perhaps prevent its development. This constraint is that the right can only be an easement if enjoyed in respect of a window or other aperture on the dominant land (*Colls* v *Home and Colonial Stores Ltd* (1904)).

A recent decision makes it clear that the right to receive a television signal cannot generally be an easement. In *Hunter* v *Canary Wharf Ltd* (1994) Estate Times, 15 September, it was held that such enjoyment was analogous to an enjoyment of a view rather than enjoyment of light. The former receives no protection under English law either as a natural right or an as easement. It is too early to speculate on the outcome of this litigation except to remark that perhaps commercial interests in land development have been promoted over those of domestic land enjoyment.

Next, given that the subject matter is eligible, it must be considered whether the relationship between the two pieces of land concerned conforms with the legal rules. In *Re Ellenborough Park* these were classified. There must be dominant and servient land, the latter accommodating the former in the sense of making it more convenient. In the present case these requirements are clearly satisfied. The dominant land is Sunnyside and the garden pool is the servient land. The right to use the pool improves the amenity and value of Sunnyside. The dominant and servient lands must not be owned and occupied by the same person. This rule is also satisfied. An owner-occupier cannot have an easement over part of his own land. An easement is an interest in land belonging to or occupied by another person. Thus John can swim in the pool because he owns and occupies it. Easements must also be capable of forming the subject matter of a grant, and it has been preferred to deal with this already under 'subject matter' when it was considered that the subject matter was capable of reasonable definition.

Finally, an easement can only come into existence if created in one of the four ways countenanced by the common law or statute. These are by statute, express grant, implied grant or presumed grant.

The question states that the right to use the pool was granted to the owners of both Conway and Sunnyside. This satisfies the classical method of creation by deed. The length of period of enjoyment is not restricted. The result, therefore, is two legal easements for the equivalent in time of a fee simple absolute. The benefit and burden of these easements will pass automatically to future owners of the properties without mention (Law of Property Act 1925 s 62). No registration is needed for their protection.

No express or implied grant of a right of light was given by Angela as against that land upon which the pool stands. Nevertheless s 3 of the Prescription Act must be examined in order to ascertain whether such a right has arisen through prescription. The section provides that, where light has been enjoyed in respect of building for a period of 20 years without interruption, the right shall be considered absolute unless enjoyed by some written consent. This period of enjoyment at the time of the dispute, 1996, falls short of the statutory period. It will be open to John, therefore, to interrupt the enjoyment by registering a notional obstruction under the Rights of Light Act 1959. If he fails to do so, however, before the final year of the period has commenced, he will be too late to prevent the acquisition of the easement. Under the Act nothing counts as 'interruption' unless it has lasted for at least one year.

In summary, Rajni has an easement to use the swimming pool but not for the protection of his house against weather or for reception of television. His rights as to light will depend upon future developments, as indicated above.

AN ALGORITHM OR METHODOLOGY FOR PROBLEM-SOLVING FOR EASEMENTS

1 Is the subject matter eligible?
If the activity or restriction satisfies all the following conditions answer 'yes' and continue to next stage. Otherwise exit, since there can be no easement.
- (a) No positive act or expenditure is required of the dominant owner, though note exceptions.
- (b) No substance is to be taken from the land, water being an exception.
- (c) There is to be no exclusive possession of the dominant land.
- (d) The activity is reasonably precise.

2 Are the conditions appropriate?
- (a) There are two relevant 'tenements' or lands.
- (b) The servient land accommodates the dominant land.
- (c) The dominant and servient lands are not both owned and occupied by the same person.
- (d) There is a capable grantor and grantee.

If all these conditions are satisfied answer 'yes' and continue.

3 There must be one of the following acts of creation:
- (a) Statute
- (b) Express grant
- (c) Implied grant
- (d) Presumed grant

4 There is an easement, but was it effectively protected?
If it is a legal easement it requires no protection.
If it is an equitable easement was it registered if created after 1925?

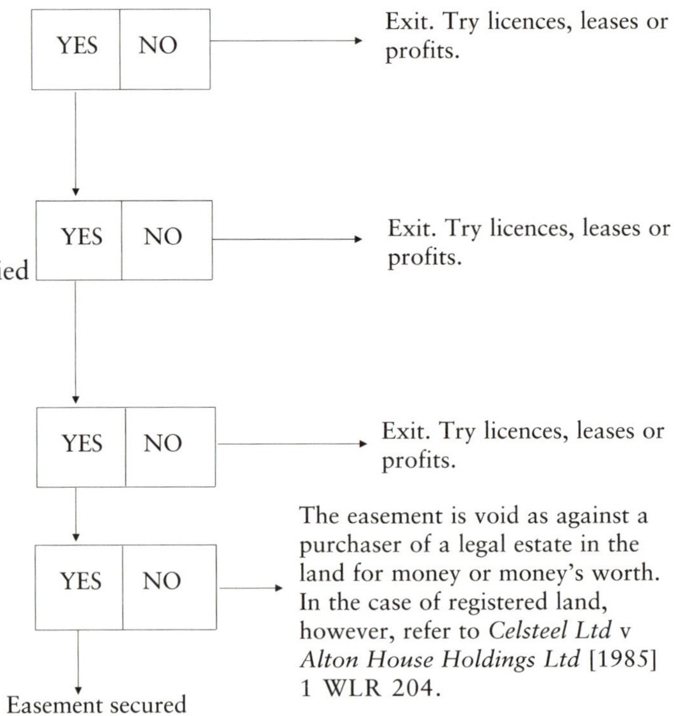

CHAPTER 13

PROFITS À PRENDRE

INTRODUCTION

A *profit à prendre* is an interest in the land of another person which gives the right to remove from that land something derived from it. Like easements, profits are means rather than ends, so that the circumstances and mode of creation are the true distinguishing factors. Since many of the principles applying have already been discussed under the subject of easements, they will be mentioned only briefly here unless there is some variation.

Profits, like easements, can be created to endure for any of the interests for which land can be held, and the same rules apply as to whether these interests are legal or equitable.

Subject matter may be dealt with swiftly, for it is much more exclusive than that of easements. It is essential that the matter to be taken from the land should be a product of the land. Examples are the rights to take turf or peat (turbary); game; fish (piscary); sand; wood (estovers); ice though not water – for water can only be the subject matter of an easement – and, of course, the right of pasture. When a profit is enjoyed by one person alone, it is called a *several profit*; when enjoyed along with other persons it is called a *profit in common* or simply a 'common'. The most important classification of profits is into profits *appurtenant* and profits *in gross*.

A profit appurtenant is one which exists in favour of dominant land. We have already met this principle of dominancy and serviency between two pieces of land in connection with easements, and this class of profits is governed by rules similar to those of easements. Unlike easements, however, profits can also exist in gross, for a person may have the right to enjoy a profit in the land of another person even though he owns no land himself.

The four conditions necessary to the existence of easements apply to profits appurtenant: there must be a dominant and a servient tenement; the profit must accommodate the dominant tenement; those tenements must not be both owned and occupied by the same person and the profit must be capable of forming the subject matter of a grant. The first three of these rules clearly cannot apply to profits in gross because no dominant tenement exists. The fourth does apply.

Thus, in the case of an appurtenant profit the quantity of the profit which can be taken is limited to the needs of the dominant tenement, for the right must accommodate this property. It cannot therefore be founded upon commercial interests (*Harris* v *Chesterfield* [1911] AC 623). A profit in gross, however, is not confined in this way and may be 'without stint'.

CREATION OF PROFITS

Profits may owe their creation to one of the following methods.

Statute

No explanation of this is necessary. The Inclosure Acts provide examples.

Express grant

The same principles apply to the express creation of profits as to the express creation of easements, including those relating to agreements, reservations and the Law of Property Act 1925 s 62.

Implied grant

The doctrines of necessity and *Wheeldon* v *Burrows* do not apply to profits, for their subject matter is not apt to invoke them, but in olden times, before the Statute *Quia Emptores* of 1290, a conveyance of land would sometimes include by implication of law the right to pasture certain animals on the manorial waste land. Such *profits appendant* are perhaps best classified under implied grant. Their ancient derivation renders them of no practical importance today.

Presumed grant

Once again the same principles apply as in the case of easements, and profits can be acquired by prescription at common law, under the doctrine of lost modern grant, or under the Prescription Act 1832 (see *Tehidy Minerals Ltd* v *Norman* [1971] 2 All ER 475). The following variations apply, however.

1 In the case of profits in gross, prescription at common law or under the doctrine of lost modern grant may be proved to accumulate in successive persons irrespective of land ownership, because there is no dominant tenement.

2 Profits in gross cannot be prescribed for under the Prescription Act because enjoyment of the advantage in question is required to be in favour of a tenement (s 5).

3 The prescription periods for profits appurtenant under the Act are 30 and 60 years, instead of 20 and 40 years as in the case of easements. No longer

period is necessary to raise the presumption of the lost grant of a profit than in the case of the lost grant of an easement (*Tehidy Minerals Ltd* v *Norman* [1971] 2 All ER 475).

4 Under the Commons Registration Act 1965 s 16, the period during which a right of common was not exercised because of animal health or because the land was requisitioned is to be left out of account in determining whether there has been an interruption within the meaning of the Prescription Act and also in computing the 30 or 60 years period. This provision could clearly be useful where, for instance, movements of stock are restricted because of foot-and-mouth disease.

The recommendations of the Law Reform Committee Report on Acquisition of Easements by Prescription, noted in the discussion of prescription in regard to easements in Chapter 12, apply also to profits.

Extinguishment of profits

Profits can be extinguished in the following ways.

Statute

1 *Approvement.* Approvement is the release of part of the land from the profit of pasture by the servient owner. This was permitted even in the early law provided that sufficient land was left for the satisfaction of the commoners. Approvement is now regulated by the Law of Commons Act 1893, and government consent is required.

2 *Inclosure.* Inclosure of land has the effect of discharging the whole of the servient tenement from all rights of common. It was achieved through private Acts of Parliament and later under the provisions of general legislation. The impetus of the movement towards inclosures was the desire to put land to better commercial use which was obviously obstructed by the existence of profits. Compensation was awarded to the profit owners. The loss of open space through inclosure in the eighteenth and early nineteenth centuries led to a reversal of this trend. Inclosures are now regulated by the Commons Act 1876, which requires government and Parliamentary confirmation, and the Commons Amendment Act 1893.

3 *Registration.* Under the Commons Registration Act 1965, most rights of common had to be registered with the local authority within a certain time which has now expired. Failure to register extinguished the right. The term *rights of common* has a wide meaning in the Act. The purpose of the legislation is to establish accurately the boundaries of large areas of land, mainly in the north and west of England which are subject to such rights, preparatory to the introduction of further legislation aimed at its better utilisation and the preservation of public amenity.

Release

The owner of a profit may release it, expressly by deed or impliedly by clearly showing an intention to release it by such alteration in the use of the dominant tenement as to raise a presumption of abandonment. Mere non-user is probably not enough, although, if lasting a long time, it is no doubt a strong contributory factor (see *Re Yateley Common, Hampshire* [1977] 1 All ER 505). If the dominant owner allows the servient owner to incur expense in the belief that the profit has been abandoned, this would also be strong evidence of abandonment.

Unity of ownership and possession

This method of extinguishment has been discussed in relation to easements.

Rights to be distinguished from profits

Because of their more exclusive subject matter profits are less likely to be confused with other rights than easements are. Nevertheless, the following rights must be carefully distinguished.

Licences

A person may be given a right by contract to take the produce of another person's land. Even if this is done by deed, the resultant advantage will not amount to a profit unless the constituent elements of a profit as described above are present. An example of such a right is a grazing licence authorising a person to graze cattle upon land.

Public rights

An example of a public right is that of fishing in the sea. This is clearly not a profit since there is no dominant tenement to constitute an appurtenant profit, and no grant to any particular individual, express or presumed, so as to establish a profit in gross.

Rights of indefinite classes

We have already seen that indefinite classes of people cannot own an easement, but that a customary right to similar effect can sometimes be proved on their behalf. A similar problem exists where a fluctuating body of people claim the right to take something from land. The recourse to custom here, however, is not possible since it was ruled a very long time ago that the effect of allowing customary profits would be to exhaust the land. Nevertheless, the law has outflanked this rule in two cases in its eagerness to protect advantages which have been long and peacefully enjoyed.

1 *Presumed incorporation of the class by the Crown.* The Crown can incorporate a fluctuating class of persons such as the inhabitants of a town. If long enjoyment of the advantage is proved, and if it is shown that the

persons in the class have always considered themselves as a corporation and acted as one, by holding meetings for example, then the courts will presume that they were incorporated by the Crown at some date for the particular purpose of enjoying the privilege in question (see *Willingdale* v *Maitland* (1866) LR 3 Eq 103). The presumption, of course, operates fictionally. In reality few such incorporations have been carried out in this way.

2 *Presumed charitable trust.* Where the indefinite class of persons cannot claim directly for some reason, such as that they have not acted as a corporation, but where the advantage has long been enjoyed along with an incorporated body such as a local authority, it may be presumed by the court that the advantage was granted to the incorporated body subject to a trust that the indefinite class should be allowed to enjoy it (*Goodman* v *Saltash Corporation* (1882) 7 App Cas 633).

CHAPTER 14

RESTRICTIVE COVENANTS

THE ROLE OF COVENANTS IN LAND LAW

In Chapter 4 we noticed some of the principal controls and restrictions upon the enjoyment of land. The most important of these, town and country planning law, is of comparatively recent origin. Its purposes are many but include the protection of amenity. However, during the hundred years before the Town and Country Planning Act 1947, landowners had resorted to private covenants to restrain land use, in an effort to preserve local amenity against the urban squalor of the industrial revolution. The purposes of the Act and the landowner who employed such restrictive covenants had much in common.

Since the 1947 Act had a revolutionary effect on land enjoyment, so universal and far reaching were its effects, it might be expected that the restrictive covenant would decline in importance, its aims being achieved through a more powerful agent. This has not been the case. It has been noted that in the ten-year period ending in 1965 more than 600 000 sets of new restrictive covenants were entered in the Land Charges Registry in respect of unregistered land alone.

The use of land after sale on such estates is almost invariably restrained by restrictive covenants. Such restrictions are designed to make ownership of property on the estate a more attractive or profitable proposition. The restrictive covenant can achieve many objectives which planning law generally cannot reach. A commonplace example might illustrate this.

'Oakesacre' is a new residential estate near Birmingham, one hundred acres in extent. It is a mile away from shops, so the developer applied for and received planning permission to build five retail shops on the estate. In Chapter 4, it was explained that under planning law it is generally lawful to change the use of a shop from one retail trade to another, with certain exceptions (see p 63). If the control of activities on the various residential and business premises on 'Oakesacre' had been left to the protection of planning law alone, the properties might have been less desirable than if restrictive covenants had been entered into by the purchasers. The developer wished to provide a balance of shops for the sale of goods of ordinary domestic kind. The intention was that each shop should restrict sales to one of five purposes. These were to be grocery, butchery, ironmongery, off-licence, and newsagency. There is a clear advantage both to the shopowners as a group and to the residents that no shopowner should change his business range to that of one of the other shopowners. If the grocer, for instance, changes his business to ironmongery, not only is the estate deprived of an amenity, but the ironmonger is likely to go out of business.

In fact the estate developer would find it more difficult to sell the shops if some permanent restriction upon the type of sales permitted by each shopowner could not be imposed. Yet under planning law each of the five shopowners could take up the trade of each of the others. Similar problems would arise in regard to the residential population. Indeed, restrictive covenants affect residential premises just as often as business property, and represent one of the most common restrictions on land use. There are many activities which might be undesirable on a particular kind of residential estate which would be permitted under planning law. Examples are the building of fences and small structures and the keeping of farm animals.

In short, restrictive covenants can control areas of activity which are generally beyond the reach of planning law on one side, or the law of tort on the other. Furthermore, enforcement can be more readily available to the private individual. No complaint to a public authority is necessary as in the case of breaches of planning law. This avoids the question of *locus standi*.

Before studying the detailed rules of restrictive covenants, we should first consider the general scheme of covenants affecting land. An owner or occupier of land frequently contracts with someone who may or may not have an interest in that land or other land. The subject matter of such contracts varies considerably. It may, for instance, be that the occupier shall paint the property at certain intervals, or that he shall refrain from selling intoxicating drinks on the premises. Such duties are often enforceable without reference to the law of restrictive covenants. Our particular enquiry is to discover what role restrictive covenants play which cannot be achieved by ordinary covenants that is, where there is neither privity of contract nor privity of estate between the person seeking to enforce and the person against whom he is seeking to enforce: to illustrate this position, a few examples of the circumstances under which this arises might be given. Firstly, *L* might lease land to *T*, who then might sub-lease to *S*. Between *L* and *S* there is neither privity of contract nor privity of estate. If *L* then wishes to enforce covenants in the lease against *S* rather than *T*, he cannot do so on any principle mentioned above. Secondly, if *V* sold the fee simple in land to *P*, who covenanted to perform some act, and then *P* himself sold the land to *X*, we must look for some further route through which *V* might enforce the covenant against *X*. Thirdly, if *A* either sold or leased land to *B*, and *B* covenanted to do something, and either a licensee *L* or a trespasser *T* came into occupation of the land and ignored the covenant, a similar problem would exist as to the enforcement of the covenant against either *L* or *T*. Finally, it should be noticed that covenants may be imposed on the owners and occupiers

AN ALGORITHM ILLUSTRATING THE ENFORCEMENT OF COVENANTS

The following algorithm illustrates the role of restrictive covenants when one person is seeking to enforce a covenant concerning land against another.

1 Is there privity of contract between the parties?

NO | YES → Exit. Ordinary rules of contract prevail. All covenants are enforceable by the parties

↓

2 Is there privity of estate between the parties?

NO | YES → Exit. Enforceability depends upon the law of landlord and tenant which is explained in Chapter 6. The range of enforceable covenants is smaller than in 1 above.

↓

3 Given that there is neither privity of contract nor estate between the parties, has the benefit of the covenant passed to the plaintiff because it 'touches and concerns' the land of the plaintiff?

YES | NO → Exit. Claim for enforcement fails.

↓

4 Given that there is neither privity of contract nor estate, as decribed above, has the burden of the covenant passed to the defendant under the law relating to restrictive covenants?

YES | NO → Exit. Claim fails.

↓

Claim succeeds

of land by independent transactions without any proprietary interest in the land passing. Thus owner *A* might covenant with owner *B* not to build on his land. *A* might then sell to *P*, and *B* might wish to enforce against *P*. Briefly, the question is how can one enforce covenants against persons with whom there is neither privity of contract nor privity of estate? In such cases, the conditions for enforcement are more stringent and a distinction must be made between the benefit and the burden of the covenant.

The benefit of the covenant will pass under the following conditions: (a) it touches and concerns the land of the covenantee; (b) the covenant must be created for the benefit of the legal estate of the covenantee ; and (c) the assignee must have the same legal estate as the covenantee, though in the case of covenants entered into after 1925 it is enough that he has an estate derived from this.

If such conditions are fulfilled the covenant is enforceable both at law and in equity. It does not matter whether this covenant is positive or negative (see *Smith and Snipes Hall Farm Ltd v River Douglas Catchment Board* [1949] 2 KB 500).

The burden of the covenant, apart from the exceptional cases mentioned below, will pass only if the rules relating to restrictive covenants have been conformed with, and then only in equity (*Rhone* v *Stephens* [1994] 2 All ER 65). Certain types of negative covenants alone qualify. Thus the cases which the law will assist when there is neither privity of contract nor privity of estate and when the burden is sought to be enforced are still more select.

When there is a question of enforcing a covenant concerning land the order of attack should be as outlined above. First, using the algorithm on p 330, check whether the covenant falls within the class of cases in 1; if so, proceed no further, for this is the zone most favourable for enforcement in that fewer rules have to be conformed with. If it does not, then move to 2; then to 3. If in the last case, however, it is a question of the burden being transmitted, then the law of restrictive covenants must be invoked.

The place of restrictive covenants in the law relating to covenants is that they achieve something no other covenant can. Under them not only the benefits but also the burdens will be enforceable as between persons who are are in neither privity of contract nor privity of estate.

The exceptional cases referred to above are as follows:

Chain of covenants

If *A* sells land to *B* who covenants to do some act and then *B* sells to *C*, *A* will not be able to enforce that covenant against *C* because there will be neither privity of contract nor privity of estate between him and *C*. He will, however, be able to enforce it against *B*, with whom he enjoys continuous privity of contract. *B* could have protected himself against such breaches of covenant by *C* by taking from him a covenant of indemnity when he sold him the land. By this means, the liability may be passed indirectly to the person who has broken the covenant. In theory, the chain might grow to indefinite length through subsequent sales of the land. The device is not a satisfactory means of imposing an enduring duty. It can only result in the remedy of damages and not an injunction and its clumsiness might obviously lead to a break in the chain of liability as the years go by.

Enlargement of long leases

The Law of Property Act 1925 s 153 provides for the enlargement of certain uncommon types of long leases into fee simple estates in the circumstances described there. The lease must have been originally granted for at least 300 years, of which not less than 200 years must still be unexpired. There must be no trust or right of redemption, no rent of any value payable and no right reserved for re-entry for condition broken. The owner of such a lease is clearly substantially in the position of a fee simple owner anyway, so that the section is not performing any real act of confiscation from the reversioner.

The importance of the power for our present purposes is that the resultant fee simple is made subject to all the covenants of the lease before enlargement. Since these covenants might have been positive in nature, the Act provides a means by which the burden of positive covenants might exceptionally be enforceable between persons enjoying neither privity of contract nor privity of estate. The Leasehold Reform Act 1967 provides a similar machinery in those cases to which the Act applies (*see* s 8(3)).

The doctrine of Halsall *v* Brizell *[1957] Ch 169*

A person who wishes to enjoy an advantage under some agreement must also perform any obligation of a reciprocal nature. Thus if a conveyance permits owners to use a road or sewer on an estate and also obliges them to contribute to the cost of its maintenance, the enjoyment of the use of the facility will be conditional upon the payment of the costs. This obligation will affect successors in title who were not parties to the agreement.

Public law obligations

Positive obligations are sometimes imposed by statute upon owners and occupiers of property. The burden of these duties affects successive owners. They are not, however, of a contractual nature.

The Land Registration Act 1925 s 58

This provides a technical device, using the entry of a restriction on the register, in the case of estate development. The Act should be consulted for details.

RULES OF RESTRICTIVE COVENANTS

We have just seen that where neither privity of contract nor privity of estate exists between the parties, the benefit of covenants may nevertheless be enforceable at law in certain circumstances. Equity generally followed the law in this but applied looser rules in certain circumstances, for the person seeking to enforce the benefit in such cases was not required to hold a legal estate in the dominant land. An equitable interest was enough. These rules may have fulfilled the needs of our society in the past, for they ensured that the most important covenants in leases were enforceable despite assignments of both leases and reversions. They even enabled the benefits of other covenants to be enforced by assignees of the dominant land if they 'touched and concerned' that land.

As towns grew rapidly in the nineteenth century, and the desire to maintain privacy and amenity for land became more urgent, the shortcomings of these rules were felt. If a landowner sold some of his land to *P* and continued to live on the rest, he might wish to impose some restriction on the land sold, such as that no building should be erected near to his boundaries. As between himself and *P*, a covenant to this effect would be enforceable on the ordinary principles of privity of contract. Furthermore, a purchaser of the rest of his land could enforce the covenant because, as explained earlier, the benefit was capable of passing. If *P*, however, sold his land to *X*, then not even the original vendor could enforce the covenant against *X* because before the nineteenth century the burden was only capable of being enforced where there was either privity of contract or privity of estate.

It has sometimes come about in our legal history that where some reasonable human aim could not be achieved under existing legal rules, the law has grown to accommodate that objective. Today it usually falls to Parliament to enact an appropriate statute. In the nineteenth century, the shortcomings in the law of covenants were mitigated by an organic development through cases decided in equity. The new doctrine, which went far beyond the existing law, is traditionally traced to the case of *Tulk* v *Moxhay* (1848) 2 Ph 744, but its origins lie before that date and its principles have developed much since then. Further developments may be expected. The remark of Megarry J, in *Brunner* v *Greenslade* [1970] 3 All ER 833, at 842, that perhaps 'this is one of those branches of equity which work best when explained least' hints that the law, like the human personality, sometimes develops more quickly behind a mask of shyness. During its development as an interest in land, some of its concepts shadowed those of easements. The requirement of a dominant and servient tenement and the general rule that the servient owner should not be obliged to spend money in the performance of his duty are examples. This relation of restrictive covenants to the ancient law of easements conferred organic status on what was a radical law reform outside Westminster. Although the new element concerns the passing of the burden of a covenant, the law of restrictive covenants has now become a self-sufficient branch of law so that the rules governing the passing of the benefit will be dealt with too. These rules will now be considered.

THE PASSING OF THE BENEFIT

First, irrespective of the rules given below, a person may take the benefit of a covenant even though he is not named as a party to it, provided that he falls within a class of persons named as parties. Such persons must be in existence at the date of the contract. If they are not in existence at that time they cannot take any benefit as parties, but they might do so as assignees. This is permitted by the Law of Property Act 1925 s 56, as explained in *Beswick* v *Beswick* [1968] AC 58. In the present context it means that, if a covenant touches and concerns land belonging to such a third party, then both he and his successors in title may enforce it. In such a case, the land must, of course, be adequately identified. In *Re Ecclesiastical Commissioners for England's Conveyance* [1936] Ch 430, *V* sold land to *P*, who entered covenants expressed to be for the benefit, not only of land retained by *V*, but also of adjacent land owned by *X*, who was not a party to the deed. It was held that the benefit was effectively conferred. The conditions necessary for the passing of the benefit to persons other than the original beneficiaries under the covenant must now be considered. We shall see that restrictive covenants concern the relationship between two or more pieces of land. One of these, the *dominant*, enjoys the benefit of the covenant; the other, the *servient*, suffers the duty of obedience to it.

The covenant must benefit the dominant land

This means that the value, amenity or convenience of the land is either preserved or increased in some way. If the covenant is contained in a lease and it is the landlord's reversion that is to be protected, it must concern the way in which the demised land is enjoyed. Examples are covenants by a neighbouring landowner either not to build at all or not to erect buildings of a particular description, or not to use premises for particular purposes. These may clearly enhance the amenities of the dominant land. It has been held that a covenant not to sell certain types of goods on the servient premises so as to allow the owner of the dominant land a greater monopoly of the trade satisfies the requirement (*Newton Abbot Co-operative Society Ltd* v *Williamson & Treadgold Ltd* [1952] Ch 286).

The assignee of the dominant land must be able to show that the benefit of the covenant has passed to him

This can be done in one of three alternative ways:

By original annexation of the covenant to the dominant land

The benefit of a covenant touching and concerning land will run with the land, provided that the language used shows a clear intention of bestowing a benefit upon the land as such, and not merely upon a particular covenantee. This is a question of construction. A formula that leaves no room for doubt is 'with intent that the covenant may enure to the benefit of the vendors their successors and assigns and others claiming under them to "Blackacre"'. It is enough, however, if it is expressed to be made with the dominant owner in his capacity as owner of the dominant land. In *Renals* v *Cowlishaw* (1878) 9 ChD 125, *P*, a purchaser, covenanted with the vendors and 'their heirs, executors, administrators and assigns' not to build. The vendors later sold the dominant land without mention of the covenant. It was held that the new owners could not sue. The word 'assigns' was taken to mean assignees of the covenant, which remained a separate entity from the land. Thus its benefit would only pass if assigned as such. If the language used had made it part of the land then it would pass with the land as an adjunct to it and without special mention. In *Rogers* v *Hosegood* [1900] 2 Ch 388 a covenant was expressed to be for the benefit of the dominant owners, 'their heirs and assigns and others claiming under them to all or any lands adjoining'. It was held that, when the dominant land was later conveyed, the benefit of the covenant passed naturally with it.

These two cases can be distinguished in the following way. Consider the benefit of the covenant to be quite a separate thing from the dominant land. In *Renals* v *Cowlishaw* the dominant owner had, so to speak, the land in his right hand and the covenant in his left. When he conveyed the land in his right hand he made no reference to the covenant in his left. So there it remained and did not pass to the purchaser. In *Rogers* v *Hosegood* the words in the covenant were such as to impress it as part of the very land, so that land and covenant were a single entity held in one hand. A later conveyance of that land therefore carried the benefit of the covenant as naturally as it carried the soil, the hedges and the ditches upon it. All this may be achieved by making the intention clear.

The words of annexation must, of course, identify the dominant land. The rules as to identification, however, have been relaxed in recent years and an implied reference will serve this purpose, provided that extrinsic evidence is available to complete this identification (*Newton Abbot* case, above).

There can be no annexation of the benefit of a covenant to land if the area of the alleged dominant land is greater than can reasonably receive some advantage from it. The original covenantee can enforce, but a purchaser from him cannot. In *Re Ballard's Conveyance* [1937] Ch 473 annexation was attempted in favour of an estate of 1700 acres. It was held that an alienee of the land could not enforce even in favour of those parts which could derive benefit, for other parts were too remote to enjoy any advantage. In short, the court refused to sever the covenant and attach its benefit to parts of the land. Yet if the parties themselves sever the covenant, as in *Zetland* v *Driver* [1939] Ch 1, so that it is expressed to be for the benefit not only of the whole but also of 'each and every part' of the land, then it may be enforced by alienees of any part which in fact benefits from it. It must not be concluded from this, however, that a restrictive covenant imposed upon a very small area is never capable of benefiting the whole of a large estate. It is a question of fact to be decided on all the evidence. Unless it is very clear that a covenant is incapable of benefiting particular land there is a presumption that the covenant is capable of doing so. (*Wrotham Park Estate Company* v *Parkside Homes Ltd* [1974] 1 WLR 798 at 808).

Following *Marten* v *Flight Refuelling Ltd* [1962] Ch 115, it has been suggested that annexation can be implied from the circumstances in which a covenant is made and without the assistance of language. This decision, however, does not seem to justify such an extension of the rules (*see* 36 Conveyancer 20).

The Court of Appeal has held that the benefit of a covenant is automatically annexed to land, irrespective of the use of words of annexation, by force of the Law of Property Act 1925 s 78, provided that the covenantee has land to which the covenant relates. Moreover, annexation is to every part of the land as well as to the whole. Intention is apparently irrelevant (*Federated Homes Ltd* v *Mill Lodge Properties Ltd* [1980] 1 All ER 371 (CA)).

Subsection 78(1) enacts

> A covenant relating to any land of the covenantee shall be deemed to be made with the covenantee and his successors in title and the persons deriving title under him or them, and shall have effect as if such successors and other persons were expressed . . .

Brightman LJ was impressed by the clarity of these words as a free standing enactment. This view however perhaps undervalues other factors:

1 This part of the 1925 Act is a consolidating measure and should be construed as changing the law as little as possible. Section 78 replaces the Conveyancing Act 1881 s 58 and passed through its Parliamentary Committee with no discussion. Section 58 was never held to annex the benefit of a covenant to land, merely to save the addition of the words 'his executors, administrators and assigns'. It is true that the wording of s 78 differs from that of s 58, but this difference was only intended to accommodate the changed rules of inheritance introduced by the 1925 Act (see 1982 JPL p 295). Statute law, like common law, loses its innocence with age.

2 Words of annexation perform an important policy function. They separate cases where there is a real intention to benefit land from those where there is no such intention, but where prolongation of a covenant's effect would achieve nothing but the unwanted incumbrance of land. *Kingsbury* v *Anderson* [1979] 40 PCR 136 had earlier emphasised that, even in the case of *building schemes*, in regard to which, we shall see, more flexible rules apply, whatever concessions are made in other respects, there must initially

> have been a covenant, not merely an allusion to one. This restraint is in the tradition of restrictive covenants. Enforcement of covenants where there is neither privity of contract nor privity of estate is a privilege. The *Mill Lodge* case loosens this tradition. Words of annexation acted as a corset on the proliferation of covenants. If the new doctrine prevails the principle of express assignment, discussed below, will become unnecessary.
>
> In *Roake* v *Chadha* [1984] 3 All E R 503 it was held however that annexation of the benefit under the section is still an arguable issue depending upon the circumstances of each individual case. The House of Lords has now interpreted its companion s 79, which deals with the running of the burden of covenants, in a less liberal way. See *Rhone* v *Stephens* [1994] 2 All ER 65. Perhaps the restrictive covenant, perceived in the nineteenth century as the protector of the property owner, might now be seen as a restriction on freedom of property and enterprise. Thus our judges have accelerator and brake at their feet.

Once annexed in accordance with the rules given above, the benefit of a covenant runs in favour of subsequent owners of any interests in the land without express mention and even if the parties are unaware of it.

By an express assignment of the benefit

If no annexation takes place in the ways just described, the covenant's benefit remains separate from the land. If it is to be passed to a purchaser of the land it must therefore be assigned independently, and this can be achieved by a statement in the conveyance that the benefit is to pass. It is, however, probably enough that all the circumstances show that this was intended. In fact, such an assignment may even occur by operation of law and the benefit may thus pass to the executors of a deceased dominant owner, and, since they would be bare trustees of the benefit, the devisee would be entitled to sue upon it in equity and to assign the benefit to purchasers without joining the personal representatives (*Earl of Leicester* v *Wells UDC* [1972] 3 All ER 77). Once the dominant land has been sold, it is too late to assign the benefit; the rather unconvincing reason being that if the land was saleable without it, then its purpose is spent. On the other hand, the covenant can be severed and dealt with in parts – in equity, though not at law – so if only part of the land has been sold, the benefit can be assigned with the parts retained on their eventual sale.

Whether the benefit of a covenant not originally annexed but contemporaneously assigned with the land passes on all future sales without express mention is open to doubt (see *Re Pinewood Estate, Farnborough* [1958] Ch 280 and *Renals* v *Cowlishaw*, above, at p 335).

By the existence of a building scheme

Since the law of restrictive covenants developed to fulfil a social need, its growth was more precocious where that need was most pronounced. This was the case where a developer wished to build an estate and impose restrictions on the purchasers of the plots for their mutual benefit and to the general advantages of the estate. Such a scheme may be highly desirable in an area of intensive development. In such cases, even some of the new equitable rules, concessionary though they are, were somewhat too confining, so that further relaxations were made. Private law was aspiring to be public law at a time before town and country planning had received the attention of Parliament.

The result is that special rules apply if a *building scheme* exists and these affect not only the passing of the benefit of covenants but also the burden, which is dealt with below. In fact, given that the covenant is negative these rules are almost self-supporting. Formerly, it was considered that some fairly rigid rules laid down by Parker J in *Elliston* v *Reacher* [1908] 2 Ch 374 must be observed. Today it is enough that the outer perimeter of a scheme shall be defined and that the purchasers or lessees within the scheme shall purchase, or take leases, on the footing that the restrictions were to enure for the benefit of other plots in the scheme. The restrictions need not, however, apply equally to all the plots. The modern principles can be found in *Baxter* v *Four Oaks Properties Ltd* [1965] Ch 816 and *Re Dolphin's Conveyance* [1970] Ch 654.

The first of these requirements is to some extent subjective in nature and the difficulty of proving it may vary according to the availability of evidence. An express declaration that a scheme is intended or that the purchasers expect mutual enforceability is not necessary, though such 'internal' evidence is clearly a great advantage. It was explained in *Re Wembley Park Estate Co Ltd's Transfer* [1968] 1 All ER 457 that, if 'external' circumstances sufficiently suggest a scheme, the inference will be readily drawn. Thus, if there is no express declaration to its effect, proof that the purchasers saw a plan of the estate might be given; but ignorance by them of the position will be fatal to a scheme. Failing an expressed intention, if no land is retained by the vendor, the intention of mutual benefit to the plots will be more readily inferred than if it is, for the latter might lead to the conclusion that he simply wished to benefit his own land. Yet the retention or otherwise of land by the vendor is by no means conclusive. Neither is the mere similarity of the covenants affecting the various plots. In short, rules of thumb should be spurned and all the circumstances considered when answering the broad question whether the developer intended and the purchasers expected reciprocal obligations and benefits within a defined estate.

The benefit and burden of covenants may even be transmitted under the doctrine to subpurchasers where the original plot from which their own subplots are derived was part of a scheme of development. If the common vendor *V* of the plots *A*, *B* and *C* shown in Figure 14.1 intended a scheme of development for the three plots, aimed at preventing the erection of more than four houses on each, and took covenants to this effect from the purchasers, then when the purchaser of *A* has sold subplots *A2* and *A3*, the owners of these subplots may enforce the covenants between themselves, just as the owners of *A*, *B* and *C* can (*Brunner* v *Greenslade* [1970] 3 All ER 833).

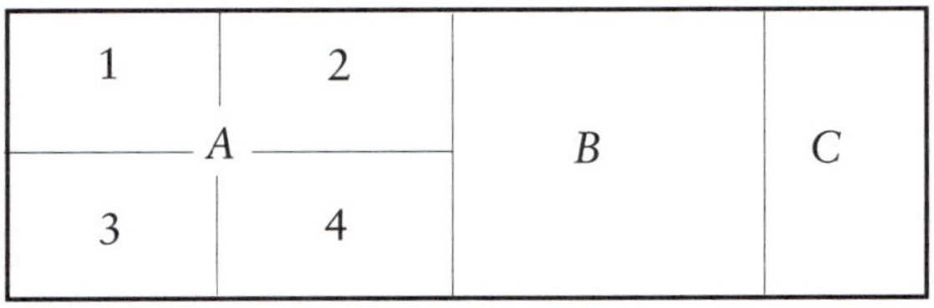

Fig. 14.1

The same principle applies if some of the plots come into common ownership at a later stage by purchase and are then again sold to separate owners. The covenants remain enforceable by the new purchasers as between themselves, though it is open to the parties to show that the restriction is no longer to apply between them, either by express provision or by the circumstances of the transaction. It will, of course, still be enforceable by the owners of the other original plots and subplots in the scheme (*Texaco Antilles Ltd* v *Kernochan* [1973] 2 All ER 118 at 126).

THE PASSING OF THE BURDEN: CONDITIONS

If neither privity of contract nor privity of estate exists between the person seeking to enforce and the person against whom he is seeking to enforce, the burden of a covenant benefiting other land is enforceable if the following conditions prevail.

The covenant must be negative in substance

This means that the covenant must not oblige the covenantor to carry out any act. Whether it is positive or negative in its language is immaterial. Thus in *Tulk* v *Moxhay*, p 333 above, the covenant was to keep certain land uncovered with buildings. Though positive in form, this obviously amounted merely to an undertaking not to build. On the other hand, a covenant not to allow property to fall into disrepair is positive since it imposes a duty to repair. The test whether it involves expenditure of money is usually sound but not necessarily conclusive, for, while a covenant involving expenditure can never be negative, the reverse is not true. If the covenant contains both negative and positive elements, the positive part may be severed, leaving the negative part only enforceable. This occurred in *Tulk* v *Moxhay*. Finally, a positive duty merely ancillary to a substantially negative obligation may be indirectly enforceable, as, for instance, in the case of a covenant not to build without first submitting plans.

There must be dominant land

This will normally mean that the covenantee must retain land to take the benefit of the covenant. In the case of building schemes, and cases such as *Re Ecclesiastical Commissioners for England's Conveyance*, p 334 above, where the benefit is bestowed upon another person's land, this need not necessarily be so. In all cases there must be dominant land for the benefit of which the covenant was taken, for the whole rationale of the doctrine is the protection of land as such. In *Formby v Barker* [1903] 2 Ch 539, *X* sold all his land, the purchaser entering a covenant restricting its use. It was held that *X*'s executors could not enforce against an assignee from that purchaser. If the covenantee does retain land, but later sells it, he cannot enforce the covenant against the servient owner in equity and so cannot obtain an injunction, for he cannot claim that it is protecting land. He could sue at law because privity of contract exists, but this would probably result in nominal damages only. We shall see, however, that a purchaser of such retained land can enforce the covenant in certain circumstances. The retention of a reversion behind a lease is equivalent to the retention of land, so that a landlord may enforce a restrictive covenant against a sublessee. There are, moreover, some statutory exceptions to the requirement that land must be retained, in favour of certain public authorities (e.g. Housing Act 1985 s 609).

Finally, the land or reversion retained must derive benefit from the covenant. It was said in *Kelly* v *Barrett* [1924] 2 Ch 379, at p 440, that 'covenants binding land in Hampstead will be too remote to benefit land in Clapham', but considering that a business interest in land is one which can be protected by restrictive covenants, physical proximity alone is a test to be applied carefully.

THE EFFECTIVENESS OF RESTRICTIVE COVENANTS

It is clear that a restrictive covenant conforming to the principles described above is more than a personal right. It is an interest in land. It is capable not merely of running with an estate in land, as certain covenants made between landlord and tenant may do, but with the very land itself, so as to be capable of binding anyone who comes to that land whether as a purchaser of the fee simple, lessee, sublessee, mortgagee, licensee or trespasser. One might say that whereas landlord and tenant covenants having reference to the subject matter of the lease, though lacking the ingredients of restrictive covenants, are 'pinned' to the lease and affect only persons who take that very lease, restrictive covenants are nailed to the gatepost on the land itself, so as to be capable of affecting anyone who comes to the land, whatever his interest in it may be. Landlord and tenant covenants may and quite frequently do qualify as restrictive covenants also. These principles are illustrated by *Mander* v *Falcke* [1891] 2 Ch 554, where a lessee covenanted not to disturb the enjoyment of the lessor's neighbouring property and then subleased. The reversion and sublease eventually came to *R* and *S* respectively. *S* did not occupy the property himself but allowed his father to use it as an oyster bar. In fact, the latter caused disturbance by using it as a brothel. It was held that the father was bound by the covenant, even though a mere licensee.

On the other hand, being creatures of equity, restrictive covenants create equitable and not legal interests in land, and, like all such interests, they have a frailty. A covenant created before 1926 cannot be enforced against a purchaser of a legal estate in the servient land for value without notice of it, nor against any person claiming through him. A covenant created after 1925 is void against a purchaser for money or money's worth of a legal estate unless it is registered under the Land Charges Act 1972, or on the charges register if the land is registered, before that legal estate is taken. Covenants made before 1926 and covenants between landlord and tenant whenever made, however, cannot be registered. A covenant in a lease may still come within this exception, even though the servient land is not the lease or the reversion but separate land altogether (*Dartstone Ltd* v *Cleveland Petroleum Co Ltd* [1969] 3 All ER 668). As to the former of these two exceptions, the old rules governing notice apply; as to the latter, a sublessee is taken to have notice of the covenants in the lease. The difference between 'valuable consideration' and 'money or money's worth' is that 'valuable consideration' includes marriage.

Unless otherwise agreed, a restrictive covenant is normally binding for ever. Nevertheless, even if it is perfectly valid under the rules described above, the court may refuse a remedy where it would be contrary to the principles of equity as, for instance, where the covenant has been openly breached for so long as to give the impression that it is no longer binding, or where it has become obsolete through changed surroundings and the action is not in good faith. Mere delay does not constitute acquiescence. The circumstances must be such that as a result of the delay, it would be unconscionable or dishonest for the person having the benefit of the covenant to seek to enforce it (*Shaw* v *Applegate* [1977] 1 WLR 970). It is clear, both from this and from the demanding nature of the rules applying to restrictive covenants, that whether a covenant is enforceable may sometimes be very uncertain. Important and expensive decisions may depend on the answer, such as whether to erect buildings. It is therefore provided by the Law of Property Act 1925 s 84 that the court has power to make a declaration as to whether an alleged covenant affects freehold land. This power should be distinguished from the power, dealt with below, of discharging an admittedly binding covenant.

THE EXTINGUISHMENT AND MODIFICATION OF RESTRICTIVE COVENANTS

Power is given to the Lands Tribunal by the Law of Property Act 1925 s 84, as amended by the Law of Property Act 1969 s 28, on the application of any person interested in freehold land affected by a restrictive covenant, to discharge or modify the restriction in any of the following cases:

1 where the restriction ought to be deemed obsolete;

2 where it would impede some reasonable user and does not give any practical benefit or substantial value to the land, or is contrary to the public interest;

3 where those entitled to the benefit have expressly or impliedly agreed to the discharge;

4 where discharge will not injure anyone entitled to the benefit of the covenant. There is a provision for compensation under this head. This was somewhat paradoxical in view of the requirement that discharge shall not cause injury.

Modern Lands Tribunal decisions should be consulted for an appreciation of the operation of these provisions. The provision regarding the 'public interest' under 2, for instance, has not been generously interpreted. In *Re Osborn's and Easton's Application* [1978] 38 P&CR 251 the President commented: 'It is one thing to say that a development is in the public interest and another to say that it would be contrary to the public interest if such development did not take place'. This view is significant in the inevitable conflict between private and public interests. Perhaps the central government might advise higher density residential development to ease the housing shortage; perhaps planning permission has been granted for such development in a particular case after consideration of this and other public and private considerations. Nevertheless, such development could be blocked by the refusal of the Lands Tribunal to discharge a covenant in restraint of that development. The *Estates Gazette* regularly reports decisions.

Limited powers to modify the effects of restrictive covenants are given by the Housing Act 1985 s 610(1) and the Town and Country Planning Act 1990 s 237 to county courts and to local planning authorities respectively.

GENERAL

The future

Eugen Ehrlich, an Austrian jurist, remarked that the centre of legal gravity lies in society itself rather than in the formal legal rules prevailing at a particular time. Thus law chases but does not always catch up with the aspirations of contemporary society. The development of the law of restrictive covenants shows both a bold chase and a weakened finish.

The development following *Tulk* v *Moxhay* (1848) during the industrial revolution responded to the individualistic aims of the propertied classes to protect the amenity of their homes against otherwise uncontrolled building and land use. At the turn of the century a more community-based aspiration came with estate development. The law responded again with the building scheme (*Elliston* v *Reacher*, 1908). These advances had however been achieved under the safe and ancient cover of easements, frequently used as an analogy in the cases.

Yet the law of easements was itself showing strain in the face of the social challenges of the twentieth century. In *Liverpool City Council* v *Irwin* [1976] AC 239 it created an exception to one of its most steadfast principles, that the servient owner could not be obliged to expend money in the cause of the easement. The law of covenants affecting freehold property has been stranded at this point. The burden of a positive covenant would not pass to a successor in title of the servient land.

Meanwhile the social need for the passage of such burden increased not only with the proliferation of estates of detached and semi-detached accommodation but also of flatted or *flying freeholds*. Such planned community living called for duties of a positive kind, such as maintaining standards of repair and decoration, contribution to common facilities and even to management schemes. The study materials at the end of this chapter are extracted from the recommendations of the Law Commission in 1984. The government has promised legislation to implement these in the early future. *See also* MLR July, 1995, 486, for a discussion of the associated question of *commonhold title*.

STUDY MATERIAL

Neighbour obligations and development obligations

(Extract from the Law Commission recommendations 1984)

6.1 Our scheme is in essence designed for the simple case of two neighbouring landowners, but we have already given our reasons for thinking that it must also be capable of accommodating the more complicated cases involving property development.[1]

6.2 After prolonged consideration it has seemed to us that a better and simpler result is obtained if these two types of caes are to some extent kept seperate – both conceptually and in the provisions of the draft Bill. This separation starts at an early stage, because in its first clause the Bill establishes and distinguishes between two classes of land obligation: 'neighbour obligations' and 'development obligations'.

Neighbour obligations

6.3 Neighbour obligations are land obligations intended for use in the simple case mentioned above – the case, that is to say, where the obligation simply imposes a burden on one piece of land (the servient land) for the benefit of another piece of land (the dominant land).

[1] Paras 4.29–4.36 above.

6.4 It would of course be wrong to allow a landowner to make use of the new law of land obligations in order to impose an obligation of any kind which might happen to take his fancy. If, for example, a garage owner sold part of the garden attached to his house, he should not be allowed to impose on the purchaser a land obligation – enforceable in perpetuity against the purchaser's successors in title – to buy a certain quantity of petrol from his garage every month. The old rule that a covenant must 'touch and concern' (or be for the benefit of) the dominant *land* was established for good reason and we wish to reproduce it in our scheme.

6.5 There is also a need (for reasons which will become clearer as this report proceeds) to distinguish one kind of land obligation from another.

6.6 Putting these two requirements together, we recommend that obligations of the following kinds, and those only, should be capable of existing as neighbour obligations:

(a) An obligation imposing a restriction which benefits the whole or part of the dominant land on the doing of some act on the servient land.

This obligation we propose to call a *restrictive obligation*. Its purpose is the same as that of restrictive covenants under the existing law.

(b) An obligation requiring the carrying out on the servient land or the dominant land of works which benefit the whole or any part of the dominant land.
(c) An obligation requiring the provision of services for the benefit of the whole or any part of the dominant land.

These obligations – one requiring works to be carried out, the other requiring services to be provided – we propose to call *positive obligations*. They are of course akin to positive covenants under the present law. An example of the first type of obligation would be one to maintain a boundary wall (and the wall might be on the servient or on the dominant land or partly on both). An example of the second would be one to provide heating (which might be desirable if a house had been divided into two flats and a central heating boiler installed in one to supply them both). And we recommend that the provision of insurance should be specifically included amongst 'services'.

(d) An obligation requiring the making of payments in a specified manner (whether to a person or a specified description or otherwise) on account of expenditure which has been or is to be incurred by a person in complying with a positive obligation (that is, an obligation of type (b) or (c) above).

We propose to call obligations of this kind *reciprocal payment obligations*. The simplest illustration is, perhaps, to be found in a case where there are two neighbours and one of them accepts a positive obligation to maintain the boundary wall while the other accepts a reciprocal payment obligation to meet half the cost. Illustrations may be found also in the case of a house divided into two flats: the upper owner might agree to maintain the roof if the lower owner met half the cost, or the lower owner might agree to insure the whole house if the upper owner paid half the premiums.

Development obligations

6.7 Development obligations, as we have indicated, are a species of land obligation designed primarily for use in cases where a substantial area of land (including a block of flats, because 'land' extends upwards as well as sideways) is or is to be divided into a number of separately owned but interdependent units.

6.8 In such a case, development obligations may be imposed on the units, and any unit on which such an obligation is imposed will be the servient land in relation to that obligation. Looked at from the point of view of the servient owner, therefore, development obligations do not differ greatly from neighbour obligations: and the rules which we propose about their burden and its devolution are virtually identical. The differences appear mainly in two ways.

6.9 First, they differ in relation to the benefit. The enforceability of development obligations, unlike that of neighbour obligations, is not confined to the owner of the dominant land for the benefit of which they were imposed. In relation to development obligations, indeed, there is no dominant land as such. The concept of the dominant land is replaced by that of 'the development land', and development obligations may be made enforceable either by owners of other parts of the development land or by a 'manager' acting on their behalf. A full discussion of these points must be postponed until the next part of this report.

6.10 Second, they differ in relation to their scope, which is wider in the case of development obligations. We set out below the obligations which, we recommend, should be capable of imposition as development obligations. It may be compared with the list of neighbour obligations which we set out earlier.[2] The descriptions of these obligations appear in the form of subheadings:

Restrictive

(a) An obligation imposing a restriction which benefits the whole or part of the development land on the doing of some act on the servient land or any other part of the development land.

Positive

(b) An obligation requiring the carrying out on the servient land or any other part of the development land of works which benefit the whole or any part of the development land.
(c) An obligation requiring the provision of services for the benefit of the whole or any part of the development land.
(d) An obligation requiring the servient land to be used in a particular way which benefits the whole or part of the development land.

Reciprocal payment

(e) An obligation requiring the making of payments in a specified manner (whether to a person of a specified description or otherwise) on account of expenditure

---

[2] Para 6.6 above.

which has been or is to be incurred by a person in complying with an obligation of type (b) or (c) above.

Reimbursement

(f) An obligation requiring the making of payments to the manager of a development scheme in respect of expenditure incurred or to be incurred in the provision of works or services provided by him in pursuance of the scheme.

(g) An obligation requiring the making of payments to the manager of a development scheme by way of contribution towards fees, costs or expenses charged or incurred by him in discharging his functions under the scheme, which costs and expenses may include costs or expenses incurred in accordance with the scheme in connection with any application (whether made by the manager or another) to the court or the Lands Tribunal under any provision of this Act.

Access

(h) An obligation requiring access to the servient land to be afforded, in such circumstances and for such purposes as may be specified, to the manager, to any servant or agent of his or to any other person authorised in writing by him.

Some brief comments on this list may be made at this stage.

6.11 Obligations of types (a), (b), (c) and (e) are broadly analogous to neighbour obligations of the same types, the most notable difference being that references to the development land appear in place of references to the dominant land.

6.12 Obligations of type (d) are obligations requiring some particular and positive use to be made of the servient land. They are therefore positive obligations and are to be distinguished from restrictive obligations of a kind which merely require the land *not* to be used in some specified manner.[3] One of our objects in framing this list of development obligations is to make provision for all the types of obligation which are reasonably imposed upon tenants as covenants in a leasehold development, and we think that positive user obligations of this kind have a legitimate place here – for example, to ensure that premises are actively used to provide proper shopping facilities of certain kinds. We think, however, that such obligations could be used oppressively if they were included in our list of neighbour obligations. We also recommend that the court should be specifically enjoined to look at their substance rather than their form, and that if their real object is not to require land to be used in some particular way, but merely to prevent it being used in some other way, they should be treated as restrictive obligations.[4]

6.13 Obligations of type (f) and (g) (reimbursement obligations) are designed for the case where there is a mananger of the development land. A further explanation must be postponed until the next part of this report, where the idea of the 'development scheme' is explained.

---

[3] For an example. see *London Chatham and Dover Railway Company* v *Spiers and Pond Ltd* (1916) 32 TLR 493.

[4] See the draft Bill, Sch 1 para 20.

6.14 Obligations of type (h) (access obligations) are also designed only for the case where there is a manager. It may at first seem strange that such obligations are not available in any other case: but the reason is that a right of access can normally be given by means of an easemnet imposed on one piece of land in favour of another: it is only in favour of a manager, who may not own any land, that the right needs to be available as a land obligation.

Supplementary provisions

6.15 Our recommendations as to the types of primary obligation which should be capable of creation, as neighbour obligations and development obligations respectively, appear above. We are conscious, however, that obligations of these kinds are nowadays commonly reinforced (especially in the landlord and tenant setting) by what might be called supplementary provisions.

6.16 For this and other reasons we recommend that it should be possible for the instrument creating the land obligation to make certain supplementary provisions of this kind and that, if it does so, these provisions should take effect as part of the land obligation. The provisions in question are set out in full in Part III of Schedule 1 to the Bill and we confine ourselves here to giving a general indication of their nature:

(a) *Information.* A provision giving a right to information (for example, as to the current ownership of the servient land) or to the production of documents (for example, those dealing with changes in its ownership).
(b) *Inspection.* A provision enabling anyone entitled to enforce a land obligation to inspect the servient land in order to see whether it has been complied with.
(c) *Self-help.* A provision enabling any person entitled to enforce a land obligation requiring the carrying out of works to enter the servient land and carry them out himself in the event of non-compliance. (More will be said about this provision in a later part of the report.[5])
(d) *Fund.* A provision relating to the keeping of a fund out of which expenditure on the carrying out of works, or the provision of services, is to be met. A provision of this kind can be made whenever a works or services obligation is coupled with a reciprocal payment obligation, and can be made to take effect as part of either obligation.
(e) *Interest.* A provision requiring the payment of interest if default is made in complying with a reciprocal payment or reimbursement obligation.
(f) *Charge.* A provision imposing a charge on the servient land for certain money which becomes due as a result of the non-performance of a reciprocal payment or reimbursement obligation or of an obligation requiring the carrying out of works. (This provision, too, will receive detailed treatment later in the report.[6])

The uses of neighbour and development obligations

6.17 Neighbour obligations may be imposed as simply, broadly speaking, as easements may be imposed under the present law. The detailed formalities for their

[5] Paras.13.28–13.31.
[6] Part XIV of this report.

creation are considered later in this report, but a few lines in a document will normally be sufficient.

6.18 Development obligations, though they must be imposed in the same way, are valid only if they are imposed in pursuance of a pre-existing 'development scheme'. Development schemes are dealt with in the next part of the report and we do not want to anticipate that discussion, but we are concerned to emphasise here that development obligations, unlike neighbour obligations, must necessarily entail a fairly elaborate scheme (the development scheme) covering a defined area of land. Those who opt to create a development scheme will find that it affords them many other facilities and advantages as well as the ability to impose development land obligations, and we think that the development scheme concept will be of great benefit to those who want these things. But those who find that all their needs are met by neighbour obligations will not wish to venture into these waters.

6.19 In what cases will neighbour obligations be sufficient? Obviously enough they include the simple case of two pieces of land side by side: if for example, a landowner sells off part of his garden to a purchaser who intends to build on it, all the obligations which the parties are likely to wish to impose on one another may be imposed as neighbour obligations. But the uses of neighbour obligations are not confined to cases of this kind. We think they will normally extend, for example, to the case of a house divided into two flats: we see no need, in such a case, for the creation of a development scheme and development obligations. It may well be possible also to complete the development of a small housing estate by means of neighbour obligations alone. Each case must be considered according to its particular circumstances.

QUESTIONS

1 Has the amendment to the Law of Property Act 1925 s 84 provided by the Law of Property Act 1969 s 28 been futile?

2 Discuss the divergences between restrictive covenants and negative easements.

3 In what ways does the decision in *Federated Homes Ltd* v *Mill Lodge Properties Ltd* [1980] 1 ER 371 (CA) run contrary to the established principles of restrictive covenants?

4 Martak, property developers, wish to build an estate on which no residents shall own motor cars. Their purposes are to increase the density of housing by saving driveway and garage space, to increase amenity areas on the estate and to minimise noise and motor accidents. Martak have a policy of selling only freehold estates and wonder whether their aims can be achieved by the use of restrictive covenants in the conveyances to purchasers.

Advise Martak.

CHAPTER 15

MORTGAGES

INTRODUCTION

A mortgage is an interest in land created in favour of a creditor as a security for a debt or the performance of an obligation.

Any creditor may sue for the recovery of a debt, but he might be frustrated if the debtor has not enough assets to satisfy the claims of his creditors. In the case of substantial loans, therefore, some form of security is desirable, out of which the debt can be satisfied in preference to other creditors. It might take the form of a pawn, when possession of a chattel is given to the lender on the understanding that he may retain it until the loan is repaid and sell it if it is not. This is not a completely satisfactory solution, because the borrower might be deprived of a very useful or beautiful thing. Yet it would be inviting trouble to allow the debtor to remain in possession of it since he might sell it.

An interest in land, however, is particularly well suited to being a security. The act of constituting an interest in land as a security is a mortgage. It is carried out by the borrower, called the mortgagor, creating a long lease in favour of the creditor, the mortgagee, or, alternatively, by what amounts to the same thing, a *charge* over the land. However, this lease provides that when the debt is paid the interest in the land shall terminate. If created in the proper way, such an interest is enforceable against the whole world, so that even if the mortgagor later sells the fee simple, the mortgage will, like any lease, adhere to that land as a barnacle sticks to the bottom of a ship wherever that ship goes. The mortgagee, therefore, will be able to enforce the mortgage against the new owner who would have expected to pay a reduced price for the land according to the amount of the mortgage. Usually when land subject to a mortgage is sold, the vendor discharges the debt at the time of completion by repaying the mortgagee out of the purchase money.

Since the mortgage may thus be made enforceable against the whole world, the mortgagee need not protect his security by taking possession under the lease and so the mortgagor may continue to enjoy his property. Indeed, the mortgagee will not be interested in taking possession, because he is only looking for a security. Nevertheless, he has an estate, and is entitled to possession if he wishes. While the very existence of his interest secures the debt against all who come to the land, the mortgagee will require some ready means of raising the amount due to him, and this is achieved by providing that the mortgagee shall have power to sell the interest of the mortgagor, satisfy his debt and costs from the proceeds of sale and pay the balance of the money to the mortgagor. In most cases there is statutory power to do this, irrespective of agreement.

The law of mortgages has been greatly influenced by history and by the intervention of equity and this has resulted in the application of certain rules, irrespective of the agreement of the parties, once it is clear that a transaction is in essence a mortgage. Consequently, the true rights of the parties may be very different than appears from the terms of their agreement. Equity interfered to protect the mortgagor, who in the past had frequently been open to exploitation. The wastrel landowner gambling into the night and putting himself at the mercy of unscrupulous moneylenders has existed in fact as well as in romantic fiction. Equity intervened in his favour. The doctrines equity evolved in doing so apply today, even though in modified form. The majority of mortgages nowadays are transacted in very different circumstances, for the mortgagor is usually a well advised commercial firm or a newly-wed couple with feet firmly on the ground, and the mortgagee a building society with a high and regulated standard of conduct.

When a house is purchased with the aid of a mortgage, the two transactions of purchase and mortgage are telescoped. After negotiating a loan, the purchaser buys the property with the loan and immediately afterwards, on the same day, mortgages it to the mortgagee as security for the loan. Nevertheless, the two transactions are quite separate, a factor which may have important consequences (*Church of England Building Society* v *Piskor* [1954] 2 All ER 85).

Whether a transaction is a mortgage or not is a matter of substance and not one of form, so that if in essence a conveyance is for the purpose of security, then it is a mortgage, even though it is called by some other name. Thus if *A* sells land to *B* and at the same time an option is given to *A* to repurchase upon repayment of the purchase money, the transaction might be a mortgage. It is a question of the intentions of the parties.

Perhaps more than any other topic in land law, therefore, the mortgage needs a prologue to any discussion of its principles. The following preliminary comments are thus necessary.

1 The legal forms which mortgages take might give a false impression of the true legal position of the parties and also of the practices they are likely to follow.

2 The legal rules have been shaped by equity over several centuries so that they justly respond, age by age, to contemporary social and economic considerations. In contrast to the chameleon, the exterior form has remained fairly constant, while the real body has changed. Some of the older authorities are thus no longer reliable. We must curtail history and concisely discuss the judicial restatements for our own generation.

3 The social background informing a modern account is of enormous importance. The mortgage is no longer merely a means of raising a personal loan. It is the means through which millions of homes are provided for families and by which mighty finance is raised for commercial ventures. In times of recession the financial hardship of borrowers brings problems of breakdown of the mortgage agreement and potential homelessness.

4 In the present century, statute has supplemented equity in the task of containing the bargains of enthusiastic lenders and borrowers within some imposed bounds. This interference with free will is not new. In modern terms, however, its habitat is within *consumer protection*. The Law of Property Act 1925 s 103, recognised the principle in regard to mortgages as it did elsewhere for other transactions. Later examples are the Administration of Justice Act 1973 s 8 and the Consumer Credit Act 1974 s 137.

5 The inflation of property prices during the 1970s and 1980s promoted house purchase for the purposes of both home ownership and investment for income. Many buyers undertook large mortgage debts, anticipating further growth in values. A general recession then not only depressed house prices but left their owners out of work and unable to keep up their mortgage repayments. Even the desperate remedy of sale offered no satisfactory solution since the house might then be worth less than the outstanding mortgage debt. This condition of *negative equity* produced hardship and loss of homes through repossession by mortgagees.

Considering these factors, the order of treatment of the subject will be as follows. First the classical theory of mortgages will be discussed, since this still underlies all forms of the transaction. This discussion will include: the creation of mortgages; the rights of the mortgagor; the rights of the mortgagee. Then the priority of competing mortgages will be considered. Finally there will follow discussion of some modern mortgage transactions in their contexts with reference to sample documents. References to sections will be to the Law of Property Act 1925 unless otherwise stated.

CREATION OF MORTGAGES

Mortgages, like leases and certain other interests in land, may exist either as legal or equitable interests. The ways in which legal and equitable mortgages are created will be considered separately. If a legal mortgage is to be created, the estate which is to be mortgaged must itself be legal, that is, either a fee simple absolute in possession or a term of years absolute, and the transaction must be carried out by deed. Equitable mortgages are created when there is only a contract to create a mortgage of a legal estate, when such a mortgage is not accompanied by the required formalities or when the interest itself, which is the subject matter of the mortgage, is equitable.

Legal mortgages

Given that the subject matter of the mortgage is a legal estate, there are two ways of creating a legal mortgage, first, by a lease *subject to a provision for cesser on redemption* and second, by a *charge by way of legal mortgage* (ss 85–87). Although the mortgage by lease has now in practice been almost completely replaced by the charge by way of legal mortgage, the mortgage by lease will be discussed first, since the Act explains the effect of a legal charge by reference to it.

By a lease

If the estate to be mortgaged is a fee simple, the lease may be of any duration. It must be by deed. This deed will contain the terms of the mortgage and will also contain a clause known as the provision for cesser on redemption. This states that if the loan is repaid in accordance with the terms of the deed and the mortgage thus satisfied or *redeemed*, the term of years shall thereupon cease. Thus, if a term of 3000 years is created with an agreement that the debt shall be repaid in one year's time and the debt is satisfied at the end of that year, the mortgage term ends then.

If the mortgagor wishes to borrow more money on the security of the same property, he may make a second mortgage, and this is done by creating a second lease in favour of the second mortgagee, usually of one day's greater duration than the first. Third and subsequent mortgages may also be made in the same way. Thus, an indefinite number of legal mortgages may be created on the same property. We shall see later that the rights of these subsequent mortgagees are substantial and are not properly reflected in the fact that nominal reversions only are reserved to them. Subsequent mortgagees should ascertain before advancing their money that the value of the property is enough to support the loans they are to make, as well as the loans of prior mortgagees, because provided that the latter have protected their securities properly, they will have prior right to be satisfied. If the mortgagor's estate is a lease and not a freehold, then a legal mortgage is created by a sublease in favour of the mortgagee, with a provision for cesser upon redemption. Again the transaction must be by deed. The length of the sublease will, of course, be restricted by the length of the lease out of which it is created, for it must be of less duration. A period of one day less would satisfy this legal requirement, but in practice the mortgage term is made several days less in duration, for second and subsequent mortgages are created by subleases of one or more days' longer duration than prior mortgages, and sufficient room in the reversion is thereby provided for these later transactions. Figure 15.1 shows the operation of this procedure in the case of the successive mortgages of a ten-year lease. Once again, an indefinite number of legal mortgages may be created in the same property.

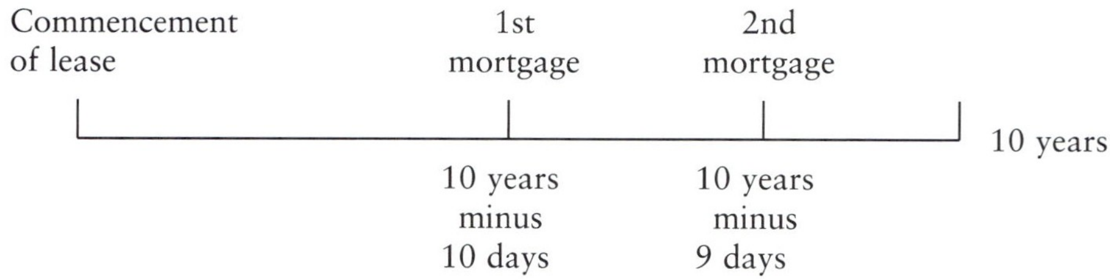

Fig. 15.1

Before 1926, a fee simple was mortgaged by a conveyance of the fee simple itself to the mortgagee, with a provision that when the loan was repaid the estate would be reconveyed to the mortgagor. The mortgagor was left in possession of the property just as he is nowadays. Even leaseholds were occasionally mortgaged by an assignment of the whole term with a similar proviso. Both these methods are now impossible under ss 85 and 86. If an attempt is made to make mortgages in either of these ways, the sections provide what the effect shall be.

A purported mortgage of an estate in fee simple by a conveyance of the fee simple operates as a lease for 3000 years without impeachment for waste, but subject to cesser on redemption, or, in the case of a second mortgage, as a lease on similar terms for a period of 3000 years plus one day, or, in the case of subsequent mortgages, of one day's greater duration than the previous mortgage. A purported mortgage of a lease by assignment takes effect as a sublease of ten days' less duration than the lease, subject to cesser on redemption. The term taken by second or subsequent mortgagees is one day longer than the mortgage immediately prior to it.

A mortgage term together with its attendant rights is clearly property and as such can itself be mortgaged by the mortgagee if, for instance, he wishes to raise a short term loan without going against the mortgagor to recover his own money. When a mortgage is itself mortgaged, as opposed to being transferred, the transaction is called a submortgage. It is created by the grant of a sublease out of the mortgage term or by a charge by way of legal mortgage, which is dealt with below (s 87). The general effect of a submortgage is to place the submortgagee in the position of the mortgagee so far as rights of enforcement of repayment of the original mortgage debt are concerned.

By a charge by way of legal mortgage

An alternative way of creating a legal mortgage which applies identically to both the fee simple and to leaseholds is by a *charge by way of legal mortgage*. After dealing with mortgages by means of leases, the nature of a charge might seem rather elusive. No estate is created and we seem to meet a new concept. In fact, it is a more rational and elegant means of achieving the desired effect of a security than is the grant of a leasehold, which is a makeshift use of an estate really designed to endow a person with possession of land for a definite period.

The legal charge, as it is usually called, is really easy to understand now that we have discussed mortgages by leasing. Section 87 enacts that a mortgagee by charge of a fee simple shall have the same protection, powers and remedies as if he held a mortgage term of 3000 years without impeachment of waste, and that a mortgagee by legal charge of a lease shall have the same protection, powers and remedies as if he held a sublease of one day's duration less than the lease which was charged. In short, although the charge is different in form from a mortgage by lease, bringing to the mortgage transaction clothing of its own, unborrowed from other wardrobes, its effect is the same (see *Regent Oil Co Ltd* v *J A Gregory (Hatch End) Ltd* [1966] Ch 402).

The legal charge has grown in popularity amongst practitioners since 1926 and has now largely superseded the lease. The Act provides a short model form of the charge which, however, is optional only. Additional provisions are usually included in practice (Fifth Schedule). The charge must be created by deed.

This new form of legal mortgage has certain advantages over a mortgage by lease besides that of simplicity of appearance. First, since it applies in the same way to both freehold and leasehold estates, both kinds of property can be mortgaged together by a legal charge. Second, if a lease contains a covenant against subletting, then a mortgage by means of a legal charge, since it does not create a term of years, probably does not constitute a breach of that covenant, even though the landlord's consent is not sought (*Grand Junction Co Ltd* v *Bates* [1954] 2 QB 160, at 168). In the case of a mortgage by lease, consent is clearly required, although it is enacted that such consent shall not be unreasonably refused (s 86).

Equitable mortgages

Mortgages may exist as equitable interests in land and are created in the following circumstances.

Mortgage of an equitable interest

If the subject matter of the mortgage is an equitable interest, then the mortgage itself must necessarily be equitable. A mortgage of an equitable interest is created by assigning the interest to the mortgagee with a provision for redemption and reassignment. No deed is necessary, but the transaction must be in writing, signed by the mortgagor or his agent (s 53(1)(c)). It may also be created by will.

Agreement for mortgage

We discussed in relation to leaseholds how equity looks on that as done which ought to be done. Thus a contract for a lease is treated as a lease, provided that certain conditions are satisfied. The same principle applies to agreements to create mortgages. If the agreement is made after 26 September 1989 it must be in writing, signed by the parties to satisfy the Law of Property (Miscellaneous Provisions) Act 1989 s 2.

A deposit of title deeds with the intention that they shall be retained as a security for a loan creates an equitable mortgage (*Russel* v *Russel* (1783) 1 Bro CC 269). Even if created after 26 September 1989 mortgages by deposit of deeds are exempted from the provisions of the Law of Property (Miscellaneous Provisions) Act 1989 so that they are not required to be in writing. In *United Bank of Kuwait* v *Sahib and Others* [1995] 2 All ER 973, however, it was proposed that this method of creation was not of independent standing and was based in contract. It must therefore be made in writing in accordance with s 2. In practice, such a deposit is usually accompanied by a deed containing the terms of the mortgage. This makes the transaction a mortgage 'by deed' which, we shall see, enables the mortgagee to exercise certain statutory powers and remedies. The deed might also include a power of attorney or a declaration of trust so as to empower the mortgagee to pass the legal estate in the event of the sale of the security by him. This would otherwise be impossible, because he only holds an equitable interest.

Equitable charge

When a person expresses the intention in signed writing that certain land is to stand responsible for the payment of some debt or other obligation, without intending to create or agreeing to create any legal or equitable interest in that land, an equitable charge results. Such a charge would be created, for example, if a man signed a written contract agreeing to charge his land with the payment of a sum of money to another (see *Matthews* v *Goodday* (1861) 31 LJ Ch 282, at 282).

THE RIGHTS OF THE MORTGAGOR

The principal rights of the mortgagor are his beneficial interest in the mortgaged property, the right to redeem, protection in some cases under the Consumer Credit Act 1974 and the right, in certain circumstances, to grant and accept surrenders of leases.

Beneficial interest in the mortgaged property

Since the essence of a mortgage is that it is a security, the mortgagor retains the beneficial interest in the estate or interest which is passed to the mortgagee, subject to the rights of the mortgagee under the mortgage contract. The changes made by the 1925 legislation with regard to the creation of mortgages are skin deep only, and do not affect this substantive interest of the mortgagor, which was taken for granted before the Acts (see the judgment of Lord Parker in *Kreglinger* v *New Patagonia Meat & Cold Storage Co Ltd* [1914] AC 25). This beneficial interest arises at the moment the mortgage is created and continues until its end. It explains why a mortgagee who enters into possession of the property must account strictly for the profits of the land, why he must return any surplus money to the mortgagor after his own debt and expenses have been satisfied, following a sale of the property by him, and why a mortgagor can bring actions in his own name for possession or for rents and profits (s 98), although he may only own a reversionary interest. The mortgagor also continues to own the reversion behind the term or sub-term which he has created in favour of the mortgagee.

Right to redeem

In the early days of mortgages, if the mortgagor did not repay the loan upon the very day agreed, the mortgagee was entitled to keep the mortgaged property, even though its value far exceeded the loan. The mortgagor had thus a short-lived contractual right to redeem. Equity intervened against this harsh doctrine and, emphasising that a mortgage was only a security and that a failure to repay on the agreed day could be remedied, it allowed that mortgagor to redeem at an indefinite time after the contractual right to redeem had passed, provided that the mortgagor, who was thereby invoking equitable principles, was himself prepared to act equitably. This means that, since he has not repaid upon the date agreed, he must give the mortgagee either six months' notice or six months' interest before he enforces his equitable right to redeem, because it is only fair to allow the mortgagee a reasonable time to investigate other ways in which to invest his money. If the loan is not repaid even upon this new date, then a further six months' notice or interest must be given, unless there is some good explanation to account for the failure to pay. Then reasonable notice must be given (*Cromwell Property Investment Co Ltd* v *Western* [1934] Ch 322). This equitable right to redeem lasts from the day after the contractual right to redeem has passed, until the mortgage itself ends, whether this occurs through repayment, sale of the security or other means. Figure 15.2 will illustrate the rights of the mortgagor discussed up to this point and their duration.

Terminology has not always been consistent or precise in this topic, but the expression *equity of redemption*, as distinguished from the 'equitable right to redeem', is properly reserved to describe the whole of the mortgagor's rights, so as to embrace all the three rights shown in the diagram. As such, it is an interest in land which can be conveyed or devised. Once the equitable right to redeem became established, the date stated in the deed for repayment of the loan as the contractual date for redemption lost some of its previous importance. As a result, the merely nominal date of redemption six months after the date of the mortgage, which often appears in the mortgage deed, gives no true indication of the mortgagor's right. This is but one reason why it has been remarked that no one ever understood a mortgage deed by the light of nature, or, as Maitland

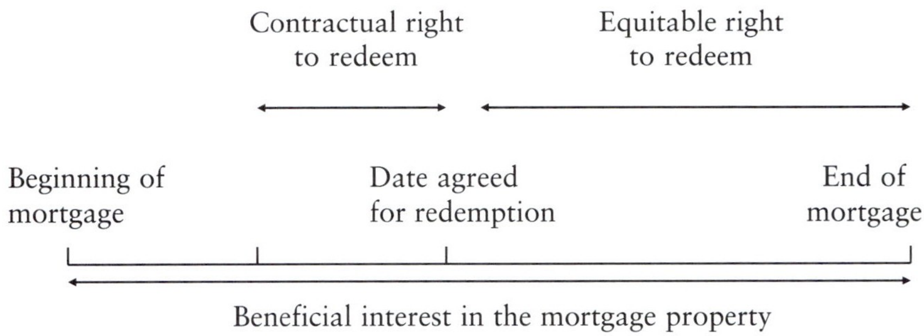

Fig. 15.2

said, it is 'one long *suppressio veri* and *suggestio falsi*'. So much for the incidence of the right of redemption, legal and equitable. We must now examine how it operates.

Historically, the mortgagor has usually been in a weak position, urgently needing money on such terms as are offered, as against the mortgagee who has generally been in such a position of strength that he could press the mortgagor into an unfair bargain. The mortgagee often took advantage of this and, demanding more than the return of his loan with interest tried to exact further profit by fettering or 'clogging' the mortgagor's right to redeem the property, either completely or substantially.

Equity, recognising the unequal positions of the parties, and affirming that the real purpose of a mortgage is simply to secure a debt, evolved the doctrine that any provision in a mortgage which directly or indirectly had the effect of clogging the right to redeem was void. In the present century, the positions of mortgagors and mortgagees have been re-examined, and it has been recognised that this degree of protection afforded to the mortgagor is not always necessary or deserved. More often, the transaction is one in which the parties are well advised and which embodies a carefully balanced contract which both parties freely entered into as a fair bargain. The repeal of the usury laws has also left the parties freer to compose their own loan terms. While such contracts will still be scrutinised when there is an allegation of fraud, oppression or unconscionable dealing, the dogmatic assertion that every provision which inhibits the right to redeem is void is nowadays too wide. Indeed, some of the older cases have lost most of their authority. We have already noted how the social context in which mortgages now generally occur has changed during recent years.

There are several ways in which a mortgagee, to achieve a bargain suitable to himself, might attempt to affect the right to redeem. First, he might try to make the mortgage irredeemable upon the happening of certain events, or delay the right to redeem for a long period. Second, he might include a term that he should be entitled to some advantage in the mortgaged property, such as that the mortgagor should for a certain period buy all his beer or petrol for sale on the mortgaged premises from the mortgagee. He might even attempt to make such a condition operative after redemption, so that although the right to redeem is not affected in theory, it is practically threatened because the mortgagor would be entitled to recover a less valuable property than he mortgaged because of the restriction. We must now discuss to what extent such provisions are enforceable.

A term must not be oppressive or unconscionable

Relief will be granted upon equitable principles against terms in a mortgage which are oppressive, unconscionable or secured by fraud (*Knightsbridge Estates Trust Ltd* v *Byrne* [1939] Ch 441, *per* Greene MR at 457). These grounds for relief are not restricted to mortgages. It was emphasised in the *Knightsbridge* case that they do not empower the courts to declare mortgage terms unenforceable merely because they are not reasonable. Freedom of contract is not affected, but when any of these elements is present, one of the parties is not really in a position of freedom. Thus it was held in *Multiservice Bookbinding Ltd* v *Marden* [1979] Ch 84 that an obligation to pay interest on the whole loan throughout the period of the loan, notwithstanding any interim repayment of capital and the linking of the obligation to repay capital and interest to the Swiss franc, was valid, even though the bargain was a hard one. There was no unconscionable behaviour in the sense of the exploitation of a young, inexperienced or ignorant person, or the striking of a bargain which no sensible well-balanced person would have entered (but see *Cityland and Property (Holdings) Ltd* v *Dabrah* [1968] Ch 166).

In *Kings North Trust Ltd* v *Bell* [1986] 1 All ER 423 it was held that there can be vicarious responsibility for undue influence. In that case a company agreed to lend money on the security of a house which was owned in equity by a husband and wife, though legally in the husband's name only. Solicitors acting for the company instructed the husband's solicitors to arrange for execution of the mortgage documents, requiring also that the wife should join in the transaction in order to charge her interest. The husband's solicitors left this task to the husband. The husband used undue influence in procuring the consent of his wife, who had no independent legal advice. It was held that the company was in no better position than the husband.

What circumstances raise a presumption of undue influence when clear evidence of duress is absent has revealed a political cleavage in judicial attitudes. In *National Westminster Bank* v *Morgan* [1985] AC 686 the House of Lords adopted a hard nosed approach in finding that there had been no undue influence on the part of the Bank upon the wife where a husband and wife, joint owners of a matrimonial home, had mortgaged it to the Bank in order to salvage the husband's financial position. The relationship of creditor and debtor is alone not sufficient to raise such a presumption. Yet the line between the roles of lender and advisor might be slim. In the latter circumstance a duty of care in negligence might arise.

When a mortgagor is not an agent for the mortgagee, as in the *Kings North Trust* case, but might have exerted undue influence upon a co-mortgagor or surety, the mortgagee's position depends upon whether he had actual or constructive notice of the co-mortgagor's or surety's susceptibility to disadvantage from the proposed transaction. This vulnerability will be evident where there is an emotional relationship between the borrowers or borrower and surety, such as exists between husband and wife or cohabitees. (*Barclays Bank* v *O'Brien* [1993] 4 All ER 417). In such circumstances, in order to escape being fixed with constructive notice, and postponement of his interest to that of the surety, he should advise the surety at a meeting not attended by the principal debtor of the extent of potential liability and the need to take independent legal advice. In *Massey* v *Midland Bank* [1995] 1 All ER 929, however, the Court of Appeal held that, even when a mortgagee had constructive notice of misrepresentation to a surety, the court was entitled to believe that independent advice had been given where this had been provided by a reputable firm of solicitors, even though that firm acted for the person who had made the misrepresentation.

Seventy years ago the 1925 legislation facilitated land transfer by the introduction of registration. This system promoted certainty at some expense to ethics. For instance, in the case of registered title, the doctrine of notice became irrelevant, except in the presence of fraud. The *O'Brien* case reintroduces the doctrine since a registered interest might now be defeated where there is constructive notice of an equity though no involvement in fraud (see *New Law Journal*, 3 June 1994, 765, and *CIBC Mortgages* v *Pitt* [1993] 3 All ER 433).

A term must not be repugnant to the right to redeem

Once decided that a transaction is a mortgage, the right to redeem is an integral part of that transaction and cannot be excluded.

Provisions, therefore, which purport to prevent the right of redemption altogether, or to restrict it to part of the property (*Davis* v *Symons* [1934] 1 Ch 442), or to a certain person or persons or time (*Salt* v *Northampton* [1892] AC 1), are void. A provision that the mortgagee shall have an option to purchase the property is similarly inconsistent with a mortgage and is void, though this is not so if the option is agreed upon in a separate and independent transaction, for then the later transaction is not a mortgage (*Reeve* v *Lisle* [1902] AC 461). Furthermore, a right of pre-emption only is always good (*London Rosemex Service Station Ltd* v *Shell Mex and BP Ltd* (1969) 20 P&CR 1).

A term postponing the contractual right to redeem for a considerable time is not repugnant to the mortgage transaction unless it has the effect of making the right to redeem merely illusory. In *Fairclough* v *Swan Brewery Co Ltd* [1912] AC 565, a lease of 20 years was mortgaged and there was a provision delaying the contractual right to redeem for the whole of this period minus six weeks. The Privy Council held that this provision was void. In substance it attempted to deprive the mortgagor of his lease, and the right to redeem was illusory. In

Knightsbridge Estates Trust Ltd v *Byrne*, above, freehold property was mortgaged and it was agreed that the loan should be repaid over a period of 40 years and that there should be no right to redeem before that time. It was held by the Court of Appeal that the mortgagors could not insist upon redemption at an earlier date, because the right to redeem was not illusory. Neither was the transaction oppressive or unconscionable. These two factors being satisfied, the court was not going to inhibit freedom of contract by making further demands such as that the transaction should be 'reasonable'.

An advantage which is restricted in duration to the time of redemption is not inconsistent with the right to redeem and is therefore enforceable. Thus if a publican mortgages his public house to a brewery, a provision that only the products of that brewery shall be sold in that house until the mortgage is redeemed is enforceable (*Biggs* v *Hoddinott* [1898] 2 Ch 307). Similarly, a provision in a mortgage by a garage proprietor (the mortgagor) to a petrol company that only the latter's petrol shall be sold during the continuance of the mortgage may be valid, even though the mortgage is to last for 19 years (*London Rosemex Service Station Ltd* v *Shell Mex and BP Ltd*, above). Once again, as in all mortgage transactions, the agreement must not be oppressive or unconscionable. Such agreements may also be void, however, on the additional ground that they are in unreasonable restraint of trade. This is a matter of the ordinary law of contract and will not be pursued here (see *Esso Petroleum Co Ltd* v *Harper's Garage (Stourport) Ltd* [1968] AC 269). Thus a mortgage may be a security not merely for the repayment of a loan and interest, but also for the performance of an act or obligation.

The final question is whether an advantage, covenanted to be enjoyed by the mortgagee not merely during the mortgage but even after redemption, is repugnant to the right to redeem in that the mortgagor would otherwise take back a less valuable property. This might amount to a partial irredeemability.

The general rule is that an advantage designed to last beyond the time when the mortgage is redeemed is repugnant to the right to redeem and unenforceable beyond that time. Thus in *Noakes* v *Rice* [1902] AC 24 a provision in a mortgage of a public house that the mortgagor should buy his liquors only from the mortgagees, who were brewers, even after redemption was held by the House of Lords to be unenforceable once the loan had been paid off. The principle was further illustrated in *Bradley* v *Carritt* [1903] AC 253. In that case, tea shares were mortgaged, the mortgagor undertaking that he would always afterwards use the controlling interest which the shares gave him to secure to the mortgagee, a tea broker, the right to sell the company's tea, or, upon failure to do so, the amount of commission which he would have earned as broker if he had sold the tea. A divided House of Lords held that this agreement was repugnant to the right to redeem because, since the value of the shares consisted in their power to secure sale of the company's tea, the agreement would have deprived them of their most desirable characteristic, even after redemption.

In two cases, however, advantages associated with mortgage transactions may remain enforceable even after redemption. The first exception is most difficult to recognise, and is represented by probably only one decided case, *Santley* v *Wilde* [1899] 2 Ch 474, a remarkable example of the dangers of sound justice unsupported by adequate conceptualisation. A lease of a theatre was mortgaged, the agreement providing that a third of the net profits of the lease should be paid to the mortgagee during the whole of the remainder of the lease, even after repayment of the loan and interest.

The Court of Appeal held that this agreement was binding. The judgment of Lindley MR proceeded mainly on the reasoning that the security of the lease was 'absolutely insufficient' and that it needed bolstering by the covenant for the payment of rents, which thus constituted part of the security. It is difficult to see, however, what purpose such a security can serve after the loan has been paid. It would, of course, be possible and reasonable to construe the payment of a third of the rents for the whole remainder of the lease as part of the price of the loan, along with the payment of interest. Yet the same could be said of the advantage of the liquor sales in *Noakes* v *Rice*, above. This case seems inconsistent with *Santley* v *Wilde* unless it can be distinguished on the grounds that in the former the covenant threatened the mortgaged property, whereas in the latter it only concerned the mortgagor's pocket.

The second case of enforceable associated advantages is not strictly an exception to the rule that an advantage designed to last beyond the time of redemption is repugnant to the right to redeem. The advantage is truly collateral to the mortgage and not part of it, even though it might have been concluded in the same instrument. It is possible that the parties, particularly if they are business men, wish to come to an agreement upon a number of matters at the same time and one of these matters might be a loan. The consideration which they give each other in respect of one particular transaction might well be partly expressed in some of the others. The collateral advantage in question might have been an independent aim irrespective of the loan. Indeed, the mortgagee might only have lent the money in order to achieve it. In such a case, that part of the transaction is not a mortgage at all.

In the leading case of *Kreglinger* v *New Patagonia Meat and Cold Storage Co Ltd* [1914] AC 25, a firm of woolbrokers agreed to lend money to a firm of meat packers. The loan was for a period of five years, though the mortgagors were entitled to end the mortgage within that period by paying the principal and interest. The security for the loan was the premises and stock of the meat company. The agreement also provided that the mortgagors would, for a period of five years, irrespective of whether the mortgage ended within that time, sell their sheepskins only to the mortgagees, who would offer the best price. The House of Lords held that the mortgagors were bound by this agreement, even though they redeemed the mortgage after two years.

The whole transaction was more than a mere loan. It was an agreement concerning several different matters, including the sale of sheepskins and the granting of a loan, both of which were independently important to the parties. The loan was no more the pivotal part of the transaction than the agreement as to the sheepskins. However, whether the advantage is truly the result of a separate transaction, even though concluded at the same time, is a question of construction and finally depends upon the form in which it is expressed. Viscount Haldane intimated this in the words

> I cannot but think that the validity of the bargain in such cases as *Bradley* v *Carritt* and *Santley* v *Wilde* might have been made free from serious question if the parties had chosen to seek what would have been substantially the same result in a different form . . . (at 43).

A short summary of the principles governing the right to redeem may now be attempted as follows. The right to redeem is an integral part of a mortgage transaction and any provision repugnant to this is void. This principle is not offended, however, by mere postponement of the right to redeem unless it renders the right illusory, or by the mortgagee obtaining an advantage which either ends upon redemption or is part of the security itself or is collateral to the mortgage transaction, provided that in each of these cases the provision has not been achieved by fraud, oppression or unconscionable behaviour.

Judicial decisions should derive directly from these sound principles, applied in the light of the practical necessities of the time and of their underlying spirit and purpose. Otherwise, there is a danger that these principles will be overlaid and obscured by the particular problems of past ages. 'The rules as to collateral advantages, for example, have been much modified by the repeal of the usury laws and by the recognition of modern varieties of commercial bargaining . . .' (per Viscount Haldane in *Kreglinger's Case*, at 38).

The act of redemption

The mortgagor redeems the mortgage by tendering the amount due. This amount includes all arrears of interest, even such arrears as would be irrecoverable under the Limitation Act 1980 s 20(5), in an action by the mortgagee (*Holmes* v *Cowcher* [1970] 1 All ER 1224). The right of redemption is also exercisable by an alienee of the equity of redemption or by any person who has an interest in it, such as second or subsequent mortgagees. In the latter case, if several persons compete to redeem, their rights to do so rank in the order in which they were created.

If there is only one mortgage and the mortgagor redeems, the mortgage is discharged and the interest of the mortgagee extinguished (s 116). The indorsement upon the deed by the mortgagee or other person in whom the mortgage is vested of a signed receipt stating the name of the person who pays the money is adequate to document this event (s 115(1)). This is known as a *vacating receipt*.

If the mortgage in question is redeemed not by the mortgagor but by a second or subsequent mortgagee, the mortgage is not discharged but is transferred to the person who redeems (s 115(2)). He thus stands in the shoes of the mortgagee whose mortgage he has redeemed. The mortgagor may in turn redeem the mortgage by paying off the transferee of the mortgagee, if he wishes to free his property of this incumbrance.

Redemption usually takes place non-contentiously, but may also take place in court if redemption is wrongfully refused. If a subsequent mortgagee seeks to redeem a prior mortgage in court, the doctrine 'redeem up, foreclose down' applies. Reference books should be consulted for further information regarding this uncommon event.

The right to redeem which arises upon the day named in the mortgage deed continues, as we have seen, for an indefinite time after that day. It is, however, extinguished by any one of four events, with the result that the mortgagor loses his right to the mortgaged property.

First, it may be extinguished by foreclosure; second, by sale. These are dealt with later in this chapter. Third, the right to redeem is lost by lapse of time under the Limitation Act 1980 s 16, which enacts that when a mortgagee has been in possession of any of the mortgaged land for 12 years, the right of redemption ceases to exist. If the mortgagee receives any payment of the sum of money due to him, or signs any acknowledgement of the mortgagor's title, the period begins afresh. Fourth, the right to redeem is ended if the mortgagor releases it to the mortgagee. This he might do, for instance, in return for a release of the debt. If the transaction is separate from the mortgage itself, it is not void as being repugnant to the right to redeem.

Protection under the Consumer Credit Act 1974

This Act protects borrowers under a wide range of credit agreements, including mortgages. It was remarked earlier that most modern mortgages are made either between building societies and home buyers or between well advised commercial firms, and that the great sensitivity, expressed in the old cases, in regard to the vulnerable position of the mortgagor is no longer appropriate in these contexts. New classes of people in need of financial protection, and novel ways of parting them from their money are always emerging, even in affluent societies. The pawn shop has gone, but the finance company is very much with us. Its agents have not waited passively in the High Street. They have knocked on doors.

The most important general provision affects all mortgages made by private individuals. Under ss 137–139, the court may reopen a credit agreement which is 'extortionate', that is if the payments to be paid under it are 'grossly exorbitant' or if the agreement 'otherwise contravenes ordinary principles of fair dealing'. In determining these matters, the court must take account of the interest rates prevailing at the time of the agreement, the age, experience, business capacity and health of the debtor and the financial pressure he suffered at the time of the bargain, the degree of risk accepted by the creditor, his relationship with the debtor and 'any other relevant considerations'. The court is empowered to set aside obligations wholly or in part, alter the agreement and to direct the return of property. Judicial application of these principles has been restrictive. In *Ketley Ltd* v *Scott* [1980] CCLR 37 it was held that an annual interest rate of almost 50 per cent was not 'extortionate' since the mortgagor had known precisely what he was doing and had not been subjected to financial pressure. Imprudence and speculation were insufficient to trigger the Act's remedies (see also *Woodstead Finance Ltd* v *Petrou* (1986) *The Times*, 23 January).

Other provisions control a wide range of activities connected with credit agreements such as advertising, licensing of business and enforcement of agreements. A mortgage will not be affected by these provisions if:

1 The credit provided exceeds £5000 (s 8), or

2 The creditor is one of the bodies specified by the Act as being exempt if the loan is made for house purchase. The most important of these bodies mentioned are building societies and local authorities.

These provisions are clearly aimed at second mortgages to finance companies.

Right to grant leases

The mortgagee, by virtue of his estate, has the right to possession of the mortgaged property, so that the mortgagor has no power, apart from his contract or statute, to grant any lease entitling the lessee to possession. Since the mortgagor is usually left in possession, however, it is settled, even at common law, that he may grant a lease which, though not binding on the mortgagee, is binding as between himself and his lessee under the doctrine of estoppel. The mortgagee may, if he wishes, accept the lessee as his own, or refuse to do so and evict him. In the latter case, the lessee may save his position by redeeming the mortgage (*Tarn* v *Turner* (1888) 39 ChD 456). Of course, if the mortgagee so agrees in writing, the mortgagor may grant leases which bind the mortgagee also (see s 99(14)).

Quite apart from these powers, a mortgagor, provided that he is in possession and that the contrary intention has not been expressed in the deed or other writing, has power under the Act to grant certain leases which bind not only himself but also the mortgagee (s 99). Such a lease must conform with the following conditions:

1 If the lease is for agricultural or occupation purposes, the maximum period is for 50 years; if for building purposes, 999 years.

2 It must be made to take effect in possession not later than 12 months after its date.

3 It must reserve the best rent reasonably obtainable, regard being paid to the circumstances, but with no fine. This provision is included to safeguard the mortgagee. If the mortgagor defaults in his payments and the mortgagee wishes to take possession of the profits of the property by the appointment of a receiver, these profits will, as a result of this enactment, be substantial.

4 It must contain a covenant by the lessee for payment of rent and a condition of re-entry on the rent not being paid within a time therein specified not exceeding 30 days.

5 A counterpart of the lease must be executed by the lessee and the mortgagor must deliver this to the mortgagee, or, in the case of several mortgages, to the first mortgagee in priority, within one month of making it.

If any of these requirements is not obeyed, the lease may be validated under s 152 upon the conditions mentioned there.

It is appropriate to note here a rule of general application. Section 172 of the Law of Property Act 1925 enacts that, with certain exceptions, conveyances made with the intention of defrauding creditors are voidable at the instance of persons thereby prejudiced. A mortgagor who exercises his powers of leasing in order to deprive the mortgagee of possession infringes this rule (*Lloyds Bank Ltd* v *Marcan* [1973] 3 All ER 754).

Even if these powers are excluded by the mortgage deed, as they frequently are, the mortgagor may still exercise his common law power of leasing described above, with its limited effect.

As a complement to his statutory power to create leases binding on the mortgagee, the mortgagor is also authorised by the Act to accept surrenders of leases in the following circumstances, provided that the contrary intention has not been expressed in the deed or in other writing (s 100). The mortgagor may, if in possession of the rents, accept a surrender for the purpose of granting a new lease under the statutory or contractual powers. The surrender is not valid unless the new lease is granted to take effect in possession within one month of the surrender for a term not shorter than the unexpired term of the surrendered lease, and at a rent no less than the original rent.

THE RIGHTS OF THE MORTGAGEE

The rights of the mortgagee are varied and formidable and make the mortgage a very desirable form of security. These rights can be exercised concurrently and consecutively insofar as they are not self-contradictory. The order in which they are discussed below is roughly that of increasing finality. The first two mentioned are in the nature of precautions which will often be exercised as a matter of course as soon as the mortgage is created. Then follow rights which are remedies to be exercised when the mortgagor defaults.

Rights to the title deeds

A first mortgagee or chargee of a legal estate, whether taking a legal or equitable mortgage, has a right to take the title deeds relating to the interest mortgaged (ss 85(1) and 86(1)). The Land Registration Act 1925 s 65 provides similarly for the deposit of the mortgagor's land certificate in the Land Registry. A mortgagee of a fee simple estate who takes, for instance, a term of 3000 years or a legal charge, will take home with him the mortgage deed itself and also the title deeds of the fee simple. This has the indirect effect of giving notice to all other persons that the mortgagor's property is subject to a mortgage, for he will have to explain the absence of the deeds to any prospective purchaser. The mortgagor, however, has the right to inspect them and make extracts or abstracts from them from time to time at his own cost (s 96(1)).

When the first mortgage is redeemed, the mortgagee must deliver the deeds to the person next entitled of whom he has notice. In the case of a single mortgage, this person will be the mortgagor; if further mortgages exist it will be the second mortgagee. Although, as we shall see, registration of a mortgage is notice of its existence for other purposes, for the purpose now being discussed it is not. The mortgagee is not required to hand deeds to the person next entitled to them unless he has actual or constructive notice of the superior right (s 96(2), as amended by the Law of Property (Amendment) Act 1926 Schedule). A subsequent mortgagee should, therefore, protect his possible future right to the deeds by giving notice in writing of his interest to prior mortgagees.

Right to insure against fire (ss 101 and 108)

If the mortgage, legal or equitable, is by deed, the mortgagee may insure the property against fire and add the cost to the mortgage debt. The amount of insurance must not exceed that mentioned in the deed, or, if none is mentioned, two-thirds of the total replacement cost. If the mortgage is not by deed, there is no such power to insure unless expressly stipulated. Even if the transaction is by deed, the mortgagee cannot exercise this right if the deed states that insurance is not required, or the mortgagor keeps it up in accordance with the deed, or, if there is no provision for insurance, the mortgagor insures with the mortgagee's consent to the amount allowed by the Act.

Right to sue for the sum due

The mortgagee may sue for the sum due as soon as the date for repayment has passed. An action to recover the principal sum is barred under the Limitation Act 1980 s 58(1), (2) after 12 years from that date unless some part-payment of principal or interest or written acknowledgement of the debt causes the time to run afresh. Only six years' arrears of interest may, however, be recovered under the Act. The right to sue belongs to both legal and equitable mortgagees.

Right to possession

> The mortgagee may go into possession before the ink is dry on the mortgage unless there is something in the contract, express or by implication, whereby he has contracted himself out of that right. He has the right because he has a legal term of years in the property or its statutory equivalent.

No default on the part of the mortgagor is necessary (*Four Maids Ltd* v *Dudley Marshall (Properties) Ltd* [1957] Ch 317, at 320, per Harman J). The right to possession is, of course, subject to the particular conditions of the mortgage.

Upon the principles expressed in *Walsh* v *Lonsdale* (1882) 21 ChD 9, an equitable mortgagee is probably similarly entitled. Generally, a mortgagee will not seek possession but there are three principal occasions when he might have a motive to do so.

The first is that he might wish to take the income of the property because the mortgage repayments are in arrears. The stringency of the rules which apply when he does so, however, discourage the exercise of this right and make the appointment of a receiver more desirable. The appointment of receivers is dealt with below, but here it may be noticed that it amounts to a vicarious possession of the premises under which the mortgagee is not affected by the strict rules just mentioned. These rules, applying to a mortgagee in possession, call him to account not only for the profits which he receives from the property, but also for those which he ought to have received had he acted as a prudent manager of that property. Thus in *White* v *City of London Brewery Co* (1889) 42 ChD 237, a mortgagee entered into possession of the property, which was a public house, and then leased it to a tenant who covenanted to buy his liquors from the mortgagee. Previously, it had been a free house. It was held that the mortgagee must account for the additional rent he would have received had it been let as a free house.

The second reason why a mortgagee might desire possession is as a preliminary to exercising his power of sale, for this is greatly facilitated if vacant possession can be offered to a purchaser. The third reason is that the mortgagee might wish to protect his security; it was held in *Western Bank Ltd* v *Schindler* [1977] Ch 1 that the mortgagee was entitled to enter possession even before the mortgagor was in default of his repayment obligations.

Mortgages have frequently contained a clause under which the mortgagor *attorns* tenant to the mortgagee, that is, constitutes himself the mortgagee's tenant. This formerly was a convenient device for the mortgagee for purposes which have now become obsolete and which need not detain us.

The plight of the dispossessed mortgagor, particularly when the property in question is his home, has caused both judges and Parliament to attenuate the harsh consequences of the mortgagee's right to possession.

Judicial relief

There is inherent jurisdiction in the court to adjourn an application for a short time to afford the mortgagor a chance of performing his obligations if there is a reasonable prospect of this occurring (*Birmingham Citizens Permanent Building Society* v *Caunt* [1962] Ch 883). An adjournment will hardly exceed 28 days. The reason for the exception is that the court will not allow a mortgagee to enforce rights in the face of a concrete offer by the mortgagor. This rule applies to all forms of mortgage (*Mobil Oil Co Ltd* v *Rawlinson* [1982] 43 P&CR

221). We shall see below that additional statutory powers are available in the case of a dwelling house.

Before examining those statutory powers, an extraordinary dictum of Lord Denning must be noted. In *Quennell* v *Maltby* [1979] 1 WLR 318 at 322, he stated that a mortgagee would be refused possession of a house when it would be contrary to the justice of the case. This statement must be considered strictly within the context of the unusual facts of the case. Space does not allow an examination of this freak authority, but Lord Denning was in effect merely saying that the machinery of mortgages cannot be used to circumvent the Rent Acts. He was saying nothing about possession by mortgagees.

Statutory relief

Under the Administration of Justice Act 1970 ss 36–39 and the Administration of Justice Act 1973 s 8, the court may, where a mortgagee claims possession of a dwelling house, adjourn the case, or stay, suspend or postpone an order for possession for such period as it thinks reasonable if the mortgagor is likely to be able to pay the sum in respect of which he is in default, or to remedy a breach of any other obligation under the mortgage within a reasonable period (see *Target Home Loans Ltd* v *Clothier* [1994] 1 All ER 439).

In *Cheltenham and Gloucester Building Society* v *Norgan* (1995) *The Times*, 8 December, the Court of Appeal provided a new perspective for the 'reasonable' period for repayment. In such cases of default, the starting point for determining the period is the outstanding period of the mortgage and the court might consider at the outset whether it would be possible for the borrower to maintain payment of the arrears by instalments over that period. Borrowers might be required to submit a detailed budget. Indeed, this was in harmony with the statement of the Council of Mortgage Lenders that members should take possession only as a last resort. Several considerations were mentioned by the Court as being influential in establishing what might be a reasonable period. Examples given were: how much the borrower could reasonably afford to pay now and in the future; how long a temporary financial difficulty of the borrower was likely to last; and the reason why the arrears had accumulated.

Mortgagees often provide professional advice such as valuation of property which, if negligently given, might found an action in damages against them, either in contract or tort. For instance, the value of the mortgaged property might have declined drastically. It has been held, however, that a mortgagee's right to possession cannot be defeated by such a cross-claim by the mortgagor, even if it is liquidated, admitted by the mortgagee and exceeds the amount of mortgage arrears (*Mobil Co Ltd* v *Rawlinson* (1981) 43 P&CR 221 and *National Westminster Bank* v *Sketton* [1993] 1 WLR 72). The rule applies equally to principal debtors and guarantors.

Where the property mortgaged is residential, relief should be sought under s 36 of the Administration of Justice Act 1970 as amended, which applies different principles (see *Solicitors Journal*, 17 November 1995 at 1155).

The fall in property values has now sometimes made it desirable for the mortgagor to sell the property, since if the mortgagee sells it in exercise of his powers (shortly to be discussed), the sale will not realise the sum owed to him. The mortgagor will then be personally liable for the deficit, which will increasingly mount with the interest. In such situations it is in the mortgagee's financial interest to delay sale. In recent years the Law of Property Act 1925 s 91 has been called into unusual service at the request of the mortgagor, whereas it has been generally perceived as empowering sale by a mortgagee. The text of the section should be studied in the light of: *Target Home Loans Ltd* v *Clothier* [1994] 1 All ER 439; *Arab Bank plc* v *Mercantile Holdings Ltd* [1993] NPC 130. In *Palk* v *Mortgage Services Funding plc* [1993] 2 All ER 481 the Court of Appeal held that it had authority under s 91 to order a sale even against the wishes of the mortgagee in order to avoid unfair advantage being taken of the mortgagor. In the case of a mortgage debt repayable by instalments, the agreement might make the whole debt become due when there is default in payment of an instalment. In such cases, the Acts do not require the likelihood of repayment of the whole as a condition of relief, but only repayment of the instalment initially due and any further sums falling due during the period of relief. A liberal interpretation of the sections has avoided the absurd possibility that relief might only be available where there has been some default and that a mortgagee might freely exercise his right to possession against a mortgagor who has performed all his obligation (*Western Bank Ltd* v *Schindler* [1976] 3 WLR 341).

A spouse who has no proprietary interest but who has registered rights of occupation as a Class F land charge or as a caution or notice must now be notified of the proceedings. The spouse can then apply to be made a party to those proceedings (Matrimonial Homes Act 1983 s 8). The mortgagee's right to possession and the associated right of sale engender some of the most difficult legal and social problems in contemporary English land law. If civil law is to do with the reconciliation of conflicting interests here is its apotheosis. The mortgagee deserves security for his loan. The mortgagor might, through national recession, be the victim of loss of income and fallen house prices. In such circumstances differences in judicial perceptions of just reconciliation can spawn uncertainty not only in the law, which is at least observable in the appellate courts, but also in the finding of facts and application of the law in the less public hearings in county court chambers.

Right to appoint a receiver

A receiver is a person who intercepts the rents and profits of property before they reach the owner. We noticed above that strict rules apply when a mortgagee takes possession, but an effect similar to that of taking possession can be achieved by the appointment of a receiver to collect the profits on behalf of the mortgagee. Such a measure would be appropriate, for instance, to intercept the rents when the mortgagor has leased the property. The advantage of this remedy is that the receiver is deemed to be the agent of the mortgagor, so that the mortgagee is not called upon to account for the receiver's acts. The power to appoint a receiver and the rules regulating his authority may be conferred by the mortgage instrument but, irrespective of this, a power so to appoint is given by the Act in the case of all mortgages, legal or equitable, which are made 'by deed' (s 101).

The power arises as soon as 'the mortgage money has become due', that is, when the contractual date for redemption has passed, or, if the mortgage debt is repayable by instalments, when an instalment is overdue. Although the power arises at this time, the mortgagee may not exercise it until one of the following has occurred:

1 notice requiring payment of the mortgage money has been served on the mortgagor and default has been made in payment of all or part of it for three months after service;

2 some interest is two months or more in arrears; or

3 there has been breach of some provision, other than for payment of the mortgage money or interest, contained in the mortgage deed or in the Act (ss 109 and 103).

In short, the 'count down' begins when the mortgage money is due, but 'blast off' cannot occur until one of the three events mentioned above happens.

Once appointed, the receiver has power to intercept the income of the property. This he may do by action, distress or otherwise. The money thus recovered must be applied by him first in discharge of rents, taxes, rates and other outgoings; second in keeping down interest on prior mortgages; third in payment of his own commission, of insurance premiums due and of the cost of proper repairs directed by the mortgagee; fourth in payment of the mortgage interest and fifth in discharging the principal sum, if so directed by the mortgagee. Any surplus must be paid to the person who would have been entitled to the income if no receiver had been appointed (s 109).

A receiver will often be appointed where the market value of the property has fallen so low as to render it unwise to enforce the remedy of sale, or where the property is tenanted.

Right to sell

A mortgagee can clearly sell the mortgage subject to the right of redemption, but here we are concerned with the right to sell the mortgaged property itself, that is the fee simple or other interest owned by the mortgagor freed of the right to redeem and other rights of the mortgagor.

This right is given by the Act in the case of every mortgage, legal or equitable, which is 'by deed', subject to any express contrary intention or variation of the right contained in the deed (s 101). The power arises and then becomes exercisable upon the same events as in the case of the appointment of a receiver (ss 103 and 109). Provided that the power of sale has arisen, however, a conveyance to a purchaser is effective even though the power has not become exercisable and therefore is wrongful on the part of the mortgagee. An action against him may be brought by a person prejudiced by it (s 104(2)). A purchaser, therefore, is only concerned to see that the power has arisen. Any purported conveyance made before the power has arisen passes no title. A contract to sell by the mortgagee after the power has arisen, but before it has become exercisable, is similarly effective, provided there is no bad faith (*Waring* v *London and Manchester Assurance Co Ltd* [1935] Ch 310).

The mortgagee may sell either by auction or by private contract subject to such conditions as he thinks fit. 'A mortgagee is strictly speaking not a trustee of the power of sale. It is a power given to him for his own benefit, to enable him the better to realise his debt' (*Warner* v *Jacob* (1882) 20 ChD 220, at 224). He has a duty, however, to take reasonable care to obtain the true market value of the property at the date of sale (*Cuckmere Brick Co Ltd* v *Mutual Finance Ltd* [1971] 2 All ER 633). He cannot 'sell' to himself, either directly or indirectly. The juridical nature of this duty remains to be settled. If it is contractual, it can be sued upon only by the mortgagor or his representatives. If it is tortious, then a wider circle of injured persons, including for instance guarantors of loans, might do so. In the latter case, the restrictions on the recovery of damages for economic loss in tort might exert influence (see *Barclays Bank* v *Thiernal* (1978) 247 EG 385, [1981] Conveyancer 329).

Building societies must take reasonable care to secure the best price reasonably obtainable, though they can sell at times convenient to themselves (Building Societies Act 1986 Sch 4).

The effect of sale when the mortgage is of a fee simple estate is to vest the fee simple in the purchaser and the conveyance may be made in the name of the mortgagor. In the case of the mortgage of a leasehold interest, the effect is to vest the whole leasehold estate in the purchaser. In both cases, the mortgage terms or charges are extinguished (ss 88 and 89), and the rights to redeem are ended.

If several mortgages exist in the property, any of the mortgagees can exercise the power of sale. The sale passes the interest of the mortgagor to the purchaser, subject to any mortgages prior to that of the mortgagee who sells, but freed from any subsequent mortgages which are overreached and are satisfied out of the purchase money. Thus, if a second mortgagee sells, the purchaser will take the property freed of the second and subsequent mortgages, but subject to the first. This first mortgagee may still exercise his power of sale, in which case the purchaser will lose the property, though he will be entitled to the surplus proceeds of sale after the first mortgagee has been satisfied. Obviously a purchaser from a second mortgagee will expect to pay a reduced price for the property. If a mortgagor has contracted to sell the mortgaged property, the mortgagee's power of sale will nevertheless predominate over the rights of the person who has contracted to buy from the mortgagor, whether or not these are registered, for the mortgagor cannot pass to a purchaser greater rights than he himself owns. The registration would affect only the mortgagor's equity of redemption (see ss 2 and 104 and *Duke* v *Robson* [1973] 1 All ER 486).

Although a mortgagee who sells is not trustee of the power of sale, he is trustee of the proceeds of sale. Under s 105, he must apply them in the following order:

1 in discharge of any prior incumbrances if the sale was made free of them. This would apply, for instance, if a second mortgagee sold and the first mortgagee agreed to the discharge of his mortgage upon that sale;

2 in payment of the expenses of sale;

3 in discharge of the money due to him under his own mortgage;

4 the residue must then be paid 'to the person next entitled to the mortgaged property'. This person will be the mortgagee next in priority or, if there is no other mortgagee, the mortgagor.

Having satisfied his own and any prior claims out of the proceeds, the mortgagee must discover whether there is a subsequent mortgagee and for this purpose registration of other mortgages as land charges constitutes notice. In turn, that subsequent mortgagee, having received the surplus proceeds, must likewise make a search and, after satisfaction of his own debt, pass any remaining money to the mortgagee next in priority, or, if there is no later mortgagee, to the mortgagor.

The power of sale extends to equitable mortgages, provided that they are 'by deed'. For this purpose, an equitable mortgage created by mere deposit of deeds is frequently accompanied by deed of memorandum, for the latter satisfies the statutory description of a mortgage by deed. Since the power of sale under s 101(1) is a power to sell 'the mortgaged property', an equitable mortgagee cannot pass the legal estate to the purchaser (*Re Hodson and Howes' Contract* (1887) 35 ChD 668). Consequently, it is common to include special machinery, such as a power of attorney, in the deed to enable him to convey the legal estate.

However, the view was expressed, by the Court of Appeal in *Re White Rose Cottage* [1965] Ch 940 that an equitable mortgagee by deed could pass the legal estate under the Act. Whether a broad or even a pedantic approach is taken to ss 101 and 104, this latter view is surely preferable. The power given is to sell 'the mortgaged property'. If this subject matter of the mortgage in the hands of the mortgagor is legal, it does not cease to become so simply because it was mortgaged in the equitable mode. The fact that the equitable mortgagee does not hold a legal estate is immaterial, for statute can accomplish anything. In any case, even a legal mortgagee upon sale disposes of an interest which he himself does not own.

Right to foreclosure

This classical remedy of the mortgagee has disadvantages which make it less desirable today than the remedy of sale.

Foreclosure is the removal by the court of the mortgagor's equitable right to redeem and the vesting of the interest of the mortgagor absolutely in the mortgagee (*see* ss 88 and 89).

The right to redeem after the contractual date for redemption has passed is given upon equitable principles and a foreclosure decree marks the termination of this indulgence, which clearly must have limits. The remedy might appear unfair if the mortgaged property is worth more than the mortgage debt, but it is hedged about by rules which protect the mortgagor against harsh results.

The right to bring foreclosure proceedings belongs to any mortgagee, legal or equitable, once the contractual date to redeem has lapsed, and with no default by the mortgagor, unless he has agreed not to do so. The effect of foreclosure is to vest the interest of the mortgagor absolutely in the mortgagee, freed from the interests of any subsequent mortgagees and the mortgagor, but subject to any prior mortgages. Since prior mortgagees are not affected, they need not be joined in a foreclosure action. Since subsequent mortgagees and the mortgagor are affected, they must be joined. The action proceeds in two stages.

First, the court issues a foreclosure *decree nisi*. This states that if the money is not paid by a certain date, usually six months ahead, the mortgagor will be foreclosed. The court now also has power to allow the mortgagor reasonable time to pay under s 36 of the Administration of Justice Act 1970 and s 8 of the Administration of Justice Act 1973, when foreclosure is sought, as it may be, when the mortgagee seeks possession. This power was described above when the mortgagee's right to possession was being considered.

If there are two or more mortgages, each mortgagee is given the chance to pay off and thus redeem the mortgage which is the subject of the action. Otherwise, they are foreclosed. If, on the appointed day, none of the parties so entitled appears and redeems, the foreclosure decree is made absolute. The court may, at the request of any of the parties to a foreclosure action, order a sale of the property (s 91). This action is clearly desirable when the property is worth more than the mortgage debts, as subsequent mortgagees and the mortgagor will be entitled to the surplus according to priority.

Sometimes, even a decree of foreclosure absolute might not be final, for the court has power to re-open the decree. The court has declined to commit to words the terms upon which its discretion to re-open the foreclosure will be exercised, for too much depends upon the circumstances of each case. The mortgagor must apply, however, within a reasonable time. Examples of matters which might weigh with the court are the mortgagor being disappointed at the last moment in his expectation of a loan of money with which to redeem, a large difference between the values of the debt and the mortgaged property, and any special value the property had for the mortgagor. Furthermore, even a purchaser from the mortgagee is deemed to know the law and that foreclosure might be re-opened (see *Campbell* v *Holyland* (1877) 7 ChD 166). Foreclosure is no longer an important remedy, though it has been used recently in falling markets where there was no prospect of the borrower being able to pay the debt. More detailed accounts may be found in the reference books.

Right to tack

The right to tack is the right to promote a mortgage debt in the order in which several mortgages in the same property must be paid. It concerns the question of priorities and will be discussed below.

Right to consolidate

The right of consolidation is the right of a person who holds two or more mortgages to refuse redemption of one unless the others are also redeemed.

It is fundamentally an illustration of the principle that he who comes to equity must do equity, but the doctrine has been developed to such a point of technicality that it does not always work justly. In its simplest and unspoilt form, it is illustrated by the following example. If *M* mortgages two properties 'Blackacre' and 'Whiteacre', to *A*, for £1000 each, and each property is worth, say, £2000, then if the value of 'Blackacre' depreciates while that of 'Whiteacre' perhaps increases, it would be unfair if *M* were allowed to redeem 'Whiteacre' and leave *A* with a security which might not cover the remaining debt. The right can only exist under the following conditions:

1. The intention to enjoy the right to consolidate must appear in the deeds of at least one of the mortgages in respect of which consolidation is claimed (s 93).

2. A mortgage cannot be the subject of consolidation unless the contractual date for redemption has passed (*Cummins* v *Fletcher* (1880) 14 ChD 699). Since the maxim that he who comes to equity must do equity is the root of the right to consolidate, a person who seeks to redeem under his contractual rights is not seeking the assistance of equity at all. Thus, if *M* mortgages three properties, *A*, *B* and *C*, to *X* and the contractual dates for redemption have passed in the cases of *B* and *C*, but not in the case of *A*, then although *X* can insist that *C* cannot be redeemed without *B* being redeemed and vice versa, *M* may redeem *A* on the date agreed for redemption without also having to redeem mortgages *B* and *C*.

3. The mortgages in respect of which consolidation is claimed must originally have been made by the same mortgagor (*Sharp* v *Rickards* [1909] 1 Ch 109). Thus, if M^1 mortgaged property *A* to *X* and M^2 mortgaged property *B* to *X* and later M^1 purchased property *B*, *X* cannot require the two mortgages to be consolidated against M^1.

4 At the date when redemption is sought, all the equities of redemption must be in one hand and at the same time all the mortgages must be in one hand, or this state of things must have occurred at some time, even though the equities of redemptions have become separated. Of course, the mortgages must always be in the same hands at the date when consolidation is sought, for otherwise there would be no purpose in the owner of a mortgage desiring it. This rule lays the limits to the doctrine of consolidation, which had been growing rankly, and was finally established in *Pledge* v *White* (1896) AC 187.

Figure 15.3 might clarify the doctrine.

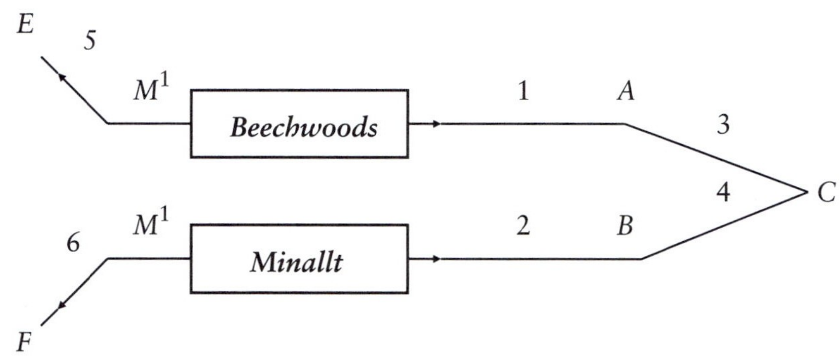

Fig. 15.3

M^1 is the original mortgagor of both properties, 'Beechwoods' and 'Minallt'. Mortgages and assignments of mortgages are shown to the right of the boxes and the assignments of the equities of redemption are shown to the left. The order in which the transactions took place is shown by the numbers placed near the lines denoting the transactions. *E* is seeking to redeem the mortgage on 'Beechwoods' by paying off *C*. But *C* may consolidate the mortgage on 'Minallt' against him, and require both mortgages to be redeemed at the same time, so that *E* may be required to redeem it as a condition of redeeming 'Beechwoods', assuming the right to consolidate was reserved in either of the mortgage deeds. The mortgages were both made by M^1 and there was a time, namely at stage 4, when the mortgages were owned by one person, *C*, and simultaneously the equities of redemption were owned by one person, M^1. If there are three or more properties concerned, the problem can be solved by playing each property against each other separately in the way described above.

The doctrine applies to both legal and equitable mortgages and against persons such as second mortgagees who have only a limited interest in the equity of redemption.

PRIORITY OF MORTGAGES

When the same property has been mortgaged more than once by the mortgagor to different mortgagees and when the mortgagor defaults in paying his debts to these mortgagees, the property might not realize enough money to pay all the mortgagees. The subject of priorities is concerned with the order in which the mortgagees shall be paid and, consequently, who shall be disappointed.

The simple solution that the mortgages should rank for payment in the order of their creation would sometimes produce unfair results, as, for instance, when a first mortgagee conspires with the mortgagor to conceal his mortgage, thus encouraging a second mortgagee to lend a further loan on the security of the property. The demands of justice have, therefore, resulted in a more complex code of rules. The rules applying before 1926 have been considerably modified by the 1925 legislation, largely because of the extension of the system of land charges. The account given below is that of the law applying to mortgages created after 1925.

There are two codes of rules, one applying to all mortgages, legal or equitable, of legal estates in land, the other to all mortgages of equitable interests in land, which, of course, must necessarily be equitable. What is important is the subject matter of the mortgage, not the mode in which it is transacted. Thus the same code applies to a legal mortgage of a legal estate as to an equitable mortgage of a legal estate, such as one by deposit of deeds. The second code only applies when an equitable interest such as a life interest is mortgaged. These two codes must now be examined separately. Then the doctrine of tacking, which empowers an admittedly prior mortgagee to swell a mortgage debt, must be considered.

Priority of mortgages of a legal estate

The law gives the mortgagee the opportunity to rank according to the order of creation, but also recognises the duty he owes to later prospective mortgagees to make the presence of his own mortgage discoverable by them. All mortgagees must, in order to preserve their priority, take certain action to make their mortgages discoverable. In the case of registered title however priority is governed by the order in which the mortgages are entered on the register (see however *Mortgage Corp Ltd* v *Nationwide Credit Corp Ltd* [1993] 4 All ER 623).

A first mortgagee, whether legal or equitable, of a legal estate has the right to call for the title deeds of the property (ss 85 and 86). If a prospective purchaser or second mortgagee later negotiates with the mortgagor, the absence of the deeds will put him on his guard. A first mortgagee should, therefore, take the deeds. Having done so, he cannot register his mortgage under the provisions mentioned below.

All other mortgagees of a legal estate can register their mortgages under the Land Charges Act 1972 (or under the Land Registration Act 1925 s 26). If such a mortgage is legal, it is registrable in Class C(i). These legal mortgages, not protected by deposit of the title deeds, are called *puisne* mortgages. If the mortgage is equitable, it is registrable under Class C(iii) (or, in the case of registered land, by a notice or caution). The Act then declares the consequences of failure to register. Since there are two ways of protecting mortgages, three types of problem might arise. First, the priority of registrable mortgages between themselves might have to be resolved; second, the same problem might occur between two unregistrable mortgages; third, there might be a dispute between a registrable mortgage and an unregistrable one. These must now be separately dealt with.

Priority of registrable mortgages as between themselves

The priority of these mortgages between themselves is controlled by two statutory provisions which, due presumably to an oversight, are contradictory.

First, the Law of Property Act 1925 s 97 enacts that a mortgage not protected by deposit of deeds shall rank 'according to its date of registration as a land charge pursuant to the Land Charges Act 1972'.

Second, the Land Charges Act 1972 s 4 states that such mortgages shall 'be void against a purchaser of the land charged therewith, or of any interest in such land, unless the land charge is registered in the appropriate register before the completion of the purchase'. Another mortgagee is, of course, a 'purchaser', provided that he gives valuable consideration (Land Charges Act 1972 s 17).

An example will illustrate their apparent incompatibility. Let us say that *M* mortgaged 'Blackacre' on 1 January to *A*, who took the title deeds, then on 2 January to *B*, and then on 3 January to *C*. Then suppose that *B* did not register his mortgage until 4 January and *C* registered on 5 January. An assessment of the priorities of the two registrable incumbrances, those of *B* and *C*, under s 97, would place *B* before *C*, because he had registered his mortgage before *C* had registered his. Yet under s 4, *C* would be placed before *B*, because *B*'s mortgage had not been registered before *C*'s mortgage had been 'completed' and would, therefore, be void as against it. This does not, of course, mean that *B*'s mortgage is void altogether; it is valid against the mortgagor and indeed any other mortgage created after it has been registered. The section merely makes it void as against interests purchased before it was registered. It makes no difference, however, that a purchaser such as *C* had actual notice of *B*'s interest. Although there is no decisive case upon the matter yet, and there are arguments in favour of the prevalence of either section, probably the better view is that s 4 predominates (see Megarry and Wade, *The Law of Real Property* (4th edn) p 972). In the case of registered land there is no such conflict, priority depending upon order of registration (Land Registration Act 1925, s 29).

Even if s 4 prevails, it is theoretically capable of producing strange results. Suppose that in June *M* makes registrable mortgages in favour of *A* on the 1st, *B* on the 2nd and *C* on the 4th. Then suppose that *A* registers on the 3rd, *C* on the 5th and *B* on the 6th. *A*'s mortgage is void against *B*'s because *B*'s was made before *A*'s was registered. Therefore *B* ranks before *A*. The mortgage of *A*, however, ranks prior to *C*'s because it was registered before *C*'s was created. Yet *C*'s must rank before *B*'s, because *B*'s was not registered when *C*'s was made. It is impossible to express the general results as any lineal order of priority, but Figure 15.4 reveals that the section is not rationally perfect.

If each mortgagee is owed £1000 and the property is worth only £2000, a

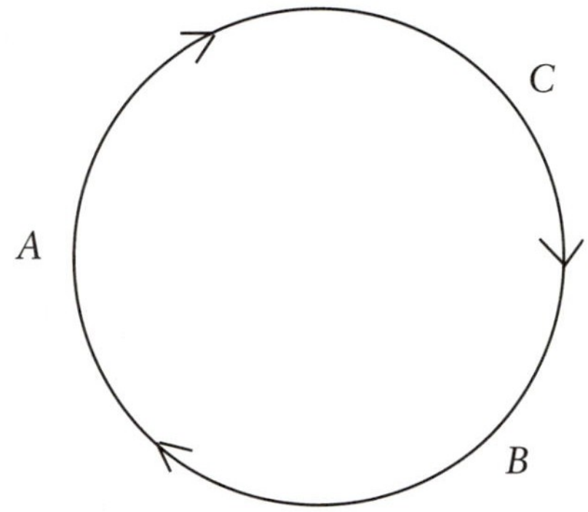

Fig. 15.4

rather desperate problem could arise should a solution be sought within the four corners of the section.

A mortgagee can, however, protect himself against the risk of a further mortgage being created before he has had time to register his own incumbrance by the registration of a priority notice before his own mortgage is created. This matter is explained more fully when land charges are discussed.

Priority of unregistrable mortgages as between themselves

Normally there should be no question of the priorities of two or more unregistrable mortgages of a legal estate, since if a mortgagee takes possession of the title deeds, he should take all of them. There would then obviously be no chance of another mortgagee taking deeds. All such later mortgages would then be registrable. There seems, however, to be no duty on a mortgagee who protects himself by taking the deeds to take them all, provided that he takes one or more which are vital to the proof of title.

Questions of the priority of mortgages protected by deposit of deeds may, therefore, arise as between themselves. These questions are resolved by the following common law principles which are expressly preserved by the Act (s 13).

The fundamental rule is that such mortgages rank in the order of creation, but this order might be displaced if either

(a) a legal mortgagee for value has no notice at the time of the creation of his interest of an earlier equitable mortgage, in which case the legal mortgage is preferred, or

(b) an earlier mortgagee has, by his conduct, deserved, in the eyes of the law, to be postponed to a later one.

These principles of displacement must now be examined. The first is, of course, a doctrine of general application and is not restricted to mortgages. Little need be added here, except to say that, in regard to notice, the law has been much more indulgent to the purchaser of the legal estate when that legal estate has been a mortgage. Thus, in *Hewitt* v *Loosemore* (1851) 9 Hare 449, *M* made an equitable mortgage by deposit of deeds in favour of *A* and later made a legal mortgage in favour of *B*, a farmer who claimed to be unversed in such legal processes. When *B* asked for the deeds, *M* told him that he was busy and would give them to him later. It was held that the legal mortgage enjoyed priority. Indeed, some of these cases seem to have been decided on the grounds of *gross negligence*, a factor which is relevant to the second of the principles mentioned above, rather than to the ordinary doctrine of notice. (See also *Oliver* v *Hinton* [1899] 2 Ch 264).

The conduct referred to in the second of the principles which will displace the fundamental rule governing the priority of unregistrable mortgages of legal estates as between themselves is constituted by fraud, gross negligence, or some act which, because it helps to deceive another person into taking a mortgage, estops the first mortgagee from claiming his priority over him. Such conduct is usually related to the title deeds. Thus a first mortgagee, who leaves the title deeds in the hands of the mortgagor to enable him to create further mortgages, will be postponed to a later mortgagee, who does not know of the first mortgage. This is because the first mortgagee has, even though in good faith, enabled the mortgagor to present himself as the owner of an unencumbered property, and will therefore be estopped from claiming the priority which otherwise would have been his (*Perry Herrick* v *Attwood* (1857) 2 DeG&J 21).

If the earlier mortgagee takes the deeds but then releases them, or fails for some other reason to retain them, and this is due to fraud or gross negligence, on principle similar results ought to follow. Yet it was decided in *Northern Counties of England Fire Insurance Co* v *Whipp* (1884) 26 ChD 482, that only fraud would cause a postponement.

It has been suggested in one case that the degree of negligence required to postpone an equitable mortgage is less than that needed to postpone a legal one (*Taylor* v *Russell* [1891] 1 Ch 1, at 17), but there seems to be no decisive authority to support this view.

Such are the principles governing the priority of unregistrable mortgages of a legal estate. As mentioned earlier, a competition between two such mortgagees could only occur if each mortgagee took some but not all the deeds; otherwise, the mortgage would be registrable. The allocation of negligence in such a case must be a difficult task. On the one hand, the first mortgagee might be considered negligent in not taking all the deeds relevant to the title, unless he had a reasonable excuse for not so doing (see *Walker* v *Linom* [1907] 2 Ch 104, which concerned a purchaser and a mortgagee). On the other hand, it could be argued that the second mortgagee can hardly claim to have been misled when the absence of some of the deeds would have occurred to him if he had taken the trouble to check (see also *Colyer* v *Finch* (1856) 5 HL Cas 905).

Priority of unregistrable mortgage as against registrable mortgage

Two types of contest are possible.

1 *The first mortgage is unregistrable and the second is registrable* – In a competition between a mortgagee, legal or equitable, who takes the deeds and a later one who does not, the common law principles described above apply, for they are expressly preserved by the Act (s 13). The earlier mortgage protected by deposit of deeds will rank first by virtue of its earlier creation, unless this order is displaced by the mortgagee's fraud, gross negligence or estoppel, or, being equitable, by the later one being a legal mortgage for value without notice of the first. 'Notice' in this context means actual or constructive notice and not notice by registration, for the earlier mortgage is, of course, unregistrable. In regard to gross negligence, this will hardly be constituted by failure to get in the deeds, for by definition the earlier mortgagee has accomplished this. Other acts of gross negligence and fraud, such as might occur through a later release of the deeds, would remain in point.

2 *The first mortgage is registrable and the second is unregistrable* – The priority of two such mortgages depends entirely upon whether the first one is registered before the second one is created (LPA 1925 s 97, and Land Charges Act 1972 s 4). If it is so registered, the first mortgage will rank first in priority. If it is not, it will be void as against the second, which will therefore rank before it in priority.

Finally, an example might illustrate the operation of these interacting rules (Table 15.1). In the following series of mortgages, all were registrable except that of *A*, who took the title deeds on the date of the creation of the mortgage and then fraudulently released them to the mortgagor, thereby inducing *B* and *C* to take subsequent mortgages. The deeds were handed back after this time, and before the mortgagor had opened negotiations for a mortgage with *D*. Our approach will be to take each mortgage in turn and test its priority against each other one individually.

Prima facie, *A* ranks first, but loses this priority to *B* and *C* on the common law principles discussed above, because his fraud has helped to deceive *B* and *C* into making mortgages. *A* will, however, rank before *D*, because as against him he has not done any act which will displace the fundamental rule that priority is

Mortgage	*Date of creation*	*Date of registration or possession of deeds*
A	1.1.96	Taken .... 1.1.96 Released .... 25.1.96 Taken back 15.2.96
B	1.2.96	15.2.96
C	14.2.96	17.2.96
D	18.2.96	

Table 15.1

governed by the order of creation of the mortgages. In all the three competitions that we have just observed, the contest has been between an unregistrable mortgage followed by a registrable mortgage.

B's mortgage ranks after *C*'s. Since it was not registered before *C*'s was created, it is void as against it, though not, of course, against the mortgagor. However, it loses no priority as against that of *D*, because it was registered before D's was created. C's mortgage ranks before *D*'s because it too was registered before *D*'s was created. *D*'s mortgage, therefore, ranks last, although, despite *D*'s failure to register, it is still good against the mortgagor. The latter will only be entitled to any part of the proceeds of a sale after all the mortgagees have been fully satisfied. These last three contests were between registrable mortgages. The question of priority notices has been deliberately ignored in the interests of clarity.

Thus, the final order of priority will be *C, B, A, D*.

Priority of mortgages of an equitable interest

The doctrine known as the rule in *Dearle* v *Hall* (1828) 3 Russ 1, which formerly only applied to the priority of successive dealings with equitable interests in pure personalty, was extended by the Act to govern the priority of successive mortgages of an equitable interest in land also (s 137). The Act made certain modifications as to the way notice may be served in accordance with the doctrine. Examples of the occasions when it applies would be successive mortgages of a life interest or an interest under a trust for sale.

Under the rule, priority depends upon the order in which notice of the mortgages is received by the owner of the legal interest in accordance with the rule, provided only that a mortgagee who has actual or constructive notice of an earlier mortgage at the time when he made his own cannot gain priority over that mortgage merely by giving notice first. Therefore the fundamental rule is that the mortgages rank not *prima facie* in order of creation, but in the order in which notice is given. The detailed operation of the rule must now be examined. It is important to note that the rule is based in equitable principles, so that a chargee who has not given consideration or has left the chargor in a position to conceal previous charges will be ranked unfavourably by the court (*see* generally *United Bank of Kuwait* v *Sahib* [1995] 2 All ER 973).

Form of notice

The notice must be in writing. Otherwise, it has no effect upon priority (s 137(3)). Provided that it is in writing, there is no requirement that it must be served by the mortgagee himself. Indeed, it has been held that notice gained by casually reading about a mortgage or assignment constitutes notice for this purpose (*Lloyd* v *Banks* (1868) LR 3 Ch 488).

Persons entitled to receive notice

The notice may be served upon the following persons:

1 in the case of a dealing with an interest in settled land, capital money, or securities representing capital money, the trustees of the settlement;

2 in the case of an interest under a trust for sale, the trustees for sale; and

3 in any other case the estate owner (s 137(2)).

Where the trustees are not persons to whom a valid notice can be given – or there are no trustees to whom notice can be given, or where for any other reason a valid notice cannot be served at all without unreasonable cost or delay – then a mortgagee may require a memorandum to be written on or annexed to the instrument creating the trust. In the case of settled land, this would be the trust instrument, and this operates in the same way as notice to the trustees (s 137(4) and (5)). There is also an alternative provision for nominating a trust corporation to receive notices.

The notice should be served upon all the trustees in existence at the time of the notice. If this is done, the notice remains permanently effective, even when these trustees have been replaced by others (*Re Wasdale* [1899] 1 Ch 163). If notice is given only to one of several trustees, it is effective against all mortgages created while that trustee remains in office, but not against those created after his trusteeship ends (*Re Phillips' Trusts* [1903] 1 Ch 183).

Tacking

Tacking is the advancement of a further sum of money by a mortgagee upon the security of his mortgage in such circumstances that it enjoys the same priority as the original debt. If, for instance, *A* lends £1000 to *X* upon the security of 'Blackacre', then *B* lends *X* £1000, taking a second mortgage of the land, and then *A* lends a further sum of £1000 to *X* upon the same security, this last loan will generally rank for payment after that of *B*. But where the doctrine of tacking operates, *A* has a right to a repayment of his total advance of £2000 in priority to that of *B*.

The process must be distinguished from that of mortgaging the property a second time to the same person. In tacking, the original mortgage debt is merely swollen at a later time. It must also be distinguished from consolidation of mortgages, which, unlike tacking, involves mortgages on different properties. The doctrine was regulated by the Law of Property Act 1925, and a mortgagee can now only tack so as to achieve the same priority for the later advances as for the original loan in any of the following circumstances (s 94). The doctrine applies irrespective of whether the property mortgaged is a legal estate or an equitable interest or whether in the former case the mortgage is legal or equitable.

If the later mortgagees agree

Suppose that *M* mortgages property to *A* for £1000 and then to *B* for £1000; then finds that he needs more money. If the land appears valuable enough to cover the total of all the loans, *B* might agree that if *A* lends a further £1000 then he shall rank first for the payment of the full sum of £2000, although only £1000 was advanced before his own loan.

If the mortgagee has no notice of the later mortgage at the time of the further advance

If the later mortgage is registered, this constitutes actual notice. If the mortgage is unregistrable, then notice will depend upon the old principles. However, if the mortgage is made expressly 'for securing a current account or other further advances', registration is not deemed to constitute notice unless it has been effected either at the time when the original mortgage was created or when the last search, if any, was made by the original mortgagee, whichever happened last (s 94(2), as amended by the Law of Property (Amendment) Act 1926 s 7).

This latter provision is to accommodate banks. If a mortgage is made to a bank to secure an overdraft, the amount owing to the bank will fluctuate from time to time as money is paid in and out. If a second mortgage is then made to another person, then it would be fair to fix the sum in respect of which the bank enjoys priority as the amount owing at that time, if the bank then knew that the second mortgage had been created. If registration were to constitute notice, it would mean that the bank, in order to ensure that the loan was adequately secured, would have to search before honouring individual cheques of the mortgagor. Otherwise, it might well find that the amount for which the cheque was drawn was postponed to the debt owed to a second mortgagee. A second or subsequent mortgagee should, therefore, send written notice to earlier mortgagees, even though his own mortgage is registered, so that the priority of such further advances can be stemmed. Such notice is also desirable to ensure that, on the repayment of the earlier mortgage, the title deeds are not returned to the mortgagor.

If the mortgage imposes an obligation to make further advances

If the mortgage does not merely empower the mortgagee to make further advances, but obliges him to do so, if required by the mortgagor, then these further advances may be tacked to the original debt, even though the mortgagee has express notice of a later mortgage at the time when the further sum is lent. Prospective second or later mortgagees, therefore, having discovered the existence of an earlier mortgage, should enquire whether further advances are made obligatory under its terms.

An example will illustrate these principles. Suppose that *M* mortgages 'Blackacre' to *A* for £1000 and then for £1000 to *B*, who registers. Then let us say *A* advances a further £1000 to *M* on the security of the same property. This second advance will take priority over *B*'s mortgage in any event if there was an obligation to advance it. If there was not, then it ranks below *B*'s debt, since the latter's mortgage was registered when the second advance was made, unless *A*'s mortgage was made expressly for securing further advances. In the latter case, the later advance will rank before *B*'s mortgage, unless at the time of that advance *A* had actual or constructive notice of *B*'s mortgage, or happens to have made a search before making the second advance and discovered *B*'s mortgage. In that case, the advance will rank below *B*'s debt.

Section 94 does not apply to registered land. The Land Registration Act (s 30 as amended by the Law of Property (Amendment) Act 1926 s 5) provides that tacking is possible only if the registered proprietor is under an obligation to make further loans or where the charge is made to secure further loans. In the latter case however priority is only achieved until such time as the Registrar notifies the mortgagee of any later mortgage proposed for registration.

THE MORTGAGE IN ITS MODERN CONTEXT

Introduction

The general law of mortgages developed in the context of business loans. Many of the cases cited in this chapter concern independently struck bargains between brewers and pub owners, large-scale property owners and those who finance them and other commercial organisations. Such transactions are still important today. Yet during the last 50 years another type of mortgage transaction has assumed enormous importance, not only in economic but in social terms, since many millions of people and their family lives are concerned. House purchase mortgages operate in a different social and financial climate from those which were scrutinised by the appellate courts a century or so ago and which helped to forge the doctrines described earlier. Furthermore, statute has intervened to protect the mortgagor as a consumer. House purchase mortgages have transformed the lives of millions of people. They have given them a real financial stake in property they cannot afford to purchase; afforded them mobility of home address; enabled them to spread their indebtedness over nearly half their life spans and thus enjoy material benefits at an earlier age than formerly. The Building Societies Act 1986 has extended the operation of building societies but also provides for their supervision and for the protection of investors and borrowers. For instance Schedule 4 places a duty upon building societies when exercising their power of sale to take reasonable care to secure the best price reasonably obtainable.

The purpose of this part of the chapter is simply to show how the classical principles of the mortgage reach down to accommodate the modern domestic mortgage. In short, the doctrines described earlier generally apply, though statutory rules provide a background control. Yet, as is so often the case with the mortgage, forms and appearances change. Examples of the domestic mortgage transaction will be given. Then some possible new developments in the financing of home purchase will be mentioned.

Examples of modern mortgage transactions

With their kind permission, the complete deed used by the National Provincial Building Society and their Mortgage Conditions (1995 Edition) are reproduced at the end of this chapter. Its simple elegance is outstanding. The following comments upon these are only intended to assist the reader in relating the transaction to the survey of mortgage doctrines attempted earlier in this chapter.

1 One matter may be disposed of quickly:

> The acknowledgement of receipt of the loan repayment is printed on the mortgage deed itself. This is done so that on final repayment the settlement of the debt can be indorsed on the loan instrument. This *vacating receipt* is thus made to keep permanent company with the contract of loan. Once executed, it cancels the mortgage.

2 Otherwise the prominent feature of the deed is that it incorporates rights and duties by reference to conditions which are contained in a separate book of conditions. Before these are examined some matters of fundamental importance to the home-buyer might be mentioned.

- **(a)** The obligation to repay the loan after a few months becomes even less a reality than earlier described. Yet for technical reasons the obligation is kept alive (see Condition 9(A)). The true position is as follows. The loan and the estimated interest accruing upon it over the agreed loan period, say 30 years, are aggregated in one sum. That sum is divided into equal monthly payments over that period. The true obligations of the borrower are expressed in the monthly payments. An alternative is the endowment mortgage in which the loan is coupled with an insurance policy. Only payments of interest are made to the building society, the payment of capital taking place on the maturity of the policy.
- **(b)** The right to change the rates of interest and therefore the total and monthly repayment sums is reserved to the Society (see Condition 3). This right should be considered in relation to the general doctrine that mortgage transactions must not be oppressive. In practice the interest rate is linked to the bank rate.

Possible new developments in mortgage transactions

Revolutionary though the impact of building society loans has been upon home ownership, some classes of people nevertheless suffer from the rather exclusive favour shown towards young couples earning good salaries. Amongst those less favoured by the mortgage market are: elderly people owning unmortgaged or lightly mortgaged property who are in need of increased income; divorced women owning the matrimonial home subject to substantial mortgage repayments but, with growing children off their hands, faced with decreasing payments from their former husbands; older people wishing to own homes for the first time.

On the other hand, safe investment is being sought for large pension funds. Mortgages are sound investments. Index-linked mortgages might provide solutions to some of these problems. These take account of the improvement of value of houses whilst taking adequate profits. A house buyer can buy at four times his annual salary, as opposed to the ordinary building society rate of two and a half times that figure. It is not unconscionable or contrary to public policy to link repayment of capital and interest to rates of exchange (see *Multiservice Bookbinding Ltd* v *Marden* [1979] Ch 84). On redemption, the advance is multiplied by a fraction of the rise in house prices, thus enabling the lender to take his benefit at that stage rather than through interest rates. (See *Nationwide Building Society* v *Registry of Friendly Societies* [1983] 3 All ER 296).

Finally, the Law Commission has made recommendations for the reform of certain aspects of the law of mortgages (1991 Law Com No 204 HC 5). The recommendations concern: the reduction of the methods of creating mortgages to two; the greater regulation of the power of sale on the part of the mortgagee; the abolition of the right of consolidation; the greater protection of the interests of non-commercial mortgagors.

STUDY MATERIAL

The legal charge and conditions of the National and Provincial Building Society

This deed secures further advances

N&P
National & Provincial Building Society

HMLR CODE: CNPRO

Account number:

NATIONAL AND PROVINCIAL BUILDING SOCIETY

Mortgage Deed

A deed of legal charge made the day of 19 between

The Borrower:-

The Society:- National and Provincial Building Society of Provincial House, Bradford, West Yorkshire BD1 1NL and its assignees and other persons from time to time entitled to exercise the powers and discretions conferred upon the Society.

1. The Borrower is a member of the Society.
2. This Mortgage incorporates the National and Provincial Building Society Mortgage Conditions 1995 Edition filed at H M Land Registry under reference MD 134A/01 and the Memorandum and Rules for the time being of National and Provincial Building Society filed at HM Land Registry under reference MD 134A/02, copies of which the Borrower has received.
3. The Borrower, acknowledges receipt of the Advance mentioned below from the Society.
4. The Borrower, with full title guarantee, charges the Mortgaged Property by way of legal mortgage with the payment of all monies payable by the Borrower to the Society under the Mortgage Conditions and agrees to observe the Borrower's obligations and agreements under the Mortgage Conditions.

Land Registry Title Number	County and District (or London Borough)	Advance

The Mortgaged Property

Signed as a deed by the Borrower in the presence of the witness. Signature(s).	Signature, name, address and occupation of witness.

337/6/95

NATIONAL AND PROVINCIAL
BUILDING SOCIETY

Mortgage Deed

National and Provincial Building Society hereby acknowledges to have received all moneys intended to be secured by the within written deed

In witness whereof the Seal of National and Provincial Building Society is hereto affixed this
day of one thousand nine hundred and
by order of the Board of Directors in the presence of:

By authority of the Board of Directors

National & Provincial Building Society
Mortgage Conditions 1995 Edition (England & Wales)

1 **Definitions and Interpretation**

(A) **'Advance'** means any sum advanced by the Society to the Borrower which is secured or is intended to be secured by the Mortgage including any further advance or re-advance.

(B) **'Assignor'** means the assignor as defined in the Mortgage.

(C) **'Borrower'** means the borrower as defined in the Mortgage.

(D) **'Interest'** means interest at the rate applicable to the Advance from time to time.

(E) **'Mortgage'** means the mortgage deed and any charge, mortgage or other document into which these Conditions are incorporated.

(F) **'Mortgage Offer'** means the offer or offers on the basis of which money is advanced to the Borrower.

(G) **'Mortgaged Property'** means the mortgaged property described in the Mortgage and includes all fixtures and additions and a reference to the Mortgaged Property includes a reference to each part of it.

(H) **'Payment'** means the monthly payment notified from time to time to the Borrower by the Society.

(I) **'Policy'** means a policy which the Society requires to be taken out as security for an Advance and any policy which replaces it or for which it is exchanged.

(J) **'Receiver'** means a receiver appointed by the Society.

(K) **'Society'** means National and Provincial Building Society, its assignees and other persons from time to time entitled to exercise the powers and discretions conferred upon the Society by the Mortgage and these Conditions.

(L) A reference to a statutory provision includes any amendment to it or replacement of it that has come into force since the provision was originally enacted.

2 **Payments**

(A) The Borrower agrees to pay to the Society:-

(i) the Payment commencing with a payment on the last day of the calendar month next following the date on which the Advance is made or such other day in the month as may be notified from time to time by the Society to the Borrower and continuing monthly thereafter until all sums secured by the Mortgage have been paid;

(ii) all sums secured by the Mortgage immediately they become due and payable in accordance with these Conditions;

(iii) all insurance premiums paid by the Society for or in relation to the Borrower, the Advance, the Mortgaged Property or its contents and all sums expended and costs and expenses incurred by the Society pursuant to Condition 15;

(iv) interest in accordance with all the terms and conditions that have been agreed between the parties.

(B) The Payment may be calculated so as to include all or any part of capital, Interest, costs, premiums, expenses and liabilities and moneys recoverable, payable or incurred and may be varied from time to time to take account to take account of any increase or decrease in any of the same.

(C) Where the Society is satisfied the Borrower is entitled to deduct income tax from interest payable, the Society will notify the Borrower in writing of the sum which the Society will accept as representing the Payment after proper allowance has been made for the amount of tax deductible.

(D) Each Payment received by the Society shall be applied towards satisfying any sums secured by the Mortgage in such order as the Society thinks fit.

365/6/95

(E) The Mortgage is continuing security for all Advances and all sums becoming due to the Society under the Mortgage and these Conditions.

3. **Interest**

(A) Where an Advance is made by instalments, Interest will not be charged on any part of an Advance until that part is advanced.

(B) Interest is payable on an Advance (or the part of it advanced) from the date on which the Advance is made. When an Advance is paid off Interest will be charged on it to the last day of the calendar month in which it is paid off.

(C) The Society may alter the rate of interest payable by the Borrower on an Advance and the Society will endeavour wherever possible to notify the Borrower in advance of the alteration becoming effective, in one or more of the following ways:-

(i) by continuing to the Borrower; and/or

(ii) by publishing notices in at least two national newspapers; and/or

(iii) by displaying notices in branches.

(D) Where the Society is unable for whatever reason to give prior notice of an alteration in accordance with Condition 3(C) above, the Society may still alter the rate of interest payable to the Borrower on an Advance without notice where there is a valid reason but the Society will inform the Borrower of the alteration at the earliest opportunity and the Borrower will be free to dissolve the contract immediately.

(E) In accordance with all the terms and conditions that have been agreed between the parties, the Borrower may redeem the Mortgage within one month of the date he is informed of any alteration.

(F) The Society may convert interest not paid on the due date into capital. Such capital will then be treated as an Advance.

(G) From the date they become due until the date they are paid, amounts payable under the Mortgage or these Conditions and not otherwise charged with interest shall carry interest at the rate applicable to the earliest Advance secured by the Mortgage of which any part remains outstanding.

(H) Interest is payable both before and after any judgement is obtained against the Borrower.

(I) Interest will be charged in each calendar year:-

(i) on all sums outstanding on the Borrower's account on the last day of the preceding calendar year;

(ii) in respect of any sums advanced by the Society during the calendar year from the date they are advanced; and

(iii) in respect of any other sums becoming payable to the Society during the calendar year from the date they become payable.

4 **Related rights**

(A) By way of further security for the sums secured by the Mortgage, the Borrower with full title guarantee will assign to the Society in such form as the Society requires the interest the Borrower may now or from time to time have in:-

(i) the freehold of the Mortgaged Property or a new lease of it or any option to acquire the same;

(ii) any damages, compensation or other money receivable in respect of the Mortgaged Property or any loss, damage or depreciation of the same including all amounts receivable in respect of blight, compulsory purchase or subsidence;

(iii) any share or membership rights in a residents' association or management company relating to the Mortgaged Property;

(iv) any insurances relating to the Mortgaged Property;

(v) any guarantees, certificates or undertakings for work done or materials supplied to the Mortgaged Property; and

(vi) any rights of action against third parties in connection with the Mortgaged Property.

(B) The Borrower will not do anything to prejudice the Society's interest in any of the interests referred to in Condition 4(A) above. Any money which the Borrower receives in respect of any such interests shall belong to the Society.

5. **Agreements by the Borrower**

The Borrower agrees with the Society:-

(i) to observe and perform the Borrower's obligations in the Mortgage Offer;

(ii) to keep the Mortgaged Property in good and substantial repair and condition;

(iii) to complete any unfinished building works upon the Mortgaged Property without delay and in a good and workmanlike manner;

(iv) to permit the Society to inspect the condition of the Mortgaged Property at any time subject to the reasonable convenience of the Borrower;

(v) to permit the Society to enter and remain upon the Mortgaged Property to repair or continue the erection and completion of buildings comprising the Mortgaged Property;

(vi) not without the approval of the Society to carry out any structural or other alterations to the Mortgaged Property;

(vii) not without the approval of the Society to change the use of the Mortgaged Property;

(viii) to comply with the Town and Country Planning Act 1990;

(ix) to send to the Society at the earliest opportunity a copy of any order or notice made in respect of the Mortgaged Property by the local authority or any other competent body and to comply with such order or notice without delay;

(x) to observe and perform all provisions affecting the title to the Mortgaged Property;

(xi) to give to the Society such information about the Mortgaged Property as the Society may reasonably require;

(xii) to pay the Society's fees in accordance with the tariff published by the Society from time to time;

(xiii) when asked to do so, to reimburse all costs, charges and expenses incurred by the Society or any Receiver in exercising any of the rights or powers conferred upon them.

6. **Leaseholds**

Where the Mortgaged Property is held by the Borrower under a lease, the Borrower agrees with the Society:-

(i) to pay the rent under the lease and any other outgoings and to produce receipts if the Society asks for them;

(ii) to comply with those covenants and agreements in the lease which are the Borrower's responsibility and to try to ensure that other parties to the lease comply with their obligations under it;

(iii) to tell the Society immediately if anyone takes or threatens to take any step which might lead to the lease being brought to an end and to do whatever the Society asks to stop this happening; and

(iv) to tell the Society if the Borrower acquires an interest in the freehold of the Mortgaged Property or a new lease or an option to do either.

7. **Insurance**

(A) The Society will not unreasonably withhold its consent to the Borrower or a third party arranging the insurance of the Mortgaged Property as long as:-

(i) the Mortgaged Property is insured with a reputable insurance company for not less than the amount required by the Society under an index-linked policy against all the risks usually covered by a comprehensive household insurance policy; and

(ii) the Society is named as a joint insured under the policy.

(B) Where the Society has given its consent under this Condition, the Borrower will:-

(i) arrange or procure that a third party arranges the insurance strictly as provided above and in accordance with the terms of the Society's consent;

(ii) where the Borrower arranges the insurance, send the Society the original insurance policy;

(iii) where a third party arranges the insurance, send the Society a copy of the insurance policy; and

(iv) send the Society evidence of the payment of the insurance premiums.

(C) The Society may withdraw its consent if any of the above requirements are not met.

(D) Where the Society has not given its consent under this Condition or such consent has been withdrawn, the Society may arrange the insurance of the Mortgaged Property. This insurance will be at the Borrower's expense for not less than the amount required by the Borrower against such risks, in such office, through such agency and in such a manner as the Society may from time to time reasonably determine.

(E) Whoever arranges the insurance of the Mortgaged Property, the Borrower will tell the Society in writing of any circumstances occurring or arising affecting or likely to affect the validity of the insurance or giving rise or likely to give rise to a claim under it.

(F) Whoever arranges the insurance of the Mortgaged Property, the Borrower will allow the Society to conduct any claim made under the policy. The proceeds of any insurance claim will be used either to make good the damage in respect of which they were received or, if the Society so requires, to reduce the amounts owing to the Society.

8. **The Borrower's power to transfer or let the Mortgaged Property**

(A) The Society will not unreasonably withhold its approval to the Borrower letting the Mortgaged Property as long as the Society has approved the tenant and has seen and approved the terms of the tenancy.

(B) The Borrower agrees that except as provided in Condition 8(A) above he will not let the Mortgaged Property or allow anyone to occupy it or share it with him.

(C) The Borrower agrees that he will not try to transfer the Mortgaged Property subject to the Mortgage.

(D) Without the Society's consent the Borrower may not redeem the Mortgage without at the same time redeeming any other mortgage it has with the Society over other property.

9. **Sums due and payable**

(A) All sums secured by the Mortgage shall become immediately due and payable without the need for the Society to demand them:-

(i) if the Borrower defaults in the payment of two consecutive Payments in whole or in part; or

(ii) if the Borrower defaults in the payment of any other sum payable to the Society for more than one month; or

(iii) if the Borrower continues to be in breach of any other obligation to the Society under these Conditions or the Mortgage which has been brought to his attention and which he has failed to remedy within a reasonable time; or

(iv) if the Borrower dies; or

(v) if the Society becomes aware of any misrepresentation or omission by the Borrower in any information provided by the Borrower in his application for the Advance or in response to the Society's enquiries; or

(vi) if any part of the Mortgaged Property the loss of which the Society reasonably considers would adversely affect the value of its security becomes subject to compulsory purchase order or is requisitioned.

10. The Society's powers as mortgagee

(A) The Society's powers as mortgagee arise the day after the date of the Mortgage and become exercisable as soon as the sums secured by the Mortgage become immediately due and payable in accordance with Condition 9.

(B) In addition to the powers conferred by statute the Society's powers as mortgagee include being able:-

(i) to perform any of the Borrower's obligations under the Mortgage or these Conditions;

(ii) to eject from the Mortgaged Property any person in possession or in occupation who does not have the Society's consent to be there;

(iii) to maintain, repair, develop, redevelop or demolish the Mortgaged Property and to apply for and obtain all consents and permissions necessary for the purpose;

(iv) to grant and accept surrenders of leases or tenancies and other rights to occupy the Mortgaged Property;

(v) to treat rent accepted from a tenant of any furnished letting of the Mortgaged Property as being a payment made exclusively in respect of the Mortgaged Property and not in any part as being made in respect of any furniture included in the letting;

(vi) to sell the Mortgaged Property for a price payable by instalments, whether or not instalments carry interest;

(vii) to remove from the Mortgaged Property any items it found there when it enters into possession. For this purpose the Society is appointed the agent of the Borrower with the Borrower's authority to deal with such items. Nothing contained in these Conditions confers upon the Society any right in respect of any such items which would make the Mortgage a bill of sale;

(viii) to do anything which the Society considers to be for the benefit, preservation or improvement of the Mortgaged Property;

(ix) at any time taking possession of the Mortgaged Property or appointing a Receiver, on giving notice to give up possession or determine the appointment of the Receiver whether or not appointing another in his place.

11. Receiver

(A) A Receiver may employ and pay agents in respect of any work incidental to the receivership.

(B) A Receiver may be either an officer or employee of the Society or any other person.

(C) A Receiver shall in addition to his statutory powers and subject to any limitation in the terms of his appointment have the same powers as those conferred upon the Society by Condition 10 above.

(D) A Receiver shall apply all money received by him in such order and in such amounts as the Society may require and section 109(8) of the Law of Property Act 1925 shall not apply.

365/6/95

12. Power of Attorney

(A) The Borrower appoints the Society to be his attorney and on his behalf to execute documents and do everything else he is required to do under the Mortgage or these Conditions.

(B) This power is irrevocable and given by way of security.

(C) This power may be delegated by the Society to any other person.

13. Consents and approvals

(A) Whether these Conditions require the Borrower to obtain the consent or approval of the Society:-

(i) it must be obtained in advance;

(ii) it is only effective if it is given in writing; and

(iii) it is only effective when the Borrower has obtained all other necessary consents and approvals.

(B) The Society may charge a fee for considering a request for its consent or approval.

(C) If the Society gives its consent or approval subject to conditions, the Society may withdraw it if the conditions are not complied with.

(D) Where the Society is not prepared to give its consent or approval it will give a reason unless to do so would require disclosing something which the Society reasonably regards as confidential.

14. Liability to account

The Society shall not be required to account to the Borrower for any sums allowed to the Society by way of commission or discount on any fire, life or other insurance.

15. The Policy

(A) The Borrower and the Assignor each agree with the Society:-

(i) to deposit or arrange the deposit of the Policy with the Society and to execute or arrange the execution of an assignment of the Policy to the Society in such a form as the Society may require as security for the obligations of the Borrower to the Society;

(ii) not do anything which might cause payment under the Policy to be refused or limited;

(iii) not to do or permit or suffer anything which might make the Policy void or cause it to become voidable;

(iv) immediately at his own cost in case the Policy becomes voidable to do all things necessary for restoring it and if the Policy does become void to do everything necessary to enable the Society to take out a new Policy on the life of the life assured in the name of the Society for the amount which would have become payable under the Policy if the life assured had died immediately before it became void;

(v) to pay all sums necessary to keep the Policy in force when they become payable and to deliver the receipt or sufficient evidence of every payment to the Society whenever the Society requires; and

(vi) to pay all sums paid and costs and expenses incurred by the Society and interest as provided for in Condition 15(B).

(B) If the Borrower or the Assignor does not pay any sums necessary to keep the Policy in force the Society may pay them and all sums so paid and all costs and expenses incurred in restoring the Policy shall be repaid to the Society by the Borrower together with Interest from the date they are paid by the Society until they are repaid by the Borrower.

(C) After the Society's powers as mortgagee have become exercisable the Society may surrender the Policy to the insurers by whom it was granted or exchange it for a fully paid up Policy or make such arrangements with the insurers as the Society may think fit.

(D) After the Society's powers as mortgagee have become exercisable the Society may apply the Policy and the full benefit thereof (including any surrender moneys) towards the discharge of the amounts secured by the Mortgage and the Policy and the full benefit of it shall constitute a continuing security and are charged accordingly.

(E) Upon the discharge of all obligations for which the Policy is security the Society will at the request and cost of the Assignor reassign it or assign it as he directs.

16. Notice

(A) Any letter to the Borrower or the Assignor is properly served if it is delivered by hand or sent by prepaid first-class post to the Mortgaged Property.

(B) Where the Borrower or the Assignor is more than one person it is sufficient if the letter is addressed to any one or more of them.

(C) In the absence of evidence to the contrary, a letter which the Society sends by prepaid first-class post shall be deemed to have been received by the person to whom it is addressed at 10a.m. on the third day after the date it is posted.

17. Conflict

(A) If the memorandum and rules for the time being of the Society conflict with the Mortgage or these Conditions, the Mortgage or these Conditions (as the case may be) shall prevail.

(B) If the Mortgage Offer conflicts with these Conditions, the Mortgage Offer shall prevail.

QUESTIONS

1 Since the essence of a mortgage is the securing of a loan on property owned by the borrower, why should it be difficult for older people and women to obtain mortgage loans despite property ownership?

2 To what extent do equity and statute law protect the modern domestic mortgagor from the possible exactions of the mortgagee?

3 Can you reconcile the raising of interest rates after the conclusion of a mortgage agreement with the right to redeem the mortgaged property?

4 What is meant by 'negative equity'? Describe a domestic mortgage situation, involving unemployment or family breakdown, to illustrate the problems which negative equity might cause.

5 'Home ownership, particularly if achieved with the aid of mortgage finance, breeds political conservatism' (Kevin Gray: *Elements of Land Law* (2nd edn) p 935). Discuss.

6 Angela and Bernard married in 1983. He was a computer engineer, temporarily out of work; she was a secretary earning £12 000 pa. They could not obtain a loan from a building society to buy their proposed home at 19 Shirley Riviera for £80 000. However, the Merchant of Warwick Bank, a private merchant bank, financed the purchase through a legal charge with interest rate charged at 15 per cent above current market rates repayable over a period of 20 years. The property was conveyed into the joint names of Angela and Bernard. Soon afterwards Bernard secured stable employment in the coal industry at a salary of £40 000 pa. In 1985 Angela gave up work to bring up her baby and two more children born in 1987 and 1989. In order to boost his earnings during this period, Bernard bought a stretch of canal for a leisure business for £20 000. This was financed by the Brum Venetian Bank, a private merchant bank, on a second mortgage of his home. The Bank insisted that Angela should receive independent, expert advice before she joined in the mortgage. This advice was provided by an accountant, Jack Cook, a water-ski partner of Bernard. This second mortgage was executed in 1993.

Late in 1995 Bernard was made redundant and the canal dried up in the drought of that year, causing the business to collapse. In February 1996, however, Angela secured a post with a newly-formed business, Jupiter Orbital Holidays, at a salary of £40 000 pa. Instalment debts of £3000 and £10 000 are owing to the Brum Venetian Bank and the Merchant of Warwick Bank respectively.

Possession proceedings have now been commenced by the Merchant of Warwick Bank. Your advice is sought on the following points:

(1) Assuming that Bernard has exerted undue influence over Angela in regard to the second mortgage of their home, to what extent will the Brum Venetian Bank be affected by this, if at all?

(2) Can the mortgage to the Merchant of Warwick Bank be set aside on the grounds that it:

(a) makes the right of redemption illusory; or

(b) is so harsh and oppressive in its terms as to be voidable on equitable or statutory principles?

(3) To what principles will the court have regard when considering a suspension of the right to possession by the Bank and the grant to Angela and Bernard of a reasonable period during which to pay off the arrears?

(4) Would the proceedings by the Merchant of Warwick Bank be affected if Angela and Bernard could prove that the Bank gave professional confirmation before purchase that their home was worth £80 000, that this advice was negligent and that it was worth only £60 000?

(5) Might the Court delay possession by the Merchant of Warwick Bank in order to afford Angela and Bernard the opportunity to sell the house themselves?

CHAPTER 16

RENTCHARGES

NATURE

A rentcharge is a periodical sum of money payable out of land and not attributable to tenure. These last words distinguish it from a rent service, which is the rent payable by a tenant to his landlord, and which derives from tenure. A rentcharge is an interest in land, the burden running with the land upon which it is charged and the benefit being enforceable by whoever owns the rentcharge for the time being. Thus its effectiveness does not depend upon either privity of contract or upon tenure. If I grant the fee simple of 'Blackacre' to *A*, subject to the payment of an annual sum of £1000 to *B*, *B* owns a rentcharge which *A* must satisfy, even though there is no relationship of contract or tenure between him and *B*.

Like other interests in or over the land of another person, rentcharges can be made to endure for the usual periods of time available for estates and interests in land, and can exist either as legal or equitable interests. They can only be legal interests, however, if they are in possession, created to last either in perpetuity or for a term of years absolute (LPA 1925 s 1(2)(b)), and made with the formalities required by the law. In all other cases they are equitable. If they are made voluntarily, or in consideration of marriage, or by way of family arrangement, for the life of any person or for less period, a settlement results (Settled Land Act 1925 s 1(1)(v)). Such an equitable rentcharge is used in a settlement to provide a jointure for a wife after the death of her husband. In Chapter 5, we noticed a common use of a legal rentcharge when a fee simple is sold and a rentcharge reserved in place of the lump sum usually taken as purchase price. These rentcharges are sometimes called fee farm rents.

A rentcharge can be charged upon or created out of another rentcharge (LPA 1925 s 122).

Rent charges can be imposed on one property for the benefit of another and attached to covenants of repair. This can be used in estate development so as to achieve mutual enforceability of positive covenants which would be impossible under the doctrine of *Tulk* v *Moxhay*.

CREATION

A legal rentcharge must be created by deed if *inter vivos*, but may be created by will. However, the doctrine of *Walsh* v *Lonsdale* (1882) 21 ChD 9 applies, so that specific performance can be demanded of a contract to create a rentcharge, provided that it is evidenced by sufficient memorandum to satisfy the Law of Property Act 1925 s 40 or the Law of Property (Miscellaneous Provisions) Act 1989 s 2. The creation of new rentcharges is prohibited by the Rentcharges Act 1977 s 2(i), with certain exceptions including those which cause or are associated with settlements, *estate* rentcharges and those arising under a statute providing for the creation of rentcharges in connection with the execution of works on land. The Act should be consulted for details.

ENFORCEMENT

If a rentcharge is not paid, the following remedies are available. If the rentcharge is created out of another rentcharge, the only one of these which is apt is an action for recovery of the money, but there is the additional remedy under the Law of Property Act 1925 s 122(2), which authorises the appointment of a receiver.

1 *Right of re-entry*. The right to forfeit the land upon which the rentcharge is imposed is only available if expressly reserved in the instrument of creation. The following remedies may be used irrespective of reservation.

2 *Action for recovery of the money*. This action may be brought against the person who is entitled to the rents and profits of the land, known in this context as the '*terre* tenant'.

3 *Distress (LPA 1925 s 121(2))*. Subject to any contrary intention expressed in the instrument of creation, the owner of a rentcharge created after 1881 can distrain on the land or part of it if the sum or any part of it is 21 days in arrears.

4 *Entry into possession (LPA 1925 s 121(3))*. Subject to any contrary intention expressed in the instrument of creation the rent owner can, if any part of the sum is 40 days in arrears, enter into possession of the land or part of it and satisfy the debt out of the profits.

5 *Lease to a trustee (LPA 1925 s 121(4))*. Subject again to any expressed contrary intention, if any part of the sum is 40 days in arrears, the owner of a rentcharge created after 1881 can lease the land or part of it to a trustee on trust to raise the sum due or to become due by creating a mortgage.

EXTINGUISHMENT

A rentcharge may be extinguished in the following ways:

1 *Release*. The owner of the rentcharge may release the land from liability either wholly or partly (see LPA 1925 s 70).

2 *Merger*. The rentcharge might disappear through merger if the rentcharge owner acquires the land upon which it is charged, but this ultimately depends upon his intention (LPA 1925 s 185).

3 *Limitation Act 1980*. If a rentcharge is unpaid for 12 years it is extinguished by the Act, though if during this time it is paid to a third party it remains recoverable by him though not by the original owner.

4 *Rentcharges Act 1977 s 3(1)*. This provides that, subject to certain exceptions, rentcharges, if not otherwise extinguished, shall cease to have effect at the expiry of 60 years beginning either with the passing of the Act or with the date on which the rentcharge first became payable, whichever is later.

5 *Statutory discharge*. Under the Rentcharges Act 1977, a landowner may discharge the land from a rentcharge upon payment of the capital value of the rentcharge (see ss 8, 9 and 10).

REGISTRATION

Certain rentcharges are capable of substantive registration; others can be protected by notice.

CHAPTER 17

REGISTRATION OF INCUMBRANCES

INTRODUCTION

It must be emphasised at the outset that this chapter is concerned with unregistered title only. As was explained in Chapter 2, the registered title system is progressively replacing the unregistered system. Where the title to land is registered, Chapter 18 deals with the questions discussed here.

We have already seen that a prospective purchaser of land not only investigates the vendor's title to the land, but also seeks to discover what interests third parties have in the land. The general principle has always been that if such interests are legal they will bind the purchaser whether he knows of them or not, and if they are equitable they will bind everyone except a purchaser in good faith of a legal estate in the land without notice of them.

This principle was greatly affected by the Land Charges Act 1925, the provisions of which, as amended, are now consolidated in the Land Charges Act 1972, except for the rules relating to local land charges. This provides that many equitable interests are registrable. Since registration constitutes actual notice of the interest to all persons (LPA 1925 s 198), these equitable interests can be endowed with all the inviolability of legal interests by the simple act of registration. On the other hand, certain legal interests are made registrable, and failure to register may cause them to fail against purchasers. The principle mentioned above, therefore, has had both its wings clipped.

Five registers are maintained at the Land Charges Registry at Plymouth. They are computerised and are concerned with the registration of incumbrances on land the title to which is unregistered. Some of these registers are of only minor importance. A sixth, the local land charges register, is kept by local authorities under the Land Charges Act 1975, for all land, registered or otherwise, in their areas. The land charges registrar does not question the validity of an interest when the owner of it applies to register, so that registration is no guarantee of its validity. Registration will not help in the enforcement of an alleged restrictive covenant, for instance, if no land or reversion was retained by the covenantee. All the register really declares is: 'If this interest is valid here is notice of it. Brief references will later be made to two further registers, one affecting companies, the other affecting common land.

The plan for this chapter will be firstly to describe the six registers and the matters which can be entered in them, and secondly, to explain the effects of registration and non-registration. References to sections are to those of the Land Charges Act 1972, unless otherwise stated.

THE REGISTERS AND THEIR CONTENTS

The registers and the matters eligible to be entered in them are as follows:

Register of pending actions (s 5)

Any action in relation to any interest in land which is pending or any petition in bankruptcy may be entered in this register. An entry is effective for five years but may be renewed (s 8). The court may order it to be 'vacated', that is struck out, if, during the pendency of the action, it believes the proceedings are not prosecuted in good faith (see *Taylor* v *Taylor* [1968] 1 WLR 378). Section 1(6) confers on the court a general power to vacate registrations and this extends to all the registers, notwithstanding this special provision. So the grounds for vacating registration of pending actions are not limited to lack of good faith (*Northern Development (Holdings) Ltd* v *UDT Securities* [1977] 1 All ER 747). The purpose of the provision is to warn any person to whom the owner of the interest may sell before the case has been decided that a case is on foot and that, if he buys, he does so at his own risk and subject to any decision the court might reach. It has been held that the claim must be to some proprietary right in the land (*Calgary and Edmonton Land Co Ltd* v *Dobinson* [1974] 1 All ER 484).

Register of annuities (s 1 and Sch 1)

This register is moribund. Before 1926 certain annuities were registrable under earlier legislation. The present section simply enacts that no more entries in that register shall be made after the Act and that, when all the existing entries have been satisfied, the register shall be closed. If such annuities, though made before 1926, were not registered, they become registrable as Class E land charges mentioned below. The days of that class also are numbered. Annuities which are created after 1925 may be registered as Class C(iii) land charges provided that they do not arise under a strict settlement or trust for sale. If they do so, they are not registrable at all but are protected by the conveyancing machinery provided for settlements and trusts for sale. They can of course be overreached.

Register of writs and orders affecting the land (s 6)

In this register may be entered writs and orders made by any court for enforcing judgments, or recognizances or any orders appointing receivers of land or receiving orders in bankruptcy. These entries expire after five years but are renewable. They are to be distinguished from the pending actions dealt with above, because they are concerned with the results and enforcements of the court's decisions. An example is an access order under the Neigbouring Land Act 1992. The Act should be consulted for details.

Register of deeds of arrangement (s 7)

Deeds of arrangement may be registered here by the trustee of the deed or by a creditor assenting to or taking the benefit of the deed. A deed of arrangement is a document under which a debtor surrenders control of his property in favour of his creditors, in return for a release from his debts (see the Deeds of Arrangement Act 1914).

Register of land changes (s 2)

The matters which can be entered in this register are divided into six classes, A, B, C, D, E and F, Classes C and D containing subdivisions. It relates only to unregistered land.

Class A consists of charges on land arising under statute when some person makes an application to have the charge created. A life tenant, who has to pay compensation under the Agricultural Holdings Act 1986 to an outgoing tenant, may apply to the Minister for the amount to be charged on the land, and the resultant charge would fall into this class.

Class B consists of charges imposed by statute without any person applying for their creation and not being registrable in the local land charges register. An example is a charge on land to cover contributions payable by a legally assisted person under the Legal Aid Act 1974 s 9.

Class C is subdivided into the following categories:

1 Puisne mortgages (legal mortgages not protected by deposit of the deeds).

2 Limited owners' charges – These are equitable charges acquired by tenants for life or statutory owners, under statute, because they have paid inheritance tax or other liabilities, and to which special priority is given by the statute. Where liabilities relate to the value of the land itself in this way, it is fair that a person having a limited interest only in it should be allowed to spread the ultimate burden of it on the settled property.

3 General equitable charges – This category sweeps up equitable charges which are not registrable in other categories, provided that they are not protected by a deposit of documents relating to the legal estate affected, and do not arise, or affect interests arising, under a settlement or a trust for sale. An example is an equitable mortgage of a legal estate in land not protected by a deposit of deeds.

4 Estate contracts – This category comprises any contract by a person who

owns a legal estate, or is entitled to have a legal estate conveyed to him, to convey or create some legal estate, any option to purchase, right of pre-emption or other like right. It has been held to include a covenant in a lease requiring the tenant to offer to surrender the lease to the landlord before seeking his consent to assignment or subletting (*Greene* v *Church Commissioners for England* [1974] Ch 467). Such contracts raise an equitable interest in the person contracting to buy the estate (see *Beesly* v *Hallwood Estates Ltd* [1960] 2 All ER 314; *Turley* v *Mackay* [1944] Ch 37). A notice of desire to purchase the reversion or to acquire a new lease under the Leasehold Reform Act 1967 comes under this head.

With regard to rights of pre-emption, a decision of the Court of Appeal has virtually denuded them of any benefit through registration. *A* granted a right of pre-emption during *A*'s life to *P*, which *P* registered. *A* later granted an option to purchase the same land to *O* which *O* registered. The intention appears to have been that *O* should be entitled to exercise his option if *P* failed to take the land through pre-emption during *A*'s lifetime. Next, *A* sold the land to *P*, though on slightly altered terms than agreed in the original agreement for pre-emption. After *A*'s death, *O* attempted to exercise his option. The Court held that he could do so, despite the facts that *P* had registered his right before *O* had negotiated his option with *A*, and that this would entitle him to take the land from *P* at a price considerably less than that which *P* had paid for it.

The reason was that a right of pre-emption is not an interest in land and therefore cannot bind a purchaser, even though the latter has notice of it. It could not be an interest in land because whether the grantee ever took any benefit under it depended entirely on the will of the grantor. Only when the latter decided to sell could the right become an interest (*Pritchard* v *Briggs* [1979] 3 WLR 868).

This reasoning is open to criticism. Contingent interests in land which depend upon the volition of the grantor can exist in the family context. An example is a settlement by *S* under which he grants the fee simple interest in land to 'such child of mine as I shall appoint'. If the land is then sold, the resultant purchase money will still remain subject to the settlement – even though *S* might never exercise his power of appointment. The example is given merely to show that the 1925 legislation protects contingent interests of all types. If they occur in the 'family' field, the machinery of the strict settlement or trust for sale shields them. If they arise in the 'commercial' field, the system of registration is available to protect them. It is difficult to see upon what grounds of justice any distinction can be drawn between the two categories. See also *Spiro* v *Glencrown Properties Ltd* [1991] 1 All ER 600; and Cheshire and Burn's *Modern Law of Real Property* (15th edn) p 128.

Class D is subdivided into the following categories:

1 Charges for inheritance tax – Any charge acquired by the Commissioners of

Inland Revenue under any statute for inheritance tax may be registered under this head.

2 Restrictive covenants – Restrictive covenants are registrable if entered into after 1925, unless made between lessors and lessees. Restrictive covenants are the second most numerous of all entries on the land charges register.

3 Equitable easements and other equitable rights or privileges over or affecting land. These are registrable if they were created after 1925. The vagueness of this class has proved troublesome to the extent that its abolition has been advocated. Identification of the equitable rights capable of registration under this head has been rendered more difficult by *Ives Investment Ltd* v *High* [1967] 2 QB 379. This was discussed in Chapter 7. The wording is probably wide enough to include equitable profits also, but has been held not to include equitable rights of re-entry (*Shiloh Spinners Ltd* v *Harding* [1973] 1 All ER 90), nor a tenant's right to remove fixtures at the end of a lease (*Poster* v *Slough Estates Ltd* [1968] 3 All ER 257). Licences, although often protected by equitable remedies and sometimes binding upon third parties, cannot be registered, unless, presumably, they amount to easements by estoppel. Even in the latter case, *Ives Investment Ltd* v *High* could present a barrier in many cases. Considering, however, that licences are frequently informal transactions, undertaken without legal advice, ineligibility to register could be helpful to the licensee. Since it will seldom occur to him to register, his failure to do so will not have the drastic effect upon his rights which failure to register eligible rights entails. It has been the story of equity to maintain a balance between certainty and justice. For a discussion of the potentially draconian effects of the land charges system, with particular reference to pending actions, see 1995 Conv 309.

Class E: this class is of little importance and has already been discussed as far as necessary.

Class F: this class was added by the Matrimonial Homes Act 1967, and in it may be registered a spouse's rights of occupation under the Act (now consolidated in the Matrimonial Homes Act 1983).

Local land charges (Local Land Charges Act 1975)

Local authorities keep registers in which they enter certain charges arising under various statutes which affect land in their area. Examples of this are refusals of planning permission and unpaid road-making charges payable by frontagers to a street which was made up at the expense of the local authority. The register covers both registered and unregistered land. Purchase of land should invariably be preceded by a search in the local land charges register as it is by a search of the registers maintained under the Land Charges Act 1972 for unregistered land.

Companies

Under the Companies Act 1985, a register is maintained by the Registrar of Companies for the registration of charges over land created by companies for securing money. If such a charge was created before 1 January 1970, or at any time in the case of a floating charge, registration shall be sufficient in place of registration under the 1972 Act (see s 3 of the 1972 Act). In other cases, registration under both schemes is required if a purchaser from the company is to be bound by it.

The alternative registration under the 1985 Act can produce a curious result in that the name registered might not be the name of the estate owner against whom registration would have been appropriate under the 1972 Act. (*Property Discount Corporation Ltd* v *Lyon Group Ltd* [1981] 1 All ER 379).

Common rights

Under the Commons Registration Act 1965, two registers are maintained for the registration of commons and town or village greens and for the ownership of and rights over them. The registration authority is the appropriate county council or, in the case of land situated in Greater London, the local Borough Council. Land may be removed from the register under the provisions of the Common Land (Rectification of Registers) Act 1989.

EFFECTS OF NON-REGISTRATION

Interests eligible for entry under Classes C(iv) or D or as local land charges are void against a purchaser of a legal estate in the land for money or money's worth unless registered before the completion of the purchase (s 4(6) and see *McCarthy & Stone Ltd* v *Julian S Hodge & Co Ltd* [1971] 2 All ER 973). All the other charges and matters registrable under the Act, with two minor exceptions, are void against a purchaser for value of any interest in the land. It was remarked earlier in this book that the statutory doctrine of notice introduced in 1925 brought certainty to conveyancing transactions where some third party rights are concerned, but that it did so at the expense of ethical standards. The House of Lords have recently underlined that there is to be no softening of this principle. In *Midland Bank Trust Co Ltd* v *Green* [1981] 1 All ER 153, *F* granted *S* an option to buy 'Blackacre'. *S* failed to register. Several years later, *F*, with the purpose of defeating the option, conveyed the land to his wife for £500, although its true value was £40 000. *S* had been in occupation of the land under a lease at all material times. It was held that the wife was a purchaser of the legal estate for money or money's worth and therefore took free of the option. Bad faith was not relevant because it was not required and had no doubt been deliberately omitted from s 4(6) and 'money or money's worth' required no adequacy of consideration. Lord Wilberforce delivered the judgment of the House. The other four Law Lords agreed unreservedly. We might note that even those in actual occupation suffer if they fail to register their rights. We shall see that in the case of registered titles, persons in actual occupation of land do enjoy particular consideration although the severe effects of failure to register prevail under that system too.

The differences between the two principles, namely the kind of interest required to be taken by the purchaser and the type of consideration necessary, should be carefully noted (see 38 Conv 8). The two exceptions separately dealt with need only be mentioned here. They concern pending actions (s 5(7) and (8)) and certain writs and orders (s 6(4) and (5)). The word 'purchaser' is given a wide definition under s 17 so as to include any person, including a lessee or mortgagee, who takes any interest or charge for valuable consideration.

If a registrable interest is created in land and is very shortly followed by the creation of another interest, there may not be time to register the first interest before the second is created. The first would therefore be void as against the purchaser of the second. Thus, if *A* makes a restrictive covenant with his neighbour *B* not to build on his land, 'Blackacre', and later the same day sells or mortgages the land to *C*, there would clearly not be time for *B* to register, and therefore the covenant would be void as against *C*. Section 11 provides a solution to this dilemma by enabling any person who intends to apply to register any contemplated charge or other matter registrable under the Act, to register a 'priority notice' at least 15 days before the registration is to take effect, that is, before the creation of the interest to be protected. If the charge or matter itself is then registered within 30 days after the priority notice, the registration takes effect as if it had been made at the time of the creation of the charge.

A prospective purchaser may discover entries on the registers by obtaining an official certificate of search. If the purchase is completed within 15 days after the date of the certificate, he will not be affected by any entry made after the date of the certificate and before completion of the purchase, unless it is made pursuant to a priority notice (s 11). If this were not so, a purchaser could never be sure that some charge had not been registered in the short time between the arrival of the certificate from the registry and the completion of the transaction. There is no priority period with company searches, local land charge searches or commons registration searches.

Incumbrances are registered against the name of the estate owner and not against the land, although the identity of the land affected is recorded with the entry (see *Oak Co-Operative Building Society* v *Blackburn* [1968] 2 All ER 117). This means that the reference for a search requested by a prospective purchaser is to a name and not land. Consequently the names of all the estate owners in the past must, in theory, be known if all the incumbrances are to be discovered. In practice this is not necessary; a search is made before every successive transaction transferring ownership and the certificates resulting from these searches are generally kept with the title deeds, so that, together with the certificate against the outgoing estate owner (the vendor), they will provide a purchaser with a complete record.

The Law of Property Act 1969, in reducing the period of commencement of titles under open contracts to 15 years, accentuates the problem because it might sometimes preclude a purchaser discovering the names of previous estate owners and perhaps old land charges which will nevertheless bind him. However, the Act does provide for compensation in certain cases where loss is occasioned by the existence of 'old land charges' (s 25).

Although the Law of Property Act 1925 s 198 fixes a purchaser with notice of all matters registered under the Land Charges Act, there was previously doubt as to whether this notice operated at the moment of the contract or at the moment of completion (see *Re Forsey and Hollebone's Contract* [1927] 2 Ch 379). However, the Law of Property Act 1969 s 24 enacted that the question whether a prospective purchaser has notice at the time of the contract of a registered land charge is to be determined by reference to his actual knowledge. An example might illustrate this.

If *P* contracts to buy 'Blackacre' from *V* and a restrictive covenant is already registered against the land at that time, and later the conveyance is completed, there is no doubt that *P* takes the land subject to the covenant. This principle remains quite undisturbed. Yet he might be able to proceed against *V* or refuse to complete on the grounds that he was, at the moment of contract, unaware of the covenant, despite the fact that it was registered at that time.

STUDY MATERIAL

Kingsnorth Trust Ltd v *Tizard* [1986] 2 All ER 56

HIS HONOUR JUDGE JOHN FINLAY QC. On 18 April 1983 the palintiffs advanced to the first defendant, Mr Tizard, the sum of £66 000 and the repayment of that sum with interest, in accordance with the provisions of the mortgage so dated and made between the plaintiffs of the first part and Mr Tizard of the second part, was secured by a charge by way of legal mortgage of the dwelling house and land known as Willowdown, Fairford Road, Lechdale in the county of Gloucester.

Willowdown was the matrimonial home of Mr Tizard and his wife, the second defendant, Mrs Tizard. The property was vested in Mr Tizard alone. Mrs Tizard claims an equitable interest in it. The plaintiffs are seeking to enforce their legal charge. The question in this action is whether that legal charge is subject to or overrides the equitable interest, if any, which Mrs Tizard has. That is the question between the plaintiffs and Mrs Tizard. Between Mr and Mrs Tizard there is also the question whether Mrs Tizard has an equitable interest and if so what it is. If their charge is subject to Mrs Tizard's equitable interest the plaintiffs are affected by that second question but they disclaim any wish to take part in the determination of it.

Mr Tizard has not appeared and is not represented. Not long after he had obtained the advance of £66 000 Mr Tizard emigrated, and it is thought that he is in America.

Mr and Mrs Tizard met in 1958. They worked in the same establishment. In 1960 they began to live together. They moved to London for a time. Both were employed. Mr Tizard had an accident and for 48 weeks could not work. Mrs Tizard maintained him. In May 1968 Mr Tizard obtained a divorce and married Mrs Tizard. On 23 March 1968 Mrs Tizard had had twins: in the event they were the only children of the marriage. Thereafter she did not work full-time for some four years but seven months after the twins were born she started working and for the rest of the four years continued to work part-time. Mr Tizard was a linesman for the local electricity board. Mrs Tizard's part-time earnings were less than his; but when she worked full-time she contributed more than half of the pooled earnings. Save when one was not working they both pooled their earnings.

When she resumed working full time Mrs Tizard was employed as a secretary in a heavy goods vehicle driving school; and in 1976 she set up her own business in that line. The business was successful, until a recession and her marital difficulties made Mrs Tizard wind it up in about 1982.

In 1966 Mr and Mrs Tizard purchased a house in Swindon. Mrs Tizard contributed to the £400 deposit. She put in £100 which she received from her parents, some money they had saved from their pooled earnings went into the deposit and so did a small part of the £600 which Mr Tizard received as compensation for his accident. Most of that £600 was spent on a car. The balance of the purchase price, which was £3 300, was raised on mortgage. The mortgage instalments were paid out of the pooled resources. This property was sold in 1973 for £10 500. Mr and Mrs Tizard purchased land at Lechlade and built a house on it, Leatherham House. Although the main building was done by contractors, both Mr and Mrs Tizard worked on it, painting, decorating and so on. Leatherham House was sold in 1979. The land on which Willowdown was built was purchased; and Willowdown was built. Bridging finance and then the proceeds of sale of Leatherham House, £44 000, were applied to the purchase and building of Willowdown.

Although Mrs Tizard did some decorating work at Willowdown House, most of the work was done by builders; the Tizards were in a better financial position then than they had been when Leatherham House was built. The Willowdown land was purchased in October 1978 and in the following year Leatherham House was sold and Willowdown House completed. The result of the property venture which I have mentioned was that Willowdown House, with its curtilage, and an adjoining building plot which had a planning permission which has now expired, but which it is hoped can be renewed (that plot having a value of about £18 000), was held free from incumbrances. All the properties had been in the sole name of Mr Tizard.

In 1982 the marriage broke down. Mr and Mrs Tizard agreed that Willowdown and the adjoining land should be sold and the net proceeds divided between them in equal shares. This was not done before Mr Tizard emigrated and it has not been done since.

Mrs Tizard moved into the spare bedroom when the marriage broke down. Willowdown had four bedrooms: the master bedroom, which until then the spouses had used and which continued to be used by Mr Tizard; two bedrooms occupied by the two children respectively; and the spare bedroom which was a room with a double bed.

In November 1982 Mrs Tizard began to sleep, not always but sometimes, at her sister's house about four miles away. She would sleep at Willowdown when Mr Tizard was not spending the night there. He was away quite often, and kept her informed when he would not be there. If she slept at her sister's, Mrs Tizard would drive over early in the morning, give the children breakfast and get them ready for school, and then make herself ready to go to work at 9 am. She returned to give the children and herself an evening meal. She would leave if Mr Tizard returned in the evening, but stay the night, sleeping in the spare bedroom, if he was not there. Sometimes he was away for several nights, occasionally even weeks. Mrs Tizard formed a relationship with a Mr Mead; and, instead of going to her sister's when she was not sleeping at Willowdown, Mrs Tizard began to go to Mr Mead's cottage, which was also not far away. Most of her wardrobe she kept at Willowdown: her clothes were in three of the four wardrobe compartments in the master bedroom. Her toiletries, her dressing gown, her nightwear and so forth were also at Willowdown. These arrangements I find continued until mid-1983 when Mrs Tizard found a note from Mr Tizard saying that he was going on holiday abroad with the boy twin. Neither he nor the boy has returned.

I find that Mrs Tizard contributed substantially to the successive property ventures by putting up money for the first deposit, by contributing through her earnings which went into the common pool out of which mortgage instalments and building costs were paid, and by her labour. No accounts were kept of the spouses' respective contributions whether in money or in labour either before or after they were married. I find that they contributed substantially equally. Mrs Tizard is entitled to half of the equity.

Furthermore, I find that Mrs Tizard remained at all material times in occupation of Willowdown House. Mr Tizard, the owner of the legal estate, was in occupation until he departed for America in about June 1983. That circumstance does not however prevent Mrs Tizard also being in occupation.

In *Williams & Glyn's Bank Ltd* v *Boland*; *Williams & Glyn's Bank Ltd* v *Brown* [1980] 2 All ER 408, [1981] AC 487 in each case the matrimonial home was registered land, the husband was the registered proprietor, the spouses lived together in the matrimonial home and the wife had an equitable interest by reason of having contributed a substantial sum to the purchase price. The House of Lords held that in each case the wife was a 'person in actual occupation' within s 70(1)(*g*) of the Land Registration Act 1925 so that her interest was protected. Although there the land was registered and here it is not, the decision illuminates the manner in which the presence of a wife in the matrimonial home is to be regarded. Lord Wilberforce says ([1980] 2 All ER 408 at 413–414, [1981] AC 487 at 505–506):

> Then, were the wives in actual occupation? I ask: why not? There was physical presence, with all the rights that occupiers have, including the right to exclude all others except those having similar rights. The house was a matrimonial home, intended to be occupied, and in fact occupied, by both spouses, both of whom have an interest in it; it would require some special doctrine of law to avoid the result that each is in occupation. Three arguments were used for a

> contrary conclusion. First, it was said that if the vendor (I use this word to include a mortgagor) is in occupation, that is enough to prevent the application of the paragraph. This seems to be a proposition of general application, not limited to the case of husbands, and no doubt, if correct, would be very convenient for purchasers and intending mortgagees. But the presence of the vendor, with occupation, does not exclude the possibility of occupation of others. There are observations which suggest the contrary in the unregistered land case of *Caunce* v *Caunce* [1969] 1 All ER 722, [1969] 1 WLR 286, but I agree with the disapproval of these and with the assertion of the proposition I have just stated by Russell LJ in *Hodgson* v *Marks* [1971] 2 All ER 684 at 690, [1971] Ch 892 at 934–935. Then it was suggested that the wife's "occupation" was nothing but the shadow of the husband's, a version I suppose of the doctrine of unity of husband and wife. This expression and the argument flowing from it was used by Templeman J in *Bird* v *Syme Thomson* [1978] 3 All 1027 at 1030, [1979] 1 WLR 440 at 444, a decision preceding and which he followed in the present case. The argument was also inherent in the judgment in *Caunce* v *Caunce* which influenced the decisions of Templeman J. It somewhat faded from the arguments in the present case and appears to me to be heavily obsolete. The appellants' main and final position became in the end this: that, to come within the paragraph, the occupation in question must be apparently inconsistent with the title of the vendor. This, it was suggested, would exclude the wife of a husband-vendor because her apparent occupation would be satisfactorily accounted for by his. But, apart from the rewriting of the paragraph which this would involve, the suggestion is unacceptable. Consistency, or inconsistency, involves the absence, or presence, of an independent right to occupy, though I must observe that "inconsistency" in this context is an inappropriate word. But how can either quality be predicated of a wife, simply *qua* wife? A wife may, and everyone knows this, have rights of her own; particularly, many wives have a share in a matrimonial home. How can it be said that the presence of a wife in the house, as occupier, is consistent or inconsistent with the husband's rights until one knows what rights she has? And if she has rights, why, just because she is a wife (or in the converse case, just because an occupier is the husband), should these rights be denied protection under the paragraph? If one looks beyond the case of husband and wife, the difficulty of all these arguments stands out if one considers the case of a man living with a mistress, or of a man and a woman (or for that matter two persons of the same sex) living in a house in separate or partially shared rooms. Are these cases of apparently consistent occupation, so that the rights of the other person (other than the vendor) can be disregarded? The only solution which is consistent with the Act (s 70(1)(*g*)) and with common sense is to read the paragraph for what it says. Occupation, existing as a fact, may protect rights if the person in occupation has rights. On this part of the case I have no difficulty in concluding that a spouse, living in a house, has an actual occupation capable of conferring protection, as an overriding interest, on rights of that spouse.

Mrs Tizard was, in my judgment, in occupation of Willowdown notwithstanding that Mr Tizard was living there also; and notwithstanding the fact that on numerous occasions she slept elsewhere. The 'physical presence' to which Lord Wilberforce refers does not connote continuous and uninterrupted presence; such a notion would be absurd. Nor, indeed, do I consider that the requisite 'presence' is negatived by regular and repeated absence. I find that Mrs Tizard was in Willowdown virtually every day for some part of the day, her life and activities were based on her presence, interrupted though it was, in Willowdown: there she prepared herself for work, there she cared for her children, there she looked after the house and the concerns of herself and the children, and she went in the morning and returned in the evening to discharge her duties as housewife and mother. It is clear that, prior to the time, November 1982, when she ceased always to sleep in the house when her husband was there, she had been in occupation; and, in my judgment, she did not cease to be in occupation simply because she made that change in her habits, significant though the change was.

Willowdown, however, is not registered land. If it were, my findings that Mrs Tizard had equitable rights in the house and was at the material time in occupation would protect those rights against the mortgagee by reason of s 70(1)(*g*) of the Land Registration Act 1925. Do these two matters bring about the like result where the land is not registered?

Counsel for the plaintiffs submits that, although in the case of registered land the fact of occupation confers protection, in the case of unregistered land it is not enough that the claimant is in occupation: she must be found to be in occupation by the purchaser or mortgagee, or, at any rate, the circumstances must be such that she would have been found had proper inspections, inquiries and searches been made.

Before I deal with that submission, I must consider what searches, inquiries and inspections were made. The plaintiffs had an association with mortgage brokers called Ian Bradshaw Financial Consultants (I will call them 'Bradshaws'). Mr Tizard went to Bradshaws.

On 12 March 1983 Mr Tizard signed a document which was a typed form intended to be completed by the insertion of what in the typescript is stated to be 'Client's Name' and 'Address' and by inserting figures in the spaces designated 'Gross Advance', 'Brokerage and Service Charges' or otherwise (none of the other indicated deductions have any figures inserted) and ending 'Your Net Cheque'. Mr Tizard's name and address were inserted, the gross advance was shown to be £66 000, the brokerage and service charges £1240 and 'Your Net Cheque' £64 760. The name and address of the client is followed by, and the particulars of the advance and deduction preceded by, the words 'We are pleased to present our offer on your loan application, the breakdown of which is as follows'. The form ends with a portion headed 'Client's Acceptance' and containing the words 'I fully understand the deductions listed above. Please accept this statement as my irrevocable authority for the lender's solicitors to remit direct to the parties concerned. Thank you for arranging this'. The typescript continues by indicating where the date should be inserted and where husband and wife should sign and contains the words '(Both Husband and Wife to sign)'. The only signature is that of Mr Tizard. The space for a wife's signature is left blank. The date inserted is 12 March 1983. The brokers, whose fee was to be £1240, were Bradshaws. They instructed a chartered surveyor, Mr Marshall, to carry out an inspection. He did so on 13 March 1983 and made a report dated 15 March. Counsel for the plaintiffs accepts that Mr Marshall must be treated as the agent of the plaintiffs. If he were not, then the plaintiffs would not have inspected the property at all and could not rely, as the plaintiffs do, on what Mr Marshall did not find. After receiving Mr Marshall's report the plaintiffs wrote to him asking him to confirm that his report could be taken as addressed to the plaintiffs, and Mr Marshall confirmed that it could.

As well as the document I have mentioned, Mr Tizard signed another: a printed form of application to the plaintiffs for an advance of £66 000. The form is filled up so as to give various particulars about Mr Tizard and about the property. *Inter alia*, it states that he is 'single', the word 'married' being deleted. Although the marriage has now been dissolved it had not been at the time of the mortgage. This form of application is signed by Mr Tizard and the date inserted is 16 March 1983.

I find that the order of events was as follows: Mr Tizard applied to the brokers to arrange a loan; he signed the document dated 12 March 1983, which, because there was no signature by a wife, indicated that no wife was concerned; Mr Marshall inspected the property on 13 March 1983, a Sunday, shortly after lunch-time; his report dated 15 March 1983 was sent to the brokers; the brokers completed or (if it had already been otherwise completed, which I think is likely) dated the application dated 16 March which I have mentioned as being signed by Mr Tizard, and sent that with Mr Marshall's report to the plaintiffs, who on 21 March made an offer of loan in the sum of £66 000, forwarding it to the brokers; and on the following day Mr Tizard accepted that offer according to its terms by signing the acceptance, and also on 22 March Mr Marshall confirmed that his report could be treated as addressed to the plaintiffs.

When Mr Marshall inspected on Sunday, 13 March there was no one at the property except Mr Tizard. Mr Tizard showed him round and then he inspected the property inside and outside on his own. He found evidence of occupation by two teenagers, a boy and a girl, from clothes, posters etc that he found in their respective rooms; he saw male clothes in the main bedroom; he had an impression that the fourth bedroom seemed to be used for storage, there were suitcases in it, but he could not in evidence recollect whether it contained a bed, dressing table, and so on; and he found no evidence at all of occupation by a female, other than the teenage daughter. Mr Tizard, in apologising for the state of the house, said to Mr Marshall that his wife had gone many months ago, that they were separated and that she was living with someone nearby.

Mr Marshall's valuation report dated 15 March 1983 was made on a printed form headed with the logo and name of Bradshaws who had provided Mr Marshall with a supply of these forms. He took one with him to do the valuation and made rough notes on it. Afterwards he produced the dated report which is completed in typescript. It gives the address of the property, and Mr Tizard's name is typed in the space for the name of the applicant. The section titled 'Occupants' contains three questions: 'Who occupies the property?', 'Are there any tenancies known to you or apparent on inspection?', 'If Yes, Please give full details, including rentals.' The second question was answered 'No', so there is no answer to the third. In answer to the first question there is typed, rather suprisingly in upper case (save for names and addresses, the remainder of the typescript uses upper and lower case in a normal way), the words 'APPLICANT, SON AND DAUGHTER'.

I was referred to the passage in 1 Halsbury's Laws (4th edn) para 833, where it states:

> Where in the course of any transaction in which he is employed on his principal's behalf, an agent receives notice or acquires knowledge of any fact material to such transaction, under such circumstances that it is his duty to communicate it to the principal, the principal is precluded, as regards the persons who are parties to such transaction, from relying upon his own ignorance of that fact, and is taken to have received notice of it from the agent at the time when he should have received it, if the agent had performed his duty with due diligence . . .

Counsel for Mrs Tizard submits that as the agent was informed that Mr Tizard was married and his wife was living nearby the fact that Mr Tizard described himself as single in his application should have put the plaintiffs on inquiry, and that in due course the plaintiffs would have discovered Mrs Tizard's occupation and thus have had notice of her rights.

To that counsel for the plaintiffs replies that the application in which Mr Tizard describes himself as single was not made until after Mr Marshall's inspection and, accordingly, that in the absence of knowledge that Mr Tizard was misdescribing his marital status there was no duty on Mr Marshall to inform his principal of what Mr Tizard told him of his marriage and his separation from his wife.

In my judgment, the fact that Mr Tizard was married was a fact material to the transaction. Was Mr Marshall under a duty to communicate it to his principal? At the time when he learned this fact, Mr Marshall did not even know who his principal was: he only learned that when he received the letter from the plaintiffs dated 21 March, but he did know that he was making a report to what the printed valuation report describes as 'The lending principals of' Bradshaws; and I think that the reality was that Mr Marshall was the agent of the plaintiffs although he did not know their identity. The name of the plaintiffs was typed in Mr Marshall's report after the report had been made by him. What was Mr Marshall's duty? The valuation report is made on a printed form; Mr Marshall's duty was to inspect the property for the purpose of completing the form. Had the form contained a section with questions about the marital status of the applicant, his duty would have been to complete it to the best of the information he acquired. There was no such section. There is nothing in the evidence to suggest that Mr Marshall was given instructions to do other than complete the form. There is a final section on the form titled 'General Observations'; and Mr Marshall has made an observation in it about the basis of his valuation. Bearing in mind that the report is a valuation report, was Mr Marshall under a duty to communicate information that he might have acquired in the course of his inspection which, however material it might be to the loan transaction, was immaterial to the purely valuation aspect of it?

In his evidence Mr Marshall made it clear that he was suspicious; he was on the lookout for signs of female occupation: not the occupation of a wife, but that of a girlfriend. He found no such signs, but his evidence made it clear that he regarded it as his duty to look for them. He drew the line, however, at opening cupboards and drawers. Mr Marshall's understanding of his duty to look for signs of occupation by anyone else accords with mine. That being the scope of his duty, I consider that he should have enlarged on his answer to the question 'Who occupies the property?' The answer that he gave was, 'Applicant, son and daughter'. That was founded in part on his own observation, in part on what Mr Tizard told him. He should, in my view, have added either in the 'Occupation' or in the 'General Observations' section, 'Applicant states that he is separated from wife who lives nearby', or something to that effect.

My reason for that view is this. It is common ground that Mr Marshall was acting as the agent of the plaintiffs. He was not instructed by the plaintiffs. He was instructed by Bradshaws. Before Mr Marshall inspected the property, Bradshaws had the document dated 12 March 1983 which Mr Tizard signed. What Mr Tizard told Bradshaws about his marital status at that stage can be inferred from what he told them later when he signed the plaintiffs' form, namely that he was 'single'. In a document which gives only one alternative to 'single', namely 'married', 'single' must signify either bachelor or spinster, as the case may be, or a widow or widower, or a person whose marriage has been dissolved. It cannot mean 'married but separated'. As Bradshaws were instructing Mr Marshall to make an inspection on behalf of the plaintiffs, they were acting as the plaintiffs' agents for that purpose. The fact that Mr Marshall was looking for evidence of the occupation of a female cohabitee, coupled with what I infer from the two documents signed by Mr Tizard was Bradshaws' understanding of Mr Tizard's marital status, implies that Mr Marshall approached his inspection on the footing that Mr Tizard was not married. When it appeared that he was, I consider that he had a duty to communicate this new information to his principals.

It follows in my judgment that the knowledge of the agent, Mr Marshall, that Mr Tizard had a wife is to be taken to be the knowledge of the principal, the plaintiffs.

The plaintiffs received Mr Tizard's application in which he described himself as single; and received Mr Marshall's report in which there was mention of a son and daughter. The application mentioned two 'Children or other dependants' who were stated to be both aged 15. The application had a space in which there fell to be inserted 'Age of spouse next birthday'. It was left blank. It also contained spaces for insertion of the spouse's name, and the name and address of the spouse's employers; and in these spaces there appeared 'N/A', not applicable. The application left it in doubt whether the two 15-year-old dependants were children or others, but Mr Marshall's report made it clear that they were the son and daughter of the applicant.

Had Mr Marshall's report indicated Mr Tizard was married, it seems to me to be clear that, bearing in mind that the application stated over Mr Tizard's signature that he was single, the plaintiffs would have been put on notice that further investigation was required. Indeed, even if I am wrong in my view that Mr Marshall should have reported what Mr Tizard said about his wife, the reference to 'Son and Daughter' in the report should have alerted the plaintiffs to the need to make further inquiries.

Primarily, the plaintiffs are to be taken to have been aware that Mr Tizard was married and had described himself as single; in these circumstances their further inquiries should have led them to Mrs Tizard.

Section 199(1) of the Law of Property Act 1925 provides:

> A purchaser shall not be prejudicially affected by notice of – (i) any instrument or matter capable of registration under the provisions of the Land Charges Act, 1925, or any enactment which it replaces, which is void or not enforceable as against him under that Act or enactment, by reason of the non-registration thereof; (ii) any other instrument or matter or any fact or thing unless – (*a*) it is within his own knowledge, or would have come to his knowledge if such inquiries and inspections had been made as ought reasonably to have been made by him; or (*b*) in the same transaction with respect to which a question of notice to the purchaser arises, it has come to the knowledge of his counsel, as such, or of his solicitor or other agent, as such, or would have come to the knowledge of his solicitor or other agent, as such, if such inquiries and inspections had been made as ought reasonably to have been made by the solicitor or other agent.

'Purchaser' in that provision, as is provided by s 205(1)(xxi) of the Act, includes mortgagee.

Although a spouse's statutory rights of occupation under s 1 of the Matrimonial Homes Act 1983 and the statutory provisions replaced by that Act are capable of protection by registration of a class F land charge, the equitable interest of such a spouse in the matrimonial home is not capable of being so protected. The plaintiffs were prejudicially affected by the knowledge of their agent, Mr Marshall, that Mr Tizard, contrary to what he had said in his application, was married (see the 1925 Act, s 199(1)(ii)(*b*)). That put them on notice that further inquiries were necessary; the inquiries which in these circumstances ought reasonably to have been made by the plaintiffs would, in my judgment, have been such as to have apprised them of the fact that Mrs Tizard claimed a beneficial interest in the property; and, accordingly, they would have had notice of such equitable rights as she had and the morgage in these circumstances takes effect subject to these rights (see the 1925 Act, s 199(1)(ii)(*a*)).

I arrive at that conclusion without having considered the question: does the occupation of Mrs Tizard affect the mortgagees with notice of her rights, or are they only so affected if, as counsel for the plaintiffs submits, they were aware of her occupation, that is if they found her in occupation?

On the balance of probabilities, I find that the reason Mr Marshall did not find Mrs Tizard in the house was that Mr Tizard had arranged matters to achieve that result. He told Mrs Tizard that on a particular Sunday, and I find in fact that it was the Sunday that Mr Marshall did inspect, he was going to entertain friends to lunch and would she take the children out for the day. She did; and having regard to the manner in which I find that the signs of her occupation were temporarily eliminated by Mr Tizard, the reasonable inference is that he made this request so that Mr Marshall could inspect and find no evidence of Mrs Tizard's occupation.

In *Caunce* v *Caunce* [1969] 1 All ER 722, [1969] 1 WLR 286 Stamp J held that where a wife who had an equitable interest in a property being mortgaged to the bank by her husband was resident with him in the property, that circumstance did not result in the bank taking the property fixed with notice of her rights because, finding her in occupation, the bank made no inquiry of her. Stamp J said ([1969] 1 All ER 722 at 728, [1969] 1 WLR 286 at 293):

> Here it is said that the wife was in possession or occupation. No enquiry was made of her and, therefore, the bank is fixed with notice of her equitable interest. In my judgment it is here that the fallacy arises for the wife in this case, unlike the deserted wife, was not in apparent occupation or possession. She was there ostensibly because she was the husband's wife and her presence there was wholly consistent with the title offered by the husband to the bank.

In *Williams & Glyn's Bank Ltd* v *Boland* [1980] 2 All ER 408 at 413, [1981] AC 487 at 505 Lord Wilberforce said, in a passage which I have already read: 'But the presence of the vendor, with occupation, does not exclude the possibility of occupation of others', but he went on to note the observations suggesting the contrary in *Caunce* v *Caunce* and agreeing with the disapproval of those expressed by Russell LJ in *Hodgson* v *Marks* [1971] 2 All ER 684 at 690, [1971] Ch 892 at 934–935. In the latter case of *Hodgson* v *Marks* Russell LJ said:

> I would only add that I do not consider it necessary to this decision to pronounce on the decision in *Caunce* v *Caunce*. In that case the occupation of the wife may have been rightly taken to be not her occupation but that of her husband. Insofar, however, as some phrases in the judgment might appear to lay down a general proposition that enquiry need not be made of any person on the premises if the proposed vendor himself appears to be in occupation, I would not accept them.

I have already stated my finding that the wife was in occupation. In the circumstances in which she was, I find that her occupation was not that of her husband. Guided by the high authority of the two passages I have just cited (i.e. from *Williams & Glyn's Bank Ltd* v *Boland* per Lord Wilberforce and *Hodgson* v *Marks* per Russell LJ) I conclude that, had Mrs Tizard been found to be in occupation by the plaintiffs or their agents and so found in the context of what had been said by Mr Tizard to Mr Marshall and stated or implied in the forms he had signed, they, the plaintiffs would clearly have either learned of her rights by inquiry of her or been fixed with notice of those rights had not inquiry of her been made.

In the light of my finding that Mr Marshall's information about Mr Tizard's wife is to be imputed to the plaintiffs and my conclusion that further inquiries should have been made by the plaintiffs because of that imputed knowledge, do I ask myself whether such an inspection as would have disclosed that Mrs Tizard was in the premises is one which ought reasonably to have been made by them, or is the proper question: can the plaintiffs show that no such inspection was reasonably necessary? The latter appears to me to be the proper way to put it. The plaintiffs did not make any further inquiries or inspections: had they done so it would have been open to them to contend that they had done all that was reasonably required and, if they still had no knowledge of Mrs Tizard's rights or claims, that they were not fixed with notice of them. But, in the absence of further inquiries or inspections, I do not think that it is open to the plaintiffs to say that if they had made a further inspection they would still not have found Mrs Tizard in occupation.

I would put it briefly thus. Mr Tizard appears to have been minded to conceal the true facts; he did not do so completely; the plaintiffs had, or are to be taken to have had, information which should have alerted them to the fact that the full facts were not in their possession and that they should make further inspections or inquiries; they did not do so; and in these circumstances I find that they are fixed with notice of the equitable interest of Mrs Tizard.

I return to the submissions made by counsel for Mrs Tizard and counsel for the plaintiffs. The submission of counsel for Mrs Tizard is that, as Mrs Tizard was in fact in occupation, that circumstance itself fixed the plaintiffs with notice of such rights as she had. To the contrary is the submission made by counsel for the plaintiffs that in the case of unregistered land it is only where the purchaser or mortgagee finds the claimant to an equitable interest in occupation that he has notice.

I accept the submission of counsel for the plaintiffs but subject to a significant qualification: if the purchaser or mortgagee carries out such inspections as ought reasonably to be made and does not either find the claimant in occupation or find evidence of that occupation reasonably sufficient to give notice of the occupation, then I am not persuaded that the purchaser or mortgagee is in such circumstances (and in the absence, which is not the case here, of other circumstances) fixed with notice of the claimant's rights. One of the circumstances, however, is that such inspection is carried out as ought reasonably to be made.

Here Mr Marshall carried out his inspection on a Sunday afternoon at a time arranged with Mr Tizard. If the only purpose of such an inspection were to ascertain the physical state of the property, the time at which the inspection is made and whether or not that time is one agreed in advance with the vendor or mortgagor appears to me to be immaterial. Where, however, the object of the inspection (or one of the objects) is to ascertain who is in occupation, I cannot see that an inspection at a time pre-arranged with the vendor will necessarily attain that object. Such a pre-arranged inspection may achieve no more than an inquiry of the vendor or mortgagor and his answer to it. In the case of residential property an appointment for inspection will, in most cases, be essential so far as inspection of the interior is concerned. How then is a purchaser or mortgagee to carry out such inspection as ought reasonably to have been made for the purpose of determining whether the possession and occupation of the property accords with the title offered? What is such an inspection as ought reasonably be made must, I think, depend on all the circumstances. In the circumstances of the present case I am not satisfied that the pre-arranged inspection on a Sunday afternoon fell within the category of 'such . . . inspections . . . as ought reasonably to have been made', the words in the Law of Property Act 1925, s 199(1)(ii), which I have already read. The plaintiffs not having established that they made such an inspection, the conclusion that I have reached by another route is, in my view, fortified.

It follows that the plaintiffs' claim for possession fails.

There was an alternative claim under s 30 of the Law of Property Act 1925 for an order for sale under that section. The parties are agreed that I need not deal with that alternative claim because both parties wish that the property should be sold and are further agreed that sale should be postponed until the spring of 1986. I have not been presented with any formulation of the agreed terms, so I will now hear counsel on the form of order which is required.

Claim for possession dismissed.

Extract reproduced by permission of the All England Law Reports

QUESTIONS

1 In *Caunce* v *Caunce* [1969] 1 All ER 722, referred to in *Kingsnorth Trust Ltd* v *Tizard*, Stamp J said:

> 'Here it is said that the wife was in possession or occupation. No enquiry was made of her and therefore the bank is fixed with notice of her equitable interest. In my judgment it is here that the fallacy arises for the wife in this case, unlike the deserted wife, was not in occupation or possession. She was there ostensibly because she was the husband's wife and her presence there was wholly consistent with the title offered by the husband to the bank.'

(*a*) Why is the equitable interest of the wife in *Tizard* not registrable as a land charge?

(*b*) Consider the attitudes to the status of women which might have influenced the judge in *Tizard* in his more liberal view of constructive notice than that which prevailed in *Caunce*.

2 What difficulties might follow as a result of charges being registered against names rather than against the land under the Land Charges Act 1972?

3 What is meant by 'money or money's worth' in the Land Charges Act 1972 s 4(6)?

4 What is the modern role of the doctrines of actual and constructive notice?

CHAPTER 18

REGISTRATION OF TITLE

INTRODUCTION

In Chapter 2 an elementary account was given of the way in which land has been conveyed in this country for several centuries. The vendor's aim has been to produce documentary evidence of past transactions over such a period of time as to raise the overwhelming inference that he owns the estate which the purchaser wishes to buy. Besides being satisfied as to the vendor's title to the land, the purchaser will also wish to know what rights exist in it in favour of third parties or the general public. This he will establish by inspecting the documents of title referred to above, by making searches in the Land Charges Register and the local land charges register, by making enquiries of the vendor and by a physical inspection of the land.

Some of the weaknesses of the system were mentioned, but outstanding amongst them is the wastefulness of making separate investigations of title on each successive occasion when the land is sold. Thus, I might take a conveyance of 'Blackacre' today in 1996 having investigated the title back to, say, 1975. If I sell the land tomorrow, the purchaser will repeat this investigation over more or less the same period of time.

The main purpose behind the introduction of registration of title is to make this repetitive work unnecessary. This is achieved by making one final proof of the title to the satisfaction of the Chief Land Registrar, who then records the title in a register in the name of the proprietor. Thereafter the register constitutes the sole proof of that title, which is guaranteed by the state. Many third-party rights may also be protected by entries in the register, so that once a title is registered the Land Charges Register has no longer any part to play in relation to it. Not all such third-party or public rights can, however, be entered in the register so that enquiries and inspections still must be made. Furthermore, searches must still be made in the local land charges register. To this extent the new system falls short of any ideal that the register should be a perfect mirror to a title. This failure to give an exhaustive record of rights in or over the land is partly due to the very nature of land enjoyment. As to proposals for improvements to the system, see Law Com No 158.

The system of registered conveyancing does not affect the pattern of estates and interests which can exist in land (see *Murray* v *Two Strokes Ltd* [1973] 3 All ER 357). Similarly, the rules as to trusts for sale, strict settlements, co-ownership and so on, remain the same as in the case of unregistered title. It is simply that the ways in which title to these estates and interests are proved, the way in which they are transferred and the way in which third party rights are protected are altered. As to this last factor, we shall see that the different means of protection in the two systems can occasionally result in an interest being better protected under one system than under the other. In the course of time, procedural rules can create substantive law, as our medieval writ system showed. Perhaps this might be so with registered land in the future.

The registered system was extended to particular districts incrementally after 1925 by Orders in Council. The Registration of Title Order 1989 completed the process so that all land is now subject to the system. Even so the obligation to register title only arises on the first sale of the fee simple, or upon the first creation or assignment of a leasehold term of 40 years or more. Once a title is registered, all subsequent dealings with the estate are carried out under the system.

The Land Registry has its headquarters at Lincoln's Inn Fields in London, but 19 district registries carry out the duties of registration in their own areas. The chief officer is called the Chief Land Registrar. The law concerning registration of title is contained in the Land Registration Acts 1925–86 and in the Rules made thereunder. The legislation, though somewhat imperfect, has not been greatly litigated.

The order in which the various topics will be discussed is as follows: the register and its contents, the procedure of registration, the transfer of interests after registration of title and the guarantee of the title. References to sections in this chapter will be to sections of the Land Registration Act 1925, unless otherwise stated.

THE REGISTER AND ITS CONTENTS

In this part, three matters must be discussed. First, there is the classification of interests in land drawn by the Act which govern whether an interest may be protected by registration, and, if so, how. Second, there is the way in which the register is structured so as to accommodate the various registrable interests. Third, there is the marriage of the two matters mentioned above, namely, the way in which registrable interests are protected by the register.

Classification of interests

The classification of interests drawn by the Act is threefold.

The legal estate

There are only two principal interests which may be registered in the sense that new sections of the register may be opened up for them, and these are the two legal estates (s 2). A fee simple absolute in possession may therefore be registered. So may certain terms of years absolute, but in this case only provided that more than 21 years are unexpired, that there is no absolute prohibition against assignment and that they are not merely mortgage terms subject to a right of redemption (s 8). Certain legal rentcharges are capable of substantive registration. We shall see below that many other interests are capable of registration in the sense of being entered on the register which has already been opened for these legal estates, but they cannot be registered independently if the legal estate is not registered. The legal estate, therefore, is the germ cell of registration and all other registrable interests are merely registered against it. These other interests are like apples hanging from a tree. The registered legal estate is the tree itself. No tree, no apples. In other words, if there is no legal estate registered other interests must look for their protection under the unregistered system.

Since more than one legal estate may exist in the same land, as where the fee simple is subject to a lease, and perhaps even a sublease, then several separate registered titles and, therefore, independent sections of the register, may exist in respect of the same land. Such separate sections may however allude to each other by cross-references on the register.

Minor interests

If a legal estate is registered, then certain third-party rights affecting the property may be entered upon that register against it. These are called minor interests. Although their definition in s 3 is oblique, they are identifiable as follows. We saw above that the legal estate is, with some exceptions, independently registrable and in this case the act of registration is the source of its protection. Below we shall find that certain interests listed by the Act are fully effective without being entered on the register, even though the legal estate which they affect is registered. Because of this characteristic, these are called *overriding interests*. All other interests – the residue left by these two classifications – are minor interests and require entry on the register for their protection. The symmetry of this threefold classification is, however, slightly marred by the fact that certain rights which are expressly rendered capable of registration such as matters which would, in the case of unregistered land, be protected under the Land Charges Act 1972 (see s 59), are also capable of being overriding interests. The classification attempted by the Act is thus imperfect since two of the categories are not mutually exclusive. The manner in which they are so entered and the nature of their protection will be discussed later.

Examples of minor interests are equitable interests such as life interests arising under strict settlements and trusts for sale and restrictive covenants. They must possess the true characteristics of interests in land, as opposed to merely personal rights, for the Act does not extend the area of rights in respect of which protection against third parties would be afforded under the unregistered system (see *Murray* v *Two Strokes Ltd* [1973] 3 All ER 357). The hallmark of these interests, however, is not their equitable nature. Generally they are characterised by not being readily discoverable from an inspection of the land, but their true identity stems from their residuary nature.

Overriding interests (ss 3, 70)

These are interests which bind a registered proprietor or his alienee irrespective of registration and irrespective of notice. They can, however, appear on the register and then they cease to be overriding interests and take their protection from the register. They are listed in s 70. The principal ones are as follows:

1 rights of common; drainage rights; customary rights (until extinguished); public rights; *profits à prendre*; rights of sheep-walk; rights of way; watercourses; rights of water, and other easements not being equitable easements required to be protected by notice on the register;

2 liability to repair highways by reason of tenure; quit-rents; crown rents; heriots, and other rents and charges (until extinguished) having their origin in tenure;

3 liability to repair the chancel of any church;

4 liability in respect of embankments, and sea and river walls;

5 [extinguished effect];

6 subject to the provisions of the Act, rights acquired or in course of being acquired under the Limitation Acts;

7 the rights of every person in actual occupation of the land or in receipt of the rents and profits thereof, save where enquiry is made of such person and the rights are not disclosed. This category will be discussed shortly;

8 in the case of a possessory, qualified, or good leasehold title; all estates, rights, interests, and powers excepted from the effect of registration. The nature of these titles is explained below;

9 rights under local land charges unless and until registered or protected on the register in the prescribed manner;

10 rights of fishing and sporting; seignorial and manorial rights of all descriptions (until extinguished), and franchises;

11 leases for any term or interest not exceeding 21 years, granted at a rent without taking a fine. A 'grant' is not constituted by an agreement to grant a lease (*City Permanent BS* v *Miller* [1952] Ch 840). If possession is taken under the agreement however, an overriding interest will occur under 7 above.

The list of overriding interests has been added to by subsequent Acts, such as rights in respect of coal vested in the National Coal Board by the Coal Act 1938 s 41.

The rights under 7 were widely drawn so as to protect persons who in terms of ordinary justice deserve protection, but whose interests are either inappropriate for registration or, if appropriate, are often informally created and thus unlikely to be registered by unsuspecting laymen. This policy led to the overlapping of categories mentioned above. It has been by far the most controversial of all the classes of overriding interests and has been subject to judicial decisions which have far-reaching consequences in the fields of both conveyancing and land enjoyment. The following elements of the provision call for some discussion: the nature of the *rights*, *actual occupation* and *inquiry*.

To ascertain what *rights* come within this provision we must have regard to the general law of land, irrespective of the Act, for the enactment does not augment but merely protects rights for what they are. Rights of a merely personal character do not, therefore, rise above their ordinary station merely because they occur where title is registered. Thus the right of a deserted wife against her husband to live in the matrimonial home is not an overriding interest, even though she is in occupation of the property, for to qualify as an overriding interest the right must be 'capable of enduring through different ownerships of the land according to normal conceptions of title to real property' (*National Provincial Bank Ltd* v *Ainsworth* [1965] AC 1175). We shall see, however, that such a right is a minor interest and may be protected by a notice.

The provision does not apply to rights of persons in occupation of land under a strict settlement, because they are designated exclusively minor interests under the Act (s 86(2)). Whether the interests of persons enjoying occupation under an express trust for sale are overriding interests is not so clear (see 22 Conv 24 and 33 Conv 254). Equitable as well as legal interests are included, so that persons in occupation under agreements for leases or options to purchase the freehold granted to a lessee in occupation are protected, even though they are capable of registration by entry on the register but have not been so registered (*Webb* v *Pollmount Ltd* [1966] Ch 584; and see *London and Cheshire Insurance Co Ltd* v *Laplagrene Property Co Ltd* [1971] 2 WLR 257).

The meaning of *actual occupation* has been the subject of two major judicial decisions. In *Hodgson* v *Marks* [1971] 2 All ER 684, *H*, a widow voluntarily conveyed her house to her lodger, *E*, on the oral understanding that though it was to be registered in his name for the purpose of his management of her affairs it was to be held upon trust for her. Both parties continued to live, sleep and eat in the house after the transfer in exactly the same way as before it. The financial arrangements for *E*'s board remained unchanged. *E* later sold the house to *M* without the knowledge of *H*. *M* mortgaged it to a building society. After

E's death, the question arose whether *H*'s rights enjoyed protection under s 70(1)(g). The Court of Appeal held that her interest was protected because she was in 'actual occupation' of the house. Such occupation was a matter of physical presence.

In *Williams and Glyn's Bank Ltd* v *Boland* [1980] 2 All ER 408, *H* was the sole registered proprietor of the home where he and his wife *W* lived. However, *W* was a part-owner in equity but had not protected her interest by any entry on the register. *H*, without *W*'s knowledge, mortgaged the house to the bank for a loan for business purposes. The bank made no inquiry as to *W*'s interest or even as to her existence. The bank later sought to enforce the loan and the question was whether *W*'s interest was an overriding one against them. This depended upon whether she was in 'actual occupation'. The House of Lords held that she was. Lord Wilberforce said:

> These words are ordinary words of plain English, and should in my opinion be interpreted as such . . . Given occupation, i.e. presence on the land, I do not think that the word "actual" was intended to introduce any additional qualification, certainly not to suggest that possession must be "adverse".
>
> (at p 412)

The criterion of physical presence, emphasised in *Hodgson* v *Marks* was confirmed. The question is one of fact not law. *Actual occupation* is not necessarily confined to one person. The expression is to be read in the context of the Act and meanings attached to 'occupation' in other Acts are not to be imported. Although occupation will usually produce visible signs, it is important to banish any trace of the doctrine of notice from the test we are discussing. That principle belongs exclusively to the unregistered system. In *Abbey National Building Society* v *Cann* [1990] 1 All ER 1085 the House of Lords held that 'actual occupation' implied 'some degree of permanence and continuity which would rule out mere fleeting presence'. Moving furniture into property by courtesy of the mortgagee prior to completion of the transaction was therefore insufficient.

Problems of construction of words are commonplace in law. The significance of the decision in *Boland* is that the House of Lords chose to prefer the interests of occupiers against those of banks, building societies and conveyancing solicitors in a field of considerable economic activity. There is nothing in the judgments which limits the decision to matrimonial homes however. The decision is thus of social importance because of the quantity of transactions it will influence.

Finally, a purchaser can take free of an otherwise overriding interest if he makes 'enquiry' and the interest is not disclosed or, of course, if the occupant agrees to the priority of the purchaser's interest. Such enquiry will only have this effect however if it is addressed to the person who owns the interest in question (see *Hodgson* v *Marks*, above). This requirement presents the principal difficulty for the purchaser, the lender and the conveyancer – the potential difficulty of discovering all the appropriate persons to whom to put enquires. The relevant date for 'actual occupation' is the date of completion of the purchase, not registration (see generally *Abbey National Building Society* v *Cann*, discussed above).

Overriding interests thus present an obstacle in conveyancing. In 1987 the Law Commission made recommendations which suggested a rebalancing of the interests of the occupier and the purchaser and some curtailment of the extent of overriding interests (Law Com No 158).

The structure of the register

The register is in three parts: the property register, the proprietorship register and the charges register. The document of title which the registered proprietor is given, known as a *land certificate*, is simply a copy of these three parts of the register relating to his land. His true proof of title, however, is the register itself and not the certificate. The register is kept on a card index system; each title is identified by title number and has a separate card. The three parts of the register concerning a particular property title all appear on that card. The Land Registration Act 1988 opened the register to public inspection. It is also possible to discover without such permission whether a particular property is registered or whether application for registration has been made in respect of it. This can be done by an appropriate search of the Index Map and Parcels Index which will not reveal the name of the owner, merely whether the land is registered or registration is pending. A prospective purchaser or chargee will clearly wish to ascertain this as a safeguard against fraud. A vendor might, for instance, represent the land as being unregistered, when it is in fact registered, in order to conceal incumbrances.

The contents of the three parts are as follows.

1 *The property register*. This describes the land and the estate for which it is held by reference to a plan or map. It also contains notes of interests, such as easements, or even covenants which exist in favour of the registered land. It may also record its freedom from the burden of certain interests such as easements. Noting of such appurtenant rights upon the register is, however, at the option of the Chief Land Registrar. The Registrar has a duty however to enter a note on first registration of any rights created by an instrument on the title which adversely affect the land (s 70(2)).

2 *The proprietorship register*. This part of the register contains the name and address of the proprietor, the nature of the title registered – that is, whether it is absolute, good leasehold, qualified or possessory – and any cautions, inhibitions and restrictions affecting the proprietor's right to deal with the estate. These matters are dealt with below.

3 *The charges register*. This contains incumbrances running against the registered land such as mortgages and restrictive covenants. Below are

fictitious examples of a land certificate and the appropriate entries on the register which are attached to it.

How registrable interests are protected by the register

We have seen that of the three classes of interests, one class, that of overriding interests, binds a purchaser, even though normally the interests are not registered. One of the two remaining classes, the legal estate, which is the subject matter of registration, receives its protection from the act of registration. We must now discuss how the third class, that of minor interests, receives its protection.

Minor interests are protected in one of two ways according to their subject matter. Some are protected by entries on the proprietorship register, in which case dealing with the land is prevented altogether for a certain time, or is only permitted if carried out in a certain way which will protect the interest in question. This is achieved through the machinery of *restrictions*, *cautions* and *inhibitions*. Others are protected by the entry of a notice on the charges register. This does not prevent dealing with the estate but fixes the world with notice of the incumbrance, so that if the incumbrance is otherwise valid, alienees of the property will take subject to it. Notices perform, therefore, the same function as registration of charges under the Land Charges Act 1972, in respect of unregistered land. The cases to which these two methods apply must now be considered.

A restriction is entered on the proprietorship register by or with the agreement of the registered proprietor, and prevents any transaction being carried out except according to the conditions or in the manner specified by the restriction (s 58). It is thus a voluntary or friendly entry and is appropriate in the case of strict settlements, express trusts for sale and co-ownership, where equitable interests arising under them require protection. A tenant for life under a strict settlement, for instance, will be the registered proprietor of the fee simple, but restrictions will be placed on the register first preventing the registration of any disposition *ultra vires* the Settled Land Act 1925, and second prohibiting any disposition involving capital money being registered unless the money is paid to the trustees. The demands of both Acts are thereby satisfied. The curtain principle is maintained, for the details of the trust are not entered on the register, and the invalidating effect of the Settled Land Act s 18 is reconciled with the confirmatory effects of registration of title.

HM LAND REGISTRY

TITLE NUMBER: XYZ123

Edition date: 29 March 1995

Entry No.	**A. PROPERTY REGISTER** containing the description of the registered land and the estate comprised in the Title
	COUNTY WEST MIDLANDS — DISTRICT SOLIHULL
1.	(4 September 1969) The Freehold land shown edged with red on the plan of the above Title filed at the Registry and being 98 WITHERED HEATH ROAD.
2.	The land has the benefit of the rights granted by but is subject as mentioned in the Transfer dated 1 July 1983 referred to in the Charges Register in the following terms:– "Together with and Subject to the rights of way drainage and other easements equivalent to those granted by and excepted from the Lease dated 28 September 1956." The following is a copy of the rights contained in the Lease referred to which is dated 28 September 1956 made between (1) Arden (Estates) Limited and (2) John Brendan Brown (Lessee) and which Lease is that referred to in the Charges Register:– "TOGETHER with the right to use the existing drains and services running to and from the property hereby demised into the street and the right if and when necessary with workmen and others to enter upon the adjoining property for the purpose of and to open cleanse and repair the said drains and services making good any damage occasioned thereby but subject to a similar right for the owners and occupiers of the adjoining property with regard to so much of the said drains and services as lie under the property hereby demised making good any damage occasioned thereby the Lessee and such owners and occupiers as aforesaid paying their due proportion of the cost of keeping the same in repair."
3.	The Transfer dated 1 July 1983 referred to above contains the following provision:– "IT IS HEREBY AGREED AND DECLARED as follows:– (1) That the Transferee shall not be entitled to any right or access of light and air over the adjoining land to the buildings erected or to be erected on the said land hereby transferred which would restrict or interfere with the use of such other adjoining land by the Transferor or any person deriving title under him for building or any other purpose. (2) That the Transferor shall be under no personal liability for either inserting or not inserting any grant lease or transfer or any part of his land comprised in title number ABC123 any covenant or restrictions similar to those herein contained or for not enforcing or attempting to enforce the performance or observance of any such covenants or restrictions or for releasing any grantee lessee or Purchaser or any part of his said land in the said title number ABC123 from any covenants or restrictions." NOTE: The land in this title with other land was formerly copyhold of the Manor of Knowle and the rights saves to the Lord by the 12th Schedule of the Law of Property Act 1922 are excepted from the registration.

HM LAND REGISTRY

TITLE NUMBER: XYZ123

Entry No	B. PROPRIETORSHIP REGISTER stating nature of the Title, name, address and description of the proprietor of the land and any entries affecting the right of disposing thereof TITLE ABSOLUTE
1.	(29 March 1995) Proprietor: Margaret Morley of 98 Withered Heath Road, Shirley, Solihull, W Midlands.

Entry No.	C.CHARGES REGISTER containing charges, incumbrances etc, adversely affecting the land and registered dwellings therewith
1.	Lease dated 28 September 1956 to John Brendon Brown for 99 years from 25 March 1956.
2.	A Transfer of the land in this title dated 1 July 1983 made between (1) Constance Helen Lee (Transferor) and (2) Peter Black and others (Transferee) contains covenants details of which are set out in the schedule of restrictive covenants hereto.
3.	(29 March 1995) REGISTERED CHARGE dated 28 February 1995 to secure the moneys including the further advances therein mentioned.
4.	(29 March 1995) Proprietor: PORTMAN BUILDING SOCIETY of Portman House, Richmond Hill, Bournemouth BH2 6EP.

Item No.	SCHEDULE OF RESTRICTIVE COVENANTS
1.	The following are details of the covenants contained in the Transfer dated 1 July 1983 referred to in the Charges Register:– "THE Transferees with the intent so as to bind the land hereby transferred and to benefit the remainder of the land comprised in title number ABC123 hereby jointly and severally for themselves and their successors in title covenant with the Transferor as follows:– a. At all times hereafter to observe and perform the covenants and restrictions and stipulations contained in the Charges Register of the said Title (so far as the same relate to and affect the property hereby transferred) and will indemnify and keep indemnified the Transferor from and against the non-observance and non-performance thereof and from all costs charges claims and demands in respect thereof b. Not to carry on or permit to be carried on upon the said premises any business trade process of manufacture whatsoever or use or permit the said premises to be used for any illegal or immoral purpose or for a Public House Inn Tavern or Beer shop or otherwise for the sale of wine malt liquors or spirituous liquors or do or suffer to be done thereon any act matter or thing

HM LAND REGISTRY

TITLE NUMBER: XYZ2123

Item No.	**SCHEDULE OF RESTRICTIVE COVENANTS (continued)**
	whatsoever which may be an annoyance or disturbance to the Transferor or her lessees or tenants or any person or persons for the time being owning or occupying any of the land adjacent to or in the neighbourhood of the land hereby transferred and not to use or permit the premises to be used for any other purpose than that of a private dwellinghouse only and (save with the previous consent in writing of the Transferor) for the occupation of the members of one family only c. Not to erect or set up or suffer to be erected or set up on any part of the said premises hereby transferred without the previous licence in writing of the Transferor any messuage or dwellinghouse or buildings other than and except the said messuage or dwellinghouse and except a garage and outbuildings to be occupied and used therewith and not to make any alteration in the plan site or elevation of such messuage or dwellinghouse without such licence as aforesaid d. That in case at any time there shall be occasioned to rebuild the said messuage or dwellinghouse and buildings or any part thereof to erect only a detached or semi-detached messuage or dwellinghouse at least two storeys in height with necessary and proper outbuildings thereto e. At all times hereafter to maintain good and substantial walls of fences on the side of the said premises hereby transferred where indicated by the Letter "T" within the boundary on the plan hereinbefore referred to f. To pay a reasonable proportion of the expense of repairing and maintaining any party walls sewers drains pipes watercourses and other easements used or to be used in common by the occupiers of the said premises hereby transferred and the occupiers of any adjoining or neighbouring premises such proportion in case of dispute to be determined by the Transferor's surveyor for the time being whose decision shall be final and binding upon all parties. NOTE: "T" marks affect the boundary of the land in this title.

***** END OF REGISTER *****

NOTE A: A date at the beginning of an entry is the date on which the entry was made in the Register.

NOTE B: This certificate was officially examined with the register on **29 March 1995**.

H.M. LAND REGISTRY			TITLE NUMBER	
			XYZ 123	
ORDNANCE SURVEY PLAN REFERENCE	COUNTY	SHEET	NATIONAL GRID	SECTION
	WEST MIDLANDS		SP1078	T
Scale: 1 1250			© Crown Copyright 1968.	

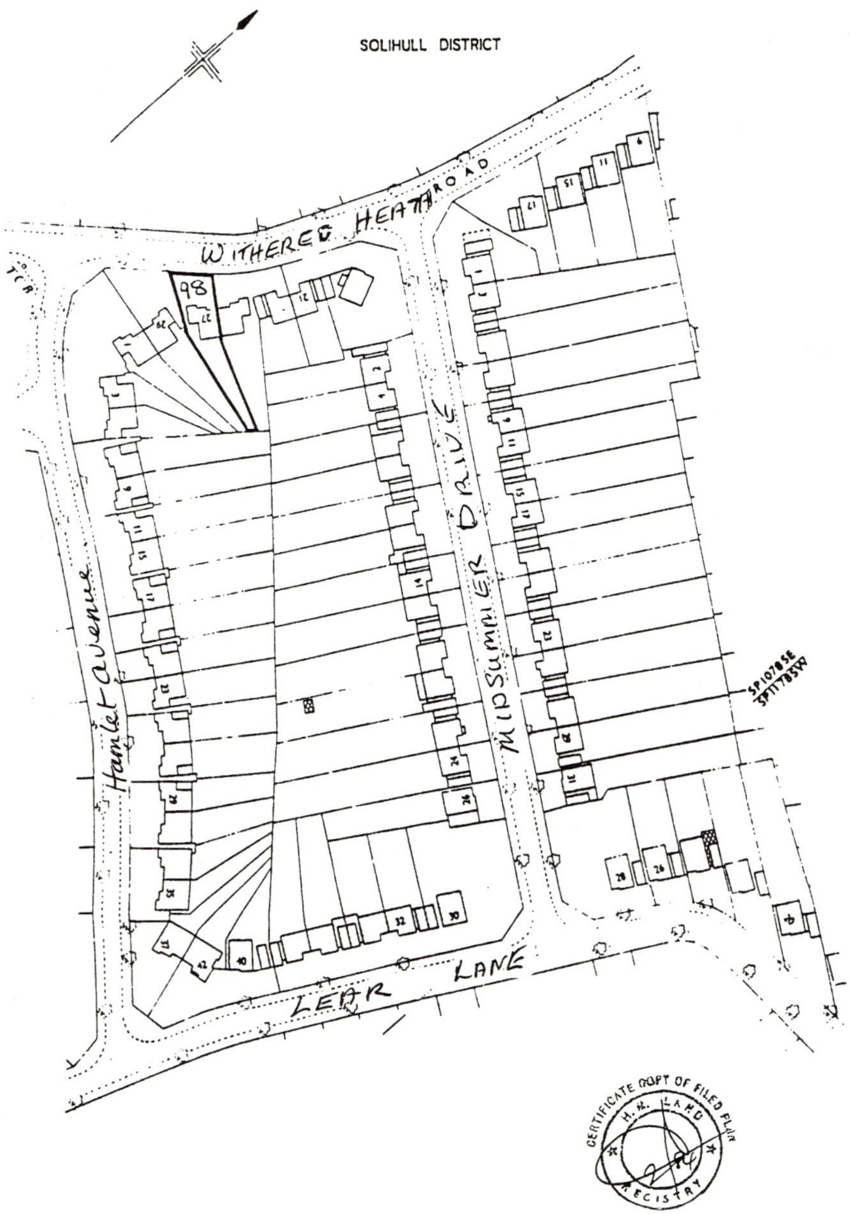

A caution has a similar effect of preventing dealings with the property until the person lodging the caution has been notified. Unlike a restriction, however, a caution has had the opportunity of disputing the right to do so when that cautioner is hostile and its purpose is to prevent dealings with the estate until the cautioner claims an interest in the land not already protected by the register (ss 53–5; and see 35 Conv 21). For instance, in *Elias* v *Mitchell* [1972] 2 All ER 153 a co-owner in equity was held entitled to enter a caution to prevent a sale of the land by the sole registered proprietor of the legal estate. Cautions may be entered against first registration of title, as where the cautioner alleges that a conveyance of unregistered property was illegally obtained from him. This is an exception to the principle mentioned earlier that title to land must be registered before third party claims can be entered on the register. The Registrar will fix a time limit within which the cautioner must dispute the right of the owner to register, or to dispose of the land if it is already registered, as the case may be.

Inhibitions also prevent dealings with the registered property until the occurrence of a certain event or until further order (s 57). They may be entered on the proprietorship register by the court or the Registrar on the application of any person interested. They are thus hostile. They are intended to be used, rather than the other methods mentioned above, in cases of emergency, since they are speedier in effect. Sometimes they are used as a matter of course, for instance, in cases of bankruptcy where inhibitions are entered to prevent the registered proprietor dealing with his land.

Many minor interests may be protected by notice. A notice is entered on the charges register and, as mentioned above, its effect is that universal notice of the interest concerned is thereby given so that dispositions take effect subject to it (see ss 48–53 and 59). Unlike registration of the title itself, entry has no confirmatory effect on the interest; if it is not otherwise valid, notice will not make it so. Matters which can be protected by notice in this way embrace all those rights which can be protected under the Land Charges Act 1972, including a spouse's right of occupation under the Matrimonial Homes Act 1983, a tenant's notice of his desire to acquire the freehold or an extended lease under the Leasehold Reform Act 1967, and even leases when they are not overriding interests and whether or not the title to the lease has been independently registered. The most common entries are restrictive covenants.

Generally, notices require the consent of the registered proprietor, but if this is not given, a caution may be lodged until it is. Figure 18.1 might help to summarise the way in which the Act provides for the protection of the three classes of interests.

THE PROCEDURE OF REGISTRATION

In this section we must discuss compulsory registration of title. The process of registration, the types of title granted on registration and the conversion of one type of title into another.

The two legal estates, with certain exceptions		*The Property Register*
Minor interests:	sometimes (a) by paralysing dealings or regulating how they are carried out, and sometimes (b) by fixing prospective alienees with notice. Sometimes there is the alternative between (a) and (b).	*The Proprietorship Register* *The Charges Register*

Overriding interests are effective irrespective of entry on the register.

Fig 18.1

Compulsory first registration

We have already noticed which estates may be registered in areas where registration is compulsory. Now we must see what estates must have their titles registered, and when registration takes place. They are as follows (s 123):

1 Title to the fee simple absolute in possession must be registered on its first sale. No doubt the use of the word 'sale' excludes transactions without consideration or where the only consideration is marriage.

2 Title to a term of years absolute must be registered on the 'grant' of a term not being less than 40 years from the date of the delivery of the grant as must every assignment on 'sale' of a term of years absolute having not less than 40 years to run from the date of the delivery of the assignment. If the title to freehold or leasehold land is already registered, a lease for more than 21 years must be registered.

An application for first registration must generally be made within two months of the transaction; otherwise the transaction becomes void so far as the passing of legal estate is concerned. Once registration has been carried out, all subsequent dealings with the estate must be effected under the system.

The process of registration

The person entitled to apply for registration is the estate owner or person entitled to have the registrable estate vested in him. In the case of settled land, for instance, this will be the tenant for life. The application is made to the appropriate district registry and must be accompanied, unless the Registrar directs otherwise, by such original deeds and documents relating to the title as the applicant has in his possession, abstract of title and sufficient particulars by which to identify the land on the registry maps. The title is then examined by the Registrar, who may make requisitions of the applicant regarding the title. There is also machinery for the making of objections to registration (Land

Registration Rules 1925 rr 34, 35). When the Registrar has completed his investigations the land certificate will be issued to the registered proprietor.

This certificate states the nature of the title which has been registered. The different types of title which may be awarded must now be explained.

Types of title

There are four types of title: absolute; qualified; possessory and good leasehold. The last only applies to leases. Qualified title cannot be applied for, but may be granted unilaterally by the Registrar. The word *absolute* here has no connection with its use in the expressions *fee simple absolute* and *term of years absolute*. It relates to the title to an estate and not to the nature of the estate itself. These titles must now be discussed individually.

Absolute title

In the case of freehold registration, an absolute title will be granted where the Registrar is satisfied that the title cannot be successfully challenged. It is the title normally sought and granted. Registration vests in the first registered proprietor the fee simple together with all rights and privileges existing in favour of the land, and subject only to any entries on the register, to overriding interests unless the contrary is stated on the register, and, where he is not entitled for his own benefit, to minor interests of which he has notice. This last proviso ensures that trustees of the legal estate hold subject to the interests of the beneficiaries (s 5). In short, registration guarantees that the person in whose name the title is registered is the owner.

Absolute title to leasehold property may be granted if the Registrar is satisfied not only as to the validity of the title to the lease, but also as to the validity of the titles to the freehold and any reversionary leases behind the lease registered. Registration vests the title to the lease in the first registered proprietor subject to those rights mentioned above subject to which a registered freeholder takes, and also to all the obligations and liabilities in the lease (see s 9).

Good leasehold title

This title is only granted for leases. Its effect is the same as that of an absolute title to a lease except that it does not guarantee that the landlord had the right to grant the lease and does not indicate matters affecting the freehold, such as restrictive covenants, which will bind the lessee. The need for such a title arises because a lessee cannot investigate the freeholder's title unless there is provision to do so in the contract (LPA 1925 s 44 (2)). If, however, unknown to the lessee, the freehold title is already registered, the Registrar may grant absolute title to a lessee even though he has only applied for good leasehold title.

Qualified title

In the case of freeholds, this title is the same as absolute title except that it is made subject to some defect specified in the register, and therefore registration does not prejudice the enforcement of the estate or right constituting the defect (s 7).

In the case of leaseholds, a qualified title has the same effect as an absolute title or good leasehold title, according to the title applied for, but again subject to some specified defect (ss 7, 12).

The grant of qualified title is of very rare occurrence.

Possessory title

In Chapter 8 it was explained that possession of land is a source of title to it. The ultimate acceptability of a title based on recent possession depends upon the passage of time and the extinction of any outstanding superior rights to possession under the Limitation Act.

Applications based only upon possession of land may be made in respect of both freeholds and leaseholds. What must be proved is possession of land or receipt of its rents and profits, and, of course, there is no investigation of title in the sense of documents, for indeed there may be no documents to support the claim. As might be expected, the registration of such a title makes no guarantee against the enforcement of any rights contrary to the title which existed or where capable of existing at the time of first registration (ss 6 and 11).

Conversion of titles

The act provides for the conversion of inferior titles into superior or absolute titles (s 77).

The Registrar has a discretion to convert a title registered as qualified, good leasehold or possessory into absolute or good leasehold title when it has been transferred for valuable consideration, and to convert a title which has been registered as good leasehold title for at least ten years into absolute title, provided that he is satisfied that the proprietor or successive proprietors have been in possession during that period.

The registrar must convert a freehold possessory title to absolute title after 15 years and a leasehold possessory title to absolute after ten years, provided that he is satisfied in both cases that the proprietor is in possession.

THE TRANSFER OF INTERESTS AFTER REGISTRATION

The title is now registered. We must next see how estates and interests are transferred to or acquired by others in future. The following cases must be considered: the transfer of the registered estate *inter vivos*, upon death, and upon bankruptcy, the loss of title under the Limitation Act 1980, and the way in which minor and overriding interests may be created or dealt with after registration.

Transfer *inter vivos*

The purchaser has no need to trace the devolution of the title as in the case of unregistered conveyancing, for registration is all that need be proved. Instead of an abstract of title, therefore, the vendor supplies him with an authority to inspect the register. The purchaser must, however, make the usual enquiries, including a search in the local land charges register, and inspection of the land, for, as we have seen, the register is not conclusive as to third party rights.

The conveyance is carried out by a form of transfer specified in the Rules. This must be deposited at the Registry with the land certificate. When the Registrar registers the necessary changes on the register, the legal estate passes (ss 19–23). The amended land certificate is then returned to the new proprietor. There is, of course, provision for the conveyance of part only of the property.

The transferee, once his name is on the register, takes the estate together with the benefit of rights existing in its favour, including those implied under the Law of Property Act 1925 s 62, so far as appropriate (ss 19(3), 20), but subject to:

1 Overriding interests.

2 Minor interests entered on the register. In the case of certain minor interests, such as restrictive covenants, the effect of entry on the register is that the transferee takes the land burdened with the interest. In the case of others, such as beneficial interests under a settlement, the effect of entry is simply that the land must be transferred in a particular way designed to safeguard the rights of the beneficiaries. If this is done, however, the interest is overreached. If the disposition is not made for valuable consideration, however, a transferee takes subject to such minor interests as bound the transferor even if they are not entered on the register (s 20).

   The effect of failure to register any registrable incumbrance which is not an overriding interest is, under the section, that the purchaser takes 'free' of it. The clear cut severity of this consequence matches that which prevails in the case of unregistered land. The doctrine of actual or constructive notice is banished in favour of the much more easily ascertainable state of the register (see also s 59(6)).

   However, a decision of the High Court has cast some doubts upon the remorselessness of this statutory policy. In *Peffer* v *Rigg* [1977] 3 All ER 745, *P* and *R* purchased a home for their mother-in-law. *R* was the sole registered proprietor but there was an agreement that it should be held on a tenancy in common beneficially. *P*'s interest was not entered on the register. The marriage of *R* and his wife *W* broke down and *R* transferred the house to *W* for £1 as part of the divorce settlement, the mother-in-law having already died. *W* was aware of all the facts mentioned above. *P* had no overriding interest. It was held that *P* was entitled to a half-share in the property. *W* could not claim the immunity from unregistered minor interests bestowed by s 20(1) upon dispositions 'for valuable consideration' since the parties had described the consideration as nominal only. A second reason was that under s 59(6), where immunity is further stated, it is expressed to run in favour of a 'purchaser'. Under s 3(xxi) 'purchaser' means a purchaser 'in good faith'. *W* could scarcely claim to possess good faith since she had knowledge of *P*'s interest. Yet a further reason was that a new trust was imposed when transfer was made to her. This was a constructive trust brought about by her knowledge of the existing trust. However just the decision, it was surely reached by doing violence to the principles of the Act. The case may be compared in this respect with *Ives Investment Ltd* v *High* [1967] 1 All ER 504, a decision discussed in relation to easements. See also *Lyus* v *Prowsa Developments Ltd* [1982] 1 WLR 1044.

Transfer on bankruptcy

When the proprietor is adjudicated bankrupt, the trustee in bankruptcy may be registered as proprietor. Before this event, creditors may be protected by a creditor's notice and a bankruptcy inhibition (see s 42).

Transfer on death

The personal representatives of a deceased proprietor may be registered in the place of the deceased, or alternatively they may have the person entitled under the will or intestacy, or purchaser, registered directly in place of the deceased (ss 37 and 41).

Loss of title under the Limitation Act 1980

Time runs against a registered proprietor under the Limitation Act 1980, in the same way that it runs in the case of unregistered land. The title of a registered proprietor, however, is not extinguished until the adverse possessor has been registered as proprietor. Until registration, which is treated as a first registration of a new title, the registered proprietor is deemed to hold the estate upon trust for the adverse possessor. This is without prejudice to the estates and interests of any other person interested in the land whose estate or interest is not extinguished by the Act.

Easements and other rights affecting land may be created in the same ways, including prescription, as in the case of unregistered land.

Dealings with interests other than the registered estate

Since the Land Registration Act 1986 the priority of beneficial interests arising under strict settlements or trusts for sale is governed by the rule in *Dearle* v *Hall* (1828) 3 Russ 1, as has always been the case in such dealings when the legal title has been unregistered. The mode of transfer of the interests mentioned above does not differ from that which prevails in the case of unregistered title and calls for no special treatment here. The same applies to the transfer of overriding interests.

A mortgage of an estate the title to which is registered may be carried out in three ways:

By registered charge (s 25)

This is created by a deed describing the land by reference to the register, or in any other manner which enables the Registrar to identify it without reference to any other document. The land certificate must be deposited at the Registry during the currency of the charge. It is protected by entry on the charges register, and the registered chargee acquires the powers of a legal mortgagee, unless the register declares otherwise (s 34). A charge certificate issued to the chargee constitutes his document of title. It carries the same information as the land certificate and the mortgage deed is bound up with it.

Successive registered charges of the same land rank for the purposes of priority in the order in which they are entered on the register and not in order of their creation (s 29). (For a discussion of the priorities of interests in registered land, see 35 Conv 100). Further advances may be tacked only if such advances are obligatory and if either the obligation is entered on the register, or if made before notice of any intended entry on the register which would affect the priority of a further advance, sent by the registrar by registered post, ought to have been received by the chargee (s 30 as amended by the Law of Property (Amendment) Act 1926).

By deposit of the land certificate (s 66)

The proprietor may create an equitable mortgage by depositing the land certificate with the person advancing the loan, who may then protect his interest by having notice of it entered on the charges register. This method of charging is favoured by banks to protect short-term or fluctuating loans secured on the property.

THE GUARANTEE OF TITLE

We have seen that it is of the essence of the registered system that the very act of registration vests the estate in the person registered as its proprietor. But there are occasions when, due to fraud or mistake, a person other than the true owner has been registered, and it would be unjust dogmatically to refuse to alter the register. There is, therefore, machinery for its rectification. The principle of guarantee of title is in such cases maintained by a right of indemnity in favour of those who suffer loss through rectification. These two matters will now be discussed.

Rectification (s 82, as amended by the Administration of Justice Act 1977 s 24)

The register may be rectified by order of the Registrar or of the court in the circumstances mentioned in the section: such as where an entry has been obtained by fraud, where there has been a mistake or omission or where a legal estate has been registered in the name of a person who, if the land had not been registered, would not have been the estate owner. The register cannot, however, be rectified, except for the purpose of giving effect to an overriding interest, so as to affect the title of the registered proprietor if he is in possession unless:

1 that proprietor has been party to or has substantially contributed to the fraud, mistake or omission which makes the rectification necessary, or

2 it would be unjust not to rectify the register against him (see generally, *Epps* v *Esso Petroleum Co Ltd* [1973] 2 All ER 465).

In *Re 139 Deptford High Street* [1951] Ch 884, the premises were described in the application for first registration simply as '139 High Street, Deptford' and no plan was provided. The Land Registry mistakenly thought the property included some adjacent land which had every appearance of being part of it, and indeed the applicant was under the same impression. Rectification was ordered on the grounds that the proprietor had contributed to the mistake as mentioned under 1 above.

For a more detailed discussion of the statutory grounds for rectification, see *Norwich and Peterborough Building Society* v *Steed* [1992] 1 All ER 330.

Indemnity (s 83)

A person *suffering loss* by reason of rectification, or by any error or omission on the register which is not rectified, or by the loss or destruction of any document lodged at the registry for inspection or safe custody, or because of an error in any official search, is entitled to be indemnified. No indemnity is payable, however,

> where the applicant or a person through whom he derives title (otherwise than under a disposition for valuable consideration which is registered or protected on the register) has caused or substantially contributed to the loss by fraud or lack of proper care (Land Registration and Land Charges Act 1971 amending s 83; see also *Re 139 Deptford High Street*, above).

In *Re Chowood's Registered Land* [1933] Ch 574 a squatter had, unknown to the purchaser of that land, acquired a predominant title to part of certain land under the Limitation Acts. The register was accordingly rectified, since the squatter's right was an overriding interest. The purchaser was held not to be entitled to an indemnity because his loss did not arise from rectification of the register but from the fact that he paid for property which was not the vendor's to sell (see also *Hodgson* v *Marks* [1971] 2 All ER 684).

STUDY MATERIAL

Williams & Glyn's Bank Ltd v *Boland and Another* [1980] 2 All ER 408

The House of Lords was unanimous in this case. The principal speech was that of Lord Wilberforce which is reproduced entirely below.

LORD WILBERFORCE. My Lords, these appeals, apart from one special point affecting only Mr Boland, raise for decision the same question: whether a husband or a wife (in each actual case a wife) who has a beneficial interest in the matrimonial home, by virtue of having contributed to its purchase price, but whose spouse is the legal and registered owner, has an 'overriding interest' binding on a mortgagee who claims possession of the matrimonial home under a mortgage granted by that spouse alone. Although this statement of the issue uses the words 'spouse', 'husband and wife', 'matrimonial home', the appeals do not, in my understanding, involve any question of matrimonial law, or of the rights of married women or of women as such. Exactly the same issue could arise if the roles of husband and wife were reversed, or if the persons interested in the house were not married to each other. The solution must be derived from a consideration in the light of current social conditions of the Land Registration Act 1925 and other property statutes.

The essential facts behind this legal formulation are as follows. Each wife contributed a substantial sum of her own money toward the purchase of the matrimonial home or to paying off a mortgage on it. This, indisputably, made her an equitable tenant in common to the extent of her contribution. Each house being registered land was transferred into the sole name of the husband who became its registered proprietor. Later, each husband mortgaged the house by legal mortgage to the appellant bank, which made no inquiries of either wife. Default being made, the bank started proceedings, in the *Boland* case in the High Court and in the *Brown* case in the Dartford County Court, for possession, with a view to sale. In each case the judge made an order for possession but his decision was reversed by the Court of Appeal ([1979] 2 All ER 697, [1979] Ch 312). So the question is whether the legal and registered mortgage takes effect against the matrimonial home, or whether the wife's beneficial interest has priority over it.

The legal framework within which the appeals are to be decided can be summarised as follows. Under the Land Registration Act 1925, legal estates in land are the only interests in respect of which a proprietor can be registered. Other interests take effect in equity as 'minor interests', which are overridden by a registered transfer. But the Act recognises also an intermediate, or hybrid, class of what are called 'overriding interests'; though these are not registered, legal dispositions take effect subject to them. The list of overriding interests is contained in s 70 and it includes such matters as easements, liabilities having their origin in tenure, land tax and tithe rentcharges, seignorial and manorial rights, leases for terms not exceeding 21 years, and, finally, the relevant paragraph being s 70(1)(*g*)–

> The rights of every person in actual occupation of the land or in receipt of the rents and profits thereof, save where enquiry is made of such person and the rights are not disclosed.

The first question is whether the wife is a 'person in actual occupation', and, if so, whether her right as a tenant in common in equity is a right protected by this provision.

The other main legal element arises out of the Law of Property Act 1925. Since that Act, undivided shares in land can only take effect in equity, behind a trust for sale on which the legal owner is to hold the land. Dispositions of the land, including mortgages, may be made under this trust, and provided that there are at least two trustees, or a trust corporation, 'overreach' the trusts. This means that the 'purchaser' takes free from them, whether or not he has notice of them, and that the trusts are enforceable against the proceeds of sale: see s 2(2) of the Law of Property Act 1925, and s 2(3) which lists certain exceptions.

The second question is whether the wife's equitable interest under the trust for sale, if she is in occupation of the land, is capable of being an overriding interest, or whether, as is generally the rule as regards equitable interests, it can only take effect as a 'minor interest'. In the latter event a registered transferee, including a legal mortgagee, would take free from it.

The system of land registration, as it exists in England, which long antedates the Land Registration Act 1925, is designed to simplify and to cheapen conveyancing. It is intended to replace the often complicated and voluminous title deeds of property by a single land certificate, on the strength of which land can be dealt with. In place of the lengthy and often technical investigation of title to which a purchaser was committed, all he has to do is to consult the register; from any burden not entered on the register, with one exception, he takes free. Above all, the system is designed to free the purchaser from the hazards of notice, real or constructive, which, in the case of unregistered land, involved him in inquiries, often quite elaborate, failing which he might be bound by equities. The Law of Property Act 1925 contains provisions limiting the effect of the doctrine of notice, but it still remains a potential source of danger to purchasers. By contrast, the only provisions in the Land Registration Act 1925 with regard to notice are provisions which enable a purchaser to take the estate free from equitable interests or equities whether he has notice or not (see, for example, s 3(xv) sv 'minor interests'.) The only kind of notice recognised is by entry on the register.

The exception just mentioned consists of 'overriding interests' listed in s 70. As to these, all registered land is stated to be deemed to be subject to such of them as may be subsisting in reference to the land, unless the contrary is expressed on the register. The land is so subject regardless of notice actual or constructive. In my opinion, therefore, the law as to notice as it may affect purchasers of unregistered land, whether contained in decided cases or in a statute (e.g. the Conveyancing Act 1882 s 3 and the Law of Property Act 1925 s 199) has no application even by analogy to registered land. Whether a particular right is an overriding interest, and whether it affects a purchaser, is to be decided on the terms of s 70, and other relevant provisions of the Land Registration Act 1925, and on nothing else.

In relation to rights connected with occupation, it has been said that the purpose and effect of s 70(1)(*g*) of the Land Registration Act 1925 was to make applicable to registered land the same rule as previously had been held to apply to unregistered land (see *National Provincial Bank Ltd* v *Ainsworth* [1964] 1 All ER 688 at 697,

[1964] Ch 665 at 689 (per Lord Denning MR) and [1965] 2 All ER 472 at 501–502, [1965] AC 1175 at 1259 (in this House)).

I adhere to this, but I do not accept the argument which counsel for the appellant sought to draw from it. His submission was that, in applying s 70(1)(*g*), we should have regard to and limit the application of the paragraph in the light of the doctrine of notice. But this would run counter to the whole purpose of the Act. The purpose, in each system, is the same, namely, to safeguard the rights of persons in occupation, the method used differs. In the case of unregistered land, the purchaser's obligation depends on what he has notice of, notice actual or constructive. In the case of registered land, it is the fact of occupation that matters. If there is actual occupation, and the occupier has rights, the purchaser takes subject to them. If not, he does not. No further element is material.

I now deal with the first question. Were the wives here in 'actual occupation'? These words are ordinary words of plain English, and should, in my opinion, be interpreted as such. Historically they appear to have emerged in the judgment of Lord Loughborough LC in *Taylor* v *Stibbert* (1794) 2 Ves 437 at 440, 30 ER 713 at 714 in a passage which repays quotation:

> . . . whoever purchases an estate from the owner, knowing it to be in possession of tenants, is bound to inquire into the estates, those tenants have. It has been determined, that a purchaser being told, particular parts of the estate were in possession of a tenant, without any information as to his interest, and taking it for granted it was only from year to year, was bound by a lease, that tenant had, which was a surprise upon him. That was rightly determined; for it was sufficient to put the purchaser upon inquiry, that he was informed the estate was not in the *actual possession* of the person with whom he contracted; that he could not transfer the ownership and possession at the same time; that there were interests, as to the extent and terms of which it was his duty to inquire. (My emphasis.)

They were taken up in the judgment of the Privy Council in *Barnhart* v *Greenshields* (1853) 9 Moo PC 18, 14 ER 204. The purpose for which they were used, in that case, was evidently to distinguish the case of a person who was in some kind of legal possession, as by receipt of the rents and profits, from that of a person actually in occupation as tenant. Given occupation, i.e. presence on the land, I do not think that the word 'actual' was intended to introduce any additional qualification, certainly not to suggest that possession must be 'adverse': it merely emphasises that what is required is physical presence, not some entitlement in law. So, even if it were necessary to look behind these plain words into history, I would find no reason for denying them their plain meaning.

Then, were the wives in actual occupation? I ask: why not? There was physical presence, with all the rights that occupiers have, including the right to exclude all others except those having similar rights. The house was a matrimonial home, intended to be occupied, and in fact occupied, by both spouses, both of whom have an interest in it; it would require some special doctrine of law to avoid the result that each is in occupation. Three arguments were used for a contrary conclusion. First, it was said that if the vendor (I use this word to include a mortgagor) is in occupation, that is enough to prevent the application of the paragraph. This seems to be a proposition of general application, not limited to the case of husbands, and no doubt, if correct, would be very convenient for purchasers and intending mortgagees. But the presence of the vendor, with occupation, does not exclude the possibility of occupation of others. There are observations which suggest the contrary in the unregistered land case of *Caunce* v *Caunce* [1969] 1 All ER 722, [1969] 1 WLR 286, but I agree with the disapproval of these and with the assertion of the proposition I have just stated by Russell LJ in *Hodgson* v *Marks* [1971] 2 All ER 684 at 690, [1971] Ch 892 at 934–935. Then it was suggested that the wife's 'occupation' was nothing but the shadow of the husband's, a version I suppose of the doctrine of unity of husband and wife. This expression and the argument flowing from it was used by Templeman J in *Bird* v *Syme Thomson* [1978] 3 All ER 1027 at 1030, [1979] 1 WLR 440 at 444, a decision preceding and which he followed in the present case. The argument was also inherent in the judgment in *Caunce* v *Caunce* which influenced the decisions of Templeman J. It somewhat faded from the arguments in the present case and appears to me to be heavily obsolete.

The appellants' main and final position became in the end this: that, to come within the paragraph, the occupation in question must be apparently inconsistent with the title of the vendor. This, it was suggested, would exclude the wife of a husband-vendor because her apparent occupation would be satisfactorily accounted for by his. But, apart from the rewriting of the paragraph which this would involve, the suggestion is unacceptable. Consistency, or inconsistency, involves the absence, or presence, of an independent right to occupy, though I must observe that 'inconsistency' in this context is an inappropriate word. But how can either quality be predicated of a wife, simply *qua* wife? A wife may, and everyone knows this, have rights of her own; particularly, many wives have a share in a matrimonial home. How can it be said that the presence of a wife in the house, as occupier, is consistent or inconsistent with the husband's rights until one knows what rights she has? And if she has rights, why, just because she is a wife (or in the converse case, just because an occupier is the husband), should these rights be denied protection under the paragraph? If one looks beyond the case of husband and wife, the difficulty of all these arguments stands out if one considers the case of a man living with a mistress, or of a man and a woman (or for that matter two persons of the same sex) living in a house in separate or partially shared rooms. Are these cases of apparently consistent occupation, so that the rights of the other person (other than the vendor) can be disregarded? The only solution which is consistent with the Act (s 70(1)(*g*)) and with common sense is to read the paragraph for what it says. Occupation, existing as a fact, may protect rights if the person in occupation has rights. On this part of the case I have no difficulty in concluding that a spouse, living in a house, has an actual occupation capable of conferring protection, as an overriding interest, on rights of that spouse.

This brings me to the second question, which is whether such rights as a spouse has under a trust for sale are capable of recognition as overriding interests, a question to my mind of some difficulty. The argument against this is based on the structure of the Land Registration Act 1925 and on specific provisions in it.

As to structure, it is said that the Act recognises three things: (a) legal estates, (b) minor interests, which take effect in equity, and (c) overriding interests. These are mutually exclusive: an equitable interest, which is a minor interest, is incapable of being at the same time an overriding interest. The wife's interest, existing under, or behind, a trust for sale, is an equitable interest and nothing more. To give it the protection of an overriding interest would, moreover, contradict the principle according to which such an equitable interest can be overreached by an exercise of the trust for sale. As to the provisions of the Act, particular emphasis is placed on s 3(xv) which, in defining 'Minor interests', specifically includes in the case of land held on trust for sale 'all interests and powers which are under the Law of Property Act, 1925, capable of being overridden by the trustees for sale' and excludes, expressly, overriding interests. Reliance is also placed on s 86, which, dealing analogously, so it is said, with settled land, prescribes that successive or other interests created by or arising under a settlement take effect as minor interests and not otherwise, and on s 101, which, it is argued, recognises the exclusive character of minor interests, which in all cases can be overridden.

My Lords, I find this argument formidable. To reach a conclusion on it involves some further consideration of the nature of trusts for sale, in relation to undivided shares. The trusts on which, in this case, the land is to be held are defined (as 'statutory trusts') in s 35 of the Law of Property Act 1925, i.e. –

> . . . upon trust to sell the same and to stand possessed of the net proceeds of sale, after payment of costs, and of the net rents and profits until sale after payment of rates, taxes, costs of insurance, repairs, and other outgoings, upon such trusts, and subject to such powers and provisions, as may be requisite for giving effect to the rights of the persons . . . interested in the land.

In addition to this specific disposition, the general provisions as to trusts for sale in ss 23 to 31, where not inconsistent, appear to apply. The right of occupation of the land pending sale is not explicitly dealt with in these sections and the position as to it is obscure. Before the Act the position was that owners of undivided shares (which could exist at law) had concurrent rights of occupation. In *Bull* v *Bull* [1955] 1 All ER 253, [1955] 1 QB 234 it was held by the Court of Appeal, applying *Re Warren, Warren* v *Warren* [1932] 1 Ch 42, [1931] All ER Rep 702, that the conversion of these legal estates into equitable interests by the Law of Property Act 1925 should not affect the mutual rights of the owners. Denning LJ, in a judgment which I find most illuminating, there held, in a factual situation similar to that of the instant cases, that 'when there are two equitable tenants in common, then, until the place is sold, each of them is entitled concurrently with the other to the possession of the land and to the use and enjoyment of it in a proper manner' ([1955] 1 All ER 253 at 255, [1955] 1 QB 234 at 238). And he referred to s 14 of the Law of Property Act 1925 which provides that the Act 'shall not prejudicially affect the interest of any person in possession or in actual occupation of land to which he may be entitled in right of such possession or occupation'.

How then are these various rights to be fitted into the scheme of the Land Registration Act 1925? It is clear, at least, that the interests of the co-owners under the 'statutory trusts' are minor interests: this fits with the definition in s 3(xv). But I can see no reason why, if these interests, or that of any one of them, are or is protected by 'actual occupation' they should remain merely as 'minor interests'. On the contrary, I see every reason why, in that event, they should acquire the status of overriding interests. And, moreover, I find it easy to accept that they satisfy the opening, and governing, words of s 70, namely, interests subsisting in reference to the land. As Lord Denning MR points out, to describe the interests of spouses in a house jointly bought to be lived in as a matrimonial home as merely an interest in the proceeds of sale, or rents and profits until sale, is just a little unreal; see also *Elias* v *Mitchell* [1972] 2 All ER 153, [1972] Ch 652 per Punnycuick V-C, with whose analysis I agree, and contrast *Cedar Holdings Ltd* v *Green* [1979] 3 All ER 117, [1979] 3 WLR 31 (which I consider to have been wrongly decided).

There are decisions, in relation to other equitable interests than those of tenants in common, which confirm this line of argument. In *Bridges* v *Mees* [1957] 2 All ER 577, [1957] Ch 475 Harman J decided that a purchaser of land under a contract for sale, who had paid the price and so was entitled to the land in equity, could acquire an overriding interest by virtue of actual occupation, and a similar position was held by the Court of Appeal to arise in relation to a resulting trust (see *Hodgson* v *Marks* [1971] 2 All ER 684, [1971] Ch 892). These decisions following the law as it undoubtedly existed before 1925: see *Barnhart* v *Greenshields* (1853) 9 Moo PCC 18 at 32, 14 ER 204 at 209, *Daniels* v *Davison* (1809) 16 Ves 249, 33 ER 978, *Allen* v *Anthony* (1816) 1 Mer 282 at 284, 35 ER 679 per Lord Eldon LC) provide an answer to the argument that there is a firm dividing line, or an unbridgeable gulf, between minor interests and overriding interests, and, on the contrary, confirm that the fact of occupation enables protection of the latter to extend to what without it would be the former. In my opinion, the wives' equitable interests, subsisting in reference to the land, were by the fact of occupation, made into overriding interests, and so protected by s 70(1)(*g*). I should add that it makes no difference to this that these same interests might also have been capable of protection by the registration of a caution (see *Bridges* v *Mees* [1957] 2 All ER 577 at 582, [1957] Ch 475 at 487 and the Land Registration Act 1925, s 59(6)).

There was finally an argument based on s 74 of the Land Registration Act 1925. Section 74 provides:

> Subject to the provisions of this Act as to settled land, neither the registrar nor any person dealing with a registered estate or charge shall be affected with notice of a trust express implied or constructive, and references to trusts shall, so far as possible, be excluded from the register.

The argument was that, if the overriding interest sought to be protected is, under the general law, only binding on a purchaser by virtue of notice, the section has the effect of denying the protection. It is obvious, and indeed conceded, that if this is right *Hodgson* v *Marks* and *Bridges* v *Mees* must have been wrongly decided.

I am of opinion that this section has no such effect. Its purpose is to make clear, as I have already explained, that the doctrine of notice has no application to registered conveyancing, and accordingly to establish, as an administrative measure, that entries may not be made in the register which would only be appropriate if that doctrine were applicable. It cannot have the effect of cutting down the general application of s 70(1).

I would only add, in conclusion, on the appeal as it concerns the wives a brief observation on the conveyancing consequences of dismissing the appeal. These were alarming to Templeman J, and I can agree with him to the extent that whereas the object of a land registration system is to reduce the risks to purchasers from anything not on the register, to extend (if it be an extension) the area of risk so as to include possible interests of spouses, and indeed, in theory, of other members of the family or even outside it, may add to the burdens of purchasers, and involve them in inquiries which in some cases may be troublesome.

But conceded, as it must be, that the Act, following established practice, gives protection to occupation, the extension of the risk area follows necessarily from the extension beyond the paterfamilias, of rights of ownership, itself following from the diffusion of property and earning capacity. What is involved is a departure from an easy-going practice of dispensing with inquiries as to occupation beyond that of the vendor and accepting the risks of doing so. To substitute for this a practice of more careful inquiry as to the fact of occupation, and, if necessary, as to the rights of occupiers, cannot, in my view of the matter, be considered as unacceptable except at the price of overlooking the widespread development of shared interests of ownership. In the light of s 70 of the Act, I cannot believe that Parliament intended this, though it may be true that in 1925 it did not foresee the full extent of this development.

Mr Boland's appeal

The special point taken by Mr Boland arises out of the facts of this case and the nature of the bank's proceeding against him. This was brought under RSC Ord 88 for summary judgment. Mr Boland contended that there was a dispute as to the amount actually owed by him to the bank, and that until this dispute was resolved by trial, judgment for possession ought not to be granted against him before he had had an opportunity of invoking the discretion of the court under the Administration of Justice Act 1970, s 36. The judgment of Templeman J, who fully considered this point, provides a complete answer to this contention. It is clear that, on the view of the matter most favourable to Mr Boland, he owes a substantial sum, of the order of £40 000, to the bank. He has, on the other hand, put forward no material evidence as to the likelihood, or possibility, of discharging or refinancing his indebtedness, on which to invoke the court's discretion under the section, and the judge was undoubtedly right in refusing to exercise it in the absence of such material evidence. In any case, there was no basis on which the Court of Appeal could legitimately interfere with the decision of the judge, and indeed no substantial reason was given for doing so. In my opinion this part of the decision of the Court of Appeal cannot be supported.

However, on the main issue on both appeals, as they affect the wives, the decision of the Court of Appeal was, in my opinion, right, and an order for possession cannot be made in either case. I would dismiss the appeals.

QUESTIONS

In this final chapter some more general perspectives might be explored, focusing on the land certificate provided. This is a precise copy of a real certificate, except that fictitious names and numbers have been substituted for reasons of privacy. The background is briefly as follows:

The property 98 Withered Heath Road is part of a suburban estate on the southern outskirts of Birmingham. In 1956 it was conveyed as a new house on a 99-year lease to John Brendan Brown, together with various rights and duties including some restrictive and positive covenants. Later the property was enfranchised under the Leasehold Reform Act 1967. The leasehold conveyance of 1956 was carried out under the unregistered system since compulsory registration was not introduced into the district until some years later. There have been various transactions since 1956 but the property is now registered in the name of Margaret Morely. She lives there with her niece who has been contributing to the mortgage repayments regularly to the extent of about one-fifth of the total. She pays no board but is abroad for more than half the year.

Discuss the following questions:

1 Lord Knowle has recently written to Margaret Morely and many of her neighbours stating that he intends to take up his sporting rights as Lord of the Manor and to shoot deer at night in their gardens as the deer enter from the woods nearby.

2 A high boundary wall at the property recently collapsed and Margaret Morely would prefer not to replace it. She is, however, concerned about item (e) in the Schedule of Restrictive Covenants. This appears to be a positive covenant which is not generally enforceable where neither privity of contract nor privity of estate exists between parties. Who can enforce this duty?

3 Her next-door neighbour has obtained planning permission to build a studio close to her boundary. Margaret Morely wishes to prevent this, claiming that it will obstruct light to a window at 98 Withered Heath Road, through which he has acquired an easement of light on account of 20 years' unobstructed use.

4 Margaret Morely is contemplating marriage. In that event she will transfer the property into the joint names of her husband and herself. A year after the marriage she and her husband will sell the property. Consider the position of her niece in that event.

5 Speculate on the role of Margaret Morely's niece, in relation to the properties on the estate.

APPENDIX

AGREEMENT
(Incorporating the Standard Conditions of Sale (Third Edition))

Agreement date :

Seller :

Buyer :

Property (freehold/leasehold) :

Root of title/Title Number :

Incumbrances on the Property :

Title Guarantee (full/limited) :

Completion date :

Contract rate :

Purchase price :

Deposit :

Amount payable for chattels :

Balance :

The Seller will sell and the Buyer will buy the Property for the Purchase price.

The Agreement continues on the back page.

WARNING

This is a formal document, designed to create legal rights and legal obligations. Take advice before using it.

Signed

Seller/Buyer

STANDARD CONDITIONS OF SALE (THIRD EDITION)
(NATIONAL CONDITIONS OF SALE 23rd EDITION, LAW SOCIETY'S CONDITIONS OF SALE 1995)

1. GENERAL

1.1 Definitions

1.1.1 In these conditions:

(a) "accrued interest" means:

(i) if money has been placed on deposit or in a building society share account, the interest actually earned

(ii) otherwise, the interest which might reasonably have been earned by depositing the money at interest on seven days' notice of withdrawal with a clearing bank

less, in either case, any proper charges for handling money

(b) 'agreement' means the contractual document which incorporates these conditions, with or without amendment

(c) 'bankers draft' means a draft drawn by and on a clearing bank

(d) 'clearing bank' means a bank which is a member of CHAPS Limited

(e) 'completion date', unless defined in the agreement, has the meaning given in condition 6.1.1

(f) 'contract' means the bargain between the seller and the buyer of which these conditions, with or without amendment, form part

(g) 'contract rate', unless defined in the agreement, is the Law Society's interest rate from time to time in force

(h) 'lease' includes sub-lease, tenancy and agreement for a lease or sub-lease

(i) 'notice to complete' means a notice requiring completion of the contract in accordance with condition 6

(j) 'public requirement' means any notice, order or proposal given or made (whether before or after the date of the contract) by a body acting on statutory authority

(k) 'requisition' includes objection

(l) 'solicitor' includes barrister, duly certificated notary public, recognised licensed conveyancer and recognised body under sections 9 or 32 of the Administration of Justice Act 1985

(m) 'transfer' includes conveyance and assignment

(n) 'working day' means any day from Monday to Friday (inclusive) which is not Christmas Day, Good Friday or a statutory Bank Holiday.

1.1.2 When used in these conditions the terms 'absolute title' and 'office copies' have the special meaning given to them by the Land Registration Act 1925.

1.2 Joint parties

If there is more than one seller or more than one buyer, the obligations which they undertake can be enforced against them all jointly or against each individually.

1.3 Notices and documents

1.3.1 A notice required or authorised by the contract must be in writing.

1.3.2 Giving a notice or delivering a document to a party's solicitor has the same effect as giving or delivering it to that party.

1.3.3 Transmission by fax is a valid means of giving a notice or delivering a document where delivery of the original document is not essential.

1.3.4 Subject to conditions 1.3.5 to 1.3.7, a notice is given and a document delivered when it is received.

1.3.5 If a notice or document is received after 4.00pm on a working day, or on a day which is not a working day, it is to be treated as having been received on the next working day.

1.3.6 Unless the actual time of receipt is proved, a notice or document sent by the following means is to be treated as having been received before 4.00pm on the day shown below:

(a) by first-class post:	two working days after posting
(b) by second-class post:	three working days after posting
(c) through a document exchange:	on the first working day after the day on which it would normally be available for collection by the addressee.

1.3.7 Where a notice or document is sent through a document exchange, then for the purposes of condition 1.3.6 the actual time of receipt is:
(a) the time when the addressee collects it from the document exchange or, if earlier
(b) 8.00am on the first working day on which it is available for collection at that time.

1.4 **VAT**
1.4.1 An obligation to pay money includes an obligation to pay any value added tax chargeable in respect of that payment.
1.4.2 All sums made payable by the contract are exclusive of value added tax.

2. **FORMATION**
2.1 **Date**
2.1.1 If the parties intend to make a contract by exchanging duplicate copies by post or through a document exchange the contract is made when the last copy is posted or deposited at the document exchange.
2.1.2 If the parties' solicitors agree to treat exchange as taking place before duplicate copies are actually exchanged, the contract is made as so agreed.

2.2 **Deposit**
2.2.1 The buyer is to pay or send a deposit of 10 per cent of the purchase price no later than the date of the contract. Except on a sale by auction, payment is to be made by banker's draft or by a cheque drawn on a solicitors' clearing bank account.
2.2.2 If before completion date the seller agrees to buy another property in England and Wales for his residence, he may use all or part of the deposit as a deposit in that transaction to be held on terms to the same effect as this condition and condition 2.2.3.
2.2.3 Any deposit or part of a deposit not being used in accordance with condition 2.2.2 is to be held by the seller's solicitor as stakeholder on terms that on completion it is paid to the seller with accrued interest.
2.2.4 If a cheque tendered in payment of all or part of the deposit is dishonoured when first presented, the seller may, within seven working days of being notified that the cheque has been dishonoured, give notice to the buyer that the contract is discharged by the buyer's breach.

2.3 **Auctions**
2.3.1 On a sale by auction the following conditions apply to the property and, if it is sold in lots, to each lot.
2.3.2 The sale is subject to a reserve price.
2.3.3 The seller, or a person on his behalf, may bid up to the reserve price.
2.3.4 The auctioneer may refuse any bid.
2.3.5 If there is a dispute about a bid, the auctioneer may resolve the dispute or restart the auction at the last undisputed bid.

3. **MATTERS AFFECTING THE PROPERTY**
3.1 **Freedom from incumbrances**
3.1.1 The seller is selling the property free from incumbrances, other than those mentioned in condition 3.1.2.
3.1.2 The incumbrances subject to which the property is sold are:
(a) those mentioned in the agreement
(b) those discoverable by inspection of the property before the contract
(c) those the seller does not and could not know about
(d) entries made before the date of the contract in any public register except those maintained by HM Land Registry or its Land Charges Department or by Companies House
(e) public requirements.
3.1.3 After the contract is made, the seller is to give the buyer written details without delay of any new public requirement and of anything in writing which he learns about concerning any incumbrances subject to which the property is sold.
3.1.4 The buyer is to bear the cost of complying with any outstanding public requirement and is to indemnify the seller against any liability resulting from a public requirement.

3.2 **Physical state**

3.2.1 The buyer accepts the property in the physical state it is in at the date of the contract unless the seller is building or converting it.

3.2.2 A leasehold property is sold subject to any subsisting breach of a condition or tenant's obligation relating to the physical state of the property which renders the lease liable to forfeiture.

3.2.3 A sub-lease is granted subject to any subsisting breach of a condition or tenant's obligation relating to the physical state of the property which renders the seller's own lease liable to forfeiture.

3.3 **Leasing affecting the property**

3.3.1 The following provisions apply if the agreement states that any part of the property is sold subject to a lease.

3.3.2 (a) The seller having provided the buyer with full details of each lease or copies of the documents embodying the lease terms, the buyer is treated as entering into the contract knowing and fully accepting those terms

(b) The seller is to inform the buyer without delay if the lease ends or if the seller learns of any application by the tenant in connection with the lease; the seller is then to act as the buyer reasonably directs, and the buyer is to indemnify him against all consequent loss and expense

(c) The seller is not to agree to any proposal to change the lease terms without the consent of the buyer and is to inform the buyer without delay of any change which may be proposed or agreed

(d) The buyer is to indemnify the seller against all claims arising from the lease after actual completion; this includes claims which are unenforceable against a buyer for want of registration

(e) The seller takes no responsibility for what rent is lawfully recoverable, nor for whether or how any legislation affects the lease

(f) If the let land is not wholly within the property, the seller may apportion the rent.

3.4 **Retained land**

3.4.1 The following provisions apply where after the transfer the seller will be retaining land near the property.

3.4.2 The buyer will have no right of light or air over the retained land, but otherwise the seller and the buyer will each have the rights over the land of the other which they would have had if they were two separate buyers to whom the seller had made simultaneous transfers of the property and the retained land.

3.4.3 Either party may require that the transfer contain appropriate express terms.

4. **TITLE AND TRANSFER**

4.1 **Timetable**

4.1.1 The following are the steps for deducing and investigating the title to the property to be taken within the following time limits:

Step	**Time Limit**
1. The seller is to send the buyer evidence of title in accordance with condition 4.2	Immediately after making the contract
2. The buyer may raise written requisitions	Six working days after either the date of the contract or the date of delivery of the seller's evidence of title on which the requisitions are raised whichever is the later
3. The seller is to reply in writing to any requisitions raised	Four working days after receiving the requisitions
4. The buyer may make written observations on the seller's replies	Three working days after receiving the replies

The time limit on the buyer's right to raise requisitions applies even where the seller supplies incomplete evidence of his title, but the buyer may, within six working days from delivery of any further evidence, raise further requisitions resulting from that evidence. On the expiry of the relevant time limit the buyer loses his right to raise requisitions or make observations.

4.1.2 The parties are to take the following steps to prepare and agree the transfer of the property within the following time limits:

Step	**Time Limit**
A. The buyer is to send the seller a draft transfer	At least twelve working days before completion date
B. The seller is to approve or revise that draft and either return it or retain it for use as the actual transfer	Four working days after delivery of the draft transfer
C. If the draft is returned the buyer is to send an engrossment to the seller	At least five working days before completion date

4.1.3 Periods of time under conditions 4.1.1 and 4.1.2 may run concurrently.

4.1.4 If the period between the date of the contract and completion date is less than 15 working days, the time limits in conditions 4.1.1 and 4.1.2 are to be reduced by the same proportion as that period bears to the period of 15 working days. Fractions of a working day are to be rounded down except that the time limit to perform any step is not to be less than one working day.

4.2 **Proof of title**

4.2.1 The evidence of registered title is office copies of the items required to be furnished by section 110(1) of the Land Registration Act 1925 and the copies, abstracts and evidence referred to in section 110(2).

4.2.2 The evidence of unregistered title is an abstract of the title, or an epitome of title with photocopies of the relevant documents.

4.2.3 Where the title to the property is unregistered, the seller is to produce to the buyer (without cost to the buyer):
(a) the original of every relevant document, or
(b) an abstract, epitome or copy with an original marking by a solicitor of examination either against the original or against an examined abstract or against an examined copy.

4.3 **Defining the property**

4.3.1 The seller need not:
(a) prove the exact boundaries of the property
(b) prove who owns fences, ditches, hedges or walls
(c) separately identify parts of the property with different titles further than he may be able to do from information in his possession.

4.3.2 The buyer may, if it is reasonable, require the seller to make or obtain, pay for and hand over a statutory declaration about facts relevant to the matters mentioned in condition 4.3.1. The form of the declaration is to be agreed by the buyer, who must not unreasonably withhold his agreement.

4.4 **Rents and rentcharges**

The fact that a rent or rentcharge, whether payable or receivable by the owner of the property, has been or will on completion be, informally apportioned is not to be regarded as a defect in title.

4.5 **Transfer**

4.5.1 The buyer does not prejudice his right to raise requisitions, or to require replies to any raised, by taking any steps in relation to the preparation or agreement of the transfer.

4.5.2 If the agreement makes no provision as to title guarantee, then subject to condition 4.5.3 the seller is to transfer the property with full title guarantee.

4.5.3 The transfer is to have effect as if the disposition is expressly made subject to all matters to which the property is sold subject under the terms of the contract.

4.5.4 If after completion the seller will remain bound by any obligation affecting the property, but the law does not imply any covenant by the buyer to indemnify the seller against liability for future breaches of it:
(a) the buyer is to covenant in the transfer to indemnify the seller against liability for any future breach of the obligation and to perform it from then on,
(b) if required by the seller, the buyer is to execute and deliver to the seller on completion a duplicate transfer prepared by the buyer.

4.5.5 The seller is to arrange at his expense that, in relation to every document of title which the buyer does not receive on completion, the buyer is to have the benefit of:

(a) a written acknowledgement of his right to its production, and
(b) a written undertaking for its safe custody (except while it is held by a mortgagee or by someone in a fiduciary capacity).

5. PENDING COMPLETION

5.1 Responsibility for property

5.1.1 The seller will transfer the property in the same physical state as it was at the date of the contract (except for fair wear and tear), which means that the seller retains the risk until completion.

5.1.2 If at any time before completion the physical state of the property makes it unusable for its purpose at the date of the contract:
(a) the buyer may rescind the contract
(b) the seller may rescind the contract where the property has become unusable for that purpose as a result of damage against which the seller could not reasonably have insured, or which it is not legally possible for the seller to make good.

5.1.3 The seller is under no obligation to the buyer to insure the property.

5.1.4 Section 47 of the Law of Property Act 1925 does not apply.

5.2 Occupation by buyer

5.2.1 If the buyer is not already lawfully in the property, and the seller agrees to let him into occupation, the buyer occupies on the following terms.

5.2.2 The buyer is a licensee and not a tenant. The terms of the licence are that the buyer:
(a) cannot transfer it
(b) may permit members of his household to occupy the property
(c) is to pay or indemnify the seller against all outgoings and other expenses in respect of the property
(d) is to pay the seller a fee calculated at the contract rate on the purchase price (less any deposit paid) for the period of the licence
(e) is entitled to any rents and profits from any part of the property which he does not occupy
(f) is to keep the property in as good a state of repair as it was in when he went into occupation (except for fair wear and tear) and is not to alter it
(g) is to insure the property in a sum which is not less than the purchase price against all risks in respect of which comparable premises are normally insured
(h) is to quit the property when the licence ends.

5.2.3 On the creation of the buyer's licence, condition 5.1 ceases to apply, which means that the buyer then assumes the risk until completion.

5.2.4 The buyer is not in occupation for the purposes of this condition if he merely exercises rights of access given solely to do work agreed by the seller.

5.2.5 The buyer's licence ends on the earliest of: completion date, rescission of the contract or when five working days' notice given by one party to the other takes effect.

5.2.6 If the buyer is in occupation of the property after his licence has come to an end and the contract is subsequently completed he is to pay the seller compensation for his continued occupation calculated at the same rate as the fee mentioned in condition 5.2.2(d).

5.2.7 The buyer's right to raise requisitions is unaffected.

6. COMPLETION

6.1 Date

6.1.1 Completion date is twenty working days after the date of the contract but time is not of the essence of the contract unless a notice to complete has been served.

6.1.2 If the money due on completion is received after 2.00 pm, completion is to be treated, for the purposes only of conditions 6.3 and 7.3, as taking place on the next working day.

6.1.3 Condition 6.1.2 does not apply where the sale is with vacant possession of the property or any part and the seller has not vacated the property or that part by 2.00 pm on the date of actual completion.

6.2 **Place**
Completion is to take place in England and Wales, either at the seller's solicitor's office or at some other place which the seller reasonably specifies.

6.3 **Apportionments**
6.3.1 Income and outgoings of the property are to be apportioned between the parties so far as the change of ownership on completion will affect entitlement to receive or liability to pay them.
6.3.2 If the whole property is sold with vacant possession or the seller exercises his option in condition 7.3.4, apportionment is to be made with effect from the date of actual completion; otherwise, it is to be made from completion date.
6.3.3 In apportioning any sum, it is to be assumed that the seller owns the property until the end of the day from which apportionment is made and that the sum accrues from day to day at the rate at which it is payable on that day.
6.3.4 For the purpose of apportioning income and outgoings, it is to assumed that they accrue at an equal daily rate throughout the year.
6.3.5 When a sum to be apportioned is not known or easily ascertainable at completion, a provisional apportionment is to be made according to the best estimate available. As soon as the amount is known, a final apportionment is to be made and notified to the other party. Any resulting balance is to be paid no more than ten working days later, and if not then paid the balance is to bear interest at the contract rate from then until payment.
6.3.6 Compensation payable under condition 5.2.6 is not to be apportioned.

6.4 Amount payable
The amount payable by the buyer on completion is the purchase price (less any deposit already paid to the seller or his agent) adjusted to take account of:
(a) apportionments made under condition 6.3
(b) any compensation to be paid or allowed under condition 7.3.

6.5 Title deeds
6.5.1 The seller is not to retain the documents of title after the buyer has tendered the amount payable under condition 6.4.
6.5.2 Condition 6.5.1 does not apply to any documents of title relating to land being retained by the seller after completion.

6.6 Rent receipts
The buyer is to assume that whoever gave any receipt for a payment of rent or service charge which the seller produces was the person or the agent of the person then entitled to that rent or service charge.

6.7 Means of payment
The buyer is to pay the money due on completion in one or more of the following ways:
(a) legal tender
(b) a banker's draft
(c) a direct credit to a bank account nominated by the seller's solicitor
(d) an unconditional release of deposit held by a stakeholder.

6.8 Notice to complete
6.8.1 At any time on or after completion date, a party who is ready able and willing to complete may give the other a notice to complete.
6.8.2 A party is ready able and willing:
(a) if he could be, but for the default of the other party, and
(b) in the case of the seller, even though a mortgage remains secured on the property, if the amount to be paid on completion enables the property to be transferred freed of all mortgages (except those to which the sale is expressly subject).
6.8.3 The parties are to complete the contract within ten working days of giving a notice to complete, excluding the day on which the notice is given. For this purpose, time is of the essence of the contract.
6.8.4 On receipt of a notice to complete:
(a) if the buyer paid no deposit, he is forthwith to pay a deposit of 10 per cent

(b) if the buyer paid a deposit of less than 10 per cent, he is forthwith to pay a further deposit equal to the balance of that 10 per cent.

7. REMEDIES

7.1 Errors and omissions

7.1.1 If any plan or statement in the contract, or in the negotiations leading to it, is or was misleading or inaccurate due to an error or omission, the remedies available are as follows.

7.1.2 When there is a material difference between the description or value of the property as represented and as it is, the injured party is entitled to damages.

7.1.3 An error or omission only entitles the injured party to rescind the contract:

(a) where it results from fraud or recklessness, or

(b) where he would be obliged, to his prejudice, to transfer or accept property differing substantially (in quantity, quality or tenure) from what the error or omission had led him to expect.

7.2 Rescission

If either party rescinds the contract:

(a) unless the rescission is a result of the buyer's breach of contract the deposit is to be repaid to the buyer with accrued interest

(b) the buyer is to return any documents he received from the seller and is to cancel any registration of the contract.

7.3 Late completion

7.3.1 If there is default by either or both of the parties in performing their obligations under the contract and completion is delayed, the party whose total period of default is the greater is to pay compensation to the other party.

7.3.2 Compensation is calculated at the contract rate on the purchase price, or (where the buyer is the paying party) the purchase price less any deposit paid, for the period by which the paying party's default exceeds that of the receiving party, or, if shorter, the period between completion date and actual completion.

7.3.3 Any claim for loss resulting from delayed completion is to be reduced by any compensation paid under this contract.

7.3.4 Where the buyer holds the property as tenant of the seller and completion is delayed, the seller may give notice to the buyer, before the date of actual completion, that he intends to take the net income from the property until completion. If he does so, he cannot claim compensation under condition 7.3.1 as well.

7.4 After completion

Completion does not cancel liability to perform any outstanding obligation under this contract.

7.5 Buyer's failure to comply with notice to complete

7.5.1 If the buyer fails to complete in accordance with a notice to complete, the following terms apply.

7.5.2 The seller may rescind the contract, and if he does so:

(a) he may

(i) forfeit and keep any deposit and accrued interest

(ii) resell the property

(iii) claim damages

(b) the buyer is to return any documents he received from the seller and is to cancel any registration of the contract.

7.5.3 The seller retains his other rights and remedies.

7.6 Seller's failure to comply with notice to complete

7.6.1 If the seller fails to complete in accordance with a notice to complete, the following terms apply.

7.6.2 The buyer may rescind the contract, and if he does so:

(a) the deposit is to be repaid to the buyer with accrued interest

(b) the buyer is to return any documents he received from the seller and is, at the seller's expense, to cancel any registration of the contract.

7.6.3 The buyer retains his other rights and remedies.

8. LEASEHOLD PROPERTY

8.1 Existing leases

8.1.1 The following provisions apply to a sale of leasehold land.

8.1.2 The seller having provided the buyer with copies of the documents embodying the lease terms, the buyer is treated as entering into the contract knowing and fully accepting those terms.

8.1.3 The seller is to comply with any lease obligations requiring the tenant to insure the property.

8.2 New leases

8.2.1 The following provisions apply to a grant of a new lease.

8.2.2 The conditions apply so that:
"seller" means the proposed landlord
"buyer" means the proposed tenant
"purchase price" means the premium to be paid on the grant of a lease.

8.2.3 The lease is to be in the form of the draft attached to the agreement.

8.2.4 If the term of the new lease will exceed 21 years, the seller is to deduce a title which will enable the buyer to register the lease at HM Land Registry with an absolute title.

8.2.5 The buyer is not entitled to transfer the benefit of the contract.

8.2.6 The seller is to engross the lease and a counterpart of it and is to send the counterpart to the buyer at least five working days before completion date.

8.2.7 The buyer is to execute he counterpart and deliver it to the seller on completion.

8.3 Landlord's consent

8.3.1 The following provisions apply if a consent to assign or sub-let is required to complete the contract.

8.3.2 (a) The seller is to apply for the consent at his expense, and to use all reasonable efforts to obtain it.
(b) The buyer is to provide all information and references reasonably required.

8.3.3 The buyer is not entitled to transfer the benefit of the contract.

8.3.4 Unless he is in breach of his obligation under condition 8.3.2, either party may rescind the contract by notice to the other party if three working days before completion date:
(a) the consent has not been given or
(b) the consent has been given subject to a condition to which the buyer reasonably objects.
In that case, neither party is to be treated as in breach of contract and condition 7.2 applies.

9. CHATTELS

9.1 The following provisions apply to any chattels which are to be sold.

9.2 Whether or not a separate price is to be paid for the chattels, the contract takes effect as a contract for sale of goods.

9.3 Ownership of the chattels passes to the buyer on actual completion.

SPECIAL CONDITIONS

1. (a) This Agreement incorporates the Standard Conditions of Sale (Third Edition). Where there is a conflict between those Conditions and this Agreement, this Agreement prevails.

   (b) Terms used or defined in this Agreement have the same meaning when used in the Conditions.

2. The Property is sold subject to the Incumbrances on the Property and the Buyer will raise no requisitions on them.

3. Subject to the terms of this Agreement and to the Standard Conditions of Sale, the seller is to transfer the property with the title guarantee specified on the front page.

4. The chattels on the Property and set out on any attached list are included in the sale.

5. The Property is sold with vacant possession on completion.

(or) 5. The Property is sold subject to the following leases or tenancies:

Seller's Solicitors :

Buyer's Solicitors :

Standard Conditions of Sale

GLOSSARY

Absolute	Free from determining factors; commonly used in expression 'fee simple absolute'.
Abstract of title	A summary of documents of title; abstracts of title are used to prove title to land of unregistered title.
Acquiescence	A failure to resist the infringement of a right.
Administrator	See **'Personal representatives'**.
Alienation	A transfer of property, whether by sale gift or other transaction.
Appurtenant	Attached to land by agreement of parties; an example of an appurtenant right is an easement; contrast 'appendant' which means attached by operation of law; appendant rights are an archaic class, principally affecting *profits à prendre*.
Assent	A transfer of property by personal representatives to beneficiaries under a will or intestacy; a deed is not necessary here; hence the special term.
Assignment	A transfer of property; commonly used in the transfer of a lease.
Beneficial owner	An owner of interest who does not hold it on trust for others. 'Beneficial' is sometimes used to mean 'equitable'.
Charge	An interest in land created either by act of parties or by operation of law for securing a debt or other obligation; for example, a mortgage.
Chattel	Any property other than freehold land; 'personal' chattels are movable items of property.
Consolidation	An obligation, arising on the right to redemption of one mortgage, to redeem one or other mortgages of other properties.
Contingent	Not presently owned; a key term in the rule against perpetuities.
Conversion	Treating land as money, or money as land; the topic gains most of its importance in the context of express and statutory trusts for sale.
Conveyance	A document transferring property during the lifetime of the transferor.

Co-ownership	Ownership shared by two or more persons at the same time.
Corporeal	Tangible: e.g. soil, bricks; see also **'Incorporeal'**.
Covenant	A contract by deed.
Deed	A document signed by the persons executing it; it is the principal means through which interests in land are transferred.
Demise	A grant of a lease.
Devise	A grant of a freehold interest by will.
Dominant tenement	Land benefiting from a burden placed upon other land; usually an easement or restrictive covenant is concerned.
Entail	An interest in land which lasts as long as descendant heirs of the original grantee of the interest are born.
Estate	Generally an interest giving the right to the land itself; particularly applied to legal interests having this effect.
Estoppel	Preclusion from denying facts which have been stated or inferred and upon which another person has acted.
Execute	Sign a deed.
Executor	See **'Personal representatives'**.
Fee simple	Ownership.
Fine	A capital payment.
Foreclosure	The lifting of the right of redemption from mortgaged property.
Freehold	A fee simple, absolute ownership.
Hereditament	Land.
Incumbrance	A burden upon property.
Incorporeal hereditament	Intangible 'land'; e.g. an easement.
Indenture	Archaic word to describe a deed.
Instrument	Any legal document.
Intestacy	Failure to dispose of property by will.
Jus accrescendi	See **'Survivorship'**.
Land	A word of variable meaning – see Chapter 2.
Licence	Permission.
Minor interest	An interest in registered land which requires entry on the Register for its protection against purchasers.
Negative equity	Shortfall of value of land on sum still outstanding on a mortgage.
Next of kin	Persons entitled to the property of an intestate person.

Oral	By word of mouth; distinguish 'verbal' which means by words, whether written or oral; a common confusion.
Overreach	To convert an interest in land to an interest in purchase money upon sale of the land.
Override	To defeat an interest in land.
Overriding interest	An interest in registered land which is binding upon purchasers even though it is not entered on the Register.
Personal representatives	Executors or administrators; both types of personal representatives deal with the property of deceased persons; the former are appointed by the will and confirmed by the court (normally a merely administrative procedure); the latter receive their authority from the court because of close relationship to the deceased.
Personalty	All property except freehold land not subject to a trust for sale. Personalty is the antonym of 'realty'.
Possession	Occupation of land or receipt of its rents and profits.
Prescription	The process of acquiring easements and profits by long use.
Privity of contract	The relationship of contracting parties.
Privity of estate	The relationship of landlord and tenant.
Probate	Grant of approval of a will by the court (normally an administrative procedure).
Puisne mortgage	A legal mortgage not protected by deposit of deeds.
Purchaser	One who acquires property by act of parties rather than operation of law; e.g. a donee.
Remainder	An interest in land which follows another interest; e.g. *B*'s interest in a grant to *A* for life and *B* in fee simple.
Resulting trust	A trust arising in favour of a grantor whose attempted transfer fails or partially fails.
Rent service	A rent due from a tenant to a landlord.
Rentcharge	A rent payable where there is no landlord/tenant relationship.
Reversion	A remainder retained by a grantor of a prior interest.
Restrictive covenant	A covenant not to use land in a particular way; such agreements are capable of binding land permanently as do easements.
Root of title	The earliest of the series of documents upon which proof of title to land is based in the case of unregistered title.
Seisin	Possession by a freeholder.

Settlement	A structure of consecutive interests in land other than those of landlord and tenant but including absolute ownership by a minor.
Survivorship	The coalescence of property on the death of one joint owner into the hands of the other joint tenants.
Tenure	Holding land of another – usually relating to landlord and tenant.
Term of years	A lease or tenancy.
Trust for sale	A duty to sell land derived either from the terms of an instrument or of an Act of Parliament; the former is called an 'express trust for sale'; the latter is a 'statutory trust for sale'.
Words of limitation	Formal words legally required for the creation of interests in land; the doctrine now applies only to entailed interests.

INDEX